Weirong Chen
A Grammar of Southern Min

Sinitic Languages of China

Typological Descriptions

Edited by
Hilary Chappell

Volume 3

Weirong Chen

A Grammar of Southern Min

The Hui'an Dialect

European Research Council
Established by the European Commission

DE GRUYTER
MOUTON

ISBN 978-1-5015-2683-1
e-ISBN (PDF) 978-1-5015-1186-8
e-ISBN (EPUB) 978-1-5015-1150-9
ISSN 2365-8398

Library of Congress Control Number: 2019948127

Bibliographic information published by the Deutsche Nationalbibliothek
The Deutsche Nationalbibliothek lists this publication in the Deutsche Nationalbibliografie;
detailed bibliographic data are available on the Internet at http://dnb.dnb.de.

© 2021 Walter de Gruyter GmbH, Inc., Boston/Berlin
This volume is text- and page-identical with the hardback published in 2020.
Cover image: Wang Jian
Printing and binding: CPI books GmbH, Leck

www.degruyter.com

Preface

In the second volume to appear in this new series on *Sinitic languages of China*, Weirong Chen brings to our attention, for the first time, an exceptionally detailed grammar of one of the main varieties of Southern Min, the Hui'an dialect.

The heartland of the Min dialect group, to which Hui'an belongs, is the coastal province of Fujian in southeastern China. A branch of Sinitic which counts over 50 million speakers yet represents just 4% of the Han Chinese population, it is well-known for its heterogeneous nature, not to mention for its retention of various Archaic Chinese features. Southern Min, is in fact, the largest and most widely distributed subgroup of dialects within Min. It extends south into Guangdong and Hainan, and also over the straits to Taiwan. Furthermore, due to a centuries-long diaspora, large concentrations of Southern Min speakers are to be found in Southeast Asia, for example, in Singapore where more than half of the Chinese population has a Min dialect such as Hokkien 福建话, Teochew 潮州话, or Hainanese 海南话, as their heritage language. Communities are also to be found in Thailand, Malaysia and Indonesia. Therefore, a comprehensive grammar of Southern Min is more than timely.

After obtaining her PhD at the University of Hong Kong, Weirong Chen was invited to take up a position as a postdoctoral researcher on the ERC SINOTYPE team in Paris from 2011 to 2013. During this period, she began work on the present volume on Hui'an Southern Min, impressive in its novel and original approach to a large array of topics that cover all the major aspects of its grammar.

Sinitic languages of China: Typological descriptions is a new series specializing in the description of the grammar of Sinitic languages, 'Sinitic' being the technical term for the Chinese branch of the Sino-Tibetan language family. As such, it includes well-known examples such as Cantonese 广东话, Hokkien 闽南话, Shanghainese 上海话 and Hakka 客家话, lesser-known ones such as Hunanese Xiang 湘语 or the Jin languages of Shanxi 晋语, and, importantly, the national language of China, *Pǔtōnghuà* 普通话, known as Standard Chinese or Mandarin in English. Even Mandarin comes in many non-standard forms including Sichuanese in the southwest, or the unusual varieties spoken in Gansu and Qinghai in northwestern China and the Central Plains region, to name but a few.

The primary goal of this series is to promote scientific knowledge of Chinese languages and their typological characteristics through the publication of high calibre linguistic research, based on empirical fieldwork, close analysis of the data and solid theoretical interpretations. The grammatical descriptions, written in a functionalist framework, are illustrated by linguistic examples presented in a 'value-added' four-line format that includes romanization, glossing, the idiomatic English translation, and also the Chinese characters to cater to historical and comparative interests, as well as our sinophone readers.

The specific objective is to reveal the great structural diversity found in Sinitic languages and to dispel many recurrent linguistic myths about Chinese. The authors involved in this series are all highly trained fieldwork linguists with a background in both typology and Chinese linguistics.

The series thus aims to reach an international readership for the first time, given that most literature available on Chinese languages other than Mandarin, up until now, has been mainly written in the medium of (Standard Written) Chinese.

The large-scale research project, *The hybrid syntactic typology of Sinitic languages* (SINOTYPE), provided the initial impetus behind this series. SINOTYPE benefitted from funding in the form of an Advanced Grant (No. 230388) awarded by the European Research Council (ERC) for the period 2009 – 2013 which included a generous publication subsidy for this series. The host institute, the Ecole des Hautes Etudes en Sciences Sociales (EHESS), graciously provided managerial support and accounting resources, not to mention the spacious premises for the SINOTYPE research centre in inner-city Paris for the entire period of the project. We take this opportunity to express our many thanks to both the ERC and the EHESS.

The other volumes planned for this series are:

Volume 2: *A Grammar of Nanning Pinghua*, by Hilário de Sousa

Volume 4: *A Grammar of Central Plains Mandarin*, by Yujie Chen

Volume 5: *A Grammar of Shaowu*, by Sing Sing Ngai

Volume 6: *A Reference Grammar of Jixi Hui*, by Wang Jian

Volume 7: *A Grammar of Waxiang*, by Hilary Chappell

H.M. Chappell
Series Editor
Paris, 2020

List of abbreviations

The abbreviations for grammatical glosses basically follow the Leipzig Glossing Rules. A square symbol is used in place of a Chinese character when neither the etymology is clear nor a Mandarin equivalent can be found. Tones are not given when a morpheme is realized with different tones when used with different morphemes.

□	Symbol for unidentifiable characters
1SG	First person singular
2SG	Second person singular
3SG	Third person singular
1PL	First person plural
2PL	Second person plural
3PL	Third person plural
ADJ	Adjective
ADV	Adverb
AUX	Auxiliary verb
BEN	Benefactive marker
C	Complement
CL	Classifier
CM	Complement marker
COM	Comparee
COMP	Complementizer
COMT	Comitative marker
COP	Copula
DELIM	Delimitative aspect
DEM	Demonstrative
DIM	Diminutive
DIR	Directional
DM	Discourse marker
DMC	Dependent-marker of comparison
DO	Direct object

DUR	Durative aspect
EVC	Extent verbal complement
EXP	Experiential aspect
FOC	Focus
FUT	Future
GEN	Genitive marker
HAB	Habitual aspect
HMC	Head-marker of comparison
INDEF	Indefinite
IO	Indirect object
LOC	Locative
MAL	Malefactive marker
MOD	Modifying marker
MW	Measure word
NEG	Negative marker
NM	Noun marker
NMLZ	Nominalizer
NOM	Nominative
N	Noun
NP	Noun phrase
NUM	Numeral
O	Object
OM	Object marker
PASS	Passive marker
PFV	Perfective aspect
PHA	Phase
PL	Plural
PN	Place name/Person name
POSS	Possessive
PP	Prepositional phrase
PRED	Predicate
PREF	Prefix

PRO	Pronoun
PROG	Progressive
PRT	Particle
PVC	Phase verbal complement
QW	Question word
RC	Relative clause
RECP	Reciprocal
RES	Resultative
RM	Relativization marker
RP	Relative pronoun
RVC	Resultative verbal complement
S	Subject/Sentence
SFP	Sentence-final particle
STA	Standard of comparison
TENT	Tentative aspect
TM	Topic marker
V	Verb
VP	Verb phrase

Content

Preface —— v

List of abbreviations —— vii

1 Introduction —— 1
1.1 The Hui'an dialect and its classification —— 1
1.1.1 Southern Min —— 1
1.1.2 Hui'an —— 2
1.1.3 Characteristics of the Hui'an dialect —— 2
1.2 Previous studies on Southern Min —— 5
1.3 Data collection —— 6
1.4 Presentation of examples in this reference grammar —— 8
1.5 Language usage in Hui'an —— 9

2 Phonology —— 10
2.1 Introduction —— 10
2.2 Initials —— 10
2.3 Finals —— 12
2.4 Tone —— 14
2.4.1 Citation tones —— 14
2.4.2 Tone sandhi —— 15
2.4.3 Tonemic representation of citation and sandhi tones —— 17
2.4.4 Neutral tone and stress —— 17
2.5 Syllable fusion —— 19
2.6 Summary —— 20

Part I Nominal structure

3 Affixation and compounding —— 25
3.1 Introduction —— 25
3.2 Affixation —— 25
3.2.1 Prefixes —— 25
3.2.1.1 *a*-阿 in kinship terms and names —— 25
3.2.1.2 Prefix *lau*-老 —— 28
3.2.1.3 Other prefixes —— 28
3.2.2 Suffixes —— 29

3.2.2.1	Diminutive suffix *a³* 仔 —— 29	
3.2.2.2	Diminutive suffix *a⁰* 仔 —— 32	
3.2.2.3	Suffix *sai¹* 師 < 'master' —— 33	
3.2.2.4	Suffix *sen¹* 仙 < 'celestial being, immortal' —— 33	
3.2.2.5	Suffix *sen²* 神 < 'god, deity' —— 33	
3.2.2.6	Suffix *tsin¹* 精 < 'spirit, demon' —— 34	
3.2.2.7	Suffix *tsiau³* 鳥 < 'bird' —— 34	
3.2.2.8	Suffix *kui³* 鬼 < 'ghost' —— 34	
3.2.2.9	Suffix *thau* 頭 < 'head' —— 34	
3.3	Compounding —— 35	
3.3.1	Coordinate —— 35	
3.3.2	Modifier-head/head-modifier —— 36	
3.3.3	Subject-predicate —— 37	
3.4	Summary —— 37	
4	**Pronouns —— 38**	
4.1	Introduction —— 38	
4.2	Personal pronouns —— 38	
4.2.1	Singular personal pronouns —— 39	
4.2.1.1	Syntactic distributions —— 39	
4.2.1.2	Referential functions —— 43	
4.2.2	Plural personal pronouns —— 45	
4.3	Reflexive pronouns —— 49	
4.4	Reciprocal pronouns —— 52	
4.5	The pronouns *laŋ⁴* 'other' and *pat⁸⁻⁴laŋ²* 'other people' —— 52	
4.6	Summary —— 56	
5	**Nominal demonstratives —— 57**	
5.1	Introduction —— 57	
5.2	Syntactic functions and semantic features —— 62	
5.2.1	Basic adnominal demonstratives: *tsit⁷* 即/*hit⁷* 迄 —— 62	
5.2.2	Singular demonstratives: *tsat⁸*/*hat⁸* —— 71	
5.2.3	Plural demonstratives: *tsuai²* 撮/*huai²* 懷 —— 75	
5.2.4	Generic demonstratives: *tse²/hə²* —— 80	
5.2.5	Generic demonstratives: *tsiɔŋ³⁻²e²* 種其/*hiɔŋ³⁻²e²* 向其 —— 84	
5.2.6	Interim summary —— 85	
5.2.7	Further discussion on the semantic features of Hui'an demonstratives —— 88	
5.3	The pragmatic uses of Hui'an demonstratives —— 89	

5.3.1	Language-external functions —— 89	
5.3.2	Language-internal functions —— 93	
5.4	Summary —— 96	

6	**Numerals and quantifiers —— 99**	
6.1	Introduction —— 99	
6.2	Numerals —— 99	
6.2.1	Cardinal numbers —— 99	
6.2.2	Ordinal numbers —— 104	
6.2.3	Approximate numbers —— 108	
6.3	Quantifiers —— 109	
6.4	Summary —— 113	

7	**Classifiers —— 115**	
7.1	Introduction —— 115	
7.2	Syntactic distributions —— 115	
7.2.1	Numeral + classifier —— 115	
7.2.2	Quantifier + classifier —— 119	
7.2.3	Demonstratives *tsitʔ*/*hitʔ* + classifier —— 121	
7.2.4	Classifier + noun —— 122	
7.2.5	Adjective + classifier —— 123	
7.3	Semantic properties —— 127	
7.4	Referential functions —— 136	
7.5	Sources and extensions —— 139	
7.6	Summary —— 140	

8	**Possessive constructions —— 141**	
8.1	Introduction —— 141	
8.2	Attributive possessive constructions —— 144	
8.2.1	The zero-marked possessive construction: possessor + ∅ + possessee —— 145	
8.2.1.1	Pronoun possessor + ∅ + possessee —— 145	
8.2.1.1.1	Possessee=kinship terms —— 145	
8.2.1.1.2	Possessee=social relations or location —— 148	
8.2.1.1.3	Possessee=spatial orientation —— 149	
8.2.1.1.4	Possessee=body parts —— 150	
8.2.1.1.5	Possessee=common nouns —— 152	
8.2.1.1.6	Interim summary —— 153	
8.2.1.2	Noun possessor + ∅ + possessee —— 153	

8.2.2	The demonstrative possessive construction: possessor + demonstrative (+ numeral + classifier) + possessee —— 155	
8.2.3	The classifier possessive construction: possessor + classifier + possessee —— 158	
8.2.4	The possessive construction with the genitive marker e^2 其: possessor + e^2 其 + possessee —— 159	
8.2.4.1	Personal pronoun + e^2 + noun —— 159	
8.2.4.2	Noun + e^2 + noun —— 161	
8.3	Predicative possessive constructions —— 161	
8.3.1	Semantic functions —— 162	
8.3.2	Pragmatic differences —— 162	
8.4	Summary —— 164	

Part II Predicate structure

9	Reduplication —— 167	
9.1	Introduction —— 167	
9.2	Form —— 167	
9.3	Functions —— 170	
9.3.1	Word formation through reduplication —— 170	
9.3.2	Repeated or continued event —— 171	
9.3.3	Increased quantity of participants —— 173	
9.3.4	Increased intensity —— 173	
9.4	Summary —— 175	

10	Verb complement constructions —— 176	
10.1	Introduction —— 176	
10.2	Directional verb complement constructions: V_1-V_{2DIR} —— 178	
10.2.1	Directional complements —— 180	
10.2.1.1	Monosyllabic directional complements —— 180	
10.2.1.2	Disyllabic directional complements —— 182	
10.2.2	Relative order of verb, complement and object —— 185	
10.2.3	Negative forms —— 187	
10.2.4	Other functions —— 188	
10.3	Resultative verb complement constructions: V_1-V_{2RES} —— 188	
10.3.1	Resultative complements —— 189	
10.3.1.1	Adjectives —— 189	
10.3.1.2	Directional verbs —— 190	
10.3.1.3	u^4 'have' and bo^2 'not have' —— 192	

10.3.1.4	*liau³* 'finish' and *sak⁷* 'push' —— **194**	
10.3.2	Relative order of verb, complement and object —— **195**	
10.3.3	Negative forms —— **196**	
10.4	Verb-phase complement constructions: V₁-V₂PHA —— **197**	
10.5	Verb-manner complement constructions: V-CM-C —— **200**	
10.5.1	With the complement marker *a⁵* 遘 —— **200**	
10.5.2	With the complement marker *leʔ⁷* 得 —— **201**	
10.6	Verb-extent complement constructions: V-*a⁵*-C; V-*si³*/*a³* —— **202**	
10.7	Verb-quantitative complement constructions: V-Quantitative expression —— **204**	
10.8	Potential verb complement constructions: V-*e⁴*/*bue⁴*-C; V-*leʔ⁷*-C; *e⁴*/*bue⁴* -V- *leʔ⁷*- C —— **206**	
10.9	Summary —— **210**	

11	**Aspect —— 212**	
11.1	Introduction —— **212**	
11.2	Perfective aspect —— **213**	
11.2.1	*liau³* 'finish' —— **213**	
11.2.2	*khw⁵* 去 —— **216**	
11.2.3	*u⁴* 'have, exist' —— **217**	
11.3	Imperfective aspect —— **219**	
11.3.1	Progressive aspect —— **219**	
11.3.2	Durative aspect —— **221**	
11.3.3	Habitual aspect —— **222**	
11.4	Experiential aspect —— **223**	
11.5	Summary —— **225**	

12	**Modality —— 226**	
12.1	Introduction —— **226**	
12.2	Possibility —— **227**	
12.2.1	Ability —— **229**	
12.2.2	Root possibility —— **231**	
12.2.3	Non-deontic possibility —— **233**	
12.2.4	Permission —— **234**	
12.2.5	Epistemic possibility —— **234**	
12.3	Necessity —— **236**	
12.4	Volition —— **237**	
12.5	Summary —— **238**	

13	**Negation — 240**	
13.1	Introduction — 240	
13.2	General and volitional negatives m^5 唔 and $m^{5\text{-}4}ai^5$ 唔愛 — 241	
13.3	Perfective negative bo^2 無 — 245	
13.4	Imminent negative $bə^5$ 未 — 250	
13.5	Irrealis negative bue^4 燴 — 251	
13.6	General prohibitive $baŋ^1 \sim m^{5\text{-}4}thaŋ^1$ 唔通 — 254	
13.7	'Lack of necessity' imperatives $(m^{5\text{-}4})ben^3$ (唔)免 — 255	
13.8	Injunctive negative $buan^3$ — 255	
13.9	Summary — 256	

14	**Adpositions — 258**	
14.1	Introduction — 258	
14.2	Spatial and temporal relations — 259	
14.2.1	Location — 259	
14.2.2	Source — 263	
14.2.3	Goal — 265	
14.2.4	Perlative — 266	
14.3	Patient — 267	
14.4	Agent — 271	
14.5	Benefactive — 272	
14.6	Comitative — 273	
14.7	Standard of comparison — 274	
14.8	Instrument — 275	
14.9	Basis — 276	
14.10	Summary — 276	

15	**Adverbs — 278**	
15.1	Introduction — 278	
15.2	Manner adverbs — 279	
15.3	Degree adverbs — 280	
15.3.1	Basic degree adverbs — 280	
15.3.2	Comparative degree adverbs — 282	
15.4	Time adverbs — 284	
15.5	Adverbs of quantity and scope — 285	
15.6	Attitude and epistemic adverbs — 290	
15.7	Summary — 291	

Part III Clause structure

16 The $ka\text{?}^7$- and ka^5- constructions —— 295
16.1 Introduction —— 295
16.2 Relevant semantic roles —— 296
16.3 The functions of $ka\text{?}^7$ —— 297
16.4 The functions of ka^5 —— 299
16.4.1 As an oblique marker —— 299
16.4.2 As an object marker —— 304
16.4.3 ka^5 + personal pronoun —— 307
16.5 Summary —— 309

17 Comparative constructions of inequality —— 311
17.1 Introduction —— 311
17.1.1 Three main types of comparative proposed in Ansaldo (1999) —— 312
17.1.2 Six main types of comparative in the Hui'an dialect —— 314
17.2 Double-marking/hybridized comparatives: A$_{COM}$ pi^3 B$_{STA}$ $kha\text{?}^7$ PRED (MW) —— 315
17.3 Absolute comparatives: A$_{COM}$ $kha\text{?}^7$ PRED (MW) —— 321
17.4 Head-marking comparatives with $kha\text{?}^7$: A$_{COM}$ $kha\text{?}^7$ PRED B$_{STA}$ (MW) —— 324
17.5 Zero-marked comparatives: A$_{COM}$ PRED B$_{STA}$ (MW) —— 327
17.6 Comparatives with the marker khu^5: A$_{COM}$ PRED khu^5 B$_{STA}$ —— 330
17.7 Dependent-marking comparatives with pi^3: A$_{COM}$ pi^3 B$_{STA}$ PRED (MW) —— 334
17.8 Summary —— 335

18 The 'give' construction —— 337
18.1 Introduction —— 337
18.2 As a ditransitive verb and perspective marker —— 337
18.2.1 As a ditransitive verb —— 337
18.2.2 As a perspective marker —— 338
18.3 As a dative marker —— 339
18.4 As a (permissive) causative verb —— 341
18.5 As a purposive marker —— 343
18.6 As a passive and speaker-affectedness marker —— 344
18.7 As a concessive marker —— 345
18.8 Summary —— 346

19 Interrogatives — 347

- 19.1 Introduction — 347
- 19.2 Alternative interrogatives — 347
- 19.3 Polar interrogatives — 349
- 19.3.1 Interrogatives with disjunctive structures — 349
- 19.3.1.1 VP-or-NEG-VP — 350
- 19.3.1.2 VP-NEG-VP — 351
- 19.3.1.3 VP-or-NEG — 351
- 19.3.2 Particle interrogatives — 352
- 19.3.2.1 a^o 啊 — 352
- 19.3.2.2 m^o 唔 — 353
- 19.3.2.3 $bə^o$ 未 — 355
- 19.3.2.4 bo^o 無 — 356
- 19.3.2.5 bue^o 燴 — 357
- 19.3.2.6 Status of particles m^o, $bə^o$, bo^o and bue^o — 358
- 19.3.2.7 Interrogatives via intonation — 359
- 19.3.3 Tag questions — 360
- 19.4 Constituent interrogatives — 361
- 19.4.1 $siəm^{3\text{-}2}bi\tilde{\imath}^{\gamma}$ and $si\tilde{a}^2$ 'what' — 362
- 19.4.2 $si\tilde{a}^2laŋ^2$ and $siaŋ^2$ 'who' — 365
- 19.4.3 ti^4si^2/tu^4si^2 and $siəm^{3\text{-}2}bi\tilde{\imath}^{\gamma\text{-}8}\ si^{2\text{-}4}tsam^4$ 'when' — 366
- 19.4.4 to^3 'which' — 366
- 19.4.5 to^3 and $to^{3\text{-}2}ta\tilde{\imath}^{\gamma}$ 'where' — 367
- 19.4.6 kui^3, lua^4tsue^5 and lua^4 'how many/much' — 368
- 19.4.7 $tsiũ^5$ and $kŋ^5$ 'how' — 369
- 19.4.8 $l\tilde{a}^5$ and $ui^{5\text{-}4}siəm^{3\text{-}2}bi\tilde{\imath}^{\gamma}$ 'why' — 370
- 19.5 Summary — 370

20 Topic-comment constructions — 372

- 20.1 Introduction — 372
- 20.2 Forms of topics — 373
- 20.3 Semantic relations between topic and comment — 378
- 20.3.1 Coreferential (pseudo-)argument topic — 378
- 20.3.2 Frame-setting topic — 382
- 20.3.2.1 Time/location frame-setting topic — 383
- 20.3.2.2 Possession frame-setting topic — 384
- 20.3.2.3 Background frame-setting topic — 385
- 20.3.3 Identical topic — 387
- 20.3.4 Clause topic — 390

20.3.5	Split argument topic —— 391	
20.4	The position of topic —— 393	
20.5	Patient topicalization —— 395	
20.6	Topic marker —— 398	
20.7	Contrastive function of topic —— 399	
20.8	Summary —— 400	

Part IV Complex sentences

21	Coordination —— 405	
21.1	Introduction —— 405	
21.2	Conjunction —— 406	
21.3	Disjunction —— 411	
21.4	Adversative coordination —— 412	
21.5	Summary —— 413	

22	Relative clauses —— 415	
22.1	Introduction —— 415	
22.2	The relativization markers —— 417	
22.2.1	Attributive marker e^2 其 —— 419	
22.2.2	Demonstratives —— 420	
22.2.3	Demonstrative complexes —— 423	
22.2.4	Classifiers —— 427	
22.2.5	Zero-marked —— 428	
22.2.6	Interim summary —— 431	
22.3	Position of the head noun —— 431	
22.3.1	Head-final and head-initial types —— 432	
22.3.2	Is there a head-internal type? —— 435	
22.3.3	Interim summary —— 437	
22.4	The role and encoding of the head noun in the relative clause —— 438	
22.4.1	Argument relative clauses —— 441	
22.4.2	Adjunct relative clauses —— 442	
22.4.3	'aboutness' relative clauses —— 443	
22.5	The role and encoding of the head noun in the main clause —— 444	
22.5.1	The role of the head noun in the main clause —— 444	
22.5.2	The encoding of the head noun in the main clause —— 445	
22.6	Summary —— 447	

23	**Adverbial clauses** —— 449
23.1	Introduction —— 449
23.2	Time clauses —— 449
23.3	Cause clauses —— 455
23.4	Purpose clauses —— 457
23.5	Conditional clauses —— 458
23.6	Summary —— 464

24	**Complement clauses** —— 466
24.1	Introduction —— 466
24.2	Utterance verbs —— 467
24.3	Verbs of perception and cognition —— 474
24.4	Modal verbs of volition —— 481
24.5	Causative (or manipulative) verbs —— 482
24.6	Summary —— 483

25	**Conclusion** —— 484

References —— 485

Index —— 511

Appendix —— 515

1 Introduction

Southern Min (also known as Hokkien or Minnan 閩南) is a major branch of Chinese spoken mainly in Fujian 福建 and Taiwan 臺灣, but also in Guangdong 廣東, Hainan 海南, Zhejiang 浙江, Jiangxi 江西 and Hong Kong 香港, as well as in many countries of Southeast Asia. Highly conservative in its linguistic profile, it is considered by many scholars to be a living language fossil due to the preservation of many archaic features that reflect its long-lasting history and culture. Despite this, there has to date been no comprehensive study of any Southern Min variety using a typological framework. This grammar therefore aims to fill this gap by presenting a systematic description of the Hui'an 惠安 dialect, mainly based on data collected during naturally occurring conversation. The volume includes four parts: nominal structure, predicate structure, clause structure and complex sentences, in addition to a brief overview of phonology. This first introductory chapter includes the classification of Min 閩 dialects and the place of Hui'an within this important branch of Chinese as well as an overview of previous studies on Southern Min. We also highlight some of the special and unique features of this dialect, followed by information on the documentation methods used, presentation of examples and language usage in Hui'an.

1.1 The Hui'an dialect and its classification

In the following two sections, we consider the classification of the Hui'an dialect within the Min branch of Chinese.

1.1.1 Southern Min

The Min branch, one of the major Chinese branches, can be classified into five or six subgroups (cf. Pan et al. 1963, Yuan 1989, Zhou and Ouyang 1998). For example, Zhou and Ouyang (1998:3) point out that the Min branch in Fujian falls into six subgroups: (a) Eastern Min 閩東, with the Fuzhou 福州 variety as representative; (b) Southern Min 閩南, with the Xiamen 廈門 variety as representative; (c) Northern Min 閩北, with the Jian'ou 建甌 variety as representative; (d) Puxian 莆仙, with the Putian 莆田 variety as representative; (e) Central Min 閩中, with the Yong'an 永安 variety as representative; and (f) Shaojiang 邵將, with the Shaowu 邵武 variety as representative.

As mentioned above, Southern Min is not only spoken in the south of Fujian province, but also in Guangdong province, southern Hainan Island, the south of Zhejiang province, Jiangxi province, Hong Kong and Taiwan, and also in some other countries such as Singapore, Brunei, Indonesia, the Philippines, Thailand and Malaysia. According to Yuan (1989:236), Southern Min can be further classified into four areas: (a) South Fujian 福建 area, the varieties spoken in Xiamen 廈門, Quanzhou 泉州, Zhangzhou 漳州 and Taiwan 臺灣, with the Xiamen variety as representative; (b) Chaoshan 潮汕 area, with the Chaozhou 潮州 variety as representative; (c) Hainan 海南 area, with the Wenchang 文昌 variety as representative; and (d) South Zhejiang 浙江 area, with the Pingyang 平陽 and Cangnan 蒼南 varieties as representative. According to *the Language Atlas of China* published in 2012, however, Southern Min is divided into five subgroups: (a) the Quan (Quanzhou) – Zhang (Zhangzhou) subgroup 泉漳小片; (b) the Datian subgroup 大田小片; (c) the Chao (Chaozhou) – Shan (Shantou) subgroup 潮汕小片; (d) the Southeastern Zhe (Zhejiang) subgroup 浙東南小片; and (e) the Northeastern Gan (Jiangxi) subgroup 贛東北小片.

1.1.2 Hui'an

Hui'an, a County administered by Quanzhou City, is situated in the southeastern part of Fujian province between Meizhou 湄洲 Bay and Quanzhou 泉州 Bay. Hui'an County was established in the sixth year of the Taiping Xingguo 太平興國 Period of the Northern Song Dynasty (AD 981) (Chen and Wang 1998:1). With the government seat housed in Luocheng 螺城 Town, Hui'an governs twelve towns, namely Luocheng 螺城, Luóyáng 螺陽, Huangtang 黃塘, Zishan 紫山, Chongwu 崇武, Shanxia 山霞, Tuzhai 塗寨, Dongling 東嶺, Dongqiao 東橋, Jingfeng 淨峰, Xiaozuo 小岞 and Wangchuan 輞川, with a total area of about 489.42 square kilometers and a population of about 779,000 people up to 2014. Hui'an is a famous hometown for numerous overseas Chinese and Taiwan compatriots.

1.1.3 Characteristics of the Hui'an dialect

In this book, the term 'the Hui'an dialect' is used to refer to the variety of Southern Min spoken in Luocheng Town, where the government seat of Hui'an County is located. According to *the Language Atlas of China*, the Hui'an dialect is grouped into the Quan (Quanzhou) – Zhang (Zhangzhou) subgroup of the Southern Min branch.

The Hui'an dialect shares much in common with other Southern Min varieties in Fujian and Taiwan, especially the Quanzhou variety, with, however, subtle differences. In terms of phonological properties, there are in total fourteen initial phonemes in the Hui'an dialect: the initial /z/[dz] attested in some other Southern Min varieties such as Zhangzhou and Taiwan has merged with the initial *l* in Hui'an. As with other Southern Min varieties, the Hui'an dialect has three sets of plosives: voiceless unaspirated (*p, t, k*), voiceless aspirated (*ph, th, kh*) and voiced (*b, l, g*), among which, the plosives *b, l* and *g* are only followed by non-nasalized finals, in complementary distribution with the nasals *m, n* and *ŋ*, respectively, which only occur before nasalized finals. The Hui'an dialect has developed a 7-tone system like most of other Southern Min varieties in Fujian and Taiwan, even though in different ways. The system of tone sandhi is complex: besides the general tone sandhi rules, reduplicated forms of adjectives have their own rules (see chapter 2).

In terms of morphology, as in other Chinese varieties, the Hui'an dialect has no inflectional morphology, but exhibits derivational processes such as reduplication, affixation and compounding. Unlike Mandarin Chinese, reduplication in Hui'an is neither used to form kinship terms, nor applied to classifiers to express the meaning of 'every'. It is common for a reduplication process to be applied twice, that is, forming a triplicated form, or even three or four times, to express increased intensity (an increased amount of emphasis) (see chapters 3 and 9).

The plural personal pronouns in general have singular meanings when they function as possessors in genitive constructions. Both the exclusive gun^3 阮 'we' and the inclusive lan^3 'we' can also have a singular meaning when functioning as a subject or an object (see chapter 4). Compared to some other Chinese varieties such as Mandarin and Yue, the Hui'an dialect (also other Min varieties) shows a relatively complicated nominal demonstrative system: five sets of nominal demonstratives are attested, and probably all involve syllable contraction (see chapter 5).

Besides the common function of modifying a noun with(out) a numeral, quantifier or nominal demonstrative, classifiers in Hui'an, just as in some other Southern Min varieties including the Taiwan variety, can also be used with an adjective such as tua^5 大 'big' and sue^5 細 'small' to form compound adjectives (see chapter 7).

As in other Chinese varieties, verb complement constructions are common in Hui'an. However, unlike Mandarin Chinese and many other Chinese dialects where potential verb complement constructions are marked by DE 得 and its cognates derived from the 'get' verb, the Hui'an dialect (also other Southern Min varieties) uses the auxiliary verb e^4 'can' and its negative form bue^4 'cannot' for potential verb complement constructions (see chapter 10).

In terms of aspect system, the Hui'an dialect has no typical perfective aspect marker. There are two experiential aspect markers: pat^7 八 (< 'know') and $tioʔ^8$ 著 'touch, get', unlike Mandarin Chinese which uses the verb $guò$ 過 'pass' as an experiential aspect marker (see chapter 11). Compared with prepositions in Mandarin Chinese, prepositions are not commonly used in daily conversation in Hui'an: many noun phrases which have to be introduced by a preposition in Mandarin Chinese can be used without any marking in Hui'an (see chapter 14).

The morphemes $ka(ŋ)$共 and $kaʔ/kap$ 合 are two important multifunctional function words in Southern Min. They overlap with each other in terms of their functions in some Southern Min varieties: for example, they both function as an oblique marker for goal in Taiwan Southern Min (cf. Cheng and Tsao 1995, Tsao 2005). In Hui'an, however, $kaʔ^7$ 合 functions as a connective or comitative marker, whereas ka^5 共 typically takes on a range of other functions: (a) it functions as an oblique marker, marking source, goal, beneficiary and maleficiary; (b) it also functions as an object marker; and (c) it can precede a (non-)referential personal pronoun to express the speaker's subjective attitude (see chapter 16).

The head-marking (or surpass) type of comparative (A_{COM} –PRED – HMC –B_{STA}) and the dependent-marking type of comparative (or similar ones) (A_{COM} – DMC – B_{STA} –PRED) are two predominant comparative construction types in contemporary Chinese. By contrast, in the Hui'an dialect (also other Southern Min varieties), the main type of comparative is the double-marking type (A_{COM} – DMC – B_{STA} – HMC – PRED). In addition, head-marking comparatives with the marker $khaʔ^7$ 恰 (A_{COM} + $khaʔ^7$ + PRED + B_{STA} (+ MW)), zero-marked comparatives (A_{COM} + PRED + B_{STA} (+ MW)) and comparatives with the marker $khuɪ^5$ 去 (A_{COM} + PRED + $khuɪ^5$ 去 + B_{STA}) are also attested in the Hui'an dialect, among which, the last type has not been reported in the literature on other Southern Min varieties, although it can be found in the Fuzhou variety of Northeastern Min (see chapter 17).

The 'give' verb in Hui'an, $khɔ^5$, can not only be used as a ditransitive verb, dative marker, permissive verb, causative verb and passive marker, but also as a perspective marker, concessive marker, purposive marker and speaker-affectedness marker (see chapter 18). Polar interrogatives in Hui'an can be marked by a series of strategies such as interrogative particles, interrogative intonation, disjunctive structures and the addition of tags, among which, the disjunctive is not common in the languages of the world, though widely used in Chinese. The 'VP-NEG' pattern of polar interrogative, which is widely used in Chinese, especially Southern Chinese, is not attested in Hui'an (see chapter 19).

The main word order in Hui'an is SVO. However, topicalization, especially patient topicalization, is quite normal in certain constructions. The topic in Hui'an typically occurs after the subject and before the main verb in the comment, especially when both the topic and the subject are present in the sentence. Unlike some Chinese varieties such as Wu, the topic in Hui'an is not basically followed by either an obvious pause or a pause particle, and is rarely used for contrast. In other words, the topic in Hui'an is more like an unmarked constituent (see chapter 20).

As in other Chinese varieties, the modifier in the Hui'an dialect usually precedes the modified. For example, the possessor in the attributive possessive construction invariably precedes the possessee (see chapter 8); the adverb typically precedes the verb which it modifies (see chapter 15). Similarly, the relative clauses mainly belong to the head-final type. However, the head-initial type is also attested (see chapter 22).

Unlike some European languages such as English where adverbial clauses are usually marked by subordinating conjunctions, the Hui'an dialect tends to juxtapose the clauses, with the relevant semantic relation between the clauses inferred, or else an adverb is used in the main clause to mark the semantic relation between the clauses (see chapter 23). Complement clauses in Hui'an typically function as an object of the main clause, that is, constitute object clauses. Utterance verbs and some verbs of perception and cognition such as $kam^{3\text{-}2}kak^7$ 感覺 'feel' and $siū^4$ 想 'think' can occur with the complementizer $sə\textipa{?}^7$ (< 'say') and/or $khuā^5$ 看 (< 'look'), among which the complementizer $khuā^5$ is typically used to introduce an interrogative complement clause and is used in the context which inquires about something or looks for an answer (see chapter 24).

1.2 Previous studies on Southern Min

During the past 88 years since the publication of Luo (1930), studies on Southern Min have developed significantly. Early works on Southern Min, however, show a strong tendency to focus on phonological phenomena. Morphosyntax of Southern Min in general has not received much attention prior to the past three decades.

Comparatively speaking, much work has been done on morphosyntax in the case of Taiwan Southern Min (e.g. Yang 1991; Cheng 1997a; Tang 1999a; Lien 2016; Lin 2011, 2016; Lee 2009, 2010, 2012), which involves a series of perspectives, such as comparative (e.g. Tsao 1988; Wang and Lien 1995; Lien 2010), historical (e.g. Lien 1994, 2003c, 2013, 2014; Chang 1996, 2009), typological (e.g. Lien 1999b, 2003c), psycholinguistic (e.g. Lien and Wang 1999), sociolinguistic (e.g. Lien 1999a), cognitive and/or pragmatic (e.g. Chang 2002; Li and Wang 2003; Lien

2003b, 2005a, 2007; Chang and Su 2012), and construction grammar (e.g. Lien 2001, 2003a, 2005b, 2008).

Much less work has been done on Southern Min varieties in Fujian, the birthplace of Southern Min (also other varieties in Guangdong, Hainan and Zhejiang). Previous research on Southern Min varieties in Fujian tends to stay mainly on a descriptive level (e.g. Chen 1992, 1993, 1994; Wang and Zhang 1994; Zhou and Ouyang 1998). In addition, the description is typically based on the framework of Mandarin Chinese, which, in fact, is not always applicable as the framework for research on Southern Min. Other research perspectives such as comparative and historical perspectives are mainly attested in a few studies during the recent years, e.g. Li (2005a), Shi (2012, 2013), Chen (2011, 2017), Zeng and Li (2013) and Xu (2017).

Note also that existing works on Southern Min mainly examine linguistic phenomena in a minority of varieties, especially those spoken in major cities, such as the Xiamen variety. Little attention has been paid to the varieties in the counties (or villages), such as Hui'an County, the focus of this book. Previous works on Southern Min in Hui'an County can only be found in the publications by Chen Fajin (e.g. Chen 1982, 1984, 1991) and his daughter Chen Manjun (e.g. Chen 2004, 2005, 2006, 2008, 2013). They do not indicate which specific variety their research is based on, except for Chen (2013:5, 14) who points out that her research is based on that spoken in the town of Luoyang 洛陽 (which belonged to Hui'an County before 2010). Moreover, her data is mainly collected from her parents and herself. This book, however, focuses on the variety spoken in the town of Luocheng 螺城 where the county seat of Hui'an is located, as mentioned above.

1.3 Data collection

The data used in this book are collected from the town of Luocheng, which is the county seat of Hui'an County. The town of Luocheng is around 24.5 kilometers away from the Licheng 鯉城 District, which is the political, economic and cultural center of Quanzhou City, as shown in Fig. 1-1 above.

The data for our analysis are mainly collected from the following three sources from 2005 to 2008:

(i) Naturally occurring conversation on diverse topics by native speakers who are representative of the Luocheng population. Total duration of the recordings is around 32.21 hours. People involved in conversations are the author's relatives and their friends of different generations, occupations and gender.

These conversations were collected via MP3 and first transcribed only into Chinese characters, due to the size of the corpus. In total 34 informants with different degrees of participation are involved in our data. A list of fourteen of these main informants are given in Table 1-1. For ethical reasons, all the names and personal information have been substituted by letters of the alphabet so that the participants cannot be identified from these data. For all the examples chosen in this grammar, names and personal information are changed to preserve anonymity. An example of transcription is given in (1) below.

Tab. 1-1: Major informants in 2019

Number	Age	Gender	Occupation
1	67	Male	Teacher
2	64	Female	Worker
3	39	Female	Officer
4	68	Female	Worker
5	69	Male	Worker
6	41	Female	Teacher
7	59	Male	Worker
8	54	Female	Freelance
9	83	Female	Farmer
10	69	Male	Teacher
11	67	Male	Officer
12	37	Female	Officer
13	69	Male	Worker
14	38	Male	Teacher

(1) An example of transcription
A: 阿三　汝　　無　　　　買　　啊
　　a¹sã¹　luɯ³　bo²⁻⁴　　bue³　aº
　　PN　　2SG　not.have　buy　SFP
　　'Ah-San, you didn't buy (anything)?'

B: 無　　　　買
　　bo²⁻⁴　　bue³
　　not.have　buy
　　'I didn't.'

C: 伊　　一直　　　　　說　　　　姆　　　買
　　i¹　　et⁷⁻⁸tet⁸⁻⁴　　sə ʔ⁷⁻⁸　m⁵⁻⁴　bue³
　　3SG　always　　　　say　　　not　　buy
　　'She'd been saying that she didn't want to buy (anything).'

This kind of data is able to largely reflect the daily usage of the Hui'an dialect and show the most natural way of expressing grammatical or semantic categories at the time when the fieldwork was conducted;

(ii) Systematic field elicitation via two questionnaires, i.e. Yue-Hashimoto (1993) and Liu and Tang (2003). The informants are asked to translate Mandarin words/sentences in the questionnaires into the Hui'an dialect version, or provide the usages of a morpheme or construction in the Hui'an dialect. It should be noted that it is easy to generate unnatural usages with this method, due to the influence of the language used in the questionnaires. The data collected by the questionnaires, however, can be used to supplement the data from conversations to a certain extent, since the conversations may not be able to cover all usages of a morpheme or syntactic construction;

(iii) Targeted investigations. We check a specific linguistic phenomenon with the native speakers during our research on a specific topic. For ethical reasons, no personal data are collected.

1.4 Presentation of examples in this reference grammar

Examples of the Hui'an dialect are generally given in a four-line format: their Chinese characters, IPA transcription (see §2.1 for a discussion on the transliteration practices for Southern Min), morpheme-by-morpheme gloss, and English translation. A homophonic character or the square symbol □ is used when no corresponding character is available. Round brackets are used in the case of syllable fusion, and for characters not used in contemporary Mandarin Chinese that are written from left to right with two vertical components and thus cannot be typed as a single character for Southern Min. For example, *khai⁰*（起來）is a fused form of *khi³lai⁰* 起來, while *bai⁵*（目賣）can be a verb meaning 'visit', in which '目賣' represents the single character which is written from left to right with the two vertical components '目' and '賣'. The gloss basically follows the Leipzig Glossing Rules.

Mandarin examples are also given in a four-line format unless reproduced from other sources, but are transcribed in *pīnyīn* with tone marks, rather than in IPA. Examples of other sources are basically quoted in their original forms, unless a four-line format is applicable.

1.5 Language usage in Hui'an

The elder generation basically uses only the Hui'an dialect in their daily lives, and some of them, especially women, can only speak the Hui'an dialect, that is, have no knowledge of Mandarin Chinese. The middle-aged adults normally can speak both the Hui'an dialect and Mandarin Chinese, but tend to use the Hui'an dialect both in and outside the family. On the contrary, the younger generation, especially those students in school, uses much more Mandarin Chinese than the other two generations mentioned above, especially at school and when they chat with their friends. Nowadays, young parents and even some grandparents use Mandarin Chinese with their children, although they speak the Hui'an dialect among themselves.

Most of the TV programs are broadcast and transmitted in Mandarin Chinese, though there is a program named *huin⁵⁻⁴uã¹ kaŋ³⁻²kɔ³* 惠安講古 telling stories using the Hui'an dialect.

A chapter on phonology is next presented which precedes the first major part of the grammar, Part I, on Nominal Structure.

2 Phonology

2.1 Introduction

This chapter aims to provide an outline of the main phonological properties relevant to the grammatical description. Thus, we will only give a brief introduction of phonology in Hui'an and make a simple comparison with other Southern Min varieties, especially those in Fujian, but do not present a detailed analysis of the phonetic and phonological features. This chapter is organized as follows. Sections 2.2 and 2.3 describe the initials and finals, respectively, followed by a discussion of tone and tone sandhi in §2.4. Section 2.5 presents examples of syllable fusion.

Before proceeding to this discussion, we say something about the transliteration of Southern Min. As mentioned by Cheng and Cheng (1994:5), at least more than ten sets of symbols have been put forward for the transliteration of Taiwan Southern Min or Amoy, of which Church Romanization has the longest history and is the most widely used, particularly in Taiwan in the domain of Southern Min linguistics, cultural anthropology and literature. As Lien (2001:174, note 1) explains, the transliteration of Taiwan Southern Min has been based on the Church Romanization given in Douglas (1873) with certain modifications, such as tone numbers instead of diacritics. As for the literature on Southern Min written by linguists in Mainland China such as Zhou and Ouyang (1998) and Qian (2002), the transliteration is mainly based on the International Phonetic Alphabet (IPA). In this book, we use a phonemic orthography based on IPA for the Hui'an dialect.

2.2 Initials

There are fourteen initial phonemes in Hui'an, which are shown in Table 2-1.

Tab.2-1: Initials in the Hui'an dialect

	Labial			Dental/Alveolar			Velar		Glottal
Plosive	p	ph	b	t	th	l	k	kh	g	ø
Affricate				ts(tɕ)	tsh(tɕh)					
Fricative					s(ɕ)				h
Nasal		(m)			(n)			(ŋ)	

The initials in Hui'an are similar to those in other Southern Min varieties in terms of inventory except that there is one more initial, i.e. the voiced affricate /z/[dz] (or /j/[dz])[1] in Zhangzhou, Shantou, Jieyang and Taiwan (except for some varieties such as the Taibei variety), which has merged with the initial *l* in Hui'an, Quanzhou and Xiamen (also Taibei and Tainan in Taiwan), or has merged with the initial *g* in Jiayi and Pingdong in Taiwan (Zhou 2006:15, Lin and Chen 1996:13-14, Xu 2007:19, Cheng 1997b:10).

As in other varieties of Southern Min, there exist three sets of initial plosives: voiceless unaspirated (*p*, *t*, *k*), voiceless aspirated (*ph*, *th*, *kh*) and voiced (*b*, *l*, *g*). The nasals *m*, *n* and *ŋ* only occur before either nasalized vowels or finals with a nasal coda, in complementary distribution with the plosives *b*, *l* and *g*, respectively, which are never followed by nasalized vowels or finals with a nasal coda. This suggests that *m* and *b*, *n* and *l*, *ŋ* and *g* constitute one initial phoneme, respectively. Following previous works on Southern Min such as Yang (1991), these initials are phonemically transcribed as /b/, /l/ and /g/ as, for example, in *bua²* 磨 'rub' and *buã³*[muã³] 滿 'full', respectively. Thus, *m*, *n*, and *ŋ* are placed in round brackets in Table 2-1.

In the speech of younger generation, the plosive *g* is lost in some words, e.g. *gua³* -> *ua³* 我 'I', or is pronounced as *b*, e.g. *gu²* -> *bu²* 牛 'cattle'. A similar phenomenon is noted by Cheng (1997b:10) in Taiwan Southern Min: not only the plosive *g* but also *b* are being lost as in *oá* and *sīn-ūn* which are originally *goá* 我 'I' and *sīn-būn* 新聞 'news', respectively.

The nature of *l* is controversial in previous works on Southern Min. It is regarded as a lateral approximant in Luo (1956[1930]), but regarded as a plosive (or stop) in Zhong (2002) and Zhu (2010), or as a flap in Lin (1989) and Cheng (1997b).

---

[1] Note that /z/[dz] is used by Zhou (2006), Lin and Chen (1996) and Xu (2007), while /j/[dz] is used by Cheng (1997b).

Those who regard *l* as a lateral approximant usually also mention the similarity between *l* and *d*. For example, Luo (1956[1930]) points out that *l* in Xiamen has a tendency to approach *d*. Due to the fact that *b*, *l*, and *g* are in complementary distribution with the nasals *m*, *n* and *ŋ*, we regard *l* as a plosive in this book, following previous works such as Zhong (2002) and Zhu (2010), one advantage of which is that the system of consonant initials constitutes a neat parallelism.

When occurring before the front vowel *i*, the initials *ts*, *tsh* and *s* are pronounced like the alveo-palatal obstruents *tɕ*, *tɕh* and *ɕ*, respectively. In other words, they undergo palatalization. This palatalization phenomenon is also noted by Luo (1956[1930]:7), Dong (1974:279) and Yang (1991:24). However, Dong (1974:279) observes that, in Xiamen, palatalization also happens when *ts*, *tsh* and *s* occur before the front vowel [e].

The symbol ø in Table 2-1, realized as a glottal stop [ʔ], is traditionally used to refer to zero initials occurring before syllables beginning with a vowel. Note that the glottal stop [ʔ] is regarded as a feature of entering tone, but not a segment in Zhong (2002:18-31). The place of articulation of the initial *h* in Hui'an is further back than the fricative *x* in Mandarin Chinese.

2.3 Finals

Zhu (2010:319) classifies the finals in Xiamen into four main categories in terms of their codas, subcategories of which are represented as follows.
(a) finals without a consonantal coda
    (i) without a coda: oral and nasal vowels
    (ii) with a glide coda: oral and nasal vowels
(b) finals with a glottal plosive coda
    (i) with a single glottal plosive coda: oral and nasal vowels
    (ii) with a glide and a glottal plosive coda: oral and nasal vowels
(c) finals with a nasal coda *m/n/ŋ*
(d) finals ending with an unreleased plosive *p/t/k*

Following this classification of Zhu (2010), the finals in Hui'an are presented in Table 2-2. There are eighty-one altogether.

Tab. 2-2: Finals in the Hui'an dialect

	Non-consonantal coda				Glottal plosive coda				Nasal coda			Plosive coda		
	no coda		glide coda[2]		glottal plosive coda		glide+ glottal plosive coda		-m	-n	-ŋ	-p	-t	-k
	OV[3]	NV	OV	NV	OV	NV	OV	NV						
	1	2	3	4	5	6	7	8	9	10	11	12	13	14
1	i				iʔ	ĩʔ				in[4]	iŋ		it	
2	u				uʔ					un				
3	a	ã	au		aʔ	ãʔ	auʔ	ãuʔ	am	an	aŋ	ap	at	ak
4			ai	ãi										
5	e	ẽ			eʔ	ẽʔ				en			et	
6	o				oʔ									
7	ɔ	ɔ̃			ɔʔ	ɔ̃ʔ					ɔŋ			ɔk
8	ɯ													
9	ə				əʔ					ən				
10	iu	iũ			iuʔ									
11	ia	iã	iau	iãu	iaʔ	iãʔ	iauʔ	iãuʔ			iaŋ		iat	iak
12	io				ioʔ									
13											iɔŋ			iɔk
14									iəm			iəp		
15	ui				uiʔ					uin				
16	ua	uã	uai	uãi	uaʔ			uãiʔ		uan	uaŋ		uat	
17	ue				ueʔ								ut	
18								mʔ ŋʔ	m		ŋ			

The frequencies of words found with the finals above differ widely. The following finals: *ĩʔ, ãi, ẽ, ẽʔ, ɔʔ, ɔ̃ʔ, iuʔ, iãu, iauʔ, iãuʔ, uai, uãiʔ* and *uaŋ*, only exist in a few

---

2 *u* and *i* at the medial or final position as in *au* and *uai*, are transcribed as *w* and *j*, as in *aw* and *waj* in Zhu (2010). In this volume however, we use *u* and *i* as in *au* and *uai*, following most other descriptions of related Southern Min varieties.
3 'OV' and 'NV' refer to oral vowel and nasal vowel, respectively.
4 Note that in our recent fieldwork with a new elder informant (January 2019), the pronunciation is more like *ĩ*. A similar phenomenon is also attested in the final *uin* (i.e. *uin* vs. *uĩ*).

words, some of which are onomatopoeic syllables, or just in one word. For example, there is only one word for the final *uaŋ*: *huaŋ¹* 風 'wind'.

2.4 Tone

2.4.1 Citation tones

There are seven citation tones in Hui'an, as shown in Table 2-3 below.

Tab. 2-3: Citation tones in the Hui'an dialect

Tone number	Classical tone categories[5]	Pitch description	Examples
1	*yīn píng* 陰平	33 mid level	*hue¹* 花 'follower'
2	*yáng píng* 陽平	24 low rising	*kiŋ²* 窮 'poor'
3	*yīn shǎng* 陰上	53 high falling	*kɔ³* 古 'old'
4	*yáng shǎng* 陽上	22 low level	*si⁴* 是 'yes'
5	*yīn qù* 陰去	31 mid falling	*si⁵* 四 'four'
6	*yáng qù* 陽去	31 mid falling	*hai⁵* 害 'harm'
7	*yīn rù* 陰入	<u>54</u> high falling checked	*kiəp⁷* 急 'urgent'
8	*yáng rù* 陽入	3 mid rising checked	*liəp⁸* 入 'enter'

Southern Min in Fujian and Taiwan has generally developed a 7-tone system, but in different ways. For example, as shown in Table 2-3 above, Tones 5 (*yīn qù*) and 6 (*yáng qù*) have merged into one tone in Hui'an, as in Quanzhou (Zhou 2006:17), while Tone 4 (*yáng shǎng*) has merged with Tone 6 (*yáng qù*) in Xiamen and Zhangzhou (Zhou 2006:17), and Tone 3 (*yīn shǎng*) has generally merged with Tone 4 (*yáng shǎng*) in Taiwan (Cheng 1997b:26). However, Southern Min in Guangdong such as Chaozhou, Shantou and Jieyang generally retains an 8-tone system (Ma 2002:53-54, Xu 2007:24). The Longyan variety in Fujian and the Lugang variety in Taiwan also have an 8-tone system (Ma 2002:51, 74).

---

5 In the history of Chinese phonology, the four tone categories *píng* 平 'level', *shǎng* 上 'rising', *qù* 去 'departing' and *rù* 入 'entering' established since Middle Chinese (AD 200-900) have undergone various splits and merges. For example, each of the four tone categories may be split into a high and a low register, i.e. *yīn* 陰 and *yáng* 陽, which thus yields a symmetrical eight-tone system (cf. Chen 2000:5-7).

2.4.2 Tone sandhi

Tone sandhi is a tonal alternation in connected speech, in which the tones assigned to individual morphemes or words change, based on their adjacent tones. As with other Chinese varieties, tone sandhi is triggered in Hui'an when syllables with specific tone values are juxtaposed in a word or phrase. Different tone systems in Southern Min present tone sandhi according to different sets of rules. Tone sandhi in Hui'an is similar to that in Quanzhou as shown by the examples in Zhou (2006). In this section, we will first give a brief introduction to the general tone sandhi rules, followed by an introduction to special tone sandhi rules in reduplicated forms of adjectives.

In Hui'an, the last morpheme or word in a word or phrase, usually retains its citation tone, while the preceding morpheme(s) or word(s) have to undergo tone sandhi unless the last morpheme or word is in a neutral tone (see §2.4.4). The general tone sandhi rules are shown in Table 2-4 below.

Tab. 2-4: General tone sandhi rules in the Hui'an dialect

Classical tone categories	yīn píng 陰平	yáng píng 陽平	yīn shǎng 陰上	yáng shǎng 陽上	yīn qù 陰去	yáng qù 陽去	yīn rù 陰入	yáng rù 陽入
Citation tone	T1(33)	T2(24)	T3(53)	T4(22)	T5(31)	T5(31)	T7(54)	T8(3)
Sandhi tone	T1(33)	T4(22)	T2(24)	T4(22)	T3(53)	T4(22)	T8(3)	T4(22)

It can be seen from Table 2-4 that:
(a) T1 (33) remains unchanged preceding other tones, e.g. $tshia^{33}lɔ^{31}$ -> $tshia^{33}lɔ^{31}$ 車路 'road';
(b) T2 (24) changes to T4 (22) preceding other tones, e.g. $si^{24}kan^{33}$ -> $si^{22}kan^{33}$ 時間 'time';
(c) T3 (53) changes to T2 (24) preceding other tones, e.g. $pun^{53}lai^{24}$ -> $pun^{24}lai^{24}$ 本來 'originally';
(d) T4 (22) remains unchanged preceding other tones, e.g. $u^{22}si^{24}$ -> $u^{22}si^{24}$ 有時 'sometimes';

(e) As mentioned in §2.4.1, the classical tone categories *yīn qù* and *yáng qù* have the same citation tone, i.e. T5 (31) in Hui'an, however, their sandhi tones are different: *yīn qù* changes to T3 (53) preceding other tones as in *kaŋ³¹ke²²* -> *kaŋ⁵³ke²²* 降低 'lower', while *yáng qù* changes to T4 (22) as in *ben³¹kən³³* -> *ben²²kən³³* 面巾 'towel';
(f) T7 (54) changes to T8 (3) preceding other tones, e.g. *peʔ⁵⁴pak⁵⁴* -> *peʔ³pak⁵⁴* 憋腹 'worry';
(g) T8 (3) changes to T4 (22) preceding other tones, e.g. *bak³tsiu³³* -> *bak²²tsiu³³* 目珠 'eye'.

In other Southern Min varieties such as Xiamen and Taiwan, triplicated adjectives do not follow the general tone sandhi rules (Zhou and Ouyang 1998:25, Cheng 1997b:28). In Hui'an, not only the triplicated adjectives but also other reduplicated forms of adjectives depart from the general tone sandhi rules. In addition, tone sandhi rules applied to triplicated adjectives in Hui'an are different from those in Xiamen or Taiwan. The tone sandhi rules for reduplicated adjectives are shown in Table 2-5 below.

Tab. 2-5: Tone sandhi rules of reduplicated adjectives

Citation tone	T1(33), T2(24), T3(53), T4(22)	T5(31)	T7(54)	T8(3)
Sandhi tone	T2(24)	T2(24)/55	T8(3)	T8(3)

The first adjective in reduplicated adjectives undergoes tone sandhi as indicated in Table 2-5 above, while the second adjective retains its citation tone. It can be seen from Table 2-5 that:
(a) non-entering tones change to T2 (24), unless T2 (24) is the original tone which remains unchanged. Note that T2 (24) is also the general sandhi form of T3 (53);
(b) T5 (31) can also change to a tone with a value of 55;
(c) T7 (54) changes to T8 (3), which is the same as its general tone sandhi rule;
(d) T8 (3) retains its citation tone.

Examples are given in (1) below.

(1) a. $ɔ^{33}$ 烏 'black' -> $ɔ^{24}$ + $ɔ^{33}$ 烏烏 'a state of being black'
b. $kuin^{24}$ 懸 'high' -> **$kuin^{24}$** + $kuin^{24}$ 懸懸 'a state of being high'
c. pa^{53} 飽 'full' -> **pa^{24}** + pa^{53} 飽飽 'a state of being full'
d. lau^{22} 老 'old' -> lau^{24} + lau^{22} 老老 'a state of being old'
e. $tshau^{31}$ 臭 'smelly' -> **$tshau^{24}$**/$tshau^{55}$ + $tshau^{31}$ 臭臭 'a state of being smelly'
f. $theʔ^{54}$ 澈 'clean' -> **$theʔ^{3}$** + $theʔ^{54}$ 澈澈 'a state of being clean'
g. $peʔ^{3}$ 白 'white' -> $peʔ^{3}$ + $peʔ^{3}$ 白白 'a state of being white'

Triplicated adjectives are formed by inserting one more adjective with T4 (22), as in $ɔ^{33}$ 烏 'black' -> $ɔ^{24}$ + $ɔ^{22}$ + $ɔ^{33}$ 烏烏烏 'a state of being black' and $peʔ^{3}$ 白 'white' -> $peʔ^{3}$ + **$peʔ^{22}$** + $peʔ^{3}$ 白白白 'a state of being white'. The same adjective with T4 (22) can be further inserted to strengthen the degree of the state indicated by the adjective, as in $ɔ^{33}$ 烏 'black' -> $ɔ^{24}$ $ɔ^{22}$ $ɔ^{22}$ $ɔ^{33}$ 烏烏烏烏 and $ɔ^{33}$ 烏 'black' -> $ɔ^{24}$ $ɔ^{22}$ $ɔ^{22}$ $ɔ^{22}$ $ɔ^{33}$ 烏烏烏烏烏.

2.4.3 Tonemic representation of citation and sandhi tones

In our phonemic representation, tones are represented by numbers referring to tone categories as shown in Table 2-3. The citation tone is followed by the sandhi tone (if any), separated by a hyphen. Take $bo^{2\text{-}4}$ 無 'not have' for example, *2* refers to the second tone (i.e. T2 (24)) standing for the citation tone, while *4* refers to the fourth tone (i.e. T4 (22)) indicating the sandhi tone (see also Tables 2-3 and 2-4).

2.4.4 Neutral tone and stress

In Southern Min including the Hui'an dialect, there exist some morphemes whose tones are short and light, and cannot be grouped into one of the seven/eight citation tones since they do not possess any of the tone contours for the citation tones. Tones of these morphemes are traditionally regarded as neutral tone. It should be noted that the term 'neutral tone' here is different from the term *qīngshēng* 輕聲 in the literature on Chinese linguistics, since *qīngshēng* is at least used in two ways, meaning either (a) an unstressed syllable or (b) the neutral tone (Lu and Wang 2005:107) in the sense we are using it.

As for the neutral tone in Southern Min, Wang (1996), Zhou and Ouyang (1998:33-36) and Cheng (1997b, 1997c) present detailed discussions on neutral tone in Quanzhou, Xiamen and Taiwan, respectively, which suggest a high degree of similarity in different Southern Min varieties in Fujian and Taiwan. Neutral tone can be divided into two types: (a) neutral tone involving lexical items and (b) neutral tone involving grammatical morphemes. Type (a) neutral tone is rare in Taiwan Southern Min (Cheng 1997b:105), which is also true for the Hui'an dialect. The following are some examples from Hui'an, which are also found in other Southern Min varieties such as Taiwan, Quanzhou and Xiamen.

(2) a. let^8si^0 日時 'day time'; bin^2si^0 暝時 'night'
   b. $tso?^8let^0$ 昨日 'the day before yesterday'; au^4let^0 後日 'the day after tomorrow'
   c. $lua?^8laŋ^0$ 熱冬 'summer'; $ku\tilde{a}^2laŋ^0$ 寒冬 'winter'
   d. ho^3tshu^0 好處 'advantage'; $phai^3tshu^0$ 否處 'disadvantage'

Type (b) neutral tone involves grammatical morphemes such as sentence-final particles and some aspect markers. For example, all sentence-final particles in Hui'an are in the neutral tone (see Chen and Wu 2015 for details of type (b) neutral tone).

Languages in the world are traditionally classified into two types: tone languages and stress/accent languages. Chinese is regarded as a typical example of tone languages. Whether there exists 'stress' and how 'stress' is indicated in Chinese are controversial issues in the literature. Most linguists nowadays agree that at least some Chinese varieties have 'stress'. The strongest evidence comes from changes of tone (e.g. Cheng and Zeng 1997:244). Cheng and Zeng (1997:244-248) suggest that changes of tone indicating stress fall into five types: (a) the original tone becomes more prominent, e.g. the first syllable in triplicated adjectives; (b) the stressed syllable retains its citation tone while the mid-stressed syllable undergoes tone sandhi[6]; (c) unstressed syllables do not have a tonal contrast (i.e. they have neutral tone); and (d) tonal spread occurs from stressed syllables to unstressed syllables.

Unlike the classification of Cheng and Zeng (1997), stress in Hui'an is divided into two main categories: (a) stressed; and (b) unstressed. Stressed syllables can be classified into three types: (a) stressed syllables which retain their citation tones; (b) syllables with contrastive stress which retain their citation tone contours with an increased intensity; and (c) the first syllable in a duplicated adjective whose tone changes to the mid-rising tone T2 (24) or the high level tone with

---

[6] In Cheng and Zeng (1997), citation tone, sandhi tone and neutral tone are associated with stressed, mid-stressed and unstressed syllables, respectively.

a value of 55. Unstressed syllables fall into three types: (a) unstressed syllables which undergo tone sandhi; (b) unstressed syllables whose tones are shorter and lighter than their citation tones, but retain their original tone contour, as opposed to syllables with contrastive stress; and (c) unstressed syllables which are in neutral tone.

Neutral tone is generally regarded as a result of syllables being unstressed (e.g. Xu 1980, Liu 2002, Lu and Wang 2005). Our classification of unstressed syllables above, however, suggests that (a) unstressed syllables do not necessarily result in neutral tone; and (b) unstressed syllables are only one factor in the emergence of neutral tone. In other words, the emergence of neutral tone needs more in-depth explanation(s).

2.5 Syllable fusion

Syllable fusion refers to the phenomenon whereby two syllables are reduced to one with loss of the boundary between the original two syllables. Zhong (2002:121-155) presents a detailed discussion on syllable fusion in Taiwan Southern Min. This section does not attempt to examine syllable fusion in detail, but gives some examples regarded as instances of syllable fusion in Hui'an, as shown in (3) and (4), which are obligatory and optional, respectively (see also Chen and Wu 2015).

(3) Frozen fused forms
   a. m^5 唔 'not' + a^0 啊 'SFP' -> ma^0 ($b\tilde{a}^0$) 'interrogative particle'
   b. $sa^1 tan^2$ 相同 -> san^2 'same'; then sa^1 is added before san^2 again to form $sa^1 san^2$
   c. $kin^1 a^{3\text{-}2} let^8$ 今仔日 -> $ki\tilde{a}^1 let^8$ 'today'
   d. $bin^{2\text{-}4} a^{3\text{-}2} let^8$ 明仔日 -> $bin^{2\text{-}4} a^{3\text{-}2} let^8$ -> $bi\tilde{a}^{2\text{-}4} let^8$ 'tomorrow'
   e. $tsit^{8\text{-}4} e^4$ 蜀下 'once, one time' -> tse^0 'delimitative marker'

(4) Optionally fused forms
   a. $si^4 m^5 a^0$ 是唔啊 -> $si^4 ma^0$ -> $si\tilde{a}^0$ 'right?'
   b. $m^{5\text{-}4} lɔŋ^3$ 唔攏 -> $bɔŋ^3$ 'possibly'
   c. $li^{5\text{-}4} tsap^8$ 二十 -> $liəp^8$ 'twenty'
   d. $khi^3 lai^0$ 起來 -> $khai^0$ 'come up'
   e. $m^{5\text{-}4} thaŋ^1$ 唔通 -> $m^{5\text{-}4} baŋ^1$ -> $baŋ^1$ 'should not'

2.6 Summary

This chapter has provided an outline of the main phonological properties relevant to grammatical description including initials, finals, tone and syllable fusion. There are fourteen initial phonemes, eighty-one finals and seven citation tones. Several examples of syllable fusion are given in §2.5.

Initials in Hui'an are the same as those in Quanzhou and Xiamen in terms of inventory. The voiced affricate /z/ [dz] in Zhangzhou, Shantou and Jieyang has merged with the initial /l/ in Hui'an. As in other Southern Min varieties, there exist three sets of plosives: voiceless unaspirated (*p, t, k*), voiceless aspirated (*ph, th, kh*) and voiced (*b, l, g*). In the speech of the younger generation, the plosive [g] is lost in some words or pronounced as [b]. The nature of [l] is controversial in the literature. In this book, [l] is grouped among the plosives, one advantage of which is that the initial system is thus constituted by a neat parallelism. The initials *ts*, *tsh* and *s* undergo palatalization to form a corresponding set of allophones when they occur before the front vowel *i*.

Following Zhu (2010), finals are classified into four main types as shown in Table 2-2: (a) finals without a consonantal coda; (b) finals with a glottal plosive coda; (c) finals with a nasal coda; and (d) finals ending with a unreleased plosive *p/t/k*.

Southern Min in Fujian and Taiwan has generally developed a 7-tone system, but in different ways. The classical tone categories *yīn qù* and *yáng qù* have merged into one tone in Hui'an, as in Quanzhou. In Hui'an, the last morpheme or word in a word or phrase, usually retains its citation tone, while the preceding morpheme(s) or word(s) have to undergo tone sandhi unless the last morpheme or word is in a neutral tone. As with other varieties such as Xiamen and Taiwan, triplicated adjectives in Hui'an depart from the general tone sandhi rules, according to a different set. In addition, other reduplicated forms of adjectives in Hui'an also do not follow the general tone sandhi.

Neutral tone falls into two types: (a) involving lexical items and (b) involving grammatical morphemes. The application of stress divides syllables in Hui'an into two main categories: (a) stressed and (b) unstressed.

Stressed syllables are classified into three types: (a) stressed syllables which retain their citation tones; (b) syllables with contrastive stress which retain their citation tone contours with an increased intensity; and (c) the first syllable in a duplicated adjective whose tone changes to the mid-rising tone T2 (24) or the high level tone with a value of 55. Unstressed syllables also fall into three types: (a) unstressed syllables which undergo tone sandhi; (b) unstressed syllables whose tones are shorter and lighter than their citation tones, but retain their original tone contour, as opposed to contrastive stress syllables; and (c) unstressed syllables which are in neutral tone. Neutral tone is generally regarded as a result of syllables being unstressed. However, our classification of unstressed syllables may suggest that (a) unstressed syllables do not necessarily result in neutral tone; and (b) unstressed syllables are only one factor in the emergence of neutral tone.

Part I: **Nominal structure**

In this part, we examine the following aspects of nominal structure: affixation and compounding (chapter 3), pronouns (chapter 4), nominal demonstratives (chapter 5), numerals and quantifiers (chapter 6), classifiers (chapter 7) and possessive constructions (chapter 8). Chapter 4 focuses on personal pronouns, reflexive pronouns, reciprocal pronouns and words meaning 'other, other people', while demonstrative pronouns are examined separately under the heading of nominal demonstratives in chapter 5. Note, however, that in Hui'an there is no independent reciprocal pronoun, and the reciprocal meaning is encoded by the reciprocal prefix *sa¹* 相.

3 Affixation and compounding

3.1 Introduction

Morphology traditionally refers to the study of the internal structure of words. As with other Chinese varieties, words in Hui'an fall into two main categories: (a) simple words consisting of one free morpheme and (b) complex words consisting of at least two morphemes. Processes of complex word formation are traditionally classified into three types, that is, reduplication, affixation and compounding, of which, affixation and compounding are involved in noun formation in Hui'an.

3.2 Affixation

3.2.1 Prefixes

Commonly used prefixes include *a* 阿, *lau* 老, *sio^3* 小, *tshue^1* 初 and *te^5* 第, of which *lau* 老, *sio^3* 小, *tshue^1* 初 and *te^5* 第 are similar to their counterparts, not only in other Southern Min varieties, but also in Mandarin Chinese. A description of the most commonly used prefix *a* 阿 is given in §3.2.1.1. Note that this prefix is realized with different tones when used with different morphemes.[1] Similarly, the prefix *lau* 老 is realized with different tones, as will be shown in §3.2.1.2. Other prefixes will be briefly mentioned in §3.2.1.3.

3.2.1.1 *a*-阿 in kinship terms and names

The prefix *a* 阿 is normally used to form a kinship term or nickname, both of which (with a few exceptions, see below) function as address terms and reference terms.

The kinship terms formed with *a* are listed in Table 3-1 below, noting that not all kinship terms are formed on this model.

---

[1] The reason for these tone differences requires further investigation.

Tab. 3-1: Kinship terms with the prefix *a* 阿

a¹kɔŋ¹ 阿公 'grandfather'	*a¹bã³* 阿媽 'grandmother'
a¹pa⁵ 阿爸 'father'	*a¹bu³* 阿母 'mother'
a¹kɔ¹ 阿姑 'father's sister'	*a¹i²* 阿姨 'mother's sister'
a¹peʔ⁷ 阿伯 'father's elder brother'	*a¹ku⁴* 阿舅 'mother's brother'
a¹tsiak⁷ 阿叔 'father's younger brother'	
a¹m³ 阿姆 'father's elder brother's wife'	*a¹kiam⁴* 阿妗 'mother's brother's wife'
a¹tsiəm³ 阿嬸 'father's younger brother's wife'	
a¹hiã¹ 阿兄 'elder brother'	*a¹tsi³* 阿姊 'elder sister'
a¹ko¹ 阿哥 'elder brother'	
a¹so³ 阿嫂 'elder brother's wife'	*a¹tiũ⁴* 阿丈 'elder sister's husband'

All the kinship terms in Table 3-1 are used as both address and reference terms. Among these terms, both *a¹hiã¹* and *a¹ko¹* are used to refer to 'elder brother'. However, according to older native speakers, *a¹ko¹* has come into use under the influence of Mandarin Chinese. Another point to be noted is that both *a¹pa⁵* 'father' and *a¹bu³* 'mother' are typically used by the older generation, while the younger generation tends to use *pa²a⁰* 爸仔 and *bã²a⁰* 媽仔² with the suffix *a⁰* 仔 (see §3.2.2.2) instead. These kinship terms with prefix *a¹* may also be followed by the diminutive suffix *a³* 仔 (see §3.2.2.1) when the addressee is not much older or even younger than the speaker. For example, if person A is in the same age group as person B, but has to call person B *a¹kɔ¹* 阿姑 'aunt' according to their position in the family tree, then they use *a¹kɔ¹a³* 阿姑仔 instead of *a¹kɔ¹*, as both a term of address and a term of reference.

Other kinship terms are not formed with the prefix *a*, such as *sio³⁻²ti⁴* 小弟 'younger brother'³, *sio³⁻²tsiəm³* 小嬸 '(husband's) younger brother's wife', *sio³⁻²bə⁵* 小妹 'younger sister', *bə⁵⁻⁴sai⁵* 妹婿 'younger sister's husband', *kɔ¹tiũ⁴* 姑丈 'father's sister's husband' and *i²⁻⁴tiũ⁴* 姨丈 'mother's sister's husband', among which *sio³⁻²ti⁴*, *sio³⁻²tsiəm³* and *sio³⁻²bə⁵* use the prefix *sio³* 小 (see §3.2.1.3) instead of *a¹*. The terms *sio³⁻²tsiəm³* and *bə⁵⁻⁴sai⁵* are only used as a reference term, whereas others can be used as both a reference term and an address term.

Besides constituting part of kinship terms, the prefix *a* can be used to form a nickname with a given name (when the given name has only one syllable) or the

---

2 Note that the kinship term *bã²* 媽 'mother' has come into use under the influence of Mandarin Chinese.

3 Note that *a-ti* 阿弟 'younger brother' as a term of address can be attested in the Xiamen, Quanzhou and Zhangzhou varieties of Southern Min (Zhou et al. 2006: 63).

last syllable of a given name (when the given name has more than one syllable). To briefly digress, Chinese names are composed of the family name followed by the given name which can be composed of one or two syllables, each representing a morpheme. For example, a girl named $ɔŋ^{2-4}$ $suat^{7-8}buin^2$ 王雪梅, in which $ɔŋ^2$ 王 and $suat^{7-8}buin^2$ 雪梅 are the surname and the given name respectively, would usually have a nickname a^1buin^2 阿梅 in which $buin^2$ is the last syllable of the given name $suat^{7-8}buin^2$. However, the first syllable of the given name, i.e. $suat^7$ 雪, can also be used for a nickname when the first syllable is considered to sound better or to be easier to pronounce than the last syllable: a^1suat^7 阿雪.

A nickname may also be formed by the prefix a and the position of a person in the family tree, such as $a^{3-2}tua^5$ 阿大, $a^{3-2}li^5$ 阿二 and $a^1sã^1$ 阿三, referring to a person who is the first, second and third child in a family, respectively. As with nicknames mentioned above, the nickname $a^1sã^1$ can be used as both an address term and a reference term, while $a^{3-2}tua^5$ and $a^{3-2}li^5$ with a different tone from a^1 in $a^1sã^1$ are typically used as reference terms (see kinship terms above for the corresponding terms of address).

A nickname may also consist of a^1 combined with any noun desired, e.g. someone may be called a^1kau^3 阿狗 in which kau^3 means 'dog', which is not associated with the person's formal name. Nicknames such as a^1kau^3 usually involve people's desire for their child to grow up healthy.[4] However, nicknames of this type are uncommon nowadays.

Besides kinship terms and nicknames, the prefix a^1 can also be used with words indicating a characteristic of a person or a group of people to form a reference term. For example, a^1pak^7 阿北, usually followed by the diminutive suffix a^3 仔, refers to someone who comes from the north.

The terms formed with the prefix a discussed above, with the exception of $a^{3-2}tua^5$ 阿大, $a^{3-2}li^5$ 阿二 and $a^1pak^{7-8}a^3$ 阿北仔, are used as both address and reference terms with exactly the same pronunciation a^1. This is different from the Quanzhou variety, where the prefix a 阿 has to be pronounced respectively as a^1 or a^3 when used for address or reference terms (Wang and Zhang 1994:92). Wang and Zhang also mention that this prefix can be traced back to the Han, Wei and Six Dynasties Periods (BC 206 –AD 581).

---

4 According to an earlier custom of Southern Min speakers, people believe that it is easier for children to grow up with a nickname formed by the prefix a^1 and an animal name, especially in difficult times to ward off evil influences or bad luck, for example, not only a^1 kau^3 阿狗 (prefix + dog) but also a^1 tu^1 阿豬 (prefix + pig).

There is another prefix *an¹* 安 used before some kinship terms such as *kɔŋ¹* 公 'grandfather' in Xiamen, Quanzhou and Zhangzhou (Zhang and Ouyang 1998: 266; Zhou et al. 2006:387), which is not found in Hui'an.

3.2.1.2 Prefix *lau*- 老

The uses of the prefix *lau* 老, originally an adjective meaning 'old', are basically the same as the prefix *lǎo* 老 in Mandarin Chinese, that is, it can be used with the kinship terms *pe⁴* 爸 'father' and *bu³* 母 'mother', morphemes indicating persons or animals as in *lau⁴su¹* 老師 'teacher' and *lau³⁻²hɔ³* 老虎 'tiger', or a surname as in *lau³⁻²tiũ¹* 老張 'Mr. Zhang', or the position in the family tree as in *lau³⁻²tua⁵* 老大 'the first child'. This, however, is slightly different from its use in Taiwan Southern Min where the prefix *lau²* 老 normally precedes a surname or the position in a family tree, which has to be further followed by the suffix *e⁰*, as in *lau² ong⁵ e⁰* 老王其 'Mr. Wang' (Yang 1991: 163-164).

Note that *lau* is realized as *lau⁴* with a fourth tone when functioning as an adjective meaning 'old', or as a prefix in words such as *lau⁴pe⁴* 老爸 'father', *lau⁴bu³* 老母 'mother', *lau⁴su¹* 老師 'teacher' and *lau⁴bə³* 老尾 'the last child'. However, *lau* is realized as *lau³* with a third tone when functioning as an adjective meaning 'experienced; long standing', or as a prefix in words such as *lau³⁻²pan³* 老闆 'boss', *lau³⁻²hɔ³* 老虎 'tiger', *lau³⁻²tiũ¹* 老張 'Mr. Zhang' and *lau³⁻²tua⁵* 老大 'the first child'.

3.2.1.3 Other prefixes

The prefix *sio³* 小 < 'little, small' can be followed by a noun as in *sio³⁻²piŋ²⁻⁴iu³* 小朋友 'little friend' and *sio³⁻²tshia¹* 小車 'car', a kinship term as in *sio³⁻²ti⁴* 小弟 'younger brother' and *sio³⁻²bə⁵* 小妹 'younger sister', or a surname as in *sio³⁻²ɔŋ²* 小王 'Mr. Wang'. The prefix *sio³* is also often used as the first syllable of a given name as in *sio³⁻²ui³* 小偉 and *sio³⁻²en⁵* 小燕 where *ui³* and *en⁵* mean 'great' and 'swallow', respectively.

Like the prefix *chū* 初 < 'beginning, first' in Mandarin Chinese, the prefix *tshue¹* 初 in Hui'an precedes the numerals *et⁷* 一 'one' through *tsap⁸* 十 'ten' to denote the first ten days of a lunar month.

The prefix *te⁵* 第 < 'order' is followed by whole numbers to form ordinal numbers such as *te⁵⁻⁴et⁷* 第一 'first' (<*te⁵* + *et⁷* 'one'), like its counterparts in Mandarin Chinese and other Southern Min varieties. In addition, *te⁵* can be followed by *bə³* 尾 'tail; end' to express 'the last', as in *i¹ tsau³⁻² te⁵⁻⁴bə³⁻² biã²* 伊走第尾名 'he ran last'.

3.2.2 Suffixes

Suffixes outnumber prefixes in Southern Min. Commonly used suffixes in Hui'an include the following forms with their lexical sources: a^3/a^0 仔 < 'child', sai^1 師 < 'master', sen^1 仙 < 'celestial being, immortal', sen^2 神 < 'god, deity', $tsin^1$ 精 < 'spirit, demon', $tsiau^3$ 鳥 < 'bird', kui^3 鬼 < 'ghost', and $thau$ 頭 < 'head'.

3.2.2.1 Diminutive suffix a^3 仔

Cross-linguistically, the semantic category of the diminutive may involve a range of senses such as small size, affection, approximation and imitation (cf. Jurafsky 1996, among others). The basic marker of the diminutive in Hui'an is the suffix a^3. Like other Southern Min varieties, this is also the most commonly used suffix in Hui'an. Much work has been done on its counterparts in other Southern Min varieties in terms of semantic, morphological and phonological features, sources and grammaticalization (e.g. Chen 1997, Lien 1998, Yang 2000, Xu 2000, Li 2005a, Zheng and Chen 2005). In this section, we focus on syntactic distribution and semantic/pragmatic senses. As for syntactic distribution, a^3 仔 can be attached to a noun, 'NUM + CL', a verb(phrase), a reduplicated adjective, or a temporal word, as shown in the following examples. In other words, what the suffix a^3 follows is cross-categorial. Furthermore, it shows a variety of functions which are described below. For convenience of analysis, the use of a^3 仔 in non-noun formation has also been included.

Attached to a noun
(a) attached to a kinship term
   (i) to express 'young'
   As mentioned in §3.2.1.1, this suffix can be preceded by the prefix a^1 阿 and a kinship term as in $a^1ko^1a^3$ 阿姑仔 'little aunt' when the addressee is not much older or even younger than the speaker, which suggests that the suffix a^3 仔 expresses the meaning of 'young'. As in other Southern Min varieties such as Xiamen and Taiwan (Zhou and Ouyang 1998: 266; Yang 2000: 117-118), this suffix can be preceded by a kinship term without the prefix a^1 阿 to refer to siblings of a person's spouse as in $i^{2-4}a^3$ 姨仔 'wife's sister', in which i^2 means 'aunt'. This usage of the suffix a^3 仔 is much more common in the elder generation than in the younger generation. The kinship term formed with the prefix sio^3 小 (e.g. $sio^{3-2}i^2$ 小姨 'wife's sister'), rather than with the suffix a^3 仔 such as $i^{2-4}a^3$ 姨仔, tends to be used by the younger generation.

(ii) to express 'affection'
The suffix a^3 can also be used with kinship term(s) to express affection, as in sun^1a^3 孫仔 'grandson' and $tsi^{3\text{-}2}bə^{5\text{-}4}a^3$ 姊妹仔 'sisters', in which tsi^3 and $bə^5$ mean 'elder sister' and 'younger sister', respectively.

(b) attached to a monosyllabic personal name to express 'affection'
The suffix a^3 can also be preceded by a monosyllabic personal name to form a nickname in which the monosyllabic personal name is usually the last syllable of a person's given name, as in $kiɔŋ^{2\text{-}4}a^3$ 強仔, to which the prefix a^1 can be further added before $kiɔŋ^2$, i.e. $a^1kiɔŋ^{2\text{-}4}a^3$ 阿強仔.

(c) attached to a common noun
  (i) to express 'small'
  e.g. $tshu^5$ 厝 'house' -> $tshu^{5\text{-}3}a^3$ 厝仔 'small house'
     $uã^3$ 碗 'bowl' -> $uã^{3\text{-}2}a^3$ 碗仔 'small bowl'

  (ii) to form a disyllabic word with the function of a noun marker
  e.g. $tə^5$ 袋 'bag' -> $tə^{5\text{-}4}a^3$ 袋仔 'bag'
  The morpheme $tə^5$ usually cannot be used alone, so that the suffix cannot be treated as a diminutive here. In fact, to refer to a small bag, the disyllabic word $tə^{5\text{-}4}a^3$ 'bag' is normally preceded by $sue^{5\text{-}3}khia^1$ 細奇 'small' (consisting of the adjective sue^5 'small' and the classifier $khia^1$), that is, to form the attributive phrase $sue^{5\text{-}3}khia^1\ tə^{5\text{-}4}a^3$ 細奇袋仔. In other words, the suffix a^3 here can be regarded as a nominalizer or noun marker. Similar examples of noun formation can be found in $haŋ^4a^3$ 巷仔 'alley', $lai^{2\text{-}4}a^3$ 梨仔 'pear', $tho^{2\text{-}4}a^3$ 桃仔 'peach', $bo^{5\text{-}4}a^3$ 帽仔 'hat', and hi^4a^3 耳仔 'ear'.

  (iii) to refer to a different object
  e.g. $thŋ^2$ 糖 'sugar' (noun) -> $thŋ^{2\text{-}4}a^3$ 糖仔 'candy' (noun)
     pau^1 包 'bag' (noun) -> pau^1a^3 包仔 'steamed stuffed bun' (noun)

Attached to 'numeral + classifier': to express 'small'
When following 'numeral + classifier', a^3 indicates that something is small in terms of size or length, etc.
e.g. $tsit^{8\text{-}4}\ tə^{5\text{-}3}\ baʔ^7$ 蜀垛肉 'a piece of meat' -> $tsit^{8\text{-}4}\ tə^{5\text{-}3}\ a^{3\text{-}2}\ baʔ^7$ 蜀垛仔肉 'a small piece of meat'
In this example, the suffix a^3, preceded by the numeral $tsit^8$ 'one' and the classifier $tə^5$, means that the meat is small in size.

Attached to a verb (phrase): to form a noun
e.g. *giəp⁷* 夾 'nip' (action verb) -> *giəp⁷⁻⁸a³* 夾仔 'clamp' (noun)
　　thiʔ⁷⁻⁸thau² 剃頭 'cut hair' (verb phrase) -> *thiʔ⁷⁻⁸thau²⁻⁴a³* 剃頭仔 'barber' (noun)
　　ue³ 矮 'short' (adjective) -> *ue³⁻²a³* 矮仔 'dwarf' (noun)
In this case, the suffix *a³* changes the category of the base, and thus can be regarded as a nominalizer. In addition, the nouns, derived from a verb (phrase) followed by *a³*, indicating a kind of person, as in *thiʔ⁷⁻⁸thau²⁻⁴a³* 'barber' above, usually express contempt when referring to other people, or function as humble forms when referring to speakers themselves.

Attached to a reduplicated adjective: to form an adverb
e.g. *khen¹⁻²khen¹* 輕輕 'light' (adjective) -> *khen¹⁻²khen¹a³* 輕輕仔 'slightly' (adverb)
　　ban⁵⁻²ban⁵ 慢慢 'slow' (adjective) -> *ban⁵⁻²ban⁵⁻⁴a³* 慢慢仔 'slowly' (adverb)

Attached to a temporal word: exactness
e.g. *tsit⁷⁻⁸tsam⁴* 即站 'now' -> *tsit⁷⁻⁸tsam⁴a³* 即站仔 'just now'
　　hit⁷⁻⁸tsam⁴ 迄站 'then' -> *hit⁷⁻⁸tsam⁴a³* 迄站仔 'just then'
In these two examples, the suffix *a³* follows the temporal words *tsit⁷⁻⁸tsam⁴* 'now' and *hit⁷⁻⁸tsam⁴* 'then' to denote an exact point in time.

The suffix *a³* can be classified into two subtypes, according to whether it can change the categorial property of the base:

(a) The suffix *a³* that changes the categorial property of the base, e.g. changes a verb (phrase) into a noun as in *giəp⁷* 'nip' (action verb) -> *giəp⁷⁻⁸a³* 'clamp' (noun), and changes a reduplicated adjective to an adverb as in *khen¹⁻²khen¹* 輕輕 'light' (adjective) -> *khen¹⁻²khen¹a³* 'slightly' (adverb).

(b) The suffix *a³* that does *not* change the categorial property of the base, e.g. *a³* preceded by a noun such as *tə⁵* 'bag', the complex [numeral + classifier] such as *tsit⁸⁻⁴ tə⁵* 'a piece of', or a temporal word such as *tsit⁷⁻⁸tsam⁴* 'now'. Some of the elements that the suffix *a³* follows can be independently used without *a³*, such as the complex [numeral + classifier] and temporal words, while other elements to which *a³* attaches may not generally be used alone without *a³*, such as *tə⁵* in *tə⁵⁻⁴a³* 袋仔.

Jurafsky (1996) presents a detailed discussion of the synchronic and diachronic semantics of the diminutive category and proposes a universal structure for the semantics of the diminutive (see Figure 5 in Jurafsky (1996:542) for details). Following Jurafsky's proposal, the sources of and relationships among the functions

of expressing 'small', 'affection', 'contempt or modesty' and 'exactness' can be represented as the following semantic changes.
(i) child -> small -> contempt (or modesty)
(ii) child -> small -> extactness
(iii) child -> affection

Although it is often written as 仔 in the literature of Southern Min, the suffix a^3 is also represented by 囝 in earlier works such as Yang (1991), Chen (1997) and Li (2005a). In addition, several scholars have proposed that the source of this suffix is 囝, a noun meaning 'child' (cf. Chen 1997, Lien 1998, Li 2005a, among others). The character 囝 in Hui'an is pronounced as $kã^3$, as in Quanzhou, but is pronounced as $kiã^3$ in some other Southern Min varieties such as Xiamen and Zhangzhou (Zhou 2006:524). In other words, the development from the noun $kã^3$ to the suffix a^3 involves phonological reduction (cf. Lien 1998).

3.2.2.2 Diminutive suffix a^0 仔

The counterparts of this suffix in other Southern Min varieties such as Taiwan and Xiamen have been regarded as a separate suffix (cf. Yang 1991:167, Lu 1999:26-27), or as a weak form of the suffix a^3 仔 (see §3.2.2.1 above) (cf. Yang 2000:117-119, Zhou 2006:65). The question arises as to whether the suffix a^0 in Hui'an is a separate suffix or a weak form of a^3 仔.

As mentioned in §3.2.1.1, the younger generation uses pa^2a^0 and $bã^2a^0$ with the suffix a^0 to refer to 'father' and 'mother', respectively. However, this suffix cannot be preceded by other kinship terms. This is different from Taiwan Southern Min where the suffix a^0 can be placed after kinship terms such as ku^7 舅 'mother's brother', i^5 姨 'mother's sister' and so^2 嫂 'brother's wife' (Lu 1999:27).[5]

As in Taiwan, a^0 in Hui'an can also be used after the last syllable of a given name to form a nickname as in $liŋ^2a^0$ 玲仔 'Ah Ling', where the prefix a^1 阿 can also be added before $liŋ^2$ 玲, that is, $a^1liŋ^2a^0$ 阿玲仔 'Ah Ling'. However, a^0 in Taiwan takes on other functions, such as being preceded by a monosyllabic localizer to form a disyllabic one ($pinn^1a^0$ 'side'), being preceded by a reduplicated adjective (e.g. $phang^1phang^1a^0$ 'fragrant') or verb (e.g. $chio^3chio^3a^0$ 'with a smile') to form an adjective or adverb (Lu 1999[6]: 27; Yang 1991: 192). Even though a^0 in Hui'an bears different functions from Taiwan, we tend to agree with Yang (2000:

---

[5] The romanization given here is based on Dong (2001).
[6] Lu also mentions that a^0 can be preceded by a reduplicated adverb to form a new adverb. However, no example is given, and such usage is not found in the Hui'an dialect.

117-119) and Zhou (2006: 65) that a^0 is a weak form of the diminutive suffix a^3 仔, since (a) a^0 expresses intimacy and affection, which is one of the main functions of the suffix a^3; and (b) the phenomenon that an affix has a weak form or is realized with different tones is not uncommon amongst the affixes in Hui'an, which can be supported by the prefixes *a* 阿 (§3.2.1.1) and *lau* 老 (§3.2.1.2), and the suffixes *thau* 頭 (§3.2.2.9). Thus, the character 仔 is also adopted for representing the suffix a^0 in this book.

3.2.2.3 Suffix *sai¹* 師 < 'master'

This suffix typically changes the preceding verb phrase or noun into terms of respect referring to people who are skilled in a certain profession, as in *khui¹tshia¹sai¹* 開車師 'driver', *thiʔ⁷⁻⁸thau²⁻⁴sai¹* 剃頭師 'barber' and *tau⁵⁻⁴hu⁵⁻⁴sai¹* 豆腐師 'people who make bean curd', in which both *khui¹tshia¹* 'drive (vehicle)' and *thiʔ⁷⁻⁸thau²* 'cut hair' are verb phrases in form, while *tau⁵⁻⁴hu⁵* 'bean curd' is a disyllabic noun. However, there are also a few examples of derogatory terms with *sai¹* as a suffix, as in *peʔ⁸⁻⁴tshat⁸⁻⁴sai¹* 白賊師 'people who like to lie, people who like to play tricks on other people', and *hɔŋ¹ku¹sai¹* 風龜師 'people who like to talk big', in which *peʔ⁸⁻⁴tshat⁸* can be a noun meaning 'lie', and *hɔŋ¹ku¹* is a verb meaning 'brag, talk big'. Note also that in the modern Hui'an dialect, the suffix *sai¹* tends to be replaced by the disyllabic word *sai¹hu⁴* 師傅 'master', which is the counterpart of *shīfu* 師傅 'master' in Mandarin Chinese. Lien (2001) discusses their usage and semantics in terms of stratification for Taiwan Southern Min.

3.2.2.4 Suffix *sen¹* 仙 < 'celestial being, immortal'

Nouns formed by a noun or verb with the suffix *sen¹* may refer to people in a certain occupation or people who possess a certain skill, as in *khuã⁵⁻³biã⁵⁻⁴sen¹* 看命仙 'fortune-teller' and *kun²⁻⁴thau²⁻⁴sen¹* 拳頭仙 'boxer', in which *khuã⁵⁻³ biã⁵* is a verb phrase meaning 'tell fortune', and *kun²⁻⁴thau²* is a noun meaning 'fist'. These nouns (with the suffix *sen¹*) tend to function as derogatory terms, unlike the nouns with the suffix *sai¹* such as *thiʔ⁷⁻⁸thau²⁻⁴sai¹* 'barber' mentioned above. The nouns with the suffix *sen¹* are more often used to refer to people who have a certain hobby, especially a bad hobby, as in *sio¹tsiu³⁻²sen¹* 燒酒仙 'wine bibber' and *puaʔ⁸⁻⁴kiau³⁻²sen¹* 跋繳仙 'hardened gambler', in which *sio¹tsiu³* is a noun meaning 'alcohol' and *puaʔ⁸⁻⁴kiau³* is a verb meaning 'gamble'.

3.2.2.5 Suffix *sen²* 神 < 'god, deity'

As with *sai¹* and *sen¹* above, the suffix *sen²* can follow a verb or noun to form a noun referring to a kind of person, as in *hɔŋ¹ku¹sen²* 風龜神 'people who like to talk big' and *peʔ⁸⁻⁴tshat⁸⁻⁴sen²* 白賊神 'people who like to lie, people who like to play tricks on other people'. Comparatively speaking, the suffix *sen²* is less used than *sai¹* and *sen¹*. However, unlike *sai¹* and *sen¹*, the suffix *sen²* can follow a verb to form a noun denoting a state, as in *tshio⁵⁻³sen²* 笑神 'smile', in which *tshio⁵* is a verb meaning 'laugh, smile'.

3.2.2.6 Suffix *tsin¹* 精 < 'spirit, demon'
The noun with the suffix *tsin¹* is always a derogatory term referring to a kind of person, as in *ku¹tsin¹* 龜精 'people who are crafty' in which *ku¹* is originally a noun meaning 'turtle', and *puaʔ⁸⁻⁴kiau³⁻²tsin¹* 跋繳精 'people who are good at gambling'.

3.2.2.7 Suffix *tsiau³* 鳥 < 'bird'
The noun with the suffix *tsiau³* is also usually a derogatory term referring to a kind of person, as in *phai³⁻²tsiau³* 否鳥 'bad egg, bad apple' and *puã⁵⁻³bin²⁻⁴tsiau³* 半暝鳥 'people who always return home or go out at midnight'[7], in which, *phai³* is an adjective meaning 'bad' and *puã⁵⁻³bin²* is a noun meaning 'midnight'.

3.2.2.8 Suffix *kui³* 鬼 < 'ghost'
This suffix often follows an adjective to form a derogatory term referring to a kind of person, as in *a¹tsam¹kui³* 醃臢鬼 'people who are unhygienic' and *pan²⁻⁴tuã⁴kui³* 貧惰鬼 'lazybones', in which *a¹tsam¹* and *pan²⁻⁴tuã⁴* are adjectives meaning 'dirty' and 'lazy', respectively. There are also some examples of the suffix *kui³* preceded by a verb or noun, as in *hɔŋ¹ku¹kui³* 風龜鬼 'people who like to talk big' and *tsiu³⁻²kui³* 酒鬼 'wine bibber', respectively.

3.2.2.9 Suffix *thau* 頭 < 'head'
The suffix *thau* 頭 in Hui'an can be preceded by a noun, an adjective, a localizer or an action verb. It typically functions as a noun marker or forms a disyllabic localizer by following a monosyllabic localizer. Here are some examples:
(a) following a nominal morpheme, e.g. *i³⁻²thau²* 椅頭 'stool' and *tsha²⁻⁴thau²* 柴頭 'firewood';
(b) following an adjective, e.g. *am⁵⁻³thau²* 暗頭 'dusk', in which *am⁵* 暗 is originally an adjective meaning 'dark';

---

[7] This term is used to refer to people who normally do not return home until midnight or people who like going out at midnight, contrasting with people who normally stay at home with their family at night.

(c) following an action verb to form a noun, e.g. *tshaʔ²⁻⁸thau²* 插頭 'plug' and *tui⁵⁻³thau²* 對頭 'both sides', in which *tshaʔ⁷* 插 and *tui⁵* 對 are verbs meaning 'insert' and 'face', respectively;
(d) following a monosyllabic localizer, e.g. *bə³thau⁰* 尾頭 'back', *tiɔŋ¹thau⁰* 中頭 'middle' and *pin¹thau⁰* 邊頭 'side'.

The suffix *thau* preceded by an action verb is not reported in Xiamen (cf. Zhou and Ouyang 1998: 267).

3.3 Compounding

The inner structures within nominal compounds in Hui'an can have the following three types of relation: coordinate, modifier-head/head-modifier, and subject-predicate.

3.3.1 Coordinate

This type of nominal compound typically involves two nominal or adjectival morphemes which refer to similar lexical domains, as in (1) and (2), respectively.

(1) 衫褲
 sã¹-khɔ⁵
 shirt-pant
 'clothes'

(2) 鹹口
 kiəm²⁻⁴-tsiã³
 salty-tasteless
 'taste'

In (1), the nominal morphemes *sã¹* 'shirt' and *khɔ⁵* 'pant' are juxtaposed to form the nominal compound *sã¹khɔ⁵* 'clothes'. In (2), the adjectival morphemes *kiəm²* 'salty' and *tsiã³* 'tasteless' are juxtaposed to form the nominal compound *kiəm²⁻⁴tsiã³* 'taste'.

3.3.2 Modifier-head/head-modifier

Two nominal morphemes can also form a modifier-head type of nominal compound, as in (3), where the nominal morpheme *tshu⁵* 厝 'house' can be regarded as a modifier of the nominal morpheme *tsu³* 主 'host'.

(3) 厝主
 tshu⁵⁻³-tsu³
 house-host
 'landlord'

The modifier-head type of nominal compound can also be formed by two morphemes of different parts of speech, as in (4) and (5).

(4) 大儂
 tua⁵⁻⁴-laŋ²
 big-person
 'adult'

(5) 滾水
 kun³⁻²-tsui³
 boil-water
 'boiled water'

In (4), the adjective *tua⁵* 'big' and the noun *laŋ²* 'person' together form a nominal compound meaning 'adult'. In (5), the verb *kun³* 'boil' precedes the noun *tsui³* 'water' to form the nominal compound *kun³⁻²tsui³* 'boiled water'.

The head-modifier type is also attested in Hui'an, as in (6) and (7).

(6) 鞋拖
 ue²⁻⁴-thua¹
 shoe-pull
 'slippers'

(7) 豬母
 tu¹-bu³
 pig-female
 'sow'

In (6), the verb *thua¹* 'pull' can be regarded as a modifier of the noun *ue²* 'shoes'. In (7), *bu³* 'female' can be interpreted as a modifier of the noun *tu¹* 'pig'.

3.3.3 Subject-predicate

As shown by the following example, the inner structures of nominal compounds in Hui'an can also have a subject-predicate relation.

(8) 地震
    te⁵⁻⁴-tsen³
    earth-quake
    'earthquake'

3.4 Summary

This chapter has focused on affixation and compounding involved in noun formation in Hui'an.

We have first examined the two main prefixes *a* 阿 and *lau* 老 (< 'old'), followed by a brief introduction to a further group of prefixes such as *sio³* 小 (< 'little, small') and *tshue¹* 初 (< 'beginning, first'), which share similar functions with their counterparts in both other Southern Min varieties and Mandarin Chinese. Next, we focused on the much larger set of suffixes, including *a³/aº* 仔 (< 'child'), *sai¹* 師 (< 'master') and *thau* 頭 (< 'head'). Note that the prefixes *a* 阿 and *lau* 老, and the suffix *thau* 頭 are realized with different tones when attached to different sets of morphemes. We have also argued that the suffix *aº* is actually a weak form of the diminutive suffix *a³* 仔.

Finally, it was shown that the inner structure of nominal compounds in Hui'an involves three types of relation: coordinate, modifier-head/head-modifier and subject-predicate, which have been briefly illustrated by examples.

4 Pronouns

4.1 Introduction

The term 'pronoun' is traditionally defined as a word that can stand for a noun, and is often used to refer to different paradigms of words such as personal pronouns, possessive pronouns, and demonstrative pronouns (Crystal 2008:391-392; Bhat 2004:1, among others). In this chapter, we will focus on personal pronouns, reflexive pronouns, reciprocal pronouns and words meaning 'other, other people' (i.e. the opposite of reflexive pronouns).

4.2 Personal pronouns

The personal pronouns in Hui'an are shown in Table 4-1 below.

Tab. 4-1: Personal pronouns in the Hui'an dialect

	Singular	Plural
First-person	$(g)ua^3$ 我	$(g)un^3$ 阮 (exclusive) lan^3 伯 (inclusive)
Second-person	lu^3 汝	len^3 恁
Third-person	i^1 伊	en^1 個

Cross-linguistically, the person marker can be formed by independent words, clitics, affixes, or be covert (i.e. zero forms) (Siewierska 2004:4, 16-39). This is also the reason why Siewierska (2004) adopts the term 'person marker' (and 'person form'), instead of 'personal pronoun'. In terms of the morpho-phonological form, all the person markers in Hui'an are independent personal pronouns, like Mandarin Chinese and other Chinese dialects. By 'independent', 'free' or 'non-bound' is intended here.

It is clear that the Hui'an dialect is not rich in pronominal person markers. According to Siewierska (2004:2), Fijian has as many as 135 person forms, though there also exist languages which have fewer person markers than the Hui'an dialect, e.g. Madurese, an Austronesian language now mainly spoken in Java, has only two person markers.

According to Table 4-1, the personal pronouns in Hui'an involve a three-way distinction, that is, first-person, second-person, and third-person. This is also true for most Chinese varieties. However, not all languages in the world have markers for all the persons. For example, some languages such as Basque do not have third-person markers and use demonstrative pronouns instead (Siewierska 2004:5-6). Note that kinship terms, and other forms such as occupational titles, can be used in place of pronouns for direct address, as is typical in Chinese. Some of these have been described in §3.2 above.

4.2.1 Singular personal pronouns

4.2.1.1 Syntactic distributions

The singular personal pronouns in Hui'an can be used alone as a subject of a main clause, subordinate clause or relative clause, as illustrated by (1) and (2) below.

(1) 我　　感覺　　　　我　　無　　　　愛　　去
    gua³　*kam³⁻²kak⁷⁻⁸*　*gua³*　*bo²⁻⁴*　*ai⁵⁻³*　*khu⁵*
    1SG　feel　　　　　　1SG　not.have　like　go
    'I don't feel like going (there).'

(2) [汝　呣　　穿]　　[迄領]
    lu³　*m⁵⁻⁴*　*tshiŋ⁵*　*hit⁷⁻⁸-liã³*
    2SG　not　wear　that-CL
    'the item (of clothing) that you don't want to wear'

In (1), the first and second occurrences of *gua³* 'I' are the subject of the main clause *gua³ kam³⁻²kak⁷* and the subordinate clause *gua³ bo²⁻⁴ ai⁵⁻³ khu⁵* 'I don't like going (there)', respectively. In (2), the clause *lu³ m⁵⁻⁴ tshiŋ⁵* 'you don't want to wear' functions as a relative clause, modifying the demonstrative phrase *hit⁷⁻⁸liã³* 'that item of' (see chapter 22 for details of relative clauses). In this case, the second-person pronoun *lu³* functions as a subject of a relative clause. The personal pronouns in the subject position illustrated by (1) and (2) can be omitted when they are sufficiently salient in the context to avoid any misunderstanding, as in *kam³⁻²kak⁷⁻⁸ bo²⁻⁴ ai⁵⁻³ khu⁵* '(I) don't feel like going (there)', where both occurrences of the first person pronoun *gua³* are omitted.

The subjects of imperative clauses are usually encoded by a second-person pronoun such as *lu³* 汝 in (3).

(3) 汝　　暗暝　　　過來
    lu³　*am⁵⁻³bin²*　*kə⁵lai⁰*
    2SG　evening　come.over
    'Come over tonight.'

The second-person subject in imperative clauses, such as *lu³* in (3), is however usually omitted, since it is usually sufficiently salient in the context.

The subject of an imperative clause can also be the first person, or even the third person. In these two cases, the subject usually cannot be omitted, since the second person is the default one as in (3) above. The following is an example of an imperative clause with a first-person subject.

(4) 我　　合　　　汝　　做做　　　　　去
    gua³　*kaʔ⁷⁻⁸*　*lu³*　*tsue⁵⁻³tsue⁵*　*khu⁵*
    1SG　COMT　2SG　together　go
    'Let me go with you.'

Example (4) is an imperative clause used to put forward a suggestion, and the first-person pronoun *gua³* here functions as a subject.

The singular personal pronouns can also be preceded by a preposition or verb, as in (5) – (7), that is, as an object complement.

(5) 伊　　其　　　骹　　　比　　　我　　　恰　　　　短
    i¹　*e²⁻⁴*　*kha¹*　*pi³⁻²*　*gua³*　*khaʔ⁷⁻⁸*　*tə³*
    3SG　GEN　leg　DMC　1SG　HMC　short
    'Her legs are shorter than mine.'

(6) 我　　無　　　嫌　　　伊
    gua³　*bo²⁻⁴*　*hiəm²*　*i⁰*
    1SG　not.have　dislike　3SG
    'I don't dislike him.'

(7) 無　　　　與　　　汝
    bo²⁻⁴　*khɔ⁵*　*lu⁰*
    not.have　give　2SG
    '(I) didn't give (it to) you.'

In (5), *gua³* 'I' follows the comparative marker *pi³* 比 'compared to', which is a preposition. In (6), *i⁰* 'he' is preceded by the verb *hiəm²* 嫌 'dislike' functioning as its object. In (7), *luɯ⁰* 'you' follows the ditransitive verb *khɔ⁵* 與 'give' and functions as its indirect object. Note that the personal pronouns functioning as an object of a verb such as *i⁰* and *luɯ⁰* in (6) and (7) respectively are in a neutral tone, unless they are the semantic focus. For example, the pronoun *i⁰* 'he' in (6) retains its citation tone if the speaker aims to emphasize that the person she does not dislike is 'him', rather than others. In addition, the personal pronouns in object position as in (5) – (7) tend to be overt, rather than to be omitted, unlike the personal pronouns in subject position as in (1) and (2) above.

The following example shows that the singular personal pronoun can be connected to a noun via the genitive marker *e²* 其, forming a genitive construction (see §8.2.4).

(8) 伊 其 意見
i¹ *e²⁻⁴* *i⁵⁻³ken⁵*
3SG GEN opinion
'his opinion'

In (8), the third person singular pronoun *i¹* and the noun *i⁵⁻³ken⁵* 'opinion' function as a possessor and possessee respectively, while *e²* functions as a genitive marker linking the possessor and possessee. In this case, the personal pronoun cannot be omitted.

A nominal demonstrative or noun phrase can directly follow the singular personal pronoun, as illustrated by (9) and (10).

(9) 我 口 氣管炎
gua³ *tse²* *khi⁵⁻³kŋ³⁻²iəm⁵*
1SG this tracheitis
'My kind (of disease) is tracheitis.'

(10) 汝 口 皮膚 合 食 藥 有 關係
luɯ³ *tsat⁸⁻⁴* *phə²⁻⁴hu¹* *kaʔ⁷⁻⁸* *tsiaʔ⁸⁻⁴* *ioʔ⁸* *u⁴* *kuan¹he⁵*
2SG this skin COMT eat medicine have connection
'(The situation of) your skin has something to do with taking medicine.'

In (9), the personal pronoun *gua³* together with the demonstrative *tse²* functions as a subject, while the noun *khi⁵⁻³kŋ³⁻²iəm⁵* 'tracheitis' serves as a predicate in a classifying construction. In (10), the personal pronoun *luɯ³* precedes the noun phrase *tsat⁸⁻⁴ phə²⁻⁴hu¹* 'this skin'. These two examples also express possession.

However, the personal pronouns functioning as a possessor in these two examples, i.e. *gua³* and *lw³*, can be omitted, when they are sufficiently salient in the context, unlike the pronoun *i¹* in example (8) above.

The singular personal pronouns can be followed by 'numeral + classifier', as in (11).

(11) 我　　兩　　個　　計　　𣍐　　讀冊
　　 gua³　*lŋ⁴*　*e²*　*ke⁵⁻³*　*bue⁴*　*thak⁸⁻⁴tsheʔ⁷*
　　 1SG　two　CL　all　cannot　study
　　 'Neither of my two (kids) are good at studying.'

In (11), *lŋ⁴ e²* 'two (kids)', consisting of the numeral *lŋ⁴* 'two' and the classifier *e²*, is preceded by the personal pronoun *gua³* 'I' to express possession. The noun *ken³⁻²a³* 囝仔 'child, kid' can be added after *lŋ⁴ e²*.

The singular personal pronouns can also be followed by a reflexive pronoun such as *kai⁵⁻⁴ki⁵* 家己 in (12), or by a locative word such as *hit⁷⁻⁸taʔ⁷* 迄搭 'there' in (13). Personal pronouns in these two positions can also be omitted, if they are sufficiently salient in the context.

(12) 我　　家己
　　 gua³　*kai⁵⁻⁴ki⁵*
　　 1SG　self
　　 'myself'

(13) 汝　　迄搭
　　 lw³　*hit⁷⁻⁸-taʔ⁷*
　　 2SG　that-LOC
　　 'your place'

The first-person singular pronoun *gua³* and the third-person singular pronoun *i¹* can occur with the pronoun *laŋ⁴* 儂 'other', as exemplified by (14) and (15).

(14) 儂　　我　　毋　　愛　　食
　　 laŋ⁴　*gua³*　*m⁵⁻⁴*　*ai⁵⁻³*　*tsiaʔ⁸*
　　 other　1SG　not　like　eat
　　 'I don't like to eat (it).'

(15) 儂　　伊　卜　　　綴　　　伯
　　 laŋ⁴　i¹　boʔ⁷⁻⁸　tə⁵⁻³　lan³
　　 other　3SG　want　follow　1PL
　　 'He wants to follow us.'

The pronoun *laŋ⁴* 'other' is originally used to refer to a third party excluding the speaker and the hearer(s). In (14), however, *laŋ⁴* is used with the first-person singular pronoun *gua³* to form an appositive construction referring to the speaker him/herself. In (15), the third-person singular pronoun *i¹* preceded by *laŋ⁴* refers to a third party. The appositive constructions *laŋ⁴ gua³* and *laŋ⁴ i¹* usually occur in clause-initial position.

Wang and Zhang (1994:134) provide an example of the second-person singular pronoun following *laŋ⁴* 'other' in Quanzhou, in which the pronoun *laŋ⁴* is co-referential with the second-person pronoun. This is not totally unacceptable in Hui'an, but cannot be found in our spoken data. This at least suggests that the second-person singular pronoun with *laŋ⁴* 'other' is much less prevalent than the first- and third-person singular pronouns.

To sum up briefly, the singular personal pronouns can not only be used alone as a subject, an object complement, or a possessor, but can also be used with a reflexive pronoun, a locative word or the pronoun *laŋ⁴* 'other'.

4.2.1.2 Referential functions

The basic pragmatic function of singular personal pronouns in Hui'an is for reference. For example, *gua³* 'I' is used by the speaker to refer to him/herself, while *luɯ³* 'you' is used to refer to the hearer(s) to whom the speaker is talking, and *i¹* refers to the third party including person(s) and thing(s).

The third party that the pronoun *i¹* refers to is usually singular, as shown by the examples given above. In daily conversation, the pronoun *i¹* can also refer to a category of person, as in (16), or even refer to plural entities, as in (17).

(16) 男其　　　　伊　無　　　　抹
　　 lam²-e⁰　　i¹　bo²⁻⁴　　　buaʔ⁷
　　 male-NMLZ　3SG　not.have　smear
　　 'As for men, they don't use (skin products).'

(17) 伯　　也　著　　　　綴　　　伊
　　 lan³　a⁴　tioʔ⁸⁻⁴　tə⁵⁻³　i¹
　　 1PL　also　should　follow　3SG
　　 'We also need to follow their (habits).'

In (16), *i¹* refers to its preceding noun *lam²e⁰* 'men' which defines a category of person. The noun *lam²e⁰* does not form a noun phrase with *i¹* since the pronoun *i¹* cannot be the head of a noun phrase, that is, cannot be modified. In fact, *lam²e⁰* and *i¹* function as the topic and subject, respectively. The context of (17) concerns family members who are discussing marriage traditions, since one of them is going to get married to a man who lives in another place with different marriage traditions, and so the father points out that they will have to follow the marriage traditions of the other family in this case. The pronoun *i¹* here refers to the other family, rather than a certain person. Note that *i¹* is used, since, in both cases, it refers to a group of persons regarded as a whole unit, that is, to a kind of person: *lam²e⁰* 'men' in (16) or to another family in (17). Zhou (2006:24) also mentions that the personal pronoun *i¹* in Xiamen, Quanzhou and Zhangzhou sometimes can be "temporarily" used as a third-person plural pronoun.

Besides a person, the third-person singular pronoun *i¹* can refer to a thing, while *gua³* and *lu³* can only refer to a person. Yang (1991:216) points out that in Taiwan Southern Min, the pronoun *i¹* referring to a thing, can only be used in object position, but not subject position. This is basically true of *i¹* in Hui'an. However, we find that *i¹* in Hui'an can in fact be used in this way in a subject/topic position when followed or preceded by a demonstrative, noun or noun phrase. The following is an example of the pronoun *i¹* followed by a noun phrase containing a demonstrative.

(18) ［伊］　［迄個　　水空］　　仵咧　　半中間
　　　i¹　　*hit⁷⁻⁸-e²⁻⁴　tsui³⁻²khaŋ¹*　*tu⁴leʔ⁷⁻⁸*　*puã⁵⁻³-tiɔŋ¹uin¹*
　　　3SG　that-CL　drain　　be.at　half-middle
　　　'That drain is in the middle.'

In (18), the pronoun *i¹* is followed by the noun phrase *hit⁷⁻⁸e²⁻⁴ tsui³⁻²khaŋ¹* 'that drain' to form an appositive construction to make it clear to the hearer(s) what the speaker is talking about. The pronoun *i¹* thus refers unequivocally to its following noun phrase *hit⁷⁻⁸e²⁻⁴ tsui³⁻²khaŋ¹* which denotes an inanimate object. The string *i¹ hit⁷⁻⁸e²⁻⁴ tsui³⁻²khaŋ¹* as a whole cannot be used in an object position unless *i¹* is regarded as denoting a person, which suggests that *i¹ hit⁷⁻⁸e²⁻⁴ tsui³⁻²khaŋ¹* in (18) does not form a noun phrase.

4.2.2 Plural personal pronouns

In terms of syntactic distributions, plural personal pronouns have much in common with singular ones. One difference is that the plural ones are more often directly followed by a noun without the genitive marker e^2 to form a genitive construction (see §8.2.1.1), in which case, plural pronouns can have singular meanings, as in (19).

(19) 阮　　小妹
　　 gun$^{3\text{-}2}$　sio$^{3\text{-}2}$bə^5
　　 1PL　Y.sister
　　 'my/our little sister'

In (19), the noun sio$^{3\text{-}2}$bə^5 'little sister' directly follows the exclusive first-person plural pronoun gun^3 'we' without the genitive marker e^2. The pronoun gun^3 here may be interpreted as a plural one (i.e. 'we') or a singular one (i.e. 'I'), depending on the context. Note that the latter interpretation is more common in daily conversation.

Another difference is that the plural pronouns, when followed by 'numeral + classifier', are not restricted to a possessive interpretation, as illustrated by (20).

(20) 伵　　兩　　個　　計　　大學生
　　 en^1　lŋ^4　e^2　ke$^{5\text{-}3}$　tua$^{5\text{-}4}$oʔ$^{8\text{-}4}$siŋ^1
　　 3PL　two　CL　all　university.student
　　 a. 'His/Their two (kids) are both university students.'
　　 b. 'The two of them are both university students.'

In (20), the third-person plural pronoun en^1 followed by lŋ^4 e^2 'two' can be interpreted as expressing possession, that is, meaning 'his/their two (kids)', or can be interpreted as an appositive construction meaning 'the two of them'. Note that there is usually a pause between the pronoun en^1 and lŋ^4 e^2 'two' in the former interpretation, but not in the latter interpretation.

As shown in Table 4-1 above, the Hui'an dialect has a distinction between exclusive 'we' and inclusive 'we', as in (21) and (22), where gun^3 in (21) excludes the person being spoken to, whereas lan^3 in (22) includes the person being spoken to.

(21) 伊　　綴　　　阮　　　做做　　　　上
　　　i¹　　tə⁵⁻³　　gun³⁻²　tsue⁵⁻³tsue⁵　siɔŋ⁵
　　　3SG　follow　1PL　　together　　take
　　　'She takes lectures with us.'

(22) 個　　卜　　　做做　　　　來　　　伯搭
　　　en¹　boʔ⁷⁻⁸　tsue⁵⁻³tsue⁵　lai²⁻⁴　lan³-taʔ⁷
　　　3PL　want　together　　come　1PL-LOC
　　　'They want to come to our place together.'

However, in daily conversation, the referential functions of these two plural pronouns, especially the inclusive one, are more complicated. As mentioned above, the plural personal pronouns functioning as possessors in genitive constructions can have singular meanings, as in examples (19) and (20) above. The following two examples illustrate that the pronouns *gun³* and *lan³* can have a singular meaning when functioning as a subject or an object.

(23) 阮　　　唔　　　愛　　　去
　　　gun³　m⁵⁻⁴　ai⁵⁻³　khɯ⁵
　　　1PL　not　　like　　go
　　　a. 'I don't want to go (there).'
　　　b. 'We don't want to go (there)'

(24) 伊　　無　　　　與　　　伯
　　　i¹　　bo²⁻⁴　khɔ⁵　lan⁰
　　　3SG　not.have　give　1PL
　　　a. 'He didn't give (it) to us.'
　　　b. 'He didn't give (it) to me.'

In (23), the pronoun *gun³* functioning as a subject can have a singular meaning, as shown in (23a), or have a plural meaning, as shown in (23b). In (24), the pronoun *lan⁰*, functioning as an object of the verb *khɔ⁵* 'give', is usually interpreted as referring to a group of persons as shown in (24a), but sometimes can also refer to the speaker him/herself, as shown in (24b).

The pronoun *lan³* can also sometimes be used like *gun³* as in (25), or refer to the hearer(s), as in (26).

(25) 伊　　共　　伨　　　相共　　　　搬
　　　i¹　　*ka⁵⁻⁴*　*lan³⁻²*　*saŋ¹-kaŋ⁵⁻⁴*　*puã¹*
　　　3SG　for　　1PL　　RECP-help　move
　　　'He helped us move.'

(26) 伨　　　早　　　無　　　　抾
　　　lan³　*tsa³*　*bo²⁻⁴*　*thue?⁸*
　　　1PL　before　not.have　take
　　　'You didn't take (the money) before.'

The context for (25) is one where a mother is telling her sister that someone helped them move, and *lan³* here refers to the family of mother, not including her sister who belongs to another family. The pronoun *lan³* is used maybe because the mother in question takes her sister as a family member to convey an intimate feeling. The context of (26) is of a daughter persuading her parents to accept her money, so *lan³* here refers to the hearers, i.e. her parents.

These uses of *lan³* as mentioned above can also be found for the inclusive first-person pronouns in Taiwan and in Beijing (Cheng 1997h:3-10). Cheng (1997h:7) suggests three reasons why the inclusive first-person pronoun is used, while in terms of the real world knowledge, it is the exclusive first-person pronoun that would be normally expected for referring to the hearer(s): (a) the speaker wants to show his/her loving care for the hearer(s) or wants to please the hearer(s); (b) to create an intimate feeling; and (c) the speaker wants to lessen the distance with the hearer(s). We suggest that, in examples (25) and (26), the use of *lan³* may also be a natural and sincere expression of an intimate feeling of warmth on the part of the speaker, that is, there is no distinction between you and me, self and others, or us and others in the speaker's mind, and it is not necessarily deliberately used to lessen the distance with the hearer(s) or to please the hearer(s), as Cheng suggests.

Unlike *lan³*, the use of the second-person plural pronoun *len³* 'you' is much simpler, that is, it only refers to the hearers, or the hearer him/herself, or the hearer and other persons in the hearer's group, without other extensions. An example is given in (27).

(27) 恁　　　大儂　　　　家己　　　　去　　　　講
　　　len³　*tua⁵⁻⁴laŋ²*　*kai⁵⁻⁴ki⁵*　*khui⁵⁻³*　*kaŋ³*
　　　2PL　adult　　　　self　　　　go　　　say
　　　'You adults discuss (it) yourselves.'

The context of example (27) is that a daughter is suggesting to her parents and her boyfriend's parents to discuss the marriage arrangement themselves. In fact, her boyfriend's parents are not present when the conversation occurs. Thus, the second person plural pronoun len^3 is used to refer to the hearers, that is, her parents, and her boyfriend's parents who are not on the spot, but considered as members of the hearers' group.

The third-person plural pronoun en^1 'they' basically refers to a third party including one person and a group of persons, which means, unlike the third-person singular pronoun i^1, en^1 usually refers to people, but not things. However, as with i^1, the pronoun en^1 can also refer to its preceding noun(phrase), that is, be used anaphorically, as in (28).

(28) 阿舅 阿姨 佢 底時 來
  a^1-ku^4 a^1-i^2 <u>en^1</u> ti^4si^2 lai^2
  PREF-uncle PREF-aunt 3PL when come
  'When will uncle and aunt come (here)?'

In (28), the pronoun en^1 is co-referential with a^1ku^4 a^1i^2 'uncle and aunt'. Note that a^1ku^4 a^1i^2 en^1 here can be regarded as an appositive noun phrase, since a^1ku^4 a^1i^2 en^1 as a whole can be used in an object position, as in (29), where a^1ku^4 a^1i^2 en^1 functions as an object of the verb $hi^{3-2}hua^1$ 喜歡 'like'.

(29) 我 無 喜歡 阿舅 阿姨 佢
  gua^3 bo^{2-4} $hi^{3-2}hua^1$ a^1-ku^4 a^1-i^2 en^1
  1SG not.have like PREF-uncle PREF-aunt 3PL
  'I don't like uncle and aunt.'

As for the source of plural personal pronouns (other than the inclusive first-person plural) in Southern Min, two kinds of proposal have been put forward in the literature: (a) these pronouns are formed by adding an ending [n] after the singular personal pronouns, e.g. gua^3 我 'I' + [-n] -> $guan^3$ 阮 'we' (e.g. Wang and Zhang 1994:86, Yang 1991:216); and (b) these pronouns are contracted forms of the singular personal pronouns and lan^2 儂 'person' (e.g. Li 1999:265, Mei 2002:5). Wang and Zhang (1994:86) also observe that proposal (b) is plausible. Interestingly, the plural personal pronouns formed by the singular forms with lan^2 儂 can still be found in some Southern Min varieties such as Shantou (Shi 1999:291). In fact, proposal (a) can be regarded as a surface observation in phonetic form, while (b) explains how the surface observation, as shown by (a), comes about. These observations and explanations are applicable to the Hui'an dialect, though the phonetic forms are not exactly the same.

4.3 Reflexive pronouns

Semantically speaking, the reflexive pronoun refers to somebody him/herself, as opposed to other people. The main reflexive pronoun in Hui'an is $kai^{5\text{-}4}ki^5$ 家己 'self' (cf. Quanzhou $kai^{5\text{-}4}ki^5$ and Xiamen $ka^{1\text{-}6}ki^6$ (Zhou 2006:55), Taiwan ka^1ki^7 (Yang 1991:216)[1]. The reflexive pronoun $kai^{5\text{-}4}ki^5$ can be further preceded by a personal pronoun, such as $gua^3\ kai^{5\text{-}4}ki^5$ 'myself' and $en^1\ kai^{5\text{-}4}ki^5$ 'themselves', as will be shown in the following examples.

The basic function of reflexive pronouns is their anaphoric use. For example, $kai^{5\text{-}4}ki^5$ (with or without a preceding personal pronoun), functioning as a direct object of a verb (or a modifier of the direct object of a verb), can anaphorically refer to the subject of the same verb, as in (30) and (31).

(30) 伊　　罵　　　（伊）家己
　　 i^1　　$bã^{5\text{-}4}$　　$(i^1)\ kai^{5\text{-}4}ki^5$
　　 3SG　scold　(3SG) self
　　 'He scolded himself.'

(31) 我　　無　　　看　　　著　　　（我）家己　　其　　包
　　 gua^3　$bo^{2\text{-}4}$　$khuã^{5\text{-}3}$　$tio?^{8\text{-}4}$　$(gua^3)\ kai^{5\text{-}4}ki^5$　$e^{2\text{-}4}$　pau^1
　　 1SG　not.have　look　PVC　(1SG) self　GEN　bag
　　 'I didn't see my own bag.'

In (30), the reflexive pronoun $kai^{5\text{-}4}ki^5$ (or $i^1\ kai^{5\text{-}4}ki^5$ 'himself'), functioning as a direct object of the verb $bã^5$ 'scold', is co-referential with the subject i^1 伊. In (31), $kai^{5\text{-}4}ki^5$ (or $gua^3\ kai^{5\text{-}4}ki^5$ 'myself'), functioning as a modifier of the noun pau^1 'bag' (the direct object of the verb phrase $khuã^{5\text{-}3}\ tio?^8$), refers back to the subject gua^3 我.

---

[1] The Hui'an and Quanzhou forms diverge from Xiamen/Taiwan in both segmental form (kai vs. ka) and tone (5 vs. 1). The tone probably indicates that kai^5 originated through fusion of the syllable ka with ki^5 (see §2.5 for syllable fusion).

The reflexive pronouns can also occur in a subordinate clause, as illustrated by (32), where the reflexive pronoun $kai^{5\text{-}4}ki^5$ (or $i^1\ kai^{5\text{-}4}ki^5$) in the subordinate clause is used to refer back to the subject of the main clause, that is, the first i^1.

(32)　伊　　感覺　　　　（伊）家己　　無　　　　夠　　　　努力
　　　i^1　　$kam^{3\text{-}2}kak^{7\text{-}8}$　(i^1) $kai^{5\text{-}4}ki^5$　$bo^{2\text{-}4}$　$kau^{5\text{-}3}$　$lɔ^4liak^8$
　　　3SG　feel　　　　(3SG) self　　not.have　enough　endeavour
　　　'He felt that he didn't work hard enough.'

The reflexive pronouns can be used alone without their antecedents, as in (33) and (34).

(33)　卜　　　　拍　　　　我，　　春　　　　著　　　　（伊）家己
　　　$boʔ^{7\text{-}8}$　$phaʔ^{7\text{-}8}$　gua^3　$tsin^1$　$tioʔ^{8\text{-}4}$　(i^1) $kai^{5\text{-}4}ki^5$
　　　want　　hit　　　　1SG　　strike　　PVC　　(3SG) self
　　　'He wanted to hit me, but hit himself.'

(34)　感覺　　　　　　家己　　　　有　　失　　　　身份
　　　$kam^{3\text{-}2}kak^{7\text{-}8}$　$kai^{5\text{-}4}ki^5$　u^4　$set^{7\text{-}8}$　sen^1hun^5
　　　feel　　　　　　self　　　　have　lose　　　dignity
　　　'He felt that he lost his dignity.'

In (33), $kai^{5\text{-}4}ki^5$ (or $i^1\ kai^{5\text{-}4}ki^5$), functioning as a direct object of the verb phrase $tsin^1\ tioʔ^8$, is used to refer back to the omitted subject i^1 伊. The context of example (34) is that people are discussing the behavior of one participant of the conversation. The pronoun $kai^{5\text{-}4}ki^5$ here is used to refer to this participant, that is, it refers to one of the people who are present when the conversation happens. The antecedent of $kai^{5\text{-}4}ki^5$ in this example is covert.

Note that $kai^{5\text{-}4}ki^5$ is also used as an intensifier, that is, there is no formal difference between the reflexive pronoun $kai^{5\text{-}4}ki^5$ and the intensifier $kai^{5\text{-}4}ki^5$ (see König and Gast 2002 for the distinction between these two categories). The intensifier $kai^{5\text{-}4}ki^5$ can follow a personal pronoun (or noun phrase) to form an appositive construction to emphasize the personal pronoun (or noun phrase). Examples are given in (35) and (36).

(35)　我　　　家己　　　　　卜　　　　讀
　　　gua^3　$kai^{5\text{-}4}ki^5$　$boʔ^{7\text{-}8}$　$thak^8$
　　　1SG　　self　　　　　want　　study
　　　'I myself want to study.'

(36) 卜　　　創　　　　甚物,
　　 boʔ⁷⁻⁸　*tshɔŋ⁵⁻³*　*siəm³⁻²biʔ⁷*
　　 want　　do　　　what
　　 兩　　家　　儂　　家己　　　講　　　(目賣)
　　 lŋ⁴　*ke¹*　*laŋ²*　<u>*kai⁵⁻⁴ki⁵*</u>　*kaŋ³⁻²*　*bai⁵*
　　 two　family　person　self　　say　　TENT
　　 'As for what (we) want to do, (our) two families try to discuss it by ourselves.'

In (35), *kai⁵⁻⁴ki⁵* follows the personal pronoun *gua³* '1SG' to emphasize that it is I, myself, who has decided to study. In (36), *kai⁵⁻⁴ki⁵* is preceded by the noun phrase *lŋ⁴ ke¹laŋ²* 'two families' to emphasize that the main participant of the discussion is the two families.

The intensifier *kai⁵⁻⁴ki⁵* can also modify a verb expressing the manner of an action, as shown by (37) and (38).

(37) 家己　　　試　　　(目賣)
　　 <u>*kai⁵⁻⁴ki⁵*</u>　*tshi⁵⁻³*　*bai⁵*
　　 self　　　try　　　TENT
　　 'Try by yourself.'

(38) 兩　　個　　有　　相口　　　　來　　抑是　　　家己　　　來
　　 lŋ⁴　*e²*　*u⁴*　*saˡtshua⁵⁻⁴*　*lai²*　*aʔ⁸⁻⁴-si⁴*　<u>*kai⁵⁻⁴ki⁵*</u>　*lai²*
　　 two　CL　have　RECP-lead　come　or-be　　self　　come
　　 'They two came together or (he) came alone?'

In (37), *kai⁵⁻⁴ki⁵*, modifying the verb phrase *tshi⁵⁻³ bai⁵* 'have a try', means 'try by yourself, without the help of others'. In (38), *kai⁵⁻⁴ki⁵* modifies the verb *lai²* 'come' to express 'come alone, without a companion'.

The intensifier *kai⁵⁻⁴ki⁵* in examples (35) – (38) can be simply substituted by *kai⁵*. In other words, *kai⁵* alone can be used as an intensifier, which may be a weak form of *kai⁵⁻⁴ki⁵*. Note that in other Southern Min varieties such as Xiamen, Zhangzhou and Taiwan, the reflexive pronoun and intensifier 家己 is pronounced as *KA KI*, rather than *KAI KI*. This may suggest that *kai⁵* in Hui'an (also in Quanzhou) is a fused form of *KA KI*. Nonetheless, further investigation would be needed to clarify this diachronic issue.

4.4 Reciprocal pronouns

There is no independent reciprocal pronoun in Hui'an, and the reciprocal meaning is encoded by the reciprocal prefix *sa¹* 相, as in (39) where *sa¹* is attached to the verb *phaʔ⁷* 拍 'hit', or by the reciprocal adverb *hɔ⁵⁻⁴siɔŋ¹* 互相 'mutually', as in (40) where *hɔ⁵⁻⁴siɔŋ¹* modifies the verb phrase *bo²⁻⁴ li³⁻²kai³* 無理解 'do not understand'.

(39) 相拍
sa¹-phaʔ⁷
RECP-hit
'fight with each other'

(40) 互相　　無　　　理解
hɔ⁵⁻⁴siɔŋ¹　*bo²⁻⁴*　*li³⁻²kai³*
mutually　not.have　understand
'(They) don't understand each other.'

Note that *sa¹* 相 is much more widely used than *hɔ⁵⁻⁴siɔŋ¹* 互相, the latter preferentially used by the younger generation.

4.5 The pronouns *laŋ⁴* 'other' and *pat⁸⁻⁴laŋ²* 'other people'

Like the personal pronouns mentioned above, in terms of syntax, the pronoun *laŋ⁴* can be (a) used as a subject; (b) preceded by a preposition or verb; (c) found in genitive constructions where the genitive marker *e²* 其 is needed; and can be (d) followed by a demonstrative or noun phrase. As mentioned in §4.2.1.1, *laŋ⁴* can also be (e) followed by a personal pronoun.

Semantically, *laŋ⁴* can refer to a third party excluding the speaker and the hearer(s) in general, as in (41), or a thing in general, as in (42).

(41) 儂　　計　　卜　　　共　　　恁　　借　　　錢
laŋ⁴　*ke⁵⁻³*　*boʔ⁷⁻⁸*　*ka⁵⁻⁴*　*len³⁻²*　*tsioʔ⁷⁻⁸*　*tsin²*
other　all　want　from　2PL　borrow　money
'People all want to borrow money from you.'

(42) 儂　　橙　　食　　繪　　否
　　 laŋ⁴　 *tshiaŋ²*　 *tsiaʔ⁸*　 *bue⁴*　 *phai³*
　　 other　 orange　 eat　 cannot　 bad
　　 'Eating oranges is not bad.'

In (41), *laŋ⁴* refers to a third party without specific person(s) being intended. In (42), *laŋ⁴* is coreferential with its following generic noun *tshiaŋ²* 橙 'orange', and signals thereby that a noun denoting a thing, and not a person, is required to follow *laŋ⁴*. Note that *laŋ⁴* referring to a third party in a general way as in (41) is pronounced as *laŋ²*, its original tonal value which now can only be found in idioms, as in (43).

(43) 拍　　　儂　　家己　　吼
　　 phaʔ⁷⁻⁸　 *laŋ²*　 *kai⁵⁻⁴ki⁵*　 *hau³*
　　 hit　 other　 self　 cry
　　 'Hit another, and cry oneself.'

Example (43) literally means that someone hits another person but cries themselves. Two possibilities are involved here: (a) they cry because they are scared after hitting someone else; (b) they cry in order to avoid punishment to induce the parents to think it is their own child who has been hit. In this example, the pronoun referring to a third party in a general way is pronounced as *laŋ²* (with a second tone, rather than a fourth tone).

The morpheme *laŋ²* 儂 is originally a generic noun meaning 'person, human being' and has a sandhi form '*laŋ⁴*'. In other words, the sandhi form of the noun *laŋ²* is used to distinguish the meaning of 'other' from the meaning of 'person, human being', of which the former is an extension (see also Li 1999:267).

The following examples show that, when referring to a third party, *laŋ⁴* can also be used for specific reference, that is, refer to specific person(s) and thing(s).

(44) 汝　　去，　儂　　也　　呣　　別　　汝
　　 lɯ³　 *khu⁵*　 *laŋ⁴*　 *a⁴*　 *m⁵⁻⁴*　 *pat⁷*　 *lɯ⁰*
　　 2SG　 go　 other　 also　 Not　 know　 2SG
　　 'She won't know you, if you go (there).'

(45) 等　　　儂　　說　　清楚
　　 tan³⁻²　 *laŋ⁴*　 *səʔ⁷⁻⁸*　 *tshiŋ¹tshɔ³*
　　 wait　 other　 say　 clear
　　 'wait for them to make (it) clear'

(46) 儂　　伯　　口　　相機　　也佫　　泛泛
　　 laŋ⁴　 lan³　hat⁸⁻⁴　siɔŋ⁵⁻³ki¹　a⁴koʔ⁷⁻⁸　hamˢ⁻³hamˢ
　　 other　1PL　that　　camera　　 fairly　　 OK
　　 'Our camera is quite O.K.'

(47) 儂　　懷　　厝　　卜　　起　　了　　咯
　　 laŋ⁴　 huai²　tshu⁵　boʔ⁷⁻⁸　khi³⁻²　liau³　lɔ⁰
　　 other　those　house　want　build　finish　SFP
　　 'Those houses are going to be finished.'

The pronoun *laŋ⁴* in (44) and (45) refers cataphorically to a specific person and a specific group of people, respectively. In (46) and (47), *laŋ⁴* refers to the referents of its following noun phrases, i.e. *lan³ hat⁸⁻⁴ siɔŋ⁵⁻³ki¹* 'our camera' and *huai² tshu⁵* 'those houses', respectively, which are specific in the given context.

The pronoun *laŋ⁴* alone can also be associated with a fourth party as in (48), since a third party encoded by *iⁱ* 伊 exists in the context. It may also refer to the speaker him/herself as in (49).

(48) 儂　　卜　　與　　伊　　其
　　 laŋ⁴　boʔ⁷⁻⁸　khɔ⁵⁻⁴　iⁱ　e⁰
　　 other　want　give　3SG　FOC
　　 'It is him to whom that person wants to give (it).'

(49) 汝　　家　　去，　儂　　唔　　愛　　去
　　 lu³　kai⁵⁻⁴　khuɨ⁵　*laŋ⁴*　m⁵⁻⁴　ai⁵⁻³　khuɨ⁵
　　 2SG　self　go　　other　not　like　go
　　 'You go (there) by yourself; I don't want to go (there).'

In (48), besides the speaker and the hearer, *iⁱ* and *laŋ⁴* are used to denote a third party and a fourth party, respectively.

The pronoun *laŋ⁴* is also preferred in the following two circumstances:
(a) when the identity of the person(s) is not so important, as in (50)

(50) 口　　是　　儂　　咧　　共　　阮　　唱　　歌
　　 tse²　si⁴　*laŋ⁴*　leʔ⁷⁻⁸　ka⁵⁻⁴　gun³⁻²　tshiũ⁵⁻³　kua¹
　　 this　be　other　PROG　BEN　1PL　sing　song
　　 'This is (when) the person was singing for us.'

In (50), the speaker is showing her parents one of her pictures taken during her travels, in which someone is singing for her and her friends. The speaker uses *laŋ⁴* to refer to that person since who they are is not important.

(b) when the speaker does not want to talk about someone directly, as in (51)

(51) 儂　　也　　無　　　　說　　口　　是　　阮　　厝裡
　　 <u>laŋ⁴</u>　 a⁴　 bo²⁻⁴　 səʔ⁷⁻⁸　hat⁸　si⁴　gun³　tshu⁵⁻³-lai⁴
　　 other　also　not.have　say　　that　be　　1PL　 house-inside
　　 'He didn't say that is my home.'

In (51), the person encoded by *laŋ⁴* is actually on the spot when the conversation happens. However, the speaker deliberately uses *laŋ⁴* to avoid explicitly referring to that person. This is an example of using *laŋ⁴* to refer to a third party indirectly. In fact, the use of *laŋ⁴* to refer to the speaker himself as in (49) above can also be sometimes regarded as a way of avoiding referring to the speaker himself directly.

The pronoun *pat⁸⁻⁴laŋ²* 別儂 'other people' is the opposite in meaning to the reflexive pronoun *kai⁵⁻⁴ki⁵* 家己 'self', as in (52).

(52) 無　　　　別儂，　　　　阿姨　　　　　家己
　　 bo²⁻⁴　 <u>pat⁸⁻⁴-laŋ²</u>　 a¹-i²　　　　 kai⁵⁻⁴ki⁵
　　 not.have　other-person　PREF-aunt　self
　　 'There is nobody else here, only me, auntie.'

As illustrated by (52), the use of *pat⁸⁻⁴laŋ²* is very straightforward, that is, it is typically used together with the reflexive pronoun *kai⁵⁻⁴ki⁵*, while *laŋ⁴* has more complex functions as mentioned above. Another difference between *pat⁸⁻⁴laŋ²* and *laŋ⁴* is that *pat⁸⁻⁴laŋ²* generally refers to a group of persons, whereas *laŋ⁴* may also refer to one person, that is, it can have a singular meaning.

According to Lü (1985:90), in the history of Chinese, there mainly exist four words meaning 'other' and involving *rén* 人 'person': *rén* 人, *rénjiā* 人家, *biérén* 別人 and *biérénjiā* 別人家. Among these, *rén* means 'other' and functions as the opposite of *jǐ* 己 'self'. For example, in the Classical Chinese text of *Lun Yu* 論語, there are nine instances of *rén* 'other' co-occurring in the same context with *jǐ* 'self', while *rénjiā*, *biérén* and *biérénjiā* are used in later periods to contrast with *zìjǐ* 自己, the disyllabic form for 'self' (Lü 1985:90-91). Among modern Chinese dialects, Min mainly uses the counterpart of *rén* 'other', while Wu, Gan and Hakka mainly use the counterparts of *rénjiā*, *biérén* and *biérénjiā* (cf. Li and Chang 1999), which may suggest that Min preserves earlier characteristics of Chinese than the other three Chinese dialects for this feature.

4.6 Summary

This chapter focuses on personal pronouns, reflexive pronouns, reciprocal pronouns and words meaning 'other, other people'. The personal pronouns involve a three-way distinction, that is, first-person, second-person, and third-person. Unlike the first- and second-person singular pronouns (gua^3 and lu^3) which only refer to a person, the third-person singular pronoun i^1 can refer to a person or thing. When referring to a thing, the pronoun i^1 can be used not only in object position, but also in subject/topic position when followed or preceded by a demonstrative, noun or noun phrase.

There is a distinction between exclusive 'we' and inclusive 'we'. The plural person pronouns in general can have singular meanings when they function as possessors in genitive constructions. Similarly, both the exclusive gun^3 'we' and the inclusive lan^3 'we' can have a singular meaning when functioning as a subject or an object. The inclusive lan^3 'we' can also sometimes be used like the exclusive gun^3, or refer to the hearer(s).

The main reflexive pronoun is $kai^{5\text{-}4}ki^5$ 家己 'self', whose basic function is its anaphoric use. The pronoun $kai^{5\text{-}4}ki^5$ is also used as an intensifier, that is, there is no formal difference between the reflexive pronoun $kai^{5\text{-}4}ki^5$ and the intensifier $kai^{5\text{-}4}ki^5$.

There is no independent reciprocal pronoun, and the reciprocal meaning is encoded by the reciprocal prefix sa^1 相, or by the reciprocal adverb $hɔ^{5\text{-}4}siɔŋ^1$ 互相 'each other'.

The pronoun $laŋ^4$ 'other' has its source in $laŋ^2$, a noun with a different tonal value meaning 'person, human being'. In other words, the sandhi form of the noun $laŋ^2$ is used to distinguish the meaning of 'other' from the meaning of 'person, human being', of which the former is an extension. The pronoun $pat^{8\text{-}4}laŋ^2$ 別儂 'other people' is the opposite in meaning to the reflexive pronoun $kai^{5\text{-}4}ki^5$ 家己 'self'.

5 Nominal demonstratives

5.1 Introduction

The term 'demonstrative' is traditionally used to refer to a class of items whose function is to point to an entity in the situation or elsewhere in a sentence (cf. Crystal 2008: 135). In English, for example, the demonstratives include *this/that* and their plural forms *these/those*, which serve as independent pronouns, as in (1), or co-occur with a noun, as in (2).

(1) *This tastes good.*

(2) *That bag is mine.*

The demonstrative *this* in (1) is used alone as an independent pronoun, whereas the demonstrative *that* in (2) is used to modify the following noun *bag*. Based on these two different syntactic functions, the demonstratives in English are traditionally called 'demonstrative pronouns' and 'demonstrative adjectives/determiners', respectively (cf. Thomson, 1986:14; Greenbaum, 1996:195; Downing & Locke, 2006:414, 424; Crystal, 2008:135, among others).

Unlike its traditional usage, the term 'demonstrative' is thus used in a broader way in studies such as Lyons (1977), Diessel (1999) and Dixon (2003). Besides demonstrative pronouns and demonstrative adjectives as in examples (1) and (2) above, the adverbs such as *here* and *there* in English are also grouped among the demonstratives and called 'demonstrative adverbs' in Lyons (1977:646).[1]

Diessel (1999:3-5) distinguishes the distribution and categorical status of demonstratives and puts forward the following four different syntactic contexts in which demonstratives may occur:
(a) Pronominal

Note: A preliminary version of this chapter also appeared in Chen (2013).

---

1 Diessel (1999:2) takes a similar line on the scope of the demonstrative: 'Many studies confine the notion of demonstrative to deictic expressions such as English *this* and *that*, which are used either as independent pronouns or as modifiers of a co-occurring noun, but the notion that I will use is broader. It subsumes not only demonstratives being used as pronouns or noun modifiers but also locational adverbs such as English *here* and *there*'.

Demonstratives are used as independent pronouns in argument positions of verbs and adpositions, such as English *this* in example (1) above.
(b) Adnominal
Demonstratives co-occur with a noun in a noun phrase, such as English *that* in example (2).
(c) Adverbial
e.g. the locational adverbs *here* and *there* in English
(d) Identificational
Many languages use special demonstrative forms in copular and nonverbal clauses to identify a referent in the speech situation, as in (3), an example from French.

(3) *C'*   *est*   *Pascal.*
     this/it   is   Pascal
     'It/this is Pascal.'   (Diessel, 1999:5)

Diessel uses the terms 'demonstrative pronoun', 'demonstrative determiner', 'demonstrative adverb' and 'demonstrative identifier' to indicate the categorial status of demonstratives in these four syntactic contexts, respectively.

In his cross-linguistic study on demonstratives, Dixon (2003:62) identifies three main types of demonstrative: (a) nominal, (b) local adverbial; and (c) verbal. Nominal demonstratives are those that can occur in an NP with a noun or pronoun such as *this* in *this stone is hot*, or, in most languages, can make up a complete NP such as *this* in *this is hot*. In other words, demonstrative pronouns and demonstrative adjectives/determiners in previous studies such as Lyons (1977) and Diessel (1999) are grouped together and labeled 'nominal demonstratives'. Type (b) corresponds to the demonstrative adverb in Lyons (1977) and Diessel (1999). A small number of languages have a subclass of verbs with demonstrative meaning, involving deictic reference to an action, such as the verb *'ene(ii)* in the Boumaa dialect of Fijian, which can be glossed 'do like this' (see Dixon, 2003:72-74 for more details). Besides these three main types, Dixon (2003:62, 78, 88) also mentions manner adverbial demonstratives meaning '(do) like this, (do) in this way/manner' and temporal adverbial demonstratives such as *i-ppa* 'now' and *a-ppa* 'then' in Tamil.

In the field of Chinese linguistics, the term *dàicí* 代詞 (lit. substitute word) is typically used to refer to the items that take on the function of substitution, which are usually further classified into three subtypes, that is, *rénchēng dàicí* 人稱代詞 'personal pronoun' such as *wǒ* 我 'I' in Mandarin Chinese, *zhǐshì dàicí* 指示代詞 'demonstrative pronoun' such as Mandarin *zhè* 這 'this', and *yíwèn dàicí* 疑問

代詞 'interrogative pronoun' such as Mandarin *shuí* 誰 'who' (cf. Ding et al., 1961:141; Zhu, 1982:80; Wang, 1984:260; Shi, 1999:85, among others). The term used for deictic demonstratives (*zhǐshì dàicí* 指示代詞) usually involves the following five subtypes: (a) the items that can either modify a noun or make up a complete NP by themselves, such as Mandarin *zhè* 這 'this' and *nà* 那 'that'; (b) the items that indicate location, such as Mandarin *zhèr* 這兒 'here' and *nàr* 那兒 'there'; (c) the items that indicate time, such as Mandarin *zhèhuìr* 這會兒 'now' and *nàhuìr* 那會兒 'then'; (d) the items that indicate the manner of an action, such as Mandarin *zhème* 這麼 '(do) in this way' and *nàme* 那麼 '(do) in that way'; and (e) the items that indicate degree, such as Mandarin *zhème* 這麼 in *zhème lěng* 這麼冷 'this cold, cold like this, such a cold weather' (cf. Ding et al., 1961:150; Zhu, 1982:85; Wang, 1984:299-303, among others). Most of the *zhǐshì dàicí* 指示代詞 in Chinese take on both the substitution function and the deictic function. So far, it is clear that the Chinese term *zhǐshì dàicí* 指示代詞 is used in the field of Chinese linguistics in a meaning which is quite close to the term 'demonstrative' in Dixon's terms (Dixon, 2003). In this chapter, we will however focus on subtype (a) of *zhǐshì dàicí* 指示代詞, i.e. the type of demonstrative that Dixon (2003) calls 'nominal demonstrative'.

As mentioned above, the nominal demonstratives *zhè* 'this' and *nà* 'that' in Mandarin Chinese can either modify a noun such as *chē* 車 'car' in (4) below, or make up a complete NP by itself, as in (5).

(4) 這　車
    zhè　*chē*
    this　car
    'this car'

(5) 那　是　我　媽
    nà　*shì*　*wǒ*　*mā*
    that　be　1SG　mother
    'That is my mother.'

Note, however, that *zhè* and *nà* also often co-occur with a classifier such as *ge* 個 in (6), or the complex [numeral + classifier] such as *liǎng běn* 兩本 'two' in (7)

(6) 這　個　（人）
    zhè　*ge*　*(rén)*
    this　CL　(person)
    'this (person)'

(7) 那　　兩　　本　　（書）
　　 nà　　liǎng　běn　 (shū)
　　 that　two　　CL　　(book)
　　 'those two (books)'

The demonstrative *zhè* in (6) is followed by the classifier *ge*, whereas *nà* in (7) precedes the complex *liǎng běn* 'two' which consists of the numeral *liǎng* 'two' and the classifier *běn*. As shown by these two examples, a noun such as *rén* 'person' and *shū* 'book' in (6) and (7) respectively can be further added after the classifier.

In other Chinese varieties such as some varieties of Min, Yue and Wu, there exist some items which, unlike the Mandarin demonstratives *zhè* and *nà*, can neither directly modify a noun nor make up a complete NP by themselves, and must be followed by a classifier or the complex [numeral + classifier]. Examples include tsi^{53}/hu^{53} 'this/that' in the Jieyang 揭陽 variety of Southern Min (Xu, 2007:85), tsi^{33} 只/xi^{33} 許 'this/that' in the Fuzhou 福州 variety of Eastern Min (Chen, 1999:254), ni^{55} 呢/$kɔ^{35}$ 嗰 'this/that' in Hong Kong Cantonese (Chang, 1999:353) and $gaʔ^{13}$ 個/e^{53} 哀 'this/that' in Shanghai Wu (Pan & Tao, 1999:26-27). An example from Shanghai Wu is given in (8) below, where e^{53} 哀 'that' cannot directly modify the noun $sɿ^{53}$ 書 'book'. Strictly speaking, these items can neither be grouped among demonstrative pronouns nor determiners in Diessel's sense of the term (1999), nor be grouped among nominal demonstratives in Dixon's sense of the term (2003). Interestingly, Diessel (1999:33) points out that '[t]hough the stems of most demonstratives are monomorphemic, there are demonstratives whose stems are composed of multiple morphemes. The stems of demonstrative pronouns may consist of a deictic root and a nominalizer, a third person pronoun or a noun classifier'. If we follow this point of view, the Southern Min morphemes mentioned above may be termed 'deictic roots'. For convenience, in this chapter, they will be examined together with the regular kind of nominal demonstratives.

(8) a.　哀　　　本　　　書
　　　 e^{53}　　$pəŋ^{55}$　$sɿ^{53}$
　　　 that　　CL　　book
　　　 'that book'
　*b.　哀　　書
　　　 e^{53}　　$sɿ^{53}$
　　　 that　　book
　　　 'that book'

As illustrated above, there is basically only one set of nominal demonstratives in Mandarin Chinese, i.e. *zhè* 'this' and *nà* 'that'. The plural forms 'these/those' in Mandarin Chinese are formed by *zhè/nà* and the indefinite measure word *xiē* 些 'some', i.e. *zhèxiē* 這些 'these' and *nàxiē* 那些 'those', as in *zhèxiē shū* 這些書 'these books' and *nàxiē huār* 那些花兒 'those flowers', respectively. Compared with Mandarin Chinese and some other Chinese dialects such as Yue, Wu and Hakka (cf. Chang, 1999; Lin, 1999, Pan & Tao, 1999), Min exhibits a relatively more complex nominal demonstrative system, partially due to a large inventory of nominal demonstrative forms that are differentiated according to a variety of semantic and syntactic parameters. In the Fuzhou variety of Eastern Min, for example, there are three separate sets of nominal demonstratives for 'this/that', i.e. $tsui^{53}/xui^{53}$, tsi^{33}/xi^{33} and $tsia^{33}/xia^{33}$ (Chen, 1999:254-258). Similarly, there are four separate sets of nominal demonstratives in Shantou 汕頭 and Jieyang 揭陽, two varieties of Southern Min spoken in the Guangdong 廣東 province of China (Shi, 1999:304-309; Xu, 2007:84; see the following sections for more details). In Hui'an, we have identified five sets of nominal demonstratives with a two-way distinction (i.e. proximal and distal), presented in Table 5-1 together with their phonological forms and basic meanings.

Tab. 5-1: Nominal demonstratives in the Hui'an dialect

		Proximal	Distal
1	Basic adnominal demonstratives	$tsit^7$ 即 (this)	hit^7 迄 (that)
2	Singular demonstrative pronouns	$tsat^8$ (this one)	hat^8 (that one)
3	Plural demonstrative pronouns	$tsuai^2$ 撮 (these) (this)	$huai^2$ 懷 (those) (that)
4	Generic demonstratives (i)	tse^2 (this kind of) (generic)	ha^2 (that kind of) (generic)
5	Generic demonstratives (ii)	$tsiŋ^{3\text{-}2}e^2$ 種其 (this kind of) (generic)	$hiɔŋ^{3\text{-}2}e^2$ 向其 (that kind of) (generic)

The nominal demonstrative system in Min raises a series of questions. For example, why is the inventory of nominal demonstrative forms larger in Min than in other Chinese varieties? Are the various sets of nominal demonstratives really separate sets, or are they related to each other in some way? How do they differ from each other? In the following sections, we explore the interesting issue of the relatively complex system of nominal demonstratives found in Min. We illustrate this discussion with examples from Hui'an, and use both the approach of linguistic typology and that of comparative dialectology. Nominal demonstratives in

Hui'an will be examined in terms of their syntactic functions and semantic features (in §5.2), and of their pragmatic uses (in §5.3).

Before doing this, we briefly clarify some terms related to semantic features of nominal demonstratives in Hui'an, as shown in Table 5-1 above and in §5.2.7 below. These include 'category', 'generic' and 'specific'. In this chapter, the term 'category' is roughly equivalent to '(sub)type, (sub)class', as opposed to 'token, individual'. For example, 'the apple' in English can refer to a class of fruit, while 'the apple I ate just now' refers to an individual item. In the first case, it is used to refer to a whole class (or an entire category), and thus is generic, while, in the second case, it can be specific, that is, be used to refer to a particular apple. The fruit itself involves many different varieties (subtypes), such as Fuji and Gala with each regarded here as a member of the entire category 'apple'.

5.2 Syntactic functions and semantic features

In this section, we describe one by one the five sets of nominal demonstratives presented above in Table 5-1, in terms of their syntactic functions and semantic features.

5.2.1 Basic adnominal demonstratives: *tsit⁷* 即 / *hit⁷* 迄

Unlike the demonstratives *zhè* and *nà* in Mandarin Chinese, the morphemes *tsit⁷* 'this' and *hit⁷* 'that' in Hui'an can neither be directly followed by a noun, as in (9), nor be used independently, as in (10).

(9) *即　　桌
　　$tsit^{7-8}$　$to?^{7}$
　　this　　table
　　'this table'

(10) *即　是　我　　其
　　$tsit^{7}$　si^{4}　gua^{3}　e^{2}
　　this　be　1SG　POSS
　　'This is mine.'

In Hui'an, *tsit⁷* 'this' and *hit⁷* 'that' typically precede a classifier, as in (11) and (12). They may also precede the complex [numeral + classifier] with plural items, as in (13).

(11) 即隻　　　無　　　甜
　　 tsit⁷⁻⁸-tsiaʔ⁷　boʔ²⁻⁴　tin¹
　　 this-CL　　not.have　sweet
　　 'This (chicken) is not sweet.'

(12) 即種　　　　否看
　　 tsit⁷⁻⁸-tsiɔŋ³　phaiʔ³⁻²-khuã⁵
　　 this-kind　　bad-look
　　 'This kind (of clothes) looks terrible.'

(13) 買　　迄兩套
　　 bue³⁻²　hit⁷⁻⁸-lŋ⁴-thoˀ⁵
　　 buy　　that-two-set
　　 'buy those two (houses)'

In (11), *tsit⁷* 'this' is followed by the classifier *tsiaʔ⁷*, a specific classifier typically for animals. In (12), *tsit⁷* 'this' precedes the measure word *tsiɔŋ³* 'kind'. In (13), *hit⁷* 'that' is followed by the numeral *lŋ⁴* 'two' and then the measure word *thoˀ⁵* 'set'. Semantically speaking, *tsit⁷⁻⁸tsiaʔ⁷* in (11) refers to a specific and individualized entity, *tsit⁷⁻⁸tsiɔŋ³* in (12) refers to a member of an entire category, while *hit⁷⁻⁸lŋ⁴thoˀ⁵* in (13) denotes a plural entity. As shown by examples (11) and (12), the numeral *tsit⁸* 蜀 'one' is typically covert, unlike the plural numeral *lŋ⁴* 'two' in example (13). In the following section, we discuss the hypothesis that demonstratives *tsit⁷* and *hit⁷* already contain numeral *tsit⁸* 'one'. If *tsit⁸* 'one' is overtly expressed, as in *tsit⁷⁻⁸tsit⁸⁻⁴tsiɔŋ³*, an emphasis is put on 'this kind of clothes' that I am talking about, as opposed to another kind. A similar phenomenon has been reported for Jinjiang 晉江 (a county-level city in Quanzhou City, see Lin, 2012:33).

The complex [*tsit⁷*/*hit⁷* (+ numeral) + classifier] often functions as a subject/topic denoting inanimate objects or animals in daily conversation, such as *tsit⁷⁻⁸tsiaʔ⁷* 'this (chicken)' and *tsit⁷⁻⁸tsiɔŋ³* 'this kind (of clothes)' in examples (11) and (12). It is also well attested that the complex [*tsit⁷*/*hit⁷* (+ numeral) + classifier] can function as the object of a verb such as *bue³* 'buy' in example (13), or as the object of a preposition such as the dependent marker of comparison *piˀ³* 比 in (14) below.

(14) 灰色　　比　　即領　　　恰　　　好看
　　 hə¹siak⁷　piˀ³⁻²　tsit⁷⁻⁸-liã³　khaʔ⁷⁻⁸　ho³⁻²-khuã⁵
　　 gray　　 DMC　 this-CL　　 HMC　　 good-look
　　 'The gray one looks better than this piece (of clothing).'

Example (14) is a typical comparative construction of inequality in Hui'an. The standard of comparison $tsit^{7\text{-}8}li\tilde{a}^3$ 'this piece (of clothing)' serves as an object of the comparative marker pi^3. The complex $tsit^{7\text{-}8}li\tilde{a}^3$ here denotes an inanimate object.

The complex [$tsit^7/hit^7$ + numeral + classifier] can also refer to human being(s), as in (15) and (16), though this usage is relatively less frequent in daily conversation.

(15) 叫　　即兩個　　來
  $kio^{5\text{-}3}$　$tsit^{7\text{-}8}\text{-}lŋ^4\text{-}e^2$　lai^2
  call　this-two-CL　come
  'ask these two (persons) to come here'

(16) 迄孤　　畢業　　咯
  $hit^{7\text{-}8}\text{-}kɔ^1$　$pet^{7\text{-}8}giəp^8$　$lɔ^0$
  that-CL　graduate　SFP
  'That (person) has graduated.'

The complex $tsit^{7\text{-}8}lŋ^4e^2$ 'these two (persons)' in (15) functions as the object of the verb kio^5 'call', whereas the complex $hit^{7\text{-}8}kɔ^1$ 'that (person)' in (16) serves as a subject of the sentence.

A noun, or a pronoun such as i^1 伊 'he' in (17) below, may be added before the complex [$tsit^7/hit^7$ + numeral + classifier] to express possession.

(17) 伊　　即領
  i^1　$tsit^{7\text{-}8}\text{-}li\tilde{a}^3$
  3SG　this-CL
  'his piece (of clothing)'

In (17), the third person singular pronoun i^1 serves as a possessor, whereas the complex $tsit^{7\text{-}8}li\tilde{a}^3$ 'this piece (of clothing)' functions as a possessee.

As illustrated by examples (18a) and (19a) below, the complex [$tsit^7/hit^7$ + numeral + classifier] may serve as the head noun of a relative clause.

(18) a. ［伯　　買］　　即套
  　lan^3　bue^3　$tsit^{7\text{-}8}\text{-}tho^5$
  　1PL　buy　this-set
  　'this (house that) we bought'

b. 伫　　［買　　即套］
   lan³　bue³⁻²　tsit⁷⁻⁸-tho⁵
   1PL　buy　this-set
   'Let's buy this (house).'

(19) a. ［恁　　爸　　掠］　　迄隻
   len³⁻²　pa²　liaʔ⁸　hit⁷⁻⁸-tsiaʔ⁷
   2PL　father　catch　that-CL
   'that (duck) your father took (home)'

b. 恁　　爸　　［掠　　迄隻］
   len³⁻²　pa²　liaʔ⁸⁻⁴　hit⁷⁻⁸-tsiaʔ⁷
   2PL　father　catch　that-CL
   'your father took that (duck)'

Examples (18) and (19) both have two possible interpretations. In (18a), the complex *tsit⁷⁻⁸tho⁵* 'this (house)' (lit. 'this CL (house)') serves as a head noun, following the relative clause *lan³ bue³* 'we buy'. Similarly, the complex *hit⁷⁻⁸tsiaʔ⁷* 'that (duck)' in (19a) is preceded by the relative clause *len³⁻² pa² liaʔ⁸* 'your father took (home)' and functions as the head noun of the relative clause. In terms of this usage, the distal demonstrative *hit⁷* found in (19a) is much more common than the proximal demonstrative *tsit⁷* found in (18a). In (18b) and (19b), however, *tsit⁷⁻⁸tho⁵* 'this (house)' and *hit⁷⁻⁸tsiaʔ⁷* 'that (duck)' function as the object of the main verbs *bue³* 'buy' and *liaʔ⁸* 'catch', respectively. The difference between these two readings relies on the presence or absence of tone sandhi on the verbs *bue³* 'buy' and *liaʔ⁸* 'catch', realized in a citation tone in (18a) and (19a), vs. a sandhi tone in (18b) and (19b) (see §22.5.2 for details of light-headed relative clauses).

The complex [*tsit⁷/hit⁷* + numeral + classifier] can function as a modifier, in its turn, of a noun. More specifically, a noun can be further added at the end of the complex to produce [*tsit⁷/hit⁷* + numeral + classifier + noun] which shares the syntactic functions of [*tsit⁷/hit⁷* + numeral + classifier] in examples (11) – (19). Here are three more examples, the first two of which involve the omitted numeral for 'one' (see below).

(20) 即個　　　燈　　共　　伊　　開　　（起來）
   tsit⁷⁻⁸-e²⁻⁴　tiŋ¹　ka⁵⁻⁴　i¹　khui¹　khai⁰
   this-CL　light　OM　3SG　open　RVC
   'Switch on the light!'

(21) 伊　　唔　　是　　迄種　　　　儂
　　　i¹　　m⁵⁻⁴　si⁴　hit⁷⁻⁸-tsiɔŋ³⁻²　laŋ²
　　　3SG　not　be　that-kind　person
　　　'He is not that kind of person.'

(22) 汝　　迄兩隻　　　　鴨
　　　lu³　hit⁷⁻⁸-lŋ⁴-tsiaʔ⁷⁻⁸　aʔ⁷
　　　2SG　that-two-CL　duck
　　　'your two ducks'

In (20), the demonstrative *tsit⁷* with the classifier *e²* modifies the noun *tiŋ¹* 'light', and *tsit⁷⁻⁸e²⁻⁴tiŋ¹* 'this light' serves as a topic. In (21), *hit⁷⁻⁸tsiɔŋ³* 'that kind' is further followed by the noun *laŋ²* 'person', and *hit⁷⁻⁸tsiɔŋ³⁻² laŋ²* 'that kind of person' is linked to the subject *i¹* 'he' by the negative form of the copula verb *si⁴* 'be' (i.e. *m⁵⁻⁴ si⁴* 'not be'). In (22), the complex *hit⁷⁻⁸lŋ⁴tsiaʔ⁷* 'those two' modifies the noun *aʔ⁷* 'duck', and the second person singular pronoun *lu³* is further added before the demonstrative *hit⁷* to denote possession.

An adjective or adjective phrase may be further added before the noun, as in (23) and (24).

(23) 迄兩雙　　　　新　　襪
　　　hit⁷⁻⁸-lŋ⁴-saŋ¹　sen¹　bəʔ⁸
　　　that-two-pair　new　sock
　　　'those two new pairs of socks'

(24) 迄領　　　口　　口　　　羊毛衫
　　　hit⁷⁻⁸-liã³　huaʔ⁷　thiak⁷　iũ²⁻⁴bŋ²⁻⁴sã¹
　　　that-CL　that　beautiful　sweater
　　　'that quite beautiful sweater'

In (23), the adjective *sen¹* 'new' is inserted between the complex *hit⁷⁻⁸lŋ⁴saŋ¹* 'those two pairs' and the noun *bəʔ⁸* 'sock'. In (24), the adjective phrase *huaʔ⁷ thiak⁷* 'that beautiful' consisting of the degree adverbial demonstrative *huaʔ⁷* and the adjective *thiak⁷* 'beautiful', is placed between the complex *hit⁷⁻⁸liã³* 'that piece of' and the noun phrase *iũ²⁻⁴bŋ²⁻⁴sã¹* 'sweater'.

As illustrated by the examples given so far, in terms of their semantics, demonstrative phrases and noun phrases where the demonstratives *tsit⁷* and *hit⁷* occur usually represent a specific and individualized entity, as in examples (11) and (14) above, or they can refer to plural entities when a plural numeral is used, as in (13) and (15), if not denote a member of an entire category when a measure word such as *tsiɔŋ³* 'kind' is used, as in (12) and (21).

The following examples, however, show that the complex [*tsit⁷/hit⁷* + numeral + classifier] may involve non-specific reference.

(25) 即個　　也　　卜挃,　　迄個　　也　　卜挃
　　 tsit⁷⁻⁸-e²⁻⁴　a⁴　boʔ⁷⁻⁸tiʔ⁸　hit⁷⁻⁸-e²⁻⁴　a⁴　boʔ⁷⁻⁸tiʔ⁸
　　 this-CL　also　want　　that-CL　also　want
　　 'Everyone wants (it).' (lit. 'this (person) wants (it), that (person) also wants (it)')

(26) 買　　　即口　　　買　　　迄口
　　 bue³⁻²　tsit⁷⁻⁸-khan¹　bue³⁻²　hit⁷⁻⁸-khan¹
　　 buy　　this-item　　buy　　that-item
　　 'buy different items' (lit. 'buy this item, buy that item')

In (25), *tsit⁷⁻⁸e²* 'this (person)' is followed by *hit⁷⁻⁸e²* 'that (person)' to imply that different persons are interested in the same object, in this case demonstratives do not point out a specific person but rather serve a use similar to indefinite pronouns. In (26), *tsit⁷⁻⁸khan¹* co-occurs with *hit⁷⁻⁸khan¹* to express that different items are bought by somebody, without pointing out a specific item. The two examples also show that this usage is valid no matter whether the complex [*tsit⁷/hit⁷* + numeral + classifier] functions in a sentence as a subject as in (25), or as an object as in (26). It should also be noted that the complex *tsit⁷⁻⁸/hit⁷⁻⁸ khan¹* is the most commonly heard in this use in daily conversation.

According to Dixon (2003:65-66), in many languages where nominal demonstratives may be full NPs, this usage is relatively infrequent and is subject to restrictions, as illustrated by English *this* and *that*, which can only be used as a full NP in limited circumstances, for example, an NP *this* or *that* with an animate reference is restricted to being a copular subject in an identity clause (e.g. *That's my wife*). If the complex [*tsit⁷/hit⁷* + numeral + classifier] in Hui'an is as a whole regarded as a nominal demonstrative, its behaviour would be contrary to the typological tendency observed in Dixon (2003), since in daily conversation the use of Hui'an [*tsit⁷/hit⁷* + numeral + classifier] as a full NP is relatively more frequent than its use as a noun modifier. In the following discussion, we attempt to provide some explanations for the current status of *tsit⁷~hit⁷* in Hui'an.

Huang & Lien (2007) note that in a play that reflects early stages of the Chaozhou and Quanzhou varieties of Southern Min, the 1581 *Wan Li* 萬曆 version of the *Li Zhi Ji* 荔枝記 (The Romance of the Lichi), only two nominal demonstratives can be attested, i.e. *tsi⁵³* 只 and *huɯ⁵³* 許.² These demonstratives take on a range of syntactic functions similar to those of Mandarin *zhè* and *nà*, that is, they may (a) directly modify a noun; (b) function as a noun modifier with the complex [numeral + classifier], or with only a classifier or a numeral; (c) co-occur with the complex [numeral + classifier] or just a classifier, without a noun; (d) make up a complete NP by themselves; and (e) modify an adjective to mark degree (see Huang & Lien 2007 for details). In addition, function (a), that is, to directly modify a noun, is much more common than function (d) where demonstratives are used independently as a complete NP, as well as with respect to the other functions. All these clearly show that in early Southern Min (e.g. the 1581 *Wan Li* version of the *Li Zhi Ji*), nominal demonstratives used to function quite similarly to modern Mandarin demonstratives *zhè* and *nà*, which also accords better with the typological observation on nominal demonstratives made in Dixon (2003) that we mentioned above.

Now, why and how did the syntactic functions of these nominal demonstratives become restricted in the modern Hui'an dialect? By comparing several varieties of Southern Min, we discovered that the counterparts of Hui'an *tsit⁷* and *hit⁷* are also pronounced as *tsit⁷* and *hit⁷* in Quanzhou, Jinjiang, Xiamen and Zhangzhou in Fujian (cf. Zhou & Ouyang 1998:358; Li 1999:270; Zhou 2006:583, 588; Lin 2012:32), as well as in Taiwan (cf. Yang 1991:198; Lien 1999; Liu X. 2005:133). However, in some other varieties spoken in Guangdong, such as Shantou, Jieyang and Chenghai 澄海, the counterparts of Hui'an *tsit⁷* and *hit⁷* are pronounced as *tsi* and *huɯ/hə* respectively, without the plosive ending *t* (cf. Shi 1995:201, 1999:304; Lin 1996:226; Xu 2007:84). More interestingly, both *tsit~hit* (with the stop ending *t*) and *tsi~hi* (without the stop ending *t*) are attested in the Qionglin 瓊林 variety of Southern Min, a conservative variety spoken on the island of Quemoy or Jinmen 金門 (Liu X. 2005). Both pronunciations are also given in Douglas (1990[1873]:38, 127, 134), a Chinese-English dictionary that reflects the early Xiamen variety (also cited in Liu X. 2005:138), and in *Putonghua Minnan Fangyan Cidian* 普通話閩南方言詞典 (1982:553, 880, 994), a Mandarin-Southern Min dictionary. Note, however, that in Qionglin, the two sets *tsit~hit* and *tsi~hi* are in complementary distribution in terms of their syntactic functions, as shown in (i).

(i) The complementary distribution of *tsit~hit* and *tsi~hi* in Qionglin
    a. *tsi/hi* + plural numeral + classifier + noun

---

2 This observation is made about a version of the Wan Li period of Ming dynasty, i.e. late 16th or early 17th century. The pronunciations *tsi⁵³* and *huɯ⁵³* given here are based on the modern Shantou variety of Southern Min, as described by Zeng (1991).

b. *tsit/hit* + classifier + noun (cf. Liu X., 2005:142)

On the contrary, these two sets seem to share similar syntactic functions in the early Xiamen variety noted in Douglas (1990[1873]). In *Putonghua Minnan Fangyan Cidian* (1982), the set *tsi~hi* (without the stop ending) seems to be only attested in the idiom *khua tsi khua hi* 看皆看許 'look around' (lit. 'look at this look at that'), in which the demonstratives *tsi* and *hi* seem to involve non-specific reference. This idiom probably preserves and reflects an earlier usage of Southern Min nominal demonstratives. In addition, the set *tsi~hi* can be found in some minor varieties of modern Southern Min spoken in Fujian, such as the Datian 大田 and Youxi 尤溪 varieties spoken in Sanming 三明, and in varieties spoken in several counties of Zhangzhou and in a few townships of the Nan'an 南安 County in Quanzhou (Huang 1961:23; Chen & Li 1991:94).

Based on some of the facts mentioned above, previous studies such as Mei & Yang (1995), Li (1999), Lien (1999), Mei (1999), and Liu X. (2005) have argued that demonstratives *tsit~hit* are in fact fused forms of the demonstratives *tsi* 只~*hi* 許 and the numeral 'one', i.e. it^7 一 'one' (e.g. Mei & Yang 1995; Mei 1999), or $tsit^8$ 蜀 'one' (e.g. Lien 1999). Liu X. (2005) further argued that the two sets of demonstratives *tsit~hit* and *tsi~hi* co-existed in earlier Southern Min, and that modern varieties preserve either *tsit~hit* or *tsi~hi*, as a result of the competition between them. The fusion hypothesis would convincingly explain why demonstratives *tsit* and *hit* typically require a classifier. This syntactic constraint can be accounted for by the fact that numeral 'one' is still retained in the demonstratives *tsit* and *hit*, even though these forms seem to have undergone a certain amount of grammaticalization in that they can be followed by a plural numeral in modern Southern Min. It is also possible that other nominal demonstratives have taken over partial functions of these earlier demonstratives, *tsi~hi*. We examine these other demonstratives in the following sections.

From the point of view of the interface between phonology and grammar, the analysis proposed so far also shows how a phonological process (i.e. syllable fusion) has affected the nominal demonstrative system and has impacted on the syntactic functions of Southern Min nominal demonstratives.

It should be noted that syllabic coalescence is also attested in Mandarin Chinese: the nominal demonstratives 這 and 那 both have two forms, *zhè~nà* and *zhèi~nèi*. The latter forms result from the fusion of *zhè* and *nà* with numeral *yī* 一 'one' (cf. Zhu 1982:85). However, the fused forms *zhèi~nèi* in Mandarin Chinese are more grammaticalized than the fused forms *tsit~hit* in modern Southern Min, since *zhèi~nèi* can directly modify a noun, and be used independently as the subject of a sentence to denote a human being or an object, even though their syntactic functions are more restricted than *zhè~nà* (Zhu 1982:86; Zhang & Fang 1996:159-160).

Another interesting phenomenon associated with Hui'an complex [*tsit^7*/*hit^7* + numeral + classifier] can be observed in a context where three, or more than three entities, are involved. Suppose that there are in total four entities present in the context (e.g. A, B, C, D), of which A and B are relatively close to the speaker, while C and D are relatively far from the speaker. A and B will be conceived of as one group, and each will be randomly represented by the complexes *tsit$^{7\text{-}8}$ e^2* (with tone sandhi) and *tsit^7 e^2* (without tone sandhi) without the two, A and B, being distinguished by any particular semantic parameters (that is, depending on the subjective viewpoint of the speaker, rather than the relative distance between A/B and the speaker). Similarly, C and D will be conceived of as another group, and be referred to by the complexes *hit$^{7\text{-}8}$ e^2* (with tone sandhi) and *hit^7 e^2* (without tone sandhi) in a random choice (also depending on the speaker's viewpoint). For example, *tsit$^{7\text{-}8}$ e^2* (with tone sandhi) and *tsit^7 e^2* (without tone sandhi) may be used to distinguish two entities which are both close to the speaker. Among these two forms, *tsit$^{7\text{-}8}$ e^2* follows the general tone sandhi rule in Hui'an, whereas *tsit^7 e^2* does not. The first syllable *tsit^7* in *tsit^7 e^2* is stressed, whereas the second syllable *e^2* is relatively unstressed, even though its tone contour is retained. The classifier (for instance, *e^2* in *tsit$^{7\text{-}8}$ e^2*) depends on the items referred to, and the relative order of A and B (also, C and D) depends on the order in which the speaker wishes to introduce the two entities, e.g. their relative importance. The relative distance between the two entities and the speaker may also play a role in some cases.

A similar phenomenon is also attested in other Southern Min varieties such as the Jinjiang and Xiamen varieties spoken in Fujian (Zhou & Ouyang 1998:359; Li 1999:277; Lin 2012:36-37), and in the Shantou variety spoken in Guangdong (Li 1999:277). However, in these varieties, the second syllable in the form without tone sandhi (e.g. the classifier *e^2*) is reported to have lost its tone contour and undergone tonal neutralization, as in (27), an example from Xiamen, where the general classifier *e^2* 個 is in a neutral tone (i.e. *e^0*) in the second occurrence of *tsit$^{7\text{-}8}$ e^2* 即個 'this one'.

(27) 即個　　　較　　　　　　否，(the Xiamen variety)
　　 tsit$^{7\text{-}8}$-e^2　kha?$^{7\text{-}3}$　　phai^3
　　 this-CL　comparatively　bad
　　 即個　　　較　　　　　　好
　　 tsit^7-e^0　kha?$^{7\text{-}3}$　　ho^3
　　 this-CL　comparatively　good
　　 'This one is comparatively bad, this one is comparatively good.'

It should be noted, however, that the case of four entities mentioned here is an idealized one. The use of forms without tone sandhi such as *tsit^7 e^2* is not obligatory. In some situations, for example, the speaker may point out different entities and use only a form with tone sandhi such as *tsit$^{7\text{-}8}$ e^2*. For instance, the speaker walks over to entity A and uses the form *tsit$^{7\text{-}8}$ e^2* to refer to A, then walks across to B and uses the same form (*tsit$^{7\text{-}8}$ e^2*) to refer to B.

5.2.2 Singular demonstratives: *tsat^8/hat^8*

Hui'an demonstratives *tsat^8* 'this' and *hat^8* 'that' differ from the demonstratives *tsit^7~hit^7* examined in the preceding section in that they may be used independently, as in (28), but may also directly modify a noun, as in (29).

(28) 口/口　　　　 今年　　　　幾　　　　　歲　　啊
　　 tsat^8/hat^8　ken^1-lin^2　kui$^{3\text{-}2}$　　hə^5　a^0
　　 this/that　this-year　how.many　year　SFP
　　 'How old is this/that one (child) this year?'

(29) 口/口　　　　　　老師　　　野　　　　好
　　 tsat$^{8\text{-}4}$/hat$^{8\text{-}4}$　lau^{4}su^1　ia$^{3\text{-}2}$　ho^3
　　 this/that　　teacher　quite　good
　　 'This/that teacher is quite good.'

Demonstratives *tsat^8* and *hat^8* make up a complete NP by themselves in (28), and directly modify the following noun *lau^{4}su^1* 'teacher' in (29). Unlike demonstratives *tsit^7* and *hit^7*, they cannot be followed by a classifier or by the complex [numeral + classifier]. These two examples also show that both the demonstratives *tsat^8~hat^8* and the complex [*tsat^8/hat^8*+ noun] can refer to a specific person and function as the subject/topic of the sentence. All this suggests that Hui'an demonstratives *tsat⁸* and *hat⁸* may have incorporated both numeral *tsit⁸* 'one' and general classifier *e²* 個.

The following two examples illustrate the use of *tsat⁸~hat⁸* as the subject of the sentence to denote a specific and individualized inanimate object. Demonstratives *tsat⁸* and *hat⁸* are used independently in (30), and modify the following noun *thua¹len⁵* 拖鏈 'towline' in (31).

(30) 口/口　　啥　　啊
　　 tsat⁸/hat⁸　siã²　aº
　　 this/that　what　SFP
　　 'What is this/that?'

(31) 口/口　　　　拖鏈　　　否　　去
　　 tsat⁸⁻⁴/hat⁸⁻⁴　thua¹len⁵　phai³　khuº
　　 this/that　　　towline　　bad　　PVC
　　 'This/that towline has gone bad.'

The demonstratives *tsat⁸~hat⁸* and the noun phrases in which they occur can also be used as the object of a preposition, such as the benefactive marker *ka⁵* 共 in (32), or of a verb, such as *kia²* 攑 'take' in (33).

(32) 共　　　口　　買　　　衫
　　 ka⁵⁻⁴　tsat⁸　bue³⁻²　sã¹
　　 BEN　this　buy　　clothes
　　 'buy clothes for this one (child)'

(33) 我　　攑　　　口
　　 gua³　kia²⁻⁴　hat⁸
　　 1SG　take　　that
　　 'I take that (one).'

Proximal demonstrative *tsat⁸* is in (32) preceded by benefactive marker *ka⁵*, and functions as the beneficiary of the action 'buy', while distal demonstrative *hat⁸* in (33) serves as the object of *kia²* 'take'. These two examples also illustrate that demonstratives *tsat⁸~hat⁸*, when they syntactically function as an object, can denote a specific human being as in (32), or a specific and individualized object as in (33). Nouns such as *ken³⁻²a³* 囝仔 'child' and *to²⁷* 桌 'table' can be further added after demonstratives *tsat⁸* and *hat⁸* in (32) and (33), respectively. It should be noted, however, that even if the proximal demonstrative *tsat⁸* and the noun phrases in which it occurs may be used as objects, they are more typically used as the subject of the sentence in daily conversation, as shown in examples (28) – (31). By way of contrast, both uses as subject and object turn out to be frequent in the case of the distal demonstrative *hat⁸* and the noun phrases in which it occurs.

Demonstratives *tsat⁸* and *hat⁸*, especially *hat⁸*, may be modified by a personal pronoun such as *gua³* 我 'I' as in (34), a noun such as *a¹i²* 阿姨 'aunt' as in (35), or a relative clause such as *i¹ le?⁷⁻⁸ iŋ⁵* 伊咧用 'he is using' as in (36).

(34) 我　　口　　三　　萬
　　　gua³　*tsat⁸*　*sã¹*　*ban⁵*
　　　1SG　this　three　ten.thousand
　　　'(The renovation) of my (house) cost thirty thousand CNY.'

(35) 伯　　口　　沙發　　比　　阿姨　　口　　恰　　好料
　　　lan³　*tsat⁸⁻⁴*　*sa¹huat⁷*　*pi³⁻²*　*a¹-i²*　*hat⁸*　*kha?⁷⁻⁸*　*ho³⁻²liau⁵*
　　　1PL　this　sofa　DMC　PREF-aunt　that　HMC　good
　　　'Our sofa is better than that at auntie's place.'

(36) [[伊　咧　用]　口]　是　我　其　其
　　　i¹　*le?⁷⁻⁸*　*iŋ⁵*　*hat⁸*　*si⁴*　*gua³*　*e²*　*e⁰*
　　　3SG　PROG　use　that　be　1SG　POSS　SFP
　　　'The (knife) that he is using is mine.'

(34) is used in a context where people are talking about the renovation of their houses. Proximal demonstrative *tsat⁸* is preceded by the first person singular pronoun *gua³* to refer to 'mine' ('my house'). In (35), distal demonstrative *hat⁸*, co-referential with the noun *sa¹huat⁷* 'sofa', is modified by the noun *a¹i²* 'aunt'. In (36), the subject is encoded by the distal demonstrative *hat⁸* which serves as a head noun and is modified by the relative clause *i¹ le?⁷⁻⁸ iŋ⁵* 'he is using' (cf. chapter 22). Distal demonstrative *hat⁸* tends to be modified, maybe because proximal *tsat⁸* is typically used to refer to a person or an object that is present, whereas *hat⁸* also often refers to something or someone not visible in the context of speech, so the modifier helps the hearer to identify the referent. Nouns such as *tshu⁵* 厝 'house', *sa¹huat⁷* 'sofa' and *to¹* 刀 'knife' can be added directly after the demonstratives *tsat⁸*~*hat⁸* in examples (34) – (36), respectively.

In some cases, demonstratives *tsat⁸* and *hat⁸* are co-referential with the preceding personal pronoun, e.g. with personal pronoun *i¹* 伊 'he' in (37), or with the following noun, e.g. with *a¹sã¹* 阿三 'Ah-San' in (38).

(37) 伊　口　四　個　姑姑
　　 i^1　$tsat^8$　$si^{5\text{-}3}$　$e^{2\text{-}4}$　$kɔ^1kɔ^1$
　　 3SG　this　four　CL　aunt
　　 'He has four aunts.'

(38) 口　阿三　考　博士
　　 hat^8　$a^1sã^1$　$khɔ̃^{3\text{-}2}$　$phɔk^{7\text{-}8}suɯ^4$
　　 that　PN　take.exam　doctor
　　 'Ah-San took an entrance examination for PhD course.'

Both the examples above are found in our spoken data. Example (37) was used in a context where the referent of the pronoun i^1 'he' had been mentioned in the preceding discourse. The pronoun i^1 'he' and its following demonstrative $tsat^8$ 'this' form an appositive construction, which helps the hearer to identify its referent. In (38), the person coded by demonstrative hat^8 is mentioned for the first time, and the noun $a^1sã^1$ is used to make it clear to the hearer who the speaker is talking about.

As shown by the examples above, Hui'an demonstratives $tsat^8$~hat^8 and the noun phrases in which they occur typically denote a specific person or object, showing a semantic correspondance with Mandarin *zhè/zhèi ge* 這個 'this (one)' and *nà/nèi ge* 那個 'that (one)' respectively, which are composed of demonstratives *zhè~nà* (or *zhèi~nèi*) 'this/that' and the general classifier *ge*. Thus, although Hui'an demonstratives $tsat^8$ and hat^8 are monosyllabic words, they share many characteristics with Mandarin *zhè/zhèi ge* and *nà/nèi ge*.[3]

---

[3] We have contemplated the possibility that Hui'an demonstratives $tsat^8$ and hat^8 might result from the fusion of demonstratives $tsit^7/hit^7$ 'this/that' and the general classifier e^2. However, we lack internal phonological evidence to support this hypothesis. In §5.2.4 below, we discuss another set of demonstratives used in Hui'an, tse^2~$hə^2$, which makes the issue even more complicated. Thus, the source of Hui'an demonstratives $tsat^8$~hat^8 requires further investigation. Comparatively speaking, their semantic counterparts in other Southern Min varieties such as Xiamen, Qionglin and Taiwan might seem to be more clearly related to a fused form [tsit/hit + e] or [tsi/hi + e], since they are typically pronounced as *tse~he* (cf. *Putonghua Minnanhua Fangyan Cidian* 1982:553, 994; Yang 1991:218; Zhou & Ouyang 1998:358-359; Lien 1999:76; Liu X. 2005:134, 137). However, these forms also require futher investigation.

5.2.3 Plural demonstratives: *tsuai*² 撮/*huai*² 懷

Demonstratives *tsuai*² 'these' and *huai*² 'those' differ from *tsat*⁸ and *hat*⁸ only in that *tsuai*² and *huai*² denote either plural entities, as in (39), or a mass entity such as *kun*³⁻²*tsui*³ 滾水 'boiled water' in (40) which is treated like a plural, while they may not refer to a specific, individualized person or object. In (39) and (40) they are both used independently as the subject of a copular sentence to denote an inanimate object.

(39) 撮　　是　　阮　　　學堂　　　其　　　樓
　　　 *tsuai*²　*si*⁴　*gun*³　*oʔ*⁸⁻⁴*tŋ*²　*e*²⁻⁴　*lau*²
　　　 these　be　1PL　school　GEN　building
　　　 'These are the buildings of our school.'

(40) 懷　　是　　滾水
　　　 *huai*²　*si*⁴　*kun*³⁻²-*tsui*³
　　　 those　be　boil-water
　　　 'That is boiled water.'

Like *tsat*⁸ and *hat*⁸, *tsuai*² and *huai*² may be the subject/topic of a sentence where the copula is covert, as shown in (41). At the same time, *tsuai*² and *huai*² are often used alone as the object of a verb such as *kuã*⁴ 捾 'carry' in (42), or of a preposition such as the comitative marker *kaʔ*⁷ 合 'with' in (43).

(41) 撮　　阮　　　老師
　　　 *tsuai*²　*gun*³⁻²　*lau*⁴*su*¹
　　　 these　1PL　teacher
　　　 'These are my teachers.'

(42) 我　　捾　　撮
　　　 *gua*³　*kuã*⁴　*tsuai*²
　　　 1SG　carry　these
　　　 'Let me take these.'

(43) 合　　　懷　　創　　做蜀下
　　　 *kaʔ*⁷⁻⁸　*huai*²　*tshɔŋ*⁵　*tsue*⁵⁻³*tsit*⁸⁻⁴*e*⁴
　　　 COMT　those　do　together
　　　 'Put (these) together with those.'

The use of demonstratives *tsuai²~huai²* to denote human beings, illustrated in example (41), is however relatively less frequent than their use to denote inanimate objects.

Demonstratives *tsuai²* and *huai²*, like *tsat⁸* and *hat⁸*, can also modify nouns, or be modified themselves, as in the examples below.

(44) 伫　厝裡　　　合　　　懷　　孫
　　 ti⁴　tshu⁵⁻³-lai⁴　kap⁷⁻⁸　huai²　sun¹
　　 at　house-inside　look.after　those　grandchild
　　 '(She is) at home looking after those grandchildren.'

(45) 汝　撮　　恰　　　　　好
　　 lu³　tsuai²　khaʔ⁷⁻⁸　ho³
　　 2SG　these　comparatively　good
　　 'These ones of yours are better (than mine).'

(46) [[恁 買]　懷]　無　　　　貴
　　 len³　bue³　huai²　bo²⁻⁴　kui⁵
　　 2PL　buy　those　not.have　expensive
　　 'Those you bought are not expensive.'

In (44), distal demonstrative *huai²* modifies the following noun *sun¹* 'grandchild' denoting a human being, and the noun phrase *huai² sun¹* 'those grandchildren' serves as the object of the verb *kap⁷* 'take care'. In (45), the proximal demonstrative *tsuai²* is modified by the second person singular pronoun *lu³* to denote possession. In (46), the distal demonstrative *huai²* functions as a head noun modified by the relative clause *len³ bue³* 'you buy', and *len³ bue³ huai²* 'those you bought' as a whole functions as the subject of the sentence, followed by the predicate *bo²⁻⁴ kui⁵* 'not expensive'.

The examples above show that demonstratives *tsuai²* and *huai²* basically correspond to demonstratives *zhèxiē* 這些 'these' and *nàxiē* 那些 'those' in Mandarin Chinese. However, according to Lü (1980:360, 593), in Mandarin *zhèxiē* 'these' and *nàxiē* 'those', when they function as the subject of an interrogative sentence, usually denote inanimate objects rather than human beings, as shown in the following two examples. Demonstrative *zhèxiē* 這些 'these' is infelicitous in (47a), and must be followed by a noun, to become *zhèxiē rén* 這些人 'these people' as in (47b).

(47) a. *这些   是   谁 (Mandarin Chinese)
    zhèxiē shì shuí
    these   be   who
    'Who are these?'

   b. 这些   人   是   谁/什麽人 (Mandarin Chinese)
    zhèxiē rén   shì shuí/shénme-rén
    these   person be   who/what-person
    'Who are these people?'

(48) a. 撮   啥儂   啊 (Hui'an)
    tsuai² siã²-laŋ²   a⁰
    these   what-person   SFP
    'Who are these?'

   b. 撮   儂   啥儂   啊 (Hui'an)
    tsuai² laŋ² siã²-laŋ²   a⁰
    these   person what-person SFP
    'Who are these people?'

In Hui'an, however, both *tsuai² laŋ²* 'these people' and *tsuai²* 'these', the counterparts of Mandarin *zhèxiē rén* 'these people' and *zhèxiē* 'these', can be used in this context, as shown in (48). It should also be mentioned that in this context the copula is usually covert in Hui'an, as opposed to Mandarin *shì* 'be' in (47).

Besides the use of *tsuai²* and *huai²* alone, a few examples of these plural demonstratives accompanied by a classifier, *tsuai²e²* 'these-CL' and *huai²e²* 'those-CL', are also attested in daily conversation in Hui'an, as in (49) and (50).

(49) 撮其   菜   著   五   口
    tsuai²e²⁻⁴   tshai⁵   tioʔ⁸⁻⁴   gɔ⁴   khɔ¹
    these   dish   need   five   YUAN
    'These dishes cost five yuan.'

(50) 懷其   儂   一直   卜   差   伊
    huai²e²⁻⁴   laŋ² et⁷⁻⁸tet⁸⁻⁴   boʔ⁷⁻⁸   tshe¹   i⁰
    those   person always   want   order.about 3SG
    'Those people always like to order him about.'

Demonstratives $tsuai^2e^2$ 'these' and $huai^2e^2$ 'those' are followed by the noun $tshai^5$ 'dish' and $laŋ^2$ 'person' in (49) and (50), respectively. The e^2 found in Hui'an $tsuai^2e^2$ and $huai^2e^2$ is most likely a case of the general classifier e^2, as our glossing shows. It should also be mentioned that $tsuai^2e^2$ and $huai^2e^2$ are attested in the speech of the elder generation, rather than that of the younger generation.

Tab. 5-2: The demonstratives for 'these' and 'those' in different Southern Min varieties

	Series A		Series B		Series C	
	Proximal 'these'	Distal 'those'	Proximal 'these' + CL	Distal 'those' + CL	Proximal 'these' + CL	Distal 'those' +CL
Hui'an 惠安	$tsuai^2$	$huai^2$	$tsuai^2e^2$	$huai^2e^2$		
Jinjiang 晉江	$tsuai^{24}$	$huai^{24}$	$tsuai^{55\text{-}24}e^{24}$	$huai^{55\text{-}24}e^{24}$		
Quanzhou 泉州	$tsia^2$	$huai^2$	$tsuai^2e^2$	$huai^2e^2$		
Xiamen 廈門	$tsia^2/$ $tsia?^7$	$hia^2/$ $hia?^7$	$tsia(?^{7\text{-}})^3e^2$	$hia(?^{7\text{-}})^3e^2$		$hit\ ku\bar{a}$
Zhangzhou 漳州	$tsia?^7$	$hia?^7$	$tsia(?^{7\text{-}})^3e^2$	$hia(?^{7\text{-}})^3e^2$		
Taiwan 臺灣	$tsia/tsiai$	$hia/hiai$	tse	he		
Qionglin 瓊林	$tsiai^{35}$	$hiai^{35}$	$tsi^{35}tsiai^{35}$	$hi^{35}hiai^{35}$	tse^5tsiai^{35}	he^5hiai^{35}
Shantou 汕頭			$tsi^3tsho?^7$	$hɯ^3tsho?^7$		
Jieyang 揭陽	$tsio^{53}$	hio^{53}	$tsi^{53\text{-}35}ko^{213}$	$hɯ^{53\text{-}35}ko^{213}$	$tsio^{53\text{-}35}$ $ko^{213}/tsho?^2$	$hio^{53\text{-}35}$ $ko^{213}/tsho?^2$

Table 5-2 shows the various counterparts of the Hui'an demonstratives $tsuai^2$ 'these' and $huai^2$ 'those' in eight other Southern Min varieties.[4] Table 5-2 clearly shows that Hui'an demonstratives for 'these/those' are basically parallel to those used in Jinjiang and Quanzhou. Lin (2012:33) considers that Jinjiang $tsuai^{24}$ and

---

4 The demonstratives in other Southern Min varieties listed in Table 5-2 are based on previous studies such as *Putonghua Minnanhua Fangyan Cidian* (1982), Yang (1991), Zhou & Ouyang (1998), Lien (1999), Liu X. (2005), Zhou (2006) and Xu (2007).

huai^{24} are contracted forms of *tsuai*$^{55\text{-}24}e^{24}$ and *huai*$^{55\text{-}24}e^{24}$, respectively. If we follow this analysis, Hui'an demonstratives *tsuai*^{2} and *huai*^{2} as shown in examples (39) – (46) should also be considered as contracted variants of the dissyllabic demonstratives *tsuai*$^2e^2$ and *huai*$^2e^2$ illustrated in (49) and (50), respectively.

Plural demonstratives in Taiwan Southern Min are basically in line with those used in the Xiamen and Zhangzhou varieties spoken in Fujian. Lien (1999:76) observes that plural demonstratives *tsia/hia* 'these/those' in Taiwan Southern Min are actually fused forms originating in demonstratives *tsit/hit* and the plural classifier *koa*, while plural demonstratives *tse/he* 'these/those' are fused forms which result from the contraction of plural demonstratives *tsia/hia* and the classifier *e*, as shown in (ii).

(ii) Fusion processes accounting for Taiwan Southern Min plural demonstratives
    a. *tsia* 這括 'these' < *tsit + *koa; *hia* 許括 'those' < *hit + *koa
    b. *tse* 這個 'these' < *tsia + *e; *he* 許個 'those' < *hia + *e

The disyllabic form *hit + *koa proposed in (ii) is still attested in the modern Xiamen variety (cf. *Putonghua Minnanhua Fangyan Cidian*, 1982:553). Similarly, Huang (1961:24-25) has also suggested that plural demonstratives in Southern Min are fused forms of demonstratives *tsit~hit* and the plural classifier *kua* 介/*kuã* 幹 or *kuaʔ* 葛, as shown in (iii). This results in two plural series as each demonstrative has a pronunciation with and without the glottal stop ending.

(iii) Fusion processes accounting for Southern Min plural demonstratives in Huang (1961)
    a. *tsia* 'these' < *tsit* + *kua/kuã*; *hia* 'those' < *hit* + *kua/kuã* (Xiamen and Zhangzhou)
    b. *tshiaʔ* 'these' < *tsit* + *kuaʔ*; *hiaʔ* 'those' < *hit* + *kuaʔ* (Xiamen and Zhangzhou)
    c. *tsua* 'these' < *tsit* + *kua/kuã*; *hua* 'those' < *hit* + *kua/kuã* (Quanzhou)
    d. *tsuaʔ* 'these' < *tsit* + *kuaʔ*; *huaʔ* 'those' < *hit* + *kuaʔ* (Quanzhou)

A similar fusion is also attested in Jieyang. According to Xu (2007:88), plural demonstratives *tsio*^{53} and *hio*^{53} are the fused forms of demonstatives *tsi*^{53}~*hu*^{5} and the collective classifier *ko*^{213}, i.e. *tsio*^{53}/*hio*^{53} < *tsi*^{53}/*hu*^{53} + *ko*^{213}. In addition, the disyllabic forms *tsi*$^{53\text{-}35}$/*hu*$^{53\text{-}35}$ *ko*^{213} are still used in the modern Jieyang variety.

Plural demonstratives followed by a classifier are also found in Mandarin Chinese. According to Lü (1980:360, 593), *zhè/zhèi xiē ge* 這些個 and *nà/nèi xiē ge* 那些個, consisting of the demonstratives *zhè/zhèi xiē* 這些~*nà/nèi xiē* 那些 and the general classifier *ge* 個, are used in the spoken language and share the functions of *zhè/zhèi xiē* 這些 and *nà/nèi xiē* 那些.

So far, we consider that it is safe to say that Hui'an *tsuai²* and *huai²* may be accounted for by the fusion of demonstratives *tsit⁷* and *hit⁷* with a plural or collective classifier, and that the following morpheme *e²* is the general classifier, though the detailed process of this fusion needs to be further explored.

5.2.4 Generic demonstratives: *tse²/hə²*

Demonstratives *tse²* 'this kind of' and *hə²* 'that kind of' show the same syntactic distribution that was described in §5.2.2 and §5.2.3 above for demonstratives *tsat⁸~hat⁸* and *tsuai²~huai²*. For example, *tse²~hə²* can either be used independently, as in (51), or be immediately followed by a noun and serve as a modifier, as in (52).

(51) 伊　　驚　　寒，　伊　　愛　　　穿　　　口
  i¹　 *kiã¹*　*kuã²*　*i¹*　*ai⁵⁻³*　*tshiŋ⁵⁻⁴*　*hə²*
  3SG　fear　cold　3SG　like　wear　that
  'She likes wearing that kind (of clothes since) she is sensitive to cold.'

(52) 口　　　桌　　食　　　恰　　　　　　好　　　食
  tse²　*to?⁷*　*tsiaʔ⁸*　*khaʔ⁷⁻⁸*　　*ho³⁻²*　*tsiaʔ⁸*
  this　table　eat　comparatively　good　eat
  'This kind of table is better for meals (than other kinds of tables).'

Distal demonstrative *hə²* in (51) is used independently as the object of the verb phrase *ai⁵⁻³ tshiŋ⁵* 'like wearing', whereas the proximal demonstrative *tse²* in (52) modifies the following noun *to?⁷* 'table', the resulting noun phrase *tse² to?⁷* functions as the subject of the sentence. Unlike demonstratives *tsat⁸~hat⁸* denoting a specific and individualized entity, demonstratives *tse²~hə²* in (51) and (52) represent a member of an entire category. Specifically, *hə²* in (51) is not used to refer to the specific piece of clothing she is wearing, but refers to a type of clothes, i.e. warm clothes, like the one that she is wearing. Similarly, *tse² to?⁷* in (52) is not used to refer to the specific and individuated table around which people are sitting, but refers to a type of table which shares some characteristic features with the one in question. In other words, demonstratives *tse²~hə²* in (51) and (52) are semantically similar to English *this kind of* or *that kind of*.

The following two examples show that *tse²~hə²* may also represent an entire category.

(53) 口　橙　　　無　　　敗害
　　　tse² tshiaŋ² bo²⁻⁴ pai⁵⁻⁴hai⁵
　　　this orange not.have harm
　　　'It is not bad (for you to eat) oranges.'

(54) 口　繪做　　　搭
　　　hə² bue⁴tsue⁵⁻³ taʔ⁷
　　　that cannot   stick
　　　'That (i.e. the scotch tape) cannot be stuck (to clothes).'

Example (53) is used in a context where the host is suggesting to the guest to eat some oranges, and *tse² tshiaŋ²* 'orange' is used to refer to the category 'orange' as a whole, rather than a specific set of oranges. This is because the host is making a generic statement about oranges. Example (54) was used in a situation where two people were getting rid of some cotton fibres stuck on their clothes by using scotch tape. The speaker wanted to stop them from doing so, as he mistakenly thought they were trying to stick scotch tape to the clothes. Thus, the distal demonstrative *hə²* in (54) is used to refer to the entire category 'scotch tape', rather than a specific token of scotch tape.

Sometimes, the use of *tse²* seems similar to that of *tsat⁸*, as in (55), emitted in a context where the speaker is showing her parents one of her photos taken during a trip, in which someone is singing for her and her friends.

(55) 口　是　儂　　咧　　　共　　阮　　　唱　　　　歌
　　　tse² si⁴ laŋ⁴ leʔ⁷⁻⁸ ka⁵⁻⁴ gun³⁻² tshiũ⁵⁻³ kua¹
　　　this be other PROG BEN 1PL sing song
　　　'This is (when) the person was singing for us.'

In (55), the proximal demonstrative *tse²* refers to the photo which the speaker is talking about. In this case, *tse²* seems to refer to a specific and individualized entity, just like demonstrative *tsat⁸*.

Demonstratives *tse²~hə²* differ from *tsat⁸~hat⁸* and *tsuai²~huai²* in that, acting as the head noun, they can be modified by the complex [numeral + classifier], as in (56) and (57).

(56) 伊　　也　蜀　　　條　　　口　　(鏈仔)
　　　i¹ a⁴ tsit⁸⁻⁴ tiau²⁻⁴ tse² (len⁵⁻⁴-a³)
　　　3SG also one CL   this (chain-NM)
　　　'She has a (necklace) like this too.'

(57) 阮   買   兩   垺   口   長   其
    gun³ bue³⁻² lŋ⁴ tə⁵⁻³ hə² tŋ²   e⁰
    1PL   buy   two CL   that long NMLZ
    'We bought two of the kind (of table) that is long.'

In (56), *tse² (len⁵⁻⁴a³)* refers to a kind of necklace, and is modified by *tsit⁸⁻⁴ tiau²*, which consists of numeral *tsit⁸* 'one' and classifier *tiau²*. In (57), *tŋ² e⁰* serves as a relative clause, while the head noun is encoded by the distal demonstrative *hə²* 'that' referring to the category of table. The noun phrase *hə² tŋ² e⁰* is further modified by the complex *lŋ⁴ tə⁵*, consisting of numeral *lŋ⁴* 'two' and classifier *tə⁵*.

In terms of their forms, all of the proximal demonstratives mentioned in §5.2.1-5.2.3 above differ from the distal ones only by their initials (i.e. *ts* for the proximal one, vs. *h* for the distal one). Proximal demonstrative *tse²*, however, differs from distal *hə²* both by the initial (i.e. *ts* vs. *h*) and the final (i.e. *e* vs. *ə*). Final *ə* regularly corresponds to final *e* in some other Southern Min varieties. For example, Hui'an *hə²* 回 'decline' and *hə³* 火 'fire' are pronounced as *he²* and *he³* respectively in Xiamen (Zhou 2006: 177-178). Thus, Hui'an *hə²* might be a late development from an earlier form *he²*. That is, it is possible that the proximal and distal forms may have shared the same final in an earlier stage of the Hui'an dialect.

Demonstratives with the phonetic shape of *tse~he* have been reported in other Southern Min varieties such as the Xiamen and Qionglin varieties and in Taiwan Southern Min (cf. Zhou & Ouyang 1998; Mei 1999; Lien 1999; Liu X. 2005). However, in these varieties *tse* and *he* typically express 'this/that one' and thus usually denote a specific and individualized entity, rather than a category. In other words, in these varieties *tse* and *he* are semantic counterparts of Hui'an *tsat⁸* and *hat⁸* (described in §5.2.2 above). In addition, in these varieties *tse* and *he* have been regarded by previous studies as fused form of demonstratives *tsit* and *hit* combined with the general classifier *e*. Thus, there may be a possibility that Hui'an demonstratives *tse²* and *hə²* originally expressed 'this/that one', that is, were used to denote a specific and individualized entity, and that later their use was extended to denote an entire category or a member of a category. In the meantime, the (new) forms *tsat⁸* and *hat⁸* developed as demonstratives for specific and individualized entities, thus accelerating the decline of demonstratives *tse²* and *hə²* in their original usage.

Another possibility is that *tse²* and *hə²* are contracted variants of demonstratives *tsiɔŋ³⁻²e²* 'this kind of' and *hiɔŋ³⁻²e²* 'that kind of' respectively, to be discussed in the following section. In some other Southern Min varieties, to denote a member of a category as in Huai'an examples (51) and (52), one typically uses the complex consisting of the demonstrative and the classifier for 'kind', for instance, *tsit⁷⁻⁸khuan³* 即款 'this kind of' and *hit⁷⁻⁸khuan³* 迄款 'that kind of' in Xiamen. This corresponds to Mandarin *zhèzhǒng* 這種 'this kind of' and *nàzhǒng* 那種 'that kind of', and to *this kind of* and *that kind of* in English. However, in the Qionglin variety of Southern Min spoken in Jinmen, and the Shantou and Jieyang varieties of Southern Min spoken in Guangdong, a special form is also attested to denote a representative of a category or an entire category, just like Hui'an *tse²~hə²*. Table 5-3-Table 5-5 shows this correspondence (data are taken from Shi 1999:289-324; Liu X. 2005:138, 143; and Xu 2007:84).

Tab. 5-3: Demonstratives denoting 'category' in Hui'an and Qionglin[5]

	Proximal	Distal
Hui'an	*tse²* 'this kind of' (generic)	*hə²* 'that kind of' (generic)
Qionglin	*tsɤ³⁵* 'this kind of' (generic)	*hɤ³⁵* 'that kind of' (generic)

Tab. 5-4: Demonstratives denoting 'category' in Shantou

Proximal	Distal
tsia⁵³⁻²⁴khi⁵³ 'this kind of' (generic)	*hia⁵³⁻²⁴khi⁵³* 'that kind of' (generic)
tsia⁵³(⁻²⁴khi⁵³)kai⁵⁵ 'this kind of' (generic)	*hia⁵³(⁻²⁴khi⁵³)kai⁵⁵* 'that kind of' (generic)
tsia⁵³ 'this kind of' (generic)	*hia⁵³* 'that kind of' (generic)

Tab. 5-5: Demonstratives denoting 'category' in Jieyang

Proximal	Distal
tsia⁵³ 'this kind of' (generic)	*hia⁵³* 'that kind of' (generic)
tsia⁵³⁻³⁵kai⁵⁵ 'this kind of NP'	*hia⁵³⁻³⁵kai⁵⁵* 'that kind of NP'

Demonstratives *tsɤ³⁵~hɤ³⁵* in Qionglin can denote a specific member of a category or just to the category itself, as shown in Table 5-3. Like Hui'an *tse²~hə²*, Qionglin

---

[5] We exclude here those forms consisting of a demonstrative meaning 'this/that' and a measure word meaning 'kind, category'.

$tsɤ^{35}$~$hɤ^{35}$ can be used independently or as a noun modifier (Liu X. 2005: 143). Table 5-4 shows that in Shantou there are three sets of demonstratives denoting a representative of a category or an entire category, of which $tsia^{53-24}khi^{53}$ and $hia^{53-24}khi^{53}$ can only be used as a noun modifier, $tsia^{53}(^{-24}khi^{53})kai^{55}$ and $hia^{53}(^{-24}khi^{53})kai^{55}$ can only be used as an independent pronoun, while $tsia^{53}$ and hia^{53} can be either a noun modifier or an independent pronoun (Shi 1999). In Jieyang, as stated in Table 5-5, $tsia^{53}/hia^{53}$ denote either a member of a category or an entire category, whereas $tsia^{53-35}kai^{55}/hia^{53-35}kai^{55}$ only denote a member of a category. In addition, $tsia^{53}/hia^{53}$ can be used independently, or as a noun modifier, whereas $tsia^{53-35}kai^{55}/hia^{53-35}kai^{55}$ may only be used independently.

This generic use of demonstratives to denote an entire category is also attested for *zhè~nà* in Beijing Mandarin. Zhang and Fang (1996:156-157) point out that Beijing Mandarin *zhè~nà* can be followed by a noun and denote an entire category, and consider that in this use, *zhè~nà* is a kind of generic marker. However, it is obvious that unlike Hui'an tse^2~$hə^2$ and other demonstratives shown in Tables 5-3, 5-4 and 5-5, Beijing *zhè~nà* do not constitute specialized forms used to exclusively to denote an entire category (see, e.g. (4) and (5) above; Lü 1980).

5.2.5 Generic demonstratives: *tsiɔŋ³⁻²e²* 種其/*hiɔŋ³⁻²e²* 向其

Demonstratives *tsiɔŋ³⁻²e²* and *hiɔŋ³⁻²e²* can either co-occur with a noun such as $tsin^{3-2}tsui^3$ 井水 'well water' in (58), or be used independently, as in (59). We show that they not only denote a specific representative of a category, but also an entire category. This distribution is similar to that of the other demonstratives described above, except for $tsit^7$ and hit^7.

(58) 種其 井水 恰 好
 $tsiɔŋ^{3-2}e^{2-4}$ $tsin^{3-2}$-$tsui^3$ $khaʔ^{7-8}$ ho^3
 this well-water comparatively good
 'Well water is better (than running water).'

(59) 向其 恰 酸
 $hiɔŋ^{3-2}e^2$ $khaʔ^{7-8}$ $sŋ^1$
 that.kind.of comparatively sour
 'That kind (of apple) tastes sourer than (this kind of apple).'

In (58), people are comparing well water and running water, and thus $tsiɔŋ^{3-2}e^{2-4}$ $tsin^{3-2}tsui^3$ 'well water' is used to denote the entire category of 'well water'. In (59), people are talking about two kinds of apple they bought, and the demonstrative *hiɔŋ³⁻²e²* is used to denote a specific member of the category 'apple'.

As illustrated by examples (58) and (59), demonstratives *tsiɔŋ³⁻²e²~hiɔŋ³⁻²e²* show the same basic syntactic functions and semantic features as demonstratives *tse²~hə²* described in §5.2.4 above, but their usage is quite limited. In other words, in everyday speech, *tse²~hə²* are much more common than *tsiɔŋ³⁻²e²~hiɔŋ³⁻²e²*. As mentioned above, we hypothesize that *tse²~hə²* may represent the fused forms of *tsiɔŋ³⁻²e²~hiɔŋ³⁻²e²*. In addition, demonstratives *tsiɔŋ³⁻²e²~hiɔŋ³⁻²e²* may be contracted forms of *tsit⁷⁻⁸tsiɔŋ³⁻²e²* 'this kind of' and *hit⁷⁻⁸tsiɔŋ³⁻²e²* 'that kind of', in which demonstratives and the measure word *tsiɔŋ³* 種 'kind' both keep their full original phonetic shape, and *e²* is the general classifier. More investigation is required to ground this hypothesis. It should be mentioned, however, that unlike the two sets of *tse²~hə²* (discussed in §5.2.4) and *tsiɔŋ³⁻²e²~hiɔŋ³⁻²e²* (discussed here), the full demonstrative phrases *tsit⁷⁻⁸tsiɔŋ³(⁻²e²)* 'this kind of' and *hit⁷⁻⁸tsiɔŋ³(⁻²e²)* 'that kind of' may only denote a specific representative of a category, and not an entire category.

Demonstratives *tsiɔŋ e~hiɔŋ e* are so far also attested in Jinjiang (Lin 2012), but not in other Southern Min varieties. In addition, in Hui'an *tse²~hə²* tend to be used in the examples provided in Lin (2012) for Jinjiang *tsiɔŋ e~hiɔŋ e*, even if *tsiɔŋ³⁻²e²~hiɔŋ³⁻²e²* are also acceptable. It should be mentioned that demonstratives *tse~hə* are not attested in Jinjiang. This may further support our hypothesis that Hui'an demonstratives *tse²~hə²* are contracted forms of *tsiɔŋ³⁻²e²~hiɔŋ³⁻²e²*.

5.2.6 Interim summary

A brief summary of the syntactic distributions and semantic features of the five sets of nominal demonstratives in Hui'an is given in Table 5-6.

Tab. 5-6: Syntactic distributions and semantic features of nominal demonstratives in the Hui'an dialect

	before [NUM + CL]	after [NUM + CL]	directly before a noun	main syntactic structure	alone as the subject or topic	alone as the object	modified by a personal pronoun, etc.	animacy	plurality and genericity
$tsit^7/hit^7$	+	-	-	$tsit^7/hit^7$(+NUM)+CL(+NP)	-	-	-	animate & inanimate	singular entity; plural entities; a member of an entire category
$tsat^8/hat^8$	-	-	+	$tsat^8/hat^8$(+NP)	+	+	+	animate & inanimate	singular entity
$tsuai^2/huai^2$	-	-	+	$tsuai^2/huai^2$(+NP)	+	+	+	animate & inanimate	plural entities; mass entity

Syntactic functions and semantic features — 87

	before [NUM+CL]	after [NUM+CL]	directly before a noun	main syntactic structure	alone as the subject or topic	alone as the object	modified by a personal pronoun, etc.	animacy	plurality and genericity
tse^2/ha^2	-	+	+	(NUM+CL+)tse^2/ha^2(+NP)	+	+	+	animate & inanimate	a member of an entire category; an entire category
$tsiɔŋ^{3\text{-}2}e^2/hiɔŋ^{3\text{-}2}e^2$		(+)[1]	+	(NUM+CL+)$tsiɔŋ^{3\text{-}2}e^2/hiɔŋ^{3\text{-}2}e^2$(+NP)	+	+	+	animate & inanimate	a member of an entire category; an entire category
tse^2/ha^2	-	+	+	(NUM+CL+)tse^2/ha^2(+NP)	+	+	+	animate & inanimate	a member of an entire category; an entire category

5.2.7 Further discussion on the semantic features of Hui'an demonstratives

Diessel (1999:35) classifies the meanings of demonstratives into two kinds: deictic features and qualitative features. Qualitative features 'provide classificatory information about the referent [...] for instance, whether the referent is animate or inanimate, female or male, or human or non-human'. In this section, we focus on the qualitative features of Hui'an nominal demonstratives by making a comparison with other Chinese varieties.

The qualitative features fall into six categories: ontology, animacy, humanness, sex, number and boundedness (Diessel, 1999:47). Hui'an nominal demonstratives are marked only for number, not for any of the other five categories, that is, they distinguish two number features: singular and plural. This is the case for most languages described in Diessel's (1999) sample: 'Most languages distinguish between singular and plural forms only' (Diessel, 1999:49).

Hui'an nominal demonstratives, however, show two further qualitative features which are not mentioned in Diessel (1999:47). They mark:

(a) type/category, that is, whether the referent is a type/category or token(s)/individual(s)

e.g. tse^2~$hə^2$ and $tsiɔŋ^{3\text{-}2}e^2$~$hiɔŋ^{3\text{-}2}e^2$ 'this/that kind of' serve as special forms indicating that the referent is a type/category, either an entire category or a specific member of a category, whereas other nominal demonstratives indicate that the referent is a token or a set of tokens.

(b) genericity, that is, whether the referent is generic or specific

e.g. tse^2~$hə^2$ (also $tsiɔŋ^{3\text{-}2}e^2$~$hiɔŋ^{3\text{-}2}e^2$) have two main functions: either tse^2~$hə^2$ 'this/that' (also $tsiɔŋ^{3\text{-}2}e^2$~$hiɔŋ^{3\text{-}2}e^2$ 'this/that') denote an entire category which is generic, or tse^2~$hə^2$ 'this/that kind of' (also $tsiɔŋ^{3\text{-}2}e^2$~$hiɔŋ^{3\text{-}2}e^2$ 'this/that kind of') denote a member of an entire category, whereas all the other nominal demonstratives indicate that the referent is specific.

As mentioned in §5.2.4 above, special forms for denoting 'category' are also attested in the Qionglin, Shantou and Jieyang varieties of Southern Min, whereas the use of the demonstratives as a generic marker is also attested in the Shantou and Jieyang varieties of Southern Min, and in Beijing Mandarin.

5.3 The pragmatic uses of Hui'an demonstratives

Based on Diessel's (1999:6) classification, we may distinguish two categories of pragmatic uses for demonstratives: (a) language-external functions and (b) language-internal functions. Language-external functions include exophoric use and recognitional use, of which exophoric use means that the demonstratives are "used with reference to entities in the surrounding situation", and recognitional use indicates that "speaker and hearer are familiar with the referent due to shared experience". Language-internal functions include anaphoric use and discourse deictic use, of which anaphoric use means that the demonstrative is "coreferential with a noun phrase in the preceding discourse", and discourse deictic use means the demonstrative refers to "a chunk of the surrounding discourse" (Diessel, 1999:6). Note that exophoric use and recognitional use are considered as more basic than anaphoric use and discourse deictic use. In this section, we examine these pragmatic uses and some other uses of Hui'an demonstratives.

5.3.1 Language-external functions

In Hui'an, the basic pragmatic use of both proximal and distal demonstratives is exophoric, that is, referring to a specific and individualized entity, to plural entities, to a member of a category, or to an entire category, via an object which is present in the surrounding situation. This usage is attested for all the five sets of demonstratives presented is §5.2. Let us take $tsit^7$~hit^7 as an example.

(60) 汝　搬　即垛
　　 lu^3　$pu\tilde{a}^1$　$tsit^{7\text{-}8}\text{-}tə^5$
　　 2SG　move　this-CL
　　 'You move this (chair)!'

(61) 我　穿　迄領
　　 gua^3　$tshiŋ^{5\text{-}4}$　$hit^{7\text{-}8}\text{-}li\tilde{a}^3$
　　 1SG　wear　that-CL
　　 'I will wear that piece (of clothing).'

In examples (60) and (61), $tsit^{7\text{-}8}tə^5$ 'this (chair)' and $hit^{7\text{-}8}li\tilde{a}^3$ 'that piece (of clothing)' both refer to an entity which is present in the speech situation and is visible to both the speaker and the hearer.

The exophoric use implies that demonstratives are restricted to a local context, that is, a context where the referent should be present in the surrounding situation. This is then extended to a broader context in which the referent can be absent from the surrounding situation but has to be familiar both to the speaker and the hearer. This gives rise to the recognitional use, illustrated in (62) and (63).

(62) 伫   厝裡   合   懷   孫
    ti⁴   tshu⁵⁻³-lai⁴   kap⁷⁻⁸   huai²   sun¹
    at   house-inside   look.after those   grandchild
    '(She is) at home looking after those grandchildren.'

(63) 我   感覺   口   工作   也   獪   否
    gua³   kam³⁻²kak⁷⁻⁸   tsat⁸⁻⁴   kaŋ¹tsɔk⁷   a⁴   bue⁴   phai³
    1SG   feel   this   job   also cannot bad
    'I think this job of mine is not bad.'

The context of (62) involves people talking about one of their relatives and her grandchildren, neither being present in the surrounding situation. In this example, *huai² sun¹* 'those grandchildren' is mentioned for the first time and used to refer to children who are known by both the speaker and the hearer. The distal demonstrative *huai²* 'those' indicates that the speaker believes that the hearer will be able to identify the referent, due to their shared knowledge. The context of (63) is one where people are talking about whether to go back to school for a PhD degree. In this example, *tsat⁸⁻⁴ kaŋ¹tsɔk⁷* 'this job' is also mentioned for the first time and does not exist in the surrounding situation. Proximal demonstrative *tsat⁸* 'this' indicates here that the speaker believes that the hearer knows the referent, and illustrates that a proximal demonstrative may have a recognitional use too. In other words, in examples (62) and (63) the referents of *huai² sun¹* 'those grandchildren' and *tsat⁸⁻⁴ kaŋ¹tsɔk⁷* 'this job' are not present in the surrounding situation, but are identifiable by both the speaker and the hearer. Like the exophoric use, the recognitional use is also attested for each of the five sets of Hui'an demonstratives. Comparatively speaking, however, proximal demonstratives tend to be associated with the exophoric use, whereas distal demonstratives tend to have a recognitional use.

From a context where the referent is not in the surrounding situation, but whose knowledge is shared by the speaker and the hearer, the use of these demonstratives may be further extended to contexts in which the speaker and the hearer do not share any common knowledge about a given referent at all, as in (64) and (65) where the referent is similarly not present in the speech context.

(64) 迄搭   口   儂   咧   拍   伊   其   手機
    hit⁷⁻⁸-taʔ⁷   hat⁸⁻⁴   laŋ²   leʔ⁷⁻⁸   phaʔ⁷⁻⁸   i¹   e²⁻⁴   tshiu³⁻²ki¹
    that-LOC   that   person   PROG   hit   3SG   GEN   cell.phone
    'That person there was calling him on his cell phone.'

(65) 阮   老爸   老實,   去   交,
    gun³⁻²   lau⁴-pe⁴   lau³⁻²set⁸   khu⁵⁻³   kau¹
    1PL   PREF-father   honest   go   hand.in
    伓   懷   計   無   交
    en¹   huai²   ke⁵⁻³   bo²⁻⁴   kau¹
    3PL   those   all   not.have   hand.in
    'My father handed (it) in since he is a honest man, while others didn't hand (it) in.'

The context for (64) is that the speaker is explaining to her sister why her husband does not come along with her, the reason being that someone ('that person') was looking for her husband just when they were leaving home, which stopped her husband from going out. In fact, the hearer, i.e. the speaker's sister, does not know the referent of *hat⁸⁻⁴ laŋ²* 'that person' at all, which is mentioned for the first time and who does not appear in the speech situation. In (65), the speaker is talking about a past experience to someone whom he meets for the first time, *en¹ huai²* 'they' is mentioned for the first time and is not identifiable by the hearer. In this example, *en¹ huai²* 'they' is used in contrast with *gun³⁻² lau⁴pe⁴* 'my father', and whether it is identifiable for the hearer or not is not important to the speaker. Such a use of demonstratives, illustrated in examples (64) and (65), is typically found for distal demonstratives *hat⁸* 'that' and *huai²* 'those', and is relatively limited, compared to their exophoric and recognitional uses.

While all uses mentioned so far are associated with specific reference, Hui'an demonstratives may also involve non-specific reference, especially when the proximal and distal demonstratives co-occur in the same sentence, as in examples (25) and (26) discussed in §5.2.1 above. Two further examples that do not involve co-occurrence of the proximal and distal demonstratives in the same sentence are given in (66) and (67) below.

(66) 即隻   來,   即隻   去
    tsit⁷⁻⁸-tsiaʔ⁷   lai²   tsit⁷⁻⁸-tsiaʔ⁷   khu⁵
    this-CL   come   this-CL   go
    'This (bus) comes here, and then this same (bus) leaves here.'

(67) 蜀   垃   樓   蜀   垃   樓   離   蠻   遠
    tsit⁸⁻⁴   tə⁵⁻³   lau²   tsit⁸⁻⁴   tə⁵⁻³   lau²   li⁵⁻⁴   ban²⁻⁴   hŋ⁴
    one   CL   building one   CL   building apart.from   rather   far
    即垃   樓,   停   蜀   把   車,
    tsit⁷⁻⁸-tə⁵⁻³   lau²   thiŋ²⁻⁴   tsit⁸⁻⁴   pe³⁻²   tshia¹
    this-CL   building stop   one   CL   vehicle
    佫   兩   個   車位
    koʔ⁷⁻⁸   lŋ⁴   e²⁻⁴   tshia¹ui⁵
    still   two   CL   parking.space
    'There is much space between buildings. Take this building, even if there is a car there, there are still two parking spaces.'

In (66), the speaker is talking about the bus operation system, that is, the same bus arrives and then leaves soon after, which is in contrast with another system, where one bus arrives at the given location, and then another bus (rather than the one which just arrived) leaves in its place. In this sentence, the demonstrative phrase *tsit⁷⁻⁸tsiaʔ⁷* ([this + classifier]) refers to any of many possible items, by way of example, rather than to a specific one. This example also illustrates that the same demonstrative phrase used twice in the same sentence may nonetheless still involve non-specific reference. In (67), the speaker is describing how much space there is between buildings in her residence community. The noun phrase *tsit⁷⁻⁸tə⁵⁻³ lau²* 'this building' also refers to any one of many possible items, by way of example, rather than to a specific building.

Due to one of their basic semantic features, distal demonstratives *hə²* and *hiɔŋ³⁻²e²* can introduce a general category which is mentioned for the first time, even when the referent is not present in the speech situation, if the knowledge is shared by everyone, that is, if it belongs to general knowledge, as exemplified by (68).

(68) 阿姨   合   口   外國仔   照
    a¹-i²   kaʔ⁷⁻⁸   hə²   gua⁵⁻⁴kɔk⁷⁻⁸-a³   tsio⁵
    PREF-aunt   COMT   that   foreign-NM   snap
    'Auntie took a picture with the foreigners.'

In (68), *gua⁵⁻⁴kɔk⁷⁻⁸a³* 'the foreigners' refers to a type of person, which is neither mentioned in the preceding discourse nor present in the speech situation. It is not privately shared knowledge either, but general knowledge known to everyone in the community.

Distal demonstratives $hə^2$ and $hiɔŋ^{3\text{-}2}e^2$ (especially $hə^2$) are also often used when the speaker is not willing to say something directly, as in (69).

(69) 伯　　也　　無　　迄種　　　　　口，　伯　　唔免
　　 lan³　a⁴　 bo²⁻⁴　hit⁷⁻⁸-tsiɔŋ³⁻²　hə²　lan³　m⁵⁻⁴ben³
　　 1PL　also　not.have　that-kind　that　1PL　no.need
　　 'We don't have that kind (of diseases/problems), (so) we don't need (a massage).'

In (69), the speaker is sharing with her mother her opinions on massage, explaining to her why massage is not necessary. However, she does not want to say it directly for reasons of delicacy. The demonstrative $hə^2$ here may refer to some diseases or problems, and is probably non-identifiable to the hearer.

Example (70) below shows that distal demonstrative $hə^2$ may be used when the speaker cannot find the right words to express something.

(70) 恁　　工作　　　會　　口　　 繪,　　會　　辛苦　　　繪
　　 len³　kaŋ¹tsɔk⁷　e⁴　hə²　 bue⁰　e⁴　sen¹khɔ³　bue⁰
　　 2PL　work　　　can　that　SFP　can　hard　　　SFP
　　 'Is your job like that? Do you need to work hard?'

The context of example (70) is one where the speaker is asking the hearer whether the job is hard or not. Unlike (69), the speaker in this example temporarily cannot think of the word $sen^1khɔ^3$ 'painstaking, hard', and thus uses the demonstrative $hə^2$ instead, partially in order to avoid pausing too long.

5.3.2 Language-internal functions

In this section, we discuss two language-internal functions observed for Hui'an demonstratives, that is, anaphoric use and discourse deictic use. All demonstratives have anaphoric uses, illustrated in (71) and (72).

(71) 伊   迄個   組   其   組長
    en¹   hit⁷⁻⁸-e²⁻⁴   tsɔ³   e²⁻⁴   tsɔ³⁻²tiũ³
    3PL   that-CL   team   GEN   group.leader
    按   北京   過來,
    an⁵⁻³ pak⁷⁻⁸kiã¹   kə⁵lai⁰
    from   PN   come.over
    迄孤   儂   能力   野   懸
    hit⁷⁻⁸-kɔ¹ laŋ²   liŋ²⁻⁴liak⁸   ia³⁻²   kuin²
    that-CL   person ability   quite   high
    'Their team leader came from Beijing. That person is very competent.'

(72) 我   有   看   著   搭   張   口   咧,
    gua³   u⁴   khuã⁵⁻³ tsioʔ⁸⁻⁴ taʔ⁷⁻⁸   tiũ¹   tse²   leʔ⁰
    1SG   have look   PVC   stick   CL   this   SFP
    搭   張   口   是   超市   其,   是   呣
    taʔ⁷⁻⁸   tiũ¹   hə²   si⁴   tshiau¹tshi⁴   e²   si⁴   m⁰
    stick   CL   that   be   supermarket   GEN   be   SFP
    'I saw a piece of (label) like this stuck (on the bag). The fact that a piece of (label) like that is stuck (on the bag) shows that it is (bought) from the supermarket, doesn't it?'

In (71), *hit⁷⁻⁸kɔ¹ laŋ²* 'that person' is co-referential with the noun phrase *en¹ hit⁷⁻⁸e²⁻⁴ tsɔ³ e²⁻⁴ tsɔ³⁻²tiũ³* 'their team leader'. In (72), the proximal demonstrative *tse²* is used to refer to a label like the one present in the surrounding context, while the distal demonstrative *hə²* can be interpreted as being co-referential with proximal demonstrative *tse²*.

The following examples illustrate the discourse deictic use of Hui'an demonstratives.

(73) A: 著　　　等　　正月　　則　　　佮　　　賣
　　　 tioʔ⁸⁻⁴　tan³⁻²　tsiã¹gəʔ⁸　tsiaʔ⁷⁻⁸　koʔ⁷⁻⁸　bue⁴
　　　 have.to　wait　January　then　again　sell
　　　 'We may not finish selling (the furniture) until the first month of the lunar year.'
　　 B: 即條　　　　　有影，
　　　 tsit⁷⁻⁸-tiau²　u⁴iã³
　　　 this-CL　right
　　　 今年　　　逐個　　　趕　　遘　　呀
　　　 ken¹-lin²　tak⁸⁻⁴-e²　kuã³　a³　ia⁰
　　　 this-year　every-CL　busy　EVC　SFP
　　　 'You're right. Everyone is so busy this year.'

(74) A: 買　　蜀點仔，　　　　豬牢仔
　　　 bue³　tsit⁸⁻⁴tiəm³⁻²a³　tu¹tiau²⁻⁴-a³
　　　 buy　a.bit　　　　　　pigsty-DIM
　　　 '(They) bought a small (house), like a small pigsty.'
　　 B: 說　　懷
　　　 səʔ⁷　huai²
　　　 say　those
　　　 'You should not talk like that.' (lit. 'say those')

The context of example (73) is that the furniture business has been not good during the past months. Speaker A says that the business may be better during the first month of the lunar year, when Chinese people will have a long vacation and will buy some furniture for the New Year. Speaker B agrees with speaker A, since she thinks that everybody has been quite busy and thus has had no time to buy any furniture in the past months. In this example, the demonstrative phrase *tsit⁷⁻⁸tiau²* 'this' ([demonstrative + classifier]) refers to what speaker A said, that is, *tioʔ⁸⁻⁴ tan³⁻² tsiã¹gəʔ⁸ tsiaʔ⁷⁻⁸ koʔ⁷⁻⁸ bue⁴* 'may not finish selling until the first month of the lunar year'. The discourse deictic use of the demonstratives *tsit⁷~hit⁷* is limited to demonstrative phrases such as *tsit⁷⁻⁸tiau²* in (73), and *tsit⁷⁻⁸/hit⁷⁻⁸tsiɔŋ³* 'this/that kind of', which can refer to a proposition or an event. In (73), *tiau²* is a classifier for invisible and abstract entities, though is also used for concrete objects with a long shape such as *kau¹* 溝 'ditch' and *len⁵⁻⁴a³* 鏈仔 'necklace'. Other demonstrative phrases such as *tsit⁷⁻⁸tə⁵* 即垛 'this piece of' usually denote a specific and individualized entity, and thus do not have this kind of discourse deictic use. The context of example (74) is that people are talking about the new house that the speaker A's daughter has just bought. Speaker A speaks in a modest way, and says that her daughter bought a small one, like a small pigsty. Speaker B is unhappy about this expression, and replies rhetorically with *sə?⁷ huai²* which literally means 'say those', but actually means 'you should not say things like that'. In this example, demonstrative *huai²* is used to refer to what speaker A said, that is, *tui¹tiau²⁻⁴a³* 'a small pigsty'. Examples (73) and (74) also illustrate that both proximal and distal demonstratives can have a discourse deictic use. In addition, in these two examples, demonstratives both refer to a chunk of the preceding discourse.

The discourse deictic use is also found for demonstratives *tse²~hə²* and *tsiɔŋ³⁻² e²~hiɔŋ³⁻² e²*, especially *tse²~hə²*, which are actually the most prevalent in discourse deictic use in Hui'an. They can be used cataphorically as well to refer to a chunk of the following discourse, as in (75).

(75) 即瓶　　　是　口　　呀,
 tsit⁷⁻⁸-pan²　si⁴　hə²　ia⁰
 this-bottle　be　that　SFP
 是　個　老爸　　　廣州　　　帶　來
 si⁴　en¹　lau⁴-pe⁴　kŋ³⁻²tsiu¹　tua⁵　lai⁰
 be　3PL　PREF-father　PN　　bring　come
 'This bottle (of coffee) is like that: …It's been brought back by their father from Guangzhou.'

In (75), the speaker is explaining to the hearer why there is a bottle of coffee at home, and the distal demonstrative *hə²* refers to the clause *en¹ lau⁴pe⁴ kŋ³⁻²tsiu¹ tua⁵ lai⁰* 'their father brought (it) from Guangzhou' . In other words, *hə²* here is used to introduce a proposition.

5.4 Summary

This chapter first clarified the terms 'demonstratives' and 'nominal demonstratives', and how they differ from the term *zhǐshì dàicí* 指示代詞 (lit. 'deictic substitute word') widely used in Chinese linguistics. We have also shown that compared to some other Chinese varieties such as Mandarin, Yue, Wu and Hakka, Min shows a relatively complicated nominal demonstrative system. The discussion then focused on five sets of nominal demonstratives observed for the Hui'an dialect, i.e. (i) *tsit⁷~hit⁷*; (ii) *tsat⁸~hat⁸*; (iii) *tsuai²~huai²*; (iv) *tse²~hə²*; and (v) *tsiɔŋ³⁻² e²~hiɔŋ³⁻² e²*. Four out of these five sets can both directly modify a noun and be used independently. One of these sets, *tsit⁷~hit⁷*, has however to co-occur with the complex [numeral + classifier], i.e. these demonstratives cannot directly modify a noun, nor be used independently. Furthermore, spoken data show that demonstratives tse^2~$hə^2$, unlike other demonstratives, can be preceded by the complex [numeral + classifier], due to their ability to refer to a category or a member of an entire category.

Similar to nominal demonstratives in other Southern Min varieties, nominal demonstratives in Hui'an, probably involve syllable contraction: (a) $tsit^7$~hit^7 are probably fused forms of the demonstrative tsi 只~hi 許 and the general classifier e^2; (b) $tsat^8$~hat^8 are probably fused forms of $tsit^7$~hit^7 and the general classifier e^2; (c) $tsuai^2$~$huai^2$ are probably fused forms of $tsit^7$~hit^7 and a plural/collective classifier; (d) tse^2~$hə^2$ are probably fused forms of $tsiɔŋ^{3\text{-}2}e^2$~$hiɔŋ^{3\text{-}2}e^2$; and (e) $tsiɔŋ^{3\text{-}2}e^2$~$hiɔŋ^{3\text{-}2}e^2$ are probably fused forms of $tsit^{7\text{-}8}tsiɔŋ^{3\text{-}2}e^2$~$hit^{7\text{-}8}tsiɔŋ^{3\text{-}2}e^2$. Although the details of the fusion process have to be further documented for some cases, evidence gathered from cross-dialectal comparison within the Min groups, as well as from a semantic and syntactic analysis of these demonstrative forms, show that the five sets of Hui'an nominal demonstratives are likely to be closely related to each other.

Semantically speaking, the demonstrative phrases involving $tsit^7$~hit^7 usually refer to a specific entity, to plural entities, or to a member of an entire category, depending on the following complex [numeral + classifier]. The demonstratives $tsat^8$~hat^8 only refer to a specific and individualized entity, whereas $tsuai^2$~$huai^2$ usually refer to plural entities or to a mass entity. Both tse^2~$hə^2$ and $tsiɔŋ^{3\text{-}2} e^2$~$hiɔŋ^{3\text{-}2} e^2$ can denote a specific member of an entire category or a general category.

Nominal demonstratives in Hui'an distinguish two number features: singular and plural, like most languages observed in Diessel (1999)'s sample. Interestingly, however, tse^2~$hə^2$ and $tsiɔŋ^{3\text{-}2} e^2$~$hiɔŋ^{3\text{-}2} e^2$ serve as special forms indicating that the referent is a type/category, no matter whether they denote an entire category or a specific member of a category. This usage has been so far attested also in some other Southern Min varieties such as the Qionglin, Shantou and Jieyang varieties, but not in other Chinese varieties. When denoting a general category, tse^2~$hə^2$ function as a generic marker, a use which is also found in the Shantou and Jieyang varieties of Southern Min, and in Beijing Mandarin.

In terms of their pragmatic uses, Hui'an nominal demonstratives involve (a) exophoric use: with reference to entities in the surrounding situation; (b) recognitional use: speaker and hearer are familiar with the referent due to shared experience; (c) anaphoric use: coreferential with a noun phrase in the preceding discourse; and (d) discourse deictic uses: with reference to a chunk of the surrounding discourse. Besides these various uses, Hui'an nominal demonstratives may also refer to entities which are not in the surrounding situation, no matter whether they are shared by the speaker and the hearer or not, or may refer to entities which are not in the surrounding situation, but are shared by everyone's general knowledge. Distal demonstrative *hə²* can also be used as a substitute to replace a word that the speaker is not willing to speak out, or when the speaker cannot find the proper word for (s)he wants to say.

6 Numerals and quantifiers

6.1 Introduction

This chapter aims to give a brief introduction to numerals and quantifiers in Hui'an.

6.2 Numerals

As with other Chinese varieties, the Hui'an dialect uses a decimal system.

6.2.1 Cardinal numbers

The numbers 0 through 10 are shown in Table 6-1 below.

Tab. 6-1: The numbers 0 through 10 in the Hui'an dialect

	Colloquial reading	Literary reading
0	liŋ² 零	
	khɔŋ⁵ 空	
1	et⁷ 一	
	tsit⁸ 蜀	
2	li⁵ 二	
	lŋ⁴ 兩	liɔŋ³ 兩
3	sã¹ 三	sam¹ 三
4	si⁵ 四	sɯ⁵ 四
5	gɔ⁴ 五	gɔ³ 五
6	lak⁸ 六	liɔk⁸ 六
7	tshet⁷ 七	
	tshiak⁷ 七	
8	pueʔ⁷ 八	pat⁷ 八
9	kau³ 九	kiu³ 九
10	tsap⁸ 十	siəp⁸ 十

Basically speaking, compound numbers in Hui'an are formed in the same order as in English, with multiples of ten preceding the units, as illustrated by (1) – (3).

(1) 二十一
 li$^{5\text{-}4}$tsap$^{8\text{-}4}$et^{7}
 twenty.one
 'twenty one'

(2) 三百　　　　四十五
 sã^{1}paʔ^{7}　　si$^{5\text{-}3}$tsap$^{8\text{-}4}$gɔ^{4}
 three.hundred　forty.five
 'three hundred and forty five'

(3) 五千　　　　三百　　　　六十六
 gɔ^{4}tshiŋ^{1}　sã^{1}paʔ^{7}　lak$^{8\text{-}4}$tsap$^{8\text{-}4}$lak^{8}
 five.thousand　three.hundred　sixty.six
 'five thousand three hundred and sixty six'

Though the tens may precede the units in both English and the Hui'an dialect as shown by (1) – (3), multiples of ten in Hui'an are morphologically transparent, e.g. li$^{5\text{-}4}$tsap^{8} 'twenty' literally means 'two tens'.

As in other Chinese varieties, there are special forms for 'ten thousand' ban^{5} 萬 and 'hundred million' iak^{7} 億. Examples are given in (4) and (5). By way of contrast, there is no word for a million (nor for a billion). These are formed by respectively using paʔ$^{7\text{-}8}$ban^{5} 百萬 (lit. hundred ten.thousand) and tsap$^{8\text{-}4}$iak^{7} 十億 (lit. ten hundred.million), as shown in Table 6-2 below, a summary of the main forms greater than 'ten'.

(4) 蜀萬　　　　　兩千　　　　三百　　　　二十二
 tsit$^{8\text{-}4}$ban^{5}　lŋ^{4}tshiŋ^{1}　sã^{1}paʔ^{7}　li$^{5\text{-}4}$tsap$^{8\text{-}4}$li^{5}
 one.ten thousand　two.thousand　three.hundred　twenty.two
 'twelve thousand three hundred and twenty two'

(5) 六億　　　　　　五千萬
 lak$^{8\text{-}4}$iak^{7}　　gɔ^{4}tshiŋ^{1}ban^{5}
 six.hundred million　five thousand.ten thousand
 'six hundred and fifty million'

Tab. 6-2: The main forms above 'ten' in the Hui'an dialect

Numerals	Hui'an	English
100	paʔ⁷ 百	hundred
1,000	tshiŋ¹ 千	thousand
10,000	ban⁵ 萬	ten thousand
100,000	tsap⁸⁻⁴ban⁵ 十萬	hundred thousand
1,000,000	paʔ⁷⁻⁸ban⁵ 百萬	million
10,000,000	tshiŋ¹ban⁵ 千萬	ten million
100,000,000	iak⁷ 億	hundred million
1000,000,000	tsap⁸⁻⁴iak⁷ 十億	billion

The intermediate zero before the final digit is usually spelt out explicitly, as exemplified by (6), where *liŋ²* or *khɔŋ⁵* is inserted between *tshet⁷⁻⁸paʔ⁷* 'seven hundred' and *pueʔ⁷* 'eight'. Note that *khɔŋ⁵* is more commonly used than *liŋ²*, the latter found in Mandarin Chinese.

(6) 七百　　　　零/空　　　八
　　tshet⁷⁻⁸paʔ⁷　*liŋ²⁻⁴/khɔŋ⁵⁻³*　*pueʔ⁷*
　　seven.hundred　zero　　eight
　　'seven hundred and eight'

As with other Southern Min varieties, there are two sets of numerals for 1 and 2 in Hui'an, that is, *et⁷* 一 'one'/*li⁵* 二 'two' and *tsit⁸* 蜀 'one'/*lŋ⁴* 兩 'two', for which Zhou and Ouyang (1998:361) suggest different lexical sources. Both sets can be used for counting. For the numbers 'one' and 'two', *tsit⁸* and *lŋ⁴* are more commonly used than *et⁷* and *li⁵*. The latter set is typically used by the younger generation. Moreover, only *tsit⁸* and *lŋ⁴*, but not *et⁷* and *li⁵*, can co-occur with a classifier (see chapter 7). For the numbers 'eleven' through 99, *et⁷* and *li⁵*, instead of *tsit⁸* and *lŋ⁴*, are used. For example, *li⁵⁻⁴tsap⁸⁻⁴et⁷* is used for 'twenty one', as shown by (1) above. For numbers larger than 99, *tsit⁸* and *lŋ⁴* occur as modifiers before *paʔ⁷* 'hundred', *tshiŋ¹* 'thousand' and *ban⁵* 'ten thousand', etc., whereas *et⁷* and *li⁵* occur in other positions, as shown in example (4) above.

For the numbers 'eleven' through 19, the numeral *et⁷* before *tsap⁸* is usually omitted, as illustrated by (7). However, for numbers larger than 100, the numeral *et⁷* before *tsap⁸* is usually *not* omitted, as in (8).

(7) (一)十三
    (et⁷⁻⁸)tsap⁸⁻⁴sã¹
    Thirteen
    'thirteen'

(8) 七百　　　　一十二
    tshet⁷⁻⁸paʔ⁷　et⁷⁻⁸tsap⁸⁻⁴li⁵
    seven.hundred　twelve
    'seven hundred and twelve'

For numbers which end in *tsap⁸* 'ten', *paʔ⁷* 'hundred' or *tshiŋ¹* 'thousand', the ending *tsap⁸*, *paʔ⁷* and *tshiŋ¹* sometimes can be omitted, as in (9) and (10).

(9) 三百　　　　五(十)
    sã¹paʔ⁷⁽⁻⁸⁾　　gɔ⁴(tsap⁸)
    three.hundred　fifty
    'three hundred and fifty'

(10) 五千　　　　六(百)
     gɔ⁴tshiŋ¹　　lak⁸(⁻⁴paʔ⁷)
     five.thousand　six.hundred
     'five thousand and six hundred'

If the first digit is *tsit⁸* 'one', *tsit⁸* can be omitted too, as in (11) and (12).

(11) (蜀)百　　　五(十)
     (tsit⁸⁻⁴)paʔ⁷　gɔ⁴(tsap⁸)
     one.hundred　fifty
     'one hundred and fifty'

(12) (蜀)千　　　六(百)
     (tsit⁸⁻⁴)tshiŋ¹　lak⁸(⁻⁴paʔ⁷)
     one.thousand　six.hundred
     'one thousand and six hundred'

When followed by a digit from 'one' to 'nine', the numbers *li⁵⁻⁴tsap⁸* 'twenty', *sã¹tsap⁸* 'thirty' and *si⁵⁻³tsap⁸* 'forty' are often contracted, as in (13), in which, for example, *li⁵⁻⁴tsap⁸* becomes *liəp⁸*, whereas the numbers *gɔ⁴tsap⁸* 'fifty', *lak⁸⁻⁴tsap⁸* 'sixty', $tshet^{7\text{-}8}tsap^8$ 'seventy', $pueʔ^{7\text{-}8}tsap^8$ 'eighty' and $kau^{3\text{-}2}tsap^8$ 'ninety' often leave out $tsap^8$ 'ten', as in (14).

(13) a. 二十一 'twenty one': $li^{5\text{-}4}tsap^{8\text{-}4}et^7$ -> $liəp^{8\text{-}4}et^7$
b. 三十一 'thirty one': $sã^1tsap^{8\text{-}4}et^7$ -> sam^1et^7
c. 四十一 'forty one': $si^{5\text{-}3}tsap^{8\text{-}4}et^7$ -> $siəp^{8\text{-}4}et^7$

(14) a. 五十一: $gɔ^4tsap^{8\text{-}4}et^7$ -> $gɔ^4et^7$
b. 六十一: $lak^{8\text{-}4}tsap^{8\text{-}4}et^7$ -> $lak^{8\text{-}4}et^7$
c. 七十一: $tshet^{7\text{-}8}tsap^{8\text{-}4}et^7$ -> $tshet^{7\text{-}8}et^7$
d. 八十一: $pueʔ^{7\text{-}8}tsap^{8\text{-}4}et^7$ -> $pueʔ^{7\text{-}8}et^7$
e. 九十一: $kau^{3\text{-}2}tsap^{8\text{-}4}et^7$ -> $kau^{3\text{-}2}et^7$

As with other Southern Min varieties (also some other Chinese varieties such as Wu), the Hui'an dialect possesses two different pronunciations for many Chinese characters: one is the colloquial reading, and the other, the literary reading. The former is normally used in vernacular speech, whereas the latter is generally found in formal settings. As shown in Table 6-1 above, numerals 'two' through 'ten' except 'seven' all have a literary reading, as shown by (15).

(15) 2: $lŋ^4$ (colloquial); $liɔŋ^3$ (literary): $liɔŋ^{3\text{-}2}tsuan^2ki^{2\text{-}4}bi^3$ 兩全其美 'kill two birds with one stone'
3: $sã^1$ (colloquial); sam^1 (literary): $\underline{sam^1}tsan^{2\text{-}4}baʔ^7$ 三層肉 'marbled meat'
4: si^5 (colloquial); su^5 (literary): $\underline{su}^{5\text{-}3}tshuan^1$ 四川 'Sichuan' (Place Name)
5: $gɔ^4$ (colloquial); $gɔ^3$ (literary): $\underline{gɔ}^{3\text{-}2}et^7$ 五一 '1 May'
6: lak^8 (colloquial); $liɔk^8$ (literary): $bi^{3\text{-}2}\underline{liɔk}^{8\text{-}4}gɔ^3$ 米六五 '165 cm (tall)'
8: $pueʔ^7$ (colloquial); pat^7 (literary): $sam^1\underline{pat}^7$ $hu^4lu^{3\text{-}2}tsueʔ^7$ 三八婦女節 '8 March International Women's Day'
9: kau^3 (colloquial); kiu^3 (literary): $et^{7\text{-}8}\underline{kiu}^3$ $\underline{kiu}^{3\text{-}2}li^5$ 一九九二 '1992'
10: $tsap^8$ (colloquial); $siəp^8$ (literary): $\underline{siəp}^{8\text{-}4}li^{5\text{-}4}lɔ^{5\text{-}4}khau^3$ 十字路口 'crossroad'

Unlike the numeral 'seven' in Xiamen and Zhangzhou which has only one pronunciation (Zhou and Ouyang 1998:361, Zhou 2006:586), the numeral 'seven' in Hui'an has two pronunciations: (a) $tshet^7$, which bears the same functions as the colloquial reading of the numerals in (15); (b) $tshiak^7$, which is mainly used by the elder generation. This may suggest that $tshiak^7$ emerged earlier than $tshet^7$, while noting that both belong to the colloquial layer. An example of $tshiak^7$ is found in $tshiak^{7\text{-}8}gəʔ^8$ 七月 'July'.

6.2.2 Ordinal numbers

Ordinal numbers can be formed by adding the prefix *te⁵* 第 before the cardinal number, as in (16) and (17).

(16) 第一, 汝 是 大學生
 te⁵⁻⁴-et⁷ *lu³* *si⁴* *tua⁵⁻⁴oʔ⁸⁻⁴siŋ¹*
 PREF-one 2SG be university.student
 'Firstly, you are a university student.'

(17) 第二日 阮搭 請
 te⁵⁻⁴-li⁵⁻⁴-let⁸ *gun³-taʔ⁷* *tshiã³*
 PREF-two-day 1PL-LOC feast
 'The second day, (we) feast (our relatives and friends) at our place.'

As shown by examples (16) and (17), *et⁷* and *li⁵*, rather than *tsit⁸* and *lŋ⁴*, are used with the prefix *te⁵* for ordinal numbers. In (16), *te⁵⁻⁴et⁷* is used alone meaning 'firstly'. In this case, the prefix *te⁵* can also be omitted, that is, *et⁷* can be used alone to express the same meaning. In (17), *te⁵⁻⁴li⁵* 'second' is followed by the noun *let⁸* 'day'. However, in this case, the prefix *te⁵* cannot be omitted.

The morpheme *thau²* 頭, rather than *te⁵* 第, is used to express 'first', when the ordinal number is followed by other elements such as the noun *let⁸* 'day' in (18) below.

(18) 頭蜀日 恁搭 請
 thau²⁻⁴-tsit⁸⁻⁴-let⁸ *len³-taʔ⁷* *tshiã³*
 PREF-one-day 2PL-LOC feast
 'The first day, (you) feast (your relatives and friends) at your place.'

Note that the numeral *tsit⁸*, rather than *et⁷*, is used with *thau²*. The numeral *tsit⁸* here can also be omitted, that is, *thau²⁻⁴let⁸* can be used alone to express the same meaning. When occurring with other numerals, *thau²* expresses a different meaning from the prefix *te⁵*. For example, *thau²⁻⁴lŋ⁴let⁸* 頭兩日, where *thau²* is followed by the numeral *lŋ⁴* 'two' and the noun *let⁸* 'day', means 'the first two days', rather than 'the second day'.

The prefix *te⁵* can be followed by *bə³* 尾 to express 'the last', as in (19).

(19) 第尾名
    te$^{5\text{-}4}$-*bə*$^{3\text{-}2}$-*biã*^{2}
    PREF-end-place
    'the last place'

In fact, the prefix *te*^{5} in (19) can be omitted, that is, *bə*^{3} 尾 alone can express 'the last', as illustrated by (20) and (21).

(20) 尾名
    bə$^{3\text{-}2}$-*biã*^{2}
    end-place
    'the last place'

(21) 尾二名
    bə$^{3\text{-}2}$-*li*$^{5\text{-}4}$-*biã*^{2}
    end-two-place
    'the last but one'

There are also other ways to express ordinal numbers. For example, a cardinal number can be followed by the noun *lau*^{2} 樓 'floor' to express the number of floors in a building, as in (22).

(22) 二樓
    li$^{5\text{-}4}$-*lau*^{2}
    two-floor
    'the second floor'

A similar example can be found in (23), where the cardinal numer *si*^{5} 四, followed by *ho*^{5} 號 'number' and *lau*^{2} 樓 'building', expresses the number of building.

(23) 四號樓
    si$^{5\text{-}3}$-*ho*$^{5\text{-}4}$-*lau*^{2}
    four-number-building
    'No.4 building'

A cardinal number can also occur before *tiɔŋ*^{1} 中 and *sio*^{3} 小 to express the names of middle schools and primary schools, such as 'No. 1 Middle School' in (24) and 'No. 2 Primary School' in (25).

(24) 一中
    et^{7-8}-$tiɔŋ^1$
    one-middle.school
    'No.1 Middle School'

(25) 二小
    li^{5-4}-sio^3
    two-primary.school
    'No. 2 Primary School'

In these two examples, $et^{7-8}tiɔŋ^1$ and $li^{5-4}sio^3$ can be regarded as abbreviations of $te^{5-4}et^{7-8}\ tiɔŋ^1oʔ^8$ and $te^{5-4}li^{5-4}\ sio^{3-2}oʔ^8$, respectively, in which, $tiɔŋ^1oʔ^8$ and $sio^{3-2}oʔ^8$ mean 'middle school' and 'primary school', respectively.

The following is an example where a cardinal number is followed by a kinship term.

(26) 三姊
    $sã^1$-tsi^3
    three-sister
    'the third oldest sister'

In (26), the cardinal number $sã^1$ 'three' is placed before tsi^3 'sister' to refer to 'the third oldest sister'.

When referring to the eldest or the youngest, however, the kinship terms are usually formed in a different way, as illustrated by (27) and (28), respectively.

(27) 阿姨   /   大姨
    a^1-i^2 / tua^{5-4}-i^2
    PREF-aunt /   big-aunt
    'the eldest aunt'

(28) 尾姑
    $bə^{3-2}$-$kɔ^1$
    end-aunt
    'the youngest aunt'

In (27), the prefix a^1 阿 or tua^5 'big' precedes i^2 姨 to refer to the eldest aunt (the eldest sister of one's mother), whereas in (28), $bə^3$ 'end' occurs before $kɔ^1$ 姑 to refer to the youngest aunt (the youngest sister of one's father).

There are three main ways to express the ranking of children in a family: (a) the prefix a^1 阿 + cardinal number, such as $a^1s\tilde{a}^1$ 阿三 in (29); (b) the prefix lau 老 + cardinal number, such as $lau^4s\tilde{a}^1$ 老三 in (30); and (c) cardinal number + e^0 其, such as $s\tilde{a}^1e^0$ 三其 in (31). Note that when referring to the first child in a family, the adjective tua^5 大, rather than the cardinal number et^7 一, is used, as shown by (32).

(29) 阿三
 a^1-$s\tilde{a}^1$
 PREF-three
 'the third child'

(30) 老三
 lau^4-$s\tilde{a}^1$
 PREF-three
 'the third child'

(31) 三其
 $s\tilde{a}^1$-e^0
 three-PRT
 'the third child'

(32) 老大
 $lau^{3\text{-}2}$-tua^5
 PREF-big
 'the first child'

The prefix $tshue^1$ 初 is used with the cardinal numbers from et^7 一 'one' through $tsap^8$ 十 'ten' to denote the first ten days of a lunar month, as illustrated by (33).

(33) 初六
 $tshue^1$-lak^8
 PREF-six
 'the sixth day of a lunar month'

The following example shows that a cardinal number such as $gɔ^4$ 五 'five' can occur before the noun $gaʔ^8$ 月 'month' (without a prefix) to express one of the twelve months of the year.

(34) 五月
    $gɔ^4$-$gəʔ^8$
    five-month
    'May'

According to the examples above, ordinal numbers in Hui'an are normally formed by adding the prefix te^5 第 before the cardinal number, that is, 'ordinal number = te^5 第 + cardinal number'. In some cases, a cardinal number is able to precede a noun without the prefix te^5 第 to express an ordinal meaning, as in $li^{5\text{-}4}lau^2$ 二樓 'the second floor' in (22) above. The morpheme $bə^3$ 尾 (< 'tail') can also be used before a cardinal number or noun to express 'last', while $tshue^1$ 初 is used with cardinal numbers to denote the first ten days of a lunar month. In contrast to this, cardinal numbers are based on a decimal system. Thus, multiples of ten are formed with the multiplier preceding the multiplicand: *number x multiple of ten* 三百 $sã^1paʔ^7$ 'three hundred' while for the units which follow the multiples of ten, the process is additive: *ten + number* 十三 $tsap^{8\text{-}4}sã^1$ ten-three 'thirteen'.

6.2.3 Approximate numbers

In Hui'an, the most common way to express approximate numbers is the juxtaposition of two adjacent numbers, as exemplified by (35) and (36).

(35) 蜀　　兩　　千
    $tsit^{8\text{-}4}$　$lŋ^4$　$tshiŋ^1$
    one　two　thousand
    'around one to two thousand'

(36) 煮　　兩　　三　　碗
    tsu^3　$lŋ^4$　$sã^1$　$uã^3$
    cook　two　three　bowl
    'cook two to three bowls (of noodles)'

In (35), the two adjacent numbers $tsit^8$ 'one' and $lŋ^4$ 'two' are juxtaposed to express an approximate number. Note that when expressing approximate numbers, $tsit^8$ and $lŋ^4$, rather than et^7 'one' and li^5 'two', are used. In (36), the two adjacent numbers $lŋ^4$ 'two' and $sã^1$ 'three' are juxtaposed to express an approximate number. As shown by these two examples, the number with a smaller value usually precedes the number with a larger value. However, there are also counterexamples to this, as in (37) below, where the number *sã¹* 'three' precedes *lŋ⁴* 'two'.

(37) 無　　三　　兩　　日　　咯
　　 bo²⁻⁴　sã¹　 lŋ⁴　 let⁸　 lɔ⁰
　　 not.have three two day SFP
　　 'There is little time left.' ('lit. not have three or two days')

The juxtaposition of two non-adjacent numbers involves *sã¹* 'three' and *gɔ⁴* 'five', as in the fixed expression illustrated by (38).

(38) 三　　五　　分鐘
　　 sã¹　 gɔ⁴　 hun¹tsiŋ¹
　　 three five minute
　　 'around three to five minutes.'

A whole number can be followed by *gua⁵* 外 or *thɔ³* 吐 to express approximate numbers, as in (39) and (40).

(39) 百　　　外　　　斤
　　 paʔ⁷⁻⁸　gua⁵⁻⁴　 kən¹
　　 hundred around MW
　　 'one hundred-something catty'

(40) 三十　　　　吐　　　　歲
　　 sã¹tsap⁸⁻⁴　thɔ³⁻²　 hə⁵
　　 thirty around year
　　 'thirty-something years old'

6.3 Quantifiers

Quantifiers in Hui'an mainly include *kui¹* 規 'whole', *sɔ³⁻²u⁴* 所有 'all', *tak⁸* 逐 'every', *kɔk⁷* 各 'each', *ia³⁻²tsue⁵* 野儕 'many', *ban²⁻⁴tsue⁵* 蠻儕 'many', *kui³* 幾 'several', *kui³⁻²loʔ⁸* 幾落 'several, quite a few', *u⁴e⁰* 有其 'some' and *tsuai²* 'some'.

When modifying a noun, the quantifier *kui¹* is typically used with a classifier such as *liã³* 領 in (41), or a measure word such as *uã³* 碗 in (42). Note that in daily conversation, the nouns modified by the quantifier *kui¹* and its following classifier or measure word, such as *sã¹* 衫 'clothes' and *thŋ¹* 湯 'soup' in (41) and (42) respectively, are usually omitted, since the semantic properties of the classifier or measure word allow for the correct inference.

(41) 規　　領　　衫
　　 kui¹　*liã³⁻²*　*sã¹*
　　 whole　CL　clothes
　　 'the whole piece of clothing'

(42) 規　　碗　　湯
　　 kui¹　*uã³⁻²*　*thŋ¹*
　　 whole　bowl　soup
　　 'the whole bowl of soup'

The quantifier *kui¹* can be directly followed by some nouns such as *let⁸* 日 'day' and *bin²* 暝 'night'. An example of *kui¹let⁸* 規日 'all day long, all the time' is given in (43).

(43) 規日　　　　落雨
　　 kui¹-let⁸　*loʔ⁸⁻⁴-hɔ⁴*
　　 whole-day　fall-rain
　　 'It rained all the time.'

The quantifier *sɔ³⁻²u⁴* 所有 'all', which is commonly used in Mandarin Chinese, can also be found in Hui'an, as shown by (44), where *sɔ³⁻²u⁴* directly modifies the noun *tai⁵⁻⁴tsi⁵* 代志 'thing'. Note, however, that this quantifier is uncommon, and, when used, it is typically by the younger generation.

(44) 按　　　所有　　代志　　　說　　與　　　伊　　清楚
　　 an⁵⁻³　*sɔ³⁻²u⁴*　*tai⁵⁻⁴tsi⁵*　*saʔ⁷*　*khɔ⁵⁻⁴*　*i¹*　*tshiŋ¹tshɔ³*
　　 OM　　all　　　thing　　　say　　give　　3SG　clear
　　 'Make all things clear.'

Like *kui¹* mentioned above, the quantifier *tak⁸* 逐 'every', is typically used with a classifier such as *e²* 個 in (45), or a measure word such as *sen¹* 身 in (46), when modifying a noun.

(45) 逐　　個　　儂
　　 tak⁸⁻⁴　e²⁻⁴　laŋ²
　　 every　CL　person
　　 'every person'

(46) 逐　　身　　衫褲
　　 tak⁸⁻⁴　sen¹　sã¹khɔ⁵
　　 every　MW　clothes
　　 'every suit of clothes'

Note that the classifier *e²* in (45) can be omitted, that is, the quantifier *tak⁸* can be used alone with the noun *laŋ²* 'person' to express the same meaning. Other nouns which can directly follow the quantifier *tak⁸* are typically the class of temporal nouns, as in (47), where *tak⁸* directly modifies the noun referring to a period of time, *let⁸* 日 'day'.

(47) 逐日
　　 tak⁸⁻⁴-let⁸
　　 every-day
　　 'every day'

The quantifier *tak⁸* with its following classifier (or measure word) is often used alone, without a head noun, as in (48).

(48) 逐個　　　都　有　厝
　　 tak⁸⁻⁴-e²　tɔ¹　u⁴　tshu⁵
　　 every-CL　all　have　house
　　 'Every one has a house.'

As shown by (48), the quantifier *tak⁸* is often used with the adverb *tɔ¹* 都 'all'. The adverb *tɔ¹* here is an important way to express quantification, and thus can be regarded as a quantifier in a broader sense.

In Hui'an, 'each person' is encoded by *kɔk⁷⁻⁸ laŋ²* 各儂, as in (49).

(49) 各　　　儂　　做　　　各　　　儂　　其　　代志
　　 kɔk⁷⁻⁸　laŋ²　tsue⁵⁻³　kɔk⁷⁻⁸　laŋ²　e²⁻⁴　tai⁵⁻⁴tsi⁵
　　 each　person　do　each　person　GEN　thing
　　 'Each person does his own thing.'

The Hui'an dialect uses $ia^{3-2}tsue^5$ 野儕 and $ban^{2-4}tsue^5$ 蠻儕 to express 'many', as illustrated by (50) and (51).

(50) 野儕　　學堂　　來　　招　　儂
　　 $ia^{3-2}tsue^{5-4}$　$oʔ^{8-4}tŋ^2$　lai^{2-4}　$tsio^1$　$laŋ^2$
　　 many　　school　come　recruit　person
　　 'Quite a lot of schools come to (our university) to recruit our students.'

(51) 車頂　　　有　　蠻儕　　　位置
　　 $tshia^1\text{-}tiŋ^3$　u^4　$ban^{2-4}tsue^{5-4}$　$ui^{5-4}ti^5$
　　 vehicle-up　have　many　　　place
　　 'There are quite a lot of seats on the train.'

Both $ia^{3-2}tsue^5$ and $ban^{2-4}tsue^5$ are originally formed by a degree adverb (i.e. ia^3 'quite' and ban^2 'rather', respectively) and the adjective $tsue^5$ 'many', which form compounds meaning 'many, quite a few'. They can both directly modify a noun such as $oʔ^{8-4}tŋ^2$ 'school' in (50) and $ui^{5-4}ti^5$ 'place' in (51).

　　 The quantifiers kui^3 幾 'several' and $kui^{3-2}loʔ^8$ 幾落 'several, quite a few' are used with a classifier (or measure word) such as $tiau^2$ 條 to modify a noun such as $pan^1tshia^1suã^5$ 班車線 'shuttle bus line' in (52).

(52) 幾(落)　　　　　條　　　　班車線
　　 $kui^{3-2}(loʔ^{8-4})$　$tiau^{2-4}$　$pan^1tshia^1\text{-}suã^5$
　　 (quite) a few　　CL　　　shuttle.bus-line
　　 '(quite) a few shuttle bus lines'

Like kui^1 and tak^8 mentioned above, the quantifiers kui^3 and $kui^{3-2}loʔ^8$ can directly modify some nouns such as lin^2 年 'year' in (53).

(53) 教　　幾(落)　　　　　年
　　 ka^5　$kui^{3-2}(loʔ^{8-4})$　lin^2
　　 teach　(quite) a few　　year
　　 '(He) has been a teacher for (quite) a few years.'

The quantifiers u^4e^0 有其 and $tsuai^2$ both mean 'some', and can both directly modify a noun such as $laŋ^2$ 儂 'person' in (54) and $te^{2-4}hioʔ^8$ 茶葉 'tea' in (55).

(54) 有其　儂　　規日　　　卜　　　食魚食肉
　　 u^4e^0　$laŋ^2$　$kui^1\text{-}let^8$　$boʔ^{7\text{-}8}$　$tsiaʔ^{8\text{-}4}\text{-}hu^2\text{-}tsiaʔ^{8\text{-}4}\text{-}baʔ^7$
　　 some　person　whole-day　want　eat-fish-eat-meat
　　 'Some people always want to live the high life.'

(55) 帶　　　口　　　茶葉　　　　去
　　 $tua^{5\text{-}3}$　$tsuai^{2\text{-}4}$　$te^{2\text{-}4}hioʔ^8$　$khɯ^5$
　　 take　some　tea　go
　　 'Take some tea.'

The co-occurrence of each quantifier with or without a classifier (or measure word) is summarized in Table 6-3 below.

Tab. 6-3: The co-occurrence of each quantifier with or without a classifier (or measure word)

	With CL/MW	Without CL/MW
kui^1 規 'whole'	+	+ (temporal nouns such as let^8 日 'day')
$sɔ^{3\text{-}2}u^4$ 所有 'all'	-	+
tak^8 逐 'every'	+	+ (temporal nouns; the noun $laŋ^2$ 儂 'person')
$kɔk^7$ 各 'each'	-	+ (the noun $laŋ^2$ 儂 'person')
$ia^{3\text{-}2}tsue^5$ 野儕 'many' $ban^{2\text{-}4}tsue^5$ 蠻儕 'many'	-	+
kui^3 幾 'several' $kui^{3\text{-}2}loʔ^8$ 幾落 'several, quite a few'	+	+ (temporal nouns)
u^4e^0 有其 'some' $tsuai^2$ 'some'	-	+

6.4 Summary

In this chapter, we have examined numerals and quantifiers in Hui'an, among which numerals fall into three subtypes: cardinal numbers, ordinal numbers and approximate numbers.

As with other Chinese varieties, the Hui'an dialect uses a decimal system. There are special forms for 'ten thousand' (i.e. ban^5 萬) or 'hundred million' (i.e. iak^7 億). There is, however, no word for a 'million' nor for a 'billion'.

Similar to other Southern Min varieties, there are two sets of numerals for 1 and 2 in Hui'an, that is, et^7 一 'one'/li^5 二 'two' and $tsit^8$ 蜀 'one'/$lŋ^4$ 兩 'two'. Numerals 'two' through 'ten' except 'seven' have both a colloquial reading and a literary reading. Unlike some other Southern Min varieties (e.g. Xiamen and Zhangzhou) where the numeral 'seven' has only one pronunciation, the numeral 'seven' in Hui'an has two colloquial pronunciations, i.e. $tshet^7$ and $tshiak^7$, the latter of the two being mainly used by the elder generation.

Ordinal numbers are typically formed by adding the prefix te^5 第 before the cardinal number, that is, 'ordinal number = te^5 第 + cardinal number'. In some cases, a cardinal number precedes a noun without the prefix te^5 第 to express an ordinal meaning, as in $li^{5-4}lau^2$ 二樓 'the second floor'. The morpheme $bə^3$ 尾 (< 'tail') can also be used before a cardinal number or noun to express 'last', while $tshue^1$ 初 is used with cardinal numbers to denote the first ten days of a lunar month. The most common way to express approximate numbers is the juxtaposition of two adjacent numbers. The juxtaposition of two non-adjacent numbers is also possible. In addition, a whole number can be followed by gua^5 外 or $thɔ^3$ 吐 to express approximate numbers.

Quantifiers have also been examined: some of which require a classifier, while others not.

7 Classifiers

7.1 Introduction

As with other Chinese varieties, numerals (and some quantifiers) cannot directly modify a noun: a classifier (if not a measure word) is needed between a numeral (or a quantifier) and a noun to enable the operation of enumeration. The classifiers categorize the referents of nouns in terms of their inherent properties such as animacy and shape, as opposed to measure words, which denote quantities of an item. In other words, the terms 'classifier' and 'measure word' here refer to 'sortal classifier' and 'mensural classifier' respectively in studies such as Matthews and Yip (2011:109) and Aikhenvald (2000:114-115). Unlike measure words which can be compared with measure terms (or quantifiers) in non-classifier languages and thus are common in a majority of the languages of the world, classifiers do not have a direct equivalent in non-classifier languages, being mainly attested in South, East and South-East Asia, Oceania and the Americas (cf. Aikhenvald 2000; Kilarski 2013). Thus, this chapter focuses on classifiers in Hui'an and will be examined in terms of their syntactic distributions (§7.2), semantic properties (§7.3), referential functions (§7.4), and sources and extensions (§7.5).

7.2 Syntactic distributions

7.2.1 Numeral + classifier

Classifiers in Hui'an usually appear together with a numeral, as in (1) and (2), and can act as a predicate.

(1) 浴室　　　蜀　　間
　　$iɔk^{8-4}siak^7$　$tsit^{8-4}$　$kuin^1$
　　bathroom　one　CL
　　'one bathroom'

(2) 骹踏車　　　　　四　　五　　把
　　$kha^1tah^{8-4}tshia^1$　si^{5-3}　$gɔ^4$　pe^3
　　bike　　　　　　　four　five　CL
　　'(There are) four or five bikes.'

The context of example (1) is that the speaker is introducing a house. The classifier *kuin¹* with the preceding numeral *tsit⁸* 'one' functions as a predicate denoting the number of the subject *iɔk⁸⁻⁴siak⁷* 'bathroom'. In (2), the classifier *pe³*, preceded by two adjacent numbers (i.e. *si⁵* 'four' and *gɔ⁴* 'five'), denotes an approximate number of the subject *kha¹tah⁸⁻⁴tshia¹* 'bike'.

The [numeral + classifier] complex can also function as a subject or topic, as in (3), or as an object, as in (4).

(3) 兩　垤　無　　　夠
    lŋ⁴　*tə⁵*　*bo²⁻⁴*　*kau⁵*
    two　CL　not.have　enough
    'Two (chairs) are not enough.'

(4) 加　　穿　　蜀　　　領
    ke¹　*tshiŋ⁵*　*tsit⁸⁻⁴*　*liã³*
    more　wear　one　CL
    'Wear one more piece (of clothing).'

In (3), *lŋ⁴ tə⁵* 'two (chairs)', consisting of the numeral *lŋ⁴* 'two' and the classifier *tə⁵*, functions as a subject or topic. The noun *i³* 椅 'chair', modified by *lŋ⁴ tə⁵*, is omitted. In (4), *tsit⁸⁻⁴ liã³* 'a piece (of clothing)', consisting of the numeral *tsit⁸* 'one' and the classifier *liã³*, functions as an object of the verb phrase *ke¹ tshiŋ⁵* 'wear more'. When overtly expressed, the noun *sã¹* 衫 'clothes' associated with the modifying classifier phrase *tsit⁸⁻⁴ liã³*, but omitted in this particular extract from discourse, tends to occur before the verb phrase *ke¹ tshiŋ⁵* and thus functions as a topic.

In the following example, the noun *tshŋ²* 床 'bed', modified by the [numeral + classifier] complex *lŋ⁴ tiũ¹* 兩張, is overtly expressed.

(5) 買　　　兩　　張　　床
    bue³⁻²　*lŋ⁴*　*tiũ¹*　*tshŋ²*
    buy　two　CL　bed
    '(He) bought two beds.'

In (5), *lŋ⁴ tiũ¹tshŋ²* 'two beds' functions as an object of the verb *bue³* 'buy'. Note that the numeral *tsit⁸* 蜀 'one' tends to be omitted, if it is used in the same postverbal context. In other words, *bue³⁻² tiũ¹ tshŋ²* 買張床 '(he) bought a bed', rather than *bue³⁻² tsit⁸⁻⁴tiũ¹ tshŋ²* 買蜀張床, is more common in daily conversation.

As shown by example (5) above, the [numeral + classifier] complex can directly modify a noun. In daily conversation, we also find some examples where e^0 其 is inserted between the [numeral + classifier] complex and a noun such as $a\textit{ʔ}^7$ 鴨 'duck' in (6).

(6) 今日　　蜀　　日　　刣　　四　　隻　　其　　鴨
    $kiã^1let^8$　$tsit^{8\text{-}4}$　let^8　$thai^2$　$si^{5\text{-}3}$　$tsiaʔ^7$　e^0　$aʔ^7$
    today　one　day　kill　four　CL　FOC　duck
    '(I) killed *four* ducks within one day today.'

The [numeral + classifier] complex $si^{5\text{-}3} tsiaʔ^7$ 四隻 'four' normally occurs directly before the noun $aʔ^7$ 'duck' to denote the number of ducks. In (6), the speaker aims to emphasize the number of ducks, since a family usually kills only one duck a day. The morpheme e^0 其 in Hui'an is multifunctional, e.g. it can function as a modifying marker and a genitive marker. In (6), however, it can be interepreted as a focus marker, used to emphasize the number $si^{5\text{-}3} tsiaʔ^7$ 'four'.

The [numeral + classifier] complex can be preceded by a personal pronoun such as gun^3 阮 in (7) to express possession.

(7) 阮　　兩　　隻　　佫　　未　　刣　　咧
    gun^3　$lŋ^4$　$tsiaʔ^7$　$koʔ^{7\text{-}8}$　$bə^{5\text{-}4}$　$thai^2$　$leʔ^0$
    1PL　two　CL　still　not.yet　kill　SFP
    'Our two ducks have not yet been killed.'

When the classifier is the general classifier e^2 個, the [numeral + classifier] complex with the preceding plural personal pronoun may form an appositive construction, as in (8).

(8) 恁　　兩　　個　　明日　　著　　來
    len^3　$lŋ^4$　e^2　$biã^{2\text{-}4}let^8$　$tioʔ^{8\text{-}4}$　lai^2
    2PL　two　CL　tomorrow　should　come
    a. 'Your two (kids) should come here tomorrow.'
    b. 'You two should come here tomorrow.'

In (8), $lŋ^4 e^2$ 'two' with the preceding second-person plural pronoun len^3 can denote possession, that is, meaning 'your two (kids)', or form an appositive construction meaning 'you two'.

The following two examples illustrate that the [numeral + classifier] complex can also follow the interrogative word to^3 底 to express 'which', as in (9), or follow the nominal demonstratives $tsit^7$ 即 'this'/hit^7 迄 'that', as in (10).

(9) 底　　蜀　　間　　買　　其
$to^{3\text{-}2}$　$tsit^{8\text{-}4}$　$kuin^1$　bue^3　e^0
which　one　CL　buy　NMLZ
'From which (store) did you buy (it)?'

(10) 迄兩領　　薄　　遘
$hit^{7\text{-}8}\text{-}lŋ^4\text{-}liã^3$　$poʔ^{8\text{-}4}$　a^3
that-two-CL　thin　EVC
'Those two pieces (of clothing) are very thin.'

Note that, when the numeral is $tsit^8$ 蜀 'one', it may be omitted, in which case, the classifier directly follows the nominal demonstratives $tsit^7$ 'this'/hit^7 'that' (see §5.2.1 for details).

The [numeral + classifier] complex can also be preceded by $thau^2$ 頭 'head, first', as in (11), or by the prefix te^5 第, as in (12).

(11) 頭兩個
$thau^2\text{-}lŋ^4\text{-}e^2$
head-two-CL
'the first two (watches)'

(12) 第二垛
$te^{5\text{-}4}\text{-}li^{5\text{-}4}\text{-}tə^5$
PREF-two-CL
'the second (house)'

Example (11) means the first two (watches), while (12) expresses an ordinal number, that is, the second (house). Note that different numeral systems are used in (11) and (12). 'two' is encoded by $lŋ^4$ in (11), which is the same form as that used in other classifier constructions, whereas it is encoded by li^4 in (12) to express an ordinal number (see §6.2 for details of numerals).

7.2.2 Quantifier + classifier

Classifiers in Hui'an can appear together with some quantifiers, such as *kui¹* 'whole', *tak⁸* 'every', *kui³* 'several', and *kui³⁻²loʔ⁸* 'several, quite a few'.

The [quantifier + classifier] complex can modify a noun such as *huɯ²* 魚 'fish' in (13) and *tshia¹* 車 'vehicle , car' in (14).

(13) 規　　尾　　魚
    kui¹　*bəˀ³⁻²*　*huɯ²*
    whole　CL　fish
    'the whole fish'

(14) 逐　　把　　車
    tak⁸⁻⁴　*pe³⁻²*　*tshia¹*
    every　CL　vehicle
    'every car'

Note that the quantifiers *kui¹* 'whole' and *kui³⁻²loʔ⁸* 'several, quite a few' (especially *kui³⁻²loʔ⁸*) imply a great number, thus the focus marker *e⁰* 其 can be used to emphasize the number when they modify a noun, as shown by (15).

(15) 我　　共　　伊　買　幾落　　　　領　其　　衫　　咯
    gua³　*ka⁵⁻⁴*　*i¹*　*bue³*　*kui³⁻²loʔ⁸⁻⁴*　*liã³*　*e⁰*　*sã¹*　*lɔ⁰*
    1SG　BEN　3SG　buy　quite.a few　CL　FOC　clothes　SFP
    'I have bought him quite a few pieces of clothing.'

In (15), the speaker not only describes a fact that she has bought him some items of clothing, but also emphasizes the number of clothes. In other words, due to the use of the focus marker *e⁰* 其, the subjective attitude of the speaker is also involved.

The quantifier *tak⁸* usually requires a classifier when modifying a common noun, as shown by example (14) above. The following example, however, shows that *tak⁸* can occur directly before the noun *laŋ²* 儂 'person'.

(16) 逐儂　　　　都　著　　檢查
    tak⁸⁻⁴-laŋ²　*tɔ¹*　*tioʔ⁸⁻⁴*　*kiəm³⁻²tsa¹*
    every-person　all　should　examine
    'Everyone has to be checked.'

The general classifier e^2 can also be inserted between the quantifier tak^8 and the noun $laŋ^2$, that is, forming $tak^{8\text{-}4} e^{2\text{-}4} laŋ^2$ 逐個儂, which is more common than $tak^{8\text{-}4} laŋ^2$ (without the classifier e^2) in daily conversation. The latter may be a contracted form of $tak^{8\text{-}4} e^{2\text{-}4} laŋ^2$, due to an omission of the classifier e^2 個.

In daily conversation, the [quantifier + classifier] complex is often used alone (without a noun) functioning as a subject as in (17), or as an object as in (18).

(17) 逐垛　　都　　相同
 $tak^{8\text{-}4}\text{-}tə^5$　$tɔ^1$　$sa^1 saŋ^2$
 every-CL　all　same
 'Every (table) is the same.'

(18) 買　　幾　　粒
 bue^3　$kui^{3\text{-}2}$　$liəp^8$
 buy　several　CL
 'buy several (apples)'

As with the [numeral + classifier] complex, the quantifier kui^3 with the following classifier can be preceded by a personal pronoun such as gun^3 'we' in (19), by the nominal demonstratives $tsit^7$ 'this'/hit^7 'that' as in (20), by the interrogative word to^3 'which', as in (21), or by $thau^2$ 'head, first' as in (22).

(19) 阮　　幾　　個
 gun^3　$kui^{3\text{-}2}$　e^2
 1PL　several　CL
 'we, the few of us'

(20) 即　　幾　　垛
 $tsit^{7\text{-}8}$　$kui^{3\text{-}2}$　$tə^5$
 this　several　CL
 'these few (tables)'

(21) 底　　幾　　領
 $to^{3\text{-}2}$　$kui^{3\text{-}2}$　$liã^3$
 which　several　CL
 'Which pieces (of clothing)?'

(22) 頭　　幾　　把
　　 thau² kui³⁻² pe³
　　 head several CL
　　 'the first few (cars)'

7.2.3 Demonstratives *tsit⁷/hit⁷* + classifier

Classifiers in Hui'an can also be preceded by the nominal demonstratives *tsit⁷* 'this' and *hit⁷* 'that', as in (23), where the classifier *tə⁵* 垛 directly follows the nominal demonstrative *tsit⁷* 即 'this' and *tsit⁷⁻⁸tə⁵* 即垛 functions as a subject of the sentence.

(23) 即垛　　　無　　　好
　　 tsit⁷⁻⁸-tə⁵　bo²⁻⁴　ho³
　　 this-CL　not.have　good
　　 'This (table) is not good.'

The [*tsit⁷/hit⁷* + classifier] complex can also function as an object as in (24), where *hit⁷⁻⁸liã³* 迄領 'that piece' is an object of the verb *tshiŋ⁵* 穿 'wear'.

(24) 穿　　　　迄領
　　 tshiŋ⁵⁻⁴　hit⁷⁻⁸-liã³
　　 wear　　that-CL
　　 'Wear that piece (of clothing).'

As illustrated by the following two examples, [*tsit⁷/hit⁷* + classifier] can modify a noun such as *kau³* 狗 'dog' in (25), or be modified as in (26) where *hit⁷⁻⁸ki¹* 迄枝 'that' is modified by the adjective *sen¹* 新 'new', which calls for the modifying marker *e⁰* 其.

(25) 去　　　看　　　迄隻　　　　　狗
　　 khu⁵⁻³　khuã⁵⁻³　hit⁷⁻⁸-tsiaʔ⁷⁻⁸　kau³
　　 go　　　look　　　that-CL　　　　dog
　　 '(We) went to see that dog.'

(26) 新   其   迄枝
    sen¹   *e⁰* *hit⁷⁻⁸-ki¹*
    new   MOD   that-CL
    'the new (mop)'

Note that the nominal demonstratives *tsit⁷* 'this' and *hit⁷* 'that' require a classifier since they are probably fused forms of demonstratives and the numeral for 'one' (see §5.2.1 for details).

7.2.4 Classifier + noun

Classifiers in Hui'an can modify a noun without a numeral, quantifier or nominal demonstrative. This [classifier + noun] complex typically occurs in postverbal position in a transitive (S) VO clause and denotes indefiniteness, as in (27) and (28), where *tsiaʔ⁷⁻⁸ aʔ⁷* 隻鴨 'a duck' and *təˤ⁻³ huɪ²* 垛魚 'a piece of fish' function as an object of the verbs *bue³* 買 'buy' and *tsiaʔ⁸* 食 'eat', respectively. This property of classifiers is extensively discussed in Wang (2013, 2015).

(27) 買   隻   鴨
    bue³⁻²   *tsiaʔ⁷⁻⁸*   *aʔ⁷*
    buy   CL   duck
    'buy a duck'

(28) 食   垛   魚
    tsiaʔ⁸⁻⁴ *təˤ⁻³*   *huɪ²*
    eat   CL   fish
    'eat a piece of fish'

When the classifier occurs after a verb and denotes, on the contrary, definiteness, we have a case of a different syntactic structure altogether: in this situation, the [classifier + noun] complex functions as a head noun of the relative clause in which the verb occurs, as in (29).

(29) [Noun – Verb]_RC [CL – Noun]_SUBJECT – Predicate
    恁   爸   掠   隻   鴨   加   珍   遘
    len³⁻²   *pa²*   *liaʔ⁸*   *tsiaʔ⁷⁻⁸* *aʔ⁷*   *ke¹*   *tin¹*   *a³*
    2PL   father   catch   CL   duck   more   sweet   EVC
    'The duck your father took (home) is more tasty (than this one).'

In (29), *tsia?⁷⁻⁸ a?⁷* 'the duck' functions as a head noun, modified by the relative clause *len³⁻² pa² lia?⁸* 'your father took'. Note that the verb *lia?⁸* is in its citation tone, that is, it does not undergo tone sandhi (see chapter 22 for details of relative clauses).

Similarly, the [classifier + noun] complex can be used in genitive constructions, functioning as a possessee and denoting definiteness, as in (30), where *pun³⁻² tshe?⁷* 本冊 'the book' is preceded by the first-person singular pronoun *gua³* 我 to form a genitive construction.

(30) 我   本   冊   咧
     gua³ pun³⁻² tshe?⁷ le?⁰
     1SG   CL   book   SFP
     'Where is my book?'

The [classifier + noun] complex can also follow a preposition such as the object-marking preposition *tsiɔŋ¹* 將 in (31) to denote indefiniteness.

(31) 將   本   冊   共   伊   拆   破   去
     tsiɔŋ¹ pun³⁻²   tshe?⁷ ka⁵⁻⁴ i¹   thia?⁷⁻⁸ phua⁵   khu⁰
     OM   CL   book   OM   3SG   tear   broken   PVC
     '(He) tore a book.'

Unlike some other Chinese varieties such as Yue and Wu (cf. Wang 2015), the [classifier + noun] complex in Hui'an normally cannot occur before a verb in a transitive SVO clause to function as a subject or topic.

7.2.5 Adjective + classifier

Classifiers in Hui'an can be preceded by an adjective, especially the adjectives *tua⁵* 大 'big' and *sue⁵* 細 'small'. The complex [adjective + classifier] can modify a noun such as *hu²* 魚 'fish' in (32) and *pan³⁻²tshai²* 板材 'panel' in (33).

(32) 大尾   魚
     tua⁵⁻⁴-bə³⁻²   hu²
     big-CL   fish
     'big fish'

(33) 蜀　　垛　　大垛　　　其　　　板材
　　 tsit⁸⁻⁴　tə⁵⁻³　tua⁵⁻⁴-tə⁵　e²⁻⁴　pan³⁻²tsai²
　　 one　　CL　　big-CL　　MOD　panel
　　 'one big panel'

In (32), the classifier ba^3 is preceded by the adjective tua^5 'big' to form the complex $tua^{5\text{-}4}ba^3$ 'big', which modifies the noun hu^2 'fish'. In (33), the classifier ta^5 follows the adjective tua^5 to form $tua^{5\text{-}4}ta^5$ 'big', which functions as a modifier of the noun $pan^{3\text{-}2}tshai^2$ 'panel'. Note that the modifying marker e^2 其 is inserted between the modifier $tua^{5\text{-}4}ta^5$ and the noun $pan^{3\text{-}2}tsai^2$ in (33), but not between $tua^{5\text{-}4}ba^3$ and hu^2 in (32). In other words, the modifying marker e^2 is not obligatory when [adjective + classifier] modifies a noun.

When functioning as the modifier of a noun, the complex [adjective + classifier] can be further modified by a degree adverb such as ban^2 蠻 'rather' in (34).

(34) 蜀　　垛　　蠻　　　大垛　　　其　　肉
　　 tsit⁸⁻⁴　tə⁵⁻³　ban²⁻⁴　tua⁵⁻⁴-tə⁵　e⁰　baʔ⁷
　　 one　　CL　　rather　big-CL　　MOD　meat
　　 'quite a big piece of meat'

In (34), the adverb ban^2 'rather' modifies the complex $tua^{5\text{-}4}ta^5$, and $ban^{2\text{-}4}\ tua^{5\text{-}4}ta^5$ 蠻大垛 'quite a big piece' as a whole functions as a modifier of the noun $baʔ^7$ 'meat'.

The complex [adjective + classifier] is also often used as a predicate. When functioning as a predicate, the [adjective + classifier] unit is often modified by a degree adverb such as $tsue^5$ 最 'most' in (35), or by a negative adverb such as bue^4 獪 'cannot' in (36).

(35) 迄叢　　　　最　　　　細枝
　　 hit⁷⁻⁸-tsaŋ²　tsue⁵⁻³　sue⁵⁻³-ki¹
　　 that-CL　　most　　small-CL
　　 'That (mop) is the smallest.'

(36) 即間　　　　獪　　　細間
　　 tsit⁷⁻⁸-kuin¹　bue⁴　sue⁵⁻³-kuin¹
　　 this-CL　　cannot　small-CL
　　 'This (room) is not small.'

In (35), the complex $sue^{5\text{-}3}ki^1$ is modified by the degree adverb $tsue^5$ 'most', and $tsue^{5\text{-}3} sue^{5\text{-}3}ki^1$ treated as a whole functions as the predicate, preceded by the subject $hit^{7\text{-}8}tsaŋ^2$ 'that (mop)'. In (36), the complex $sue^{5\text{-}3}kuin^1$ is modified by the negative adverb bue^4 'cannot', and $bue^4 sue^{5\text{-}3}kuin^1$ similarly functions as a predicate.

The examples above suggest that the [adjective + classifier] complex functions syntactically like an adjective: it not only directly modifies a noun, but also functions as a predicate. In other words, the complex [adjective + classifier] constitutes a compound adjective.

Interestingly, we also find a few examples in which the complex [adjective + classifier] seems to function as the object of a verb, as in (37) below, where $tua^{5\text{-}4}liã^3$ 大領 'big (quilt)' functions as an object of the verb bue^3 買 'buy'.

(37) 無　　　買　　大領
$bo^{2\text{-}4}$　　$bue^{3\text{-}2}$　$tua^{5\text{-}4}\text{-}liã^3$
not.have　buy　big-CL
'(She) didn't buy a big (quilt).'

Other adjectives that can be followed by a classifier are quite limited in number, and vary with their following classifiers and sometimes the nouns they modify. For example, the classifier $kuin^1$ 間 can co-occur with a series of adjectives such as tua^5 'big', sue^5 'small', $tshiəm^1$ 深 'deep', $tshen^3$ 淺 'shallow', $khuaʔ^7$ 闊 'wide', $ueʔ^8$ 狹 'narrow', $tŋ^2$ 長 'long' and $tə^3$ 短 'short'. Examples of $kuaʔ^{7\text{-}8}kuin^1$ 'wide' and $ueʔ^{8\text{-}4}kuin^1$ 'narrow' are given in (38).

(38) 即間　　　房　　恰　　　　　闊/狹間
$tsit^{7\text{-}8}\text{-}kuin^1$　$paŋ^2$　$khaʔ^{7\text{-}8}$　$khuaʔ^{7\text{-}8}/ueʔ^{8\text{-}4}\text{-}kuin^1$
this-CL　room　comparatively　wide/narrow-CL
'This room is wider/narrower than (that one).'

In (38), the compound adjectives $khuaʔ^{7\text{-}8}kuin^1$ 'wide' and $ueʔ^{8\text{-}4}kuin^1$ 'narrow' are further modified by the comparative marker $khaʔ^7$.

Though the adjectives mentioned above can all be used with the classifier $kuin^1$ to form compound adjectives, they are not commonly used in daily conversation, except for the compound adjectives involving tua^5 'big' and sue^5 'small' (i.e. $tua^{5\text{-}4}kuin^1$ and $sue^{5\text{-}3}kuin^1$). The compound adjectives $kuaʔ^{7\text{-}8}kuin^1$ 'wide' and $ueʔ^{8\text{-}4}kuin^1$ 'narrow' in (38) can be replaced by the monosyllabic adjectives $kuaʔ^7$ and $ueʔ^8$, respectively. In fact, the compound adjectives are in general less common than their corresponding monosyllabic adjectives, excepting, again, those involving tua^5 'big' and sue^5 'small'. For example, the compound adjectives with *tua⁵* and *sue⁵* in examples (32) – (37) above cannot usually be substituted by the monosyllabic ones (i.e. *tua⁵* and *sue⁵*). Although in some cases, *tua⁵* and *sue⁵* used alone may also be acceptable for some native speakers, the compound ones are undoubtedly more natural. Some further examples are discussed below.

The classifier *tiau²* 條 can be preceded by a series of adjectives such as *tua⁵* 'big', *sue⁵* 'small', *tŋ²* 長 'long', *ta³* 短 'short', *tshɔ¹* 粗 'thick' and *iu⁵* 幼 'thin' when they modify a noun such as *soʔ⁷* 索 'rope' in (39).

(39) 蜀   條   粗條   索
     tsit⁸⁻⁴ *tiau²⁻⁴* *tshɔ¹-tiau²⁻⁴* *soʔ⁷*
     one   CL   thick-CL   rope
     'a thick rope'

However, only the adjectives *tua⁵* 'big' and *sue⁵* 'small' can be naturally followed by the classifier *tiau²* 條 when they modify a noun such as *lɔ⁵* 路 'road' and *kau¹* 溝 'ditch'. Examples are given in (40) and (41).

(40) 蜀   條   大條   路
     tsit⁸⁻⁴ *tiau²⁻⁴* *tua⁵⁻⁴-tiau²⁻⁴* *lɔ⁵*
     one   CL   big-CL   road
     'a big road'

(41) *蜀   條   粗條   路
     tsit⁸⁻⁴ *tiau²⁻⁴* *tshɔ¹-tiau²⁻⁴* *lɔ⁵*
     one   CL   thick-CL   road
     'a thick road'

The compound adjectives consisting of an adjective and a classifier are also reported in some other Chinese varieties such as Taiwan Southern Min (cf. Liu 2010). Liu (2010) argues that the classifier in the compound adjective functions to provide a dimension (i.e. scale) along which the relevant property of the noun (phrase) is predicated or by which it is modified or measured, while the adjective in the compound adjective denotes an ordering function that orders the sets of points toward the upper or lower end of the scale denoted by the classifier (see Liu 2010 for more details).

7.3 Semantic properties

As with Mandarin Chinese, the Hui'an dialect has a general classifier, that is, e^2 個, which can be used for person-denoting nouns such as $ken^{3\text{-}2}a^3$ 囝仔 'child' in (42).

(42) 兩　　個　　囝仔
　　　$l\eta^4$　$e^{2\text{-}4}$　$ken^{3\text{-}2}a^3$
　　　two　CL　child
　　　'two children'

As shown by example (42), there is no specific classifier for human beings, which usually take the general classifier e^2, whose lexical source is unclear, but may be associated with the modifying marker e^2 其.

This general classifier can also be used for nouns which can take a specific classifier, such as $o\textrm{?}^{8\text{-}4}t\eta^2$ 學堂 'school' in (43).

(43) 蜀　　　間/個　　　學堂
　　　$tsit^{8\text{-}4}$　$kuin^1/e^{2\text{-}4}$　$o\textrm{?}^{8\text{-}4}t\eta^2$
　　　one　　CL/CL　　school
　　　'a school'

The noun $o\textrm{?}^{8\text{-}4}t\eta^2$ is usually used with its specific classifier $kuin^1$, but can also be used with the general classifier e^2 個. In other words, the general classifier e^2 can susbstitute for some specific classifiers.

The general classifier e^2 is also used for nouns which do not have a specific classifier, such as the abstract noun $k\partial^{5\text{-}3}thi\eta^2$ 過程 'process' in (44).

(44) 蜀　　　個　　過程
　　　$tsit^{8\text{-}4}$　$e^{2\text{-}4}$　$k\partial^{5\text{-}3}thi\eta^2$
　　　one　CL　process
　　　'a process'

As mentioned above, person-denoting nouns usually take the general classifier e^2. However, there are two more classifiers for person-denoting nouns: $k\textrm{ɔ}^1$ 孤 and ui^5 位. The former one usually shows a derogatory sense, as in (45), whereas the latter is used to show respect for somebody (that is, used as a polite form for human beings), as in (46).

(45) 迄孤　　　男其
　　 hit⁷⁻⁸-kɔ¹　lam²-e⁰
　　 that-CL　 male-NMLZ
　　 'that guy'

(46) 蜀　　位　　領導
　　 tsit⁸⁻⁴　ui⁵⁻⁴　liŋ³⁻²tɔ⁵
　　 one　　CL　　leader
　　 'a leader/boss'

Animals are basically distinguished from human beings and inanimate objects. The general classifier for animals is *tsiaʔ⁷* 隻 < 'a bird', as in (47).

(47) 蜀　　　隻　　　　馬
　　 tsit⁸⁻⁴　tsiaʔ⁷⁻⁸　be³
　　 one　　 CL　　　　horse
　　 'a horse'

This classifier can also be used for some inanimate objects such as vehicles, as in (48). Note that vehicles such as *tshia¹* 車 'vehicle, car' in (48) have their own specific classifier *pe³* 把, as illustrated by (49).

(48) 蜀　　　隻　　　　車
　　 tsit⁸⁻⁴　tsiaʔ⁷⁻⁸　tshia¹
　　 one　　 CL　　　　vehicle
　　 'a car'

(49) 蜀　　　把　　　車
　　 tsit⁸⁻⁴　pe³⁻²　tshia¹
　　 one　　 CL　　 vehicle
　　 'a car'

In Quanzhou, Xiamen and Zhangzhou, the general classifier for animals (i.e. *tsiaʔ* 隻) is also used for vehicles (Zhou 2006). In Hui'an, however, *tsiaʔ⁷* is also used with some home appliances such as *tshai³⁻²ten⁵* 彩電 'color TV', *piŋ¹siũ¹* 冰箱 'fridge', *sue³⁻²sã¹ki¹* 洗衫機 'washing machine', and the noun *ki²⁻⁴a³* 棋仔 'chessman'. An example of *sue³⁻²sã¹ki¹* 'washing machine' is given in (50) below. The reason why these inanimate objects use *tsiaʔ⁷* as their classifiers may be that they can 'move', e.g. a washing machine rotates when it works.

(50) 蜀　　隻　　　洗衫機
　　 tsit⁸⁻⁴　tsiaʔ⁷⁻⁸　sue³⁻²-sã¹-ki¹
　　 one　　CL　　　wash-clothes-machine
　　 'a washing machine'

There is a specific classifier *bə³* 尾 (derived from *bə³* 'tail') for fish or reptiles such as *tsua²* 蛇 'snake' and *gia²⁻⁴kaŋ¹* 蜈蚣 'centipede'. An example of *hu²* 魚 'fish' is given in (51).

(51) 蜀　　尾　　魚
　　 tsit⁸⁻⁴　bə³⁻²　hu²
　　 one　　CL　　fish
　　 'a fish'

Inanimate objects usually have a specific classifier besides the general classifier *e²*. For example, the specific classifier *tiau²* 條 is mainly used for three-dimensional objects with a long shape such as *kau¹* 溝 'ditch', *i³⁻²tiau²* 椅條 'bench', *khɔ⁵⁻³tua⁵* 褲帶 'waistband', *len⁵⁻⁴a³* 鏈仔 'necklace', *soʔ⁷* 索 'rope' and *hun¹* 薰 'cigarette'. An example is given in (52).

(52) 蜀　　條　　　鏈仔
　　 tsit⁸⁻⁴　tiau²⁻⁴　len⁵⁻⁴a³
　　 one　　CL　　　chain-NM
　　 'a necklace'

This classifier is also used for two-dimensional objects with a long shape such as *lɔ⁵* 路 'road' in (53), or for one-dimensional objects with a long, thin shape such as *hun²* 痕 'scratch' in (54), which forms when the skin is scraped by something.

(53) 蜀　　條　　　路
　　 tsit⁸⁻⁴　tiau²⁻⁴　lɔ⁵
　　 one　　CL　　　road
　　 'a road'

(54) 蜀　　條　　　痕
　　 tsit⁸⁻⁴　tiau²⁻⁴　hun²
　　 one　　CL　　　scratch
　　 'a scratch'

The following example illustrates that the classifier *tiau²* can also function as a classifier for invisible and abstract entities such as *sen¹bun²* 新聞 'news' in (55).

(55) 蜀　　條　　新聞
　　 tsit⁸⁻⁴　tiau²⁻⁴　sen¹bun²
　　 one　　CL　　news
　　 'an item of news'

The classifier *tsua⁵* < 'line' is also used for inanimate objects with a long shape. Unlike *tiau²*, however, the classifier *tsua⁵* is mainly used with linear-form objects (that is, one-dimensional objects with a long shape) such as *hun²* 'scratch' mentioned above and *li⁵* 字 'character' which are written in a line, as in (56).

(56) 蜀　　囗　　字
　　 tsit⁸⁻⁴　tsua⁵⁻⁴　li⁵
　　 one　　CL　　character
　　 'a line of characters'

The classifier *tsua⁵* can also be used for two-dimensional objects with a long profile such as *lɔ⁵* 路 'road' in (57), or for three-dimensional objects with a long shape such as *kau¹* 溝 'ditch' in (58).

(57) 蜀　　囗　　路
　　 tsit⁸⁻⁴　tsua⁵⁻⁴　lɔ⁵
　　 one　　CL　　road
　　 'a road'

(58) 蜀　　囗　　溝
　　 tsit⁸⁻⁴　tsua⁵⁻⁴　kau¹
　　 one　　CL　　ditch
　　 'a ditch'

However, *tsua⁵* cannot be used for three-dimensional objects such as *i³⁻²tiau²* 椅條 'bench', *khɔ⁵⁻³tua⁵* 褲帶 'waistband' and *len⁵⁻⁴a³* 鏈仔 'necklace' which take the classifier *tiau²* 條 as mentioned above.

The classifier *tiũ¹* 張 < 'to draw a bow' is mainly used for two-dimensional objects which have a flat surface, e.g. *tsua³* 紙 'paper', *phio⁵* 票 'ticket', *siɔŋ⁵* 相 'picture' and *phue¹* 批 'letter'. An example of *tsua³* 'paper' is given in (59).

(59) 蜀　　張　　紙
 tsit⁸⁻⁴　tiũ¹　tsua³
 one　　CL　　Paper
 'a piece of paper'

The following example shows that *tiũ¹* is also used for three-dimensional objects which have a flat surface such as *tshŋ²* 床 'bed'.

(60) 蜀　　張　　床
 tsit⁸⁻⁴　tiũ¹　tshŋ²
 one　　CL　　Bed
 'a bed'

The classifier *tə⁵* 垛, originally a noun denoting a lump or chunk, is mainly used for three-dimensional objects with a lumpy shape such as *o²* 蠔 'oyster', *piã³* 餅 'biscuit' and *thŋ²⁻⁴a³* 糖仔 'candy', but also extended to further three-dimensional objects with a chunky shaped component such as *toʔ⁷* 桌 'table', *tshŋ²* 床 'bed' and *tshu⁵* 厝 'house'. Two examples are given in (61) and (62).

(61) 蜀　　垛　　糖仔
 tsit⁸⁻⁴　tə⁵⁻³　thŋ²⁻⁴-a³
 One　　CL　　sugar-NM
 'a candy'

(62) 蜀　　垛　　桌
 tsit⁸⁻⁴　tə⁵⁻³　toʔ⁷
 one　　CL　　table
 'a table'

The classifier *tə⁵* is also the specific classifier for the abstract noun *kua¹* 歌 'song', as shown by (63). This may involve an extension of the use of *tə⁵* from concrete objects with a lumpy/chunky shape to abstract things.

(63) 蜀　　垛　　歌
 tsit⁸⁻⁴　tə⁵⁻³　kua¹
 one　　CL　　song
 'a song'

The classifier *bɔ²* 模, originally meaning 'mould', is a specific classifier for *tau⁵⁻⁴hu⁵* 豆腐 'bean curd', as in (64).

(64) 蜀　　模　　豆腐
    tsit⁸⁻⁴　*bɔ²⁻⁴*　*tau⁵⁻⁴hu⁵*
    one　　CL　　bean.curd
    'a piece/cake/square of bean curd'

The bean curd is typically encountered in a chunk-like shape. The classifier *bɔ²* also suggests that the bean curd has a fixed size which is determined by the mould with which the bean curd is made.

The classifiers *hut⁸* 核 and *liəp⁸* 粒 are both used for roundish objects regardless of size, e.g. *ki⁵* 痣 'mole', *phiŋ²⁻⁴kɔ³* 蘋果 'apple' and *kiu²* 球 'ball'. Two examples are given in (65) and (66).

(65) 蜀　　核　　蘋果
    tsit⁸⁻⁴　*hut⁸⁻⁴*　*phiŋ²⁻⁴kɔ³*
    one　　CL　　apple
    'an apple'

(66) 蜀　　粒　　球
    tsit⁸⁻⁴　*liəp⁸⁻⁴*　*kiu²*
    one　　CL　　ball
    'a ball'

The classifier *hut⁸*, originally a noun meaning 'core', is typically used for objects with a core such as *phiŋ²⁻⁴kɔ³* 'apple' in (65), and then extended to other roundish objects. The classifier *liəp⁸*, originally a noun meaning 'grain', is fundamentally used as a classifier for grain-like objects such as *ki⁵* 'mole', and then extended to objects such as *phiŋ²⁻⁴kɔ³* 'apple' and *kiu²* 'ball' in (66). A similar extension from small to large in size can also be attested for the classifier *tə⁵* 垛 mentioned above. The classifiers *hut⁸* 核 and *liəp⁸* 粒 overlap with each other. However, *hut⁸* was used more than *liəp⁸* in earlier times, while *liəp⁸* is used more than *hut⁸* at present (according to older native speakers).

The classifiers *ki¹* 枝 < 'branch of a plant' and *tsaŋ²* 叢 < 'assemble' are both used for stick-like objects regardless of size: the object can be a small one like *tsam¹* 針 'needle', *so³⁻²si²* 鎖匙 'key', *pet⁷* 筆 'pen' and *to¹* 刀 'knife', or a large one like *tshiŋ⁵* 銃 'gun', *thua¹pa²* 拖把 'mop' and *sau⁵⁻³tshiu³* 掃帚 'broom'. Two examples are given in (67) and (68).

(67) 蜀　　枝　　針
　　 tsit⁸⁻⁴　ki¹　tsam¹
　　 one　CL　needle
　　 'a needle'

(68) 蜀　　叢　　銃
　　 tsit⁸⁻⁴　tsaŋ²⁻⁴　tshiŋ⁵
　　 one　CL　gun
　　 'a gun'

Zhou (2006) mentions that in Quanzhou, Xiamen and Zhangzhou, not all nouns that can occur with *ki¹* 枝 can be used with *tsaŋ²* 叢, and gives the example of *hue¹* 花 'flower'. In Hui'an, however, *hue¹* can be used with both of these classifiers.

The classifier *khia¹/khã¹* 奇, originally meaning 'singular' as in *khia¹sɔ⁵* 奇數 'singular', is used for one of a pair such as *ue²* 鞋 'shoe' and *tɯ⁵* 箸 'chopstick' which exist in pairs. An example is given in (69).

(69) 蜀　　奇　　鞋
　　 tsit⁸⁻⁴　khia¹　ue²
　　 one　CL　shoe
　　 'a shoe'

This classifier is also used for container-like objects with a hollow interior, e.g. *tə⁵* 袋 'sack', *siũ¹* 箱 'suitcase' and *piŋ¹siũ¹* 冰箱 'fridge', as in (70), and for annular objects with a hollow interior such as *tshiu³⁻²tsi³* 手指 'ring' in (71).

(70) 蜀　　奇　　袋仔
　　 tsit⁸⁻⁴　khia¹　tə⁵⁻⁴-a³
　　 one　CL　sack-NM
　　 'a sack'

(71) 蜀　　奇　　手指
　　 tsit⁸⁻⁴　khia¹　tshiu³⁻²tsi³
　　 one　CL　ring
　　 'a ring'

The classifier *tso⁴* 座 is always used for big and stable objects, e.g. *suã¹* 山 'hill', *lau²* 樓 'building' and *tshu⁵* 厝 'house'. An example of *suã¹* 'hill' is given in (72).

(72) 蜀　　座　　山
     tsit$^{8\text{-}4}$　tso^4　suã^1
     one　CL　hill
     'a hill'

The classifier *liã^3* 領 is mainly used for something which can cover people's body, including clothes, quilts and blankets, but is also used for mats. An example is given in (73).

(73) 蜀　　領　　羊毛衫
     tsit$^{8\text{-}4}$　liã$^{3\text{-}2}$　iũ$^{2\text{-}4}$bŋ$^{2\text{-}4}$sã^1
     one　CL　sweater
     'a sweater'

The classifier *kuin^1* 間 < 'crack of the door' is used for a room of a building or the whole building, e.g. *paŋ^2* 房 'room', *iɔk$^{8\text{-}4}$ siak^7* 浴室 'bathroom', *tshai$^{5\text{-}3}$kuan^3* 菜館 'restaurant', *tshu^5* 厝 'house' and *oʔ$^{8\text{-}4}$tŋ^2* 學堂 'school'. An example of *paŋ^2* 'room' is given in (74).

(74) 蜀　　間　　房
     tsit$^{8\text{-}4}$　kuin^1　paŋ^2
     one　CL　room
     'a room'

The classifier *pun^3* 本 < 'root of a plant' is used for objects such as books, notebooks and account books, all of which are made of paper and used for reading or writing. An example is given in (75).

(75) 蜀　　本　　冊
     tsit$^{8\text{-}4}$　pun$^{3\text{-}2}$　tsheʔ^7
     one　CL　book
     'a book'

The classifier *lui^3* 蕊 < 'flower bud' is mainly used for flowers, but also used for *tshai$^{5\text{-}3}$hue^1* 菜花 'cauliflower' (which looks like a flower), and for *bak$^{8\text{-}4}$tsiu^1* 目珠 'eye'. An example of *tshai$^{5\text{-}3}$hue^1* 'cauliflower' is given in (76).

(76) 蜀　　蕊　　菜花
　　 tsit⁸⁻⁴　lui³⁻²　tshai⁵⁻³hue¹
　　 one　 CL　 cauliflower
　　 'a cauliflower'

The classifier *sin⁵* 扇 < 'door leaf' is mainly used for objects such as doors, windows and walls, as in (77).

(77) 蜀　　扇　　窗
　　 tsit⁸⁻⁴　sin⁵⁻³　thaŋ¹
　　 one　 CL　 window
　　 'a window'

A summary of the major classifiers and the semantic domain of nouns classified is shown in Table 7-1.

Tab. 7-1: Major classifiers and the semantic domain of nouns classified in the Hui'an dialect

Classifiers	Semantic domain of nouns classified
e² 個	general classifier
kɔ¹ 孤	human beings (derogatory)
ui⁵ 位	human beings (respect)
tsiaʔ⁷ 隻	animals, some inanimate objects such as vehicles and home appliances
ba³ 尾	fish and animals which are flexible, long and creeping
pe³ 把	vehicles
tiau² 條	mainly three-dimensional objects with a long shape but also one- and two-dimensional objects with a long shape
tsua⁵	mainly linear form objects but also two/three-dimensional objects with a long shape
tiū¹ 張	two/three-dimensional objects which have a flat surface
ta⁵ 垛	three-dimensional objects with a lumpy/chunky shape also *kua¹* 'song'
bɔ² 模	*tau⁵⁻⁴hu⁵* 'bean curd'
hut⁸ 核/*liap⁸* 粒	roundish objects regardless of size
ki¹ 枝/*tsaŋ²* 叢	stick-like objects regardless of size
khia¹/*kha¹* 奇	one of a pair container-like objects with a hollow interior

Classifiers	Semantic domain of nouns classified
	annular objects with a hollow interior
tso⁴ 座	big and stable inanimate objects
liã³ 領	coverings such as clothes, quilts, blankets and mats
kuin¹ 間	a room of a building or the whole building
pun³ 本	inanimate objects which are made of paper and used for reading or writing
lui³ 蕊	objects such as flowers, cauliflower and eyes
sin⁵ 扇	objects such as doors, windows and walls

7.4 Referential functions

When occurring with a demonstrative, classifier constructions are mainly used for referring to something that exists in the speech context, as in (78), or something that is easy for both the speaker and hearer to recognize and understand, as in (79).

(78) 即隻　　　小妹　　　其　　老虎
　　　tsit⁷⁻⁸-tsiaʔ⁷　*sio³⁻²bə⁵*　*e²⁻⁴*　*lau³⁻²hɔ³*
　　　this-CL　　Y.sister　　GEN　tiger
　　　'This is little sister's tiger.'

(79) 按　　　新　　其　　迄枝　　　洗
　　　an⁵⁻³　*sen¹*　*e⁰*　*hit⁷⁻⁸-ki¹*　*sue³*
　　　with　　new　　MOD　that-CL　　wash
　　　'wash with the new (mop)'

The context of example (78) is that the family is cleaning up things in a room, and the elder sister finds a tiger toy and tells her parents that it is her little sister's tiger. The complex *tsit⁷⁻⁸tsiaʔ⁷* 'this' here refers to an entity that is present in the surrounding situation. In (79), the complex *hit⁷⁻⁸ki¹* 'that' refers to the mop that both the speaker and hearer can identify, though it is mentioned for the first time and does not exist in the surrounding situation.

When functioning as the possessee of a genitive construction or as the head noun of a relative clause, the complex [classifier + noun] is typically used to refer to something that is not present in the surrounding situation but can be identified by both the speaker and the hearer, as in (80). That is, pragmatically, it has a recognitional use (see also recognitional use of demonstratives in §5.3).

(80) 阮　垛　厝　呣免　拆
　　 gun³　*tə⁵⁻³*　*tshu⁵*　*m⁵⁻⁴ben³⁻²*　*thiaʔ⁷*
　　 1PL　CL　house　no.need　pull.down
　　 'Our house doesn't need to be pulled down.'

In (80), the complex *tə⁵⁻³ tshu⁵* 'the[1] house' functions as a possessee of the genitive construction *gun³ tə⁵⁻³ tshu⁵* 'our house', referring to the house that is easy for both the speaker and hearer to recognize.

When used with a numeral or demonstrative, classifier constructions can also refer to something mentioned in the preceding context, as in (81) and (82).

(81) A: 伊　請　別儂　　　做
　　　　 i¹　*tshiã³⁻²*　*pat⁸⁻⁴-laŋ²*　*tsue⁵*
　　　　 3SG　hire　other-person　do
　　　　 'He hired other people to do (it).'
　　 B: 底　其　儂
　　　　 to³⁻²　*e²⁻⁴*　*laŋ²*
　　　　 where　GEN　person
　　　　 'Where does he come from?'
　　 A: 山頭　　其　儂
　　　　 suã¹thau²　*e²⁻⁴*　*laŋ²*
　　　　 PN　GEN　person
　　　　 '(He) comes from Suã-thau (Shantou).'
　　 A: 卜　　知，　直接　　叫　　即個　　　來　　做
　　　　 boʔ⁷⁻⁸　*tsai¹*　*tet⁸⁻⁴tsiap⁷*　*kio⁵⁻³*　*tsit⁷⁻⁸-e²⁻⁴*　*lai²⁻⁴*　*tsue⁵*
　　　　 want　know　directly　call　this-CL　come　do
　　　　 'If (we) had known (this situation), (we) would've contacted him directly for the job.'

---

[1] In this case, the complex *tə⁵⁻³tshu⁵* (CL + N) has a definite reading and means 'the house'.

(82) A: 迄兩隻　　　鴨　伯　其　口
　　　 hit⁷⁻⁸-lŋ⁴-tsiaʔ⁷⁻⁸　*aʔ⁷*　*lan³*　*e²*　*siã⁰*
　　　 that-two-CL　duck　1PL　GEN　SFP
　　　 'Are those two ducks ours?'

B: 蜀　　隻　　　伯　其，
　　tsit⁸⁻⁴　*tsiaʔ⁷⁻⁸*　*lan³*　*e²*
　　one　CL　1PL　GEN
　　蜀　　隻　　　佮　同事　　　其
　　tsit⁸⁻⁴　*tsiaʔ⁷⁻⁸*　*en¹*　*tɔŋ²⁻⁴suɯ⁵*　*e²*
　　one　CL　3PL　colleague　GEN
　　'One (duck) is ours, and the other one belongs to his colleague.'

In (81), speaker A uses *tsit⁷⁻⁸ e²* 'this' in the last turn to refer back to *pat⁸⁻⁴ laŋ²* 'another person' in the first turn. In (82), speaker B uses *tsit⁸⁻⁴ tsiaʔ⁷* 'one' to refer to one of two ducks speaker A is talking about.

Classifiers can also be used alone to take on an anaphoric function, as in (83). Note, however, that this usage of classifiers is not common, and is not well-described as yet in the literature.

(83) A: 今日　　蜀　　　日　刣　　四　　隻　　　其　　鴨
　　　 kiã¹let⁸　*tsit⁸⁻⁴*　*let⁸*　*thai²*　*si⁵⁻³*　*tsiaʔ⁷*　*e⁰*　*aʔ⁷*
　　　 today　one　day　kill　four　CL　FOC　duck
　　　 '(I) killed four ducks within one day today.'

B: 刣　　去　　四　　隻？
　　thai²　*khuɯ⁵⁻³*　*si⁵⁻³*　*tsiaʔ⁷*
　　kill　RVC　four　CL
　　伯　　兩　　隻　　　做做　　　　洘　　哦？
　　lan³　*lŋ⁴*　*tsiaʔ⁷*　*tsue⁵⁻³tsue⁵*　*khuʔ⁸*　*o⁰*
　　1PL　Two　CL　together　cook　SFP
　　'(You) killed four (ducks)? Did we cook two of them (ducks) together?'

A: 做做　　　　　刣，　　隻　　　搭　　　佮　　凍
　　tsue⁵⁻³tsue⁵　*thai²*　*tsiaʔ⁷⁻⁸*　*taʔ⁷⁻⁸*　*en¹*　*taŋ⁵*
　　together　kill　CL　entrust　3PL　freeze
　　'(I) killed (the ducks) together, and asked someone to freeze one (for us).'

In (83), speaker B uses *lŋ⁴ tsiaʔ⁷* 兩隻 to refer to two of the four ducks speaker A is talking about, while in the second turn, speaker A uses *tsiaʔ⁷* 隻 alone to refer to one of these two ducks speaker B is talking about in her second sentence. The phenomenon that the classifier is used alone may be the result of deletion of its preceding numeral 'one'. Interestingly, a similar use of lone classifiers is also found in Nanning Cantonese and Northern Zhuang (Tai-Kadai) spoken in Guangxi for subject/topic and object positions (see de Sousa 2015). As de Sousa observes, Standard Mandarin, Standard Cantonese and Nanning Pinghua only allow this use in postverbal position.

7.5 Sources and extensions

There are basically two sources of classifiers: nouns and verbs. Classifiers derived from nouns may represent a part-whole relation: that is, the classifier may refer to just a part of the object it classifies. Examples include the classifiers pun^3 本, lui^3 蕊, sin^5 扇, $liã^3$ 領, $bə^3$ 尾 and ki^1 枝, as explained next:

– Pun^3 本 is originally a noun meaning the root of a plant, and then is used as a classifier for plants. After that, pun^3 is extended to bound and printed items such as books and notebooks.[2]
– Lui^3 蕊 originally refers to a flower bud, and then is used as a classifier for flowers. As explained above, in Hui'an, lui^3 is extended to something which looks like a flower, e.g. $tshai^{5\text{-}3}hue^1$ 菜花 'cauliflower' and $bak^{8\text{-}4}tsiu^1$ 目珠 'eye'.
– Sin^5 扇, a noun meaning a door leaf, is used as a classifier for doors, and then extended to windows, which is similar to the door since both of them can be opened or closed. In Hui'an, this classifier is also used for walls. This may be because door, window and wall are all parts of a room, all possessing a flat surface which is located in a vertical plane.
– $Liã^3$ 領 originally means the neck of a person, which then refers to the part of clothes close to the neck of a person. From here, $liã^3$ extends its use as a classifier for clothes: firstly only for upper, outer garments which have a collar, then for different kinds of clothes. In Hui'an, $liã^3$ can also be used for objects such as $tshio?^8$ 席 'mat', $phə^4$ 被 'quilt', $than^{3\text{-}2}a^3$ 毯仔 'blanket' and $baŋ^3$ 網 'net', all of which can be spread out to cover a surface.
– $Bə^3$ 尾, a noun meaning 'tail', is used as a classifier for fish, and then extended to animals which are long and flexible in shape and which move by slithering or creeping.

---

[2] The classifiers we discussed in this section may show a different picture for semantic extensions or show more extensions when treated in terms of the history of Chinese. We only focus on those that are associated with classifiers in the Hui'an dialect. In addition, our discussion is based on previous studies on the historical development of classifiers in the history of Chinese, e.g. Wang (1984b), Wang (1992), Jiang and Cao (1997), Wei (2000), Hong (2004), Li (2004), Sun (2005), Ye (2005) and Zhang (2012).

- *Ki¹* 枝, originally meaning a branch of a plant or tree, is used as a classifier for plants which have branches. The classifier *ki¹* is further extended to items of a stick-like shape, such as pens.

A noun may also serve as its own classifier. Examples include *tsiaʔ⁷* 隻 and *liəp⁸* 粒:
- *Tsiaʔ⁷* 隻, originally a noun meaning a bird, later comes to be used as a classifier for birds. From here, *tsiaʔ⁷* is extended to inanimate objects such as vehicles and home appliances.
- *Liəp⁸* 粒, originally a noun meaning 'grain', is used as a classifier of grains, and then extended to small and roundish objects. In Hui'an, this classifier is further extended to roundish objects regardless of size.

All the examples above show a grammaticalization path from noun to classifier, undergoing both category change and semantic generalization. The following two examples represent another grammaticalization path, that is, from verb to classifier:
- *Tiũ¹* 張, originally a verb meaning 'to draw a bow', came to be used as a classifier for bows. From here, it generalized in meaning to be used as a classifier for objects with a flat extension of one of their surfaces.
- *Tsaŋ²* 叢, originally a verb meaning 'assemble', becomes a classifier for plants which grow up together, such as bushes, and then for single plants. In Hui'an, this classifier is further extended to items of a stick-like shape.

7.6 Summary

In this chapter, classifiers, which categorize the referents of nouns in terms of their inherent properties such as animacy and shape, have been examined in terms of their syntactic distributions, semantic properties, referential functions, sources and extensions. Classifiers are usually preceded by a numeral, quantifier or by the nominal demonstratives *tsit⁷* and *hit⁷*, but can also modify a noun without any of these in certain, specific constructions. Classifiers can also be used with an adjective such as *tua⁵* 大 'big' and *sue⁵* 細 'small' to form compound adjectives. Semantic domains of nouns classified by major classifiers and their referential functions have also been examined. Finally, we discussed the sources of classifiers and showed that they involve both nouns and verbs.

8 Possessive constructions

8.1 Introduction

According to previous studies on the linguistic notion of possession such as Taylor (1989a, b), Heine (1997) and Stassen (2009), the 'prototypical' or 'canonical' case of possession is alienable possession, which is characterized by the presence of two entities (the possessor and the possessee) such that the possessor and the possessee are in some relatively enduring locational relation, and the possessor exerts control over the possessee (and is therefore typically human) (Stassen 2009:15), as in (1).

(1)   *I have a bicycle.*

In (1), the possessor, *I*, exerts control over the possessee, *a bicycle*. For example, other people cannot use the bicycle unless it is permitted by the possessor, *I*, whose rights over the possessee, *bicycle*, may be transferred to other people via an act of selling or lending. In addition, the possessive relation in this case is relatively time-stable, rather than temporary.

Besides alienable possession, the concept of possession in the literature on possession also usually involves another two categories, that is, inalienable possession and temporary or physical possession (Stassen 2009:16). Taylor (1989a, b) and Heine (1997) further distinguish a fourth category, that is, abstract possession. These four categories of possession can be distinguished from each other in terms of the following two parameters: permanent contact and control, as shown in (i).

(i)
Possessive subtype	Permanent contact	Control
Alienable	+	+
Inalienable	+	-
Temporary	-	+
Abstract	-	-

(Stassen 2009:17)

Examples of inalienable, temporary and abstract possession are given in (2) – (4) below, reproduced from Stassen (2009:18-19).

(2)   *Long John Silver had only one eye.* (Inalienable possession)

(3)   *Look out! That guy has a knife.* (Temporary/physical possession)

(4) *Listen! I have a great idea!* (Abstract possession)

In the case of inalienable possession, the possessor such as *Long John Silver* in example (2) does not exert any control over the possessee, *one eye*. This example involves body parts and illustrates one of the prototypical cases of inalienable possession. Languages may differ as to the semantic scope of inalienable possession. Cross-linguistically, however, besides terms for body parts, kinship terms, spatial orientation (locatives), part-whole relations and social relations such as 'friend' and 'colleague' may also be grouped among cases of inalienable possession. Nonetheless, body parts and kinship terms are typically considered to form the core of inalienable possession (cf. Chappell and McGregor 1989:26-27; Stassen 2009:18). Examples like (3) are usually associated with a fight or robbery. In this case, the possessor *that guy* exerts control over the possessee, *a knife*, at a certain point in time, while whether he owns the knife or not is not important. In other words, the relation between the possessor (*that guy*) and the possessee (*a knife*) is temporary, rather than relatively time-stable (cf. Stassen 2009:19). In example (4), the possessee *a great idea* is an abstract concept, and thus the possession involved is labeled 'abstract possession'.

As mentioned above, these four categories of possession may involve different semantic subtypes in individual languages. In general, the major semantic subtypes which languages may or may not morphologically or syntactically distinguish include ownership, body parts, kinship terms, part-whole relations, spatial orientation, social relations and abstract possession. Chinese usually does not show a one-to-one relationship between these four categories of possession (and their semantic subtypes) and possessive constructions (syntactic structures). In fact, a certain syntactic structure usually expresses different types of possession. For example, the possessive construction with the genitive marker *de* 的 in Mandarin Chinese can express ownership, as in (5), possession of the body part, as in (6), or other types of possession such as abstract possession, as in (7) (see also Chappell and Thompson 1992).

(5) 我　　的　　車 (ownership)
　　 wǒ　de　Chē
　　 1SG　GEN　Car
　　 'my car'

(6) 我　　的　　頭 (body part)
   wǒ　　de　　tóu
   1SG　GEN　head
   'my head'

(7) 我　　的　　想法 (abstract possession)
   wǒ　　de　　xiǎngfǎ
   1SG　GEN　idea
   'my idea'

When the possessee is a kin term, location noun or a term for spatial orientation, the zero-marked possessive construction (without the genitive marker *de*), as in (8) below, tends to be used in Mandarin Chinese (Chappell and Thompson 1992).

(8) 我　　大哥 (kinship term)
   wǒ　　dà-gē
   1SG　big-brother
   'my older brother' (cf. Chappell and Thompson 1992:203)

The encoding of possession in a language typically take two forms: attributive possession (or adnominal possession) and predicative possession, of which the former refers to constructions in which the possessee and possessor form a noun phrase as in the English sentence *Mary's house* and examples (5) – (8) above from Mandarin Chinese, while the latter refers to structures in which the relation of possession between possessor and possessee is the main assertion of the sentence, as illustrated by examples (1) – (4) from English (cf. Heine 1997, Stassen 2009:26, McGregor 2009:2). However, previous studies such as Payne and Barshi (1999) mention another type of possessive construction, that is, the external possessive construction, in which 'a semantic possessor-possessum relation is expressed by coding the possessor (PR) as a core grammatical relation of the verb and in a constituent separate from that which contains the posessum (PM)' (Payne and Barshi 1999:3), as in (9), an example from IlKeekonyokie dialect of Maasai, reproduced from Payne & Barshi (1999:4).

(9) áa-yshú　　en-titó
   3>1-be.alive　FEM.SG-girl.NOM
   'My girl is alive (with presumably positive effect on me).'
   Subject = Possessed Patient & source of impact on possessor;
   Object = Affected Possessor.

In traditional Chinese linguistics, the attributive possessive construction is typically examined under studies on *jiégòu zhùcí* 結構助詞 [structural particles or structural auxiliary words] and/or *piānzhèng jiégòu* 偏正結構 [modifier-modified constructions], while the predicative possessive structure is examined under *dòngcí* 動詞 [verbs] and/or *shùbīn jiégòu* 述賓結構 [predicative structures with object complements]. In addition, people tend to associate the term *lǐngshǔ jiégòu* 領屬結構 [possessive construction] solely with the attributive possessive construction, but do not include the predicative possessive construction or the external possessive construction. However, a certain number of systematic works on possessive constructions in Chinese, especially Mandarin Chinese, can be found during the past three decades. For example, Chappell and Thompson (1992) examine the factors influencing the choice of the Mandarin genitive marker *de* 的, while Chappell (1996, 1999) focuses on double subject constructions and double unaccusative constructions, respectively, both of which are regarded as external possessor constructions. See also Teng (1974), Modini (1981) and Shen (1987) *inter alia* which also treat double subject constructions.

Following the semantic and syntactic subtypes of possession mentioned above, this chapter examines both the attributive and predicative possessive constructions in Hui'an, but not the external possessive construction (qv. Chappell 1999 on this construction in seven Chinese varieties).

8.2 Attributive possessive constructions

As shown in (ii) below, the attributive possessive construction in Hui'an falls into four types in terms of whether or not there exists a linking morpheme between the possessor and the possessee, and if yes, the form of the linking morpheme.

(ii) Four types of attributive possessive construction in the Hui'an dialect
    a. Possessor + ∅ + possessee
       i.e. zero-marked possessive construction
    b. Possessor + demonstrative (+ numeral + classifier) + possessee
       i.e. possessive construction with a demonstrative or demonstrative phrase
    c. Possessor + classifier + possessee
       i.e. possessive construction marked by a classifier
    d. Possessor + e^2 其 + possessee
       i.e. possessive construction with the genitive marker e^2 其

These types of attributive possessive construction can also be found to varying extents in other Chinese varieties. In addition, all four types can be simultaneously attested in certain other Chinese varieties, such as in Yue (cf. Matthews & Yip 2011:128). It is clear that the possessee (=the head) in the attributive possessive construction in Hui'an invariably follows the possessor (=the dependent/modifier), as is the case in Mandarin Chinese and other Chinese dialects. This is, however, not compatible with Greenberg's Universal 2 as shown in (iii).
(iii) In languages with prepositions, the genitive almost always follows the governing noun, while in languages with postpositions it almost always precedes.

It is well known that Chinese is usually regarded as a language with a majority of prepositions, while, as mentioned above, the possessor (the genitive) in Chinese tends to precede the possessee (the governing noun). This is one of several instances of disharmony in word order correlations for the syntactic typology of Chinese (see Chappell, Li and Peyraube 2007; Djamouri, Paul and Whitman 2013).

8.2.1 The zero-marked possessive construction: possessor + ∅ + possessee

8.2.1.1 Pronoun possessor + ∅ + possessee
In the zero-marked possessive construction in Hui'an, the possessor is usually expressed by a pronoun, or sometimes by a noun. In this section, we focus on the zero-marked possessive construction with a pronoun possessor, which is the most common possessive construction in daily conversation of the Hui'an dialect. Generally speaking, the pronoun possessor, especially the plural form, directly precedes the possessee when the possessee is encoded by kinship terms, social relations, location or spatial orientation terms. In addition, the plural form often has a singular meaning, as also described in §4.2.2 above. However, the genitive marker e^2 其 tends to be used when the possessee is encoded by a body part or a common noun, and, in this case, the plural form of the personal pronoun will tend to express a plural meaning (see §8.2.4.1).

8.2.1.1.1 Possessee=kinship terms
In this first structural type, the personal pronoun is usually a plural one such as gun^3 'we' and len^3 'you', but typically expresses a singular meaning, as in (10) and (11).

(10) 伊　　小妹
　　 en¹　 *sio³⁻²bə⁵*
　　 3PL　 Y.sister
　　 'her/their younger sister'

(11) 阮　　媽仔
　　 gun³⁻²　 *bã²-aº*
　　 1PL　 mother-NM
　　 'my/our mother'

In (10), the possessor is encoded by the third person plural pronoun *en¹*, which preferentially expresses a singular meaning when followed by a kinship term such as *sio³⁻²bə⁵* (see chapter 4 on pronouns). In other words, the possessive structure *en¹ sio³⁻²bə⁵* usually means 'her younger sister', rather than 'their younger sister', though the latter interpretation is also acceptable. A plural demonstrative such as *tsuai²* 'these' and *huai²* 'those' and the genitive marker *e²* 其 are usually inserted between the possessor *en¹* and the possessee *sio³⁻²bə⁵*, when the speaker aims to clearly express 'their younger sister' rather than 'her younger sister', that is, *en¹* **tsuai²/huai²** *e²⁻⁴ sio³⁻²bə⁵* (lit. 3PL **these/those** GEN younger sister). Similarly, the possessive structure *gun³⁻² bã²aº* in (11) usually means 'my mother', rather than 'our mother'. When the speaker's sibling(s) is/are present during such a conversation, *gun³⁻² bã²aº* may mean 'our mother'. In other words, in this case, the plural pronoun *gun³* expresses a plural meaning. It should be mentioned that, unlike Mandarin Chinese, in the Hui'an dialect, no possessive structure can directly express distributive notions such as 'their younger sisters' and 'our mothers', in which more than one family are involved. A comparison between Mandarin Chinese and the Hui'an dialect is given in (12) and (13).

(12) Mandarin Chinese
　　 我們　　 的　　 媽媽們　　 都　　 會　　 來
　　 wǒmen　 *de*　 *māma-men*　 *dōu*　 *huì*　 *lái*
　　 1PL　 GEN　 mother-PL　 all　 will　 come
　　 'Our mothers will all come here.'

(13) The Hui'an dialect
阮　　媽仔　　　　卜　　　來,
$gun^{3\text{-}2}$　$bã^2\text{-}a^0$　　$boʔ^{7\text{-}8}$　lai^2
1PL　mother-NM　want　come
個　媽仔　　　也　　卜　　　來
en^1　$bã^2\text{-}a^0$　a^4　$boʔ^{7\text{-}8}$　lai^2
3PL　mother-NM　also　want　come
'My mother will come here, his mother will also come here.'= 'our mothers will all come here.'

In (12), *men* is a plural suffix attached to the noun *māma* 'mother' to form a plural form expressing 'mothers', and the possessive structure *wǒmende   māmamen* 'our mothers' involves different mothers. In Hui'an, there is no plual suffix like -*men* in Mandarin Chinese. To express 'our mothers', more than one possessive structure has to be used: as in example (13), different possessive structures are adopted to express 'my mother' and 'his mother', which allows the whole sentence to thus express the meaning of 'our mothers'.

In daily conversation for the Hui'an dialect, the inclusive first person plural pronoun lan^3倌 usually does not function as a possessor. The main reason is that the possessor is not required to be overt when the hearer belongs to the same kinship circle. As in (14), the kinship term $a^1kɔŋ^1$ 阿公 'grandfather' is used alone without a possessor.

(14) 阿公　　　　食　　　　了　　　咯
　　 $a^1kɔŋ^1$　$tsiaʔ^{8\text{-}4}$　$liau^3$　$lɔ^0$
　　 grandfather　eat　　　 finish　SFP
　　 'Grandfather has finished his (meal).

In addition, a person's name or nickname, rather than a kinship term, is used when the speaker addresses or refers to someone from the same/younger generation in the same kinship circle. An example is given in (15), where $a^1sã^1$ 阿三 'Ah-San' is the nickname of the speaker's daughter.

(15) 阿三　　　去　　　　學堂
　　 $a^1sã^1$　$khu^{5\text{-}3}$　$oʔ^{8\text{-}4}tŋ^2$
　　 PN　　　go　　　　School
　　 'Ah-San went to school.'

Two examples of *lan³* as a possessor followed by a kinship term are given in (16) and (17).

(16) 伯　　　阿公　　　　　早　　是　　教冊　　　　其
　　 lan³　*a¹kɔŋ¹*　　　*tsa³*　*si⁴*　*ka⁵⁻³tsheʔ⁷*　*e⁰*
　　 1PL　grandfather　before　be　teach　　　　SFP
　　 'Our/your grandfather was a teacher.'

(17) 伯　　　新婦　　　　　合　　　　儕　　無　　　　同
　　 lan³　*siəm¹pu⁴*　　*kaʔ⁷⁻⁸*　*laŋ⁴*　*bo²⁻⁴*　*saŋ²*
　　 1PL　daughter-in-law　COM　　other　not.have　same
　　 'Our/my daughter-in-law is different from other people.'

In daily conversation, the inclusive first person plural pronoun *lan³* may refer to just the hearer, or function like the exclusive first person plural pronoun *gun³* 阮. For example, *lan³ a¹kɔŋ¹* in (16) may refer to the grandfather of both the speaker and the hearer (i.e. meaning 'our grandfather'), or refer to the grandfather of the hearer (i.e. meaning 'your grandfather'). The possessive structure *lan³ siəm¹pu⁴* in (17) may refer to the daughter-in-law of both the speaker and the hearer (i.e. meaning 'our daughter-in-law'), or refer to the daughter-in-law of the speaker (i.e. meaning 'my daughter-in-law'). The different interpretations are associated with the multiple functions of the inclusive pronoun *lan³* (see §4.2.2).

8.2.1.1.2 Possessee=social relations or location

In these two cases, the pronoun functioning as the possessor is also usually a plural one, and usually expresses a singular meaning. Three examples are given in (18) – (20).

(18) 恁　　　老師
　　 len³⁻²　*lau⁴suɪ¹*
　　 2PL　　teacher
　　 'your teacher'

(19) 恁　　學堂
　　 len³　*oʔ⁸⁻⁴tŋ²*
　　 2PL　School
　　 'your school'

(20) 阮　　厝裡
　　 gun³　tshu⁵⁻³-lai⁴
　　 1PL　 house-inside
　　 'my home'

The possessee lau⁴su¹ 'teacher' in (18) is associated with social relations, while the possessee in (19) and (20), i.e. oʔ⁸⁻⁴tŋ² 'school' and tshu⁵⁻³lai⁴ 'home', are examples of location. More specifically, the possessee oʔ⁸⁻⁴tŋ² 'school' in (19) is an example of the collective, unit or organization that someone belongs to. These examples share their special usage of the plural pronoun with examples (10) and (11) above, where the possessee is encoded by a kinship term, which will not be repeated here. Nevertheless, we may distinguish the two following subtypes of the zero-marked possessive construction, based on both the semantic category of the possessee, NP_2, and the tone value of the possessor, NP_1.

Comparatively speaking, the relation between the possessor and the possessee is closer in zero-marked possessive constructions which denote kinship and social relations as opposed to those which denote location, including denoting collectives, units or organizations to which the 'possessor', NP_1, belongs. This is clear when the tones of the pronoun possessor involved are compared. On the one hand, the pronoun possessor in the possessive construction denoting kinship and social relations is typically in its sandhi tone, as in gun³ 阮 in (11) and len³ 恁 in (18) respectively, which both change from third to the second tone. The only exception is the inclusive plural pronoun lan³ 伯, which may be treated as a special case, since, as mentioned above, the usage of lan³ itself is quite complicated. On the other hand, the pronoun possessor in the zero-marked possessive construction denoting a location as the head noun typically does not undergo any tone sandhi, as in len³ 恁 in (19) and gun³ 阮 in (20), which are in their citation tone (i.e. the third tone), rather than in their sandhi tone (i.e. the second tone).

8.2.1.1.3 Possessee=spatial orientation
The personal pronoun can be directly followed by a spatial orientation term, as in (21) and (22).

(21) 汝　　頭前
　　 lu³　 thau²⁻⁴tsuin²
　　 2SG　front
　　 'in front of you'

(22) 阮　　後尾
　　 gun³　au⁴bə³
　　 1PL　back
　　 'behind us'

As with possessive constructions denoting location, the possessor in this subtype of zero-marked possessive construction, such as *lu³* 'you' in (21) and *gun³* 'we' in (22), normally retains its citation tone, rather than undergoing any tone sandhi. However, compared with possessive constructions denoting location, this subtype is uncommon in daily conversation. Furthermore, examples such as (21) and (22) can be interpreted in another way: the personal pronoun and the spatial orientation term function as the subject and the predicate, respectively. More specifically, *lu³ thau²⁻⁴tsuin²* in (21) has a meaning of 'you go first, after you', while *gun³ au⁴bə³* in (22) can express 'we will follow'.

8.2.1.1.4 Possessee=body parts

The personal pronoun as a possessor usually cannot directly precede the possessee encoded by a body part, unless the whole possessive construction is used in a sentence or clause, especially in a postverbal position. Further morphological and semantic constraints are that the possessee, NP₂, is typically encoded by a disyllabic noun, while second and third person plural pronoun possessors usually only expresses a plural meaning. This contrasts distinctly from the case for kinship terms as the possessee, discussed just above. Examples are given in (23) – (25).

(23) 是　　阮　　腹肚，　　唔　　是　　汝　　腹肚
　　 si⁴　gun³　pak⁷⁻⁸tɔ³　m⁵⁻⁴　si⁴　lu³　pak⁷⁻⁸tɔ³
　　 be　1PL　belly　　 not　be　2SG　belly
　　 'It is my belly, not your belly.'

(24) 拍　　　伊　　頭殼
　　 phaʔ⁷⁻⁸　i¹　thau²⁻⁴khak⁷
　　 hit　　 3SG　head
　　 'hit his head'

(25) *唔通　　　 動　　 阮/我　　　手
　　 m⁵⁻⁴-thaŋ¹　taŋ⁴　gun³/gua³　tshiu³
　　 not-can　　touch　1PL/1SG　　hand
　　 'Don't touch my hand.'

In (23), the possesessive construction $gun^3\ pak^{7\text{-}8}tɔ^3$ means 'my belly', in which the exclusive first person plural pronoun gun^3 expresses a singular meaning. However, the second person singular pronoun lu^3, rather than the plural form len^3, is required when expressing 'your belly' in its singular meaning. The two possessive constructions $gun^3\ pak^{7\text{-}8}tɔ^3$ 'my belly' and $lu^3\ pak^{7\text{-}8}tɔ^3$ 'your belly' are both used in a clause and involve contrastive focus. The genitive marker e^2 其 can be added after the possessor (i.e. gun^3 and lu^3) to emphasize the possessor. However, when used alone (rather than in a clause as in (23)), neither $gun^3\ pak^{7\text{-}8}tɔ^3$ 'my belly' nor $lu^3\ pak^{7\text{-}8}tɔ^3$ 'your belly' are acceptable. In this case, the genitive marker e^2 其 is required (rather than being optional) to be inserted between the possessor and the possessee, that is, forming $gun^3\ e^{2\text{-}4}\ pak^{7\text{-}8}tɔ^3$ 'my belly' and $lu^3\ e^{2\text{-}4}\ pak^{7\text{-}8}tɔ^3$ 'your belly', respectively. Example (23) also shows that the possessor in this subtype of zero-marked possessive construction normally does not undergo tone sandhi. In (24), the possessive construction $i^1\ thau^{2\text{-}4}khak^7$ with the third person singular pronoun i^1 as the possessor, functions as an object of the verb $pha\mathrm{?}^7$ 'hit'. The singular meaning of the possessor here cannot be expressed by the plural form en^1 'they'. Note that both $pak^{7\text{-}8}tɔ^3$ 'belly' in (23) and $thau^{2\text{-}4}khak^7$ 'head' in (24) are disyllabic, while $tshiu^3$ 'hand' in (25) is monosyllabic, which is probably the reason why it cannot immediately follow a personal pronoun such as gun^3 'we' in sentences such as (25). It would be more natural if the genitive marker e^2 其 were added, i.e. $gun^3/gua^3\ e^{2\text{-}4}\ tshiu^3$ 'my hand'.

These syntactic and morphological constraints and the absence of tone sandhi may suggest that the relation between the possessor and the possessee in this type of possessive construction is, relatively speaking, not close, compared with that in possessive constructions denoting kinship, social relations, location and spatial orientation mentioned above (especially the former two). It should be mentioned, however, that the 'relation' here typically involves the structural relationship between the possessor and the possessee, rather than their semantic relation. In fact, in some languages, the relationship between human beings and their body parts may be much coded as being closer than that between human beings and the kinship system, social relations, location and spatial orientation with which they are associated. However, the different structural and prosodic characteristics attested in different types of possessive construction may reflect the cognition of the speakers of the Hui'an dialect concerning alienability. In the continuum of inalienability, the speakers of the Hui'an dialect may tend to place the kinship and social relations toward the end where inalienable possession is located, location and spatial orientation in the middle, and body parts at a relative distance from the end for inalienable possession, shown as follows.

Inalienable ←--→ Alienable
kinship/social relations > location > spatial orientation > body parts
Fig.8-1: Inalienability Hierarchy I

This is interesting, since cross-linguistically, body parts tend to be treated as one of the core members of inalienable possession, as mentioned above. This apparently atypical treatment may undoubtedly be associated with the different cultural views reflected in the relevant structures of different languages (see Ameka 1996 on Ewe (Niger-Congo), Haiman 1985 on Menya (Papuan), Chappell and Thompson 1992 on Mandarin Chinese for other cases of alienable treatment of body part terms).

8.2.1.1.5 Possessee=common nouns

The possessive construction denotes ownership when the possessee is encoded by other common nouns such as $bak^{8\text{-}4}kiã^5$ 目鏡 'glasses' in (26) and $tshiu^{3\text{-}2}tho^5$ 手套 'glove' in (27). Similar to the subtype of the zero-marked possessive construction denoting body parts, in the possessive construction denoting ownership, the personal pronoun as a possessor can only sometimes be directly followed by the possessee. This is when the whole possessive construction is used in a clause, as in (26) and (27).

(26) 汝   目鏡   咧
     lu^3 $bak^{8\text{-}4}kiã^5$ $leʔ^0$
     2SG glasses   SFP
     'Where are your glasses?'

(27) 將   我   手套   收   咧   屜咧
     $tsiɔŋ^1$ gua^3 $tshiu^{3\text{-}2}tho^5$ siu^1 $leʔ^{7\text{-}8}$ $thuaʔ^7\text{-}leʔ^0$
     OM   1SG glove   tidy.up at   drawer-LOC
     '(He) put my glove in the drawer.'

In (26) and (27), the possessive constructions lu^3 $bak^{8\text{-}4}kiã^5$ 'your glasses' and gua^3 $tshiu^{3\text{-}2}tho^5$ 'my glove' denote ownership. In (26), the construction lu^3 $bak^{8\text{-}4}kiã^5$ 'your glasses' is followed by the sentence-final particle $leʔ^0$ to form an interrogative, while gua^3 $tshiu^{3\text{-}2}tho^5$ 'my glove' in (27) is placed between the object marker $tsiɔŋ^1$ and the predicate siu^1 $leʔ^{7\text{-}8}$ $thuaʔ^7leʔ^0$ 'put in the drawer'. A linking morpheme such as the genitive marker e^2 is normally required when these two possessive constructions are used alone (rather than in a sentence or clause), as in

lu^3 $e^{2\text{-}4}$ $bak^{8\text{-}4}kia^5$ 'your glasses' and gua^3 $e^{2\text{-}4}$ $tshiu^{3\text{-}2}tho^5$ 'my glove'. A similar phenomenon can also be attested in other Chinese varieties such as Mandarin Chinese (cf. Zhu 1982:142-143).

8.2.1.1.6 Interim summary

In terms of the zero-marked possessive construction, when the possessee NP_2 encodes kinship, social relations and location, the plural form of the personal pronoun is typically used for the possessor NP_1 and can express a singular meaning. The singular forms of the personal pronouns combined with terms of spatial orientation and body parts or common nouns can also function as a possessor and possessee, respectively, in the zero-marked possessive construction, but evince a low frequency in daily conversation. In terms of semantics, the zero-marked possessive construction with a pronoun possessor, that is, [pronoun possessor + possessee], is thus preferentially used to denote kinship, social relations and location with which the possessor pronoun, NP_1, is associated. As we have seen, this type of possessive construction can also denote spatial orientation, body parts and ownership, but is quite limited, and does not constitute one of its main semantic functions. The inalienability hierarchy mentioned above can be further revised as follows.

Inalienable ←--→ Alienable
kinship/social relations > location > spatial orientation > body parts > ownership
Fig.8-2: Inalienability Hierarchy II

In addition, the zero-marked possessive construction normally expresses definite or referential possession, that is, the speaker believes that the hearer is clear about the specific person or object that the speaker refers to. However, note also that in the case of the possessive construction denoting social relations, it may not be used to identify a specific individual, as in example (18) above.

8.2.1.2 Noun possessor + Ø + possessee

The possessor in the zero-marked possessive construction can be, albeit less frequently, encoded by a noun. When the possessor is encoded by a noun denoting a human being, the whole possessive construction is normally acceptable only when used in a clause, as in (28), an example of a possessive construction in which the possessee is expressed by a common noun.

(28) 將   囝仔   衫褲   共   伊   收   (起來)
    tsiɔŋ¹   ken³⁻²a³   sã¹khɔ⁵   ka⁵⁻⁴   i¹   siu¹   khai⁰
    OM   child   clothes   OM   3SG   tidy.up   RVC
    'Gather up the clothes of the children.'

In (28), the object marker *tsiɔŋ¹* is followed by the possessive construction *ken³⁻²a³ sã¹khɔ⁵* 'the clothes of the children', in which the possessor *ken³⁻²a³* is a noun denoting a human being. When used alone (rather than in a sentence or clause), the genitive marker *e²* 其 is normally required to be inserted between the possessor *ken³⁻²a³* and the possesssee *sã¹khɔ⁵*, i.e. *ken³⁻²a³ e²⁻⁴ sã¹khɔ⁵* 'the clothes of the children'. This is also true for possessive constructions in which the possessee is encoded by a body part, as in *tiũ¹biŋ² e²⁻⁴ kha¹* 張明其骹 'Zhang Ming's foot'.

When the possessee is encoded by a noun denoting kinship, social relations or location, the third person plural pronoun *en¹* 'they', rather than the genitive marker *e²* 其, is the preferred form for insertion between the possessor and the possessee to form an independent possessive construction, e.g. *tiũ¹biŋ² en¹ bã²a⁰/piŋ²⁻⁴iu³/oʔ⁸⁻⁴tŋ²* 張明individuals 媽仔 / 朋友 / 學堂 'Zhang Ming's mother/friend/school' (lit. Zhang Ming 3PL mother/friend/school). These examples can also be interpreted as being formed by the possessive construction [personal pronoun + noun] following the noun denoting a human being, e.g. *tiũ¹biŋ²* 張明 + *en¹ bã²a⁰* 個媽仔 > *tiũ¹biŋ² en¹ bã²a⁰* 張明個媽仔. Note that, however, the slot for the personal pronoun here can in fact only be filled by the third person plural pronoun *en¹* 個: Noun_HUMAN + 3PL + Noun_KINSHIP/SOCIAL RELATIONS/LOCATION.

Spatial orientation terms seem to be the only exception in that they can directly follow a person-denoting noun possessor without a linking morpheme, as in *tiũ¹biŋ² au⁴bə³* 張明後尾 'Zhang Ming's back', where *tiũ¹biŋ²* and *au⁴bə³* are the person's name and the spatial orientation term meaning 'back', respectively. However, as with 'pronoun possessor + spatial orientation term', the construction 'person-denoting noun possessor + spatial orientation term' is uncommon in daily conversation, and can be interpreted as a clause in which the person-denoting noun possessor and the spatial orientation term function as the subject and the predicate, respectively. For example, *tiũ¹biŋ² au⁴bə³* 張明後尾 can be used to express 'Zhang Ming will follow'.

Comparatively speaking, the spatial orientation term tends to follow a noun denoting location (or locative word), as in (29), though this is also not common in daily conversation, compared with other subtypes of zero-marked possessive construction, such as those denoting kinship and location.

(29) 電影院　　　邊頭
　　 ten$^{5\text{-}4}$iã$^{3\text{-}2}$in^{5}　*pin^{1}thau^{0}*
　　 cinema　　　side
　　 'the place next to the cinema'

The following are two examples of possessive constructions in which both the possessor and the possessee are encoded by a noun denoting an inanimate object.

(30) 桌骹
　　 toʔ$^{7\text{-}8}$-kha^{1}
　　 table-leg
　　 'the leg of the table'

(31) 桌屜
　　 toʔ$^{7\text{-}8}$-thuaʔ^{7}
　　 table-drawer
　　 'the drawer of the table'

In (30), the possessor and the possessee are encoded by the noun *toʔ^{7}* 'table' and *kha^{1}* 'leg', respectively. In (31), the possessor and the possessee are encoded by the noun *toʔ^{7}* 'table' and *thuaʔ^{7}* 'drawer', respectively. This type of possessive construction denotes a part-whole relationship. In addition, constructions such as (30) and (31) are in fact compound words in which the possessor and the possessee are in a close relationship with each other, and the possessor *toʔ^{7}* undergoes tone sandhi, iconically reflecting their closeness.

8.2.2 The demonstrative possessive construction: possessor + demonstrative (+ numeral + classifier) + possessee

In Hui'an, all nominal demonstratives or demonstrative phrases, except *tsiɔŋ$^{3\text{-}2}$e^{2}/hiɔŋ$^{3\text{-}2}$e^{2}* 'this/that kind of', can be used to link the possessor and the possessee. This type of possessive construction can denote various kinds of possession, including property or association in general, abstract possession, body parts, location, social relations and kinship, in which, property or association in general constitutes one of the main functions. In addition, this type of construction typically denotes definite possession, that is, refers to specific entities.

We may first look at the construction in which the personal pronoun functions as a possessor. As with the zero-marked possessive construction mentioned above, the plural personal pronoun as a possessor in this type of possessive construction often has a singular meaning, which will not be repeated here. The following are two examples of possessive constructions denoting property or association in general.

(32) 汝　　迄兩隻　　　鴨
　　 lu³　 hit⁷⁻⁸-lŋ⁴-tsiaʔ⁷⁻⁸　aʔ⁷
　　 2SG　that-two-CL　　duck
　　 'your two ducks'

(33) 伯　　懷　　桌
　　 lan³　huai²　toʔ⁷
　　 1PL　 those　table
　　 'our tables, those tables of ours'

As mentioned above, the possessee denoting the owned object cannot immediately follow the possessor to form an independent possessive construction. In (32), the demonstrative phrase *hit⁷⁻⁸lŋ⁴tsiaʔ⁷* 'those two' is inserted between the possessor *lu³* 'you' and the possessee *aʔ⁷* 'duck'. In (33), the demonstrative *huai²* 'those' is inserted between the possessor *lan³* 'we' and the possessee *toʔ⁷* 'table'. The demonstrative phrase *hit⁷⁻⁸lŋ⁴tsiaʔ⁷* and the demonstrative *huai²* not only function like a linking marker, but also, and more importantly, denote definiteness and involve the number of the possessee.

Examples of possessive constructions denoting abstract possession and body parts are given in (34) and (35).

(34) 伊　 口　　　　 觀念
　　 i¹　 hə²　　　　kuan¹liəm⁵
　　 3SG　that.kind.of　idea
　　 'his idea, that kind of idea of his'

(35) 汝　　口　　　皮膚　　　合　　 食　 藥　　　　有　　 關係
　　 lu³　 tsat⁸⁻⁴　phə²⁻⁴hu¹　kaʔ⁷⁻⁸　tsiaʔ⁸⁻⁴　ioʔ⁸　u⁴　 kuan¹he⁵
　　 2SG　this　　 skin　　　 COM　　eat　 medicine　have　connection
　　 '(The situation of) your skin has something to do with taking medicine.'

The possessee denoting abstract possession usually cannot be immediately preceded by the possessor to form an independent possessive construction. In (34), the demonstrative *hə²* is inserted between the pronoun possessor *i¹* 'he' and the abstract possessee *kuan¹liəm⁵* 'idea', and the whole construction refers to a specific kind of idea. As mentioned in §8.2.1.1.4 above, the possessee denoting body parts normally does not directly follow a pronoun possessor in preverbal position to form an independent possessive construction. Thus, in (35), the demonstrative *tsat⁸* is inserted between the pronoun possessor *lu³* 'you' and the possessee *phə²⁻⁴hu¹* 'skin' to refer to a specific state of the skin of the hearer during a certain period. The demonstratives *hə²* and *tsat⁸* in these two examples not only denote definiteness, but also function like a linking marker. This syntactic property provides further evidence of their status as being closer to the alienable end of the continuum for possession.

Two examples of demonstrative possessive constructions in which the possessee is encoded by a noun denoting a unit or organization are given in (36) and (37). This subtype is uncommon in daily conversation, since, as mentioned in §8.2.1.1.2 above, the possessee denoting units or organizations normally immediately follows the pronoun possessor.

(36) 佢　　口　　公司
　　 en¹　 *hat⁸⁻⁴*　 *kɔŋ¹si¹*
　　 3PL　 that　 company
　　 'the company he works at'

(37) 佢　　口　　單位
　　 en¹　 *hə²*　 *tuã¹ui⁵*
　　 3PL　 that.kind/of　 unit
　　 'the kind of unit like that he works in'

Similarly, there are also few examples of possessive constructions in which the demonstrative functions as a linker and the possessee is encoded by a noun denoting kinship. Compared to the zero-marked possessive construction, the demonstrative possessive construction denoting kinship is usually followed by a negative evaluation, as in (38).

(38) 佢　　口　　大家　　　　真　　否死
　　 en¹　 *hat⁸⁻⁴*　 *ta¹ke¹*　 *tsen¹*　 *phai³⁻²si³*
　　 3PL　 that　 mother.in.law　 really　 evil
　　 'That mother-in-law of hers is really evil.'

The following is an example of demonstrative possessive constructions denoting social relations. The demonstrative *tsat⁸* 'this' is placed between the pronoun possessor *len³* 恁 'you' and the possessee *taŋ²⁻⁴oʔ⁸* 同學 'classmate' to refer to a specific classmate.

(39) 恁   口   同學
      len³ *tsat⁸⁻⁴* *taŋ²⁻⁴oʔ⁸*
      2PL   this   schoolmate
      'this classmate of yours'

The personal pronoun as a possessor in the examples above can all be replaced by a noun denoting human being such as *tiũ¹biŋ²* 張明 'Zhang Ming' and *ken³⁻²a³* 囝仔 'child'. In addition, the person-denoting noun can be added before the personal pronoun in the examples above to create an even more complex possessive construction. For example, the noun *a¹buin²* 阿梅 'Ah-Mei' can be added before the personal pronoun 佢 'they' in example (38), that is, forming *a¹buin² en¹ hat⁸⁻⁴ ta¹ke¹* 阿梅佢口大家 'that mother-in-law of Ah-Mei's' (lit. Ah-Mei they that mother-in-law).

8.2.3 The classifier possessive construction: possessor + classifier + possessee

It is well known that classifiers in most Chinese varieties such as Mandarin Chinese usually require a preceding demonstrative or numeral in order to form a classifier phrase. In Yue, however, classifiers can be used alone without a demonstrative or numeral in the structure 'classifier + noun' known as 'bare classifiers' (cf. Matthews & Yip 2011; Liu 1997). A similar phenomenon is also attested in Wu, but it does not seem to be reported for Southern Min in earlier studies. In fact, Wang (2015) argues that in general the Min group forms a type on their own with respect to the phenomenon of bare classifiers, since they do not allow this structure even in postverbal position. Nonetheless, we showed in chapter 7 above, that bare classifiers are indeed possible in Hui'an in the postverbal position.

In Hui'an, as in Yue, classifiers have a further function as a linker connecting the possessor and the possessee in the structure 'possessor + classifier + possessee'. In addition, the possessee in this type of possessive construction is typically encoded by a common noun, as in (40) and (41) and has a singular interpretation.

(40) 我　　本　　冊
　　 gua³　pun³⁻²　tsheʔ⁷
　　 1SG　 CL　　book
　　 'my book'

(41) 伊　　條　　　鏈仔
　　 i¹　 tiau²⁻⁴　len⁵⁻⁴-a³
　　 3SG　CL　　chain-NM
　　 'her necklace'

In (40), the possessive construction *gua³ pun³⁻² tsheʔ⁷* refers to a specific book. Similarly, *i¹ tiau²⁻⁴ len⁵⁻⁴a³* in (41) refers to a specific necklace. As shown by these two examples, singular personal pronouns such as *gua³* 'I' in (40) and *i¹* 'she' in (41), rather than their plural counterparts, are used to express the singular meaning.

The possessee in this type of possessive construction can also be encoded by a noun denoting social relations, as in (42).

(42) 恁　　　孤　　老師
　　 len³　 kɔ¹　 lau⁴su¹
　　 2PL　 CL　　teacher
　　 'your teacher'

In (42), the classifier *kɔ¹* usually shows a derogatory sense. The classifier *ui⁵* 位, a polite form for a human being, is usually not used in this type of construction. In addition, the plural personal pronoun *len³* 'you' has a singular interpretation.

8.2.4 The possessive construction with the genitive marker *e²* 其: possessor + *e²* 其 + possessee

8.2.4.1 Personal pronoun + *e²* + noun

As mentioned above, the personal pronoun, especially its plural form, can precede a noun to form a zero-marked possessive construction. However, the genitive marker *e²* 其 tends to be used when the possessee is encoded by a body part or a common noun, while the plural form of the personal pronoun tends to express a plural meaning in this structure. In addition, the singular form, rather than the plural form, of the personal pronoun tends to be used in daily conversation. Two examples are given in (43) and (44).

(43) 伊　其　骹
　　　i¹　e²⁻⁴　kha¹
　　　3SG　GEN　foot
　　　'his foot'

(44) 我　其　車
　　　gua³　e²⁻⁴　tshia¹
　　　1SG　GEN　vehicle
　　　'my car'

In (43), the possessee *kha¹* denotes a body part, and the possessor is encoded by the third person singular pronoun *i¹*. In (44), the possessee *tshia¹* is a common noun, and the possessor is encoded by the first person singular pronoun *gua³*. In these two examples, the possessor and the possessee are linked by the genitive marker *e²* 其.

The possessive construction with the genitive marker *e²* may be used, when the zero-marked possessive construction is ambiguous. An example is given in (45).

(45) 我　其　媽仔
　　　gua³　e²⁻⁴　bã²-aº
　　　1SG　GEN　mother-NM
　　　'my mother'

In Hui'an, 'my mother' is usually expressed by the possessive construction *gun³⁻² bã²aº* 阮媽仔 (lit. our mother-NM), in which the possessor is encoded by the first person plural pronoun *gun³* (see §8.2.1.1.1). However, *gun³⁻² bã²aº* may also mean 'our mother' in some contexts. Thus, example (45) may be used when the speaker aims to avoid misunderstanding, or wishes to emphasize the referent of the possessor. A similar phenomenon is also attested in the possessive construction denoting social relations, location and spatial orientation: the genitive marker *e²* may be employed to disambiguate number of the possessor.

The possessee of this type of possessive construction is typically encoded by a common noun, as in (44). In addition, this type of possessive construction is not limited to definite singular possession, e.g. (44) may refer to a specific car, or may generally refer to the car(s) that belong(s) to me.

8.2.4.2 Noun + e^2 + noun

There are few examples of this type of possessive construction in our recordings of daily conversation. However, in terms of acceptability, all kinds of noun are able to occur in this type of construction which can semantically express various kinds of possession, as shown by examples (46) – (48).

(46) 張明　　其　　車 (ownership)
　　 tiũ¹biŋ²　$e^{2\text{-}4}$　tshia¹
　　 PN　　　GEN　vehicle
　　 'Zhang Ming's car'

(47) 張明　　其　　媽仔 (kinship)
　　 tiũ¹biŋ²　$e^{2\text{-}4}$　bã²-a⁰
　　 PN　　　GEN　mother-NM
　　 'Zhang Ming's mother'

(48) 張明　　其　　態度 (abstract possession)
　　 tiũ¹biŋ　$e^{2\text{-}4}$　thai⁵³tɔ⁵
　　 PN　　　GEN　attitude
　　 'Zhang Ming's attitude'

The genitive marker in Southern Min shares its pronunciation with the general classifier. For example, in Hui'an, they are all pronounced as e^2. Cross-linguistically, this is probably a case of the same morpheme associated with multiple functions. Similar phenomena can be attested in other Chinese varieties such as the Chaozhou variety of Southern Min (cf. Xu & Matthews 2011).

8.3 Predicative possessive constructions

The predicative possessive construction in Hui'an falls into two categories: (a) possessee (+si^4 'be') + possessor + e^2 其; (b) possessor + u^4 'have' + possessee. In type (a), the copula si^4 is usually omitted, and the possessee may be omitted too. The possessor in type (b) may be omitted. The predicative possessive construction, especially type (a), is not common in daily conversation, compared with the attributive possessive construction. This may be one of the reasons why the predicative possessive construction has not yet attracted much attention in Chinese linguistics. In the following, we focus on the semantic functions of the predicative possessive construction, and its differences from the attributive possessive construction in terms of pragmatic usage.

8.3.1 Semantic functions

The type (a) predicative possessive construction typically denotes property in daily conversation, as in (49).

(49) Possessee + possessor + e^2 其
迄領　　　恁　　阿姊　　　其　　呀
$hit^{7\text{-}8}\text{-}liã^3$　$len^{3\text{-}2}$　$a^1\text{-}tsi^3$　e^2　ia^0
that-CL　2PL　PREF-sister　GEN　SFP
'That piece of (clothes) is your sisters.'

The type (b) predicative possessive construction normally denotes property too as in (50), but also often expresses abstract possession, as in (51).

(50) Possessor + u^4 'have' + possessee
我　　有　　目鏡 (property)
gua^3　u^4　$bak^{8\text{-}4}kiã^5$
1SG　have　glasses
'I have glasses.'

(51) Possessor + u^4 'have' + possessee
伊　　有　　壓力 (abstract possession)
i^1　u^4　$ap^{7\text{-}8}liak^8$
3SG　have　pressure
'He feels some pressure.'

8.3.2 Pragmatic differences

The possessor and the possessee in the attributive possessive construction usually function together as background information. Two examples are given in (52) and (53).

(52) 㑩　　翁　　　愛　　啉　　　燒酒
en^1　$aŋ^1$　$ai^{5\text{-}3}$　$liəm^1$　sio^1tsiu^3
3PL　husband　like　drink　alcohol
'Her husband likes drinking alcohol.'

(53) 汝　　其　　　相　　　與　　恁　　　爸仔　　　　看
　　 lu³　 e²⁻⁴　siɔŋ⁵　khɔ⁵⁻⁴　len³⁻²　pa²-a⁰　khuã⁵
　　 2SG　GEN　picture　give　 2PL　 father-NM　look
　　 'Let your father look at your pictures.'

The possessive constructions en¹ aŋ¹ 'her husband' and lu³ e²⁻⁴ siɔŋ⁵ 'your pictures', functioning as a subject and topic in (52) and (53) respectively, provide background information, while the predicates, ai⁵⁻³ liəm¹ sio¹tsiu³ 'like drinking alcohol' and khɔ⁵⁻⁴ len³⁻² pa²a⁰ khuã⁵ 'let your father take a look at (it)', involve new information.

The attributive possessive construction usually involves new information when it functions as (part of) predicate, as in (54) and (55).

(54) 即個　　　　阿三　　其　　　朋友
　　 tsit⁷⁻⁸-e²⁻⁴　a¹sã¹　e²⁻⁴　piŋ²⁻⁴iu³
　　 this-CL　　 PN　　GEN　friend
　　 'This is a friend of Ah-San.'

(55) 恁　　 著　　　　學　　 我　　 其　　　態度
　　 len³　tioʔ⁸⁻⁴　oʔ⁸⁻⁴　gua³　e²⁻⁴　thai⁵⁻³tɔ⁵
　　 2PL　should　learn　1SG　 GEN　attitude
　　 'You should learn my attitude.'

In (54), the possessive construction a¹sã¹ e²⁻⁴ piŋ²⁻⁴iu³ 'Ah-San's friend' functions as a predicate and provides new information. In (55), the possessive construction gua³ e²⁻⁴ thai⁵⁻³tɔ⁵ 'my attitude' functions as an object of the verb oʔ⁸ 'learn', and provides new information too.

In the type (b) predicative possessive construction, the possessee is the background information, while the possessor is the new information, as shown by (56), in which, the possessor gun³ is the background information, while the possessee ui²⁻⁴kən¹ represents new information.

(56) 阮　　 有　　圍巾
　　 gun³　u⁴　 ui²⁻⁴kən¹
　　 1PL　 have　scarf
　　 'I have a scarf.'

In contrast to this, the type (a) predicative possessive construction is sometimes used to emphasize the possessor, as in (57).

(57) 是   我   其，   唔   是   汝   其
     si⁴ gua³ e²   m⁵⁻⁴ si⁴ lu³   e²
     be   1SG   GEN   not   be   2SG   GEN
     '(This) is mine, not yours.'

8.4 Summary

In this chapter, we have examined two types of possessive construction: the attributive possessive construction and the predicative possessive construction.

The attributive possessive construction falls into four categories in terms of whether or not there exists a linking morpheme between the possessor and the possessee, and if yes, the form of the linking morpheme: (a) the zero-marked possessive construction: possessor + possessee; (b) the possessive construction with a demonstrative or demonstrative phrase: possessor + demonstrative (+ numeral + classifier) + possessee; (c) the classifier possessive construction: possessor + classifier + possessee and (d) the possessive construction with the genitive marker e^2 其: possessor + e^2 其 + possessee. These four types of construction differ from each other in terms of their forms and semantic functions. In addition, note that the common shared feature is that the possessor invariably precedes the possessee.

The predicative possessive construction can be divided into two types: (a) possessee (+si^4 'be') + possessor + e^2 其; and (b) possessor + u^4 'have' + possessee, among which, type (a) is commonly used to denote property in colloquial registers of speech such as daily conversation, while type (b) normally denotes property, but also often expresses abstract possession.

Part II: **predicate structure**

This part, Part II, focuses on predicate structure. In the following chapters, we examine reduplication, verb complement constructions, aspect, modality, negation, adpositions and adverbs. Reduplication constitutes an important aspect of verbal morphology, though it is not confined to verbs. For reasons of convenience, reduplication involving other word classes is also mentioned.

9 Reduplication

9.1 Introduction

Reduplication is traditionally regarded as a morphological process (or word formation process) in which a word or part of a word (e.g. the root or stem) is repeated,[1] and can be found in a wide range of language families, e.g. the Austronesian family in South-East Asia and the Salish family in North America (Rubino 2005; Nadarajan 2006; among others). In many languages, reduplication is used to convey grammatical functions (e.g. plurality, diminution and intensity), and to derive word classes or new lexemes (cf. Rubino 2005; Nadarajan 2006).

Reduplication is also widespread and diversified in Chinese. As mentioned in Zhang (1997:38), the range of reduplication types is greater outside of Mandarin Chinese. Unlike Mandarin Chinese, reduplication in Hui'an is neither used to form kinship terms, nor applied to classifiers to express the meaning of 'every'. However, reduplication in Hui'an is often applied more than once to express increased intensity (an increased amount of emphasis), and constitutes an important aspect of verbal morphology, though it is not confined to verbs, as can be seen in the following.[2]

9.2 Form

Two types of reduplication are distinguished based on the size of the reduplicant (the reduplicated element): full vs. partial, both of which types are pervasive in the languages of the world (cf. Rubino 2005, 2007). In Hui'an, however, reduplication typically takes the form of full reduplication, while partial reduplication is rare. This means that base and reduplicant are essentially represented by the same form, although the new reduplicated form is subject to tone sandhi rules, which will not be discussed here (see chapter 2).

The reduplicant involves lexical items with a range of parts of speech, especially verbs, such as the action verb *bua?⁷* 抹 'smear' in (1) and the qualitative adjective *tshiŋ¹tshɔ³* 清楚 'clear' in (2).

(1) *bua?⁷* 抹 'smear' (action verb) -> *bua?⁷⁻⁸~bua?⁷* 抹抹 'smear repeatedly'

---

[1] Note also that reduplication is often treated as a phonological phenomenon in Generative Grammar.
[2] For convenience, reduplication involving non-verbs is also examined here.

(2) *tshiŋ¹tshɔ³* 清楚 'clear' (qualitative adjective) -> *tshiŋ¹~tshiŋ¹tshɔ³⁻²~tshɔ³* 清清楚楚 'a state of clarity' (stative adjective)

In (2), the reduplicant *tshiŋ¹tshɔ³* usually denotes a property, 'clear', whereas the reduplicated form *tshiŋ¹tshiŋ¹tshɔ³⁻²tshɔ³* typically describes a state of clarity.

The reduplicant can be a common noun such as *bu⁵* 霧 'fog' in (3), or an adverb such as *tshɔ¹* 初 'just' in (4).

(3) *bu⁵* 霧 'fog' (noun) -> *bu⁵⁻²~bu⁵* 霧霧 'foggy' (stative adjective)

(4) *tshɔ¹* 初 'just, a short time ago' (adverb) -> *tshɔ¹~tshɔ¹* 初初 'just, a very short time ago'

In (3), the reduplication of the noun *bu⁵* creates a stative adjective *bu⁵⁻²bu⁵* describing the state of being foggy³. In (4), the reduplicated form *tshɔ¹tshɔ¹* emphasizes that an event just happened a very short time ago.

The reduplicant can also be a localizer such as *pin¹* 邊 'side' in (5), a classifier such as *liəp⁸* 粒 in (6), or the complex [numeral + classifier] such as *tsit⁸⁻⁴ e²* 蜀個 'one' in (7).

(5) *pin¹* 邊 'side' (localizer) -> *pin¹⁻²~pin¹* 邊邊 'right on the far side'

(6) *liəp⁸* 粒 (classifier < grain) -> *liəp⁸⁻⁴~liəp⁸* 粒粒 'the state of being granular' (stative adjective)

(7) *tsit⁸⁻⁴ e²* 蜀個 'one' (numeral + classifier) -> *tsit⁸⁻⁴ e²~tsit⁸⁻⁴ e²* 蜀個蜀個 'one by one'

In (6), the reduplicant, i.e. the classifier *liəp⁸*, is typically used for grain-like objects such as rice (see §7.3), while the reduplicated form *liəp⁸⁻⁴liəp⁸* functions as a stative adjective describing the state that the grain is undercooked or something that is not smooth but lumpy.

The following example shows that the reduplicant can also be a syllable without a specific meaning.

---

3 This phenomenon is also found in other Southern Min varieties (e.g. the Quanzhou, Yongchun and Xiamen varieties in Fujian and the Chaoyang and Haifeng varieties in Guangdong), not to mention other Min varieties such as Puxian 莆仙 (Wang and Zhang 1994:90, Zhang 1999:9).

(8) $bɔ̃^1$ 摸 (syllable without a specific meaning) -> $am^{5\text{-}3}\text{-}bɔ̃^1\text{~}bɔ̃^1$ 暗摸摸 'a state of darkness' (stative adjective)

In (8), $bɔ̃^1bɔ̃^1$, a reduplication of the syllable $bɔ̃^1$, is attached to the monosyllabic adjective am^5 'dark' to form a reduplicated form of the adjective, i.e. $am^{5\text{-}3}bɔ̃^1bɔ̃^1$, which describes a state of darkness.

As shown by the examples above, reduplicated forms in Hui'an fall into four types in terms of their formal properties: (a) AA, e.g. $buaʔ^{7\text{-}8}buaʔ^7$ in (1); (b) ABB, e.g. $am^{5\text{-}3}bɔ̃^1bɔ̃^1$ in (8); (c) AABB, e.g. $tshiŋ^1tshiŋ^1tshɔ^{3\text{-}2}tshɔ^3$ in (2); and (d) ABAB, e.g. $tsit^{8\text{-}4}\,e^2\,tsit^{8\text{-}4}\,e^2$ in (7). Types (a) and (b) apply to monosyllabic bases, while types (c) and (d) apply to disyllabic bases.

Cross-linguistically, the reduplicant is most often repeated only once, while in some languages, reduplication can occur more than once, that is, triplication is attested (cf. Nadarajan 2006). In Hui'an, triplication is very common, especially triplication of monosyllabic verbs, as in (9) and (10).

(9) 講講講
$kaŋ^3\text{~}kaŋ^3\text{~}kaŋ^3$
say~say~say
'talk repeatedly'

(10) 紅紅紅
$aŋ^2\text{~}aŋ^{2\text{-}4}\text{~}aŋ^2$
red~red~red
'very red'

Reduplication can even be applied three or four times (or even more than four times) to monosyllabic adjectives, as illustrated by (11) and (12) below.

(11) 紅紅紅紅
$aŋ^2\text{~}aŋ^{2\text{-}4}\text{~}aŋ^{2\text{-}4}\text{~}aŋ^2$
red~red~red~red
'extremely red'

(12) 紅紅紅紅紅
$aŋ^2\text{~}aŋ^{2\text{-}4}\text{~}aŋ^{2\text{-}4}\text{~}aŋ^{2\text{-}4}\text{~}aŋ^2$
red~red~red~red~red
'totally red'

Note that the number of occurrences of the reduplicant iconically expresses differences in degree: the more the occurrences of the reduplicant, the higher the degree of the state it describes, which will be discussed in §9.3.3.

9.3 Functions

The functions of reduplication in Hui'an fall into five categories: (a) derivational in forming a new word; (b) aspectual in expressing a repeated or continued event; (c) augmentative in expressing increased quantity of participants of an event; (d) intensifying in expressing increased intensity; and (e) distributive in expressing the meaning of 'one by one'. In the following, we focus on types (a) - (d). We just reproduce one example here of type (e), example (7) in §9.2, that is, $tsit^{8\text{-}4}\ e^2\text{~}tsit^{8\text{-}4}\ e^2$ 'one by one', which illustrates that the reduplication of the complex [numeral + classifier] has the meaning of 'one by one'.

9.3.1 Word formation through reduplication

Reduplication can be used to form a stative adjective or adverb. Examples (3) and (6) in §9.2 above illustrate that the reduplication of a noun or classifier can create a stative adjective describing a state, e.g. the reduplication of the classifier $liəp^8$ creates a stative adjective to describe the state of the grain being undercooked or something that is not smooth but lumpy. Two more examples of stative adjectives derived through reduplication are given in (13) below.

(13) Stative adjectives derived through reduplication
    a. $khui^1$ 開 'open' (action verb) -> $khui^{1\text{-}2}\text{~}khui^1$ 開開 'in the state of being open'

    b. $aŋ^2$ 紅 'red' (qualitative adjective) -> $aŋ^2\text{~}aŋ^2$ 紅紅 'a state of being red'

Examples in (13) are used to describe a state. In (13a), the monosyllabic action verb $khui^1$ 'open' is reduplicated and the reduplicated form $khui^{1\text{-}2}khui^1$ functions as a stative adjective describing the state of being open. In (13b), the reduplication of the qualitative adjective $aŋ^2$ 'red' creates a stative adjective $aŋ^2aŋ^2$ describing a state of being red and indicating the evaluation of the speaker.[4]

---

[4] Reduplication of a monosyllabic adjective such as $aŋ^2\text{~}aŋ^2$ in (13c) is regarded as expressing 'a little' in Quanzhou (Wang and Zhang 1994:128), or expressing increased or decreased quantity

The following are examples of adverbs derived through reduplication.

(14) Adverbs derived through reduplication
    a. 偷偷   去   看   迄隻   狗
       thau¹~thau¹   *khu⁵⁻³*   *khuã⁵⁻³*   *hit⁷⁻⁸-tsiaʔ⁷⁻⁸*   *kau³*
       steal~steal   Go   look   that-CL   dog
       '(We) went stealthily to see that dog.'

    b. 好好   寫
       ho³⁻²~ho³   *sia³*
       good~good   Write
       'write (it) carefully'

    c. 好好   飛   過
       ho³⁻²~ho³   *pəˡ*   *kə⁰*
       good~good   fly   pass
       'happen to fly over'

In (14a), the monosyllabic action verb *thau¹* 'steal' is reduplicated and the reduplicated form *thau¹thau¹* functions as an adverb meaning 'stealthily'. In both (14b) and (14c), the reduplicant is the monosyllabic adjective *ho³* 'good' and the reduplicated form *ho³⁻²ho³* functions as an adverb, but with different meanings: it means 'carefully' in (14b), but means 'coincidentally 'or 'happen to' in (14c).

9.3.2 Repeated or continued event

In Hui'an, the reduplicated forms of action verbs typically express a repeated event, as shown by (15).

(15) 湯   啉啉
     thŋ¹   *liəm¹~liəm¹*
     soup   drink~drink
     'Have soup (repeatedly).'

---

in Xiamen (Zhou and Ouyang 1998:270), or denoting vivification and some degree of intensification in both Taiwan Southern Min and Mandarin (Cheng 1997d:312).

In (15), the speaker wants the addressee to have more soup, in other words, to carry out the action of having soup again and again. This function can also be regarded as expressing the aspectual meaning of iterativity.

Example (15) above can be regarded as a case of a repeated event with the same participant. Reduplicated forms of action verbs can also express repeated events with different participants. This applies to the agent of an event as well as the patient. Examples are given in (16) and (17), respectively.

(16) 佢　　逐個　　　說說　　　　者
　　 en^1　tak^{8-4}-e^2　$sə\text{ʔ}^{7-8}$~$sə\text{ʔ}^7$　tse^0
　　 3PL　every-CL　say~say　　DELIM
　　 'Everyone of them had a short conversation (with me).'

(17) a. 懷　　窗　　　共　　關關　　　(起來)
　　　 $huai^2$　$thaŋ^1$　ka^{5-1}　$kuin^1$~$kuin^1$　$khai^0$
　　　 those　window　OM　close~close　RVC
　　　 'Close those windows.'

　　 b. □　　窗　　　共　　關　　(起來)
　　　 hat^{8-4}　$thaŋ^1$　ka^{5-1}　$kuin^1$　$khai^0$
　　　 that　window　OM　close　RVC
　　　 'Close the window.'

　　 c. *□　　窗　　　共　　關關　　　(起來)
　　　 *hat^{8-4}　$thaŋ^1$　ka^{5-1}　$kuin^1$~$kuin^1$　$khai^0$
　　　 that　window　OM　close~close　RVC
　　　 'Close the window.'

In (16), the event $sə\text{ʔ}^7$ 'speak' is performed by different people and the agent i.e. en^1 $tak^{8-4}e^2$ 'everyone of them' is plural. The reduplicated form $kuin^1kuin^1$ 'close repeatedly' is normally used together with a plural noun such as $huai^2$ $thaŋ^1$ 'those windows' in (17a). This is more obvious when compared with (17b) and (17c), in which the singular noun hat^{8-4} $thaŋ^1$ 'that window' is compatible with the simple verb $kuin^1$ 'close', but not the reduplicated form $kuin^1kuin^1$ 'close repeatedly'. The plural noun $huai^2$ $thaŋ^1$ 'those windows' here functions syntactically as a topic while it is semantically the patient of the reduplicated form $kuin^1kuin^1$ 'close repeatedly'.

Reduplicated forms of postural verbs typically express a continued event, as in (18).

(18) 食　　飽　　徛徛
    tsiaʔ⁸⁻⁴　paʳ³　khia⁴~khia⁴
    eat　　full　stand~stand
    'Keep standing for a while after having dinner.'

9.3.3 Increased quantity of participants

The following example shows that reduplicated forms of action verbs can also be used to emphasize the amount or the number of participants in an event, without indicating a repeated event.

(19) 走　　來　　厝裡　　　　拖拖　　　遘　蜀　　大　　堆
    tsau³　lai²⁻⁴　tshu⁵⁻³-lai⁴　thua¹~thua¹　a³　tsit⁸⁻⁴　tua⁵⁻⁴　tui¹
    run　come　house-inside　drag~drag　EVC　one　big　MW
    'Come home to buy a lot of (things).'

In (18), the event of *thua¹* 'drag', which means 'buy' in its colloquial use, typically happens only once, while the reduplicated form *thua¹thua¹* is used to emphasize the large quantity of its object, i.e. the things bought.

9.3.4 Increased intensity

Moravcsik (1978:321) points out that 'intensity appears related to quantity in that it involves quantity of energy investment or size of effect. If an action is performed with greater intensity,…what it means is that it is performed more thoroughly and/or with greater than ordinary effect'. This function of reduplication is typically found in the duplicated forms which undergo the process of reduplication more than once as in examples (9) – (12) in §9.2. One more example is given in (20) below.

(20) a. 融融融
    iũ²~iũ²⁻⁴~iũ²
    melt~melt~melt
    'all melted'

b. 融融融融
$i\tilde{u}^2 \sim i\tilde{u}^{2-4} \sim i\tilde{u}^{2-4} \sim i\tilde{u}^2$
melt~melt~melt~melt
'all thoroughly melted' (with increased intensity)

The function of expressing increased intensity can also be found in verb reduplication, adverb reduplication and localizer reduplication in which reduplication only occurs once, as in (21) – (23) below.

(21) 想想
$si\tilde{u}^4 \sim si\tilde{u}^4$
think~think
'think (things) more thoroughly'

(22) 平平
$pin^{2-4} \sim pin^2$
equally~equally
'completely equally'

(23) 中中
$ti\mathrm{ɔ}\eta^{1-2} \sim ti\mathrm{ɔ}\eta^1$
centre~centre
'the very centre'

In (21), the reduplicated form $si\tilde{u}^4si\tilde{u}^4$ means thinking about something more thoroughly. In (22), pin^2 alone also means 'equally', and the reduplicated form $pin^{2-4}pin^2$ intensifies the 'equally' meaning. The reduplicated form $ti\mathrm{ɔ}\eta^{1-2}ti\mathrm{ɔ}\eta^1$ in (23) can be regarded as an intensification of the degree of location.

9.4 Summary

In this chapter, reduplication has been examined in terms of form and function, a summary of which is given in Table 9-1 below. Reduplication typically takes the form of full reduplication. The reduplicant involves lexical items with a range of parts of speech especially verbs, but also some nouns, adverbs, localizers, classifiers, the complex [numeral + classifier] or syllables without a specific meaning. It is common for a reduplication process to be applied twice to the reduplicant in Hui'an, that is, forming a triplicated form, or even three or four times. Reduplication can be used for (a) forming a new word; (b) expressing a repeated or continued event; (c) expressing increased quantity of participants in an event; (d) expressing increased intensity; and (e) expressing the meaning of 'one by one'.

Tab. 9-1: Forms and functions concerning reduplication in the Hui'an dialect

Reduplicant	Reduplicated form		Functions	
	Hui'an	Mandarin Chinese	Hui'an	Mandarin Chinese
Verb	AA AABB ABAB AAA	AA ABAB	forming a new word (stative adjective; adverb); repeated or continued event; increased quantity of participants in an event; increased intensity	signaling the actor's doing something "a little bit", the delimitative aspect
Adjective	AA AABB ABAB AAA AAAA AAAAA ...	AA AABB A 里 AB ABAB	forming a new word (stative adjective; adverb); increased intensity	forming a new word (stative adjective, adverb); increased intensity
Noun	AA	AA	forming a new word (stative adjective)	forming kinship terms and some nouns such as xīngxing 星星 'star'
Adverb	AA	AA	increased intensity	increased intensity
Localizer	AA		increased intensity	
Classifier	AA	AA	forming a new word (stative adjective)	yielding the meaning 'every'
Numeral + classifier	ABAB	ABAB	expressing the meaning of 'one by one'.	expressing the meaning of 'one by one'.
Syllable without a specific meaning	(A)BB	(A)BB	reduplication of the syllable is attached to a monosyllabic adjective to form a stative adjective	reduplication of the syllable is attached to a monosyllabic adjective to form a stative adjective

10 Verb complement constructions

10.1 Introduction

The term 'complement' here is used to refer to modifying elements that are verb phrases (VP), sentences or quantitative expressions occurring after a main verb[1] (cf. Yue 2001:233) and which form part of the given predicate. This should be distinguished from the 'complement' in syntactic theory, which is mainly expressed by a noun phrase acting as an object of the verb or by a subordinate clause acting in the place of the core argument (the subject or the object) of a matrix clause (Dixon & Aikhenvald, 2006).

Verb complements can be classified into seven major types in terms of their semantic functions: directional, resultative, phase, manner, extent, quantitative and potential (e.g. Chao 1968, Zhu 1982, Chen 1992, Zhou and Ouyang 1998, Shi 1996c), as illustrated by the Mandarin examples in (1) below.

(1) Mandarin examples of verb complement construction
    a. directional verb complement construction
        出   來 (V_1-V_{2DIR})
        chū   *lai*
        go.out come
        'come out'

    b. resultative verb complement construction
        說   清楚 (V_1-V_{2RES})
        shuō *qīngchu*
        say   clear
        'make (it) clear'

    c. verb-phrase complement construction
        我   碰   到   一   件   怪事 (V_1-V_{2PHA})
        wǒ *pèng* *dao* *yī* *jiàn* *guài-shì*
        1SG meet PVC one CL odd-thing
        'I met with a strange event.' Chao (1968:447)

---

[1] For convenience of analysis, the term 'verb' here is used as a cover term for verb and adjective.

d. verb-manner complement construction
   跑　得　快 (V-DE-C)
   pǎo　de　kuài
   run　CM　fast
   'run fast'

e. verb-extent complement construction
   冷　死　了 (V-*sǐ*)
   lěng　sǐ　le
   cold　die　PFV
   'It's freezing.'

f. verb-quantitative complement construction
   多　看　幾　遍 (V-Quantitative phrase)
   duō　kàn　jǐ　biàn
   more　look　several　times
   'watch (it) more times'

g. potential verb complement construction
   說　得　清楚 (V-DE-C)
   shuō　de　qīngchu
   say　CM　clear
   'can make (it) clear'

In (1a), *lai* (with neutral tone), originally a verb meaning 'come' (*lái*, full-toned), functions as a directional complement indicating a direction of the action encoded by the verb *chū* 'go out' towards a given deictic reference point, often the speaker. In (1b), the adjective *qīngchu* 'clear' functions as a resultative complement of the verb *shuō* 'speak, talk' indicating the result state of the action. In (1c), *dao* (with neutral tone), originally a verb meaning 'arrive' (*dào*, citation tone), functions as a phase complement expressing a phase of the action, *pèng* 'meet, run into'. Note that phase complements denote a particular stage in the process of an action or event and differ from aspect markers in being less grammaticalized (cf. Chao 1968:446). In (1d), the adjective *kuài* 'fast' functions as a manner complement describing the way in which the action, *pǎo* 'run', is carried out. Unlike the directional, resultative and phase complements, a manner complement such as *kuài* cannot directly follow the verb, but requires the complement marker *de* (with neutral tone), which is originally a verb meaning 'get, obtain' (*dé*, citation tone). In (1e), *sǐ*, originally a verb meaning 'die', functions as an intensifier expressing the extent of the state encoded by the adjective *lěng* 'cold'. This use of *sǐ* is regarded as an extent complement in Chinese linguistics. In (1f), the complement of the verb *kàn* 'look, watch' is encoded by the quantitative phrase *jǐ biàn* 'several times' in which *biàn* is traditionally regarded as a verb classifier. In (g), the infix *de* is inserted between the verb *shuō* 'speak, talk' and the complement *qīngchu* 'clear' to express the possibility of making something clear.

Much attention has been devoted to these verb complement constructions in Chinese from both synchronic and diachronic perspectives, including for Southern Min varieties (e.g. Chao 1968; Zhu 1982; Yang 1991; Chen 1992; Shi 1996c; Wu 1996; Li and Zhang 1997; Tang 1999b; Lien 1992, 2006; Zhou and Ouyang 1998; Lamarre 2001; Shen 2003; Zhang 2003; Li 2007b; Liu Z. 2008). Studies of verb complement constructions are also found in the literature regarding languages of the ethnic minorities in China such as Zhuang, e.g. Wei and Qin (1980) and Zhang et al. (1999).

In the present chapter, we will discuss verb complement constructions in Hui'an in some detail in the order as shown by (1) above in the following sections, §10.2 to §10.8.

10.2 Directional verb complement constructions: V_1-V_{2DIR}

Directional verb complement constructions are formed by an action verb (including the directional verbs[2]) and its directional complement which is encoded by a directional (compound) verb indicating the direction of an action. In other words, this construction takes the form of V_1-V_{2DIR}, as illustrated by (2) below.

(2) a. 送　　來
　　　 saŋ⁵　lai⁰
　　　 send　come
　　　 'send (it) here'

---

2 Note that the term 'the directional verbs' here include *lai²* 來 'come' and *khu⁵* 去 'go', which are regarded as deictic verbs and distinguished from the directional words such as 入 'into' and 起 'up' by Lien (2006b:759). We agree with Lien (2006b) that there exists a difference between these two types. However, we suggest that all these words can be labeled as directional verbs which then fall into two types: deictic and non-deictic.

b. 搬　　出來
   puã¹　tshutᵒlaiᵒ
   move　come.out
   'move (it) out'

In (2a), *laiᵒ* (with neutral tone), originally a directional verb meaning 'come' (*lai²*, full-toned), follows the action verb *saŋ⁵* 'send' functioning as its directional complement indicating the direction of sending something. In (2b), *tshutᵒlaiᵒ* (with neutral tone), originally a directional compound verb meaning 'come out' (*tshut⁷laiᵒ*), follows the action verb *puã¹* 'move' functioning as its directional complement indicating the direction of moving something. Both directional complements involve phonological reduction, i.e. being in a neutral tone.

These two examples also illustrate that directional complements (i.e. V₂DIR in V₁-V₂DIR) fall into two types in terms of their forms: (i) monosyllabic or simple, as in (2a); and (ii) disyllabic or compound, which are formed by the verb meaning 'come' or 'go' preceded by another monosyllabic directional verb, as in (2b). A complete list of these complements is given in the table below:

Tab. 10-1: Directional complements in the Hui'an dialect

Monosyllabic directional complements	Disyllabic directional complements
lai² 來 'come'	
khɯ⁵ 去 'go'	*lai²⁻⁴khɯ⁵* 來去 'go'
khi³ 起 'up'	*khi³laiᵒ* 起來 'come up'/*khi³khɯᵒ* 起去 'go up'
loʔ⁸ 落 'down'	*loʔ⁸laiᵒ* 落來 'come down'/*loʔ⁸khɯᵒ* 落去 'go down'
tshut⁷ 出 'out'	*tshut⁷laiᵒ* 出來 'come out'/*tshut⁷khɯᵒ* 出去 'go out'
liap⁸ 入 'into'	*liap⁸laiᵒ* 入來 'come into' and *liap⁸khɯᵒ* 入去 'go into'
kə⁵ 過 'pass'	*kə⁵laiᵒ* 過來 'come over'/*kə⁵khɯᵒ* 過去 'go over'
	to⁵laiᵒ 倒來 'come back'/*to⁵khɯᵒ* 倒去 'go back'

In the remainder of this section, directional verb complement constructions will be examined in terms of (a) forms and meanings of directional complements; (b) the relative order of the verb, complement and object; (c) negative forms; and (d) other functions of directional complements.

10.2.1 Directional complements

10.2.1.1 Monosyllabic directional complements

Monosyllabic directional complements in Hui'an mainly involve lai^2 來 'come', khu^5 去 'go', khi^3 起 'up', $lo?^8$ 落 'down', $tshut^7$ 出 'out', $liəp^8$ 入 'into' and $kə^5$ 過 'pass', of which lai^2 and khu^5 are widely used, while the others are much less used, which may be due to their different status as suggested by Lien (2006b:759) and outlined in note 5.

Lai^2 來 'come'/khu^5 去 'go' follow the main verb to indicate that a person or thing moves to the place where the speaker is (or some other given reference point), as in (3) and (4), and from the place where the speaker is to somewhere else, as in (5). They have developed into deictic verbs on the basis of their original lexical meaning of motion (see classic studies such as Fillmore 1971).

(3) 走　　來
 $tsau^3$　lai^0
 run　come
 'come here'

(4) 錢　　　　呣免　　　　寄　　來
 $tsin^2$　$m^{5\text{-}4}ben^{3\text{-}2}$　kia^5　lai^0
 money　no.need　mail　come
 'There is no need to send (us) money.'

(5) 單　　捒　　去
 $tuã^1$　$thue?^8$　khu^0
 receipt　take　go
 'Give (you) the receipt to take with (you).'

In (3), $tsau^3$ 'run' is an intransitive verb, thus lai^0 indicates that the agent of the action $tsau^3$ moves to the place where the speaker is. In (4), kia^5 'mail' is a transitive verb and lai^0 means that the patient of the action kia^5 (i.e. $tsin^2$ 'money') ordinarily moves to the place where the speaker is. In (5), $thue?^8$ 'take' is also a transitive verb, while khu^0 expresses that both the agent and patient of the action $thue?^8$ (i.e. the omitted lu^3 'you' and $tuã^1$ 'receipt') move from the place where the speaker is to somewhere else. These illustrate that the direction indicated by directional complements involves the agent or patient of the action encoded by the verb, or both the agent and patient of the action, depending on the syntactic and semantic properties of the verb. These three examples also show that directional complements take on a neutral tone when occurring at the end of the phrase (see §20.3.3 in Chen (2011) for discussion). In addition, the patients in (4) and (5), i.e. *tsin²* and *tuã¹*, are topicalized.

Khi³ 起 'up' is used to indicate that a person or thing moves from a lower place to a higher place, as in (6) where the omitted agent with the patient of *kŋ¹* 扛 'carry' (i.e. *tsuai²* 'these') moves from a lower place to a higher place. *Loʔ⁸* 落 'down' indicates that a person or thing such as the patient of *kɔk⁸* 摑 'throw' (i.e. *tsua³* 紙 'paper') in (7) moves from a higher place to a lower place.

(6) 撮　　著　　扛　　起
　　tsuai²　tioʔ⁸⁻⁴　kŋ¹　khi⁰
　　these　should　carry　up
　　'These should be carried upstairs.'

(7) 紙　　摑　　落
　　tsua³　kɔk⁸　loʔ⁰
　　paper　throw　down
　　'Throw the paper down.'

Liəp⁸ 入 'into' and *tshut⁷* 出 'out' usually mean that a person or thing such as the agent of *kiã²* 行 'walk' in (8) moves from the outside to the inside and from the inside to the outside respectively.

(8) 行　　　出　　　行　　　入
　　kiã²⁻⁴　tshut⁷　kiã²⁻⁴　liəp⁸
　　walk　out　　walk　into
　　'walk in and out'

Note that the order of *kiã²⁻⁴ tshut⁷* and *kiã²⁻⁴ liəp⁸* in (8) is different from its counterparts in Mandarin Chinese and English which use *zǒu jìn zǒu chū* 走進走出 and *walk in and out*, respectively.

Use of *kə⁵* 過 'pass' to indicate a person or thing passing by a place can be exemplified by (9), where the agent of *len³* 輦 'stroll, walk' passes his friend's shop when he walks from one place to another.

(9) 我　　輦　　過
　　gua³　len³　kə⁰
　　1SG　walk　pass
　　'I walked past (his shop).'

10.2.1.2 Disyllabic directional complements

Disyllabic directional complements in Hui'an involve *khi³lai⁰* 起來 'come up'/*khi³khu⁰* 起去 'go up', *loʔ⁸lai⁰* 落來 'come down'/*loʔ⁸khu⁰* 落去 'go down', *liəp⁸lai⁰* 入來 'come into' and *liəp⁸khu⁰* 入去 'go into', *tshut⁷lai⁰* 出來 'come out'/*tshut⁷khu⁰* 出去 'go out', *kə⁵lai⁰* 過來 'come over'/*kə⁵khu⁰* 過去 'go over', *to⁵lai⁰* 倒來 'come back'/*to⁵khu⁰* 倒去 'go back', and *lai²⁻⁴khu⁵* 來去 'go'.³ In each set of these complements, the one with *khu⁰* 'go' is less used than the one with *lai⁰* 'come', since the functions of the disyllabic directional complements with *khu⁰* basically equal their counterparts with monosyllabic directional complements: both mean 'away from the speaker'.

The tendency is for the directional complement use of *khi³khu⁰* 起去 'go up' to be replaced by its monosyllabic counterpart *khi³* 起 'up' (see §10.2.4 for the non-spatial use of *khi³khu⁰*). The use of *khi³lai⁰* 起來 'come up' to indicate a person or thing moving from a lower place to a higher place, where the speaker is, can be exemplified by (10).

(10) 汝   共   我   帶   起來
     luɯ³ *ka⁵⁻⁴* *gua³⁻²* *tua⁵* *khi⁰lai⁰*
     2SG for 1SG bring come.up
     'Bring (it) up for me.'

The complement *khi³lai⁰* has a contracted form *khai*, which is much more used than *khi³lai⁰*, especially for functions other than as a verb or directional complement (see §10.3.1.2, Chen & Wu 2015).

Loʔ⁸lai⁰ 落來 'come down' and *loʔ⁸khu⁰* 落去 'go down' indicate that a person or thing moves toward the speaker or away from the speaker, respectively, as in (11) and (12).

(11) 行   落來
     kiã²   *loʔ⁰lai⁰*
     walk come.down
     'walk down'

---

3 The disyllabic directional complements *to⁵lai⁰* 'come back'/*to⁵khu⁰* 'go back' are not reported in Taiwan, where the monosyllabic *to³* 'back' seems to be used instead (cf. Lien 1992:382). The directional complement *lai²⁻⁴khu⁵* 'go' is also not attested in Taiwan, but can be found in other Southern Min varieties such as Quanzhou (Li 1997:131) and Chaozhou (Lin 1997:10). However, the directional complements *tng lai* 'come back'/*tng khi* 'go back' attested in Taiwan are not found in Hui'an.

(12) 倒　　落去
　　 to⁵　*loʔ⁰khu⁰*
　　 pour　go.down
　　 'pour (it) down'

Examples of *liəp⁸lai⁰* 入來 'come into' and *liəp⁸khu⁰* 入去 'go into' are given in (13) and (14), where *liəp⁰lai⁰* in (13) indicates that the omitted agent of *kiã²* 'walk' moves from the outside to the inside where the speaker is located, and the patient of *that⁷* 踢 'kick', *kiu²* 球 'ball', in (14) moves from the outside where the speaker is to the inside of the hole.

(13) 慢慢　　　　行　　入來
　　 ban⁵⁻²~ban⁵　*kiã²*　*liəp⁰lai⁰*
　　 slow~slow　walk　come.into
　　 'slowly walk in'

(14) 球　　踢　　入去
　　 kiu²　*that⁷*　*liəp⁰khu⁰*
　　 ball　kick　go.into
　　 'kick the ball into (the hole)'

Tshut⁷lai⁰ 出來 'come out' indicates that a person or thing such as *kue¹* 雞 'chicken' (the agent of *tsau³* 走 'run') in (15) moves out of the place where it is originally located to the place where the speaker is. *Tshut⁷khu⁰* 出去 'go out' in (16) indicates that the addressee (the omitted agent in this imperative) with the patient of *puã¹* 搬 'move' (*tsit⁷⁻⁸tə⁵⁻³ toʔ⁷* 即垛桌 'this table') moves out of the place where the speaker is.

(15) 雞　　家　　　走　　出來
　　 kue¹　*kai⁵⁻⁴*　*tsau³*　*tshut⁰lai⁰*
　　 chicken　self　run　come.out
　　 'The chicken ran out by itself.'

(16) 即垛　　　　桌　　搬　　出去
　　 tsit⁷⁻⁸-tə⁵⁻³　*toʔ⁷*　*puã¹*　*tshut⁰khu⁰*
　　 this-CL　table　move　go.out
　　 'Move this table out.'

$Kə^5lai^0$ 過來 'come over' indicates a person or thing such as the agent of $thiau^5$ 跳 'jump' in (17) moving to the place where the speaker is. $Kə^5khu^0$ 過去 'go over' in (18) indicates that both the omitted agent and the patient of $puã^1$ 'move' move from the place where the speaker is to somewhere else.

(17) 跳　　過來
　　 $thiau^5$　$kə^0lai^0$
　　 jump　come.over
　　 'jump over here'

(18) 搬　　過去
　　 $puã^1$　$kə^0khu^0$
　　 move　go.over
　　 'move (it) over there'

To^5lai^0 倒來 'come back' is used to indicate that a person or thing moves to the original/starting place where the speaker is, as in (19) where both the omitted agent and patient of tua^5 帶 'bring' move from somewhere else back home, which is usually regarded as the original starting point and, furthermore, the speaker is understood to be at home at the time of speech, given the context. As illustrated by (20), to^5khu^0 倒去 'go back' indicates that a person or thing moves from the place where the speaker is to the original starting place.

(19) 帶　　倒來
　　 tua^5　to^0lai^0
　　 bring　come.back
　　 'bring (it) back'

(20) 伊　　斡　　倒去　　咯
　　 i^1　uat^7　to^0khu^0　$lɔ^0$
　　 3SG　return　go.back　SFP
　　 'He has gone back.'

$Lai^{2\text{-}4}khu^5$ 來去 'go' presents an unusual case in being formed by the lexemes lai^2 'come' and khu^5 'go', yet it only has the meaning of khu^5, i.e. the meaning of lai^2 is lost. An example is given in (21).

(21) 伉 過 來去
　　 lan³ kə⁵ lai⁰khɯ⁰
　　 1PL pass go
　　 'Let's go over there.'

10.2.2 Relative order of verb, complement and object

In daily conversation, the non-locative object tends to occur before the verb functioning as a topic, as in (4) – (7) above, or be covert, as in (18) and (19). In other words, the whole construction tends to take the form of (O)VC. One more example is given in (22) below, where the patient $toʔ^7$ 桌 'table' can be covert or occur before the verb phrase $koʔ^{7\text{-}8}\ bə^{5\text{-}4}\ saŋ^5\ lai^0$ 佮未送來 'not yet send here'.

(22) (桌) 佮 未 送 來
　　 ($toʔ^7$) $koʔ^{7\text{-}8}$ $bə^{5\text{-}4}$ $saŋ^5$ lai^0
　　 (table) still not.yet send come
　　 '(The table) has not yet arrived.' (lit. '(the table) has not yet been sent here')

When the object of an action is encoded by a quantitative expression and noun, the noun is usually placed before the verb functioning as a topic or omitted, while the quantitative expression occurs between the verb and its directional complement functioning as a quantitative object (i.e. '(O) + V + Quantitative + C'). An example is given in (23).

(23) (湯匙) 攑 (蜀) 叢 來
　　 ($thŋ^1si^2$) kia^2 ($tsit^{8\text{-}4}$) $tsaŋ^{2\text{-}4}$ lai^2
　　 (spoon) take (one) CL come
　　 'give (me) one (spoon)'

In (23), the patient $thŋ^1si^2$ 'spoon' can be omitted, or occur before the verb kia^2 'take' functioning as a topic, whereas the quantitative expression $(tsit^{8\text{-}4})\,tsaŋ^2$ (蜀) 叢 'one CL' is inserted between the verb kia^2 and its directional complement lai^2.

The non-locative object can also be placed between the verb and its directional complement (i.e. VOC), as illustrated by (24) and (25), though this is comparatively less common in daily conversation.

(24) 送　　張　　批　　去
　　 saŋ⁵⁻³ tiũ¹ phue¹ khɯ⁵
　　 send　CL　letter　go
　　 'send over a letter'

(25) 搬　　沙　　入來
　　 puã¹ sua¹ liəp⁸lai⁰
　　 move sand come.into
　　 'move the sand inside here'

The noun phrase *tiũ¹ phue¹* 'a letter' in (24) occurs between the verb *saŋ⁵* 'send' and its directional complement *khɯ⁵*. Similarly, the noun *sua¹* 'sand' in (25) is placed between the verb *puã¹* and its directional complement *liəp⁸lai⁰*.

In Quanzhou, the indefinite non-locative object can be placed after the verb complement construction (i.e. VCO$_{INDEF}$) (Li 1997:132). In Hui'an, however, such an order is typically found via elicitation, as in (26).

(26) 洞咧　　　　串　　　出來　　　　　蜀　　隻　　　虎
　　 tɔŋ⁵-leʔ⁰ tshŋ⁵⁻³ tshut⁷⁻⁸lai²⁻⁴ tsit⁸⁻⁴ tsiaʔ⁷⁻⁸ hɔ³
　　 cave-LOC emerge come.out one CL tiger
　　 'A tiger emerged from the cave.'

In (26), the indefinite object *tsit⁸⁻⁴ tsiaʔ⁷⁻⁸ hɔ³* 'one tiger' is preceded by the directional complement *tshut⁷⁻⁸lai²*. Note that this order is also not reported as possible in Taiwan Southern Min (cf. Lien 1992:388-389).

The locative object in Hui'an can either be placed after the directional complement (VCN$_{LOC}$), as in (27a), or inserted between the verb and its directional complement (VN$_{LOC}$C), as in (27b).

(27) a. 攑　　來　　搭
　　　 kia² lai²⁻⁴ taʔ⁷
　　　 take come here
　　　 'take (it) here'

　　 b. 攑　　搭　　來
　　　 kia² taʔ⁷⁻⁸ lai²
　　　 take here come
　　　 'take (it) here'

The locative word *ta?⁷* 'here' occurs after the complement *lai²* 來 in (27a), while in (27b) it is placed between the verb *kia²* 'take' and its directional complement *lai²*. This is different from both Quanzhou and Taiwan, where the locative object is only placed after the directional verb complement construction (i.e. VCN$_{LOC}$) (Lien 1992:388-389; Li 1997:132-133).

The order of verb, directional complement and object in Hui'an is summarized in Table 10-2.

Tab. 10-2: Order of verb, directional complement and object in the Hui'an dialect

Type of object	Order of verb, directional complement and object
Non-locative object	(O)VC (O=topic)
	(O) + V + Quantitative + C (O=topic)
	V + O + C
	VCO$_{INDEF}$
Locative object	VCN$_{LOC}$
	VN$_{LOC}$C

10.2.3 Negative forms

The directional verb complement construction can be negated by adding a negative adverb such as *bo²* 無 'not have', *m⁵* 唔 'not', *ba⁵* 未 'not yet' and *m⁵⁻⁴ ai⁵* 唔愛 'do not like'. The negative adverbs usually occur before the directional verb complement construction (i.e. NEG V$_1$-V$_{2DIR}$). Take *bo²* 無 and *m⁵* 唔 'not' as examples.

(28) 迄領　　　衫　　無　　　　穿　　倒來
    hit⁷⁻⁸-liã³⁻²　sã¹　bo²⁻⁴　　tshiŋ⁵　to⁰lai⁰
    that-CL　clothes　not.have　wear　come.back
    '(You) didn't come back wearing those clothes.'

(29) 伊　唔　　斡　　倒去
    i¹　m⁵⁻⁴　uat⁷　to⁰khu⁰
    3SG　not　return　go.back
    'He won't go back.' (He is unwilling to return.)

(28) is an example of *bo²* preceding the directional verb complement construction *tshiŋ⁵ to⁰lai⁰* 'come back wearing (that piece of clothes)', while (29) is an example

of m^5 negating the directional verb complement construction $uat^7\ to^0khu^0$ 'go back'.

10.2.4 Other functions

The directional complements may be extended to function as resultative or phase complements (see §10.3 and 10.4). Besides these, the directional complement khi^3khu^0 起去 'go up' can denote a movement from a lower place to a higher place in which the 'place' does not refer to a spatial place, but to an abstract position or rank, as in (30).

(30) 即幾個　　　　升　　起去
　　 $tsit^{7\text{-}8}\text{-}kui^{3\text{-}2}\text{-}e^2$　sin^1　khi^3khu^0
　　 this-several-CL　rise　go.up
　　 'These few (people) got to a higher position (in the company).'

Both $lo?^8lai^0$ 落來 'come down' and $lo?^8khu^0$ 落去 'go down' can be extended to function as temporal words meaning 'in the future' when preceded by the adverb $ko?^7$ 佫 'again', as in (31).

(31) 佫　　　落來/落去　　　　　　工作　　　否　　　（才罪）
　　 $ko?^7$　$lo?^8lai^0/\ lo?^8khu^0$　$kan^1tsɔk^7$　$phai^{3\text{-}2}$　$tshə^5$
　　 again　come.down/go.down　job　　　difficult　look.for
　　 'It will be difficult to find a job in the future.'

10.3 Resultative verb complement constructions: V₁-V₂ᴿᴱˢ

Resultative verb complement constructions refer to the constructions formed by a verb and a resultative complement which indicates a result of the action encoded by the verb, with the structure of 'V₁-V₂ᴿᴱˢ', as exemplified by (32), where the adjective $the?^7$ 㤀 'finished' follows the action verb $tsia?^8$ 食 'eat' to indicate a result of the action of eating.

(32) 食　　　　㤀
　　 $tsia?^{8\text{-}4}$　$the?^7$
　　 eat　　　finished
　　 'eat (it) up'

10.3.1 Resultative complements

As shown by example (32) above, the adjective *the?⁷* 'finished' can follow an action verb functioning as a resultative complement. Other adjectives which can function as a resultative complement include *ho³* 好 'good', *pa³* 飽 'full', *tiau²* 牢 'firm' and *tshiŋ¹tshɔ³* 清楚 'clear' (see §10.3.1.1). Resultative complements can also be encoded by the following three types of words: (a) directional verbs in an extended use, e.g. *lai²* 來 'come', *khu⁵* 去 'go', *khi³lai⁰* 起來 'come up', *kə⁵lai⁰* 過來 'come over' and *lo?⁸lai⁰* 落來 'come down' (§10.3.1.2); (b) the existential verb *u⁴* 有 'have' and its negative form *bo²* 無 'not have' (§10.3.1.3); and (c) other verbs, such as *liau³* 了 'finish' and *sak⁷* 揀 'push' (§10.3.1.4). Note that, when functioning as a resultative complement, directional verbs such as *lai²* no longer have a literal directional meaning, and their resultative meanings may vary with different types of verb they follow (see §10.3.1.2 for more details).

10.3.1.1 Adjectives

Take *ho³* 'good', *pa³* 'full' and *tshiŋ¹tshɔ³* 'clear' as examples. The resultative complement *ho³* can be used to express that something is done well, as in (33), or an action has achieved a result which implies that the action has been finished, as in (34).

(33) 做　　好　　活
　　 tsue⁵⁻³　*ho³⁻²*　*ue⁵*
　　 do　　good　Work
　　 'do a good job'

(34) 阮　　說　　好　　咯
　　 gun³　*sə?⁷⁻⁸*　*ho³*　*lɔ⁰*
　　 1PL　 say　　good　SFP
　　 'We have made a deal.'

In (33), *ho³* means that the work is well done. In (34), *ho³* indicates that the discussion has achieved a result, that is, the people involved in the discussion reach an agreement, which also suggests that the discussion has been finished.

The following is an example of *pa³* 'full' which usually follows the verb *tsia?⁸* 'eat' to indicate the result of the action *tsia?⁸*, i.e. the agent has a full stomach.

(35) 我   食   飽   咯
    gua³ tsiaʔ⁸⁻⁴ pa³   lɔ⁰
    1SG   eat   full SFP
    'I am full.'

Use of *tshiŋ¹tshɔ³* 'clear' as a resultative complement is exemplified by (36), where *tshiŋ¹tshɔ³* means that some matter gets cleared up after the discussion.

(36) 等   佢   說   清楚
    tan³⁻²   en¹ səʔ⁷⁻⁸ tshiŋ¹tshɔ³
    wait   3PL say   clear
    'Wait for them to make (it) clear.'

10.3.1.2 Directional verbs

When functioning as a resultative complement, the directional verb *lai²* 'come' does not keep its literal directional meaning, but means that something is got or obtained, as in (37), where *lai⁰* indicates that something is obtained due to a blood donation.

(37) 口   是   伊   獻血   換   來   其
    tse²   si⁴   i¹   henˢ⁻³-huiʔ⁷ uã⁵   lai⁰ e⁰
    this   be   3SG donate-blood change RVC SFP
    'She got this due to a blood donation.'

In the following exampe, *khu⁵* 去 functions as a resultative complement indicating that something moves away or disappears from its original place, i.e. something is eaten, which is a result of the action *tsiaʔ⁸* 食 'eat'.

(38) 伊   食   去
    i¹   tsiaʔ⁸   khu⁰
    3SG eat   RVC
    'He ate (it).'

Use of *kə⁵lai⁰* 過來 'come over' and *loʔ⁸lai⁰* 落來 'come down' as a resultative complement can be illustrated by (39) and (40), where *kə⁰lai⁰* in (39) indicates the result of *pen⁵* 變 'change', that is, something returns to its original state, and *loʔ⁰lai⁰* in (40) indicates the result of *tshiəm¹* 簽 'sign', i.e. something gets signed.

(39) 變　　過來
　　 pen⁵　　kə⁰lai⁰
　　 change　RVC
　　 'go back to the original state'

(40) 簽　　落來
　　 tshiəm¹　loʔ⁰lai⁰
　　 sign　　RVC
　　 'get the agreement signed'

As a resultative complement, *khai*, i.e. the reduced form of *khi³lai⁰* 起來, can be used in the context of the meanings 'separation, get rid of', as in (41) and (42).

(41) 衫　　褪　　（起來）
　　 sã¹　　thŋ⁵　khai⁰
　　 clothes　take.off　RVC
　　 'Take off that piece of clothing.'

(42) 食　　（起來）
　　 tsiaʔ⁸　khai⁰
　　 eat　　RVC
　　 'eat up'

In (41), a piece of clothing is separated from its original place, i.e. the person who wears it. In (42), the food is separated from its original place, i.e. a dish or bowl.

In example (43) below, the resultative complement *khai* means 'together', i.e. the originally separated parts of a book are brought together by the action *hap⁸* 合 'close'.

(43) 合　　（起來）
　　 hap⁸　khai⁰
　　 close　RVC
　　 'close (the book)'

The resultative complement *khai* can also be used in the context of 'gather up', 'hide' and 'take out', as illustrated by (44) – (46).

(44) 衫褲　　共　　伊　　收　　（起來）
　　 sã¹khɔ⁵　ka⁵⁻⁴　i¹　siu¹　khai⁰
　　 clothes　OM　3SG　tidy.up　RVC
　　 'gather up the clothes'

(45) 崀　　（起來）
　　 bi²⁷　khai⁰
　　 hide　RVC
　　 'go into hiding'

(46) 攑　　口　　（起來）　泡
　　 kia²⁻⁴　hat⁸　khai⁴　phau⁵
　　 take　that　RVC　brew
　　 'take that out to make tea'

In (44), *khai⁰* following the verb *siu¹* 'tidy' indicates that the clothes are gathered up and put into the closet. In (45), *khai⁰* follows the verb *bi²⁷* 'hide' and indicates that someone hides him/herself from other people. In (46), a teapot which is kept in some place and has not been used for a long period is taken out for use again. Note that *khai⁴* in (46) adopts the sandhi tone of its second component, *lai²* 'come', rather than a neutral tone as in (44) and (45), since it is separated from its preceding verb *kia²* 'take' and followed by another verb *phau⁵* 'brew'.

10.3.1.3 *u⁴* 'have' and *bo²* 'not have'

The existential and possessive verb *u⁴* 有 'have' and its negative form *bo²* 無 'not have' can be preceded by an action verb to express that a person or thing is obtained, as in (47), or lost, as in (48).

(47) （扌罪）　　有　　工作
　　 tshə⁵⁻⁴　u⁴　kaŋ¹tsɔk⁷
　　 look.for　have　job
　　 'have found a job'

(48) 喙齒　　　落　　無
　　 tshui⁵⁻³-khi³　lau⁵⁻³　bo²
　　 mouth-tooth　fall　not.have
　　 'The teeth fall out.'

The context for (47) is of someone looking for a job, and the result of his action is that he gets a job. Thus, u^4 indicates that the patient of $tshə^5$ (i.e. $kaŋ^1tsɔk^7$ 'job') is obtained. The patient $kaŋ^1tsɔk^7$ can also be topicalized as in $kaŋ^1tsɔk^7 tshə^{5\text{-}4} u^4$ (see chapter 20 for details of topics). In (48), lau^5 is an intransitive verb, and the resultative complement bo^2 means that the theme, $tshui^{5\text{-}3}khi^3$ 'teeth', falls out.

A noun (phrase) can also follow the resultative complement bo^2, as in (49) and (50).

(49) (揣罪) 無　　頭路
　　 tshə⁵⁻⁴　bo²⁻⁴　thau²⁻⁴lɔ⁵
　　 look.for　not.have　job
　　 'do not find a job'

(50) 讀　　無　　冊
　　 thak⁸⁻⁴　bo²⁻⁴　tshe?⁷
　　 study　not.have　book
　　 'do not study well' (lit. 'read/study not have book')

In (49), $tshə^{5\text{-}4} bo^{2\text{-}4} thau^{2\text{-}4}lɔ^5$ 'do not find a job' denotes the particular result of looking for a job, namely that the goal of looking for a job is not achieved. In (50), $thak^{8\text{-}4} bo^{2\text{-}4} tshe?^7$ 'do not study well' indicates that the goal of studying is not achieved.[4] Example (50) differs from (49) in that $thak^{8\text{-}4} bo^{2\text{-}4} tshe?^7$ is more like an idiom than $tshə^{5\text{-}4} bo^{2\text{-}4} thau^{2\text{-}4}lɔ^5$: $thak^{8\text{-}4} bo^{2\text{-}4} tshe?^7$ literally means 'study not have book', and is based on a separable verb compound, $thak^{8\text{-}4}tshe?^7$ 'to study', but is used to express that someone does not study well. There also exists a related expression to describe someone who does not study well, i.e. $thak^{8\text{-}4} a^{5\text{-}3} bo^{2\text{-}4} tshe?^7 aŋ^1 thak^8$ 讀遘無冊通讀 in which $bo^{2\text{-}4} tshe?^7 aŋ^1 thak^8$ (lit. 'not have book can study') functions as a manner complement of the verb $thak^8$ 'study' (see §10.5 for details of manner complement).

To our knowledge, the verb meaning '(not) have' functioning as a resultative complement is probably a distinctive usage of the Min branch.

---

4 Huang (2007) distinguishes these two uses of bo^2 in (49) and (50) and regards them as a presuppositional negative marker and a non-presuppositional negative marker, respectively. Huang (2007:163) points out that the constructions in which these two kinds of negative markers bo^2 occur have an episode reading and a generic reading, respectively: the episode reading 'expresses the lack of a desired result' and the generic reading 'is taken as an association with a potential property'.

10.3.1.4 *liau³* 'finish' and *sak⁷* 'push'

The resultative complement *liau³* 了, originally a verb meaning 'finish', follows a verb denoting a process to indicate the completion of the process, as in (51a), or the total affectedness of the object in the process, as in (51b) and (52).

(51) 拄拄　　則　　食　　了
  tu³⁻²~tu³　*tsia⁷⁻⁸*　*tsiaʔ⁸⁻⁴*　*liau³*
  just~just　just　eat　finish
  (a) '(We) just finished eating.'
  (b) '(Everything) has just been eaten up.'

(52) 懷　　創　　了　　咯
  huai²　*tshɔŋ⁵⁻³*　*liau³*　*lɔ⁰*
  those　do　finish　SFP
  'Those (rooms) have been decorated.'

In (51), *tsiaʔ⁸* 'eat' is an activity verb denoting a process situation, and *tsiaʔ⁸⁻⁴ liau³* may mean that the process of eating is just finished as shown by the interpretation (a), or that what we were eating has just been eaten up as in (b), depending on the context and the speaker's focus. In other words, the resultative complement *liau³* in (51) indicates the completion of the process itself or the total exhaustion of the object of a process. In (52), the verb *tshɔŋ⁵* 'do' is used to refer to the decoration process; the resultative complement *liau³* not only indicates that the process of decoration is finished, but also indicates that all the rooms have been decorated, that is, the total affectedness of the object of the decoration process. Note that both (51) and (52) can be transformed into a potential verb complement construction V1-E/BUE-V2 (see §10.8 below), which in turn proves that *liau³* here functions as a resultative complement.

  The resultative complement *sak⁷* 揀, originally a verb meaning 'push', usually follows a transitive verb to indicate that the patient of an action is removed or lost, as in (53) and (54).

(53) 即張　　紙　　㧒　　揀
  tsit⁷⁻⁸-tiũ¹　*tsua³*　*kɔk⁸⁻⁴*　*sak⁷*
  this-CL　paper　throw　RVC
  'Throw away this piece of paper.'

(54) 我   關   揀
    gua³   kuin¹   sak⁷
    1SG   close   RVC
    'I turn off (the light).'

In (53), the patient *tsit⁷⁻⁸tiũ¹ tsua³* 'this piece of paper' is thrown away. In (54), the omitted patient *tiŋ¹* 'light' is turned off. The verb *sak⁷* 'push' semantically implies that something is moved and ends up being away from its original place, which enables it to be used after another verb to express that something is removed.

10.3.2 Relative order of verb, complement and object

In daily conversation, the object is usually omitted, or placed before the resultative verb complement construction functioning as a topic (i.e. (O)VC, O=topic). However, patient objects can also follow the [verb + resultative complement] complex when the resultative complement is encoded by *khuɪ⁵* 去 'go', *u⁴* 有 'have', *bo²* 無 'not have' and *ho³* 好 'good' (i.e. VCO). Take *bo²* as an example.

(55) (扌罪)   無   鎖匙
    tshə⁵⁻⁴   bo²⁻⁴   so³⁻²si²
    look.for not.have key
    '(He) cannot find the key.'

In (55), the patient *so³⁻²si²* 'key' is preceded by the resultative verb complement construction *tshə⁵⁻⁴ bo²* which can be translated as 'not found'.

The following example shows that the patient object (*tsiu³* 酒 'alcohol') can be inserted between the verb (*liəm¹* 啉 'drink') and the resultative complement (*tsui⁵* 醉 'drunk') (i.e. VOC), though it acts like a fixed phrase.

(56) 啉   酒   醉
    liəm¹   tsiu³⁻²   tsui⁵
    drink   alcohol   drunk
    'get drunk'

The order of verb, resultative complement and object in Hui'an is summarized in Table 10-3.

Tab. 10-3: Order of verb, resultative complement and object in the Hui'an dialect

(O)VC	O=topic
VCO	C=*khɯ⁵* 'move away, disappear' (lit. 'go'), *u⁴* 'have', *bo²* 'not have', *ho³* 'good' O=patient
VOC	O=patient Fixed phrases

10.3.3 Negative forms

The resultative verb complement constructions can be negated by a negative adverb such as *bo²* 'not have', *bə⁵* 'not yet' and *bue⁴* 'cannot', which can be inserted between the verb and the complement (i.e. V NEG C), as in (57a) and (58a), or before the verb complement construction (i.e. NEG VC), as in (57b) and (58b). An exception is the construction with *u⁴* 'have' as a resultative complement, whose negative form is the construction with *bo²* 'not have' as its counterpart resultative complement (see §10.3.1.3).

(57) a. V NEG C
      食   無   飽
      tsiaʔ⁸⁻⁴ *bo²⁻⁴* *pa³*
      eat   not.have full
      'have not eaten one's fill' (or: have not eaten enough)

   b. NEG VC
      無   食   飽
      bo²⁻⁴ *tsiaʔ⁸⁻⁴* *pa³*
      not.have eat   full
      'have not eaten one's fill' (or: have not eaten enough)

(58) a. V NEG C
      食   未   飽
      tsiaʔ⁸⁻⁴ *bə⁵⁻⁴* *pa³*
      eat   not.yet full
      'have not yet eaten one's fill'

b. NEG VC
未 食 飽
bə⁵⁻⁴ *tsiaʔ⁸⁻⁴* *paʔ³*
not.yet eat full
'have not yet eaten one's fill'

In (57) and (58), the two constructions with the negative adverb in different positions basically mean the same thing, except that the scope of negation is different. For example, in (57), *boʔ²* in *tsiaʔ⁸⁻⁴ boʔ²⁻⁴ paʔ³* negates the complement *paʔ³*, whereas *boʔ²* in *boʔ²⁻⁴ tsiaʔ⁸⁻⁴ paʔ³* negates the whole verb complement construction *tsiaʔ⁸⁻⁴ paʔ³*. However, both *tsiaʔ⁸⁻⁴ boʔ²⁻⁴ paʔ³* and *boʔ²⁻⁴ tsiaʔ⁸⁻⁴ paʔ³* are used to describe someone who has not yet eaten sufficiently/to the full.

The resultative verb complement construction becomes a potential verb complement construction when negated by the negative adverb *bue⁴* 'cannot' (see §10.8).

10.4 Verb-phase complement constructions: V_1-V_{2PHA}

Verb-phase complement constructions are formed by a verb and its phase complement which indicates the achievement of an action or a state, with the structure of 'V_1-V_{2PHA}'. The term 'phase complement' was first introduced by Chao (1968:446) who suggested that 'There are a few complements which express the phase of an action in the first verb rather than some result in the action or goal'. An example of a Mandarin phase complement *dào* 到 < 'arrive at, reach' has been given in (1c) above. The following is an example of Mandarin phase complement *zháo* 著 < 'hit the mark'.

(59) 貓 逮 著 個 耗子
 māo *dǎi* *zháo* *gè* *hào-zi*
 cat catch PVC CL mouse-NM
 'The cat has caught [hold of] a rat.' (Chao 1968:447)

Phase complements in Hui'an mainly involve *tioʔ⁸* 著 'get' and *khu⁵* 去 'go'. An example of *tioʔ⁸* is given in (60), where *tioʔ⁰* indicates that the action of seeing something is achieved.

(60) 阮   無   看   著
    gun³ bo²⁻⁴   khuã⁵ tioʔ⁰
    1PL   not.have look   PVC
    'I didn't see (it).'

Not all verbs or verb phrases can be followed by the phase complement *tioʔ⁸*. Lien (2001:178) points out that, in Taiwan, the phase complement *tioh⁸* 著 still retains a trace of its spatial sense, since the verbs that take *tioh⁸* as their complement must denote contact such as *boe²* 買 'buy' and *liah⁴* 掠 'catch', but not detachment such as *boe⁷* 賣 'sell' and *pang³* 放 'set free', which also applies to *tioʔ⁸* in Hui'an.

Another point to be noted is that in Taiwan, only when the complement *tioh⁸* is immediately preceded by the verb and followed by a pause can it bear an unstressed tone (Lien 2001:180), whereas the phase complement *tioʔ⁸* in Hui'an is subject to a different set of conditions.

First, it is always in a neutral tone when it is immediately preceded by the verb or followed by a sentence-final particle such as *lɔ⁰*, as in (61a), or a quantitative phrase, as in (61b) and (61c).

(61) a. V+ *tioʔ⁰* + SFP
    看   著   咯
    khuã⁵ tioʔ⁰ lɔ⁰
    look   PVC   SFP
    'have seen (it)'

b. V+ *tioʔ⁰* + quantitative phrase
    看   著   蜀   個
    khuã⁵ tioʔ⁰   tsit⁸⁻⁴ e²
    look   PVC   one   CL
    'see one'

c. V+ *tioʔ⁰* + quantitative phrase
    看   著   蜀   擺
    khuã⁵ tioʔ⁰   tsit⁸⁻⁴ pai³
    look   PVC   one   time
    'see (it) once'

Second, the following two examples illustrate that the phase complement *tioʔ⁸* cannot be in a neutral tone when separated from its preceding verb by other elements such as the negation word *bue⁴* 'cannot' as in (62a), or followed by a non-quantitative phrase object such as *tsit*⁸⁻⁴ *e*²⁻⁴ *laŋ*² 'a person' as in (62b), where *tsit*⁸ acts as an indefinite article and not as the numeral 'one'.

(62) a. V + *bue*⁴ 'cannot' + *tioʔ*⁸
 看　　　 繪　　　著
 *khuã*⁵⁻³　*bue*⁴　*tioʔ*⁸
 look　　cannot　PVC
 'cannot see (it)'

 b. V + *tioʔ*⁸ + non-quantitative phrase object
 看　　　著　　　蜀　　個　　儂
 *khuã*⁵⁻³　*tioʔ*⁸⁻⁴　*tsit*⁸⁻⁴　*e*²⁻⁴　*laŋ*²
 look　　PVC　　one　　CL　　person
 'see a person'

The difference in tonal values between Taiwan Southern Min for the phase complement *tioʔ*⁸ as described by Lien (2001) and the Hui'an dialect can be shown as follows.
(i) Taiwan: Verb + *tioh*⁰ + pause
(ii) Hui'an: Verb + *tioʔ*⁰ + pause/SFP/quantitative phrase
　　　　　　Verb + *bue*⁴ + *tioʔ*⁸
　　　　　　Verb + *tioʔ*⁸ + non-quantitative phrase

Another phase complement *khu*⁵ can be illustrated by (63), where *khu*⁰ follows the adjective *kuã*² 寒 'cold' and denotes entering the new state of 'being cold', and (64), where *khu*⁰ follows the resultative verb complement construction *lau*⁵⁻³ *bo*² 落無 'fall out' to indicate entering a new state, i.e. having no teeth.

(63) 會　　寒　　去
　　 *e*⁴　*kuã*²　*khu*⁰
　　 Would　cold　PVC
　　 '(You) would get cold.'

(64) 喙齒　　　　　計　　落　　無　　　　去
　　 *tshui*⁵⁻³-*khi*³　*ke*⁵⁻³　*lau*⁵⁻³　*bo*²　*khu*⁰
　　 mouth-tooth　all　fall　not.have　PVC
　　 'All (his) teeth have fallen out.'

The phase complement *khuɨ⁵* is typically used together with predicates that have a negative meaning or indicate something unexpected, which is determined by the semantic feature of *khuɨ⁵* 'go', indicating that something moves away or disappears. A similar phenomenon can also be found in Quanzhou (Li 1996b:198). In addition, the phase complement *khuɨ⁵* is normally in a neutral tone as in (63) and (64) above.

10.5 Verb-manner complement constructions: V-CM-C

A manner complement describes the manner of the action expressed by the verb (Lamarre 2001:85), but may also describe the state of a property, or the state of the person/thing involved in an action. Unlike directional, resultative and phase complements, manner complements cannot directly follow the verb, but require a complement marker such as *a⁵* 遘 and *le?⁷* 得. In other words, the verb-manner complement construction takes the form of 'V+CM+C', as illustrated by (65) below.

(65) 發　　遘　　　無　　　　閑
　　 huat⁷　*a⁵⁻³*　*bo²⁻⁴*　*uin²*
　　 send　CM　not.have　leisure
　　 'so busy with sending (messages)'

In (65), *bo²⁻⁴ uin²* 'have no time' functions as a manner complement of the action verb *huat⁷* 'send (messages)' describing the state of the action *huat⁷*, and has its complement marker *a⁵* inserted between the verb *huat⁷* and the complement *bo²⁻⁴ uin²*. These are next described in more detail.

10.5.1 With the complement marker *a⁵* 遘

In this type of verb-manner complement construction, the verb can be a dynamic one, as in (65) above, or a stative one, as in (66) below.

(66) 烏　　　遘　　　齪齪
　　 ɔ¹　　*a⁵⁻³*　*tsak⁷⁻⁸~tsak⁷*
　　 black　CM　bored~bored
　　 'rather black'

In (66), the stative adjective *tsak⁷⁻⁸tsak⁷* follows the qualitative adjective *ɔ¹* 'black' functioning as a manner complement to indicate a state of the property *ɔ¹* 'black'.

With the complement marker a^5, a range of manner complements is possible. Besides a stative adjective as in (66) above, the complement can be a verb phrase such as $tshun^4\ hit^{7\text{-}8}tiəm^{3\text{-}2}a^3$ 'remain so few' in (67), or a clause such as $kha^1\ sŋ^1$ 骹酸 '(my) feet are sore' in (68).

(67) 尾頭　　挽　　遘　　口　　迄點仔
　　　$bə^3thau^0$　ban^3　$a^{5\text{-}3}$　$tshun^4$　$hit^{7\text{-}8}\text{-}tiəm^{3\text{-}2}a^3$
　　　back　　pluck　CM　remain　that-few
　　　'(The eyebrows) have been pulled out and only a bit is left at the back.'

(68) 輦　　　遘　　　骹　　酸
　　　len^3　$\underline{a^{5\text{-}3}}$　kha^1　$sŋ^1$
　　　stroll　CM　foot　Sore
　　　'(I) strolled about and (now my) feet are sore.'

The complement marker a^5 is probably derived from the verb kau^5 遘 'arrive' (involving phonological reduction). This complement marker is normally not pronounced as kau^5 (the pronunciation of its use as a verb) in the contemporary Hui'an dialect. However, we find examples in our data where the pronunciation is ka^5 (rather than a^5), which is typically used by the elder generation. A similar phenomenon is noted by Li (2007b:164), who points out that in Southern Min, such as Xiamen, the complement marker derived from the verb kau^{21} 遘 'arrive' is pronounced either in its sandhi tone (i.e. kau^{53}) or as a short tone (i.e. ka^5), and sometimes reduced to a^5. Kau 'arrive' functioning as a complement marker is also found in other Southern Min varieties such as Quanzhou, Zhangping 漳平, Shantou 汕頭 and Tunchang 屯昌 (cf. Chen 1992, Zhang 1992:16, Shi 1996c:158, Qian 2002:148, among others), and also in Eastern Min such as those of Fuzhou and Fuqing (Chen 2001:62, Feng 1993:130). Use of the verb meaning 'arrive' as a complement marker is also common in other branches of Chinese such as Yue, Hakka, Gan and Pinghua (Wu 2001:348). Details of the grammaticalization of the 'arrive' verb as a complement marker can be found in previous works such as Liu (2006).

10.5.2 With the complement marker *leʔ⁷* 得

This type is much less used than that with the complement marker a^5 in the preceding section. When used with $leʔ^7$ 得, the verb is usually an action verb, and the complement is usually a stative adjective phrase formed by a degree adverb and an adjective, such as *ban²⁻⁴ ken³* 蠻緊 'rather fast' in (69), where *ban²⁻⁴ ken³* indicates a state of the action *peʔ⁷* 'climb'.

(69) (足百)　　得　　　蠻　　　緊
　　　peʔ⁷　　*leʔ⁷⁻⁸*　*ban²⁻⁴*　*ken³*
　　　climb　　CM　　rather　fast
　　　'climb so fast'

The complement can also indicate a state of the agent or patient of an action as in (70) and (71), respectively, where *ban²⁻⁴ sen¹khɔ³* 蠻辛苦 in (70) describes a state of the omitted agent (i.e. *iⁱ* 伊 'he') of *kə⁵* 過 'live', and *ban²⁻⁴tsue⁵* 蠻儕 in (71) describes a state of the omitted patient noun (i.e. the dish/food) of *tsiaʔ⁸* 食 'eat'.

(70)　過　　　得　　　蠻　　　辛苦
　　　kə⁵　　*leʔ⁷⁻⁸*　*ban²⁻⁴*　*sen¹khɔ³*
　　　pass　　CM　　rather　hard
　　　'(He) lived a hard life.'

(71)　食　　　得　　　蠻儕
　　　tsiaʔ⁸　*leʔ⁷⁻⁸*　*ban²⁻⁴tsue⁵*
　　　eat　　　CM　　many
　　　'eat a lot'

The manner complement marker *leʔ⁷* 得 here is probably derived from the 'get' verb *tet⁷* 得 (see §10.8 for more details). This usage of *leʔ⁷* is not reported in other related Southern Min varieties such as Quanzhou, Xiamen and Shantou (cf. Li 2007b; Shi 1996c). However, a similar morpheme is found in the Fuzhou and Fuqing varieties of Eastern Min (Chen 2001:63-64, Feng 1993:23): the morpheme *le³¹* in Fuzhou and *le⁰* 唎 in Fuqing can both function as a manner complement marker. In fact, Chen (2001) suggests that the Fuzhou marker, *le³¹*, may be derived from the 'get' verb. The 'get' verb functioning as a manner complement marker is not uncommon in Chinese, e.g. it is widely used in Mandarin Chinese (cf. Zhu 1982, among others).

10.6 Verb-extent complement constructions: V-*a⁵*-C; V-*si³*/*a³*

Strictly speaking, extent can also be regarded as a kind of state, and some verb-manner complement constructions also imply the extent of an action or a state, especially when the manner complement describes an extreme state, as in (72), where *bo?*⁷⁻⁸ *si*³ 卜死 'up to death' can be regarded as a complement describing an extreme state for the extent of the pain.

(72) 痛　　　遘　　卜　　　死
　　 *thiã*⁵　 *a*⁵⁻³　 *bo?*⁷⁻⁸　 *si*³
　　 painful　CM　want　die
　　 '(It is) so painful (I) could die.'

In the following, we would like to focus on verb-extent complement constructions in which the extent complement directly follows a verb (i.e. without a complement marker) and is typically encoded by the verb *si*³ 死 'die' or by *a*³ 遘 (derived from the complement marker *a*⁵), i.e. with a structure of 'V + *si*³/*a*³'.

The extent complement *si*³ usually follows a stative verb such as *kiã*¹ 驚 'be scared' in (73) and *a*¹*tsam*¹ 醃臢 'dirty' in (74).

(73) 驚　　　　死
　　 *kiã*¹　　 *si*³
　　 be.scared　die
　　 'so scared'

(74) 醃臢　　死
　　 *a*¹*tsam*¹　 *si*³
　　 dirty　　 die
　　 'so dirty'

The following example shows that *si*³ can also be preceded by an action verb, but the preference is for it to occur in the [V₁+*si*³+V₁+*bo*²⁻⁴ *biã*⁵] complex, which is widely used to indicate an extent.

(75) 走　　　 死　　走　　　 無　　　　命
　　 *tsau*³⁻²　 *si*³　 *tsau*³⁻²　 *bo*²⁻⁴　 *biã*⁵
　　 run　die　run　not.have　life
　　 'run like mad'

Two examples of the extent complement *a*³ 遘 are given in (76) and (77).

(76) 紅　迲
    aŋ²　a³
    red　EVC
    'very red'

(77) 緊　迲　驚儂　迲
    ken³　a⁵⁻³　kiã¹laŋ²⁻⁴　a³
    fast　CM　frightened　EVC
    'so fast as to make people very scared'

In (76), *a³* (with the sandhi tone of *a⁵*) follows the adjective *aŋ²* 'red' and functions as an extent complement which indicates the extent of being red. In (77), we have an example of an extent complement embedded under a manner complement: *a³* (the second 迲) forms a verb-extent complement construction *kiã¹laŋ²⁻⁴ a³* 'very scared', denoting the extent to which one can be scared. This extent complement phrase then forms a larger manner complement with the adjective *ken³* 'fast', being joined to it by *a⁵* (the first 迲).

The use of *a³* here can be regarded as being derived from the complement marker *a⁵* as in (72) above, when the complement such as *boʔ⁷⁻⁸ si³* 'up to death' in (72) has been deleted. In other words, the extent complement *a³* can be regarded as a substitute of an originally longer and complete form [complement marker *a⁵* + manner complement]. Thus, the extent complement *a³* in Hui'an is usually pronounced with stress and longer duration. The 'arrive' verb used as a bare extent complement, that is, without the following intensifier phrase, is also attested in some other Southern Min varieties such as Xiamen, Quanzhou, Yongchun and Taiwan (Zhou and Ouyang 1998:393, Chen 1992:182, Lin 1995:458, Lu 2003:90). A similar phenomenon is also found in Mandarin Chinese where the complement marker *de* 得 can be used alone as in *bǎ wǒ lèi de* 把我累得 '(it) makes me so tired' in which the original complement marker *de* 得 is preceded by the verb *lèi* 'tired' but not followed by any other elements. Lü (1999:164) also mentions this use of *de* 得 where he points out that *de* is preceded by a verb or an adjective with an omission of what follows *de*, indicating a state of affairs that one cannot describe.

10.7 Verb-quantitative complement constructions: V-Quantitative expression

Verb-quantitative complement constructions are formed by a verb and a following quantitative complement which is encoded by a quantitative expression indicating the frequency or duration of an action, as in (78) and (79) respectively, or indicating the quantity of the patient of an action, as in (80). As illustrated by these examples, the whole construction takes the form of 'V + Quantitative expression'.

(78) 說　　蜀　　擺
    sɔʔ⁷　tsit⁸⁻⁴　pai³
    say　one　time
    'say once'

(79) 行　　蜀　　點鐘
    kiã²　tsit⁸⁻⁴　tiəm³⁻²tsiŋ¹
    walk　one　hour
    'walk for one hour'

(80) 搬　　遘　　蠻儕
    puã¹　a⁵⁻³　ban²⁻⁴tsue⁵
    move　CM　many
    'move a lot of (things)'

The complement *tsit⁸⁻⁴ pai³* 'once' in (78), consisting of the numeral *tsit⁸* 'one' and the verbal classifier *pai³* 'time', indicates the frequency of the action *sɔʔ⁷* 'say', while the complement *tsit⁸⁻⁴ tiəm³⁻²tsiŋ¹* 'one hour' in (79) indicates the duration of the action *kiã²* 'walk'. In (80), the complement *ban²⁻⁴tsue⁵* 'many, a lot of' denotes the quantity of the patient of the action *puã¹* 'move'. This example also shows that the complement marker *a⁵* 遘 as mentioned in §10.5.1 may be inserted between the verb (e.g. *puã¹* 'move') and its quantitative complement (e.g. *ban²⁻⁴tsue⁵* 'many, a lot of').

In the following example, *a⁵* 遘 is placed between the verb *kiã²* 行 'walk' and its quantitative complement *sã¹ tiəm³⁻²tsiŋ¹* 三點鐘 'three hours' indicating the duration of walking.

(81) 行　　遘　　三　　點鐘
    kiã²　a⁵⁻³　sã¹　tiəm³⁻²tsiŋ¹
    walk　CM　three　hour
    'walk for three hours'

10.8 Potential verb complement constructions: V-e^4/bue^4-C; V-$le\textit{?}^7$-C; e^4/bue^4 -V- $le\textit{?}^7$- C

Potential verb complement constructions refer to constructions formed by a verb and its potential complement indicating the possibility of an event. The potential verb complement constructions in Mandarin Chinese use the complement marker *de* 得 < 'get; able' to connect the verb and the complement, as in (82), where *de* is inserted between the verb *xiě* 寫 'write' and its complement *wán* 完 'finished' to express the possibility of finishing writing something.

(82) Potential verb complement construction in Mandarin Chinese
 寫　　得　　完
 xiě　 de　 wán
 write　CM　finish
 'can finish writing (it)'

In Hui'an, however, potential verb complement constructions typically use the auxiliary verb e^4 會 'can' and its negative form bue^4 獪 'cannot', which are inserted between the verb and its directional/resultative complement to change directional/resultative verb complement constructions into potential verb complement constructions (i.e. V + e^4/bue^4+ C), as illustrated by (83) and (84).

(83) 講　　　會　　清楚
 $kaŋ^{3\text{-}2}$　e^4　 $tshiŋ^1tshɔ^3$
 say　　can　clear
 'can make (it) clear'

(84) 捸　　　獪　　　出來
 $thue\textit{?}^{8\text{-}4}$　bue^4　 $tshut^7lai^0$
 take　　cannot　come.out
 'cannot get (it) out'

In (83), e^4 is placed between the action verb $kaŋ^3$ 'speak' and its resultative complement $tshiŋ^1tshɔ^3$ 'clear' to mean that something can be made clear. In (84), bue^4 is inserted between the action verb $thue\textit{?}^8$ 'take' and its directional complement $tshut^7lai^0$ 'come out' to indicate that the action of 'getting something out' cannot be achieved. Note that the negative bue^4 is more widely used than the positive e^4.

Verb-quantitative complement constructions can be changed into potential verb complement constructions by inserting the complement marker $le\textit{?}^7$ 得 (i.e.

V + *leʔ⁷* 得 + quantitative expression), as illustrated by (85). Note, however, that this usage is not very common in daily conversation.

(85) 囥　　　得　　　三　　四　　十　　日
　　　khŋ⁵　*leʔ⁷⁻⁸*　sã¹　si⁵³　tsap⁸⁻⁴　let⁸
　　　store　CM　three　four　ten　day
　　　'(It) can be stored for thirty or forty days.'

The auxiliary verbs *e⁴* and *bue⁴* can be further added before the verb *khŋ⁵* 'store' in (85), i.e. forming '*e⁴* 會/*bue⁴* 嬒 + V + *leʔ⁷* 得 + quantitative expression', as shown by (86). However, this usage is also uncommon.

(86) 會/嬒　　　　囥　　　得　　　三　　四　　十　　日
　　　e⁴/*bue⁴*　khŋ⁵　*leʔ⁷⁻⁸*　sã¹　si⁵³　tsap⁸⁻⁴　let⁸
　　　can/cannot　store　CM　three　four　ten　day
　　　'(It) can/cannot be stored for thirty or forty days.'

As shown by (87) below, *e⁴*/*bue⁴ khŋ⁵ leʔ⁰* 會/嬒囥得 can be used alone without a quantitative expression. A similar example (i.e. with the structure of *e⁴* 會/*bue⁴* 嬒 + V + *leʔ⁰* 得) is given in (88).

(87) 會/嬒　　　　囥　　　得
　　　e⁴/*bue⁴*　khŋ⁵　*leʔ⁰*
　　　can/cannot　store　get
　　　'can/cannot be stored'

(88) 會/嬒　　　　記　　　得
　　　e⁴/*bue⁴*　ki⁵　*leʔ⁰*
　　　can/cannot　remember　get
　　　'can/cannot remember (it)'

Unlike *leʔ⁷* 得 in (85) and (86) where *leʔ⁷* can be regarded as a complement marker linking the verb and its quantitative complement, *leʔ⁰* in (87) and (88) functions as a potential complement of the verbs *khŋ⁵* 'store' and *ki⁵* 'remember', respectively. Note that, in these two examples, the potential complement *leʔ⁰* is in a neutral tone.

In some other Southern Min varieties such as Quanzhou and Xiamen, the complement marker 得 can also occur in the following two potential verb complement constructions: (a) V + 會/嬒 + 得 + C, as in (89); and (b) 會/嬒 + V + 得 +

C, as in (90), where C is by contrast not confined to quantitative expressions (Li 2007b:166-167).

(89) 'V + 會 + 得 + C' in Xiamen
食　　會　　得　　落[5]
tsia$\mathrm{\Omega}^{8\text{-}5}$　e$^{6\text{-}5}$　lit$^{7\text{-}8}$　lo$\mathrm{\Omega}^8$
eat　can　CM　down
'be able to eat/be able to get an appetite'

(90) '會 + V + 得 + C' in Xiamen
會　　食　　得　　落
e$^{6\text{-}5}$　tsia$\mathrm{\Omega}^{8\text{-}5}$　lit$^{7\text{-}8}$　lo$\mathrm{\Omega}^8$
can　eat　CM　down
'be able to eat/be able to get an appetite'

When occurring in these two constructions as illustrated by (89) and (90), 得 in Xiamen can be pronounced as *lit*^{7} or *tit*^{7}, whereas when it is followed by a quantitative expression, 得 in Xiamen can be pronounced as *le*$\mathrm{\Omega}^7$, like *le*$\mathrm{\Omega}^7$ 得 in Hui'an as shown by (85) above. According to Li (2007b:167), these two constructions are formed, based on the construction 'V + 會/獪 + C' as in (83) and (84) above: V + 會/獪 + C -> V + 會/獪 + 得 + C -> 會/獪 + V + 得 + C. Li (2007b:166) also suggests that the function word 得 as illustrated by (89) and (90) is derived from the 'get' verb *tit*^{32} 得, which undergoes phonological reduction during grammaticalization as in *tit->lit->le?->le*.

The potential verb complement construction 'V + 會 + 得 + C' is also attested in Shantou, where 得 is pronounced as *tik* (see Shi 1996c: 161 for more details). However, neither 'V + 會/獪 + 得 + C' such as (89) nor '會/獪 + V + 得 + C' such as (90) is attested in common usage in Hui'an.

The 'get' verb functioning as a complement marker and potential complement is found in Mandarin Chinese as well. However, when functioning as a potential complement marker, Mandarin *de* 得 is normally inserted between a verb and its resultative or directional complement (rather than its quantitative complement) to change a resultative or directional verb complement construction into a potential verb complement construction, as in (82) above, which is reproduced in (91) below, where the complement marker *de* is inserted between the verb *xiě* 'write' and its resultative complement *wán* 'finished'.

---

5 The romanization given here is based on Zhou (2006).

(91) The potential complement marker *de* 得 in Mandarin Chinese
　　寫　　得　　完
　　xiě　*de*　*wán*
　　write　CM　finish
　　'can finish writing (it)'

Unlike *le?⁰* in Hui'an, the potential complement *de* in Mandarin Chinese does not co-occur with an auxiliary verb such as *huì* 會 'can' in the structure *e⁴* 會/*bue⁴* 燴 + V + *le?⁰* 得, i.e. it is used alone with a verb such as *chī* 吃 'eat' in (92). The negative form uses the negator *bù* 不 'not', which is inserted between the verb *chī* and its potential complement *de*, as in (93).

(92)　吃　　得
　　　chī　*de*
　　　eat　get
　　　'can be eaten'

(93)　吃　　不　　得
　　　chī　*bu*　*de*
　　　eat　not　get
　　　'cannot be eaten'

In her typological study on verb complement constructions in Chinese, Lamarre (2001) identifies four main patterns in the use of markers in potential, manner and extent complements: (a) there is no formal distinction in complement marking, e.g. the complement marker *de* 得 in Mandarin Chinese is used in all three kinds of complement; (b) potential complements versus manner and extent complements, e.g. the marker *ti⁰* 得 in Changli 昌黎 is used for manner and extent complements, while the potential complement is formed by V-C-l(i)ou; (c) extent complements versus manner and potential complements, e.g. Cantonese uses *do³* 到 as an extent complement marker and *dak¹* 得 as a manner and potential complement marker; and (d) a three-way distinction in some Min varieties, e.g. the Zhangping 漳平 variety of Southern Min uses *kau²¹* for extent, *kai¹¹* for manner, and *ei⁵³⁻²¹ tit⁵⁵* for potential. The Hui'an dialect, as shown by preceding sections, uses *a⁵* 遘 and *le?⁷* 得 for manner complements, *a⁵* 遘 for extent complements, and *e⁴* 會/*bue⁴* 燴 and *le?⁷* 得 for potential complements.

10.9 Summary

In previous sections, we have examined seven types of verb complement constructions. In this section, we focus on pointing out some important features of verb complement constructions.
(a) As with other Southern Min varieties such as the Taiwan variety, monosyllabic directional complements are much more widely used than the disyllabic directional complements, especially compared with Mandarin Chinese. Semantic functions of some disyllabic directional complements are similar to those in Mandarin Chinese;
(b) As for the relative order of verb, complement and object:
The object of a verb complement construction is usually placed before the verb as a topic (i.e. OVC). Besides this possibility, the object can be inserted between the verb and its directional complement (i.e. VOC) except for locative objects, which can not only be inserted between the verb and its complement but can also be preceded by the verb complement construction (i.e. VO-$_{LOC}$C or VCO$_{LOC}$). As for the resultative verb complement constructions, the object preferentially occurs following the verb-complement construction (i.e. VCO), but can also be inserted between the verb and its resultative complement in some fixed phrases (i.e. VOC), which suggests that VOC reflects the relative order of verb, complement and object in an earlier stage in the development of the Hui'an dialect, compared to VCO;
(c) The complement markers a^5 and le^{7} are probably derived from the verb kau^5 遘 'arrive' and the verb tet^7 得 'get', respectively.
(d) Compared with Mandarin Chinese, the most important feature of verb complement constructions in Hui'an (as also in other Southern Min varieties) is the use of the auxiliary verb e^4 'can' and its negative form bue^4 'cannot' for potential verb complement constructions, rather than the complement marker a^5 as used in verb-manner complement constructions.

The structures for verb complement constructions in Hui'an are summarized in Table 10-4.

Tab. 10-4: Structures of verb complement constructions in the Hui'an dialect

Directional verb complement constructions	V_1-V_{2DIR}	(O-)V_1-V_{2DIR}; (O-)V_1-Quantitative-V_{2DIR}; V_1-O-V_{2DIR};	VCO$_{LOC}$ VO$_{LOC}$C

		V_1-V_{2DIR}-O_{INDEF}
Resultative verb complement constructions	V_1-V_{2RES}	(O-)V_1-V_{2RES}; V_1-V_{2RES}-O V_1-O-V_{2RES} (fixed phrases)
Verb-phase complement constructions	V_1-V_{2PHA}	(O-)V_1-V_{2PHA} V_1-V_{2PHA}-O
Verb-manner complement constructions	V-a^5/$le?^7$-C	(O-)V-a^5/$le?^7$-C
Verb-extent complement constructions	V-a^5-C; V-si^3/a^3	(O-)V-a^5-C
Verb-quantitative complement constructions	V-Quantitative expression	(O-)V-Quantitative expression
Potential verb complement constructions	V-e^4/bue^4-C; V-$le?^7$-C; e^4/bue^4–V-$le?^7$-C	(O-)V-e^4/bue^4-C; (O-)V-$le?^7$-C; (O-)e^4/bue^4-V-$le?^7$-C

11 Aspect

11.1 Introduction

The term 'aspect' traditionally refers to grammaticalized viewpoints, i.e. different grammaticized ways of viewing the internal temporal constituency of a situation (Comrie 1976:3, 7; Smith 1997:1).[1] A basic aspectual distinction is that between perfective and imperfective: perfective presents a situation as a whole, without necessarily distinguishing any of its internal structure; whereas imperfective pays close attention to the internal make-up (Comrie 1976:16; Smith 1997:66, 73, among others). In some languages, imperfective may involve distinct subcategories such as habitual, progressive and continuous (or durative). In Chinese (including the Hui'an dialect), in addition to these, there exists a perfective aspect category as well as a morpheme which is used to express experiential meaning, that is, indicating that a given situation has held at least once prior to the moment of utterance (cf. Zhang 1996a). This is termed 'experiential perfect aspect' in Comrie (1976) and is traditionally regarded as a separate aspect in the literature on Chinese linguistics, i.e. *jīngyàn tǐ* 經驗體 'experiential aspect'.

The typical aspect markers attested in Hui'an are summarized in the following table (see §11.3 and 11.4 for details).

---

1 In Smith (1997), the term 'aspect' includes situation types, which constitutes one of the two independent aspectual components (the other one is viewpoint).

https://doi.org/10.1515/9781501511868-011

Tab. 11-1: Typical aspect markers in the Hui'an dialect

Progressive	le?⁷ 咧/tuɯ⁴le?⁷ 伫咧-VERB
Durative	VERB-le?⁷ 咧/tuɯ⁴le?⁷ 伫咧
Habitual	le?⁷ 咧/tuɯ⁴le?⁷ 伫咧-VERB
Experiential	pat⁷ 八-VERB-tio?⁸ 著
	pat⁷ 八-VERB
	VERB-tio?⁸ 著

In the following section, we will argue that typical perfective aspect markers do not exist in Hui'an, unlike Mandarin Chinese and other Chinese dialects, such as the Yue branch.

11.2 Perfective aspect

In Hui'an, the verbs $liau^3$ 了 'finish', khu^5 去 'go' and u^4 有 'have' may indicate the achievement of an event or a state, or that an event happened, when preceded by or followed by another verb. However, none of them has developed into a typical, conventionalized perfective aspect marker, as foreshadowed in §10.3 above on resultative verb complement constructions. Note that khu^5 去 'go' can function not only as a resultative complement, but also as a directional and phase complement. The use of u^4 有 'have' preceding a verb (u^4 + verb), rather than its use as a resultative complement, is the focus of this section.

11.2.1 $liau^3$ 'finish'

In Hui'an, $liau^3$ is originally an intransitive verb meaning 'finish', as in (1), where $liau^3$ indicates that an event is finished.

(1) 今日   則   了
    $kiã^1 let^8$ $tsia?^{7\text{-}8}$ $liau^3$
    today   just   finish
    '(It) is not finished until today.'

When followed by a noun (phrase), $liau^3$ functions as a transitive verb meaning 'cost, lose', as in (2).

(2) 了　蠻儕　　錢
    liau³　ban²⁻⁴tsue⁵⁻⁴　tsin²
    lose　much　　　money
    'lose much money'

In (2), the verb *liau³* is followed by the noun phrase *ban²⁻⁴tsue⁵⁻⁴ tsin²* 'much money'. In this syntactic context, *liau³* functions as a transitive verb meaning 'cost, lose'.

In Hui'an, *liau³* often occurs after a verb functioning as a resultative complement to indicate the completion of a process or the total affectedness of the object of a process, as illustrated by (3).

(3) 拄拄　　則　　食　　了
    tu³⁻²~tu³　tsiaʔ⁷⁻⁸　tsiaʔ⁸⁻⁴　liau³
    just~just　just　　eat　　finish
    (a) '(We) just finished eating.'
    (b) '(Everything) has just been eaten up.'

In (3), *tsiaʔ⁸* 'eat' is an activity verb denoting a process, and *tsiaʔ⁸⁻⁴ liau³* may mean that the process of eating is just finished as shown by the interpretation (a), or that what we were eating has just been eaten up as in (b), depending on the context and the speaker's focus. In other words, the resultative complement *liau³* in (3) indicates the completion of the process itself or the total exhaustion of the object of a process.

When preceded by the verb *tsiaʔ⁸* 'eat', *liau³* can also be used to indicate that an event has been achieved, when in a subordinate clause, similar to a temporal adverbial clause in English.

(4) 藥　　　食　　　了　　無　　　效果
    ioʔ⁸　　tsiaʔ⁸⁻⁴　liau³　boʔ²⁻⁴　hau⁵⁻⁴kɔ³
    medicine　eat　　finish　not.have　effect
    'There is no effect after taking this medicine.'

Unlike the resultative complement *liau³* in (3), *liau³* in (4) neither emphasizes the completion of a process, nor indicates that all the medicine has been finished. In this case, *liau³* indicates that the event encoded by the verb *tsiaʔ⁸* 'eat' is regarded as a whole without reference to its internal temporal structure, and that the action of taking the medicine has been done.

This use of *liau³* can co-occur with an instantaneous verb such as *tshio⁵* 笑 'laugh' in (5), or a stative verb such as *kiã¹* 驚 'be scared' in (6), to indicate their anticipated achievement.

(5) 笑 了 等 會 儈 堪
    tshio⁵⁻³ *liau³* *tan³* *e⁴* *bue⁴* *kham¹*
    laugh finish wait would cannot bear
    '(You) will feel uncomfortable later after (you) laugh.'

(6) 驚 了 會 死
    kiã¹ *liau³* *e⁴* *si³*
    be.scared finish would die
    '(People) may die after getting scared.'

Note that this use of *liau³* directly follows a verb, and is followed by another clause, as shown by examples (4) – (6), to background one event as taking place before the event in the main clause takes place. This appears to be an important stage in the development of gramamticalized perfectives (see Li, Thompson and Thompson 1982; Bybee et al. 1994).

In Mandarin Chinese, when the verb is followed by an object or a [numeral + classifier] complex, the perfective aspect marker *le* 了 can occur after the verb to express perfective aspectual meaning, as illustrated by (7). In Hui'an, however, the verb is used alone without *liau³* 了, as exemplified by (8).

(7) a. V + *le* 了 + O (Mandarin Chinese)
       我 買 了 張 床
       wǒ *mǎi* *le* *zhāng* *chuáng*
       1SG buy PFV CL bed
       'I bought a bed.'

    b. V + *le* 了 + NUM + CL (Mandarin Chinese)
       他 輸 了 五 百
       tā *shū* *le* *wǔ* *bǎi*
       3SG lose PFV five hundred
       'He lost five hundred yuan.'

(8) a. V + O (Hui'an dialect)
  我　　買　　張　　床
  gua³　*bue³⁻²*　*tiŭ¹*　*tshŋ²*
  1SG　buy　CL　bed
  'I bought a bed.'

  b. V + NUM + CL (Hui'an dialect)
  伊　　輸　　五　　百
  i¹　*su¹*　*gɔ⁴*　*paʔ⁷*
  3SG　lose　five　hundred
  'He lost five hundred yuan.'

Summarizing, besides functioning as a verb, *liau³* in Hui'an is normally used as a resultative complement indicating the completion of a process or the total affectedness of the object of a process. Though it can occur after a verb indicating the anticipated achievement of an event or action, or a state, which is similar to the perfective aspectual meaning, this use of *liau³* is limited to modifying verbs in the first clause of a complex sentence, and has not yet developed into a typical perfective aspect marker.

11.2.2 *khɯ⁵* 去

The word *khɯ⁵* is originally a motion verb meaning 'go', as in (9), where *khɯ⁵* functions as a main verb and is modified by the adverb *suin¹* 先 'first'.

(9)　恁　　先　　去
  len³　*suin¹*　*khɯ⁵*
  2PL　first　go
  'You go first.'

When preceded by a verb, *khɯ⁵* often functions as a directional complement, as in (10a), or as a resultative complement, as in (10b).

(10) a. *khɯ⁵* as a directional complement
  攑　　去　　迄搭
  kia²　*khɯ⁵⁻³*　*hit⁷⁻⁸-taʔ⁷*
  take　go　that-LOC
  'Take (it) there!'

b. *khuɯ⁵* as a resultative complement

糖仔	伊	食	去
thŋ²⁻⁴-a³	i¹	tsiaʔ⁸	khuɯ⁰
sugar-NM	3SG	eat	RVC

'He ate the candy up.'

In (10a), *khuɯ⁵* follows the verb *kia²* 'take' indicating the direction of the action *kia²*, which is further followed by the locative word *hit⁷⁻⁸taʔ⁷* 'there'. In (10b), *khuɯ⁵* follows the verb *tsiaʔ⁸* 'eat' to indicate that something is eaten, that is, something moves away or disappears from its original place, which can be regarded as a result of the action *tsiaʔ⁸* 'eat'. In other words, *khuɯ⁵* here functions as a resultative complement, typically with patient topicalization.

As mentioned in §10.4, when preceded by a stative verb or resultative verb complement construction, *khuɯ⁵* indicates the achievement of a state, i.e. indicating entering into a new state. Two examples are reproduced in (11) and (12).

(11)
會	寒	去
e⁴	kuã²	khuɯ⁰
would	cold	PVC

'(You) would get cold.'

(12)
喙齒	計	落	無	去
tshui⁵⁻³-khi³	ke⁵⁻³	lau⁵⁻³	bo²	khuɯ⁰
mouth-tooth	all	fall	not.have	PVC

'All (his) teeth have fallen out.'

In (11), *khuɯ⁰* follows the stative verb *kuã²* 'cold' to denote entering the new state of 'being cold'. In (12), *khuɯ⁰* follows the resultative verb complement construction *lau⁵⁻³ bo²* 'lose' to indicate entering a new state, i.e. having no teeth. This use of *khuɯ⁰* usually co-occurs with predicates which have a negative meaning or indicate something unexpected. It functions as a phase complement (see §10.4), rather than as a typical perfective aspect marker.

11.2.3 *u⁴* 'have, exist'

The word *u⁴* is originally a verb meaning 'have, exist', as in (13).

(13) 有　　燒水
　　 u^4　 sio^1-$tsui^3$
　　 have　hot-water
　　 'There is hot water.'

When followed by a verb, u^4 may indicate that an event happened, as illustrated by (14).

(14) 我　　有　　去
　　 gua^3　u^4　khu^5
　　 1SG　have　go
　　 'I went there.'

In (14), u^4 occurs before the motion verb khu^5 'go' and may be interpreted as indicating that the event of going to a place happened. This may be the reason why the complex 'u^4 + V' in Southern Min is often regarded as the counterpart of 'V + le 了 (PFV)' in Mandarin Chinese. In fact, however, the main function of u^4 in (14) is to confirm the existence of the event of going there, which then implies that the event happened.

This can be supported by the fact that not all cases of 'u^4 + V' indicate that an event happened, as illustrated by (15).

(15) 伯　　有　　抹
　　 lan^3　u^4　$bua?^7$
　　 1PL　have　smear
　　 'We (women) use (skin products).'

Example (15) aims to express that we women have the habit of using skin products, unlike men. In this case, u^4 precedes the verb $bua?^7$ 'smear' to indicate the existence of the habit of using skin products, rather than to indicate that a specific event happened.

When followed by a stative verb or an adjective, u^4 indicates the existence of a state or property, as illustrated by (16) and (17).

(16) 汝　　有　　驚　　　　無
　　 lu^3　u^4　$kiã^1$　bo^0
　　 2SG　have　be.scared　SFP
　　 'Are you scared?'

(17) 湯　　有　　甜
　　　thŋ¹　u⁴　tin¹
　　　soup　have　sweet
　　　'The soup is sweet.'

In (16), *u⁴* precedes the stative verb *kiã¹* 'be scared' to express the existence of the state of being scared. In (17), *u⁴* is used with the adjective *tin¹* 'sweet' to indicate the existence of the property *tin¹* 'sweet', rather than the non-existence of any taste.

Summarizing, when followed by a verb, *u⁴* in Hui'an is used to state the existence of an event, a state or a property, rather than to function as a perfective aspectual marker.

11.3 Imperfective aspect

As stated in §11.1, the Hui'an dialect uses the same aspect markers *leʔ⁷* 咧 and *tu⁴leʔ⁷* 仜咧 to denote progressive, durative and habitual aspect, which are three subtypes of imperfective aspect. These two markers are used interchangeably. However, in the contemporary Hui'an dialect, *tu⁴leʔ⁷* is not common in daily conversation. Thus, we will take *leʔ⁷* as an example in the following sections. It is important to note that, structurally, the progressive use of this marker occurs preverbally, whereas the durative use occurs post-verbally.

11.3.1 Progressive aspect

The progressive aspect usually denotes an ongoing event, and typically involves an agent carrying out an action, as in (18) and (19).

(18) 阮　　　咧　　　　講　　　　汝　　其　　　否話
　　　gun³　*leʔ⁷⁻⁸*　kaŋ³⁻²　lu³　e²⁻⁴　phai³⁻²-ue⁵
　　　1PL　PROG　say　2SG　GEN　bad-word
　　　'We were speaking ill of you.'

(19) 伊　　咧　　　　嗽
　　　i¹　*leʔ⁷⁻⁸*　sau⁵
　　　3SG　PROG　cough
　　　'He is coughing.'

In these two examples, the aspect marker *le?⁷* occurs before the action verbs *kaŋ³* 'speak' and *sau⁵* 'cough' to describe respectively an ongoing and involuntary event. In (18), *kaŋ³* 'speak' is a verb denoting an activity, and *le?⁷* is used to describe a continuous action. In (19), *sau⁵* 'cough' is a semelfactive verb (also called a momentary or punctual verb), and *le?⁷* is used to indicate iterations of an action.

The progressive aspect marker in Hui'an can also be used with some stative verbs such as *to³* 倒 'lie' and *tsə⁴* 坐 'sit' in (20).

(20) 咧　　　倒　　抑　　咧　　　坐
　　 le?⁷⁻⁸　 *to³*　*a?⁸⁻⁴*　*le?⁷⁻⁸*　*tsə⁴*
　　 PROG　 lie　or　 PROG　 sit
　　 '(She) was lying or sitting?'

In (20), both *le?⁷⁻⁸ to³* 'be lying' and *le?⁷⁻⁸ tsə⁴* 'be sitting' are used to describe someone's postural state at the reference time.

The progressive aspect can be used with an event or a state in the past, present or future. In daily conversation, the past, present or future is often clear in the context, without the presence of temporal words. Comparatively speaking, however, the future progressive is less used and often occurs with a temporal word, as exemplified by (21), where the progressive *le?⁷⁻⁸ siɔŋ⁵⁻⁴khɔ⁵* 咧上課 'be taking a lecture' co-occurs with the temporal word *biã²⁻⁴let⁸* 明日 'tomorrow' to describe an ongoing event in the future.

(21) 明日　　　　即站　　　　　我　　　咧　　　　上課
　　 biã²⁻⁴let⁸　*tsit⁷⁻⁸tsam⁴*　*gua³*　*le?⁷⁻⁸*　*siɔŋ⁵⁻⁴khɔ⁵*
　　 tomorrow　 now　　　　 1SG　 PROG　 take.lectures
　　 'I will be taking a lecture this time tomorrow.'

The following two examples show that the progressive aspect in Hui'an can co-occur in the same sentence with inchoatives encoded by the verb *khai¹si³* 開始 'start' as in (22), or with iteratives encoded by duplicated forms of verb such as *khaŋ⁵khaŋ⁵khaŋ⁵* 控控控 'pick one's nose over and over again' in (23).

(22) 口面　　　　開始　　　　咧　　　　口口
　　 khau³⁻²ben²　*khai¹si³⁻²*　*le?⁷⁻⁸*　*sam⁵⁻³~sam⁵*
　　 outside　　 start　　　 PROG　 drizzle~drizzle
　　 'It's started drizzling outside.'

(23) 佫　　咧　　控控控
　　 ko?⁷　le?⁷⁻⁸　khaŋ⁵~khaŋ⁵~khaŋ⁵
　　 again　PROG　pick~pick~pick
　　 '(He is) picking (his nose) over and over again.'

In (22), *le?⁷⁻⁸ sam⁵⁻³sam⁵* 'drizzling' denotes an ongoing event 'drizzling', while the verb *khai¹si³* 'start' denotes the inchoative. In (23), the triplicated form *khaŋ⁵khaŋ⁵khaŋ⁵* denotes an iterative event, that is, 'picking (his nose)' happens again and again, while *le?⁷* indicates that this iterative event is ongoing.

11.3.2 Durative aspect

The durative aspect marker *le?⁷* (also *tu⁴le?⁷*) occurs after the predicate, denoting duration of a state, as illustrated by (24) and (25).

(24) 汝　　家己　　　口　　咧
　　 lu³　kai⁵⁻⁴ki⁵　lã⁵　le?⁰
　　 2SG　self　　　stay　DUR
　　 'You stay (at home) by yourself.'

(25) 骹　　縛　　咧
　　 kha¹　pak⁸　le?⁰
　　 foot　tie　　DUR
　　 (a) 'The feet (of the chicken) are tied.'
　　 (b) 'Bind the (chicken's) feet.'

Unlike the progressive aspect which often co-occurs with an action verb, the durative aspect is often used with a stative verb. For example, the aspect marker *le?⁰* follows the stative verb *lã⁵* 'stay' in (24) to describe a continuous state of staying at home. However, the durative apsect can also co-occur with an action verb such as *pak⁸* 'tie' in (25). This example has two possible interpretations: (a) it is used to describe the state of the chicken's feet after being bound; and (b) it is used in an imperative to ask someone to bind the chicken's feet. In the second interpretation, the patient marker *ka⁵* with a resumptive pronoun (i.e. the third person pronoun *i¹*) can also be inserted between *kha¹* 'foot' and *pak⁸ le?⁰* 'tired', that is, forming *kha¹ ka⁵⁻⁴ i¹ pak⁸ le?⁰* 'bind the chicken's feet'. In the second interpretation, the final state after carrying out the action of binding is implied as part of its meaning.

The complex [V + le?] is often followed by another verb to indicate the manner of an event encoded by the following verb, as in (26).

(26) 坐　咧　　商量
　　 tsə⁴　le?⁷⁻⁸　siɔŋ¹liɔŋ²
　　 sit　DUR　discuss
　　 'have a discussion while sitting'

In (26), the aspect marker *le?⁷* follows the stative verb *tsə⁴* to mean that the situation of sitting is maintained during the simultaneous event of having a discussion, and, syntactically, *tsə⁴ le?⁷* 'sitting' occurs before the verb *siɔŋ¹liɔŋ²* 'discuss' to indicate the manner of the discussion. There is a prosodic break between *le?⁷* and the verb *siɔŋ¹liɔŋ²*. In this case, it resembles somewhat one of the uses of *-zhe* 著 in Mandarin Chinese (see Li & Thompson 1981:223-224).

11.3.3 Habitual aspect

The progressive and durative aspect markers *le?⁷* and *tui⁴le?⁷* are also used in habitual contexts, which describe a situation that is characteristic of an extended period of time (cf. Comrie 1976:27-28). In Hui'an, the habitual aspect marker *le?⁷* and *tui⁴le?⁷* are typically used for denoting the occupation of a person, as in (27).

(27) 個　咧　　賣　　家俱
　　 en¹　le?⁷⁻⁸　bue⁴　ka¹ku⁵
　　 3PL　HAB　sell　furniture
　　 (a)'They are selling furniture.'
　　 (b)'They sell furniture.'

Example (27) has two possible interpretations: (a) it can be used to describe an ongoing event at the reference time, that is, they are selling furniture, rather than doing other things such as moving house, that is, it is the progressive use; or (b) it can be used as a response to the question about their occupation. In the second interpretation, *bue⁴ ka¹ku⁵* 'sell furniture' refers to a habitual situation, that is, a state holding over a long period, rather than a specific event happening at the reference time. Note that the second interpretation is more common than the first one in daily conversation.

The following example shows that *le?⁷* can also be used in other contexts that do not necessarily refer to a person's occupation.

(28) 細漢　　咧　　討論　　甚物，
　　 sue⁵⁻³han⁵　le‍ʔ⁷⁻⁸　thoˀ³⁻²lun⁵　siəm³⁻²bĩʔ⁷
　　 child　　HAB　discuss　what
　　 口　　咧　　討論　　甚物
　　 tse⁵　le‍ʔ⁷⁻⁸　thoˀ³⁻²lun⁵　siəm³⁻²bĩʔ⁷
　　 now　HAB　discuss　what
　　 'What did you talk about when you were children, and what do you discuss now?'

In (28), *le‍ʔ⁷* is used twice before the verb phrase *thoˀ³⁻²lun⁵ siəm³⁻²bĩʔ⁷* 'discuss what' to denote the event of 'talking about something' in the way it has habitually taken place during two different periods, i.e. *sue⁵⁻³han⁵* 'as children' and *tse⁵* 'now'. This example is not a question asking about the content of the discussion, but is used to express the big difference between two different periods.

11.4 Experiential aspect

In Hui'an, the experiential aspectual meaning is indicated by two markers, i.e. *pat⁷* 八 and *tioʔ⁸* 著. These two markers often co-occur in one sentence, with the structure of *pat⁷* + V + *tioʔ⁸*, as illustrated by (29).

(29) 我　　八　　去　　著　　北京
　　 gua³　pat⁷⁻⁸　khuɯ⁵⁻³　tioʔ⁸⁻⁴　pak⁷⁻⁸kiã¹
　　 1SG　EXP　　go　　EXP　　PN
　　 'I have been to Beijing.'

In (29), together, *pat⁷* and *tioʔ⁸* indicate that I have been to Beijing at least once prior to the speech time. It is obvious that *pat⁷* differs from *tioʔ⁸* in that *pat⁷* precedes the verb, whereas *tioʔ⁸* follows the verb and may also be followed by a locative word such as *pak⁷⁻⁸kiã¹*.

The negative adverb *m⁵* 唔 'not' can be added before *pat⁷* to express an event which has not been experienced, as in (30), where *m⁵* negates the experience of seeing something. In other words, both experiential markers can be retained in the negated construction.

(30) 阮　　唔　　八　　看　　著
　　 gun³　m⁵⁻⁴　pat⁷⁻⁸　khuã⁵　tioʔ⁰
　　 1PL　not　EXP　　look　EXP
　　 'I have never seen (it).'

Both markers can be used alone to express experiential aspectual meaning. When used alone, *tioʔ⁸* normally co-occurs with the auxiliary verb *u⁴* 有 'have' or its negative form *bo²* 無 'not have', as in (31).

(31) 伊   有/無   問   著
     lan³   *u⁴/bo²⁻⁴*   *bŋ⁵*   *tioʔ⁰*
     1PL   have/not.have   ask   EXP
     'I have/have never asked (him).'

In (31), *tioʔ⁸* indicates that the event of 'asking him' has been experienced, while the auxiliary verbs *u⁴* and *bo²* are used to confirm and negate the existence of the experience, respectively.

Tioʔ⁸ 著 is originally a verb meaning 'touch, reach, get'. Use of the verb meaning 'touch, reach, get' to indicate an experiential aspectual meaning can also be found in Quanzhou (Li 1996b:206). However, in other Chinese varieties including the Xiamen, Shantou and Taiwan varieties of Southern Min, the Fuzhou variety of Min, Mandarin Chinese, the Meixian and Liancheng varieties of Hakka, the Anyi variety of Gan, Hong Kong Cantonese, and the Wenzhou, Tangxi and Hangzhou varieties of Wu, the experiential aspect marker is derived from the verb meaning 'pass, cross' (Li and Thompson 1981:226-232, Lin 1996:40, Xiang 1996:64, Wan 1996:88, Zhang 1996b:155, Matthews and Yip 2011:235, Chen 1996:236, Zhou and Ouyang 1998:373, Shi 1996d:183, Lu 2003:99). Thus, *tioʔ⁸* in Hui'an and Quanzhou suggests a different lexical source of the experiential aspect marker.

Comparatively speaking, the marker *pat⁷* alone is used more frequently than the marker *tioʔ⁸*. An example is given in (32), where *pat⁷* preceding the verb *lai²* 來 'come' is used in an interrogative sentence to ask whether the addressee has ever had the experience of coming to the reference location, 'here', prior to the speech time.

(32) 汝   八   來   唔
     luʳ³   *pat⁷⁻⁸*   *lai²*   *m⁰*
     2SG   EXP   come   SFP
     'Have you been here before?'

As suggested by Chappell (2001b) (also Lien 2007:729), the use of *pat* as an experiential marker in Southern Min is derived from its use as a lexeme meaning 'know; be acquainted with'.[2] Note also that Chappell (2001b) argues that the experiential aspect in Chinese including Southern Min such as what indicated by *pat⁷* in (32) should not be considered as an aspect marker but rather as a type of evidential.

11.5 Summary

This chapter has examined five aspectual categories in Hui'an: perfective, progressive, durative, habitual and experiential.

We suggest that there is no typical perfective aspect marker, and the counterparts of the perfective aspect markers reported in the literature of Southern Min have not been fully grammaticalized as aspect markers in Hui'an.

Following Comrie (1976), the imperfective aspect in Hui'an includes progressive, durative and habitual aspect. The Hui'an dialect uses the same aspect markers *leʔ⁷* 咧 and *tu⁴leʔ⁷* 仁咧 to denote these three subtypes of imperfective aspect. However, the progressive and habitual aspect markers *leʔ⁷* and *tu⁴leʔ⁷* precede the predicate, while the durative aspect markers *leʔ⁷* and *tu⁴leʔ⁷* follow it.

There are two experiential aspect markers, *pat⁷* 八 and *tioʔ⁸* 著, of which *pat⁷* is followed by the predicate, while *tioʔ⁸* follows it. They often co-occur within the same clause.

---

2 Chappell (2001b) uses the morpheme '別' for the experiential *pat⁴* in Southern Min, unlike Lien (2007) who uses the morpheme '八' instead.

12 Modality

12.1 Introduction

The term 'modality' traditionally refers to the speaker's subjective evaluation and attitude towards events expressed in a proposition, and normally falls into three subcategories: dynamic, deontic and epistemic (cf. Lyons 1977; Palmer 1986, 2001, Nuyts 2005; Chappell & Peyraube 2016; among others). Dynamic modality encodes ability, and sometimes volition, as in (1a); deontic modality deals with the necessity or possibility of acts performed by morally responsible agents which involve obligation and permission, as in (1b); while epistemic modality involves the speaker's belief or opinion about the validity of the proposition, as in (1c) (cf. Lyons 1977; Palmer 1986; Nuyts 2005; Chappell & Peyraube 2016).

(1) a. dynamic modality
    She can speak perfect French.
  b. deontic modality
    You must leave now.
  c. epistemic modality
    John must have been studying all night.

In (1a), the modal auxiliary verb *can* encodes the ability of speaking perfect French. The modal auxiliary verb *must* in (1b) expresses obligation, i.e. the necessity of leaving, while *must* in (1c) expresses a confident assumption, that is, the speaker believes that John has been studying all night.

The core modal notions involve a possibility-necessity contrast (Van der Auwera & Plungian 1998). For example, permission is a type of possibility, while obligation is a type of necessity, according to their different degrees of force and certainty (see Van der Auwera & Plungian 1998:82 for details). Similarly, Chappell & Peyraube (2016) classify modal auxiliary verbs in Chinese into three main semantic groups: (a) possibility, including possibility and permission, such as Mandarin *néng* 能 'can, able to' and *kěyǐ* 可以 'may, to be permitted to'; (b) necessity, obligation and certainty, such as Mandarin *yīnggāi* 應該 'ought to'; and (c) volition, such as Mandarin *yào* 要 'want to'.

This chapter aims to examine how these three semantic types of modality (i.e. possibility, necessity and volition) are encoded in Hui'an. Generally speaking, modality in Hui'an can be expressed by modal auxiliary verbs, adverbs, syntactic structures (e.g. verb complement constructions) and modal particles (i.e. sentence-final particles). In this chapter, we will focus on modal auxiliary verbs and adverbs, including (a) possibility: e^4 會 'can', e^4hiau^3 會曉 'can', u^4huat^7($^8thaŋ^1$)有法(唔^1) 'can', $e^4thaŋ^1$ 會唔 'can', $u^4thaŋ^1$ 有唔 'can', $thaŋ^1$ 唔 'can', e^4tsue^5 會做 'can', $khɔ^{3-2}liŋ^2$ 可能 'possibly' and $m^{5-4}lɔŋ^3$ 唔攏 'possibly'; (b) necessity: $tioʔ^8$ 著 'should', $iŋ^1kai^1$ 應該 'should, must', $khŋ^{3-2}tiŋ^5$ 肯定 'certainly' and $et^{7-8}tiŋ^5$ 一定 'certainly'; (c) volition: $boʔ^7$ 卜 'want', $siũ^4boʔ^7$ 想卜 'want' and ai^5 愛 'like, want'.

12.2 Possibility

Van der Auwera & Plungian (1998) classify possibility into three main subcategories: (a) participant-internal possibility; (b) participant-external possibility; and (c) epistemic possibility. Participant-internal possibility (also termed 'ability') refers to possibility as attributed internally to a participant engaged in a state of affairs. In other words, the enabling conditions for the achievement of a state of affairs exist inherently in the participant. An example from English is reproduced in (2).

(2) Participant-internal possibility
Boris can get by with sleeping five hours a night. (Van der Auwera & Plungian 1998:80)

Participant-external possibility, referring to the enabling circumstances external to the participant, falls into two subtypes: (a) non-deontic possibility: involving physical conditions, as in (3a); and (b) deontic possibility (i.e. permission): involving social conditions, as in (3b) (Van der Auwera & Plungian 1998).

(3) Participant-external possibility
   a. non-deontic possibility
      To get to the station, you can take bus 66. (Van der Auwera & Plungian 1998:80)
   b. deontic possibility (permission)
      John may leave now. (Van der Auwera & Plungian 1998:81)

Van der Auwera & Plungian (1998:84) mention that Bybee et al. (1994:178) use the term 'root possibility' in much the same sense of their term 'participant-external possibility'. Root possibility reports on general enabling conditions, such as

---

[1] The morpheme 唔 here is usually pronounced as $aŋ^1$, rather than $thaŋ^1$. This also applies to other modal auxiliary verbs involving 唔.

social or physical ones and so is not restricted to the internal condition of ability (Bybee et al. 1994:178). Both terms are thus used to include such types of external conditions while permission (involving social conditions) is regarded as a special instance of this (cf. Van der Auwera & Plungian 1998:84; Bybee et al. 1994:193). Nevertheless, the term 'root possibility' is often distinguished from 'permission' in Bybee et al. (1994). In other words, root possibility, in the narrow sense (i.e. not including permission), as in (4) below, seems to correspond to non-deontic possibility, as in (3a) above. However, as noted by Fan (2011), non-deontic possibility differs from root possibility in that the former focuses on the relative *appropriateness* of the achievement of an event, whereas the latter focuses on the *possibility* of the achievement of an event.

(4) Root possibility
 I can ride that horse. (Bybee et al. 1994:192)

According to Bybee et al. (1994:192), the enabling conditions for the agent (i.e. the speaker) to ride the horse in (4) do not lie entirely within the agent, but also depend on the external world, e.g. the properties of the horse. In other words, the external physical conditions here are of some significance in determining the agent's ability and the achievement of the event 'riding that horse'. In this case, the modal auxiliary verb *can* focuses on the *possibility* of riding that horse. In (3a) above, however, the auxiliary verb *can* does not indicate the possibility of the achievement of the event 'taking bus 66', but expresses that 'taking bus 66' is a possible way to get to the station. In other words, *can* in (3a) focuses on the *appropriateness* of taking bus 66, which is determined by external physical conditions such as the availability of a route between the station and the place where the addressee is.

Epistemic possibility refers to the speaker's judgment of the proposition as being uncertain, as illustrated by (5), where John's arrival is judged possible by the speaker.

(5) Epistemic possibility
 John may have arrived. (Van der Auwera & Plungian 1998:81)

In the remainder of this section, we will examine how these subcategories of possibility (i.e. ability, root possibility, non-deontic possibility, permission and epistemic possibility) are encoded in Hui'an.

12.2.1 Ability

Two subcategories of ability have been distinguished: physical ability and mental ability. The modal words for expressing ability in Hui'an involve e^4 會, e^4hiau^3 會曉 and $u^4huat^7(^8thaŋ^1)$ 有法(通). The most common one is e^4, which can encode mental ability as in (6), or physical ability as in (7).

(6) 我　　會　　說　　廣東話
　　 gua^3　e^4　$səʔ^{7\text{-}8}$　$kŋ^{3\text{-}2}taŋ^1ue^5$
　　 1SG　can　speak　Cantonese
　　 'I can speak Cantonese.'

(7) 伊　　手　　　長，　會　邁　　　櫥頂
　　 i^1　$tshiu^3$　$tŋ^2$　e^4　$kau^{5\text{-}3}$　$tu^{2\text{-}4}\text{-}tiŋ^3$
　　 3SG　hand　long　Can　arrive　closet-up
　　 'His hand is long and can reach the top of the closet.'

The ability such as e^4 $səʔ^{7\text{-}8}$ $kŋ^{3\text{-}2}taŋ^1ue^5$ 'can speak Cantonese' in (6) is traditionally regarded as mental ability, or ability in terms of learned skill. In (7), e^4 $kau^{5\text{-}3}$ $tu^{2\text{-}4}\text{-}tiŋ^3$ means that the subject i^1 has an 'internal' physical ability to reach the top of the closet.

As shown by the following example, e^4 is originally a verb meaning 'know, understand'.

(8) 我　　會　　廣東話
　　 gua^3　e^4　$kŋ^{3\text{-}2}taŋ^1ue^5$
　　 1SG　know　Cantonese
　　 'I know Cantonese.'

Unlike e^4 in (6) above, e^4 in (8) is immediately followed by the noun $kŋ^{3\text{-}2}taŋ^1ue^5$ 'Cantonese' and functions as a main verb meaning 'know, understand'. Example (8) normally means that someone can not only speak (some) Cantonese, but also understands (some) Cantonese, while example (6) focuses on the ability to speak Cantonese.

More often, however, the mental ability or ability in terms of learned skill is encoded by the modal auxiliary verb e^4hiau^3, as in (9).

(9) 我　　會曉　　　說　　　廣東話
　　 gua³　e⁴hiau³⁻²　saʔ⁷⁻⁸　kŋ³⁻²taŋ¹ue⁵
　　 1SG　 can　　　 speak　 Cantonese
　　 'I can speak Cantonese.'

The use of *e⁴hiau³* illustrated by example (9) is the only function of *e⁴hiau³* as a modal auxiliary verb, unlike the modal auxiliary verb *e⁴*, which expresses a series of modal meanings such as mental ability, physical ability and epistemic possibility. This may explain why *e⁴hiau³*, rather than *e⁴*, is more often used to encode mental ability.

The auxiliary verb use of *e⁴hiau³* as shown by (9) is derived from its use as a verb meaning 'know, understand', as in (10), like the auxiliary verb *e⁴*.

(10) 口　　　無　　　　味，　會曉？
　　 tse²　　bo²⁻⁴　　bi⁵　　e⁴hiau³
　　 this　 not.have　taste　understand
　　 'This is tasteless, understand?'

Unlike *e⁴hiau³*, the modal word *u⁴huat⁷(⁻⁸thaŋ¹)* encodes physical ability, rather than mental ability, as illustrated by (11).

(11) 我　　有法(通)　　　　　　　攑　　十　　斤　　米
　　 gua³　u⁴-huat⁷⁻⁸(thaŋ¹)　　kia²　tsap⁸⁻⁴　kən¹　bi³
　　 1SG　 have-method(can)　　 lift　 ten　　 MW　 rice
　　 'I can lift ten catty of rice.'

In (11), the modal word *u⁴huat⁷(⁻⁸thaŋ¹)* occurs before the verb phrase *kia² tsap⁸⁻⁴ kən¹ bi³* 'lift ten catty of rice' to express that the subject (i.e. *gua³*) has the internal physical ability to lift ten catty of rice.

As shown by example (11), *u⁴huat⁷*, literally meaning 'have method', can be used alone as a modal word expressing physical ability without the following *thaŋ¹* 'can'. Note, however, that the modal word *u⁴huat⁷⁻⁸thaŋ¹* (with the following *thaŋ¹*) is more common than *u⁴huat⁷* (without the following *thaŋ¹*) in daily conversation. In Hui'an, *thaŋ¹* itself normally occurs before a verb (phrase) to function as a modal word expressing modal meanings such as permission (see §12.2.4), while *u⁴huat⁷* is often used alone without preceding a verb (phrase), as illustrated by (12), where *u⁴huat⁷* is the main verb and the whole sentence means that we can resolve something by ourselves.

(12) 阮　　家己　　有法
　　 gun³　kai⁵⁻⁴ki⁵　u⁴-huat⁷
　　 1PL　self　　have-method
　　 'We have methods ourselves./We can resolve (it) by ourselves.'

Both *e⁴* and *u⁴huat⁷(⁻⁸thaŋ¹)* can be used to encode a recovered physical ability, as in (13).

(13) 伊　口　　會/有法(嗵)　　　　行　　咯
　　 i¹　tse⁵　e⁴/u⁴-huat⁷⁻⁸(thaŋ¹)　kiã²　lɔ⁰
　　 3SG　now　can/have-method(can)　walk　SFP
　　 'He can walk now.'

Example (13) in fact has two possible interpretations. Firstly, it may mean that a child, who could not walk before, can walk now, i.e. has learnt how to walk. Secondly, it may mean that someone broke his leg and could not walk for some time, but now he can walk again, that is, he regains the ability to walk. In the second interpretation, the modal words *e⁴* and *u⁴huat⁷(⁻⁸thaŋ¹)* are used to encode a recovered ability.

Nonetheless, normally speaking, people do not lose their mental abilities once they possess them. Hence, the following example can only mean that someone has learnt to speak Cantonese, rather than indicates that someone has regained their ability to speak it.

(14) 我　　口　　會曉　　　說　　　廣東話　　　　　咯
　　 gua³　tse⁵　e⁴hiau³⁻²　saʔ⁷⁻⁸　kŋ³⁻²taŋ¹ue⁵　lɔ⁰
　　 1SG　now　can　　　　speak　Cantonese　　　SFP
　　 'I can speak Cantonese now.'

12.2.2 Root possibility

Besides encoding ability, the modal auxiliary verbs *e⁴* and *u⁴huat⁷(⁻⁸thaŋ¹)* can also indicate root possibility, that is, they can occur in the contexts where an external condition exists for the achievement of a state of affairs, as illustrated by (15). We use the term 'root possibility' here in the sense of Fan (2011).

(15) 坐　　七　　　　路　　　車　　　會/有法(呾)　　　　　　遘　　　厝
　　 tsa⁴　tshet⁷⁻⁸　lɔ⁵⁻⁴　tshia¹　e⁴/u⁴-huat⁷⁻⁸(thaŋ¹)　kau⁵⁻³　tshu⁵
　　 sit　 seven　　road　 vehicle　can/have-method(can)　arrive　home
　　 '(We) can take the No. 7 bus to go home.'

Example (15) does not talk about someone's internal ability to get home, but rather the bus line that people can use, which can be regarded as an external physical condition for achieving this.

Root possibility can also be expressed by the modal auxiliary verbs *e⁴thaŋ¹* 會呾 and *u⁴thaŋ¹* 有呾, as in (16) and (17).

(16) 門　　　開　　　咧,　　伓　　　則　　　　會呾　　　　入來
　　 bŋ²　　khui¹　　leʔ⁰　　en¹　　tsiaʔ⁷⁻⁸　e⁴thaŋ¹　　liəp⁸lai⁰
　　 door　open　　DUR　　3PL　　then　　　can　　　　come.into
　　 'Keep the door open, so that they can come in.'

(17) 二十　　　　　口　　有呾　　　　　食　　　　　飽　　無
　　 li⁵⁻⁴tsap⁸⁻⁴　khɔ¹　*u⁴-thaŋ¹*　tsiaʔ⁸⁻⁴　pa³　bo⁰
　　 twenty　　　YUAN　have-can　　eat　　　　full　SFP
　　 'Can (you) eat enough with (the food) that costs 20 yuan?'

In (16), 'keep the door open' constitutes an external physical condition for them to come in. In (17), the speaker is asking whether food that costs 20 yuan is enough for the addressee to eat until fully satisfied. In this case, the quantity of the food constitutes an external physical condition of having a full stomach.

In Hui'an, *e⁴thaŋ¹* can be used alone functioning as a main verb meaning 'to be OK, to be acceptable', as in (18), while *u⁴thaŋ¹* is usually followed by a verb, as illustrated by (17).

(18) 口　　　會呾
　　 hə²　　*e⁴thaŋ¹*
　　 that　 OK
　　 'That is OK.'

As shown by the following example, *thaŋ¹* can be used alone to express root possibility.

(19) 明年　　倒來　　　　　 囅　　 徛　　新厝
　　 buã²⁻⁴-lin² to⁵laiº　 thaŋ¹ khia⁴ sen¹-tshu⁵
　　 next-year come.back can   live   new-house
　　 '(You) can live in the new house when (you) come back next year.'

In (19), the auxiliary verb *thaŋ¹* alone indicates the possibility of living in the new house, which is determined by the external physical condition that the new house will be ready when the addressee comes back next year.

12.2.3 Non-deontic possibility

Besides encoding ability and root possibility, the modal verb *e⁴* in Hui'an can also indicate non-deontic possibility, that is, indicate the appropriateness of a situation, which is determined by external physical conditions, as illustrated by (20).

(20) 口　 伯　 會　 食　　 得
　 tse² lan³ e⁴   tsiaʔ⁸ leʔº
　 this 1PL   can   eat   get
　 'We can eat this.'

In (20), the auxiliary verb *e⁴*, followed by the verb *tsiaʔ⁸* 'eat' and its potential complement *leʔº*, indicates that it is suitable for us to eat this (see §10.8 on potential verb complement constructions for more details). In this case, the appropriateness of eating something is determined by the properties of the food.

Non-deontic possibility can also be encoded by the modal auxiliary verbs *thaŋ¹* 囅 and *e⁴tsue⁵* 會做, as in (21) and (22), respectively.

(21) 囅　　 共　　 伊　 買　　 電腦　　　 唔
　　 thaŋ¹ ka⁵⁻⁴ i¹   bue³⁻² ten⁵⁻⁴lo³ mº
　　 can   to   3SG buy   computer   SFP
　　 'Can (I) buy her a computer?'

(22) 去　　 泉州，　　　　會做　　 坐　 汽車
　　 khu⁵⁻³ tsuan²⁻⁴tsiu¹ e⁴tsue⁵⁻³ tsə⁴ khi⁵⁻³tshia¹
　　 Go   PN   can   sit   Car
　　 'To get to Quanzhou, (you) can take the bus.'

The context of example (21) is that the speaker is asking the addressee whether it is suitable to buy her daughter a computer, because she is worried that it may be still a bit early for her daughter to use a computer. In this case, the auxiliary verb *thaŋ¹* is used to express the appropriateness of buying her daughter a computer. In (22), the auxiliary verb *e⁴tsue⁵*, followed by the verb phrase *tsə⁴ khi⁵⁻³tshia¹* 'take the bus', indicates that it is feasible to get to Quanzhou by bus, which is determined by the distance between Quanzhou and the place where the addressee is.

12.2.4 Permission

The modal auxiliary verbs *e⁴*, *thaŋ¹* and *e⁴tsue⁵* can also denote permission, as in (23), where the time to get married is conditioned by social norms.

(23) 二十　　　　歲　　則　　　　會/啯/會做　　　　　結婚
　　　li⁵⁻⁴tsap⁸⁻⁴　hə⁵　tsiaʔ⁷⁻⁸　e⁴/thaŋ¹/e⁴tsue⁵⁻³　ketʔ⁷⁻⁸hun¹
　　　twenty　　year　only.then　can/can/can　　　　marry
　　　'(People) can get married when (they) are 20 years old.'

As with *e⁴thaŋ¹*, *e⁴tsue⁵* can be used alone to mean 'to be OK', as in (24). Note also that in a declarative sentence such as (24), *e⁴tsue⁵* is more widely used than *e⁴thaŋ¹*.

(24) 紅桔　　　　食　　　就　　　會做
　　　aŋ²⁻⁴ket⁷　tsiaʔ⁸　tsiu⁵⁻⁴　e⁴tsue⁵
　　　orange　　eat　　then　　OK
　　　'It's certainly OK to eat oranges.'

12.2.5 Epistemic possibility

The Hui'an dialect normally uses the modal auxiliary verb *e⁴* to express epistemic possibility, as in (25), where *e⁴ loʔ⁸⁻⁴hɔ⁴* 會落雨 is concerned with the speaker's attitude towards a potential future event, that is, the speaker is uncertain whether it will rain.

(25) 看勢　　　　　　　會　　落雨
　　　khuã⁵⁻³-se⁵　　　e⁴　　loʔ⁸⁻⁴-hɔ⁴
　　　look-situation　can　fall-rain
　　　'It looks as if it will rain.'

The modal auxiliary verb $(u^4)thaŋ^1$(有)嗵 can also encode epistemic possibility, however, it is often used in negative sentences, as in (26), or interrogative sentences, as in (27).

(26) 今日　　　無嗵　　　　落雨
　　 $kiã^1let^8$　$bo^{2\text{-}4}\text{-}thaŋ^1$　$lo\Omega^{8\text{-}4}\text{-}ho^4$
　　 today　　 not.have-can　fall-rain
　　 'It won't rain today.'

(27) 今日　　　(有)嗵　　　落雨　　　　無
　　 $kiã^1let^8$　$(u^4)thaŋ^1$　$lo\Omega^{8\text{-}4}\text{-}ho^4$　bo^0
　　 today　　 (have)can　　fall-rain　　SFP
　　 'Will it rain today?'

In (26), $bo^{2\text{-}4}thaŋ^1$, the negative form of the auxiliary verb $(u^4)thaŋ^1$, is followed by the verb $lo\Omega^{8\text{-}4}ho^4$ 'rain' to express that the speaker thinks that it will not rain today. In (27), the auxiliary verb $(u^4)thaŋ^1$ is used in a interrogative sentence to ask whether it will rain today or not.

The Hui'an dialect also often uses adverbs, especially the adverb $kho^{3\text{-}2}liŋ^2$ 可能, to encode epistemic possibility, as in (28) and (29).

(28) 可能　　　　汝　　無　　　　看　　著
　　 $kho^{3\text{-}2}liŋ^2$　lu^3　$bo^{2\text{-}4}$　$khuã^5$　$tio\Omega^0$
　　 possibly　　2SG　not.have　look　PVC
　　 'Maybe you didn't see (it).'

(29) 伊　　可能　　　　　超市　　　　　買　　其
　　 i^1　$kho^{3\text{-}2}liŋ^2$　$tshiau^1tshi^4$　bue^3　e^0
　　 3SG　possibly　　 supermarket　buy　SFP
　　 'He may have bought (it) at the supermarket.'

In both these two examples, the adverb $kho^{3\text{-}2}liŋ^2$ is used to indicate the speaker's subjective judgment. The adverb $kho^{3\text{-}2}liŋ^2$ can occur at the sentence-initial position, as in (28), or occur between the subject and the main predicate, as in (29).

As shown by the following example, the adverb $m^{5\text{-}4}loŋ^3$ 呣攏 can also encode epistemic possibility.

(30) 唔攏　　　卜　　　讀　　　一年　　　咯
　　　m⁵⁻⁴lɔŋ³⁻²　boʔ⁷⁻⁸　thak⁸⁻⁴　et⁷⁻⁸-lin²　lɔ⁰
　　　possibly　want　study　one-year　SFP
　　　'(He) may be going into first grade.'

12.3 Necessity

In Hui'an, the modal auxiliary verbs for encoding necessity include *tioʔ⁸* 著 and *iŋ¹kai¹* 應該. The auxiliary verb *tioʔ⁸* can encode the participant's internal need, as in (31).

(31) 我　　　逐日　　　著　　　睏　　　八　　　點鐘
　　　gua³　tak⁸⁻⁴-let⁸　tioʔ⁸⁻⁴　khun⁵　pueʔ⁷⁻⁸　tiam³⁻²tsiŋ¹
　　　1SG　every-day　need　sleep　eight　hour
　　　'I need to sleep eight hours every day.'

The modal word *tioʔ⁸* can also express compelling physical conditions that are external to the participant, as in (32).

(32) 卜　　　去　　　車站，
　　　boʔ⁷⁻⁸　khu⁵⁻³　tshia¹tsam⁴
　　　want　go　station
　　　汝　　　著　　　坐　　　七　　　路　　　車
　　　lu³　tioʔ⁸⁻⁴　tsə⁴　tshet⁷⁻⁸　lɔ⁵⁻⁴　tshia¹
　　　2SG　should　sit　seven　road　vehicle
　　　'To get to the station, you have to take bus 7.'

Unlike the modal word *e⁹tsue⁵*, which expresses a possible option (that is, suggests the existence of other options), the modal word *tioʔ⁸* often suggests that there is only one option, or else the option offered by the speaker is the best one, and so the addressee should take it up.

The modal word *tioʔ⁸* can also encode deontic necessity, i.e. obligation, as illustrated by (33).

(33) 汝　　　糖仔　　　著　　　分　　　儂　　　食
　　　lu³　thŋ²⁻⁴-a³　tioʔ⁸⁻⁴　pun¹　laŋ⁴　tsiaʔ⁸
　　　2SG　sugar-NM　should　distribute　other　eat
　　　'You should share your candies with others.'

As shown by the following example, *tioʔ⁸* is originally a verb meaning 'touch, reach'.

(34) 骹　　著　　地
　　 kha¹　*tioʔ⁸⁻⁴*　*tue⁵*
　　 foot　touch　floor
　　 'The foot touches the floor.'

The modal auxiliary verb *iŋ¹kai¹* normally encodes epistemic necessity, as in (35).

(35) 伊　　應該　　是　　八　　點　　遘
　　 i¹　*iŋ¹kai¹*　*si⁴*　*pueʔ⁷⁻⁸*　*tiəm³*　*kau⁵*
　　 3SG　must　be　eight　o'clock　arrive
　　 'It must be 8 o'clock when he arrives.'

Epistemic necessity is often encoded by an adverb such as *khŋ³⁻²tiŋ⁵* 肯定 and *et⁷⁻⁸tiŋ⁵* 一定, in which *khŋ³⁻²tiŋ⁵* is typically used in positive sentences, as in (36), while *et⁷⁻⁸tiŋ⁵* is generally used in negative sentences, as in (37).

(36) 肯定　　　是　　汝　　家己　　無　　　主動
　　 khŋ³⁻²tiŋ⁵　*si⁴*　*lɯ³*　*kai⁵⁻⁴ki⁵*　*bo²⁻⁴*　*tsu³⁻²tɔŋ⁴*
　　 certainly　be　2SG　self　not.have　active
　　 'It is certain that you yourself didn't take the initiative in (this).'

(37) 儂　　也　　無　　　一定　　　卜　　來
　　 laŋ⁴　*a⁴*　*bo²⁻⁴*　*et⁷⁻⁸tiŋ⁵*　*boʔ⁷⁻⁸*　*lai²*
　　 other　also　not.have　certainly　want　come
　　 'It's not certain that he wants to come.'

12.4 Volition

The main modal auxiliary verbs of volition in Hui'an involve *boʔ⁷* 卜 and *siũ⁴boʔ⁷* 想卜. Examples are given in (38) and (39).

(38) 我　　卜　　去
　　 gua³　*boʔ⁷⁻⁸*　*khu⁵*
　　 1SG　want　go
　　 'I want to go (there).'

(39) 伊   想卜   買   厝
    i¹   siũ⁴boʔ⁷⁻⁸   bue³⁻²   tshu⁵
    3SG   want   buy   house
    'He wants to buy a house.'

In (38), the modal auxiliary verb *boʔ⁷* occurs before the motion verb *khu⁵* 'go' to express the speaker's volition to go somewhere. In (39), the auxiliary verb *siũ⁴boʔ⁷*, consisting of the verb *siũ⁴* 'think' and the verb *boʔ⁷* 'want', is followed by the verb phrase *bue³⁻² tshu⁵* 'buy a house' to express the subject's desire to buy a house. In this use, *boʔ⁷* is more common than *siũ⁴boʔ⁷*.

As illustrated by (40) below, *boʔ⁷* in Hui'an is originally a verb meaning 'want'. This is a typical lexical source for the volition modal (cf. Bybee et al. 1994; Van der Auwera & Plungian 1998).

(40) 雞翼   汝   卜   唔
    kue¹-set⁸   lu³   boʔ⁷   m⁰
    chicken-wing   2SG   want   not
    'Do you want a chicken wing?'

In (40), *boʔ⁷* is the only verb, and its object *kue¹set⁸* 'chicken wing' is placed in clause-initial position functioning as a topic.

There is another main modal auxiliary verb of volition in Taiwan, i.e. *ai³* 愛 'to want', which is derived from its use as a verb meaning 'like' (cf. Chappell & Peyraube 2016). In Hui'an, some examples of *ai⁵* 愛 seem to be able to be interpreted as a modal auxiliary verb meaning 'want', as in (41).

(41) 愛   倒來   倒來
    ai⁵⁻³   to⁵lai⁰   to⁵lai⁰
    like   come.back   come.back
    'Come back if you like/want.'

12.5 Summary

In this chapter, we have examined how the three semantic types of modality - possibility, necessity and volition - are encoded by modal auxiliary verbs and adverbs in Hui'an.

Possibility includes ability, root possibility, non-deontic possibility, permission and epistemic possibility. A series of modal auxiliary verbs is attested that encode possibility, of which e^4 會 and $thaŋ^1$ 嗵 are most common and multifunctional. The modal auxiliary verb e^4 encodes all the five subcategories of possibility, while $thaŋ^1$ expresses all the five subcategories of possibility except ability. Epistemic possibility can also be expressed by adverbs such as $khɔ^{3\text{-}2}liŋ^2$ 可能 and $m^{5\text{-}4}lɔŋ^3$ 唔攏.

The modal auxiliary verbs for encoding necessity include $tioʔ^8$ 著 and $iŋ^1kai^1$ 應該, of which, $tioʔ^8$ encodes the participant's internal need, if not the compelling physical conditions external to the participant, that is, deontic necessity (i.e. obligation), whereas $iŋ^1kai^1$ normally encodes epistemic necessity. Epistemic necessity is also often encoded by an adverb such as $khŋ^{3\text{-}2}tiŋ^5$ 肯定 and $et^{7\text{-}8}tiŋ^5$ 一定.

The main modal auxiliary verbs of volition are $boʔ^7$ 卜 and $siũ^4boʔ^7$ 想卜. The verb ai^5 愛 'like' can also be interpreted as a modal auxiliary verb meaning 'want'.

13 Negation

13.1 Introduction

In their typological study of negation in Chinese, Chappell & Peyraube (2016b) distinguish three main syntactic categories of negatives and put forward a semantic typology of negation, as shown in (i) below.

(i) Syntactic and semantic typology of negation in Chinese
   A. Negative existential and possessive verbs
   B. Standard negation: negators of declarative main clauses
      (a) Perfective negatives 'not V_{ed}': an event in a past time context did not take place
      (b) General and volitional negatives 'not (want to) V'
      (c) Imminent negatives 'not yet V_{ed}': an event or action has not taken place at the reference point of time, while nonetheless being expected or anticipated to occur in the future
      (d) Irrealis negatives 'unlikely to V/unable to V': expressing either inability of the subject to carry out an action or the unlikelihood of an event taking place, due to some external circumstance which prevents its occurrence
   C. Prohibitives: negators of imperative clauses
      (a) General prohibitives 'Don't V!'
      (b) 'Lack of necessity' negatives 'There's no need to V'/ 'You needn't V'
      (c) Injunctive negatives 'It's better not to V'/ 'You shouldn't V'

All these types of negative can be attested in Hui'an, as in Table 13-1.

Tab. 13-1: Main negatives in the Hui'an dialect

		Hui'an	Mandarin Chinese
Negative existential and possessive verb		bo^2 無	*méi(yǒu)* 沒(有)
Standard Negation	Perfective negative	bo^2 無	*méi(yǒu)* 沒(有)
	General and volitional negatives	m^5 毋; $m^{5\text{-}4}ai^5$ 毋愛	*bù* 不
	Imminent negative	$bə^5$ 未	
	Irrealis negative	bue^4 燴	
Prohibitives	General prohibitive	$baŋ^1$~$m^{5\text{-}4}thaŋ^1$ 毋通	*bùyào* 不要 ~ *bié* 別
	'Lack of necessity' negatives	$(m^{5\text{-}4})ben^3$ (毋)免	*bùyòng* 不用~ *béng* 甭
	Injunctive negatives	$buan^3$	

As shown in Table 13-1 above, there are four main negative forms in Mandarin Chinese, that is, *méi, bù, bié, béng*, of which *bié* and *béng* are fused forms of *bùyào* and *bùyòng* respectively (cf. Chappell & Peyraube 2016b). Unlike Mandarin Chinese, the Hui'an dialect possesses a comparatively large number of negatives: two general and volitional negatives m^5 毋 and $m^{5\text{-}4}ai^5$ 毋愛; an existential and perfective negative bo^2 無; the imminent negative $bə^5$ 未 'not yet'; the irrealis negative bue^4 燴 'not be able, unlikely'; the general prohibitive $baŋ^1$ 毋通 and its unfused form $m^{5\text{-}4}thaŋ^1$ 毋通; the 'lack of necessity' negatives $(m^{5\text{-}4})ben^3$ (毋)免 'do not need' and the injunctive negative $buan^3$ 'best not to, should not'. Some of these negatives, such as $m^{5\text{-}4}ai^5$, bue^4 and $baŋ^1$~$m^{5\text{-}4}thaŋ^1$, are either adverbs or modal auxiliary verbs.

13.2 General and volitional negatives m^5 毋 and $m^{5\text{-}4}ai^5$ 毋愛

The negative marker m^5 毋 in Hui'an functions as a general negative with the meaning of 'not' and often expresses lack of volition on the agent's part to carry out an action, that is, meaning 'to not want'. Similarly, the negator $m^{5\text{-}4}ai^5$ 毋愛, being the negative form of the modal auxiliary verb ai^5 愛 'want', functions as a volitional negative 'to not want'.

The negative form *m⁵* often occurs with an activity predicate over which the subject has some control to suggest that the subject does not want to do something, as illustrated by (1).

(1) 我　　呣　　食
　　 gua³　m⁵⁻⁴　tsiaʔ⁸
　　 1SG　 not　 eat
　　 'I don't want to eat (an apple).'

In (1), *m⁵* precedes the verb *tsiaʔ⁸* 'eat' to negate the speaker's willingness to eat an apple. In other words, the speaker refuses to eat an apple. In this case, *m⁵* functions as a volitional negative, and can thus be regarded as the negative form of the modal auxiliary verb *boʔ⁷* 卜 'want', which expresses volition. The use of the general negative *m⁵* to express lack of volition on the agent's part to carry out an action is also reported in other Southern Min varieties such as Xiamen, Quanzhou and Taiwan (cf. Li 1971, Teng 1990, Li 2007a, see also Chappell & Peyraube 2016b).

The negator *m⁵* is also often used to negate the copular verb *si⁴* 是 'be', as in (2) and (3). In this case, there is no component of unwillingness.

(2) 伊　　呣　　是　　大學生
　　 i¹　　m⁵⁻⁴　si⁴　 tua⁵⁻⁴oʔ⁸⁻⁴siŋ¹
　　 3SG　not　 be　 university.student
　　 'He is not a university student.'

(3) 呣　　是　　咧　　 說　　伊
　　 m⁵⁻⁴　si⁴　 leʔ⁷⁻⁸　səʔ⁷⁻⁸　i¹
　　 not　 be　 PROG　 say　 3SG
　　 '(We) are not talking about him.'

In (2), the negator *m⁵* occurs before the copular verb *si⁴*, which is further followed by the noun phrase *tua⁵⁻⁴oʔ⁸⁻⁴siŋ¹* 'university student'. In this case, the negator *m⁵* is used to negate that he is a university student. In (3), *m⁵⁻⁴ si⁴* 'not be' is not followed by a noun phrase, but followed by the verb phrase *leʔ⁷⁻⁸ səʔ⁷⁻⁸ i¹* 'talking about him', to negate that we are talking about him.

As shown by the following example, *m⁵⁻⁴ si⁴* is often used alone to deny what someone else has said.

(4) A: 即張　　呀
　　　tsit⁷⁻⁸-tiũ¹　iaº
　　　this-CL　　SFP
　　　'It is this piece (of paper).'
　　B: 唔　　是，　即張　　　　發票
　　　m⁵⁻⁴　si⁴　tsit⁷⁻⁸-tiũ¹　huat⁷⁻⁸phio⁵
　　　not　be　this-CL　　　invoice
　　　'No, this piece (of paper) is the invoice.'

In (4), m^{5-4} si^4 in turn B is used to deny what has been said in turn A. In this use, m^{5-4} si^4 is usually followed by an explanation, such as the clause $tsit^{7-8}tiũ^1$ $huat^{7-8}phio^5$ 'this piece (of paper) is the invoice' in (4).

The negator m^5 can be used with some stative verbs such as the verb of cognition pat^7 別 'know' in (5).

(5) 儂　　唔　　　別　　汝
　　laŋ⁴　m⁵⁻⁴　pat⁷　luº
　　other　not　know　2SG
　　'She doesn't know you.'

In (5), the negator m^5 precedes the verb of cognition pat^7 'know' to negate the presupposition that the subject ('she') knows the addressee. In this case, it is a fact that the subject does not know the addressee, while the willingness of the subject is not involved.

Unlike the Mandarin general negative *bù* 不 'not', the negator m^5 in Hui'an is normally not used to negate an adjective, as illustrated by (6) and (7).

(6) Mandarin general negative *bù* 不 'not'
　　這　　朵　　花　　　不　　香
　　zhè　duǒ　huā　　bù　　xiāng
　　this　CL　flower　not　fragrant
　　'This flower is not fragrant.'

(7) Hui'an general negative m^5 唔 'not'
　　*即蕊　　　　花　　　唔　　　芳
　　tsit⁷⁻⁸-lui³⁻²　hue¹　m⁵⁻⁴　phaŋ¹
　　this-CL　　　flower　not　　fragrant
　　'This flower is not fragrant.'

In (6), the general negative *bù* 'not' in Mandarin can occur before the adjective *xiāng* 'fragrant', or before other adjectives, to negate the property of being fragrant, if not some other property. In (7), however, the general negative m^5 'not' in Hui'an cannot be used with the adjective *phaŋ¹* 'fragrant'. Another negator, bo^2 無 'not have', is often required for use with the category of the adjective (see the following section for details).

The following example shows that the adjective $tioʔ^8$ 著 'right' can be negated by m^5 'not'.

(8)　吗　著
　　　$\underline{m^{5\text{-}4}}$　$tioʔ^8$
　　　not　right
　　　'not right'

Note, however, that in earlier Southern Min (19th century), it is not uncommon for the general negative m^5 to negate adjectives (see Xu 2017 for details).

The negative marker m^5 can be used to negate modal auxiliary verbs. As mentioned above, when negating the modal auxiliary verb ai^5 愛 'want', the volitional negative $m^{5\text{-}4}ai^5$ 吗愛 is created, as in (9). The negative $m^{5\text{-}4}ai^5$ is originally the negative form of the verb ai^5 'like', expressing that someone does not like to do something, as illustrated by (10).

(9)　我　口　吗愛　抹
　　　gua^3　tse^5　$\underline{m^{5\text{-}4}\text{-}ai^{5\text{-}3}}$　$buaʔ^7$
　　　1SG　now　not-like　smear
　　　'I don't want to smear (it) on now.'

(10)　伊　吗愛　聽　儂　說　爸　其　否話
　　　i^1　$\underline{m^{5\text{-}4}\text{-}ai^{5\text{-}3}}$　$thiã^1$　$laŋ^4$　$səʔ^{7\text{-}8}$　pa^2　$e^{2\text{-}4}$　$phai^{3\text{-}2}\text{-}ue^5$
　　　3SG　not-like　hear　other　say　father　GEN　bad-word
　　　'She doesn't like hearing others speak ill of her father.'

In (9), someone is suggesting to use some skin products for the speaker, while the speaker does not want to use any at that point of time. In other words, $m^{5\text{-}4}ai^5$ is used to express that the speaker is momentarily not willing to use the skin products, rather than to express that the speaker does not like to use them. Note that the counterpart of the volitional negative $m^{5\text{-}4}ai^5$ in some other Southern Min varieties such as Taiwan has undergone fusion: $m + ai > mmai$ (cf. Chappell & Peyraube 2016b).

The negative marker m^5 is also used to negate the modal auxiliary verb $thaŋ^1$ 通 to form the general negative imperative $m^{5\text{-}4}thaŋ^1$ 唔通 'do not', as discussed below. The negator m^5 can also be used to negate the experiential aspect marker pat^7 八, expressing that someone has never done the given action before, as in (11).

(11)　唔八　　穿
　　　$m^{5\text{-}4}pat^{7\text{-}8}$　$tshiŋ^5$
　　　never　　wear
　　　'have never worn (the shirt)'

Note that Lien (2007) argues that the experiential aspect marker pat^4 八 in Southern Min developed from the lexeme pat^4 meaning 'know', as exemplified by (5) above.

13.3 Perfective negative *bo²* 無

This negative has at least four syntactic uses: it can (a) function as a negative existential and possessive verb; (b) precede a verb or an adjective, functioning as a negative adverb; (c) follow a verb functioning as a resultative complement; and (d) be used alone to negate a proposition.

As a verb, *bo²* typically expresses 'not exist', as in (12), or 'not possess', as in (13). In other words, *bo²* functions as the negative form of the verb u^4 有 'exist, possess'.

(12)　即搭　　　　無　　　　風
　　　$tsit^{7\text{-}8}\text{-}taʔ^7$　$\underline{bo^{2\text{-}4}}$　$huaŋ^1$
　　　this-LOC　not.have　wind
　　　'There is no wind here.'

(13)　我　　無　　　　鎖匙
　　　gua^3　$\underline{bo^{2\text{-}4}}$　$so^{3\text{-}2}si^2$
　　　1SG　not.have　key
　　　'I don't have the key.'

In (12), the verb *bo²* is preceded by the locative word $tsit^{7\text{-}8}taʔ^7$ 'here' and followed by the noun $huaŋ^1$ 'wind', indicating that the wind does not exist here. In (13), *bo²* is preceded by the first-person singular pronoun gua^3 and followed by the noun $so^{3\text{-}2}si^2$ 'key', meaning that I am not in possession of the key.

The verb *bo²* may also mean 'be short of', as illustrated by (14).

(14) 媽仔　　　　無　　　　目眉
　　 bã²-a⁰　　 *bo²⁻⁴*　　*bak⁸⁻⁴bai²*
　　 mother-NM　not.have　eyebrow
　　 'Mother hardly has any eyebrows.' (Literally: 'Mother does not have any eyebrows.')

Example (14) literally means that mother does not have any eyebrows. However, *bo²* is not used here in this literal meaning of the non-possession of eyebrows, but rather that she does not have thick or bushy eyebrows or simply that her eyebrows are not dark enough. In other words, *bo²* is used to show that the mother's eyebrows are lacking in a certain quantity or that their color does not reach a certain degree.

The following example shows that the verb *bo²* can appear in sentences expressing comparison of inferiority.

(15) 伊　　　無　　　　我　　　巧
　　 i¹　　 *bo²⁻⁴*　　*gua³*　 *khiau³*
　　 3SG　not.have　1SG　clever
　　 'He is not as smart as me.'

In (15), his cleverness does not achieve the degree that I have, that is, he is not as smart as me. In other words, *bo²* is used in comparison of inferiority, and thus can be interpreted as meaning 'inferior to'.

The verb *bo²* can also mean 'lose, disappear', as in (16).

(16) 喙齒　　　　　無　　　　去
　　 tshui⁵⁻³-khi³　*bo²*　　*khu⁰*
　　 mouth-tooth　not.have　PVC
　　 'His teeth are all gone.'

When followed by a dynamic verb, *bo²* is used for negating a presupposition from the context that an action or event has been carried out or has happened, as in (17). This can be compared with the use of the negator *m⁵* with the same dynamic verb, as in (18).

(17) 伊　　無　　　交
　　 i¹　 bo²⁻⁴　kau¹
　　 3SG not.have hand.in
　　 'He didn't hand (it) in.'

(18) 伊　　唔　　交
　　 i¹　 m⁵⁻⁴　kau¹
　　 3SG not　 hand.in
　　 'He refuses to hand (it) in.'

As shown by these two examples, *bo²* focuses on negating the belief/presupposition by the interlocutor (or from the context) that something has occurred, while *m⁵* focuses on negating the willingness of the subject to do something.

Example (17) with *bo²* is normally interpreted as a past event, that is, the event that he hands in the document has not happened before the speech time. However, the same clause can also be used for a future event, e.g. in a hypothetical context, as in (19) below which represents the first clause in a complex conditional sentence. Example (18) with *m⁵* is normally interpreted as a present event, as shown by the English translation. However, the use of *m⁵* is not restricted by the temporal context: it can also be used for a past event, as in (20), or a future event, as in (21).

(19) 伊　　明日　　　　若　　無　　　交
　　 i¹　 biã²⁻⁴let⁸　lã⁴　bo²⁻⁴　kau¹
　　 3SG tomorrow　 if　 not.have　hand.in
　　 'If he won't have handed (it) in tomorrow …'

(20) 伊　　昨日　　　唔　　　交
　　 i¹　 tsa⁴let⁸　m⁵⁻⁴　kau¹
　　 3SG yesterday not　 hand.in
　　 'He refused to hand (it) in yesterday.'

(21) 伊　　明日　　　　若　　唔　　　交
　　 i¹　 biã²⁻⁴let⁸　lã⁴　m⁵⁻⁴　kau¹
　　 3SG tomorrow　 if　 not　 hand.in
　　 'If he refuses to hand (it) in tomorrow…'

Similarly, *bo²* and *m⁵* can both occur with some stative verbs such as *tɔŋ²⁻⁴i⁵* 同意 'agree' in (22), where *bo²* indicates that Father did not agree with the suggestion as expected by everyone, while m^5 indicates that Father refuses to agree with the suggestion. Generally speaking, when Father refused to agree with the suggestion, it is also the case that he did not agree with the suggestion. However, bo^2 and m^5 are used to describe the event from different aspectual and modal perspectives.

(22) a. 爸仔　　　無　　　同意
　　　　pa^2-a^0　　$bo^{2\text{-}4}$　　$tɔŋ^{2\text{-}4}i^5$
　　　　father-NM　not.have　agree
　　　　'Father didn't agree (with the suggestion).'

　　　b. 爸仔　　　唔　　　同意
　　　　pa^2-a^0　　$m^{5\text{-}4}$　　$tɔŋ^{2\text{-}4}i^5$
　　　　father-NM　not　agree
　　　　'Father refuses/refused to agree (with the suggestion).'

The negator bo^2 can precede the modal auxiliary verb $thaŋ^1$ 倘 'can' to form the negative counterpart of the modal auxiliary verb $u^4thaŋ^1$ 有倘 'can', which expresses a series of modal meanings such as root possibility, permission and epistemic possibility (see the preceding chapter). Two examples of $bo^{2\text{-}4}$ $thaŋ^1$ are given in (23) and (24).

(23) 往日　　　　無倘　　　　　照相
　　　$ɔŋ^{3\text{-}2}let^8$　$bo^{2\text{-}4}$-$thaŋ^1$　$tsio^{5\text{-}3}siɔŋ^5$
　　　before　　not.have-can　take.pictures
　　　'(We) could not take pictures in former days.'

(24) 媽仔　　　無倘　　　　　與　　　我　　去
　　　$bã^2$-a^0　$bo^{2\text{-}4}$-$thaŋ^1$　$khɔ^{5\text{-}4}$　$gua^{3\text{-}2}$　$khɯ^5$
　　　mother-NM　not.have-can　give　1SG　go
　　　'Mother doesn't allow me to go (there).'

In (23), the speaker is talking about the lack of opportunity to take pictures in former days, due to lack of money or a photographer. In other words, $bo^{2\text{-}4}thaŋ^1$ is used to express the lack of the necessary external conditions for people to take pictures. This is a case of root possibility, also known as participant-external possibility (see §12.2.2 above). In (24), $bo^{2\text{-}4}thaŋ^1$ is used to denote permission, that is, the subject (mother) does not permit the speaker to go to some place.

Unlike Mandarin Chinese where adjectives are normally negated by the general negative *bù* 不 'not' (rather than the perfective negative *méi(yǒu)*没(有) 'there is not, not have'), adjectives in Hui'an are normally negated by the perfective negative *bo²* 'there is not, not have' (rather than the general negative *m⁵* 'not'), as illustrated by (25), where *bo²* modifies the adjective *ho³* 好 'good' and negates the existence of a state of good health.

(25) 身體　　無　　　好
　　 sen¹the³　bo²⁻⁴　ho³
　　 body　not.have　good
　　 'be in bad health'

The negative *bo²* can also be used to negate a verb complement construction, which either precedes the verb complement construction as in (26), or is inserted between the verb and its complement, as in (27) (see also §10.3.3).

(26) 無　　　看　　了
　　 bo²⁻⁴　khuã⁵⁻³　liau³
　　 not.have　look　finish
　　 '(We) didn't finish watching (the program).'

(27) 看　　　無　　　了
　　 khuã⁵⁻³　bo²⁻⁴　liau³
　　 look　not.have　finish
　　 '(We) didn't finish watching (the program).'

In (26), *bo²* is placed before the resultative verb complement construction *khuã⁵⁻³ liau³* 'finish watching'. In (27), *bo²* is inserted between the verb *khuã⁵* 'look, watch' and its resultative complement *liau³* 'finish'. In these two cases, the scope of negation is different: *bo²* in (26) negates the whole verb complement construction, whereas *bo²* in (27) negates only the resultative complement. However, they both describe the event that the people involved did not finish watching the program.

As mentioned above, *bo²* can follow a verb such as *khuã⁵* 看 'look' in (28) to function as its resultative complement.

(28) 看　　　無
　　 khuã⁵⁻³　bo²
　　 look　not.have
　　 '(I) didn't see (it).'

The negator *bo²* can also negate a proposition, as in (29), where the first *bo²* in turn B negates what turn A says.

(29) A: 逐年　　　(嗨也)　　招　　　儂
　　　tak⁸⁻⁴-lin²　bã⁴　　　tsio¹　laŋ²
　　　every-year　also　　　recruit　person
　　　'(They) recruit new people every year.'
　　B: 無　　　呀,　幾落　　　　年　　無　　　　招　　　咯
　　　bo²　　iaº　kui³⁻²lo⁸⁻⁴　lin²　bo²⁻⁴　　tsio¹　lɔº
　　　not.have　SFP　quite.a few　year　not.have　recruit　SFP
　　　'No, (they) have not recruited any new people for quite a few years.'

13.4 Imminent negative *bə⁵* 未

The negator *bə⁵* 'not yet' typically modifies a verb to denote that something has not yet happened, as in (30), or someone/something has not yet entered a state, as in (31).

(30) 未　　　　洗
　　 bə⁵⁻⁴　　sue³
　　 not.yet　wash
　　 'have not yet been washed'

(31) 水　　　未　　　　燒
　　 tsui³　*bə⁵⁻⁴*　　sio¹
　　 water　not.yet　hot
　　 'The water has not yet become hot.'

In (30), the negator *bə⁵* precedes the verb *sue³*, indicating that the clothes have not yet been washed. In (31), *bə⁵* modifies the adjective *sio¹*, meaning that the water has not yet entered a new state, that is, of being hot.

The negative marker *bə⁵* can be placed between a verb and its resultative complement to negate the outcome (result state), as in (32).

(32) 裝修　　　　未　　　　了
　　 tsɔŋ¹siu¹　*bə⁵⁻⁴*　　liau³
　　 renovate　not.yet　finish
　　 'The house renovation has not yet been finished.'

In (32), *bə⁵* is inserted between the verb *tsɔŋ¹siu¹* 'renovate' and its resultative complement *liau³* 'finished', denoting that the house renovation has not yet been finished. In other words, *bə⁵* is used to denote that an action or event has not yet achieved a certain result, which implies that more work is required.

The negative form *bə⁵* can also be used to negate the modal auxiliary verb *thaŋ¹* 通 to express 'cannot yet', as in (33).

(33) 未通　　　　摑　　挃
　　bə⁵⁻⁴-thaŋ¹　*kɔk⁸⁻⁴*　*sak⁷*
　　not.yet-can　throw　RVC
　　'(You) cannot throw (it) away yet.'

13.5 Irrealis negative *bue⁴* 燴

The morpheme *bue⁴*, being the negative form of the verb *e⁴* 會 'know, understand', can function as a verb meaning 'not know, not understand', as in (34).

(34) 我　　燴　　　　廣東話
　　gua³　*bue⁴*　*kŋ³⁻²taŋ¹ue⁵*
　　1SG　not.know　Cantonese
　　'I don't know Cantonese.'

As suggested by previous research on Southern Min, *bue⁴* may be a fused form of the negator *m⁵* (or *bo²*) and the verb *e⁴* 'know, understand' (cf. Li 2007; Lien 2015).

When followed by a verb phrase, *bue⁴* can function as a modal auxiliary verb, expressing inability to carry out an action or the unlikelihood of an event taking place (see also Chappell & Peyraube 2016b). Two examples are given in (35) and (36).

(35) 我　　燴　　　說　　　廣東話
　　gua³　*bue⁴*　*səʔ⁷⁻⁸*　*kŋ³⁻²taŋ¹ue⁵*
　　1SG　cannot　speak　Cantonese
　　'I cannot speak Cantonese.'

(36) 看勢　　　　　燴　　　落雨
　　khuã⁵⁻³-se⁵　*bue⁴*　*loʔ⁸⁻⁴-hɔ⁴*
　　look-situation　cannot　fall-rain
　　'It looks as if it won't rain.'

In (35), *bue⁴* encodes inability due to not having learned the language. In (36), *bue⁴* indicates the speaker's attitude towards a potential future event. In other words, in the speaker's opinion, it will not rain, a case of epistemic modality (see §12.2.5).

The following example provides an illustration of the negator *bue⁴* being inserted between a verb and its resultative complement, once again to code inability due to limited stomach capacity.

(37) 食　　繪　　了
　　 tsia$\mathit{?}^{8\text{-}4}$　*bue⁴*　liau³
　　 eat　cannot　finish
　　 'cannot finish (it)'

In (37), *bue⁴* denotes that the action denoted by *tsia?⁸* 'eat' cannot achieve the result of *liau³* 'finish'.

The negative marker *bue⁴* can also be used to negate adjectives, expressing the impossibility of existence of a state, as in (38). An example of adjective negated by the perfective negative *bo²* is given in (39) for comparison.

(38) 即領　　　繪　　否看
　　 tsit$^{7\text{-}8}$-liã³　*bue⁴*　phai$^{3\text{-}2}$-khuã⁵
　　 this-CL　cannot　bad-look
　　 'This (shirt) cannot look unstylish.'

(39) 即領　　　無　　好看
　　 tsit$^{7\text{-}8}$-liã³　*bo$^{2\text{-}4}$*　ho$^{3\text{-}2}$-khuã⁵
　　 this-CL　not.have　good-look
　　 'This (shirt) doesn't look good.'

The adjective *phai$^{3\text{-}2}$khuã⁵* 'bad looking' is the antonym of *ho$^{3\text{-}2}$khuã⁵* 'good looking', and 'good looking' is normally what people expect for a shirt. In this context, the negator *bue⁴* typically occurs with *phai$^{3\text{-}2}$khuã⁵*, as in (38), rather than the adjective *ho$^{3\text{-}2}$khuã⁵*, whereas the negator *bo²* is typically used with the adjective *ho$^{3\text{-}2}$khuã⁵*, as in (39), but not with the adjective *phai$^{3\text{-}2}$khuã⁵*. In other words, *bue⁴* tends to negate adjectives with a negative meaning, whereas *bo²* tends to negate the positive ones. In addition, the negative *bue⁴* in (38) negates the possibility of being unstylish or dowdy, while the negative *bo²* in (39) negates the existence of the state of being smart and presentable (of a shirt).

These two negators may modify the same adjective with different meanings, as illustrated by (40) and (41).

(40) 水　　　 繪　　 燒　 咯
　　 tsui³　 *bue⁴*　 sio¹　 lɔ⁰
　　 water　 cannot　 hot　 SFP
　　 'The water cannot be hot.'

(41) 水　　　 無　　　 燒　 咯
　　 tsui³　 *bo²⁻⁴*　 sio¹　 lɔ⁰
　　 water　 not.have　 hot　 SFP
　　 'The water is not hot.'

In (40), *bue⁴* precedes the adjective *sio¹* 'hot', meaning that the water is not hot and thus would be suitable for drinking. In (41), however, which belongs to a completely different context, *bo²⁻⁴ sio¹* means that the water is cold and thus not suitable for drinking.

The negator *bue⁴* can precede the modal auxiliary verb *thaŋ¹* 'can' to form the negative counterpart of the modal auxiliary compound verb *e⁴thaŋ¹* 會咁 'can', which often denotes root possibility. An example is given in (42), where the subject (he) cannot go into the house due to lack of a key (i.e. the external physical condition).

(42) 無　　　　 鎖匙　　　 繪咁　　　　 入去
　　 bo²⁻⁴　 *sɔ³⁻²si²*　 *bue⁴thaŋ¹*　 *liəp⁸khuɯ⁰*
　　 not.have　 key　　　　 cannot　　　 go.into
　　 '(He) has no key and cannot go into (the house).'

Similarly, *bue⁴tsue⁵* 繪做 'cannot', being the negative form of the modal auxiliary compound verb *e⁴tsue⁵* 會做 'can', normally denotes non-deontic possibility, as in (43), or permission, as in (44).

(43) 繪做　　　　 食　　　 辣其
　　 bue⁴tsue⁵⁻³　 *tsiaʔ⁸⁻⁴*　 *luaʔ⁸-e⁰*
　　 cannot　　　 eat　　　 spicy-NMLZ
　　 '(I) cannot eat spicy food.'

(44) 獪做　　入去
　　 bue⁴tsue⁵⁻³　liəp⁸khuu⁰
　　 cannot　　 go.into
　　 '(You) cannot enter (the room).'

In (43), the speaker cannot eat spicy food, due to a sore throat. In other words, *bue⁴tsue⁵* is used to express the unsuitability of eating spicy food due to an external physical circumstance. In (44), *bue⁴tsue⁵* is used to denote that the subject is not permitted to enter the room due to some regulation and is thus connected with lack of permission.

13.6 General prohibitive *baŋ¹* ~ *m⁵⁻⁴thaŋ¹* 毋通

The general negative imperative *baŋ¹* 'do not' often modifies an action verb phrase to express the wish to stop someone from doing something, as in (45), or to suggest that someone not do something, as in (46).

(45) (毋通)　　共　　我　　　挾
　　 baŋ¹　　 ka⁵⁻⁴　gua³⁻²　gueʔ⁷
　　 do.not　　 To　　1SG　　to.pincer
　　 'Don't refill my bowl!'

(46) (毋通)　　擱　　　　揀
　　 baŋ¹　　 kɔk⁸⁻⁴　sak⁷
　　 do.not　　 throw　　RVC
　　 'Don't throw (it) away.'

The context of example (45) is that the speaker is unhappy about the addressee refilling her bowl all the time. In this case, *baŋ¹* is used with the intention of stopping the addressee from refilling her bowl again. The context of (46) is that the family is organizing belongings to prepare for a move, during which the speaker finds some things that she wants to keep for the new house. In this context, *baŋ¹* is used to suggest to the addressee not to throw away the stuff. It is clear that the exact meaning of *baŋ¹* is determined by the context where it occurs but also the intonation of the speaker may play a role.

The negative *baŋ¹* is the fused form of *m⁵⁻⁴thaŋ¹* 毋通 'do not', which is composed of the general negative *m⁵* and the modal auxiliary verb *thaŋ¹*. The compound negative *m⁵⁻⁴thaŋ¹* is nonetheless still in use: in other words, the fused form *baŋ¹* in both (45) and (46) can be substituted by the compound form *m⁵⁻⁴thaŋ¹*. In addition, $m^{5\text{-}4}thaŋ^1$ has a variant form, which is $m^{5\text{-}4}baŋ^1$. In other words, the fusion process can be represented as $m^{5\text{-}4}thaŋ^1 > m^{5\text{-}4}baŋ^1 > baŋ^1$. Both the compound form and the fused form are also attested in other Southern Min varieties in Fujian (cf. Zhou 2006; Li 2007).

13.7 'Lack of necessity' imperatives $(m^{5\text{-}4})ben^3$ (唔)免

The negatives ben^3 免 and $m^{5\text{-}4}ben^3$ 唔免 mean that there is no need to do anything, as in (47) and (48).

(47) 恁　　 (唔)免　　 落去
　　 len^3　 $(m^{5\text{-}4})ben^{3\text{-}2}$　 $loʔ^8khw^0$
　　 2PL　 no.need　 go.down
　　 'You don't need to go down (there).'

(48) (唔)免　　 插　　 伊
　　 $(m^{5\text{-}4})ben^{3\text{-}2}$　 $tshap^7$　 i^0
　　 no.need　 bother　 3SG
　　 'There is no need to interfere./Leave it alone.'

In (47), the speaker is expressing her opinion that the addressees do not need to go down to a certain place. The context of (48) is that the speaker is unhappy about what her husband is doing with the chicken on the balcony. In this context, $m^{5\text{-}4}ben^3$ can be interpreted as functioning more politely to indirectly ask someone not to do something.

13.8 Injunctive negative $buan^3$

As described in Chappell & Peyraube (2016), the injunctive negative enjoins the addressees not to do an action, implying that the outcome might not be beneficial for them or that the action in itself is unwise. This negative is formed by the use of $buan^3$ in Hui'an, as in (49) and (50).

(49) 口　　 口　　 食　　 哦
　　 tse^2　 $buan^{3\text{-}2}$　 $tsiaʔ^8$　 o^0
　　 this　 need.not　 eat　 SFP
　　 'Don't eat this.'

(50) 無　　　生日　　　就　　　囗　　　過
　　　bo²⁻⁴　　sin¹let⁸　　tsiu⁵⁻⁴　buan³⁻²　kə⁵
　　　not.have　birthday　then　need.not　pass
　　　'If (you) don't have a birthday, then don't celebrate it.'

The context of example (49) is that a mother suggests to her daughter that she give up something and eat something better. In (50), the speaker is expressing her opinion that if you do not have a birthday, then it would be wise not to celebrate it.

The negative *buan³* may be a fused form, though its fusion process is still unclear. In Taiwan, the injunctive negative is expressed by $(m^{22})mo^{53}$ (cf. Chappell & Peyraube 2016). It seems that there is no correlation between the negative *buan³* in Hui'an and the negative $(m^{22})mo^{53}$ in Taiwan.

13.9 Summary

This chapter is concerned with negative forms. A comparatively large number of negative markers is attested in Hui'an: two general and volitional negatives m^5 唔 and $m^{5\text{-}4}ai^5$ 唔愛; an existential and perfective negative bo^2 無; the imminent negative $bə^5$ 未 'not yet'; the irrealis negative bue^4 燴 'not be able, unlikely'; the general prohibitive $baŋ^1$ 唔啴 and its unfused form $m^{5\text{-}4}thaŋ^1$ 唔啴; the 'lack of necessity' negatives $(m^{5\text{-}4})ben^3$ (唔)免 'do not need' and the injunctive negative *buan³* 'best not to, should not'. Some of these negative forms, such as $m^{5\text{-}4}ai^5$, bue^4 and $baŋ^1{\sim}m^{5\text{-}4}thaŋ^1$, function as either adverbs or modal auxiliary verbs.

The negative m^5 唔 functions as a general negative and often expresses lack of volition on the agent's part to carry out an action, whereas $m^{5\text{-}4}ai^5$ 唔愛, functions as a volitional negative. Unlike Mandarin Chinese, adjectives in Hui'an are normally not negated by the general negative m^5, but are negated by the perfective negative bo^2, by the imminent negative $bə^5$ 未 'not yet', or by the irrealis negative bue^4.

The perfective negative bo^2 has at least four syntactic uses: (a) it functions as a negative existential and possessive verb; (b) it can precede a verb or an adjective, functioning as a negative adverb; (c) it can follow a verb functioning as a resultative complement; and (d) it can be used alone to negate a proposition.

The imminent negative $bə^5$ denotes that something has not yet happened, or someone/something has not yet entered into a state. The irrealis negative bue^4 can function as a verb meaning 'not know', 'not understand', or as a modal auxiliary verb expressing inability to carry out an action or the unlikelihood of an event taking place.

The general prohibitive *baŋ¹* 'do not' is the fused form of *m⁵⁻⁴thaŋ¹* 唔通 'do not', which is composed of the general negative *m⁵* and the modal auxiliary verb *thaŋ¹*. The 'lack of necessity' imperatives *ben³* 免 and *m⁵⁻⁴ben³* 唔免 express that there is no need to do anything. The injunctive negative *buan³* enjoins the addresses not to do an action, implying that the outcome might not be beneficial for them or that the action in itself is unwise.

14 Adpositions

14.1 Introduction

Adpositions refer to functional or grammatical words which occur before or after a noun phrase and mark the grammatical or semantic relationship of that noun phrase to the predicate head in the sentence (cf. Dryer 2005; Hagège 2010). When occurring before a noun phrase, the adposition is termed 'preposition', such as the English preposition *on* in *I put an egg on the kitchen table*: *on* occurs before the noun phrase *the kitchen table*. While the adposition occurring after a noun phrase is called a 'postposition', such as the classical Latin postposition *–cum* in *mecum* 'with me' (lit. 'me with'). A less common type is the circumposition, which involves two or more parts, positioned on both sides of the noun phrase, such as English *from ... on* in *from now on*.

Whether there exist postpositions and circumpositions in Chinese is a controversial question in the field of Chinese linguistics. For example, Liu (2003a) argues that there exist both types, and points out that postpositions in Chinese include grammaticalized *fāngwèicí* 方位詞 (localizer) and attributive markers such as *de* 的. Sun (2008), however, argues that there are neither postpositions nor circumpositions in Standard Modern Chinese, and that the monosyllabic localizers are actually NP enclitics, rather than postpositions. We basically agree with Liu (2003a) that some localizers in Mandarin Chinese may function like postpositions.[1] In this chapter, however, we will focus on prepositions in Hui'an.

Generally speaking, prepositions are not commonly used in daily conversation in Hui'an, when compared with prepositions in Mandarin Chinese. Many noun phrases which have to be introduced by a preposition in Mandarin Chinese can be used without any marking in Hui'an, as will be demonstrated in the following sections. The prepositions commonly used in Hui'an are given in Table 14-1 below.

---

1 However, we doubt that their counterparts in Hui'an can also be interpreted as postpositions, which will be addressed in a separate paper.

Tab. 14-1: Prepositions in the Hui'an dialect

		Prepositions	Verbal Sense
Spatial and temporal relation	location	tu⁴/ti⁴ 佇	be at
		le?⁷ 咧	(unclear)
		tu⁴/ti⁴le?⁷ 佇咧	be at
		lã⁵	stay
	source	an⁵ 按	stay
		iɔŋ⁵/iŋ⁵ 用	use
	goal	kau⁵ 遘	arrive
Patient		ka⁵ 共	share
		lia?⁸ 掠	catch
		an⁵ 按	stay
		tsiɔŋ¹ 將	take
Agent in passive		khɔ⁵ 與	give
Benefactive		ka⁵ 共	share
		thue⁵ 替	substitute for
		ui⁵ 為	do
Comitative		ka?⁷ 合	take care
		kiau¹ 交	add in
Comparative standard		pi³ 比	compare
Instrument		iŋ⁵ 用	use
		an⁵ 按	stay
Basis		an⁵ 按	stay
		tsiau⁵ 照	(unclear)
		tsue⁵ 做	do

14.2 Spatial and temporal relations

14.2.1 Location

In Hui'an, the prepositions indicating the location of a person, an object or an action in space include *le?⁷* 咧[2], *tu⁴~ti⁴* 佇[3], *tu⁴le?⁷* (or *ti⁴le?⁷*) 佇咧 and *lã⁵*. The first

---

[2] The character 咧 can be found in previous works such as Zhou (2006), while Li (2000) uses the character 嘞 instead.

[3] In some previous works such as Li (2000) and Zhou (2006), the morpheme corresponding to the character 佇 'be at' is regarded as the lexical source of *tu⁴/ti⁴* < 'be at', while other previous works such as Yang (1991) uses the character 著 'touch' (see also Li 2000:124-125 for details).

three prepositions occupy the same position in the sentence: the prepositional phrase in which they occur can either precede or follow a verb phrase. However, *leʔ⁷* is the most commonly used, while *tuɯ⁴* or *ti⁴* and *tuɯ⁴leʔ⁷*(or *ti⁴leʔ⁷*) are not common nowadays. In the following, we take *leʔ⁷* as an example.

(1) 買　　咧　　對面
    bue³　leʔ⁷⁻⁸　tui⁵⁻³ben⁵
    buy　 at　 opposite
    '(They) bought (a house) opposite ours.'

(2) 阮　　　媽仔　　　咧　　　涼臺　　　咧　　　洗　　　菜
    gun³⁻²　bã²-a⁰　(leʔ⁷⁻⁸)　iɔŋ²⁻⁴tai²　leʔ⁷⁻⁸　sue³⁻²　tshai⁵
    1PL　 mother-NM　(at)　 balcony　 PROG　 wash　 vegetable
    'My mother is washing vegetables on the balcony.'

In (1), the prepositional phrase *leʔ⁷⁻⁸ tui⁵⁻³ben⁵* 'in the opposite' is preceded by the verb *bue³* 'buy', while the prepositional phrase *leʔ⁷⁻⁸ iɔŋ²⁻⁴tai²* 'on the balcony' in (2) is followed by the verb phrase *leʔ⁷⁻⁸ sue³⁻² tshai⁵* 'washing vegetables'. Note that the second occurrence of *leʔ⁷* in (2) is a marker of progressive aspect, indicating that the action of washing vegetables is ongoing at the speech time, and is undoubtedly related diachronically to the locative use (see §11.3.1). In terms of semantic meanings, the prepositional phrase that occurs after a verb phrase tends to indicate the destination or final location of a person or an object as the outcome of an event, e.g. the prepositional phrase *leʔ⁷⁻⁸ tui⁵⁻³ben⁵* in (1) above denotes the location of the house they bought, and the action of buying the house is independent of its location. The prepositional phrase that occurs before a verb phrase, however, tends to indicate the location in which an action or event takes place, e.g. the prepositional phrase *leʔ⁷⁻⁸ iɔŋ²⁻⁴tai²* in (2) denotes the location of the action of washing vegetables, that is, the action of washing the vegetables is taking place on the balcony and is not independent of the location. The meaning contrast induced by different orders for the *leʔ⁷* phrase can be explained by the principle of temporal sequence: the location of the family or persons referred to by 'they' is determined after the action of buying the new house they will live in, while it is necessary for one to be on the balcony before washing the vegetables there (cf. Tai 1985).

These three prepositions can be attested in other Southern Min varieties with subtle differences in their syntactic distributions. For example, in Quanzhou, the preposition *tuɯ⁴* can occur both before and after the verb phrase, while *leʔ⁷* and *tuɯ⁴leʔ⁷* can only occur after the verb phrase (cf. Li 2000:124).

In fact, the prepositional phrase occurring before a verb phrase as in (2) above is not common in Hui'an. The preposition *leʔ⁷* in (2) can be omitted, i.e. forming *gun³⁻² bã²a⁰ iɔŋ²⁻⁴tai² leʔ⁷⁻⁸ sue³⁻² tshai⁵* (lit. 'my mother balcony PROG wash vegetable'). In this case, the locative word *iɔŋ²⁻⁴tai²* 'balcony' functions as a sub-topic (see chapter 20). In other words, in Hui'an, the locative word denoting the location of an action or event is normally used alone (without a preposition) in preverbal position.

As shown above, the preposition 佇 in Hui'an has two pronunciations, i.e. *tu⁴* and *ti⁴*. In other Southern Min varieties, however, 佇 normally has only one pronunciation, e.g. *tu⁴* is used in Quanzhou, while *ti⁴* is attested in Xiamen, Zhangzhou and Taiwan. The lexeme *tu⁴~ ti⁴* has its source in a verb meaning 'be at', as in (3) and (4) below, where the verb *tu⁴/ti⁴* is followed by the locative deictic *tsit⁷⁻⁸taʔ⁷* 即搭 'here' in (3), and preceded by the negator *bo²* 無 'not have' in (4). Note that this usage is very common in the current Hui'an dialect, and represents its most common function.

(3) 冊包　　　佇　　　即搭
　　 tsheʔ⁷⁻⁸-pau¹　*tu⁴/ti⁴*　*tsit⁷⁻⁸-taʔ⁷*
　　 book-bag　be.at　this-LOC
　　 'The schoolbag is here.'

(4) 伊　　無　　　佇
　　 i¹　*bo²⁻⁴*　*tu⁴/ti⁴*
　　 3SG　not.have　be.at
　　 'He is not here.'

Similarly, *tu⁴leʔ⁰* (or *ti⁴leʔ⁰*) in Hui'an is often used as a verb meaning 'be at', as in (5), where the verb *tu⁴leʔ⁰* is used in a Yes-No polar question.

(5) 阿三　　有　　佇咧　　　無
　　 a¹sã¹　*u⁴*　*tu⁴leʔ⁰*　*bo⁰*
　　 PN　　have　be.at　　SFP
　　 'Is Ah-San there?'

Note that when followed by a locative as in (3) above, the verb *tu⁴~ti⁴* is more commonly used than *tu⁴leʔ⁰* (or *ti⁴leʔ⁰*), while when used alone, the verb *tu⁴leʔ⁰* (or *ti⁴leʔ⁰*) is more often used than *tu⁴~ti⁴*.

In Quanzhou and Xiamen, the prepositional phrase containing *leʔ⁷*, *tu⁴~ti⁴* and *tu⁴leʔ⁷* (or *ti⁴leʔ⁷*) also denotes the location of an action or event in time, as in (6), an example from Xiamen (cf. Li 2000:124; Zhou and Ouyang 1998:381).

(6) The preposition *ti⁶* 佇 in Xiamen: denoting the location of an event in time

	伊	佇	舊年	八九月	破病
	i¹	ti⁶⁻⁵	kuʔ⁶⁻⁵-ni²	pueʔ⁷⁻³-kau³⁻¹-geʔ⁸	phua⁵⁻³pĩ⁶
	3SG	at	old-year	eight-nine-month	get.sick

'He got sick last August or September.' (Zhou and Ouyang 1998:381)

In (6), the prepositional phrase *ti⁶⁻⁵ kuʔ⁶⁻⁵ni² pueʔ⁷⁻³kau³⁻¹geʔ⁸* 'last August or September' indicates the time when the event *phua⁵⁻³pĩ⁶* 'get sick' happens.

In Hui'an, however, temporal words and phrases are typically used alone without an adposition, functioning as a subtopic in a sentence, as illustrated by (7) for the temporal phrase *ku⁵⁻⁴lin² pueʔ⁷⁻⁸kau³⁻²gəʔ⁸* 'last August or September'.

(7) The temporal phrase used alone without an adposition in Hui'an

	伊	舊年	八九月	破病
	i¹	ku⁵⁻⁴-lin²	pueʔ⁷⁻⁸-kau³⁻²-gəʔ⁸	phua⁵⁻³pin⁵
	3SG	old-year	eight-nine-month	get.sick

'He got sick last August or September.'

Unlike the prepositions *leʔ⁷*, *tu⁴~ti⁴* and *tu⁴leʔ⁷* (or *ti⁴leʔ⁷*), which are found in both preverbal and postverbal positions, the preposition *lã⁵* occurs only before a verb phrase, as in (8), where the prepositional phrase *lã⁵⁻⁴ tsit⁷⁻⁸kuin¹* 'in this (room)' precedes the verb *khun⁵* 睏 'sleep', denoting the location of the action *khun⁵* 'sleep'. Note that this preposition can also be omitted.

(8)

	我	口	即間	睏
	gua³	(lã⁵⁻⁴)	tsit⁷⁻⁸-kuin¹	khun⁵
	1SG	(at)	this-CL	sleep

'I sleep in this (room).'

This preposition is also attested in other Southern Min varieties such as Quanzhou and Shantou (cf. Li 2000:126; Shi 2000:164-166). As with the Hui'an dialect, *lã⁵* in Quanzhou is typically followed by a locative noun or deictic to form a prepositional phrase, and occurs in preverbal position. In Shantou, however, this preposition occurs both before and after a verb phrase, forming both location and time phrases.

The preposition $lã^5$ is originally a verb meaning 'stay', which can be followed by a locative word, as in (9), or used alone, as in (10), where $lã^5$ takes the locative object $tshu^{5\text{-}3}lai^4$ 厝裡 'home'.

(9) 口　　厝裡
    $lã^{5\text{-}4}$　$tshu^{5\text{-}3}\text{-}lai^4$
    stay　house-inside
    'stay at home'

(10) 汝　　卜　　　口，　汝　　家　　　口　　咧
     lu^3　$boʔ^{7\text{-}8}$　$lã^5$　lu^3　$kai^{5\text{-}4}$　$lã^5$　$leʔ^0$
     2SG　want　stay　2SG　self　stay　DUR
     'Stay by yourself, if you want to stay here.'

14.2.2 Source

The prepositions denoting the source in space or time include an^5 按 and $iɔŋ^5/iŋ^5$ 用, among which an^5 is more commonly used than $iɔŋ^5/iŋ^5$. The preposition an^5 can indicate the source in space (i.e. the starting place), as in (11), or indicate the source in time (i.e. the starting point in time), as in (12).

(11) 按　　北京　　　　帶　　來
     $an^{5\text{-}3}$　$pak^{7\text{-}8}kiã^1$　tua^5　lai^0
     from　PN　　　　bring　come
     '(I) brought (it) from Beijing.'

(12) 按　　舊年　　　　開始　　　工作
     $an^{5\text{-}3}$　$ku^{5\text{-}4}\text{-}lin^2$　$khai^1si^{3\text{-}2}$　$kaŋ^1tsɔk^7$
     from　old-year　start　work
     'begin to work from last year'

In (11), the preposition an^5 introduces the place from which I brought something. In (12), the temporal word $ku^{5\text{-}4}lin^2$ 'last year', preceded by the preposition an^5, denotes the time of commencement for $kaŋ^1tsɔk^7$ 'work'. As shown by these two examples, the prepositional phrase an^5 occupies a preverbal position, noting that it may be omitted in both cases.

In Hui'an, an^5 is a multifunctional morpheme: it not only denotes the source in space or time as in (11) and (12) above, but also takes on other functions, as will be shown in the following (§14.2.4 and 14.3). This preposition is also attested in other Southern Min varieties such as Xiamen and Quanzhou (Li 2000; Zhou 2006). In addition, Li (2000:127) mentions that the morpheme, cognate with an^5 can function as a verb meaning 'stay' in the suburban areas of Quanzhou, which may suggest that the preposition an^5 is probably derived from this use.

Unlike an^5, the preposition $iɔŋ^5/iŋ^5$ is normally used to introduce a locative source, as illustrated by (13) and (14).

(13) 用   北京   倒來
    $iɔŋ^{5\text{-}4}/iŋ^{5\text{-}4}$ $pak^{7\text{-}8}kiã^1$ to^5lai^0
    from   PN   come.back
    'come back from Beijing'

(14) 用   即搭   去   泉州
    $iɔŋ^{5\text{-}4}/iŋ^{5\text{-}4}$ $tsit^{7\text{-}8}\text{-}taʔ^7$ $khuɯ^{5\text{-}3}$ $tsuan^{2\text{-}4}tsiu^1$
    from   this-LOC   go   PN
    'go to Quanzhou from here'

As with an^5, the prepositional phrase to which $iɔŋ^5/iŋ^5$ belongs is placed before the verb phrase, such as to^5lai^0 'come back' in (13) and $khuɯ^{5\text{-}3}$ $tsuan^{2\text{-}4}tsiu^1$ 'go to Quanzhou' in (14). Note that in these two examples the preposition $iɔŋ^5/iŋ^5$ is omissible.

In his study on prepositions in Southern Min, Li (2000:126) also remarks on the special use of the preposition $iŋ$ in Hui'an denoting the source. Hence, this usage may be distinctive of the Hui'an dialect, while it is probably derived from the verb $iŋ^5$ 用 meaning 'use', as in (15).

(15) 錢   我   用   了   咯
    $tsin^2$ gua^3 $iŋ^{5\text{-}4}$ $liau^3$ $lɔ^0$
    money   1SG   use   finish   SFP
    'I have used up the money.'

As will be mentioned in the following, the preposition an^5 in Hui'an can be used to introduce an instrument, which is also a function of the preposition $iŋ^5$. This means that the prepositions an^5 and $iŋ^5$ in Hui'an overlap in at least these two of their functions – those of denoting the source and instrument. Thus, it is not impossible that the use of the preposition $iŋ^5$ to code source is derived from its use as a verb meaning 'use', though this may be uncommon in other languages (cf. Heine & Kuteva 2002).

As shown above, the preposition 用 in Hui'an has another pronunciation, i.e. $ioŋ^5$. This pronunciation is typically used by the younger generation and thus may be a reading pronunciation, since it is closer to that of Mandarin. Note also that this pronunciation has been attested in Zhangzhou (Zhou 2006:444).

14.2.3 Goal

In this section, we will focus on prepositions introducing the goal in space or time: $leʔ^7$ 咧 and kau^5 遘. As mentioned in §14.2.1, when following a verb phrase, the prepositional phrase where $leʔ^7$ occurs can denote the location of a person or an object, independent of the action, as illustrated by example (1) above, which focuses on the stative location of a house. In other cases, however, the preposition $leʔ^7$ is used to indicate the spatial goal of an action, as in (16) below, where the locative word $et^{7-8}tiɔŋ^1$ 一中 'No.1 Middle School' is the goal of the action $khɔ̃^3$ 考 'take an exam'.

(16) 考 咧 一中
 $khɔ̃^3$ $leʔ^{7-8}$ et^{7-8}-$tiɔŋ^1$
 take.exam To one-middle.school
 '(He) enters the No.1 Middle School by taking an entrance exam.'

Similarly, when following a verb phrase, kau^5 遘, originally a verb meaning 'arrive', can function as a preposition introducing the spatial goal of the action, $peʔ^7$ (足百) 'climb', as in (17), that is, to reach $pueʔ^{7-8}lau^2$ 八樓 'the eighth floor'.

(17) (足百) 遘 八樓
 $peʔ^7$ kau^{5-3} $pueʔ^{7-8}$-lau^2
 climb arrive eight-floor
 'climb to the eighth floor'

As shown by the following example, when following a verb phrase, the preposition kau^5 can also introduce the goal in time, that is, the endpoint in time.

(18) 拖 遘 明年
 $thua^1$ kau^{5-3} $buã^{2-4}$-lin^2
 delay arrive next-year
 'delay until next year'

The phrase consisting of *kau⁵* and a locative or temporal word can also occur before a verb phrase, as illustrated by (19) and (20).

(19) 遘　　樓骹　　拄　　著
　　 kau⁵⁻³　lau²⁻⁴khaˡ　tu³　tioʔ⁰
　　 arrive　downstairs　meet　PVC
　　 '(I) ran into (him) when (I) arrived downstairs.'

(20) 撮　　菜　　遘　　明日　　　　否食　　　　咯
　　 tsuai²　tshai⁵　kau⁵⁻³　biã²⁻⁴let⁸　phai³⁻²-tsiaʔ⁸　lɔ⁰
　　 these　dish　arrive　tomorrow　bad-eat　SFP
　　 'These dishes will taste bad, if they are left until tomorrow.'

Unlike example (17) above, the preposition *kau⁵* in (19) does not introduce the spatial goal of the event, encoded by its following verb phrase *tu³ tioʔ⁰* 'run into (someone)' but rather where the chance encounter takes place. In fact, *kau⁵* can be interpreted as introducing the spatial goal for an implied motion event of the subject, while at the same time denoting the location where the event of running into someone takes place. In (20), *kau⁵* introduces a goal in time (i.e. *biã²⁻⁴let⁸* 'tomorrow') for the event 'keeping the dishes uneaten', which in turn functions as the reference time for describing the state of the dishes, that is, the dishes will taste bad. It is clear that the phrase consisting of *kau⁵* and a locative or temporal word bears different semantic properties when following and preceding a verb phrase. In the case of preceding a verb phrase, such as in (19) and (20), *kau⁵* seems to function more like a verb, rather than a preposition.

A typical example of *kau⁵* as a verb is given in (21).

(21) 儂　　　遘，　　檔案　　　　未　　　　遘
　　 laŋ²　kau⁵　tɔŋ⁵⁻³an⁵　bə⁵⁻⁴　kau⁵
　　 person　arrive　archive　not.yet　arrive
　　 'The person has arrived, but the archive has not yet arrived.'

14.2.4 Perlative

As mentioned in §14.2.2, the preposition *an⁵* can be used to introduce a source in space or time. The following example, however, shows that *an⁵* can also introduce the place where someone or something passes through, known as a perlative use.

(22) 按   門口   經過
     <u>an⁵⁻³</u> bŋ²⁻⁴-khau³   kiŋ¹kə⁵
     from   door-mouth   pass
     'pass through the door'

In (22), the prepositional phrase *an⁵⁻³ bŋ²⁻⁴khau³* 'from the door' occurs before the verb *kiŋ¹kə⁵* 'pass' denoting the place through which someone passes, rather than the source or goal in space.

14.3 Patient

In Mandarin Chinese, a patient is normally introduced by the prepositions *bǎ* 把 and *jiāng* 將, with a structure of '(NP_AGENT +) *bǎ/jiāng* + NP_PATIENT + VP', as in (23) and (24).

(23) Mandarin Chinese: (NP_AGENT +) *bǎ* + NP_PATIENT + VP
     把   門   關   上
     bǎ   mén   guān   shang
     OM   door   close   up
     'Close the door.'

(24) Mandarin Chinese: (NP_AGENT +) *jiāng* + NP_PATIENT + VP
     他   將   錢   交   給   了   我
     tā   jiāng   qián   jiāo   gěi   le   wǒ
     3SG   OM   money   hand.over   give   PFV   1SG
     'He has handed over the money to me.'

In (23), the patient *mén* 'door' is preceded by the preposition *bǎ*, and the prepositional phrase *bǎ mén* occurs before the verb phrase *guān shang* 'close up'. Similarly, the patient *qián* 'money' in (24) is introduced by the preposition *jiāng*, and the prepositional phrase *jiāng qián* is followed by the verb phrase *jiāo gěi le wǒ* 'have handed over to me'. Sentences involving a preposition introducing a patient (also called 'patient marker' or 'object marker') such as *bǎ* and *jiāng* in (23) and (24) are termed *chǔzhìshì* 處置式 'disposal constructions' (or 'object marking constructions') in Chinese linguistics (cf. Wang 1984b). The preposition *jiāng* is more formal than *bǎ* in contemporary Mandarin Chinese.

In Hui'an, however, a patient is typically used alone as a subtopic without any adposition, as in (25), where the patient, *bŋ²* 門 'door', is preceded by the subject *gua³* 我 'I' and followed by the verb phrase *kuin¹ liau³* 關了 'have closed'.

This construction has the form SOV (see chapter 20 for more details on patients as subtopics in SOV constructions).

(25) The Hui'an dialect: the patient used alone without an adposition
我　　門　　關　　了　　咯
gua³　bŋ²　kuin¹　liau³　lɔ⁰
1SG　door　close　finish　SFP
'I have closed the door.'

This does not mean that there are no overt markers introducing a patient in Hui'an. In fact, there is a series of such prepositions, e.g. *ka⁵* 共, *liaʔ⁸* 搦, *an⁵* 按 and *tsiɔŋ¹* 將, of which *ka⁵*, *liaʔ⁸* and *an⁵* are used in daily conversation, while *tsiɔŋ¹* is mainly found via elicitation. Furthermore, *ka⁵* is much more common than *liaʔ⁸* and *an⁵*. The prepositional phrase containing these four prepositions is consistently placed before the verb phrase, as will be shown by the examples below.

Unlike Mandarin Chinese, the object marking construction with the preposition *ka⁵* in Hui'an normally involves a structure of '(NP_AGENT +) NP_PATIENT + *ka⁵* + *i¹*(3SG) + VP', as in (26).

(26) The Hui'an dialect: (NP_AGENT +) NP_PATIENT + *ka⁵* + *i¹*(3SG) + VP
門　　共　　伊　　關　　(起來)
bŋ²　ka⁵⁻⁴　i¹　kuin¹　khai⁰
door　OM　3SG　close　RVC
'Close the door.'

In (26), the patient *bŋ²* 'door' occurs before the preposition *ka⁵* functioning as a topic, and the third person singular pronoun *i¹* follows the preposition *ka⁵*, serving as a resumptive pronoun referring to the patient *bŋ²* 'door'. This corresponds to one of the five types of 'disposal' or object marking construction identified in Chappell (2007, 2013). Note that *ka⁵⁻⁴ i¹* has a contracted form, i.e. *ka¹*, which adopts the tone of the pronoun *i¹*. Syntactically speaking, *ka⁵* is used to introduce the pronoun *i¹*, which is co-referential with the patient (syntactically the topic) *bŋ²*. Thus, *ka⁵* is regarded as a preposition, rather than as a postposition.

The patient noun phrase can also be placed after the preposition *ka⁵*, as in (27), where the patient noun *bŋ²* 門 'door' occurs after *ka⁵*. Note, however, that this is seldom used in daily conversation, though it is acceptable.

(27) The Hui'an dialect: (NP_{AGENT} +) *ka⁵* + NP_{PATIENT} + VP
 共   門   關   (起來)
 ka⁵⁻⁴ *bŋ²* *kuin¹* *khai⁰*
 OM   door   close   RVC
 'Close the door.'

The preposition *ka⁵* may even co-occur with the preposition *tsiɔŋ¹* in the same sentence, as in (28).

(28) The Hui'an dialect: (NP_{AGENT} +) *tsiɔŋ¹* + NP_{PATIENT} + *ka⁵* + *i¹*(3SG) + VP
 將   門   共   伊   關   (起來)
 tsiɔŋ¹ *bŋ²* *ka⁵⁻⁴* *i¹* *kuin¹* *khai⁰*
 OM   door   OM   3SG   close   RVC
 'Close the door.'

In (28), the patient noun *bŋ²* 'door' is introduced by the preposition *tsiɔŋ¹*, and the resumptive pronoun *i¹*, being co-referential with the patient noun *bŋ²*, is introduced by the preposition *ka⁵*.

Finally, in a fourth variation of the disposal construction, we find the preposition *tsiɔŋ¹* used alone, with a structure of '(NP_{AGENT} +) *tsiɔŋ¹* + NP_{PATIENT} +VP', as illustrated by (29). Note that *tsiɔŋ¹* has a similar use in more formal registers of Mandarin Chinese.

(29) The Hui'an dialect: (NP_{AGENT} +) *tsiɔŋ¹* + NP_{PATIENT} + VP
 將   門   關   (起來)
 tsiɔŋ¹ *bŋ²* *kuin¹* *khai⁰*
 OM   door   close   RVC
 'Close the door.'

Note that *ka⁵* is a multifunctional morpheme (see chapter 16 for more details). This morpheme is also attested in quite a large number of other Southern Min varieties such as Xiamen, Quanzhou and Zhangzhou, and in the Eastern Min variety of Fuzhou (see Chappell 2007, 2013). There are evidently subtle differences in pronunciation, e.g. it is pronounced as *ka⁶* in Zhangzhou and *kaŋ⁵* in Quanzhou (cf. Wang and Zhang 1994:137; Zhou 2006:459; Yang 1991:259).

The prepositions *liaʔ⁸* and *an⁵* can be attested in daily conversations in the contemporary Hui'an dialect, though they are less common than the preposition *ka⁵*. These two prepositions are placed before the patient noun phrase, like Mandarin Chinese, as illustrated by (30) and (31).

(30) The Hui'an dialect: (NP_AGENT +) *liaʔ⁸* + NP_PATIENT + VP
　　搦　　我　　　罵
　　liaʔ⁸⁻⁴　*gua³⁻²*　*bã⁵*
　　OM　　1SG　　scold
　　'(He) scolded me.'

(31) The Hui'an dialect: (NP_AGENT +) *an⁵* + NP_PATIENT + VP
　　按　　　所有　　　　問　　清楚
　　an⁵⁻³　*sɔ³⁻²u⁴*　*bŋ⁵⁻⁴*　*tshiŋ¹tshɔ³*
　　OM　　all　　　　ask　　clear
　　'Make all things clear.'

In (30), the patient *gua³* follows the preposition *liaʔ⁸*, and the prepositional phrase *liaʔ⁸⁻⁴ gua³* occurs before the verb *bã⁵* 'scold'. This example shows that the object marking construction with the preposition *liaʔ⁸* can involve a bare verb (such as the verb *bã⁵*). This is not acceptable in most object marking constructions in Chinese (see also Teng 1982). For example, object marking constructions in Mandarin Chinese require a more complex verb phrase such as *guān shang* 'close up' in (23) and *jiāo gěi le wǒ* 'have handed over to me' in (24), rather than a bare verb. In (31), the patient noun *sɔ³⁻²u⁴* 'all' is preceded by another preposition with the same function, *an⁵*, and this prepositional phrase *an⁵⁻³ sɔ³⁻²u⁴* occurs before the verb phrase *bŋ⁵⁻⁴ tshiŋ¹tshɔ³* 'make clear'.

As shown by the following two examples, *liaʔ⁸* has its source in a verb meaning 'catch, take'. Notably, it can be found in early Southern Min texts such as the 16th century *Li Jing Ji* operas in this very function of an object marker (see Lai 2019), as also exemplified by (30) above.

(32) 明日　　　　　　搦　　　去　　　賣　　　揀
　　biã²⁻⁴let⁸　*liaʔ⁸*　*khɯ⁵⁻³*　*bue⁴*　*sak⁷*
　　tomorrow　　catch　　go　　　sell　　RVC
　　'Take (the chicken) to sell (it) tomorrow.'

(33) 伊　　說　　　　搦　　　幾落　　　　　個
　　i¹　*səʔ⁷⁻⁸*　*liaʔ⁸*　*kui³⁻²loʔ⁸⁻⁴*　*e²*
　　3SG　say　　　catch　　quite.a few　　CL
　　'He said quite a few (persons) have been caught.'

The verb *liaʔ⁸* can be used without restrictions with a patient noun denoting animals such as the chicken in (32), or with a patient noun denoting persons as in (33).

14.4 Agent

The preposition used to introduce an agent in Hui'an passives is *khɔ⁵* 與, as in (34).

(34) NP_PATIENT + *khɔ⁵* 與 + NP_AGENT + VP
冊　　與　　儂　　買　　去
tsheʔ⁷　khɔ⁵⁻⁴　laŋ⁴　bue³　khuɨ⁰
book　give　other　buy　RVC
'The book has been bought by other people.'

In (34), *khɔ⁵*, originally a verb meaning 'give', functions as a passive marker (or agent marker) introducing the agent *iⁱ* 'he'. Note that the agent here cannot be omitted, that is, the preposition *khɔ⁵* in Hui'an cannot be used in agentless passives. This is different from the preposition *bèi* 被 in Mandarin Chinese, which by way of contrast can be so used, as in (35).

(35) The agentless passive in Mandarin Chinese: NP_PATIENT + *bèi* 被 + VP
房子　　被　　燒　　了
fángzi　bèi　shāo　le
house　PASS　burn　PFV
'The house was burnt down.'

An example of *khɔ⁵* as a 'give' verb is given in (36).

(36) 與　　伊　　蜀　　分　　錢
khɔ⁵　i⁰　tsit⁸⁻⁴　hun¹　tsin²
give　3SG　one　cent　money
'give him a cent'

Apart from this lexical use as a 'give' verb, in Hui'an, *khɔ⁵* takes on a series of functions such as the causative verb, the dative marker and the speaker-affectedness marker (see chapter 18 for more details).

In terms of pronunciation, the prepositions used to introduce an agent in other Southern Min varieties (such as Quanzhou, Xiamen and Taiwan) include *hɔ* 與, *thɔ* 度, *tŋ* 傳 and *khi* 乞, of which *hɔ* is mainly used in Xiamen, Zhangzhou and

Taiwan; *thɔ* is mainly used in Quanzhou, but also Xiamen; *tŋ* is only used in Quanzhou; while *khi* is used in different Southern Min varieties (cf. Li 2000:129; Zhou & Ouyang 1998:382; Yang 1991:259; Shi 2000:159; Chappell 2000). All these four prepositions are also derived from their uses as a 'give' verb. A question arises: what is the relationship between these four prepositions and the preposition *khɔ⁵* in Hui'an? Firstly, the morpheme *tŋ* is also attested in Hui'an, however, it does not function as an agent marker. The preposition *khɔ⁵* in Hui'an is quite similar to *hɔ* and *thɔ* (especially *hɔ*) in terms of their pronunciations: they share the final (i.e. ɔ) and belong to the same tone category[4]. However, there is no general sound correspondence between [kh] in Hui'an and [h] in Taiwan. Interestingly, Zhou (2006:102,114-115) suggests that *thɔ* is a more conservative form of *hɔ*, i.e. *thɔ* -> *hɔ*. So far, we believe that it would be safer to say that *khɔ* in Hui'an and *thɔ* or *hɔ* in other Southern Min varieties are cognates, though further research is needed.

14.5 Benefactive

In Mandarin Chinese, the 'give' verb can function as a preposition introducing a benefactive, as in (37), or a malefactive, as in (38).

(37) The preposition *gěi* introducing a benefactive in Mandarin Chinese
他　　給　　我　　翻譯
tā　　gěi　　wǒ　　fānyì
3SG　give　1SG　translate
'He translated for me.'

(38) The preposition *gěi* introducing a malefactive in Mandarin Chinese
你　　給　　我　　算　　錯　　了
nǐ　　gěi　　wǒ　　suàn　　cuò　　le
2SG　give　1SG　count　wrong　PFV
'You made a mistake on me in the accounting.'

The first person singular pronoun *wǒ* in (37) acts as the beneficiary, and codes the person who benefits from the action of translating, while the pronoun *wǒ* in (38) acts as the maleficiary, who is harmed by the event of making a mistake in the accounts.

---

4 Tone 5 in Mainland notation for Hui'an and Quanzhou corresponds to Tone 7 in Taiwan.

Unlike Mandarin Chinese, the Hui'an dialect uses *ka⁵* 共, rather than *khɔ⁵* 'give', to code respectively the benefactive, as in (39), and the malefactive, as in (40).

(39) The preposition *ka⁵* coding the benefactive in Hui'an
共　　　伊　　出　　　錢
ka⁵⁻⁴　*en¹*　*tshut⁷⁻⁸*　*tsin²*
BEN　3PL　take.out　money
'pay for them'

(40) The preposition *ka⁵* coding the malefactive in Hui'an
伊　杯仔　　　共　　　我　　　拍　　　　破
i¹　*pue¹-a³*　*ka⁵⁻⁴*　*gua³⁻²*　*phaʔ⁷⁻⁸*　*phua⁵*
3SG　cup-NM　MAL　1SG　hit　broken
'He broke the cup on me.'

In addition to *ka⁵*, in Hui'an, there are another two prepositions serving as benefactive markers, i.e. *thue⁵* 替, as in (41), and *ui⁵* 爲, as in (42).

(41) 替　　　汝　　　說
thue⁵⁻³　*lɯ³⁻²*　*səʔ⁷*
replace　2SG　say
'speak for/instead of you'

(42) 為　　　逐個　　　　服務
ui⁵⁻⁴　*tak⁸⁻⁴-e²*　*hɔk⁸⁻⁴bu⁵*
for　every-CL　serve
'serve for everyone's sake'

These two prepositions are much less used than the preposition *ka⁵*. In addition, *ui⁵* is seldom used in daily conversation, that is, it is typically used in formal speech.

14.6 Comitative

The prepositions introducing the comitative role in Hui'an are *kaʔ⁷* 合 and *kiau¹* 交, as in (43) and (44), respectively.

(43) 我　　合　　　伊　　做做　　　　去
　　　gua³　ka⁷⁻⁸　i¹　tsue⁵⁻³tsue⁵　khɯ⁵
　　　1SG　COMT　3SG　together　go
　　　'I went (there) together with him.'

(44) 交　　伊　　煮
　　　kiau¹　i¹　tsɯ³
　　　COMT　3SG　cook
　　　'cook (something) together with it'

The preposition *ka?⁷* in (43) is much more common in daily conversation than the preposition *kiau¹* in (44). In Hui'an, *ka?⁷* can also function as a conjunction (see §21.2 for details).

The preposition *kiau¹* is probably derived from its use as a verb meaning 'add in', as in (45).

(45) 交　　　幾　　　　垛　　　肉
　　　kiau¹　kui³⁻²　tə⁵⁻³　ba?⁷
　　　add　several　CL　meat
　　　'add in several pieces of meat'

The development from a comitative to a NP conjunction is well-attested in Chinese, not to mention crosslinguistically (see Liu Jian & Peyraube 1994; Heine & Kuteva 2002:80-82) while we find the use of verbs meaning 'mix' as comitatives in Hakka as well (see Lai 2003).

14.7 Standard of comparison

As with Mandarin Chinese, the preposition for comparison in Hui'an is *pi³* 比, as in (46), where the third person singular pronoun following the preposition *pi³* functions as a standard of comparison.

(46) 比　　　伊　　恰　　　　水
　　　pi³⁻²　i¹　kha?⁷⁻⁸　sui³
　　　DMC　3SG　HMC　pretty
　　　'prettier than her'

It is likely that the preposition *pi³* as in (46) is borrowed from Mandarin Chinese, since the indigenous comparative construction in Hui'an, as in (47), does not use the preposition pi^3 but rather an adverbial form $kha\text{?}^7$, also present (obligatorily) in the construction with pi^3 (see chapter 17 for details, Chen 2015).

(47) 今年　　　恰　　　　　寒　　舊年
　　　$ken^1\text{-}lin^2$　$kha\text{?}^{7\text{-}8}$　　　$kuã^2$　$ku^{5\text{-}4}\text{-}lin^2$
　　　this-year　comparatively　cold　old-year
　　　'This year is colder than last year.'

In (47), the standard of comparison ku^4lin^2 'last year' follows the main predicate $kuã^2$ 'cold' without using the preposition pi^3 as in (46) above.

14.8 Instrument

As mentioned in §14.2.2 above, the prepositions $iŋ^5$ and an^5, which can introduce a source, are also used to introduce an instrument, as illustrated by (48) and (49), respectively.

(48) [$iŋ^5$ NP]$_{PP}$ - VP
　　　用　　　奇箸　　　　食
　　　$iŋ^{5\text{-}4}$　kha^1tu^5　　$tsia\text{?}^8$
　　　use　chopsticks　eat
　　　'eat with chopsticks'

(49) [an^5 NP]$_{PP}$ - VP
　　　按　　　喙　　　咧　　　　講話
　　　$an^{5\text{-}3}$　$tshui^5$　$le\text{?}^{7\text{-}8}$　$kaŋ^{3\text{-}2}\text{-}ue^5$
　　　with　mouth　HAB　say-word
　　　'speak with the mouth'

In (48), the noun kha^1tu^5 'chopsticks' preceded by the preposition $iŋ^5$ functions as the instrument for carrying out the action denoted by the verb $tsia\text{?}^8$ 'eat'. Similarly, the noun $tshui^3$ 'mouth' following the preposition an^5 in (49) functions as the means for the action of the verb phrase $le\text{?}^{7\text{-}8}$ $kaŋ^{3\text{-}2}ue^5$ 'speak' to be realized.

As with the majority of prepositions discussed so far, the prepositional phrase where $iŋ^5$ and an^5 occur is placed before the verb phrase, as shown by (48) and (49) above. Note that the preposition an^5 introducing an instrument is not reported in other Southern Min varieties, while the preposition $iŋ^5$ can be attested in Quanzhou and Taiwan (cf. Li 2000:131; Yang 1991:258).

14.9 Basis

The prepositions meaning 'according to' in Hui'an include *an⁵* 按, *tsue⁵* 做 and *tsiau⁵* 照, as shown by examples (50) – (52).

(50) 按　　　　無　　　　同　　　工齡
　　 an⁵⁻³　　 *bo²⁻⁴*　　 *saŋ²⁻⁴*　 *kaŋ¹-liŋ²*
　　 according.to not.have same work-age
　　 'according to different working years'

(51) 做　　　　兩　　碗　　煮
　　 tsue⁵⁻³　 *lŋ⁴*　 *uã³*　 *tsu³*
　　 according.to two　 bowl　 cook
　　 'cook according to two bowls'

(52) 照　　　　大　　　細　　　排
　　 tsiau⁵⁻³　 *tua⁵⁻⁴*　 *sue⁵*　 *pai²*
　　 according.to big　　 small　 place
　　 'place (them) according to the size'

The prepositions *an⁵* in (50) and *tsue⁵* in (51) are relatively more common than *tsiau⁵* in (52) in daily conversation.

As mentioned above, the preposition *an⁵* introducing a patient or an instrument is not reported in other Southern Min varieties. However, its use in the meaning of 'according to' can indeed be found in varieties such as Quanzhou and Xiamen (Li 2000:132; Zhou 2006:387). Similarly, the preposition *tsiau⁵* is common in other Southern Min varieties, while their use of the preposition *tsue⁵* is not reported.

The following example shows that *tsue⁵* is originally a verb meaning 'do'.

(53) 無　　　　代志　　　　做
　　 bo²⁻⁴　　 *tai⁵⁻⁴tsi⁵⁻³*　 *tsue⁵*
　　 not.have　 thing　　　　do
　　 'have nothing to do'

14.10 Summary

This chapter has examined in depth adpositions, especially prepositions, in Hui'an, while noting that for the time being the existence of postpositions and circumpositions is a controversial question. Comparatively speaking, prepositions in Hui'an are not commonly used in daily conversation. Many noun phrases which have to be introduced by a preposition in Mandarin Chinese can be used without any marking in Hui'an.

The prepositions indicating location in space include $le\textipa{P}^7$ 咧, tu^4 or ti^4 伫, $tu^4le\textipa{P}^7$ (or $ti^4le\textipa{P}^7$) 伫咧 and $lã^5$. The first three prepositions occur both before and after a verb phrase, whereas $lã^5$ occurs only preverbally. Temporal words are typically used alone without any marking by an adposition. The preposition $le\textipa{P}^7$ is also used to introduce spatial goals. Another preposition indicating spatial goals is kau^5 遘, which can also denote temporal goals.

The prepositions denoting source are an^5 按 and $i\text{ɔ}\eta^5/i\eta^5$ 用, neither of which is in fact required in this function in Hui'an. The preposition an^5 indicates the source in space or time, while $i\text{ɔ}\eta^5/i\eta^5$ typically denotes only locative source. In Hui'an, an^5 is a multifunctional morpheme, taking on other functions such as marking perlative, patient, instrument and basis. The preposition $i\text{ɔ}\eta^5/i\eta^5$ is also used to introduce an instrument, while there are two further prepositions indicating basis: $tsue^5$ 做 and $tsiau^5$ 照.

In Hui'an, the patient is generally used without any marking by an adposition, though a series of object markers is indeed attested, such as ka^5 共, $lia\textipa{P}^8$ 搦, an^5 按 and $tsi\text{ɔ}\eta^1$ 將. Unlike the syntactic structure using preposition $b\check{a}$ 把 in Mandarin Chinese, the preposition ka^5 in Hui'an is typically used with a different form for the object marking construction: (NP$_{\text{AGENT}}$ +) NP$_{\text{PATIENT}}$ + ka^5 + i^1(3SG) + VP, or it may co-occur with $tsi\text{ɔ}\eta^1$ in the same clause, that is, '(NP$_{\text{AGENT}}$ +) $tsi\text{ɔ}\eta^1$ + NP$_{\text{PATIENT}}$ + ka^5 + i^1(3SG) + VP'. The preposition ka^5 also functions as a benefactive and malefactive marker. The agent marker in Hui'an is encoded by a preposition derived from the verb $kh\text{ɔ}^5$ 與 'give', which cannot be used in agentless passives.

The prepositions coding comitative meaning in Hui'an are either $ka\textipa{P}^7$ 合 or $kiau^1$ 交, of which, $ka\textipa{P}^7$ also functions as a conjunction, while $kiau^1$ is probably derived from its use as a verb meaning 'add in'.

The preposition for comparison of inequality in Hui'an is pi^3 比. However, the indigenous comparative construction in Hui'an does not use the preposition pi^3 at all but rather an adverbial form $kha\textipa{P}^7$, also present (obligatorily) in the construction with pi^3.

15 Adverbs

15.1 Introduction

Adverbs are traditionally regarded as a class of words that function as modifiers of primarily non-nominal constitutents (cf. van der Auwera & O'Baoill 1998; Schachter & Shopen 2007, among others).[1] Semantically speaking, adverbs typically express manner, place, time, frequency, degree and modal meanings such as the level of certainty.

In Mandarin Chinese, adverbs typically occur after the subject or topic, and preceding the verb which they modify, as in (1); some adverbs, however, can also occur at the beginning of the sentence, as in (2b) (Li & Thompson 1981:319-322).

(1) Adverbs occurring after the subject in Mandarin Chinese
 他 很 帥
 tā hěn shuài
 3SG very handsome
 'He is very handsome.'

(2) Adverbs that can occur at the beginning of the sentence in Mandarin Chinese
 a. 張三 顯然 不 高興
  Zhāng Sān xiǎnrán bù gāoxìng
  PN obviously not happy
  'Obviously, Zhang San is unhappy.'

 b. 顯然 張三 不 高興
  xiǎnrán Zhāng Sān bù gāoxìng
  obviously PN not happy
  'Obviously, Zhang San is unhappy.'

The degree adverb *hěn* 'very' in (1), modifying the adjectival predicate *shuài* 'handsome', occurs after the subject *tā* 'he', and has just the predicate in its scope, while the attitude adverb *xiǎnrán* 'obviously', modifying the whole sentence *Zhāng Sān bù gāoxìng* 'Zhang San is unhappy', can occur after the subject *Zhāng*

---

[1] Contemporary linguists such as Jackendoff (1972) have noted that the category 'adverb' has traditionally been a catch-all term, classifying words that do not fit into any of the other available categories such as nouns and adjectives.

Sān, as in (2a), or occur at the beginning of the sentence, as in (2b). The scope relations are clearly distinct for these two classes of adverbs.

As with Mandarin Chinese, most adverbs in Hui'an typically modify the predicate and occur after the subject or topic. These include manner, degree, and time adverbs, but also adverbs of quantity and scope. Other adverbs such as attitude and epistemic adverbs modify a whole sentence and occur either after the subject (or topic) or in the sentence-initial position. These five subtypes of adverb in Hui'an will be examined in the following sections.

15.2 Manner adverbs

Manner adverbs, typically used as modifiers of verb phrases, usually indicate the manner in which an action is carried out, as exemplified by (3), where *thiau¹kaŋ¹* 超工 'especially, deliberately' modifies the verb phrase *thueʔ⁸ lai⁰* 捒來 'bring' by indicating its manner.

(3) 伊 超工 捒 來
  i¹ <u>*thiau¹kaŋ¹*</u> *thueʔ⁸* *lai⁰*
  3SG deliberately take come
  'She came here deliberately for giving (me the money).'

There is a subclass of manner adverbs formed via reduplication of an adjective, as illustrated by (4), where the adverb *ho³⁻²ho³* 好好 'well' is formed by reduplication of the adjective *ho³* 'good' (see also §9.3.1).

(4) 論文 好好 寫
  lun⁵⁻⁴bun² <u>*ho³⁻²~ho³*</u> *sia³*
  thesis good~good write
  'Write (your) thesis seriously.'

Like *thiau¹kaŋ¹* in (3), *ho³⁻²ho³* in (4) occurs before the verb *sia³* 'write' indicates the manner in which the action of writing a thesis is carried out.

The following example shows that manner adverbs in Hui'an can also be formed via reduplication of a verb, in this case, *tsue⁵* 'do'.

(5) 個 做做 來
  en¹ <u>*tsue⁵⁻³tsue⁵*</u> *lai²*
  3PL together come
  'They came here together.'

In (5), *tsue⁵⁻³tsue⁵* 'together' modifies the motion verb *lai²* 'come' signaling the manner of their coming.

As shown by these three examples, manner adverbs in Hui'an occur between the subject (or the topic) and the verb phrase. More specifically, in both (3) and (5), the manner adverb occurs between the subject and the verb phrase. For example, *thiau¹kaŋ¹* in (3) is placed between the subject *i¹* 'she' and the verb phrase *thuəʔ⁸ lai⁰* 'bring'. The manner adverb *ho³⁻²ho³* in (4), however, occurs between the topicalized patient (or direct object) noun, *lun⁵⁻⁴bun²* 'thesis', and the verb *sia³* 'write'.

15.3 Degree adverbs

Degree adverbs fall into two types: (a) those indicating the degree without an explicit comparison, e.g. *khaʔ⁷* 恰 'a bit; fairly', *pi³⁻²kau⁵* 比較 'fairly', *a⁴koʔ⁷* 也佫 'fairly', *ia³* 野 'quite', *ban²* 蠻 'rather', *tsiã²* 誠 'rather', *tsen¹* 真 'really/very', *thai⁵* 太 'too' and *kə⁵* 過 'excessively'; and (b) those denoting comparison (between two or more entities), e.g. *khaʔ⁷* 恰 'comparatively', *koʔ⁷⁻⁸khaʔ⁷* 佫恰 'even more' and *siɔŋ⁵* 上/*tsue⁵* 最 'the most'.

15.3.1 Basic degree adverbs

This type of degree adverb modifies adjectives including monosyllabic and disyllabic ones, or their negative forms. Take *ia³* 'quite' and *ban²* 'rather' as examples.

(6) 野/蠻　　久
　　ia³⁻²/ban²⁻⁴　*ku³*
　　quite/rather　Long
　　'quite/rather long'

(7) 野/蠻　　厲害
　　ia³⁻²/ban²⁻⁴　*li⁵⁻⁴hai⁵*
　　quite/rather　smart
　　'quite/rather　smart'

(8) 野/蠻　　無　　　容易
　　ia³⁻²/ban²⁻⁴　*bo²⁻⁴*　*iɔŋ²⁻⁴i⁵*
　　quite/rather　not.have　easy
　　'really not easy'

In (6) and (7), the degree adverbs ia^3 'quite' and ban^2 'rather' modify the monosyllabic adjective ku^3 'long' and the disyllabic adjective $li^{5-4}hai^5$ 'smart', respectively. In (8), ia^3 'quite' and ban^2 'rather' are used to modify $bo^{2-4}iɔŋ^{2-4}i^5$ 'not easy', the negative form of the adjective $iɔŋ^{2-4}i^5$ 'easy'.

The degree adverb $khaʔ^7$ can mean 'a bit; fairly', as illustrated by (9) and (10).

(9) 湯　　恰　　　　無　　　甜
　　$thŋ^1$　$khaʔ^{7-8}$　bo^{2-4}　tin^1
　　soup　a.bit　not.have　sweet
　　'The soup is not tasty enough.'

(10) 汝　　著　　　　恰　　　　主動
　　lu^3　$tioʔ^{8-4}$　$khaʔ^{7-8}$　$tsu^{3-2}tɔŋ^4$
　　2SG　should　fairly　active
　　'You need to be fairly active.'

In (9), the adverb $khaʔ^7$ modifies $bo^{2-4}tin^1$ 'not sweet' (the negative form of the adjective tin^1 'sweet') denoting the degree of tastiness of the soup, i.e. between tasty and non-tasty, but approaching tasty, which suggests that adding a bit, but not too much salt is enough. In this case, the speaker is talking about the degree of tastiness of the soup according to his expectation about what constitutes the right level of saltiness, i.e. some more abstract benchmark based on experience, rather than comparing the soup with other soups that might be physically present in the given context (or other objects) in terms of their degrees of tastiness. In (10), $khaʔ^7$ modifies the adjective $tsu^{3-2}tɔŋ^4$ 'active' implying that the activeness of the subject should achieve a certain degree, otherwise the subject cannot get what he wants. According to the context, the speaker is either suggesting the need for the addressee to take some initiative in doing something, rather than directly comparing the addressee with other people in terms of degrees of activeness, or else is suggesting that the addressee is not as active as he could be.

The adverb $pi^{3-2}kau^5$, as illustrated by (11), is probably borrowed from Mandarin Chinese. It is not widely used in Hui'an and typically occurs in the speech of the younger generation.

(11) 比較　　　　開朗
　　$pi^{3-2}kau^{5-3}$　$khai^1lɔŋ^3$
　　fairly　　　　optimistic
　　'fairly optimistic'

These implicitly comparative degree adverbs differ from each other in the degree they denote, as can be seen from the translation. Note that, however, the translation only shows that the difference among these adverbs is similar to the difference among the degree adverbs *a bit*, *fairly*, *quite*, *rather*, *really/very*, *too*, *excessively* in English, but not that the adverbs in Hui'an are equivalent to the corresponding English adverbs.

15.3.2 Comparative degree adverbs

As mentioned in §15.3.1 above, *khaʔ⁷* can be a degree adverb meaning 'a bit; fairly' without indicating an explicit comparison. The following example, however, shows that *khaʔ⁷* may also denote a comparison between two or more entities.

(12) 即間   恰   熱
 tsit⁷⁻⁸-kuin¹   khaʔ⁷⁻⁸   luaʔ⁸
 this-CL   comparatively   hot
 'This room is hotter (than that room).'

In (12), *khaʔ⁷* modifies the adjective *luaʔ⁸* 'hot' indicating that this room is hotter than the other room. In other words, *khaʔ⁷* here functions as a marker of overt comparison (see chapter 17 for more on comparative constructions).

The adverb *khaʔ⁷* can modify the reduplicated form of an adjective such as *siŋ³⁻²siŋ³* 省省 'cheap' in (13).

(13) 暝時   恰   省省
 bin²-si⁰   khaʔ⁷⁻⁸   siŋ³⁻²~siŋ³
 night-time   comparatively   cheap~cheap
 '(The flight) is cheaper at night (than during the day).'

In (13), *siŋ³⁻²siŋ³* is the reduplicated form of the adjective *siŋ³* 'cheap', and the adverb *khaʔ⁷* modifies *siŋ³⁻²siŋ³* signaling that the flight is cheaper at night than during the day. Note that in some other Chinese varieties such as Mandarin Chinese and Cantonese, reduplicated forms cannot be so modified.

The following example shows that the adverb *khaʔ⁷* can also modify another word in the same speech category, such as the adverb of frequency *siɔŋ²* 常 'often'.

(14) 伊　　　恰　　　　　　常　　　　倒來
　　　i¹　　kha$ʔ^{7\text{-}8}$　　siɔŋ$^{2\text{-}4}$　to⁵lai⁰
　　　3SG　comparatively　often　come.back
　　　'He comes back more often (than me).'

The adverb kha$ʔ^7$ can also precede a negator, as illustrated by (15) and (16).

(15) 即蕊　　　　　恰　　　　　　無　　　　芳
　　　tsit$^{7\text{-}8}$-lui³　kha$ʔ^{7\text{-}8}$　　bo$^{2\text{-}4}$　phaŋ¹
　　　this-CL　comparatively　not.have　fragrant
　　　'This (flower) is less fragrant (than that one).'

(16) 恰　　　　　　鱠　　　　走
　　　kha$ʔ^{7\text{-}8}$　　bue⁴　　tsau³
　　　comparatively　cannot　run
　　　'(There is) less (opportunity for the chicken to) run away.'

In (15), bo$^{2\text{-}4}$ phaŋ¹ 'not fragrant' is the negative form of the adjective phaŋ¹ 'fragrant', which is modified by the adverb kha$ʔ^7$ to indicate that this flower is less fragrant than the other flowers. In (16), bue⁴ tsau³ 'cannot run away' is the negative form of e⁴ tsau³ 會走 'can run away', and the adverb kha$ʔ^7$ modifies bue⁴ tsau³ to signal that there is less opportunity for the chicken to run away.

The adverb ko$ʔ^{7\text{-}8}$kha$ʔ^7$ 佫恰 'even more' shares its syntactic distribution with the adverb kha$ʔ^7$ 恰. In other words, ko$ʔ^{7\text{-}8}$kha$ʔ^7$ can occur in all the contexts shown by examples (12) – (16) above. One example is given in (17).

(17) 即間　　　　　佫恰　　　　　　　熱
　　　tsit$^{7\text{-}8}$-kuin¹　ko$ʔ^{7\text{-}8}$kha$ʔ^{7\text{-}8}$　lua$ʔ^8$
　　　this-CL　even.more　hot
　　　'This (room) is even hotter (than that room).'

The adverbs siɔŋ⁵ 上 and tsue⁵ 最 'the most' are followed by an adjective to denote a superlative degree, as in (18).

(18) 上/最　　　　　　　　好
　　　siɔŋ$^{5\text{-}4}$/tsue$^{5\text{-}3}$　ho³
　　　the.most/the.most　good
　　　'the best'

Note that *siɔŋ⁵* is the traditional superlative marker, while *tsue⁵* occurs in the speech of younger generation, due to the influence of Mandarin Chinese.

15.4 Time adverbs

Time adverbs in Hui'an mainly include *suin¹* 先 'first', *tsiaʔ⁷* 則 'just now, only then', and *i³⁻²kiŋ¹* 已經 'already'.

The adverb *suin¹* 'first', modifying a verb (phrase), indicates that someone does something before other people, as in (19), or something happens before other events, as in (20).

(19) 汝　　先　　食，　我　　佫　　削
　　 lu³　　suin¹　tsiaʔ⁸　gua³　koʔ⁷⁻⁸　siaʔ⁷
　　 2SG　 first　 eat　　 1SG　again　 pare
　　 'You eat first, I will pare another (apple for myself).'

(20) 暗暝　　　　先　　睏，　　明日　　　則　　　　佫　　　說
　　 am⁵⁻³bin²　suin¹　khun⁵　biã²⁻⁴letˤ⁸　tsiaʔ⁷⁻⁸　koʔ⁷⁻⁸　səʔ⁷
　　 night　　　first　 sleep　tomorrow　only.then　again　 say
　　 'Let's sleep tonight first and discuss (it) again until tomorrow.'

In (19), the adverb *suin¹* modifies the verb *tsiaʔ⁸* and has a sequencing function in indicating that the addressee is to eat an apple first, and then, after that, the speaker herself will do so. In this case, the meaning 'first' of the adverb *suin¹* is applied to the subject *lu³* 'you'. In (20), the adverb *suin¹* modifies the verb *khun⁵* 'sleep', indicating that the persons concerned should first sleep, and then continue discussing the problem the next day. In this case, the meaning 'first' of the adverb *suin¹* is applied to the event denoted by the verb *khun⁵* 'sleep'. The adverb *tsiaʔ⁷* 'only then' in (20) refers back to the temporal word *biã²⁻⁴letˤ⁸* 'tomorrow', which indicates the time when people are to continue discussing the problem.

The adverb *tsiaʔ⁷* can also mean 'just now', as illustrated by (21), where *tsiaʔ⁷* modifies the verb *kau⁵* 'arrive' signaling that he just arrived.

(21) 伊　　則　　　　迣
　　 i¹　　tsiaʔ⁷⁻⁸　kau⁵
　　 3SG　just.now　 arrive
　　 'He just arrived.'

The adverb *i³⁻²kiŋ¹* 'already', preceding a verb (phrase), denotes something has already been done, as in (22), or someone or something has already entered into a state, as in (23).

(22) 已經　　食　　澈
　　 i³⁻²kiŋ¹　*tsiaʔ⁸⁻⁴*　*theʔ⁷*
　　 already　eat　　finished
　　 'have been eaten up'

(23) 已經　　晏　　咯
　　 i³⁻²kiŋ¹　*uã⁵*　*lɔ⁰*
　　 already　late　SFP
　　 'It has become late.'

15.5 Adverbs of quantity and scope

In this section, we focus on other adverbs that modify a verb phrase, rather than a sentence, especially those involving quantity or scope in some way. More specifically, we will examine the adverbs that either denote a repeated action (or imply the number of occurrences of an action) such as *koʔ⁷* 佫 'again', or denote the quantity or scope of the person/thing involved such as *tsau²* 禕 'all', or denote the frequency of an action such as *siɔŋ²* 常 'often'.

The adverb *koʔ⁷* 'again' often denotes a repeated action when modifying a verb phrase, as in (24) - (26).

(24) 唔啅　　　佫　　　挽　　咯
　　 m⁵⁻⁴-thaŋ¹　*koʔ⁷⁻⁸*　*ban³*　*lɔ⁰*
　　 not-can　　again　　pluck　SFP
　　 'Don't pluck (your eyebrows) again!'

(25) 佫　　　咧　　　剔　　齒
　　 koʔ⁷⁻⁸　*leʔ⁷⁻⁸*　*thak⁷⁻⁸*　*khi³*
　　 again　PROG　pick　tooth
　　 'picking (his) teeth again'

(26) 伊　　昨日　　　佫　　　去
　　 i¹　*tsa⁴let⁸*　*koʔ⁷⁻⁸*　*khɯ⁵*
　　 3SG　yesterday　again　go
　　 'He went (there) again yesterday.'

In (24), the speaker suggests that the addressee should not pluck her eyebrows again. In this case, the adverb *koʔ⁷* is used in an imperative to advise against an event that has not yet happened. In (25), at the speech time, the addressee is picking his teeth again. In other words, the adverb *koʔ⁷* in (25) is used to modify an event that is occurring at the speech time. In (26), the adverb *koʔ⁷* is used for a past event as indicated by the time word *tsa⁴let⁸* 'yesterday'. Note that this is different from Mandarin Chinese, where different adverbs are used for these different contexts: the adverb *zài* 再 is used for an event that has not yet occurred, while the adverb *yòu* 又 is used for a past or for present events (cf. Li & Thompson 1981; Lǚ 1999, among others).

Besides denoting a repeated action, the adverb *koʔ⁷* can mean 'still', as in (27), or 'also', as in (28).

(27) 伊　　佫　　　未　　　遘
    i¹　　*koʔ⁷⁻⁸*　*bə⁵⁻⁴*　*kau⁵*
    3SG　still　not.yet　arrive
    'He has still not arrived.'

(28) 我　　佫　　　買　　　雙　　　鞋
    gua³　*koʔ⁷⁻⁸*　*bue³⁻²*　*saŋ¹*　*ue²*
    1SG　also　buy　pair　shoe
    'I also bought a pair of shoes.'

In (27), the adverb *koʔ⁷* occurs after the subject *i¹* and before the verb phrase *bə⁵⁻⁴ kau⁵* 'not arrive', meaning that he has still not arrived. In (28), *koʔ⁷* is placed between the subject *gua³* and the verb phrase *bue³⁻² saŋ¹ ue²* 'buy a pair of shoes', indicating that in addition to buying some other things, the speaker also bought a pair of shoes. Note that, in Mandarin Chinese, another adverb, i.e. *hái* 還 'still' (rather than *zài* or *yòu* mentioned above), is needed in both these two contexts.

The adverb *a⁴* 也 'also' can indicate that the same event happens to another person, as in (29), or that the same situation is found in another context, as in (30).

(29) 阮²　　腹肚　　　也　　　枵　　　遘
    gun³　*pak⁷⁻⁸tɔ³*　*a⁴*　*iau¹*　*a³*
    1PL　Belly　also　hungry　EVC
    'I am also so hungry.'

---

2 For plural pronouns with a singular meaning, please see §4.2.2.

(30) 學堂 也 無嘥 食
    oʔ⁸⁻⁴tŋ² a⁴ bo²⁻⁴-thaŋ¹ tsiaʔ⁸
    school   also not.have-can eat
    'There is also nothing to eat at school.'

In (29), *a⁴* is followed by the adjective phrase *iau¹ a³* 'so hungry' to suggest that the speaker is also hungry like someone else. In (30), *a⁴* precedes the phrase *bo²⁻⁴thaŋ¹ tsiaʔ⁸* 'there is nothing to eat' indicating that the situation of having nothing to eat also applies to the school's canteen, besides somewhere else.

The adverb *a⁴* may also mean that the same action is undertaken by another person, as in (31), or in a different situation, as in (32).

(31) 佢 也 去
    en¹ a⁴ khuɯ⁵
    3PL also go
    'They also went (there).'

(32) 熱冬 也 著 蓋 被
    luaʔ⁸laŋ⁰ a⁴ tioʔ⁸⁻⁴ kaʔ⁷⁻⁸ phə⁴
    summer   also have.to cover   quilt
    '(We) also need to use a quilt during the summer.'

In (31), the adverb *a⁴* suggests that the action of going to a place is also undertaken by them, besides other people. In (32), the adverb *a⁴* suggests that the action of using a quilt is also needed during the summer, besides at other times of the year, such as during the winter.

As shown by examples (29) – (32), the meaning 'also' of the adverb *a⁴* applies to the subject, while in the case of the adverb *koʔ⁷*, the meaning 'also' applies instead to the verb phrase, rather than to the subject, as illustrated by example (28).

The adverbs *kɔ¹⁻²kɔ¹* 孤孤 and *tsi³* 只 both mean 'only', as in (33) and (34), respectively.

(33) 孤孤 買 叢 銃
    kɔ¹⁻²~kɔ¹ bue³⁻² tsaŋ²⁻⁴ tshiŋ⁵
    only~only buy   CL   gun
    'only bought one gun'

(34) 只　　過　　蜀　　個　　生日
　　 tsi³⁻²　_kə⁵_　_tsit⁸⁻⁴_　_e²⁻⁴_　_sin¹let⁸_
　　 only　pass　one　CL　birthday
　　 'only celebrate one birthday'

The adverb _kɔ¹⁻²kɔ¹_ 'only' in (33) indicates that the speaker only bought a gun, but not other things. Since Chinese people may celebrate their birthday twice in a year, that is, following the solar calendar and the lunar calendar, example (34) suggests that the speaker celebrates her birthday only once in a year.

　　The following are examples of _tsau²_ 禮, _tɔ¹_ 都 and _ke⁵_ 計 meaning 'all'. The adverb _tsau²_ normally modifies action verbs, indicating that the whole set or entirety of the referents encoded by the subject/topic take on or suffer from the same action, as illustrated by (35) and (36).

(35) 佢　　禮　　倒來
　　 en¹　_tsau²⁻⁴_　_to⁵lai⁰_
　　 3PL　all　come.back
　　 'They all came back.'

(36) 衫褲　　禮　　洗　　了　　咯
　　 sã¹khɔ⁵　_tsau²⁻⁴_　_sue³⁻²_　_liau³_　_lɔ⁰_
　　 clothes　all　wash　finish　SFP
　　 'All the clothes have been washed.'

In (35), _tsau²_ indicates that the referents of the subject _en¹_ 'they' all carry out the action of coming back. In (36), _tsau²_ means that the referents of the topic _sã¹khɔ⁵_ 'clothes' have all undergone the action of washing.

　　Unlike _tsau²_, the adverb _tɔ¹_ 'all' often also occurs with an adjectival phrase such as _kə⁵⁻³ poʔ⁸_ 過薄 'too thin' in (37), or with the copular verb _si⁴_ 是, as in (38).

(37) 兩　　領　　都　　過　　薄
　　 lŋ⁴　_liã³_　_tɔ¹_　_kə⁵⁻³_　_poʔ⁸_
　　 two　CL　all　excessively　thin
　　 'These two pieces (of clothing) are both too thin.'

(38) 逐個　　都　　是　　大學生
　　 tak⁸⁻⁴-e²　_tɔ¹_　_si⁴_　_tua⁵⁻⁴oʔ⁸⁻⁴siŋ¹_
　　 every-CL　all　be　university.student
　　 'Everyone is a university student.'

In (37), the adverb $tɔ^1$ indicates that the referents of the subject $lŋ^4 liã^3$ 'two pieces (of clothing)' are both too thin. Similarly, the adverb $tɔ^1$ in (38) indicates that the referents of the subject $tak^{8-4}e^2$ 'everyone' are all university students. In other words, the adverbs $tsau^2$ and $tɔ^1$ both refer to the entire set of members denoted by the preceding subject or topic.

As with the adverbs $tsau^2$ and $tɔ^1$, the adverb ke^5 'all' can refer to its preceding subject (or topic), as illustrated by (39), where ke^5 indicates inclusively that the referents of the subject $lŋ^4 kuin^1 iɔk^{8-4}siak^7$ 兩間浴室 'two bathrooms' both have hot water.

(39) 兩　　間　　浴室　　　　計　　有
　　　$lŋ^4$　$kuin^1$　$iɔk^{8-4}siak^7$　ke^{5-3}　u^4
　　　two　CL　bathroom　all　have
　　　'Both two bathrooms have (hot water).'

However, the adverb ke^5 can also indicate that something (encoded by the verb phrase following ke^5) happens all the time, which suggests that ke^5 in this use may be regarded as an adverb of frequency. This is illustrated by (40) below, where two tokens of ke^5 both function as an adverb of frequency indicating respectively 'not studying all the time' but 'sending messages all the time'.

(40) 伊　　計　　　無　　　　讀冊,
　　　i^1　ke^{5-3}　bo^{2-4}　$thak^{8-4}tshe?^7$
　　　3SG　all　not.have　study
　　　計　　咧　　　發　　　短信
　　　ke^{5-3}　$le?^{7-8}$　$huat^{7-8}$　$tə^{3-2}\text{-}sen^5$
　　　all　HAB　send　short-message
　　　'He was sending messages all the time but not studying.'

As exemplified by (41) below, $siɔŋ^2$ 常 and $kiŋ^1siɔŋ^2$ 經常, both meaning 'often', are typically used to denote the frequency of an action.

(41) 恁　　有　　常/經常　　　　　　聯繫　　　　無
　　　len^3　u^4　$siɔŋ^{2-4}/kiŋ^1siɔŋ^{2-4}$　$len^{2-4}he^5$　bo^0
　　　2PL　have　often/often　contact　SFP
　　　'Do you often have contact (with each other)?'

15.6 Attitude and epistemic adverbs

Attitude adverbs refer to those that denote the speaker's attitude toward or evaluation of the event expressed by the sentence (cf. Li & Thompson 1981:321). Unlike the adverbs mentioned in the preceding sections, attitude adverbs are sentential adverbs, that is, they modify the whole sentence, rather than the verb phrase (i.e. the predicate). Another important difference is that attitude adverbs can not only occur in the regular position after the subject or topic and before the verb phrase, but also occur before the subject or topic, that is, in sentence-initial position. Two examples are given in (42) and (43).

(42) a. 汝 好得 無 買 迄垛 桌
 lu^3 $\underline{ho^{3\text{-}2}tet^7}$ $bo^{2\text{-}4}$ $bue^{3\text{-}2}$ $hit^{7\text{-}8}\text{-}tə^{5\text{-}3}$ $toʔ^7$
 2SG fortunately not.have buy that-CL table
 'You fortunately didn't buy that table.'

 b. 好得 汝 無 買 迄垛 桌
 $\underline{ho^{3\text{-}2}tet^7}$ lu^3 $bo^{2\text{-}4}$ $bue^{3\text{-}2}$ $hit^{7\text{-}8}\text{-}tə^{5\text{-}3}$ $toʔ^7$
 fortunately 2SG not.have buy that-CL table
 'You fortunately didn't buy that table.'

(43) a. 懷 反正 下日 著 賣 揀
 $huai^2$ $\underline{huan^{3\text{-}2}tsin^5}$ e^4let^8 $tioʔ^{8\text{-}4}$ bue^4 sak^7
 those anyway future should sell RVC
 'Those should be sold, anyway, in the future.'

 b. 反正 懷 下日 著 賣 揀
 $\underline{huan^{3\text{-}2}tsin^5}$ $huai^2$ e^4let^8 $tioʔ^{8\text{-}4}$ bue^4 sak^7
 anyway those future should sell RVC
 'Anyway, those should be sold in the future.'

The attitude adverb $ho^{3\text{-}2}tet^7$ 'fortunately' is placed after the subject lu^3 'you' in (42a), and occurs at the beginning of the sentence in (42b). Similarly, the adverb $huan^{3\text{-}2}tsin^5$ 'anyway' occurs immediately after the topic $huai^2$ 'those' in (43a), while it occurs at the beginning of the sentence in (43b).

A subclass of attitude adverbs involves the speaker's belief or opinion about the validity of the proposition, that is, it expresses epistemic modality, and is thus termed 'epistemic'. In Hui'an, these include adverbs denoting epistemic possibility such as $khɔ^{3\text{-}2}liŋ^2$ 可能 and $m^{5\text{-}4}lɔŋ^3$ 唔攏, and epistemic necessity such as $khŋ^{3\text{-}2}tiŋ^5$ 肯定 and $et^{7\text{-}8}tiŋ^5$ 一定 (see chapter 12 for more details).

15.7 Summary

This chapter has focused on adverbs. Most adverbs in Hui'an typically modify the predicate and occur after the subject or topic. These include manner, degree and time adverbs, but also adverbs of quantity and scope. Other adverbs such as attitude and epistemic adverbs modify a whole sentence and occur either in the sentence-initial position or after the subject (or topic).

Manner adverbs, occurring between the subject (or the topic) and the verb phrase, usually indicate the manner in which an action is carried out.

Degree adverbs can be classified into two subcategories: (a) those indicating the degree without an explicit comparison such as ia^3 野 'quite' and ban^2 蠻 'rather'; and (b) those denoting comparison (between two or more entities) such as $khaʔ^7$ 恰 'comparatively' and $siɔŋ^5$ 上/$tsue^5$ 最 'the most'.

Time adverbs mainly include $suin^1$ 先 'first', $tsiaʔ^7$ 則 'just now, only then', and $i^{3\text{-}2}kiŋ^1$ 已經 'already'.

In the section of adverbs of quantity and scope, we also focused on the adverbs that either denote a repeated action (or imply the number of occurrences of an action) such as $koʔ^7$ 佫 'again', or denote quantity or scope of the persons or things involved, such as $tsau^2$ 禲 'all', if not denote the frequency of an action such as $siɔŋ^2$ 常 'often'.

Attitude adverbs, such as $ho^{3\text{-}2}tet^7$ 'fortunately' and $huan^{3\text{-}2}tsiŋ^5$ 'anyway', denote the speaker's attitude toward or evaluation of an event. Epistemic adverbs, such as $khɔ^{3\text{-}2}liŋ^2$ 可能 'likely' and $khŋ^{3\text{-}2}tiŋ^5$ 肯定 'certainly', being a subclass of attitude adverbs, involve the speaker's belief or opinion about the validity of the proposition.

Part III: clausal structure

In this part, Part III, the focus will be on clausal structure. We discuss in the following order the topics of the $ka\textipa{P}^7$-construction and the ka^5-construction (chapter 16), comparative constructions of inequality (chapter 17), the 'give' construction (chapter 18), interrogatives (chapter 19) and topic-comment constructions (chapter 20).

Chapter 16 focuses on the different uses of $ka\textipa{P}^7$ and ka^5. Six main types of comparative construction of inequality are next examined in chapter 17.

Following on from this, in chapter 18, the 'give' verb in Hui'an is shown to take on quite a range of functions: as a ditransitive verb, dative marker, (permissive) causative verb, passive marker, speaker-affectedness marker, perspective marker and concessive marker, some of which prove to be typologically rare.

Three types of interrogative are next examined in chapter 19: the polar interrogative, the constituent interrogative and the alternative interrogative.

Given that the Hui'an dialect is claimed to be a highly topic-prominent language, in chapter 20, the topic-comment construction is discussed last of all in terms of six aspects: (a) forms of topics; (b) semantic relations between topic and comment; (c) positions of topics; (d) patient topicalization; (e) topic marker; and (f) contrastive function of topic.

16 The *kaʔ⁷*- and *ka⁵*- constructions

16.1 Introduction

Some Chinese varieties use one morpheme to mark different semantic roles like comitative, goal and source, e.g. *koyng²⁴²* 共 in the Fuzhou 福州 variety of Min can be used to mark comitative, goal, source, benefactive and patient (Chen Z. 2000:117-118), while others use more than one morpheme to mark these semantic roles, e.g. the Jixi 績溪 variety of Hui uses *tɤ⁰* to mark comitative and goal, *uã²²* 問 to mark source, and *po²¹³/pɤ⁰* 把 to mark patient and benefactive (Zhao 2000:86-89).

Much work has been done to investigate how these semantic roles are marked in Southern Min, especially the semantic roles marked by *ka⁷* 共 in Taiwan (cf. Yang 1991; Wang & Zhang 1994; Cheng & Tsao 1995; Zhou & Ouyang 1998; Chappell 2000; Lien 2002; Tsao 2005; Yang 2006; Lin 2012, among others). Different Southern Min varieties show different scenarios for this issue. For example, in Quanzhou 泉州, *kap⁷* 合 functions as a connective or comitative marker, while *kaŋ⁵* 共 is used as a marker of semantic roles including goal, source, benefactive and patient, besides being used as a connective marker (Wang Jianshe, pers. comm.). In Taiwan, *kap⁴/kap⁴* 合 is used not only as a connective or comitative marker, but also as a marker of the semantic role 'goal', while *ka⁷* 共 typically marks goal, source, benefactive and patient (cf. Cheng & Tsao 1995; Tsao 2005).

In the contemporary Hui'an dialect, *kaʔ⁷* 合 and *ka⁵* 共 are found to be associated with the semantic roles mentioned above and other semantic roles such as the malefactive. In addition, there is a distinction between *kaʔ⁷* and *ka⁵* in that *kaʔ⁷* functions as a connective or comitative marker, while *ka⁵* takes on a range of other functions (e.g. as an oblique marker: marking source, goal, benefactive and malefactive; and as a direct object marker, see also chapter 14). This is different from their counterparts in both Quanzhou and Taiwan mentioned above.[1]

Besides being both an oblique and object marker, *ka⁵* in Hui'an can be followed by a personal pronoun, especially a non-referential singular personal pronoun, to express the speaker's subjective attitude. Similar constructions are also reported in Taiwan in Lin (2012), who regards them as a subtype of the object marking construction. As will be shown in the following, however, this use of *ka⁵* in Hui'an is related to its use as a benefactive/malefactive marker, among which,

---

[1] There are different viewpoints about the lexical sources of 共 and 合 as well as the relationship between them in the literature such as in Chappell (2000, 2006, 2007), Lien (2002, 2013) and Cheng & Tsao (1995). This will be further explored in a separate paper.

the use as a malefactive marker in fact has not yet attracted enough attention in previous studies on both general linguistics and Chinese linguistics (including studies on Southern Min).

The remainder of this chapter is organized as follows. In §16.2, we give a brief introduction to some of the relevant semantic roles. The functions of $ka^{ʔ7}$ in Hui'an are examined in §16.3, while the functions of ka^5 are discussed in §16.4. A summary will be given in §16.5.

16.2 Relevant semantic roles

In this section, we briefly explain the main semantic roles relevant to our following discussion, such as patient, goal, source, beneficiary (benefactive), and maleficiary (malefactive). According to Saeed (2003:149-150), a patient is 'the entity undergoing the effect of some action, often undergoing some change in state', as in (1a); theme is 'the entity which is moved by an action, or whose location is described', as in (1b); goal is 'the entity towards which something moves', either literally or metaphorically, as in (1c); source is 'the entity from which something moves', either literally or metaphorically, as in (1d).

(1) Examples of the semantic roles "patient, theme, goal, source" in Saeed (2003)
    a. patient
       Enda cut back *these bushes*.
    b. theme
       Roberto passed *the ball* wide.
    c. goal
       Pat told the joke to *his friends*.
    d. source
       We got the idea from *a French magazine*.

The beneficiary is 'a participant that is advantageously affected by an event without being its obligatory participant (either agent or primary target, i.e. patient)' (Kittilä & Zúñiga 2010:1). Three subtypes of beneficiary have been identified in the literature: (a) plain beneficiary, in which the act is done for some kind of benefit for the beneficiary, such as amusement and enjoyment, as in (2a); (b) deputative beneficiary, in which the agent performs some action in place of the beneficiary, as in (2b); and (c) recipient-beneficiary, in which the beneficiary is also the recipient, as in (2c) (cf. Van Valin & LaPolla 1997:383-384; also cited in Zúñiga & Kittilä 2010).

(2) Three subtypes of beneficiary
 a. *She sang a song for <u>the child</u>*. (plain beneficiary)
 b. *He went to bank for <u>his wife</u>*. (deputative beneficiary)
 c. *He baked <u>me</u> a cake*. (recipient-beneficiary)

The maleficiary is the opposite of the beneficiary, i.e. a participant that is adversely affected by an event without being its obligatory partipant (cf. Kittilä & Zúñiga 2010:5), as exemplified by (3), an example from English.

(3) An English example of maleficiary
 My bicycle broke down on <u>me</u>.

Comparatively speaking, little attention has been paid to maleficiary in both general linguistics (cf. Kittilä & Zúñiga 2010:5) and Chinese linguistics, as mentioned above. Previous studies on the morpheme 共 in Southern Min, for example, normally focus on its use as a marker of source, goal, benefactive and patient.

16.3 The functions of *ka$ʔ^7$*

In Hui'an, *ka$ʔ^7$* can be used as a comitative marker (or preposition, see §14.6) indicating the other participant in an action which involves the co-participation of two participants. The verb phrase following the preposition phrase *ka$ʔ^7$*-NP can be one which possesses this inherent property such as *uan^{1}ke^1* 冤家 'quarrel' and *sa^{1}pha$ʔ^7$* 相拍 'fight'. An example is given in (4).

(4) 合　　伊　　相拍
 ka$ʔ^{7\text{-}8}$　i^1　sa^1-pha$ʔ^7$
 COMT　3SG　RECP-hit
 'fight with him'

In (4), *sa^1* is a reciprocal prefix (see §4.4) and *sa^{1}pha$ʔ^7$* 'fight with each other' indicates that both the subject (omitted in 4) and the object of *ka$ʔ^7$* (i.e. *i^1* 'he') are involved in fighting.

The meaning of co-participation can also be indicated by an adverb meaning 'together', as in (5), where the adverb *tsue$^{5\text{-}3}$tsue^5* 做做 'together' makes it clear that the two participants take lectures together.

(5) 合　　恁　　做做　　　　上
ka?⁷⁻⁸　len³　tsue⁵⁻³tsue⁵　siɔŋ⁵
COMT　2PL　together　take
'take (lectures) with you'

The following example shows that the verb may denote an action that carried out by an individual or more than one person.

(6) 汝　　明日　　　　合　　小妹　　　去　　買　　衫
lɯ³　biã²⁻⁴let⁸　ka?⁷⁻⁸　sio³⁻²bə⁵　khɯ⁵⁻³　bue³⁻²　sã¹
2SG　tomorrow　COMT　Y.sister　go　buy　clothes
'Go shopping with your younger sister tomorrow.'

In (6), the action encoded by the verb phrase *khɯ*⁵⁻³ *bue*³⁻² *sã*¹ 'go to buy clothes' can be done by one or more than one person. The meaning that the two participants, i.e. the subject *lɯ*³ 'you' and the object of *ka?*⁷ (i.e. *sio*³⁻²*bə*⁵ 'younger sister'), go to buy clothes together, is indicated by the whole construction. Note however, that the object governed by the comitative preposition cannot be considered to have a subject-like role. This is one criterion for distinguishing a comitative prepositional phrase clearly from a coordinate NP, a second one being that a coordinate NP would not permit a temporal noun such as 'tomorrow' to intervene between 'you' and 'younger sister'.

The comitative marker *ka?*⁷ is also used with the verb phrase *u*⁴ *kuan*¹*he*⁵/*bo*²⁻⁴ *kuan*¹*he*⁵ 有關係/無關係 'have a connection'/'have no connection' indicating that a person or thing has respectively something or nothing, to do with another person or thing, as in (7).

(7) 撮　　　合　　　　佣　　有/無　　　　　關係
tsuai²　ka?⁷⁻⁸　en¹　u⁴/bo²⁻⁴　kuan¹he⁵
these　COMT　3PL　have/not.have　connection
'These (things) have something/nothing to do with them.'

The structure *ka?*⁷ + NP + *u*⁴ *kuan*¹*he*⁵/*bo*²⁻⁴ *kuan*¹*he*⁵ as in (7) is a fixed phrase similar to English phrase *have something to do with /have nothing to do with*.

The comitative marker *ka?*⁷ can also indicate the object of a statement of comparison of equality when used in comparison of equality, as in (8), where *ka?*⁷ is used to introduce the comparee *gua*³ 我 'me'. In other words, *ka?*⁷ here can be regarded as a marker of the equative.

(8) 伊　　合　　　　我　　平　　歲
　　 i¹　　ka$ʔ$⁷⁻⁸　 gua³　pin²⁻⁴　hə⁵
　　 3SG　COMT　　1SG　same　year
　　 'He is the same age as me.'

Besides being a comitative marker, ka$ʔ$⁷ can also function as a conjunction (or connective marker) connecting nouns, noun phrases, pronouns, or verbs and verb phrases (see §21.2). An example is given in (9), where ka$ʔ$⁷ is used to connect two nouns, i.e. thŋ² 糖 'sugar' and iəm² 鹽 'salt'.

(9) 糖　　　合　　　　鹽
　　thŋ²　　ka$ʔ$⁷⁻⁸　 iəm²
　　sugar　and　　　salt
　　'sugar and salt'

The development from a comitative marker to a connective marker is widely attested not only in Chinese, but also cross-linguistically (cf. Heine & Kuteva 2002; Liu & Peyraube 1994 ; Peyraube 1996; Zhang 2011, among others). Thus, it is safe to say that the use of ka$ʔ$⁷ as a connective marker in Hui'an is derived from its use as a comitative marker.

16.4 The functions of ka⁵

As mentioned above, the morpheme ka⁵ in Hui'an takes on a range of functions (a) as an oblique marker, marking source, goal, beneficiary and maleficiary (see §16.4.1); (b) as an object marker (§16.4.2); and (c) it may precede a (non-)referential personal pronoun to express the speaker's subjective attitude (§16.4.3). For all these three uses of ka⁵, the syntactic structure can be represented as 'ka⁵ + NP + VP', where the NP involves different semantic roles and referential functions.

16.4.1 As an oblique marker

When used with ditransitive verbs of taking away such as tsio$ʔ$⁷ 借 'borrow' in (10) and tho³ 討 'ask for, beg' in (11), ka⁵ normally functions as a source marker, as shown by (10a) and (11a). In certain contexts, however, ka⁵ can also be interpreted as a benefactive marker, as in (10b) and (11b).

(10) 我　　共　　　伊　　借　　車

gua³ ka⁵⁻⁴ i¹ tsioʔ⁷⁻⁸ tshia¹
1SG from/for 3SG borrow vehicle
(a) 'I borrowed a car from him.'
(b) 'I borrowed a car (from somebody) for him.'

(11) 伊　　共　　　儂　　討　　錢
i¹　　ka⁵⁻⁴　　laŋ⁴　tho³⁻²　tsin²
3SG from/for other ask.for money
(a) 'He asked for money from somebody.'
(b) 'He asked for money for somebody.'

The borrowing event involves the borrower, the borrowed thing and the lender (i.e. the source). In Hui'an, the borrower and the borrowed thing are typically realized as a subject, *gua³* 'I' in (10) and an object, *tshia¹* 'car' in (10), respectively, while the lender (i.e. the source) is introduced by the morpheme *ka⁵*. Thus, example (10) is normally interpreted as 'I borrowed a car from him', as in (10a), in which *ka⁵* functions as a source marker, i.e. indicating the lender. In some contexts, however, a separate beneficiary may be involved. As with the source, the beneficiary in Hui'an is also introduced by the morpheme *ka⁵*. In this case, *ka⁵* NP may be interpreted as the beneficiary, with the source being underspecified, as in (10b), where *ka⁵* then serves as a benefactive marker. Similarly, example (11) has two possible interpretations: (a) *ka⁵* functions as a source marker, introducing the person from whom the money was asked for ; and (b) *ka⁵* functions as a benefactive marker, indicating the person for whom the money was asked. In the interpretation (b), the source, i.e. the person from whom the money was asked for, is not specified.

The following example shows that the benefactive and the source can both be specified in a given sentence, though this is not common in daily conversation.

(12) 共　　　我　　　共　　　㑑　　借　　　錢
ka⁵⁻⁴　gua³⁻²　ka⁵⁻⁴　en¹　tsioʔ⁷⁻⁸　tsin²
for 1SG from 3PL borrow money
'(He) borrowed money from them for me.'

In (12), the first *ka⁵* functions as a benefactive marker, indicating the beneficiary of the event 'borrow money', while the second *ka⁵* serves as a source marker, indicating the person from whom the money is borrowed.

When used with ditransitive verbs of communication such as *sə?⁷* 說 'say' in (13) and *pha?⁷⁻⁸ ten⁵⁻⁴ue⁵* 拍電話 'make a phone call' in (14), *ka⁵* normally functions as a goal marker.

(13) 汝　共　伊　說　汝　無　閑
　　 lu³　ka⁵⁻⁴　i¹　sə?⁷⁻⁸　lu³　bo²⁻⁴　uin²
　　 2SG　to　3SG　say　2SG　not.have　leisure
　　 'Tell him that you don't have time.'

(14) 伊　共　我　拍　電話
　　 i¹　ka⁵⁻⁴　gua³⁻²　pha?⁷⁻⁸　ten⁵⁻⁴ue⁵
　　 3SG　to　1SG　hit　telephone
　　 'He called me.'

The communication event involves the communicator, the transferred information and the receiver (i.e. the goal). In Hui'an, the communicator is typically realized as a subject such as *lu³* 'you' in (13) and *i¹* 'he' in (14), and the transferred information can be realized as an object in the object clause *lu³ bo²⁻⁴ uin²* 'you don't have time' in (13), or be underspecified as in (14), while the receiver (i.e. the goal) is normally introduced by the morpheme *ka⁵*, as in (13) and (14). In other words, in both (13) and (14), the morpheme *ka⁵* is used as a goal marker, indicating the receiver in a communication event.

In some cases, a beneficiary is involved and the morpheme *ka⁵* can be used to indicate the beneficiary, with the goal (i.e. the receiver) being (under)specified, as in (15) and (16).

(15) 汝　共　我　共　恁　爸　拍　電話
　　 lu³　ka⁵⁻⁴　gua³⁻²　ka⁵⁻⁴　len³⁻²　pa²　pha?⁷⁻⁸　ten⁵⁻⁴ue⁵
　　 2SG　for　1SG　to　2PL　father　hit　telephone
　　 'Make a phone call to your father for me.'

(16) 我　咧　共　伊　寫　批
　　 gua³　le?⁷⁻⁸　ka⁵⁻⁴　i¹　sia³⁻²　phue¹
　　 1SG　PROG　to/for　3SG　write　letter
　　 (a) 'I am writing a letter to him.'
　　 (b) 'I am writing a letter (to somebody) for him.'

Like example (14), (15) also involves an event of making a phone call. In this case, however, there are two tokens of the morpheme *ka⁵*: the first one is used to introduce the beneficiary *gua³* 'me', while the second one is used to introduce the goal (i.e. the receiver) *len³⁻²pa²* 'your father'. In other words, the first *ka⁵* functions as a benefactive marker, while the second *ka⁵* serves as a goal marker. In this case, both the beneficiary (*gua³* 'me') and the goal (*len³⁻²pa²* 'your father') are specified. In fact, in daily conversation, the goal is often underspecified when a beneficiary is involved, i.e. the goal *len³⁻²pa²* 'your father' in (15) can be omitted. Example (16) involves another communication event: an event of writing a letter. In this case, the morpheme *ka⁵* also functions as a goal marker, indicating the person to whom the letter is being written, as shown by (16a). However, in certain contexts (e.g. if the letter is being written for someone who is illiterate and unable to write), the morpheme *ka⁵* is used as a benefactive marker in its deputative sense, indicating the beneficiary of the letter-writing rather than the addressee. In this case, the goal, i.e. the receiver of the letter, is not specified.

When used with other verbs (especially transitive verbs) and when the NP following *ka⁵* does not serve as an argument, the morpheme *ka⁵* often functions as a benefactive marker, as in (17) and (18).

(17) 我　　共　　伊　　開　　門
  gua³　*ka⁵⁻⁴*　*i¹*　*khui¹*　*bŋ²*
  1SG　for　3SG　open　door
  'I opened the door for him.'

(18) 汝　　共　　我　　停　　車
  lu³　*ka⁵⁻⁴*　*gua³⁻²*　*thiŋ²⁻⁴*　*tshia¹*
  2SG　for　1SG　stop　vehicle
  'Park the car for me.'

In (17), the main verb *khui¹* 'open' involves two arguments: the agent *gua³* 'I' and the patient *bŋ²* 'door'. The NP following *ka⁵*, i.e. *i¹* 'him', does not function as an argument of the verb *khui¹*, and can be regarded as a beneficiary of the action 'open the door'. In other words, *ka⁵* in this case serves as a benefactive marker. Similarly, the main verb *thiŋ²* 'stop' in (18) has two arguments: the agent *lu³* 'you' and the patient *tshia¹* 'car', while *gua³* 'I' (the NP following the morpheme *ka⁵*) can be interpreted as a beneficiary of the action 'park the car'. Note that in both (17) and (18), the NP following *ka⁵* can not be regarded as a goal (the receiver).

In some cases, however, a reading of recipient-benefactive is involved, as exemplified by (19).

(19) 我　　共　　汝　　煮
　　 gua³　ka⁵⁻⁴　lɯ³⁻²　tsu³
　　 1SG　 for　 2SG　 cook
　　 (a) 'Let me cook for you (and give it to you).'
　　 (b) 'Let me cook for you (and give it to somebody else).'

The cooking event involves an agent (i.e. the cook) and a patient (i.e. the meal that is cooked). In (19), the agent is realized as the subject gua^3 'I', while the patient is not specified. The NP following ka^5, i.e. $lɯ^3$ 'you', can be regarded as a beneficiary of the cooking event, i.e. the person who will eat the meal that is cooked by the subject gua^3. After the cooking event, a giving event may be involved (though it is not necessary), that is, the agent of the cooking event gives the meal to the person who will eat it. In this context, speakers tend to interpret the beneficiary $lɯ^3$ 'you' as a goal, i.e. the receiver of the meal. In other words, a reading of recipient-benefactive seems to be involved here: 'let me cook for you and give it to you'. Example (19) has another possible interpretation. The context can be that the speaker (i.e. the subject gua^3 'I') is offering to help the addressee ($lɯ^3$ 'you', i.e. the NP following ka^5) cook the meal for the children (or someone else), since the addressee is already late for work. In this case, $lɯ^3$ 'you' is no longer a receiver of the meal, and thus can only be interpreted as a deputative beneficiary.

In examples (17) – (19), the verb phrases (i.e. $khui^1$ $bŋ^2$ 'open the door', $thiŋ^{2-4}$ $tshia^1$ 'park the car' and tsu^3 'cook') are all used in benefactive events, in which the beneficiary is indicated by the benefactive marker ka^5. In certain contexts, however, similar events can be regarded as malefactive, and the morpheme ka^5 accordingly functions as a malefactive marker, rather than a benefactive marker. For example, in a car parking event, the car may be parked in an inappropriate place or way, by which the participant encoded by the NP following ka^5 may be adversely affected. A more typical example of the malefactive marker ka^5 is given in (20).

(20) 杯仔　　　共　　　我　　　拍破
　　 puePə-a³　ka⁵⁻⁴　gua³⁻²　phaʔ⁷⁻⁸-phua⁵
　　 cup-NM　 MAL　 1SG　　 hit-broken
　　 '(He) broke the cup on me.'

In (20), the verb $phaʔ^{7-8}phua^5$ 'break' is inherently negative, and thus the event 'break the cup' is interpreted as a malefactive one. It is then obvious that gua^3 'I' (i.e. the NP following ka^5) serves as a maleficiary, and the morpheme ka^5 functions as a malefactive marker, indicating the person who is adversely affected by the even t of breaking the cup.

According to the analysis above, the morpheme ka^5 in Hui'an functions as a marker of the source or goal argument on the one hand, while on the other hand, it can function as a marker of the benefactive or malefactive adjunct. All the examples of ambiguity above show the following possible extension: the source/goal marker > the benefactive/malefactive marker. A similar extension can be found in Lai (2013), a detailed study on semantic extension of Hakka LAU, which takes on the functions that are examined in this chapter, such as the comitative, source, goal, benefactive and patient senses, though a different verbal source is involved (LAU can also be used as a verb meaning 'to mix') (see Lai 2003 for details).

16.4.2 As an object marker

When ka^5 is used as an object marker, the main verb is often encoded by a transitive action verb such as $siɔŋ^1hai^5$ 傷害 'hurt' in (21) and $thai^2$ 刣 'kill' in the imperative form given in (22), and the NP following ka^5 such as gun^3 阮 'we' in (21) and kue^1 雞 'chicken' in (22) functions as a patient of the main verb.

(21) 共　　阮　　　傷害　　　咯
$\underline{ka^{5\text{-}4}}$　$gun^{3\text{-}2}$　$siɔŋ^1hai^5$　$lɔ^0$
OM　　1PL　　hurt　　　SFP
'(He) has hurt me.'

(22) 共　　雞　　　刣　　　揀
$\underline{ka^{5\text{-}4}}$　kue^1　$thai^{2\text{-}4}$　sak^7
OM　　chicken　kill　　　RVC
'kill the chicken'

In (21), the first person plural pronoun gun^3, with a singular meaning in this context, functions as the patient of the main verb $siɔŋ^1hai^5$ 'hurt'. Similarly, the noun kue^1 'chicken' in (22) is the patient of the main verb $thai^2$ 'kill'. In both cases, the morpheme ka^5 functions as an object marker, more specifically in terms of its semantic role, as a patient marker, indicating the patient of the main verb.

Both (21) and (22) take the form of 'ka^5 + NP$_{\text{PATIENT}}$ + VP', in which the patient NP is preceded by the object marker ka^5 and encoded by a personal pronoun (gun^3

'we' in (21)) and a noun (*kue¹* 'chicken' in (22)), respectively. In fact, in daily conversation, the NP following the object marker *ka⁵* is normally encoded by a personal pronoun, as in (21), rather than by a noun, as in (22) (the patient of *ka⁷* in Taiwan is also typically pronominal, see Lien 2002). In other words, examples such as (22) are not common in contemporary Hui'an dialect. When a noun such as *kue¹* 'chicken' in (22) is involved, the noun is usually placed before the object marker *ka⁵*, functioning as a topic, while the third person singular pronoun *i¹* 伊, as a resumptive pronoun, occurs after the object marker *ka⁵*, as shown by example (23).

(23) 雞　　共　　伊　　刣　　揀
     kue¹　*ka⁵⁻⁴*　*i¹*　*thai²⁻⁴*　*sak⁷*
     Chicken　OM　3SG　kill　RVC
     'kill the chicken'

Unlike example (22), the noun *kue¹* 'chicken' in (23) occurs before the object marker *ka⁵*, functioning as a topic. The third person singular pronoun *i¹*, being coreferential with the topic *kue¹* 'chicken', is preceded by the object marker *ka⁵*. In other words, the construction takes the form of: NP$_{\text{PATIENT}}$ + *ka⁵* + 3SG + VP.

As shown by (21) – (23), the patient NP used with the object marker *ka⁵* can be animate: a person, as in (21), or an animal, as in (22) and (23). The following example shows that the patient NP can also be inanimate.

(24) 門　　共　　伊　　關　　(起來)
     bŋ²　*ka⁵⁻⁴*　*i¹*　*kuin¹*　*khai⁰*
     door　OM　3SG　close　RVC
     'close the door'

In (24), the patient NP is encoded by *bŋ²* 'door' and occurs before the object marker *ka⁵* to function as a topic. The third person singular pronoun *i¹*, being coreferential with the topic *bŋ²* 'door', occurs after the object marker *ka⁵*.

Besides marking a patient, as in (21) – (24), the object marker *ka⁵* in Hui'an is also often used to mark a theme, as in (25).

(25) 懷　　共　　伊　　下　　咧　　塗骸
     huai²　*ka⁵⁻⁴*　*i¹*　*khe⁴*　*leʔ⁷⁻⁸*　*thɔ²⁻⁴kha¹*
     those　OM　3SG　put　at　floor
     'Place those (things) on the floor.'

In (25), the location of the topic *huai²* 'those (things)' is changed to that of the floor due to the agent's action. Note that the object marker *ka⁵* is followed by the third person singular pronoun *i¹*, even though the topic *huai²* refers to plural entities.

As shown by example (26), a verb like *khuã⁵* 看 'look' can also be used with the object marker *ka⁵*.

(26) 著　　　去　　　共　　　伊　　　看　　　瞴
　　　tioʔ⁸⁻⁴　khu⁵⁻³　ka⁵⁻⁴　i¹　　khuã⁵⁻³　bai⁵
　　　should　go　　　OM　　3SG　look　　　TENT
　　　'(You) should go take a look at it.'

In (26), the object of the verb phrase *khuã⁵⁻³ bai⁵* 'take a look at' is placed before the verb phrase and indicated by the object marker *ka⁵*.

In certain contexts, additional to those discussed above for source and goal, some examples of the object marker *ka⁵* can be interpreted in three different ways, as illustrated by (27).

(27) a. 門　　　共　　　伊　　關　　　（起來）= (24)
　　　　bŋ²　　ka⁵⁻⁴　i¹　　kuin¹　khai⁰
　　　　door　OM　　3SG　close　RVC
　　　　'close the door'

　　　b. 門　　　共　　　伊　　關　　　（起來）
　　　　bŋ²　　ka⁵⁻⁴　i¹　　kuin¹　khai⁰
　　　　door　BEN　3SG　close　RVC
　　　　'close the door for him'

　　　c. 門　　　共　　　伊　　關　　　（起來）
　　　　bŋ²　　ka⁵⁻⁴　i¹　　kuin¹　khai⁰
　　　　door　MAL　3SG　close　RVC
　　　　'close the door on him'

As mentioned above, the third person singular pronoun *i¹* in this example can be coreferential with the topic *bŋ²* 'door', and the morpheme *ka⁵* functions as an object marker, as in (27a). However, when three persons are involved in the context, *ka⁵* may be used to introduce a beneficiary, as in (27b), or a maleficiary, as in (27c). The context of (27b) may be that the speaker asks the addressee to close the door for a third person who is sleeping, the beneficiary coded by 3SG *i¹* who will benefit from the action of closing the door, and attention to the need for some quiet. Accordingly, the morpheme *ka⁵* serves as a benefactive marker, rather than an object marker. When the door is closed to prevent the third person from entering the house, the third person might be adversely affected by this action (e.g. the third person is kept waiting outside the house), and so the interpretation (c) can arise. In this case, the pronoun *i¹* can refer to the maleficiary, i.e. the person who is prevented from entering the house. Accordingly, the morpheme *ka⁵* functions as a malefactive marker, rather than an object marker. This example shows the possible extension from benefactive/malefactive marker to object marker. Proposals for a similar series of semantic extensions can also be found in previous studies such as Chappell (2006, 2007) and Lai (2003).

16.4.3 *ka⁵* + personal pronoun

In Hui'an, the complex '*ka⁵* + 1SG' can be used in an imperative construction to express the speaker's subjective attitude, as in (28).

(28) 汝 共 我 出來
    lu³ *ka⁵⁻⁴* *gua³⁻²* *tshut⁷lai⁰*
    2SG KA 1SG come.out
    'Come out!'

Example (28) is normally used in the context that the speaker is very angry with the addressee for some reason and orders the addressee to come out. Without the prepositional phrase *ka⁵⁻⁴ gua³* (KA 1SG), *lu³ tshut⁷ lai⁰* also constitutes an imperative construction, used to ask or order the addressee to come out, depending on the intonation and the context. In other words, the complex *ka⁵⁻⁴ gua³* here is an adjunct, used to reinforce the imperative mood and express the speaker's subjective attitude.

This use of the complex '*ka⁵* + 1SG' may additionally be associated with the use of *ka⁵* as a benefactive marker. We can take a look at example (29).

(29) 汝 共 我 出來 者
    lu³ *ka⁵⁻⁴* *gua³⁻²* *tshut⁷lai⁰* *tse⁰*
    2SG BEN 1SG come.out DELIM
    'Come out for a while for me.'

Example (29) tends to be used in the context where the speaker wants to discuss something with the addressee and requests the addressee to come outside for his or her benefit. In this case, the first person singular pronoun *gua³* functions as a beneficiary, and *ka⁵* accordingly serves as a benefactive marker.

In fact, even in (28), *ka⁵* may be regarded as a benefactive marker, since the action of coming out meets the expectation of the speaker. However, we wish to highlight here the fact that the complex [*ka⁵* + 1SG] has become a fixed expression indicating that the speaker is very angry with the addressee over some matter and, as a result, orders the addressee to do something.

Similarly, the morpheme *ka⁵* can also be followed by a second or third person singular pronoun to express the speaker's subjective attitude. An example of this use with the second person singular pronoun is given in (30c).

(30) 伊　　賬　　　共　　　汝　　　做　　　遘　　好好
     i¹　　*tsaŋ⁵*　　*ka⁵⁻⁴*　*lu³⁻²*　*tsue⁵*　*a³*　*ho³⁻²~ho³*
     3SG　Accounts　KA　2SG　do　　　CM　good~good
     a. 'She has done well for you with the accounts.'
     b. 'She has fiddled the accounts well on you.'
     c. 'She has fiddled the accounts well.'

The utterance in (30) is a real recorded example from our spoken data and from its context has the sense of (30c). However, the interpretations (a) and (b) are also possible in certain other contexts. In both (30a) and (30b), the second person singular pronoun *lu³* refers to the addressee. The difference is that the morpheme *ka⁵* in (30a) functions as a benefactive marker indicating that the addressee benefits from the event 'she has done well with the accounts', while *ka⁵* in (30b) functions as a malefactive marker indicating that the addressee is adversely affected by the event of fiddling the accounts. Unlike (30a) and (30b), the pronoun *lu³* in (30c) does not refer to anybody. In other words, *lu³* does not function as a maleficiary, and accordingly *ka⁵* does not function as a malefactive marker. An omission of *ka⁵⁻⁴ lu³* does not change the semantic meaning of the sentence. The phrase *ka⁵⁻⁴ lu³* is used to indicate that the speaker is unhappy about the event 'she has fiddled the accounts well'. In other words, *ka⁵⁻⁴ lu³* here is used to express the speaker's disapproval, rather than indicate the precise role of a maleficiary. This example also shows the extension of *ka⁵* from a benefactive/malefactive marker to a stance marker, accompanied by a change of the second person singular pronoun following *ka⁵* from a referential one to a non-referential one.

Two more examples of the complex [*ka⁵* + 3SG] are given in (31a) and (32a).

(31) 媽仔　　　好得　　　共　伊　社保
　　 bã²-a⁰　　 ho³⁻²tet⁷　 ka⁵⁻⁴ i¹ sia⁴-po³
　　 mother-NM　fortunately　KA　3SG　social-insurance
　　 a. 'Fortunately, I (your mother) have applied for social insurance.'
　　 b. 'Fortunately, I (your mother) have applied for social insurance for him.'

(32) 阿三　　共　　伊　笑　　　出來
　　 a¹sã¹　 ka⁵⁻⁴ i¹ tshio⁵　 tshut⁰lai⁰
　　 PN　　 KA　　3SG　laugh　come.out
　　 a. 'Unfortunately, Ah-San burst out laughing.'
　　 b. 'Ah-San burst out laughing on him.'

The utterance in (31) is also a recorded example and in the context has the sense of (31a). The context of (31a) is that the speaker feels lucky that she has applied for social insurance for herself. The third person singular pronoun *i¹* here, without referring to anybody, does not function as a beneficiary, and thus *ka⁵* is not a benefactive marker. In fact, the complex *ka⁵⁻⁴ i¹* is used to indicate that the speaker feels that she has done the right thing, and thus is very happy about this. However, it is true that the interpretation in (31b) is also possible, when the speaker has applied for social insurance for someone else (e.g. her husband), and similarly feels happy about this. In this case, the pronoun *i¹* does in fact refer to a real beneficiary, i.e. the person for whom the speaker has applied for social insurance. Note that *sia⁴po³* can be a noun meaning 'social insurance', but here it is used as a verb meaning 'apply for the social insurance'. Example (32) normally means that 'unfortunately, Ah-San burst out laughing', as in (32a). In this case, the complex *ka⁵⁻⁴ i¹* is used to express the speaker's subjective attitude of disapproval, that is, the speaker believes that the subject *a¹sã¹* should not burst out laughing. Like the pronoun in (31a), the third person singular pronoun *i¹* in (32a) is empty in its reference. However, we can imagine the following context: some person has asked Ah-San to refrain from bursting out laughing on him, but Ah-San does in fact do this. In this context, the third person singular pronoun *i¹* refers to a third party and the morpheme *ka⁵* serves as a malefactive marker, as shown in (32b). These two examples show the possible extension of *ka⁵* from a benefactive/malefactive marker to a stance marker, accompanied by a change of the third person singular pronoun following *ka⁵* from a referential to a non-referential one.

16.5 Summary

This chapter examines the *kaʔ⁷* 合-construction and the *ka⁵* 共-construction in Hui'an. Unlike some other Southern Min varieties such as Xiamen and Taiwan, the morpheme *kaʔ⁷* in Hui'an functions as a connective or comitative marker, while *ka⁵* takes on a range of other functions: (a) it functions as an oblique marker, marking source, goal, beneficiary and maleficiary; (b) it also functions as an object marker; and (c) it can precede a (non-)referential personal pronoun to express the speaker's subjective attitude. We suggest that the use (c) of the morpheme *ka⁵* is related to its use as a benefactive/malefactive marker. This is different from what has been put forward by Lin (2012), where similar constructions in Taiwan are regarded as a subtype of the object marking construction.

17 Comparative constructions of inequality

17.1 Introduction

The comparative construction of inequality (hereafter termed 'comparative construction') is defined as one which 'has the semantic function of assigning a graded (i.e. non-identical) position on a predicative scale to two (possibly complex) objects' (Stassen 1985:24). Comparative constructions typically involve four constituents: the comparee (COM), the standard of comparison (STA), the (comparative) predicate (PRED) and the comparative marker (CM) (Stassen 1985:24-26; Ansaldo 1999:39; Chappell & Peyraube 2015). The term 'the (comparative) predicate' here refers to the constituent that 'states the dimension of the comparison' (Ansaldo 1999:39). This is different from 'the predicate' in traditional grammar, which functions as one of two main parts of a sentence, with the other part being the subject.

As stated in Chappell & Peyraube (2015), the predicate in comparative constructions is predominantly expressed by an adjective, but is not confined to this category in Chinese. We follow Ansaldo (1999) and Chappell & Peyraube (2015) in using the term 'comparative marker' to refer to markers applied to either the standard noun or the predicate: the former is typically used to introduce the standard of comparison, such as the comparative marker *bǐ* 比 in Mandarin Chinese; whereas the latter is generally used to modify the predicate, such as the comparative marker *gwo³* 過 in Cantonese, which functions as a verbal complement of the predicate. These two types of comparative marker are referred to respectively as a dependent-marker of comparison (DMC) and a head-marker of comparison (HMC) in Ansaldo (1999:39).

In his typological study on comparative constructions, Stassen (1985:28-47) identified six basic types of comparative in a sample of 110 languages based on the encoding of the standard NP: the separative comparative, the allative comparative, the locative comparative, the exceed comparative, the conjoined comparative, and the particle comparative. In another important typological study on comparative constructions, Heine (1997) argued that most comparative constructions in the languages of the world are derived from a limited number of conceptual source structures (or event schemas), and he identified eight main event schemas: Action, Location, Source, Goal, Polarity, Sequence, Similarity and Topic. A comparison between these two proposals is given in Chappell &

Note: Preliminary versions of this chapter also appeared in Chen (2008) and Chen (2015).

Peyraube (2015), from which a table summarizing the correspondances is reproduced as follows.

Tab. 17-1: Comparison of analytic approaches for comparative schemas of superiority

	STASSEN 1985, 2005, 2011	HEINE 997	
1	Separative	Source	'from'
2	Allative	Goal	'to'
3	Locative	Location	'at'
4	Exceed	Action	'surpass, defeat'
5	Conjoined	Polarity	'X is A, Y is not A'
6	Particle	Sequence	e.g. Germanic 'than'
7	--	Similarity	'as, like'
8	--	Topic	'X and Y, Y is A'

In terms of Chinese, much work has been done on comparative constructions during the past two decades, for example, Li & Lien 1995; Ansaldo 1999, 2010; Zhao 2002; Li 2003; Chang & Kwok 2005; Wu 2010; Chappell & Peyraube 2015, among others. Ansaldo (1999:105) identifies three main types of (target) comparative construction in Chinese: (i) Head-marking comparatives based on the Surpass or Exceed source construction; (ii) Dependent-marking based on the Similarity source construction; and (iii) Double-marking, as follows.

17.1.1 Three main types of comparative proposed in Ansaldo (1999)

(i) Head-marking/Surpass type

In the Surpass type of comparative, the standard of comparison is required to be constructed as the direct object of the main verb, noted as a property of the source construction (Ansaldo 1999:64). An example from Cantonese is given in (1), where the standard of comparison *Soeng⁶Hoi²* 上海 'Shanghai' functions as the direct object of the verb phrase *jit⁶ gwo³* 熱過 'is warmer than'.

(1) 香港 熱 過 上海
 Hoeng¹Gong² jit⁶ gwo³ Soeng⁶Hoi²
 Hongkong warm HMC Shanghai
 'Hong Kong is warmer than Shanghai.' (Ansaldo 1999:105)

This type of comparative construction is one of the two predominant comparative construction types in contemporary Chinese, and widely attested in Southern and Southwestern China, in particular Yue, Hakka and Southwestern Mandarin (cf. Li 2003). This type of comparative basically equates with the second structural type (Type II, Surpass type, NP_A – VERB – CM - NP_B), proposed by Chappell & Peyraube (2015), or the Exceed type in Stassen (1995), and is associated with the 'Action schema' in Heine (1997).

(ii) Dependent-marking/Similarity type
In this type of comparative, the standard of comparison in the source construction is marked by an element originally meaning 'to look like', 'like', 'comparatively' and 'to be compared to' (Ansaldo 1999:64, 119). An example from Mandarin Chinese is given in (2), where the comparative marker bǐ 比 'compared to' is used to introduce the standard of comparison jiějie 姐姐 'elder sister'.

(2) 弟弟   比   姐姐   聰明
    dìdi   bǐ   jiějie   Cōngmíng
    brother DMC   E.sister Smart
    'Little brother is smarter than the elder sister.' (Ansaldo 1999:105)

As mentioned in Ansaldo (1999:64), the term 'Similarity' is used in a slightly different way from that in Heine (1997:118), where, in the Similarity Schema, a relationship of similarity or equivalence is asserted between the comparee and the standard of comparison. The basic structure of the Similarity Schema in Heine (1997) is [A_{COM} is PRED (like) B_{STA}], and can be paraphrased as [A_{COM} is PRED-er compared to B_{STA}] (p.118).

Unlike Ansaldo (1999), comparative constructions such as example (2) are separately categorized as a new 'Compare' schema in Chappell & Peyraube (2015), since they claim that the comparative marker bǐ 'compared to' does not have the meaning of 'be similar to' in the comparative construction, and thus cannot, strictly speaking, be treated as a similarity comparative. This type of comparative is the most common type in Chinese: it is widely used in Northern China and has been adopted elsewhere in Chinese (cf. Ansaldo 1999; Li 2003).

(iii) Double-marking type
Double marking type refers to a comparative construction which has both a marker for the standard and a marker for the predicate. An example from Hui'an is given in (3), where the dependent-marker of comparison pi^3 比 'compared to' is used to introduce the standard of comparison i^3 椅 'chair', and the head-marker

of comparison *kha?⁷* 恰 modifies the comparative predicate *taŋ⁴* 重 'heavy' to denote comparison.

(3) 桌 比 椅 恰 重
    to?⁷ *pi³⁻²* *i³* *kha?⁷⁻⁸* *taŋ⁴*
    table DMC chair HMC heavy
    'The table is heavier than the chair.'

This type of comparative construction is termed a hybridized construction and is so far attested only in Min and Hakka (Li 2003; Chappell 2015).

So far, it is quite clear that Types (i) and (ii) among the three types of comparative proposed in Ansaldo (1999) are the two main types of comparative in Chinese, as mentioned in Chappell & Peyraube (2015), since Type (iii) has a comparatively limited distribution in Chinese. Significantly, Type (iii) is an important type of comparative construction in contemporary Southern Min (cf. Wang & Zhang 1994; Li & Lien 1995; Zhou & Ouyang 1998, among others). In addition, previous studies such as Li (2003) have shown that certain other types of comparative construction are also mainly attested in Min, while they are rarer in many other Chinese varieties. This analysis attempts to further examine these 'special' comparatives in Min, which are quite limited in their distribution, with examples from Hui'an.

We have identified six main types of comparative construction in Hui'an, as shown in §17.1.2 below.

17.1.2 Six main types of comparative in the Hui'an dialect

a. Double-marking/hybridized comparatives
   i.e. 'A$_{COM}$ + *pi³* 比 + B$_{STA}$ + *kha?⁷* 恰 + PRED (+ MW)'
b. Absolute comparatives
   i.e. 'A$_{COM}$ + *kha?⁷* + PRED (+ MW)'
c. Head-marking comparatives with the marker *kha?⁷*
   i.e. 'A$_{COM}$ + *kha?⁷* + PRED + B$_{STA}$ (+ MW)'
d. Zero-marked comparatives
   i.e. 'A$_{COM}$ + PRED + B$_{STA}$ (+ MW)'
e. Comparatives with the marker *khuɯ⁵*
   i.e. 'A$_{COM}$ + PRED + *khuɯ⁵* 去 + B$_{STA}$'
f. Dependent-marking comparatives with the marker *pi³*
   i.e. 'A$_{COM}$ + *pi³* + B$_{STA}$ + PRED (+ MW)'

Note that type (a) and type (b), i.e. the hybridized or double-marked comparative 'A$_{COM}$ + pi^3 + B$_{STA}$ + $kha?^7$ + PRED (+ MW)' and the absolute comparative 'A$_{COM}$ + $kha?^7$ + PRED (+ MW)' are the two dominant types, examples of which can be freely found in the spoken data we collected. In addition, these two types are commonly used not only by the younger generation, but also by the elder generation. Examples of type (c), i.e. the head-marking comparative 'A$_{COM}$ + $kha?^7$ + PRED + B$_{STA}$' can also be found in the spoken data. However, type (c) is more common in the speech of the elder generation than in the speech of the younger generation. The other three types, i.e. types (d), (e) and (f), are attested mainly via elicitation. Among these three types, type (d) is more common than the other two types, whereas type (f), the most common one found in Chinese, is the least common type of comparative in Hui'an.

I will now present each type of comparative construction in turn.

17.2 Double-marking/hybridized comparatives: A$_{COM}$ pi^3 B$_{STA}$ $kha?^7$ PRED (MW)

This type of comparative construction is widely used not only in Hui'an, but also in other Southern Min varieties in Fujian, Taiwan and Singapore (cf. Chen 1991a:299; Chen 1991b:458; Yang 1991:260; Wang & Zhang 1994:143; Li & Lien 1995:72; Zhou & Ouyang 1998:398; Li 2000:131; Zhou & Zhou 2000:130, among others). Ansaldo (1999) calls this type of comparative construction in Southern Min the double-marking type, given the presence of two markers: one marker for the standard of comparison (i.e. pi^3) and another for the predicate (i.e. $kha?^7$). Chappell & Peyraube (2015), however, use the term 'hybridized construction' to refer to this type, since it involves a blend of different types of comparative in Chinese, as will be mentioned later.

In Hui'an, the comparee and the standard of comparison in this type of comparative construction can be encoded by either substantive or predicative words and phrases. Two examples are given in (4) and (5).

(4) 即蕊   比   迄蕊   恰   水   蠻儕
    $tsit^{7\text{-}8}\text{-}lui^3$ $pi^{3\text{-}2}$ $hit^{7\text{-}8}\text{-}lui^3$ $kha?^{7\text{-}8}$ sui^3 $ban^{2\text{-}4}tsue^5$
    this-CL   DMC   that-CL   HMC   beautiful   much
    'This (flower) is much more beautiful than that (flower).'

(5) 有　　比　　無　　恰　　好
　　 u^4　 pi^{3-2}　 bo^2　 $kha\textrm{?}^{7-8}$　 ho^3
　　 have　DMC　not.have　HMC　good
　　 'Something is better than nothing.' (lit. have compared to not have comparatively good)

In (4), the comparee and the standard of comparison are encoded by the demonstrative phrase $tsit^{7-8}lui^3$ 'this (flower)' and $hit^{7-8}lui^3$ 'that (flower)', respectively. In (5), the comparee and the standard are expressed by the verbs u^4 'have' and bo^2 'not have', respectively. In both examples (4) and (5), pi^3 functions as a dependent-marker of comparison introducing the standard of comparison, i.e. $hit^{7-8}lui^3$ 'that (flower)' and bo^2 'not have', while $kha\textrm{?}^7$ is used as a head-marker of comparison modifying the predicate, which is encoded by the adjective sui^3 'beautiful' and ho^3 'good' respectively. Unlike (5), the adjective sui^3 'beautiful' in (4) is followed by the measure phrase $ban^{2-4}tsue^5$ 'much' denoting the degree of the difference between the comparee and the standard, indicating that the measure phrase is optional in this type of comparative construction.

The following example shows that the predicate can also be encoded by a non-monosyllabic adjective such as $u^4tshui^{5-3}tsi\textrm{?}^8$ 有喙舌 'talkative'.

(6) 伊　　比　　我　　恰　　有喙舌
　　 i^1　 pi^{3-2}　 gua^3　 $kha\textrm{?}^{7-8}$　 u^4-$tshui^{5-3}$-$tsi\textrm{?}^8$
　　 3SG　DMC　1SG　HMC　have-mouth-tongue
　　 'She is more talkative than me.'

In (6), the comparative predicate u^4 $tshui^{5-3}tsi\textrm{?}^8$, consisting of the verb u^4 'have' and the noun $tshui^{5-3}tsi\textrm{?}^8$ 'mouth and tongue', is a fixed expression functioning as an adjective to denote 'talkative'.

A topic may be involved in this type of comparative construction. The topic can be placed before the comparee, that is, the comparative construction takes the form of 'Topic A_{COM} pi^3 B_{STA} $kha\textrm{?}^7$ PRED (MW)', as in (7) below.

(7) 坐　　車　　廣州　　比　　泉州　　恰　　加　　時間
　　 $\underline{tsə^4}$　 $\underline{tshia^1}$　 $kŋ^{3-2}tsiu^1$　 pi^{3-2}　 $tsuan^{2-4}tsiu^1$　 $kha\textrm{?}^{7-8}$　 ke^1　 $si^{2-4}kan^1$
　　 sit　vehicle　PN　　DMC　PN　　HMC　more　time
　　 'It takes more time to take the bus to Guangzhou than to Quanzhou.'

In (7), the verb phrase *tsə⁴ tshia¹* 'take bus', preceding the comparee (*kŋ³⁻²tsiu¹* 'Guangzhou'), functions as a topic indicating that the comparison between the comparee and the standard of comparison is based on 'taking the bus'.

The following example illustrates that the topic can also be inserted between the comparee and the dependent-marker of comparison, that is, the comparative construction takes the form of 'A_COM Topic *pi³* B_STA *khaʔ⁷* PRED (MW)'.

(8) 我　　讀　　比　　伊　　恰　　好
　　gua³　*thak⁸*　*pi³⁻²*　*i¹*　*khaʔ⁷⁻⁸*　*ho³*
　　1SG　study　DMC　3SG　HMC　good
　　'I study better than him.'

In (8), the comparee (*gua³* 'I') and the standard of comparison (*i¹* 'he') are compared in terms of studying, which is encoded by the verb *thak⁸* 'study'. Furthermore, as noted above, the topic *thak⁸* is inserted between the comparee (*gua³*) and the dependent-marker of comparison (*pi³*).

The topic can also be placed between the standard of comparison and the head-marker of comparison, as in (9), where the topic *huaŋ¹* 風 'wind' is inserted between the standard of comparison *ku⁵⁻⁴lin²* 舊年 'last year' and the head-marker of comparison *khaʔ⁷*. In other words, the comparative construction takes the form of 'A_COM *pi³* B_STA Topic *khaʔ⁷* PRED (MW)'.

(9) 今年　　　比　　舊年　　　風　　恰　　透
　　ken¹-lin²　*pi³⁻²*　*ku⁵⁻⁴-lin²*　*huaŋ¹*　*khaʔ⁷⁻⁸*　*thau⁵*
　　this-year　DMC　old-year　wind　HMC　strong
　　'The wind of this year is stronger than that of last year.'

It is generally known that the comparative construction in Mandarin Chinese takes the form of [A_COM + *bĭ* 比 + B_STA + PRED], that is, the standard of comparison is placed between the comparative marker (*bĭ* 比) and the comparative predicate, which is disharmonic with the basic SVO word order pattern of Mandarin Chinese (cf. Dryer 1992; see also Chappell & Peyraube 2015), and not compatible with Greenberg's Universal 22 as shown in (iv).

(iv) No. 22. If in comparisons of inequality the only order, or one of the alternative orders, is standard-marker-adjective, then the language is postpositional. With overwhelmingly more than chance frequency, if the only order is adjective-marker-standard, the language is prepositional. (Greenberg 1966:89)

Similarly, in the double-marking/hybridized type of comparative construction in Hui'an as in examples (4) - (9) above, the standard of comparison is placed between the marker of the standard (dependent-marker of comparison) and the predicate, i.e. 'DMC-STA-HMC-PRED', which is also neither harmonic with its basic SVO word order pattern nor compatible with Greenberg's Universal 22.

Liu (2003c:17-18), however, points out that this double-marking/hybridized type of comparative construction satisfies the principle concerning relators put forward by Dik (1997:406): relators have their preferred position in between their two relata. According to Dik (1997:398), '(T)he class of relators contains those grammatical elements which serve to link two constituents together, and/or to mark the function(s) of a constituent as specified in underlying clause structure'. In the case of comparatives, in order to be compatible with the principle concerning the relators, the comparative marker needs to be placed between the predicate and the standard of comparison. The comparative construction [A_{COM} + *bǐ* 比 + B_{STA} + PRED] in Mandarin Chinese does not satisfy the principle concerning relators, since the marker *bǐ* 'compared to' is not placed between the standard of comparison and the predicate, whereas markers of the predicate (head markers of comparison) such as *khaʔ⁷* 恰 in the double-marking/hybridized type of comparative in Hui'an fill in the 'gap' between the standard of comparison and the predicate (Liu 2003c:17-18).

As with other Southern Min varieties, the head marker of comparison *khaʔ⁷* can be substituted by *koʔ⁷⁻⁸khaʔ⁷* 佫恰 'even more', which is similar to the adverb *gèng* 更 '(even) more' in Mandarin Chinese, as in (10).

(10) 我　　比　　伊　　佫恰　　　　懸
 　　gua³　*pi³⁻²*　*iʲ*　*koʔ⁷⁻⁸khaʔ⁷⁻⁸*　*kuin²*
 　　1SG　DMC　3SG　even.more　　tall
 　　'I am even taller than her.'

Example (10) implies that both the comparee (*gua³* 'I') and the standard of comparison (*iʲ* 'she') are tall, based on which, the comparee is taller than the standard of comparison. However, without *koʔ⁷*, i.e. *gua³ pi³⁻² iʲ khaʔ⁷⁻⁸ kuin²* 我比伊恰懸 'I am taller than her' does not imply that both the comparee and the standard of comparison are tall. In other words, it could be that both the comparee and the standard of comparison are short, while the comparee is nevertheless still taller than the standard of comparison. Note also that the English translation provided above for (10) is not semantically equivalent to the comparative construction of the Hui'an dialect, since the English sentence 'I am even taller than her' does not necessarily imply that both the comparee and the standard are tall.

The double-marking type of comparative is probably not uncommon cross-linguistically. At least, it is attested in many European languages such as German, English and Italian. An example from English is given in (11), where the comparative predicate *old* is marked by the suffix *-er*, and the standard of comparison *me* is marked by the conjunction *than*. In this case, note however that Dixon (2012, vol 3) distinguishes two grammatical functions which are 'mark' and 'index': the index is the form that carries the meaning of 'more' or 'surpass' and it modifies the parameter of comparison, while the mark is the form that introduces the standard noun, such as English *than* or German *als*.

(11) *He is older than me.*

However, unlike the double-marking type of comparative in European languages as in (11) above, the double-marking type of comparative in Chinese (e.g. Min and Hakka) tends to be a result of hybridization due to language contact (see also Li & Lien 1995; Ansaldo 1999; Chappell & Peyraube 2015). This type of comparative is not attested in the *Li Jing Ji*, and may arise due to language contact (Li & Lien 1995:74, 77). Ansaldo (1999:107, 140) suggests that the double-marking type of comparative construction may arise in Chinese as a consequence of a hybridization of two different source constructions, i.e. the Surpass type (e.g. with $kha\textrm{?}^{7}$ as a head-marker of comparison) and the Similarity type (with pi^3 as a dependent-marker of comparison), due to Northern influence.

Following this proposal, the double-marking/hybridized comparative in Southern Min, including the Hui'an dialect, may be the result of interaction of the Similarity/Compare type (i.e. A_{COM} pi^3 B_{STA} PRED) and head-marking comparatives with the marker $kha\textrm{?}^{7}$ (i.e. A_{COM} $kha\textrm{?}^{7}$ PRED B_{STA} (MW), see §17.4 below). This is also what Chappell (2015) suggests. However, we are not able to rule out another possibility: the double-marking/hybridized comparative 'A_{COM} pi^3 B_{STA} $kha\textrm{?}^{7}$ PRED (MW)' may be a blend of the Similarity/Compare type (i.e. A_{COM} pi^3 B_{STA} PRED) and absolute comparatives (i.e. A_{COM} $kha\textrm{?}^{7}$ PRED (MW), see §17.3 below), since, as will be shown in the following discussion, absolute comparatives are one of the predominant comparative construction types in both earlier Southern Min and contemporary Southern Min.

Note that unlike gwo^3 in Cantonese which functions as a verbal complement in post-verbal position as in example (1) above, $kha\textrm{?}^{7}$ functions as a comparative marker in pre-verbal position. As suggested in §17.1, $kha\textrm{?}^{7}$ can be used in three types of comparative construction (see also Ansaldo 1999:114). As shown by the following example, $kha\textrm{?}^{7}$ can also be used as a degree adverb meaning 'a bit; fairly' in non-comparative constructions with scalar adjectives (see §15.3.1).

(12) Non-comparative constructions with *khaʔ⁷* as a degree adverb
a. 湯　　恰　　　無　　　甜
   thŋ¹　*khaʔ⁷⁻⁸*　*boˀ²⁻⁴*　*tin¹*
   soup　a.bit　not.have　sweet
   'The soup is not tasty enough.'

b. 汝　　著　　　　恰　　　主動
   lɯ³　*tioʔ⁸⁻⁴*　*khaʔ⁷⁻⁸*　*tsu³⁻²tɔŋ⁴*
   2SG　should　fairly　active
   'You need to be fairly active.'

In (12a), the subject *thŋ¹* 'soup' is not explicitly compared to anything else, and the adjective phrase *khaʔ⁷⁻⁸ boˀ²⁻⁴ tin¹* 'not tasty enough' is used to denote the degree of tastiness of the soup, that is, somewhere between tasty and non-tasty, but closer to tasty, which suggests that adding a bit of salt, but not too much, will be enough. The context for (12b) is that the speaker is giving some advice on how to find a job to the addressee (i.e. the subject *lɯ³* 'you') who is about to graduate from university. The speaker neither makes a comparison between the addressee and anyone else, nor compares the present behavior of the addressee and his future behavior. The use of *khaʔ⁷* here means that the active approach of the subject in taking the initiative to look for a job should achieve a certain degree on the scale of activeness, otherwise the subject will not get what he wants. Note that *khaʔ⁷* cannot be used with non-gradable adjectives such as 'alive' or 'dead'.

The two examples in (12) take the form of [NP *khaʔ⁷* VP] with *khaʔ⁷* functioning as a degree adverb meaning 'a bit; fairly', rather than a comparative marker. This adverbial use of *khaʔ⁷* may suggest that the absolute comparatives (i.e. A$_{COM}$ *khaʔ⁷* PRED (MW), see §17.3 below) are not highly grammaticalized comparative constructions, since similar syntactic structures may be regarded as non-comparatives where *khaʔ⁷* is a degree adverb without denoting any comparison, but rather a point on a scale for the given quality or feature. However, in the examples of double-marking/hybridized comparatives above and head-marking comparatives with *khaʔ⁷* (i.e. A$_{COM}$ *khaʔ⁷* PRED B$_{STA}$ (MW)) described in §17.4 below, *khaʔ⁷* indicates comparison. This may suggest that *khaʔ⁷* in Hui'an undergoes grammaticalization from a degree adverb to a marker of comparison, although the relevant pathway remains unclear (see also Dixon 2012: 370 on diachronic sources).

The counterparts of *khaʔ⁷* in other Min varieties have also been reported to function as a degree adverb, or, if not, to also have a meaning of 'a bit, a little'. For example, Lin (1998:374) points out that *kah* found in Southern Min spoken in Fujian such as Xiamen, Zhangzhou and Quanzhou is a degree adverb meaning 'a bit, a little'. The counterpart of *khaʔ⁷* in the Singapore variety of Southern Min also has a meaning of 'a bit, a little' (Zhou & Zhou 2002:291). Zhou & Ouyang (1998:379, 398-400) and Zhou (1999:220, 222) suggest that *k'aʔ* in Xiamen is originally a degree verb meaning 'fairly', but has been gradually grammaticalized to be a marker of comparative constructions. *K'aʔ* in the Chaozhou variety of Southern Min and in the Fuzhou variety of Eastern Min similarly functions as a degree adverb meaning 'too' (cf. Cai 1991:235; Feng 1998:395).

Similar extensions from a degree adverb to a comparative marker are also attested in other Chinese varieties, although a post-verbal degree adverb, rather than a pre-verbal degree adverb as *khaʔ⁷* in Hui'an, may be involved. For example, in Xianghua, an unclassified Chinese spoken in Xiangxi in Hunan province of China, the morpheme sa^{55} 些 is originally a degree adverb meaning 'a little', but functions as a comparative marker in polarity comparatives (cf. Chappell 2015), as in example (13), where sa^{55} follows the predicate fi^{13} 肥 'fat' and ua^{55} 瘦 'thin'.

(13) 你 肥 些, 我 瘦 些
 ni^{25} fi^{13} sa^{55}, wu^{25} ua^{55} sa^{55}
 2SG fat little 1SG thin little
 'You're fatter and I'm thinner.' = 'You're fatter than me.'

In Cantonese, the morpheme *dī* 啲 can be used in the absolute comparative [A_COM PRED *dī*] to simply denote comparison, that is, where the standard of comparison is not explicitly mentioned but implied by the context, as in (14) below, although it may also mean 'rather' or 'a bit' in a similar structure (Matthews & Yip 2011:188-189).

(14) 今日 熱 啲
 gāmyaht *yiht* *dī*
 today hot a.bit
 'It's hotter today.' (Matthews & Yip 2011:189)

17.3 Absolute comparatives: A_COM *khaʔ⁷* PRED (MW)

As stated in Ansaldo (1999:43), comparatives often appear in a shortened, or truncated form without an overt standard of comparison in conversation and real language use. This comparative is called 'short comparative' in Ansaldo (1999). In traditional grammar, however, this construction is known as the absolute comparative (Huddleston & Pullum 2002: 1161ff. *inter alia*). The absolute comparative in Hui'an typically takes the form of [A_COM *khaʔ⁷* PRED], in which *khaʔ⁷* serves as a head-marker of comparison, like the comparative marker *khaʔ⁷* in the double-marking type of comparative examined in §17.2 above.

The absolute comparative is also widely used in other contemporary Southern Min varieties such as Taiwan (Lu 2003:92-93) and Jieyang 揭陽 (Xu 2007:278-279). In Taiwan, the comparative marker in the absolute comparative is the counterpart of *khaʔ⁷* in Hui'an, whereas the absolute comparative in Jieyang is syntactically indicated by markers such as *iau⁵³*, *lau⁵³* and *zu⁵³* (cf. Lu 2003:92; Xu 2007:278). Xu (2007:278) also mentions that absolute comparatives in Jieyang are 'only possible if the Sta [standard of comparison] has been mentioned before in the immediate discourse'. In Hui'an, however, the reason for the omission of the standard of comparison is because it can usually be inferred from the context. An example is given in (15).

(15) 口　　喉　　恰　　　　有聲　　　　咯
  tse⁵　*au²*　*khaʔ⁷⁻⁸*　*u⁴-siã¹*　*lɔ⁰*
  now　throat　HMC　have-voice　SFP
  '(Your) throat is better now (than before).'

In (15), the comparee *tse⁵* 'now' is compared to 'before' (the standard of comparison) which is not expressed but can be inferred from the context. Example (15) also suggests that a topic such as *au²* 'throat' can be overt in absolute comparatives. In addition, the topic *au²* is placed between the comparee *tse⁵* 'now' and the head-marker of comparison *khaʔ⁷*. The comparee *tse⁵* 'now' is a temporal word which is a substantive, and the comparative predicate *u⁴ siã¹* is a verb phrase with *siã¹* as the object of the existential verb *u⁴*.

In the following, we give an example in which the comparee is encoded by a verb phrase such as *tshiŋ⁵⁻⁴ tsit⁷⁻⁸liã³* 穿即領 'wear this piece (of clothing)', rather than a substantive word.

(16) 穿　　　　即領　　　　恰　　　　　爽
  tshiŋ⁵⁻⁴　*tsit⁷⁻⁸-liã³*　*khaʔ⁷⁻⁸*　*sɔŋ³*
  wear　this-CL　HMC　comfortable
  'Wearing this piece (of clothing) is more comfortable than (wearing that one).'

In (16), the comparee *tshiŋ⁵⁻⁴ tsit⁷⁻⁸liã³* 'wear this piece (of clothing)' is compared to *tshiŋ⁵⁻⁴ hit⁷⁻⁸liã³* 'wear that piece (of clothing)', which is not expressed but can be inferred from the context. The comparative predicate in (16) is encoded by the monosyllabic adjective *sɔŋ³* 'comfortable'.

As in the double-marking/hybridized type of comparative, the predicate in the absolute comparative in Hui'an may also be followed by a measure word, as exemplified by (17), where the comparative predicate $kiau^3$ 巧 'clever' precedes the measure word $tiəm^{3\text{-}2}a^3$ 點仔 'a bit, a little'.

(17) 伊　　恰　　　巧　　　點仔
　　　i^1　　$khaʔ^{7\text{-}8}$　$kiau^3$　$tiəm^{3\text{-}2}a^3$
　　　3SG　HMC　clever　a.bit
　　　'He is a bit cleverer (than me).'

According to Li & Lien (1995:74), the absolute comparative [A_{COM} $khaʔ^7$ PRED] can be found in the *Li Jing Ji*. They also mentioned that the predicate in the absolute comparative in the *Li Jing Ji* is more complex than that in other comparative constructions attested in the *Li Jing Ji*, such as the zero-marked comparative [A_{COM} PRED B_{STA}] and the head-marking comparative with $khaʔ^7$ [A_{COM} $khaʔ^7$ PRED B_{STA} (MW)]. This may suggest that the absolute comparative [A_{COM} $khaʔ^7$ PRED] was already in wide use in the period corresponding to the composition of the *Li Jing Ji*, that is, the Ming dynasty (1368-1644) and can be regarded as a comparative construction native to Southern Min, unlike the double-marking/hybridized type. However, as mentioned in §17.2 above, the absolute comparative [A_{COM} $khaʔ^7$ PRED] in Hui'an is probably not a highly grammaticalized comparative construction, since similar syntactic structures may be regarded as a non-comparative construction where $khaʔ^7$ is a degree adverb without denoting comparison.

We do not use the term 'short comparative' for the absolute comparative construction [A_{COM} $khaʔ^7$ PRED] in Hui'an, since we avoid suggesting that the absolute comparative [A_{COM} $khaʔ^7$ PRED] is a shortened form that has developed from a comparative with an overt standard of comparison, such as the double-marking/hybridized type [A_{COM} + pi^3 + B_{STA} + $khaʔ^7$ + PRED (+ MW)] examined in §17.2, or the head-marking comparative [A_{COM} $khaʔ^7$ PRED B_{STA} (MW)], which will be examined in the following section. Firstly, it is impossible for the absolute $khaʔ^7$ comparative [A_{COM} $khaʔ^7$ PRED] to be derived from the double-marking/hybridized comparative [A_{COM} + pi^3 + B_{STA} + $khaʔ^7$ + PRED (+ MW)]. According to previous studies such as Li & Lien (1995:74-75) and Yue-Hashimoto (1999:63), the comparative construction with the comparative marker pi^3 比, which can be found in different contemporary Southern Min varieties such as Hui'an and Taiwan, is not attested in earlier Southern Min documents such as the *Li Jing Ji* and the *Doctrina Christiana*, which dates from the early 17th century. The comparative [A_{COM} + pi^3 + B_{STA} + $khaʔ^7$ + PRED (+ MW)] is most likely a late development due to the influence of the comparative construction in Northern Chinese, as mentioned in §17.2 above. It is thus clear that the absolute comparative [A_COM *khaʔ⁷* PRED], already widely used in the *Li Jing Ji*, is not a shortened form of the double-marking comparative [A_COM + *pi³* + B_STA + *khaʔ⁷* + PRED (+ MW)] (see also Li & Lien 1995). Secondly, it is also superfluous to claim that the absolute comparative developed from the head-marking comparative [A_COM *khaʔ⁷* PRED B_STA (MW)]. The reason is that the absolute comparative [A_COM *khaʔ⁷* PRED] can directly undergo syntactic reanalysis from the non-overt comparative construction [NP *khaʔ⁷* VP] with *khaʔ⁷* functioning as a degree adverb meaning 'a bit; fairly', as in example (12) above. Another piece of evidence comes from the absolute comparative in other Chinese varieties, such as the comparative [A_COM PRED *di*] in Cantonese, as in example (14) above. The Surpass comparative in Cantonese typically takes the form of [A_COM PRED *kwo³* B_STA] and its standard noun may not be omitted. It is furthermore obvious that the absolute comparative [A_COM PRED *di*] is not a shortened form of the comparative [A_COM PRED *kwo³* B_STA].

17.4 Head-marking comparatives with *khaʔ⁷*: A_COM *khaʔ⁷* PRED B_STA (MW)

This type of comparative construction is regarded as an adverbial strategy in Chappell (2015). As mentioned in §17.1 above, it is not widely used in the contemporary Hui'an dialect compared to the double-marking type and the absolute comparative, and is more commonly used in the speech of the elder generation than in that of the younger generation, even although examples are indeed attested in contemporary daily conversation. The following is an example collected from the spoken data.

(18) 阮　　　即厝　　　　恰　　　　有嗵　　　食　　　恁　　　口面
　　 gun³　*tsit⁷⁻⁸-tshu⁵*　*khaʔ⁷⁻⁸*　*u⁴-thaŋ¹*　*tsiaʔ⁸*　*len³*　*khau³⁻²ben²*
　　 1PL　this-house　HMC　have-can　eat　2PL　outside
'We here have more things to eat than you, outside the home.'

In (18), the comparee and the standard of comparison are realized as 'pronoun + locative word', i.e. *gun³ tsit⁷⁻⁸tshu⁵* 'we here' and *len³ khau³⁻²ben²* 'you outside', respectively. The comparative predicate is encoded by the verb phrase *u⁴thaŋ¹ tsiaʔ⁸* 'have things to eat'. Not only the comparee NP and the standard NP, but also the comparative predicate, are expressed by a comparatively complex noun or verb phrase respectively, rather than a simple monosyllabic noun or adjective. This kind of evidence may indicate that the comparative construction [A_COM *khaʔ⁷*

PRED B$_{STA}$ (MW)] is, or at least once was, a very highly grammaticalized and mature comparative construction in Hui'an, even though it is not common nowadays. The morpheme *khaʔ⁷* in (18) simply denotes comparison, rather than functioning as a degree adverb meaning 'a bit; fairly'. The standard of comparison *len³ khau³⁻²ben²* syntactically functions as an object of the verb phrase *khaʔ⁷⁻⁸ u⁴thaŋ¹ tsiaʔ⁸* 'have more things to eat', that is, example (18) is a transitive construction. This shows that the comparative construction [A$_{COM}$ *khaʔ⁷* PRED B$_{STA}$ (MW)] is associated with the 'Action Schema' in Heine (1997) or the Exceed type in Stassen (1995) in terms of the transitivity of the construction, as for the comparative [A$_{COM}$ PRED *kwo³* B$_{STA}$] in Cantonese. However, unlike these, there is no verb expressing the notion 'defeat', 'exceed' or 'surpass' in the Hui'an comparative construction [A$_{COM}$ *khaʔ⁷* PRED B$_{STA}$ (MW)].

The following are more examples of this type of comparative in Hui'an.

(19) 口　　恰　　　大　　口
　　 tsat⁸　khaʔ⁷⁻⁸　tua⁵　hat⁸
　　 this　HMC　　big　　that
　　 'This one is bigger than that one.'

(20) 今年　　　　恰　　　寒　　舊年
　　 ken¹-lin²　khaʔ⁷⁻⁸　kuã²　ku⁵⁻⁴-lin²
　　 this-year　HMC　　cold　old-year
　　 'This year is colder than last year.'

(21) 阿母　　　恰　　　愛食　　　嬰仔
　　 a¹-bu³　khaʔ⁷⁻⁸　ai⁵⁻³-tsiaʔ⁸　in¹iã³
　　 PREF-mother　HMC　like-eat　child
　　 'Mother likes eating more than the child.'

Examples (19) – (21) show that the comparee and the standard of comparison in the comparative [A$_{COM}$ *khaʔ⁷* PRED B$_{STA}$ (MW)] can be encoded by demonstratives (e.g. *tsat⁸* 'this' and *hat⁸* 'that' in (19)), temporal words (e.g. *ken¹lin²* 'this year' and *ku⁵⁻⁴lin²* 'last year' in (20)), or common nouns (e.g. *a¹bu³* 'mother' and *in¹iã³* 'child' in (21)). The comparative predicate can be a monosyllabic adjective such as *tua⁵* 'big' in (19) and *kuã²* 'cold' in (20), or a disyllabic stative verb such as *ai⁵⁻³tsiaʔ⁸* 'like eating' in (21).

A topic can also be overt in this type of comparative, as in example (22) below.

(22) 我   手   恰   長   汝
    gua³   tshiu³   khaʔ⁷⁻⁸   tŋ²   lu³
    1SG   hand   HMC   long 2SG
    'My hand is longer than yours.'

In (22), the noun *tshiu³* 手 'hand' is placed between the comparee *gua³* 我 'I' and the head-marker of comparison *khaʔ⁷* 恰, and functions as a topic. Semantically speaking, the comparee *gua³* and the topic *tshiu³* function as a possessor and possessee, respectively.

As illustrated by example (23) below, a measure word can be further added after the standard of comparison, rather than after the comparative predicate as in the double-marking/hybridized type and the absolute comparative as examined in §17.2 and 17.3 respectively above.

(23) 大車   恰   緊   細車   淡薄
    tua⁵⁻⁴-tshia¹   khaʔ⁷⁻⁸   ken³   sue⁵⁻³-tshia¹   tam⁴poʔ⁸
    big-vehicle   HMC   fast   small-vehicle   a.little
    'The big car goes a bit faster than the small car.'

In (23), the measure word *tam⁴poʔ⁸* 'a little' follows the standard of comparison *sue⁵⁻³tshia¹* 'small car' to indicate the degree of difference between the comparee *tua⁵⁻⁴tshia¹* 'big car' and the standard *sue⁵⁻³thia¹* 'small car' in terms of how fast they can go. The comparee and the standard of comparison in this example are both encoded by a noun phrase, and the predicate is expressed by the monosyllabic adjective *ken³* 'fast'.

This type of comparative construction has also been reported in other Southern Min varieties in Fujian and Taiwan (cf. Chen 1982:62; Wang & Zhang 1994:143; Li & Lien 1995:72; Crosland 1995; Zhou & Ouyang 1998:198). In contemporary Taiwan Southern Min, for example, the head-marking comparative is attested in both the younger and elder generation, even though it has an extremely low frequency (Li & Lien 1995:81). In the contemporary Xiamen variety of Southern Min, it is typically attested in the speech of older and less educated informants (see Wu 1958:82-102; Crosland 1995; also cited in Li & Lien 1995:79; Ansaldo 1999:116).

Ansaldo (1999:116) also mentioned that the existence of this type of comparative construction in Southern Min can be traced back to at least the beginning of the century in, for example, the grammar of Amoy by Piñol (1928), where Piñol points out that the comparative with *khaʔ* is the primary option for comparison or superiority. According to Li & Lien (1995:73), this head-marking comparative construction [A_COM *khaʔ* PRED B_STA] is nonetheless attested in the *Li Jing Ji* and its comparative predicate can be both monosyllabic and disyllabic. It is thus clear that this type has served as one of the basic comparative constructions in early Southern Min, and can be regarded as one of the 'native' comparative constructions in this branch of Chinese, as also suggested by Li & Lien (1995:74) and Ansaldo (1999:116).

17.5 Zero-marked comparatives: A_COM PRED B_STA (MW)

Previous works on Southern Min such as Chen (1982), Li & Lien (1995), Zhou & Ouyang (1998) and Xu (2007) have all reported that there exists a type of comparative construction with the structure of 'A_COM PRED B_STA'. This type is regarded as the absent-marking type by Ansaldo (1999), and as the zero-marked type by Chappell (2015).

In the contemporary Hui'an dialect, this type of comparative construction is more commonly used by the elder generation than by the younger generation. The comparee and the standard of comparison are predominantly encoded by a simple noun or noun phrase, and the comparative predicate is typically a monosyllabic adjective, as illustrated by examples (24) – (26) below.

(24) 我　　　肥　　汝
　　 gua^3　pui^2　lu^0
　　 1SG　　 fat　　2SG
　　 'I am fatter than you.'

(25) 大車　　　　　緊　　　細車
　　 $tua^{5\text{-}4}\text{-}tshia^1$　$ken^{3\text{-}2}$　$sue^{5\text{-}3}\text{-}tshia^1$
　　 big-vehicle　fast　small-vehicle
　　 'The big car goes faster than the small car.'

(26) 即張　　　　　鋪　　　闊　　　迄張　　　　　鋪
　　 $tsit^{7\text{-}8}\text{-}tiũ^1$　$phɔ^1$　$khuaʔ^7$　$hit^{7\text{-}8}\text{-}tiũ^1$　$phɔ^1$
　　 this-CL　　bed　　wide　that-CL　　bed
　　 'This bed is wider than that bed.'

These three examples show that the comparee and the standard of comparison in this type of comparative construction can be encoded by a personal pronoun such as the first person singular pronoun gua^3 and the second person singular pronoun lu^0 in (24), a noun such as $tua^{5\text{-}4}tshia^1$ 'big car' and $sue^{5\text{-}3}tshia^1$ 'small car' in (25), or a noun phrase such as $tsit^{7\text{-}8}tiũ^1 phɔ^1$ 'this bed' and $hit^{7\text{-}8}tiũ^1 phɔ^1$ 'that bed' in (26).

The comparative predicate in all these three examples is encoded by a monosyllabic adjective, i.e. *pui²* 'fat', *ken³* 'fast' and *khuaʔ⁷* 'wide' in (24) – (26), respectively. In these examples, the standard of comparison such as *lu⁰* 'you' in example (24) serves as the object of the comparative predicate *pui²* 'fat'. In other words, like the comparative [A_COM *khaʔ* PRED B_STA] examined in §17.4 above, the comparative [A_COM PRED B_STA] is also a transitive construction and associated with the 'Action Schema' in Heine (1997).

However, the comparee in this type of comparative in Hui'an can also be a verb phrase, as in (27).

(27) 穿　　　即領　　　爽　　　迄領
    tshiŋ⁵⁻⁴　*tsit⁷⁻⁸-liã³*　*sɔŋ³*　*hit⁷⁻⁸-liã³*
    wear　this-CL　comfortable　that-CL
    'Wearing this piece (of clothing) is more comfortable than wearing that one.'

In (27), the comparee is encoded by the verb phrase *tshiŋ⁵⁻⁴ tsit⁷⁻⁸liã³* 'wear this piece (of clothing)', whereas the standard of comparison is simply expressed by the demonstrative phrase *hit⁷⁻⁸liã³* 'that piece (of clothing)', rather than the verb phrase *tshiŋ⁵⁻⁴ hit⁷⁻⁸liã³* 'wear that piece (of clothing)'. In other words, the repetition of the verb *tshiŋ⁵* is not necessary for coding the standard of comparison. A similar phenomenon is also attested in the Surpass type of comparative in Cantonese [A_COM PRED *kwo³* B_STA], but not in the Compare type of comparative in Mandarin varieties (see Chappell & Peyraube 2015). Moreover, for example (27), the construction without a second *tshiŋ⁵* is more natural than the one with it, i.e. *tshiŋ⁵⁻⁴ tsit⁷⁻⁸liã³ sɔŋ³ hit⁷⁻⁸liã³* 穿即領爽迄領 is more natural than *tshiŋ⁵⁻⁴ tsit⁷⁻⁸liã³ sɔŋ³ tshiŋ⁵⁻⁴ hit⁷⁻⁸liã³* 穿即領爽穿迄領, for native speakers of the Hui'an dialect.

Besides the monosyllabic adjectives in examples (24) – (27) above, the comparative predicate in this type of comparative can also be encoded by a disyllabic adjective such as *tua⁵⁻⁴tsiaʔ⁷* 大隻 'big' in (28), or a trisyllabic adjective such as *u⁴tshui⁵⁻³tsiʔ⁸* 有喙舌 'talkative' in (28).

(28) 鵝　　　大隻　　　　雞
    gia²　*tua⁵⁻⁴-tsiaʔ⁷⁻⁸*　*kue¹*
    goose　big-CL　chicken
    'The goose is bigger than the chicken.'

(29) 我　　有噍舌　　　　汝
　　　gua³　u⁴-tshui⁵⁻³-tsiʔ⁸　　luɨ³
　　　1SG　have-mouth-tongue　2SG
　　　'I am more talkative than you.'

In (28), the predicate is encoded by the adjective *tua⁵⁻⁴tsiaʔ⁷* 'big' which consists of the adjective *tua⁵* 'big' and the classifier *tsiaʔ⁷*. In (29), the predicate *u⁴tshui⁵⁻³tsiʔ⁸* is a fixed expression functioning like an adjective expressing 'talkative' (see also example (6) in §17.2 above).

The following are two examples with an overt topic.

(30) 我　　骹　　短　　汝
　　　gua³　kha¹　tə³　luº
　　　1SG　leg　short　2SG
　　　'My legs are shorter than yours.'

(31) 坐　　車　　　廣州　　　　加　　時間　　　泉州
　　　tsa⁴　tshia¹　kŋ³⁻²tsiu¹　ke¹　si²⁻⁴kan¹　tsuan²⁻⁴tsiu¹
　　　sit　vehicle　PN　　　more　time　　PN
　　　'It takes more time to take the bus to Guangzhou than to Quanzhou.'

The topic *kha¹* 'leg' in (30) is placed between the comparee *gua³* 'I' and the predicate *tə³* 'short', whereas the topic *tsa⁴ tshia¹* 'take the bus' in (31) is placed before the comparee *kŋ³⁻²tsiu¹* 'Guangzhou'.

A measure word following the standard of comparison such as *ban²⁻⁴tsue⁵* 蠻儕 'much' in example (32) below, is optional in Hui'an.

(32) 我　　勇　　　伊　　(蠻儕)
　　　gua³　iɔŋ³　iº　(ban²⁻⁴tsue⁵)
　　　1SG　strong　3SG　(much)
　　　'I am (much) stronger than her.'

The comparative construction [A_COM PRED B_STA (MW)]] *without* the requirement of a measure word is so far attested only in Min such as the Hui'an, Quanzhou, Xiamen and Jieyang varieties of Southern Min, and Southwestern Mandarin such as the Jishou variety in Hunan province of China, whereas the comparative [A_COM PRED B_STA MW] *with* an obligatory, overt measure word is widely used in various Chinese varieties such as Mandarin, Wu, Hakka, Yue and Xiang (cf. Li 2003:218-219; Ansaldo 1999:105-106; Xu 2007:272). It should be mentioned, however, that the zero-marked comparative with a measure word, [A_COM PRED B_STA MW], rather than the same form without, [A_COM PRED B_STA], is also attested in contemporary Taiwan Southern Min (Li & Lien 1995:77).

The zero-marked comparative [A_COM PRED B_STA] can be attested in the Ming dynasty *Li Jing Ji*, where only a monosyllabic comparative predicate is allowed in this type (see Li & Lien 1995:73-74). Across the thirteen texts including five versions of the *Li Jing Ji*, consulted in Chappell, Peyraube and Song (forthcoming), there are only two real examples out of 46 zero-marked comparatives and these are both formed with *tang⁷* 重 'be heavy', 'be important'. The remaining 44/46 all contain different *surpass* verbs as the main verb and are thus lexical comparatives. It is in fact quite marginal in the thirteen early Southern Min texts. Nonetheless, this construction type can be found as early as in Archaic Chinese texts (11ᵗʰ – 3ʳᵈ BC) and also in contemporary Chinese, as mentioned above. We suggest that the zero-marked comparative construction [A_COM PRED B_STA] can be regarded as one of the 'native' comparative constructions in Southern Min, like the head-marked comparative [A_COM *khaʔ* PRED B_STA].

17.6 Comparatives with the marker *khɯ⁵*: A_COM PRED *khɯ⁵* B_STA

This type of comparative construction is not widely used in the contemporary Hui'an dialect and, if anything, is more common in the speech of the elder generation than in the speech of the younger generation. The use of this type of comparative is more limited than the zero-marked comparative [A_COM PRED B_STA] exemplified in (24) – (32) above, not to mention than the four other types of comparative we have already examined.

The comparee and the standard of comparison in this type of comparative are typically nouns or pronouns, personal or demonstrative, rather than a VP, and the comparative predicate is typically a monosyllabic adjective, as exemplified by (33) – (35).

(33) 口   大   去   口
     tsat⁸ tua⁵⁻⁴ khɯ⁵⁻³ hat⁸
     this   big   go   that
     'This one is bigger than that one.'

(34) 我   凶   去   汝
     gua³   hiɔŋ¹ khɯ⁵⁻³ lɯ³
     1SG   ugly   go   2SG
     'I am uglier than you.'

(35) 張三　　重　　去　　李四
　　　tiũ¹sã¹　taŋ⁴　khɯ⁵⁻³　li³⁻²si⁵
　　　PN　　　heavy　go　　PN
　　　'Zhang San is heavier than Li Si.'

The examples above show that the comparee and the standard of comparison in this type of comparative can be encoded by a demonstrative such as *tsat⁸* 'this' and *hat⁸* 'that' in (33), a personal pronoun such as *gua³* 'I' and *lɯ³* 'you' in (34), or a proper noun such as *tiũ¹sã¹* 'Zhang San' and *li³⁻²si⁵* 'Li Si' in (35).

Not all monosyllabic adjectives can be used in this type of comparative, as shown by (36).

(36) a. 我　　　巧　　　汝
　　　 gua³　khiau³　lɯ⁰
　　　 1SG　 clever　 2SG
　　　 'I am cleverer than you.'

　　 b. *我　　 巧　　　 去　　　 汝
　　　　gua³　khiau³　khɯ⁵⁻³　lɯ³
　　　　1SG　 clever　 go　　　 2SG
　　　　(attempted meaning: 'I am cleverer than you.')

In (36), the monosyllabic adjective *khiau³* 'clever' can function as a comparative predicate in the zero-marked comparative construction [A_COM PRED B_STA], but not in the *khɯ⁵*-comparative [A_COM PRED *khɯ⁵* B_STA]. This may be associated with the fact that the verbal complement *khɯ⁵* in Hui'an tends to be used with a negative, rather than a positive attribute.

However, not all positive monosyllabic adjectives are excluded from this type of comparative, as seen in (37).

(37) a. 我　　 好　　　去　　　 汝
　　　 gua³　ho³　　khɯ⁵⁻³　lɯ³
　　　 1SG　 good　 go　　　 2SG
　　　 'I am better than you.'
　　 b. 我　　 否　　　去　　　 汝
　　　 gua³　phai³　khɯ⁵⁻³　lɯ³
　　　 1SG　 bad　　go　　　 2SG
　　　 'I am worse than you.'

As shown in (37), both the positive monosyllabic adjective *ho³* 'good' and its negative form *phaiⁿ³* 'bad' can serve as a comparative predicate followed by the comparative marker *khuɯ⁵*. One of the reasons may be that the adjective *ho³* 'good' is more basic and common than the adjective *khiau³* 'clever'.

In addition, not all non-positive monosyllabic adjectives can be naturally used with the comparative marker *khuɯ⁵*, as (38) shows.

(38) a. 即搭　　熱　　迄搭
　　　tsit⁷⁻⁸-taʔ⁷　luaʔ⁸　hit⁷⁻⁸-taʔ⁷
　　　this-LOC　hot　that-LOC
　　　'It is hotter here than there.'

　　b. ?即搭　　熱　　去　　迄搭
　　　tsit⁷⁻⁸-taʔ⁷　luaʔ⁸　khuɯ⁵⁻³　hit⁷⁻⁸-taʔ⁷
　　　this-LOC　hot　go　that-LOC
　　　'It is hotter here than there.'

The monosyllabic adjective *luaʔ⁸* 'hot' used with the comparative marker *khuɯ⁵* as in example (38b) can be accepted by native speakers of the Hui'an dialect. However, comparatively speaking, the zero-marked form [A$_{COM}$ PRED B$_{STA}$], without the marker *khuɯ⁵* as in (38a), is preferred in use, rather than the form with it, as in (38b). One of the reasons may be that the sequence *khuɯ⁵⁻³ hit⁷⁻⁸taʔ⁷* is ambiguous in Hui'an, having another possible, and probably more common interpretation, i.e. the locative word *hit⁷⁻⁸taʔ⁷* 'there' functions as a locative object of the motion verb *khuɯ⁵* 'go', 'to go there'.

As demonstrated by examples (39) and (40) below, it seems that the comparative predicate in this type of *khuɯ⁵*-comparative cannot be other than monosyllabic.

(39) a. 今日　　　嚨喉　　　有聲　　　昨日
　　　kiãⁿ¹let⁸　lau²⁻⁴au²　u⁴-siãⁿ¹　tsa⁴let⁸
　　　today　throat　have-voice　yesterday
　　　'(Your) throat is better today (than yesterday).'

　　b. ?今日　　嚨喉　　　有聲　　　去　　昨日
　　　kiãⁿ¹let⁸　lau²⁻⁴au²　u⁴-siãⁿ¹　khuɯ⁵⁻³　tsa⁴let⁸
　　　today　throat　have-voice　go　yesterday
　　　'(Your) throat is better today (than yesterday).'

(40) *我　　有喙舌　　　　　　去　　　汝
　　　gua³　u⁴-tshui⁵⁻³-tsi⁷⁸　　khɯ⁵⁻³　lɯ³
　　　1SG　have-mouth-tongue　go　　2SG
　　　'I am more talkative than you.'

In (39), u⁴siã¹ 'have voice' serving as a comparative predicate preceding the comparative marker khɯ⁵ is acceptable. However, the form without the marker khɯ⁵ as in (39a) is better than the form with it, as in (39b). In (40), the polysyllabic form, u⁴tshui⁵⁻³tsi⁷⁸ 'talkative', cannot occur at all in the comparative with the khɯ⁵.

Based on the analysis above, it appears to be safe to say at this point that the comparative predicate in this type of comparative in contemporary Hui'an dialect tends to be encoded by a negative monosyllabic adjective, though positive monosyllabic adjectives with high frequency such as ho³ 好 'good' are also possible.

As shown by the following example, the comparee can be encoded by a verb phrase such as tshiŋ⁵⁻⁴ tsit⁷⁻⁸liã³ 'wear this piece (of clothing)'.

(41) 穿　　　即領　　　　爽　　　　去　　　迄領
　　　tshiŋ⁵⁻⁴　tsit⁷⁻⁸-liã³　sɔŋ³　　khɯ⁵⁻³　hit⁷⁻⁸-liã³
　　　wear　　this-CL　　comfortable　go　　that-CL
　　　'Wearing this piece (of clothing) is more comfortable than wearing that one.'

This example also shows that the positive monosyllabic adjective sɔŋ³ 'comfortable' can be used with the comparative marker khɯ⁵. In other words, the positive-negative distinction may not be, after all, the most important factor in explaining the limited use of the comparative construction with the marker khɯ⁵.

Unlike the previous four types of comparative construction as examined in §17.2 – 17.5, this type of comparative construction has not been elsewhere reported in the literature on Southern Min, but can be found in the Fuzhou variety of Eastern Min (Yuan 1989:305; Zhao 2002:49). Wu Fuxiang (pers. comm.) suggests that the comparative marker khɯ⁵ here functions as a verbal complement of the predicate. As mentioned above, the head-marker of comparison gwo³ in Cantonese is also regarded as a verbal complement in the literature, including Li (1994), Mok (1998), Ansaldo (1999:121) and Chappell (2015). In other words, as with gwo³ in Cantonese, khɯ⁵ in Hui'an can also serve as a head-marker of comparison, similarly observed by Liu (2003c:14) who suggests that qù 去 in Northern Min and qǐ 起 in the Shandong variety are markers of the predicate in comparative constructions and that this function can be derived from their functions as directional complements.

Similar kinds of head-markers of comparison and comparative constructions are attested in many other Chinese varieties, including Wu, Hakka, Gan, Xiang and Mandarin (Li 2003:219). If we agree that the comparative marker *khɯ⁵* in Hui'an may also be a verbal complement of the predicate, then in this case, it would form a transitive construction with the standard of comparison as the object of the complex [PRED *khɯ⁵*], associated with the 'Action Schema' in Heine (1997). However, we also wonder whether there is another possible interpretation. The counterpart of *khɯ⁵* in Mandarin Chinese, i.e. *qù*, originally means 'leave, depart from' in earlier Chinese and can also be used as a verb showing a comparison between two places.

Thus, is there any possible connection between the comparative marker *khɯ⁵* and the Separative comparatives of Stassen (1985)? However, as pointed out by Wu Fuxiang (pers. comm.), the comparative markers associated with Separative comparatives are typically morphemes indicating cases such as adpositions or affixes, while neither *khɯ⁵* in Hui'an nor *qù* in Mandarin Chinese is used as an adposition in a dependent-marking strategy. While this suggests that comparatives with the marker *khɯ⁵* may not be a typical example of the Separative type, the possibility cannot be ruled out that they belong to the Separative type, rather than the Surpass type. Wu (2011:9) also suggests that the comparative construction with the marker *QÙ* 去 is an innovation in Eastern Min based on the zero-marked comparative construction 'A$_{COM}$ PRED B$_{STA}$'.

17.7 Dependent-marking comparatives with *pi³*: A$_{COM}$ *pi³* B$_{STA}$ PRED (MW)

It is generally known that the basic comparative construction in Mandarin Chinese is A$_{COM}$ *bǐ* 比 B$_{STA}$ PRED, which is respectively called the Similarity type by Ansaldo (1999) and the Compare type by Chappell & Peyraube (2015), as stated in §17.1 above. We have also mentioned that this type of comparative is the most common one found in Chinese. Not surprisingly, it is also attested in different Southern Min varieties. In the Jieyang variety of Southern Min, for example, the dependent-marked comparative is the most versatile and plays an important role in Jieyang syntax (see Xu 2007:277). In Taiwan, it is found across the speech of all the different age groups ranging from 15 years old to 74 years old (Li & Lien 1995:80-81). In Hui'an, however, it is not widely used and is quite limited. The double-marking/hybridized type of comparative is preferred when the comparative marker *pi³* is involved. In addition, this type of comparative construction usually requires a measure phrase following the comparative predicate, as in (42), where the measure phrase *sã¹ hə⁵* 三歲 'three years' is preceded by the predicate *tua⁵* 大 'big'.

(42) 我　　比　　伊　　大　　三　　歲
　　 gua³　pi³⁻²　i¹　tua⁵⁻⁴　sã¹　hə⁵
　　 1SG　DMC　3SG　big　three　year
　　 'I am three years older than him.'

17.8 Summary

This chapter has examined comparative constructions of inequality (termed 'comparative construction') in Hui'an. Six main types of comparative construction are attested:
(a) double-marking/hybridized comparatives
    i.e. [A_COM *pi³* B_STA *kha?⁷* PRED (MW)]
(b) absolute comparatives, i.e. [A_COM *kha?⁷* PRED (MW)]
(c) head-marking comparatives with the marker *kha?⁷*
    i.e. [A_COM *kha?⁷* PRED B_STA (MW)]
(d) zero-marked comparatives
    i.e. [A_COM PRED B_STA (MW)]
(e) comparatives with the marker *khu⁵*, i.e. [A_COM PRED *khu⁵* B_STA]
(f) dependent-marking comparatives with the marker *pi³* 'compare'
    i.e. [A_COM *pi³* B_STA PRED (MW)]]

Type (a) and Type (b), i.e. [A_COM *pi³* B_STA *kha?⁷* PRED] and [A_COM *kha?⁷* PRED] are the dominant types. Types (c), (d) and (e) are more commonly used in the speech of the elder generation than that in the speech of the younger generation. In addition, the use of Type (e) is much more restricted than that of Types (c) and (d), as we have shown. Type (f), the most common one in Chinese, however, is quite limited in Hui'an and usually requires a measure word following the comparative predicate.

A topic noun or phrase may be involved in these comparative constructions. Moreover, the position of the topic is relatively free: it may be placed before the comparee, be inserted between the comparee and the dependent-marker of comparison, or even be placed between the standard of comparison and the head-marker of comparison, especially in the comparative construction where all these relevant constituents are present such as in the double-marking/hybridized type.

The morpheme *kha?⁷* in Hui'an found in the head-marking type can also be used as a degree adverb meaning 'a bit; fairly' in non-comparative constructions, which suggests a possible grammaticalization path from a degree adverb to a marker of comparison. In fact, similar extensions from a degree adverb to a comparative marker can also be potentially attested in other Min varieties and other Chinese varieties such as Xianghua and Cantonese.

The non-comparative constructions, in which the degree adverb *khaʔ⁷* 'a bit, fairly' occurs, share the same structure with Type (b), [A_COM *khaʔ⁷* PRED (MW)], which suggests that it is not highly grammaticalized. In this construction, the standard of comparison is usually not expressed because it can be inferred from the context. This is different from the Jieyang variety which syntactically requires that the standard of comparison be mentioned in the prior discourse (see §17.3).

The head-marking Type (c), [A_COM *khaʔ⁷* PRED B_STA (MW)], was the primary option for comparison at the beginning of 20th century and is also attested in the Ming dynasty *Li Jing Ji*. Similarly, the zero-marked Type (d) is also attested in the *Li Jing Ji*, though be it marginal in nature. Such evidence may show that these two types are both 'native' comparative constructions in Southern Min. However, neither is widely used in the contemporary Hui'an dialect. In addition, these two types are both associated with the 'Action Schema' in Heine (1997) or the Exceed type in Stassen (1995) in terms of the transitivity of their forms. However, unlike the typical Exceed/Surpass type of comparative based on the 'Action Schema' such as the comparative construction [A_COM PRED *kwo³* B_STA] in Cantonese, there is no verb expressing the notion 'defeat', 'exceed' or 'surpass' in these two types.

Type (e) comparatives have not been reported in the literature on other varieties of Southern Min, but are found in the Fuzhou variety of Eastern Min. There are two possible hypotheses regarding this type of comparative construction using the marker *khu⁵*: (a) similar to the comparative marker *gwo³* in Cantonese, the marker *khu⁵* functions as a verbal complement of the predicate which means that this type of comparative construction can be classified as the Surpass type or the 'Action Schema' according to Heine (1997); and (b) the counterpart of *khu⁵* in Mandarin Chinese, i.e. *qù*, originally means 'leave, depart from' in earlier Chinese and can also be used as a verb showing a comparison between two places. This suggests that the marker *khu⁵* may be derived from its use as a verb meaning 'leave, depart from' and that it may be associated with the Separative type in Stassen (1985), if not the Source schema in Heine.

18 The 'give' construction

18.1 Introduction

The 'give' verb takes on a range of functions including those of ditransitive verb, dative marker, causative marker and passive marker in different languages (e.g. Chinese, Thai and Akan). The multifunctionality of the 'give' verb is also attested in Hui'an, where *khɔ⁵* 與 'give' can not only be used as a ditransitive verb, dative marker, permissive verb, causative verb and passive marker, but also as a perspective marker, concessive marker, purposive marker and speaker-affectedness marker. This chapter aims to give a brief introduction to the different uses of *khɔ⁵* 'give' in Hui'an.

18.2 As a ditransitive verb and perspective marker

18.2.1 As a ditransitive verb

Khɔ⁵ 'give', as a ditransitive verb, can be followed by an indirect object and a direct object, i.e. '*khɔ⁵* IO DO', as in (1), where *gua³* 我 'me' is the indirect object, while *lin²⁻⁴tau¹tsin²* 年兜錢 'gift money' is the direct object.

(1) V_{GIVE}   NP_{IO}   NP_{DO}
    伊   與   我   年兜錢
    i¹   *khɔ⁵⁻⁴*   *gua³⁻²*   *lin²⁻⁴tau¹-tsin²*
    3SG   give   1SG   New.Year-money
    'He gave me gift money.'

Only three examples of utterances with the structure of '*khɔ⁵* IO DO' are found in our spoken data. In addition, these three examples are spoken by the younger generation. Although such a [V NP NP] configuration is often taken to be the prototypical ditransitive construction, it is not at all characteristic of the Hui'an dialect, where the direct object typically appears before the verb functioning as a topic as in (2), or undergoes deletion as in (3).

Note: A preliminary version of this chapter also appeared in Chen & Matthews (2009).

(2) NP$_{DO}$ V$_{GIVE}$ NP$_{IO}$
 雞翼　　　　與　　　恁　　爸仔
 kue^1-set^8　$kho^{5\text{-}4}$　$len^{3\text{-}2}$　pa^2-a^0
 chicken-wing　give　2PL　father-NM
 'Give your father the chicken wing.'

(3) V$_{GIVE}$ NP$_{IO}$
 儂　　卜　　　與　　　伊　　其
 $laŋ^4$　$boʔ^{7\text{-}8}$　$kho^{5\text{-}4}$　i^1　e^0
 other　want　give　3SG　SFP
 'The person wants to give (it) to him.'

In (2), kue^1set^8 'chicken wing', being direct object, is fronted and placed in the preverbal position. In (3), the direct object, kue^1 'chicken', is omitted but can be found in the preceding context. The structure of these two examples can be represented as '(DO) kho^5 IO'.

Example (4) below shows that even the indirect object can be simultaneously omitted.

(4) NP$_{AGENT}$ V$_{GIVE}$ ADV ADJ
 可能　　　　個　　懷　　與　　　恰　　　　　儕
 $kho^{3\text{-}2}liŋ^2$　en^1　$huai^2$　$kho^{5\text{-}4}$　$khaʔ^{7\text{-}8}$　$tsue^5$
 possibly　3PL　those　give　comparatively　much
 'They may give (her) more (money than other people).'

As with the examples above, kho^5 in (4) is also the only verb in the utterance. Both direct object and indirect object, however, are omitted and can be found in the preceding context. Furthermore, this also indicates that the arguments of the verb are not obligatorily overt in Hui'an.

18.2.2 As a perspective marker

The ditransitive verb kho^5 can be used in a hypothetical situation, as in (5).

(5) 卜　　　 與　　 我，　 我　　 唔愛　　　 食
    boʔ⁷⁻⁸　 khɔ⁵⁻⁴　 gua³　 gua³　 m⁵⁻⁴-ai⁵⁻³　 tsiaʔ⁸
    want　　 give　　 1SG　　 1SG　　 not-like　　 eat
    (a) 'If (he) gives me (something), I would not want to eat (it).'
    (b) 'If it were me, I would not want to eat (it).'

In (5), the first clause *boʔ⁷⁻⁸ khɔ⁵⁻⁴ gua³* has two possible interpretations: (a) a 'giving' action in a hypothetical situation, in which *khɔ⁵* is used as a ditransitive verb; and (b) irrealis, expressing the meaning of 'if it were me', in which *khɔ⁵* is no longer a ditransitive verb, but can be regarded as a perspective marker (see §23.5).

The 'give' verb used as a perspective marker is also attested in Akan, as in (6) (cf. Lord et al. 2002:222).

(6) ɛ-yɛden　　　 ma　　 me
    it-is difficult　 give　 me
    'It is difficult for me.'

Lord et al. suggest that the object of 'give' in (6) is the person from whose perspective or point of view something is difficult, and consequently that the 'give' morpheme functions as a marker of perspective (or stance). They also point out that in this use of 'give', the preceding verb (i.e. *den* 'difficult') refers to a state rather than an activity.

18.3 As a dative marker

When used as the second verb in serial verb constructions of the form '(NP1) VP (NP2) *khɔ⁵* NP3', *khɔ⁵* is used to introduce the recipient and can be regarded as a dative marker. NP2, the object of the first verb, can be overt like *lŋ⁴ paʔ⁷* 兩百 'two hundred (yuan)' in (7), or omitted as in (8).

(7) (NP1) VP NP2 *khɔ⁵* NP3
    分　　　　 兩　　 百　　　 與　　 伊
    pun¹　　　 lŋ⁴　 paʔ⁷　　 khɔ⁵　 i⁰
    distribute　 two　 hundred　 give　 3SG
    'Give him two hundred (yuan).'

(8) (NP1) VP (NP2) *khɔ⁵* NP3
　　落車　　　　　　洗　　與　　伊
　　loʔ⁸⁻⁴-tshia¹　　*sue³*　*khɔ⁵*　*i⁰*
　　descend-vehicle　wash　give　3SG
　　'Wash (it) and give (it to) her after getting out of the bus.'

In (7), NP2 is *lŋ⁴ paʔ⁷* 'two hundred'. In (8), NP2 is covert and can be found from the previous context. The first verb in the serial verb construction '(NP1) VP (NP2) *khɔ⁵* NP3' can be classified into two types: (a) verbs implying a 'giving' action such as *pun¹* 'distribute' in (7); and (b) extended dative verbs without a 'giving' action such as *sue³* 'wash' in (8). The serial verb construction provides an environment for the second verb *khɔ⁵* 'give' to lose its verbhood and become decategorized as a dative marker.

In Mandarin Chinese, the dative marker *gěi* 給 (< *gěi* 'give') can occur in three different positions, as shown by the following three examples (see Zhu 1982:170).

(9) V + DO + *gěi* + IO
　　送　　一　　本　　書　　給　　他 (Mandarin Chinese)
　　sòng　*yī*　*běn*　*shū*　*gěi*　*tā*
　　send　one　CL　book　give　3SG
　　'send him a book'/ 'give him a book (as a present)'

(10) V + *gěi* + IO + DO
　　送　　給　　他　　一　　件　　毛衣(Mandarin Chinese)
　　sòng　*gěi*　*tā*　*yī*　*jiàn*　*máoyī*
　　send　give　3SG　one　CL　sweater
　　'send him a sweater'/ 'give him a sweater (as a present)'

(11) *gěi* + IO + V + DO
　　給　　他　　織　　了　　一　　件　　毛衣(Mandarin Chinese)
　　gěi　*tā*　*zhī*　*le*　*yī*　*jiàn*　*máoyī*
　　give　3SG　knit　PFV　one　CL　sweater
　　'knit a sweater for him'

In (9), the dative marker *gěi* in Mandarin Chinese occurs after 'V + DO'. In (10), *gěi* is placed immediately after the verb. In (11), the dative marker *gěi*, with its following indirect object, occurs as a prepositional phrase before the verb and the direct object, and in the majority of cases codes a benefactive meaning.

In Hui'an, however, the dative marker *khɔ⁵* typically occurs after the verb and the direct object, as shown by examples (7) and (8) above, but not in the other two positions. The development from a 'give' verb to a dative marker is not uncommon in Chinese, nor in other serial verb languages such as Vietnamese (see Newman 1996; Heine & Kuteva 2002; Lord et al. 2002; Yap & Iwasaki 2003; Chappell & Peyraube 2007, inter alia).

18.4 As a (permissive) causative verb

Khɔ⁵ can function as a permissive verb when it is the first verb in a serial construction '*khɔ⁵* NP VP', as illustrated by (12b).

(12) 唔   與   儂   食
      m^{5-4} $\underline{khɔ^{5-4}}$ $laŋ^4$ $tsia\textipa{P}^8$
      not   give   other   eat
      (a) '(He) doesn't want to give (it) to others to eat.' (NEG + *khɔ⁵*GIVE + IO +V)
      (b) '(He) doesn't allow others to eat (it).' (NEG + *khɔ⁵*PERMIT + NPCAUSEE + V)

In (12), *khɔ⁵* is vague in status between a ditransitive verb and a permissive verb, since it can be interpreted as 'giving' in (12a) or 'permit, allow' in (12b). In (12a), NP, *laŋ⁴* 'other', is interpreted as the indirect object of *khɔ⁵* and is followed by another verb *tsiaP⁸* 'eat'. In (12b), however, the same NP (i.e. *laŋ⁴* 'other') is no longer interpreted as the recipient but rather as the causee and subject of following verb, *tsiaP⁸* 'eat'. The omitted subject, and the causer, *i¹* 'he', is understood as not allowing (or let) the others to eat the food. Thus, the event of giving undergoes semantic extension in this structure with a complex predicate to the notion of permission or enabling the causee NP to carry out the action they wish to do. Note also that, though both two interpretations are possible, interpretation (b) is preferred.

Two more typical examples of *khɔ⁵* as a permissive verb are given in (13) and (14).

(13) *khɔ⁵* + NP + V
      與   伊   去
      $\underline{khɔ^{5-4}}$ i^1 $khɯ^5$
      give   3SG   go
      'Let him go.'

(14) NEG + *khɔ⁵* + NP + V
　　無通　　　　與　　　我　　　講
　　bo²⁻⁴-thaŋ¹　*khɔ⁵⁻⁴*　*gua³⁻²*　*kaŋ³*
　　not.have-can　give　1SG　say
　　'(She) doesn't allow me to say (anything).'

In both these two examples, *khɔ⁵* no longer expresses 'giving' in its original meaning, since there is no object to be passed from the giver to the recipient. In (13), *khɔ⁵* has two possible interpretations: (a) allow someone to do something by giving permission; and (b) express a suggestion, without a permissive meaning. The first interpretation implies that someone, who is not the speaker, has initially not allowed the NP *i¹* 'he' to go. The second interpretation, however, does not imply this. In (14), *khɔ⁵* is used in a negative context, and can be glossed exclusively as 'allow, permit'. Note that generally this is regarded as a type of causative known as the 'permissive causative use' (see Newman 1996; Yap & Iwsaki 2003; Chappell & Peyraube 2007).

The non-permissive causative use of *khɔ⁵* is exemplified by (15) and (16).

(15) *khɔ⁵* + NP + V$_{AGENTIVE}$
　　伯　　　唔免　　　　管,
　　lan³　*m⁵⁻⁴ben³⁻²*　*kuan³*
　　1PL　no.need　interfere
　　與　　　　伊　　家　　　去　　　努力
　　khɔ⁵⁻⁴　*i¹*　*kai⁵⁻⁴*　*khɯ⁵⁻³*　*lɔ⁴liak⁸*
　　give　3SG　self　go　endeavour
　　'There is no need for us to interfere in (his affair), let him fight for himself.'

(16) *khɔ⁵* + NP + V$_{STATE}$
　　汝　　　與　　　　我　　　否勢　　　　遏
　　lu³　*khɔ⁵⁻⁴*　*gua³⁻²*　*phai³⁻²se⁵*　*a³*
　　2SG　give　1SG　embarrassed　EVC
　　'You make me feel very embarrassed.'

The context of (15) is that family members are talking about an emotional problem of one of their relatives and the mother says that we do not need to interfere. On the one hand, while the verb *khɔ⁵* no longer has its original meaning of 'giving' in this example, yet, on the other, nor is it a case of giving permission, and as such can be regarded as a causative of the non-interference type. In addition, *i¹* 'he' here is agentive and retains volitional control over the action of fighting. In example (16), however, the causee *gua³* 'me' is not agentive and does not perform an action, as the phrase *phai³⁻²se⁵ a³* 'very embarrassed' indicates a change of state. In addition, the caused event of my being embarrassed is not expected by the causer *lu³* 'you'. This is a case of 'unintentional causation of a new state' in Chappell's classification (Chappell 1992). The difference between these two causative constructions can also be seen from the translations: *khɔ⁵* in (15) is similar to English *let*, while *khɔ⁵* in (16) functions like the English verb *make*. This means that *khɔ⁵* GIVE is very versatile as a causative verb since it may co-occur with both agentive (+ control) V2s and also non-control states and events. These are two different semantic types of causatives determined by the nature of the complex predicate among other parameters (cf. Comrie 1989; Shibatani & Pardeshi 2002; Chappell & Peyraube 2007).

18.5 As a purposive marker

When both preceded and followed by another verb (phrase), the causative verb *khɔ⁵* tends to be reinterpreted as a purpose marker, as in (17) and (18).

(17) VP + *khɔ⁵* + NP + VP
    創   歌   與   媽仔   聽
    tshɔŋ⁵⁻³ *kua¹* *khɔ⁵⁻⁴* *bã²-a⁰* *thiã¹*
    do   song   give   mother-NM listen
    'Play music for mother to listen to.'

(18) VP + *khɔ⁵* + NP + VP
    拍   與   伊   吼
    pha?⁷ *khɔ⁵⁻⁴* *i¹* *hau³*
    hit   give   3SG cry
    '(She) hits him so that he cries.'

In (17), the purpose of the action coded by the first clause, *tshɔŋ⁵⁻³ kua¹* 'play music', is to achieve the planned outcome of *khɔ⁵⁻⁴ bã²a⁰ thiã¹* 'let mother listen to (it)'. Similarly, *khɔ⁵⁻⁴ i¹ hau³* 'let him cry' in (18) can be regarded as the purpose of the action denoted by *pha?⁷* 'hit' in the preceding phrase. In both cases, *khɔ⁵* can be interpreted as a purposive marker (cf. Newman 1996: 171-181; Heine & Kuteva 2002: 154-155; Yap & Iwasaki 2003).

The VP that occurs after the purposive marker *khɔ⁵* can contain an adjective (phrase), as in (19).

(19) VP + *khɔ⁵* + 3SG + ADJ
食　　與　　伊　　飽
tsiaʔ⁸　*khɔ⁵⁻⁴*　*i¹*　*pa³*
eat　　give　　3SG　full
'Eat your fill!'

Similar structures in Southern Min and Thai are mentioned in Newman (1996:180), where the 'give' verb is translated as 'until (some state is achieved)' (see also Embree 1973:89).

18.6 As a passive and speaker-affectedness marker

The 'give' verb *khɔ⁵* in Hui'an can also function as a passive marker, as in (20).

(20) NP$_{PATIENT}$ + GIVE + NP$_{AGENT}$ + VP$_{TRANSITIVE}$
我　　與　　伊　　罵
gua³　*khɔ⁵⁻⁴*　*i¹*　*bã⁵*
1SG　give　　3SG　scold
'I got scolded by him.'

In (20), *khɔ⁵* is used to introduce the agent of the transitive verb *bã⁵* 'scold' (i.e. *i¹* 'he'). This use of *khɔ⁵* is termed 'agent marker' or 'passive marker'. As shown by this example, the passive 'give' construction in Hui'an often denotes an unexpected and unfortunate event, like passive constructions in other Chinese varieties (see Chappell 2015).

The use of 'give' verb as a passive marker is unusual typologically, but can be attested in a large number of Chinese in Central and Southeastern China, and certain Western Malay dialects and Manchu-Tungusic languages (cf. Yap & Iwasaki 2003; Chappell 2015). Previous studies have shown that the use of a 'give' verb as a passive marker has developed from its use as a causative verb, i.e. following the pathway 'causative > passive' (see Yue-Hashimoto 1976; Hashimoto 1986; Yap & Iwasaki 2003, 2007; Chappell & Peyraube 2006; inter alia).

In the passive 'give' construction, the verb phrase following the passive marker *khɔ⁵* is always a transitive one, as, for example, the transitive verb *bã⁵* 'scold' in (20). Notably, the verb phrase in Hui'an can be extended to use with intransitive unaccusative ones, as in (21).

(21) NP_{PATIENT/THEME} + *khɔ⁵* + 3SG + VP_{UNACCUSATIVE}
　　花　　與　　伊　死　去
　　hue¹　*khɔ⁵⁻⁴*　*i¹*　*si³*　*khuɯ⁰*
　　flower　give　3SG　die　PVC
　　'Unfortunately, the flower has died.'

In (21), the predicate *si³ khuɯ⁰* 'die' is unaccusative, and the whole construction denotes adversity and unexpectedness, that is, the fact that 'the flower has died' is perceived as an unfortunate and unexpected event by the speaker. The third person singular pronoun *i¹* that follows the 'give' verb (*khɔ⁵*) is obligatory. This pronoun is highly grammaticalized and pleonastic in that it is not constrained by person and number agreement, and can be incorporated into the 'give' verb to form 與伊 *khɔ⁵⁻¹* (< *khɔ⁵⁻⁴ i¹*). In this construction, *khɔ⁵⁻⁴ i¹* as a whole, or *khɔ⁵⁻¹* (with *i¹* incorporated), is used to indicate that the speaker is emotionally affected by what has happened, and is thus regarded as a marker of speaker affectedness in Chen & Yap (2018).

This use of the 'give' verb is typologically rare, but can be attested in some other Chinese varieties, especially in other Southern Min varieties and some Mandarin varieties. However, in Mandarin varieties, the third person singular pronoun that follows the 'give' morpheme is usually dispreferred and often omitted. Chen & Yap (2018) have identified two major pathways in the development of this 'give' construction, i.e. the causative pathway (e.g. the mainland Mandarin varieties) and the passive-mediated pathway (e.g. Southern Min) (For more details see Chen & Yap 2018; see also Matthews et al. 2005; Lin 2011; Huang 2013).

18.7 As a concessive marker

The permissive verb *khɔ⁵* can be used in a hypothetical situation, as in (22), which expresses permission for speaking in an irrealis context.

(22) VP, *khɔ⁵* + NP + VP
　　卜　　講，　與　　伊　講
　　boʔ⁷⁻⁸　*kaŋ³*　*khɔ⁵⁻⁴*　*i¹*　*kaŋ³*
　　want　say　give　3SG　say
　　'Let (him) speak if (he) wants.'

The following seems to be another example of *khɔ⁵* as a permissive verb in an irrealis context.

(23) VP, ADJ + *khɔ⁵⁻¹*(or *khɔ⁵* + 3SG) + ADJ
　　　装修　　　者,　　　否看　　　　　与　　　否看
　　　tsɔŋ¹siu¹　*tse⁰*　*phai³⁻²-khuã⁵*　*khɔ⁵⁻¹*　*phai³⁻²-khuã⁵*
　　　renovate　DELIM　bad-look　　give　bad-look
　　　'(It is better) to renovate (it), ugly though it may be.'

In (23), the second clause *phai³⁻²khuã⁵ khɔ⁵⁻¹ phai³⁻²khuã⁵* 'ugly though it may be' can also be interpreted as 'just allow it to be ugly, if it has to be', in which *phai³⁻²khuã⁵* 'ugly' is not the actual state at the time of speech, but refers to what may happen in the future. In other words, *khɔ⁵* can be regarded here as a permissive verb used in an irrealis context. However, unlike example (22) in which the permissive clause *khɔ⁵⁻⁴ i¹ kaŋ³* 'permit (him) to speak' is preceded by the conditional clause *boʔ⁷⁻⁸ kaŋ³* 'if (he) wants to speak', *khɔ⁵⁻¹* (< *khɔ⁵⁻⁴ i¹*) in example (23) is placed between the same two adjectives (i.e. *phai³⁻²khuã⁵* 'ugly'). More importantly, 'VP *khɔ⁵⁻¹* VP' such as (23) has become a fixed phrase expressing concession, as shown by the translation 'ugly though it may be'. In other words, *khɔ⁵* here also indicates concession, and may be regarded as a concessive marker. A similar function in Mandarin Chinese is encoded by the adverb *jiù* 就, as in (24).

(24) ADJ + *jiù* + ADJ
　　　贵　　　　　就　　　贵　　　　　　呗 (Mandarin Chinese)
　　　guì　　　*jiù*　　*guì*　　　　*bei*
　　　expensive　ADV　expensive　SFP
　　　'expensive though it may be'

18.8 Summary

This chapter focuses on the 'give' construction in Hui'an. The 'give' verb *khɔ⁵* takes on a range of functions: as a ditransitive verb, dative marker, (permissive) causative verb, purposive marker, passive marker, speaker-affectedness marker, perspective marker, and concessive marker. These functions may occur in different, though related, syntactic structures. The development pathways can be simply represented as follows:

(i)　ditransitive verb > dative marker
(ii)　ditransitive verb > perspective marker
(iii) ditransitve verb > (permissive) causative verb > purposive marker
(iv) ditransitive verb > (permissive) causative verb > passive marker > speaker-affectedness marker
(v)　ditransitive verb > (permissive) causative verb > concessive marker

19 Interrogatives

19.1 Introduction

According to Siemund (2001:1010-1011), three types of interrogatives across the world's languages can be differentiated according to the kind of information sought: (a) polar interrogatives (or Yes-No questions): 'to ask whether a proposition or its negation is true', as in (1a); (b) constituent interrogatives (or questions formed with an interrogative pronoun): 'to inquire which values (if any) instantiate the variable of an open proposition', as in (1b); and (c) alternative interrogatives: 'to query which element of a set of alternatives makes an open sentence true', as in (1c).

(1) a. *Does a platypus lay eggs?*
    b. *What is a platypus?*
    c. *Is a platypus a mammal or a bird?*

In Hui'an, polar interrogatives can be marked by a series of strategies such as interrogative particles, interrogative intonation, disjunctive structures and the addition of tags. Note that disjunctive structures are typically used for alternative interrogatives, but also function as a device for indicating polar interrogatives in Chinese (cf. Ernst 1994; Matthews & Yip 2011; Siemund 2001). In the following sections, interrogatives in Hui'an will be examined in the order of alternative interrogatives, polar interrogatives and constituent interrogatives.

19.2 Alternative interrogatives

In alternative interrogatives, 'the speaker offers the addressee a list of possible answers from which he is supposed to choose the correct one' (Siemund 2001:1012). In Mandarin Chinese, the disjuncts of alternative interrogatives are connected by the alternative marker *háishì* 還是 'or', as in (2).

(2) The alternative interrogative in Mandarin Chinese
    A + *háishì* 還是 + B
    你　去，　還是　他　去？
    nǐ　qù　háishì　tā　qù
    2SG　go　or　he　go
    'Are you going or is he?'

In Hui'an, the disjuncts of alternative interrogatives are typically connected by the alternative marker $aʔ^{8\text{-}4}si^4$ 抑是 or $aʔ^8$ 抑, as in (3) and (4), respectively. In other words, the alternative interrogative in Hui'an typically takes the form of [A + $aʔ^{8\text{-}4}si^4/aʔ^8$ + B].

(3) A + $aʔ^{8\text{-}4}si^4$ + B
    蘋果   抑是   梨仔
    $phiŋ^{2\text{-}4}kɔ^3$ $aʔ^{8\text{-}4}\text{-}si^4$ $lai^{2\text{-}4}\text{-}a^3$
    apple   or-be   pear-NM
    'Apple or pear?'

(4) A + $aʔ^8$ + B
    卜   (才罪)   工作   抑   卜   讀冊
    $boʔ^{7\text{-}8}$ $tshə^{5\text{-}4}$ $kaŋ^1tsɔk^7$ $aʔ^{8\text{-}4}$ $boʔ^{7\text{-}8}$ $thak^{8\text{-}4}tsheʔ^7$
    want   look.for   job   or   want   study
    '(Do you) want to find a job or study?'

It can be seen from these two examples that the disjuncts can be encoded by a noun, e.g. $phiŋ^{2\text{-}4}kɔ^3$ 'apple' in (3), or a verb phrase, e.g. $tshə^{5\text{-}4} kaŋ^1tsɔk^7$ 'find a job' in (4).

The first adjunct in alternative interrogatives in Hui'an may be preceded by the copular verb si^4 是, as in (5), where the first adjunct $phiŋ^{2\text{-}4}kɔ^3$ 蘋果 'apple' follows the copular verb si^4.

(5) si^4 + A + $aʔ^{8\text{-}4}(si^4)$ + B (+ a^0 啊)
    是   蘋果   抑(是)   香蕉   啊
    si^4 $phiŋ^{2\text{-}4}kɔ^3$ $aʔ^{8\text{-}4}(\text{-}si^4)$ $kiŋ^1tsio^1$ a^0
    be   apple   or(-be)   banana   SFP
    'Is (it) an apple or a banana?'

This example shows that the alternative interrogative in Hui'an can also take the form of [si^4 + A + $aʔ^{8\text{-}4}si^4/aʔ^8$ + B], which is however less common than [A + $aʔ^8/aʔ^{8\text{-}4}si^4$ + B] (without the first copular verb si^4) as illustrated by (3) and (4) above.

Furthermore, when the first adjunct is preceded by the copular verb si^4, the second adjunct tends to be preceded by the alternative marker $aʔ^{8\text{-}4}si^4$, rather than by the marker $aʔ^8$. In other words, in example (5), speakers prefer the use of $aʔ^{8\text{-}4}si^4$ (rather than $aʔ^8$) to connect the adjuncts $phiŋ^{2\text{-}4}kɔ^3$ 'apple' and $kiŋ^1tsio^1$ 'banana'. Note also that, the sentence-final particle a^0 啊 can be used in alternative interrogatives in Hui'an, as demonstrated by example (5). This particle is optional in that it could also occur at the end of the interrogative in (3) and (4).

19.3 Polar interrogatives

As mentioned above, strategies for marking polar interrogatives in Hui'an include interrogative particles, interrogative intonation, disjunctive structures and tag questions. Note that, crosslinguistically speaking, interrogative particles and interrogative intonation are two main methods of indicating that an utterance is a polar interrogative, while using disjunctive structures to express polar interrogatives as in Southern Min and other Chinese varieties is not common in the languages of the world (cf. Dryer 2005:470).

Interrogative particles in Hui'an include a^0 啊, m^0 呣, $bə^0$ 未, bo^0 無 and bue^0 獪, of which m^0, $bə^0$, bo^0 and bue^0 are derived from negative forms m^5 'not', $bə^5$ 'not yet', bo^2 'not have' and bue^4 'cannot', respectively, with tonal reduction. Note that negative forms in polar interrogatives with the disjunctive structure VP-NEG are a common source of sentence-final interrogative particles in Chinese (cf. Li 1992; Wu 1997, inter alia). For convenience of comparison, we will firstly examine polar interrogatives involving disjunctive structures.

19.3.1 Interrogatives with disjunctive structures

In Hui'an, this type of polar interrogative typically consists of an affirmative sentence followed by its negative counterpart, with or without the alternative marker $aʔ^8$ 抑 'or', more specifically, taking the form of VP-or-NEG-VP, VP-NEG-VP and VP-or-NEG.[1] The latter two forms (VP-NEG-VP and VP-or-NEG) are both shortened versions of the first one (VP-or-NEG-VP). All these three structures semantically convey an interrogative meaning which is neutral in assumption on the part of the speaker, that is, there are no expectations regarding the answer on the part of the addressee, either expressed or implied.

---

[1] In the literature, VP-NEG-VP and VP-NEG, along with ADV-VP, are often called *zhèngfǎn wènjù* 正反問句, *fǎnfù wènjù* 反復問句, the 'A-not-A' question, the 'V-not-V' question or 'neutral question' (cf. Li & Thompson 1981; Zhu 1982; Yue 1993; Matthews & Yip 1994; Zhang 2000, inter alia). The 'A-not-A' pattern (also 'V-not-V') often functions as a cover term for 'VP-NEG-VP' and 'VP-NEG'. ADV-VP is also neutral in presupposition and refers to the interrogative pattern bearing the attachment of an interrogative adverb to a VP.

The 'VP-NEG' pattern (without a disjunct marker), which is widely used in Chinese, especially Southern Chinese, is not mentioned here, since negative markers in the 'VP-NEG' pattern of the Hui'an dialect have developed into sentence-final interrogative particles, even though they show different degrees of grammaticalization (see §19.3.2).

19.3.1.1 VP-or-NEG-VP

The VP-or-NEG-VP type refers to the juxtaposition of a predicate and its syntactically negated form with the alternative marker $a\textit{ʔ}^8$ 'or', as illustrated by (6) and (7).

(6) 焦　　抑　　　無　　　　焦
　　ta^1　$aʔ^{8\text{-}4}$　$bo^{2\text{-}4}$　ta^1
　　dry　or　　not.have　dry
　　'Is it dry?'

(7) 汝　　卜　　　去　　　抑　　　　唔　　　去　　　啊
　　lu^3　$boʔ^{7\text{-}8}$　$khuɨ^5$　$aʔ^{8\text{-}4}$　$m^{5\text{-}4}$　$khuɨ^5$　a^0
　　2SG　want　go　or　not　go　SFP
　　'Do you want to go?'

In (6), VP is encoded by the predicative adjective ta^1 'dry', and the expression $bo^{2\text{-}4} ta^1$ 'not dry' functions as its negative counterpart. In (7), the VP and its negative form are encoded by the verb phrases $boʔ^{7\text{-}8} khuɨ^5$ 'want to go' and $m^{5\text{-}4} khuɨ^5$ 'not want to go', respectively.

The VPs always contain the same verb except when the copular verb si^4 is used as the copy, as in (8) below.

(8) 口　　　會　　開　　　　啤酒瓶　　　　　　　抑　　　　唔　　　是　　啊
　　tse^2　e^4　$khui^1$　$pi^{2\text{-}4}tsiu^{3\text{-}2}\text{-}pan^2$　$aʔ^{8\text{-}4}$　$m^{5\text{-}4}$　si^4　a^0
　　this　can　open　beer-bottle　or　not　be　SFP
　　'Can this be used to open the beer bottle?'

In (8), NEG-VP is encoded by $m^{5\text{-}4} si^4$ 'not be' (consisting of the general negative m^5 'not' and the copular verb si^4), rather than by $bue^4 khui^1 pi^{2\text{-}4}tsiu^{3\text{-}2}pan^2$ 繪開啤酒瓶 'cannot open the beer bottle', the typical negative counterpart of the verb phrase $e^4 khui^1 pi^{2\text{-}4}tsiu^{3\text{-}2}pan^2$. The reason for using the copular verb as the copy may be that the affirmative form is a relatively complicated verb phrase, consisting of the modal auxiliary verb e^4, the verb $khui^1$ and its three-syllable object $pi^{2-4}tsiu^{3-2}pan^2$.

19.3.1.2 VP-NEG-VP

VP-NEG-VP differs from VP-or-NEG-VP in that the predicate and its syntactically negated form are not connected by the alternative marker $a\mathit{?}^8$ 'or'. The VP here can be a verb such as the copular verb si^4 是 'be' in (9), or the adjective ho^3 好 'good' in (10).

(9) 伊　　是　　唔　　是　　野　　口　　　　啊
    i^1　　si^4　$m^{5\text{-}4}$　si^4　$ia^{3\text{-}2}$　$thiak^7$　a^0
    3SG　be　not　be　quite　beautiful　SFP
    'Is she very beautiful?'

(10) 即支　　　鼎　　好　　無　　　好
     $tsit^{7\text{-}8}$-ki^1　$tiã^3$　ho^3　$bo^{2\text{-}4}$　ho^3
     this-CL　pot　good　not.have　good
     'Is this pot good?'

The VP can also be a verb phrase such as $siɔŋ^{2\text{-}4}$ lai^2 常來 'come often' in (11).

(11) 伊　　常　　　來　　無　　　常　　　來
     i^1　$siɔŋ^{2\text{-}4}$　lai^2　$bo^{2\text{-}4}$　$siɔŋ^{2\text{-}4}$　lai^2
     3SG　often　come　not.have　often　come
     'Does he often come (here)?'

This type of interrogative is prevalent in the Northern Chinese, though it can be attested in all of the major Chinese varieties including Southern Min (cf. Yue 1993:42). In Hui'an, it is not commonly used in daily conversation: all the examples are produced via elicitation, except those with the VP being the copular verb si^4 'be', as in (9) above.

19.3.1.3 VP-or-NEG

Two examples of VP-or-NEG interrogatives are given in (12) and (13).

(12) 汝　　卜　　　按　　　即搭　　　　　去　　抑　　　呣
　　　 lu^3　$bo\text{?}^{7\text{-}8}$　$an^{5\text{-}3}$　$tsit^{7\text{-}8}\text{-}ta\text{?}^{7\text{-}8}$　$khuɯ^5$　$a\text{?}^{8\text{-}4}$　m^5
　　　 2SG　want　from　this-LOC　go　or　not
　　　 'Do you want to go from here?'

(13) 伊　　有　　　錢　　　抑　　　　無
　　　 i^1　u^4　$tsin^2$　$a\text{?}^{8\text{-}4}$　bo^2
　　　 3SG　have　money　or　not.have
　　　 'Does he have money?'

In (12), the volitional negative m^5 alone functions as the negative form of the disjunctive structure. Similarly, the perfective negative bo^2 in (13) is used alone as the negative counterpart of the verb phrase $u^4\,tsin^2$ 'have money'. In both examples, the negative form plays an equally important part as its affirmative counterpart, even though the affirmative one is encoded by a more complex verb phrase, as in (12). This is consistent with the fact that the negative forms m^5 and bo^2 in (12) and (13) are in their citation tones, unlike the interrogative particles m^0 (< the negative m^5) and bo^0 (< the negative bo^2), which are in the neutral tone, as will be shown in the following section.

19.3.2 Particle interrogatives

As with Mandarin Chinese and other Chinese dialects, polar interrogatives in Hui'an can be formed by adding an interrogative particle to a statement. As mentioned above, interrogative particles in Hui'an include a^0 啊, m^0 呣, $bə^0$ 未, bo^0 無 and bue^0 獪, of which m^0, $bə^0$, bo^0 and bue^0 are derived from negative words m^5 'not', $bə^5$ 'not yet', bo^2 'not have' and bue^4 'cannot', respectively, with tonal reduction. In the following sections, interrogatives formed by these five particles will be examined one by one, followed by a brief explanation of the status of the particles m^0, $bə^0$, bo^0 and bue^0 and their neutral tones.

19.3.2.1 a^0 啊
Polar interrogatives with the particle a^0 啊 may indicate disbelief, as in (14), or surprise, as in (15).

(14) 恁　　則　　　坐　　蜀字　　　　久　　啊
　　　len³　tsiaʔ⁷⁻⁸　tsə⁴　tsit⁸⁻⁴-li⁵⁻⁴　kuʔ³　aᵒ
　　　2PL　only　　sit　one-quarter　long　SFP
　　　'You only stayed (there) for 15 minutes?'

(15) 汝　　無　　　　共　　　儂　　　說　　啊
　　　luˀ³　boˀ²⁻⁴　kaˀ⁵⁻⁴　laŋ⁴　səʔ⁷　aᵒ
　　　2SG　not.have　to　other　say　SFP
　　　'You didn't tell him?'

The context of (14) is that the persons addressed come back home from a visit to one of their relatives, and the speaker, who has stayed at home waiting for their return, does not believe they could have stayed at the home of their relative for only 15 minutes, unaware that they also went to a supermarket. In (15), the speaker is surprised that the addressee did not tell soemthing to another person.

The following example illustrates that polar interrogatives with the particle *aᵒ* can also be used to ask for confirmation.

(16) 啰　　　食　　　啊
　　　m⁵⁻⁴　tsiaʔ⁸　aᵒ
　　　not　eat　SFP
　　　'You don't want to eat?'

In (16), the speaker guesses that the addressee does not want to eat anything, and uses the interrogative with *aᵒ* to ask for confirmation.

Note that the interrogative particle *aᵒ* is not restricted to polar interrogatives as in (14) – (16), but can also be used in alternative interrogatives (see §19.2) and constituent interrogatives (see §19.4). In other words, this particle in Hui'an is not the counterpart of the interrogative particle *ma* 嗎 in Mandarin Chinese, which is only used in polar interrogatives.

19.3.2.2 *mᵒ* 啰

Polar interrogatives with the particle *mᵒ* 啰 can be used to ask whether something is true, as in (17) and (18), or whether a course of action is desirable, as in (19).

(17) 汝　　是　　大學生　　　　　　　啰
　　　luˀ³　siˀ⁴　tuaˀ⁵⁻⁴oʔ⁸⁻⁴siŋˀ¹　mᵒ
　　　2SG　be　university.student　SFP
　　　'Are you a university student?'

(18) 好看　　唔
ho$^{3\text{-}2}$-khuã^5　m^0
good-look　SFP
'Does it look good?'

(19) 汝　卜　　食　　唔
lɯ^3　boʔ$^{7\text{-}8}$　tsiaʔ^8　m^0
2SG　want　eat　SFP
'Do you want to eat?'

In (17), the particle m^0 is used with the copular clause $lɯ^3 si^4 tua^{5\text{-}4}oʔ^{8\text{-}4}siŋ^1$ 'you are a university student', asking whether it is true that the addressee is a university student. In (18), m^0 is preceded by the adjective $ho^{3\text{-}2}khuã^5$ 'good-looking' to ask whether the existence of the property $ho^{3\text{-}2}khuã^5$ is true. In (19), m^0 is preceded by the verb phrase $boʔ^{7\text{-}8} tsiaʔ^8$ 'want to eat' to ask whether the addressee's desire to eat something is true (Compare with a similar example with a^0 in (16)). All these three examples typically convey an interrogative meaning which is neutral in presupposition.

The following two examples show two other semantic uses of the particle m^0.

(20) 汝　八　　來　　即搭　　　唔
lɯ^3　pat$^{7\text{-}8}$　lai$^{2\text{-}4}$　tsit$^{7\text{-}8}$-taʔ^7　m^0
2SG　EXP　come　that-LOC　SFP
'Have you been here?'

(21) 汝　知　　爸仔　　障　　　說　唔
lɯ^3　tsai^1　pa^2-a^0　tsiũ$^{5\text{-}3}$　səʔ^7　m^0
2SG　know　father-NM　how　say　SFP
'Do you know what father said?'

The context of (20) is that the addressee looks familiar to the speaker, even though they are meeting each other for the first time. This example is used by the speaker to invite confirmation. In (21), the father has said something earlier to the speaker, when the addressee was not on the spot, and this interrogative form is used by the speaker to attract the addressee's attention.

In Hui'an, m^5 (with Tone 5, rather than neutral tone), functions as a general negative meaning 'not', and as a volitional negative meaning 'not want, not willing to' (see chapter 13). Accordingly, the interrogative particle m^0 (with neutral tone) can follow a state which involves a verb such as the copular verb si^4 in (17) and the volitional modal verb $bo?^7$ in (19). Unlike the general negative m^5 which is basically not used to negate adjectives, the particle m^0 can occur with an adjective such as $ho^{3\text{-}2}khuã^5$ 'good-looking' in (18). In other words, compared to the general negative m^5, the interrogative particle m^0 undergoes generalization in that it can be used in more contexts. Unlike its use as the negative form in disjunctive structures (e.g. VP-or-NEG in §19.3.1.3 above), m^0 in (17) – (19) has lost its original tone and is in a neutral tone, which shows that m^0 no longer plays an equally important part as the constituents in its preceding verb phrase. In other words, m^0 in (17) – (19) neither functions as an adverb negating a predicate (see chapter 13), nor functions as the negative form in disjunctive structures (see §19.3.1.3), but functions as an interrogative particle to form a particle polar interrogative. In addition, unlike polar interrogatives with disjunctive structures which typically convey an interrogative meaning neutral in assumption, polar interrogatives with the particle m^0 can also be used to invite confirmation or to attract the addressee's attention. All these show that the morpheme m^5 in Hui'an involves an extension from a negative marker to an interrogative particle, with tonal reduction.

19.3.2.3 $bə^0$ 未

As mentioned above, the interrogative particle $bə^0$ 未 is derived from the negator $bə^5$ 'not yet'. When functioning as a particle in polar interrogatives, $bə^0$ is typically used to ask whether something has occurred, as in (22), where $bə^0$ follows the verb $ket^{7\text{-}8}hun^1$ 結婚 'marry', asking whether he has got married or not.

(22) 伊　　結婚　　　未
　　 i^1　　$ket^{7\text{-}8}hun^1$　$bə^0$
　　 3SG　marry　　　SFP
　　 'Has he got married?'

When used with $bo?^7$ ト 'want' in polar interrogatives, the particle $bə^0$ asks whether something is about to happen, as in (23). The particle $bə^0$ here is used with the expectation that the event will happen but has not yet taken place.

(23) 個　　ト　　　來　　未
　　 en^1　$bo?^{7\text{-}8}$　lai^2　$bə^0$
　　 3PL　want　　come　SFP
　　 'Are they about to come?'

19.3.2.4 bo^0 無

The particle bo^0 無, derived from the negator bo^2 'not exist, not have', is often used with the verb (or auxiliary verb) u^4 有 'exist, have', as illustrated by (24) – (26).

(24) 搭 有 插頭 無
$ta\text{ʔ}^7$ u^4 $tsha\text{ʔ}^{7\text{-}8}\text{-}thau^2$ $\underline{bo^0}$
here have plug SFP
'Is there a plug here?'

(25) 汝 後尾 有 挽 無
lu^3 $au^4bə^3$ u^4 ban^3 $\underline{bo^0}$
2SG back have pull SFP
'Did you pull out your back (teeth)?'

(26) 有 夠 燒 無
u^4 $kau^{5\text{-}3}$ sio^1 $\underline{bo^0}$
have enough warm SFP
'Is it warm enough?'

A noun, an action verb or adjective (phrase) can be inserted between the verb u^4 'have' and the particle bo^0. When there is only one noun argument such as $tsha\text{ʔ}^{7\text{-}8}thau^2$ 'plug' in (24), the polar interrogative asks whether something (e.g. a plug) exists. When it is an action verb such as ban^3 'pull' in (25), the interrogative asks whether something (i.e. pulling out the back teeth) has happened. When it is an adjective phrase such as $kau^{5\text{-}3} sio^1$ 'warm enough' in (26), the interrogative asks whether a state (i.e. warm enough) exists.

The particle bo^0 can also be used alone without u^4, as in (27) and (28).

(27) 伊 經常 來 無
i^1 $kiŋ^1siɔŋ^{2\text{-}4}$ lai^2 $\underline{bo^0}$
3SG often come SFP
'Does he come here often?'

(28) 迄搭 恰 省 無
$hit^{7\text{-}8}\text{-}ta\text{ʔ}^7$ $kha\text{ʔ}^{7\text{-}8}$ $siŋ^3$ $\underline{bo^0}$
that-LOC comparatively cheap SFP
'Is it cheaper there?/It is cheaper there, right?'

Example (27) is used to ask whether someone comes here often, without implying that the speaker has an expectation of a positive or negative answer. Example (28), however, is used to invite confirmation. In other words, this interrogative is a 'biased one' in terms of the subjectivity, that is, the speaker's stance. This use of the particle bo^0 is similar to the function of the interrogative particle *ba* 吧 in Mandarin Chinese (see Li & Thompson 1981:307-311).

As shown by these examples, unlike its use as the negative form in disjunctive structures (e.g. VP-or-NEG in §19.3.1.3 above), the particle bo^0 has lost its original tone, and no longer plays an equally important part as its preceding predicate. Unlike polar interrogatives with disjunctive structures which semantically convey an interrogative meaning which is neutral in assumption (see §19.3.1), polar interrogatives with the particle bo^0 can also be used to invite confirmation, thus implicating the attitude of the speaker, as illustrated by example (28).

19.3.2.5 *bue⁰* 獪

In Hui'an, bue^4 (with Tone 4) can be a verb meaning 'know, understand', or a modal auxiliary verb expressing possibility such as ability, permission and epistemic possibility (see chapter 12). As mentioned in §19.3.1.3 above, bue^4 can also be used alone as the negative form in polar interrogatives with disjunctive structures. When functioning as a sentence-final interrogative particle, bue^0 is in neutral tone (i.e. no longer retains its citation tone) and is often used with its affirmative counterpart e^4 'can', as in (29) and (30).

(29) 伊　　會　　說　　　廣東話　　　　獪
　　 i^1　 e^4　 $səʔ^{7-8}$　 $kŋ^{3-2}taŋ^1ue^5$　 $\underline{bue^0}$
　　 3SG   can　speak　Cantonese　　SFP
　　 'Can he speak Cantonese?'

(30) 汝　　說　　　今日　　　　會　　落雨　　　　獪
　　 $lɯ^3$　 $səʔ^{7-8}$　 $kiã^1let^8$　 e^4　 $loʔ^{8-4}\text{-}hɔ^4$　 $\underline{bue^0}$
　　 2SG   say　today　　　can　fall-rain　SFP
　　 'Do you think it will rain today?'

The following example shows that the particle bue^0 can be used without e^4.

(31) 即垛　　　　否看　　　　　　獪
　　 $tsit^{7-8}\text{-}tə^5$　 $phai^{3-2}\text{-}khuã^5$　 $\underline{bue^0}$
　　 this-CL　bad-look　　　　SFP
　　 'Would this (table) be ugly?'

19.3.2.6 Status of particles m^0, $bə^0$, bo^0 and bue^0

As mentioned above, all these four sentence-final interrogative particles are derived from their use as a negator, i.e. m^5 'not', $bə^5$ 'not yet', bo^2 'not have' and bue^4 'cannot', respectively. Unlike their use as the negative form in polar interrogatives with disjunctive structures (e.g. VP-or-NEG), these interrogative particles have all lost their original tones and are in a neutral tone, which shows that they no longer play the same role as when they occur in the preceding verb phrases. In addition, some syntactic restrictions that we saw pertain to the VP-negators do not apply to the particles. For example, the negator m^5 'not' normally does not modify a predicative adjective, while the particle m^0 (with neutral tone) can be used in this case, as shown in §19.3.2.2 above. This suggests that the relevant particles have undergone generalization in that they can be used in more contexts.

Unlike polar interrogatives with disjunctive structures which typically convey an interrogative meaning which is neutral in presupposition, polar interrogatives with some of these particles such as m^0 and bo^2 have developed new semantic uses such as inviting confirmation and attracting the addressee's attention without looking for an answer. All these suggest that the four interrogative particles have undergone grammaticalization in this sentence-final position to become interrogative particles (see also Wu 1997; Yang 2003 for NEG > Q particle in VP-NEG interrogatives in Chinese). Note that, however, these four interrogative particles seem to involve different degrees of grammaticalization. The particles $bə^0$ and bue^0 appear to be less grammaticalized than the particles m^0 and bo^0: the particle $bə^0$ maintains its original lexical meaning of 'not yet', while the particle bue^0 most frequently occurs with its positive form e^4 'can'. In addition, interrogatives with the particles $bə^0$ and bue^0 are typically neutral in assumption, just as their counterparts - the polar interrogatives with disjunctive structures. This phenomenon showing different degrees of grammaticalization is, however, entirely compatible with the continuum concept in grammaticalization which alludes to the gradual nature of this process (cf. Hopper & Traugott 2003, inter alia).

19.3.2.7 Interrogatives via intonation

According to Ultan (1978:218-219), intonation is by far the most widespread strategy for expressing polar interrogatives. More specifically, the rising contour is the most frequently occurring type, while other strategies include terminal acceleration and higher pitch toward the end of a contour. In Hui'an, the intonation pattern for indicating unbiased polar interrogatives is precisely this terminal acceleration and a higher pitch on the last word. An example is given in (32).

(32) 相機　　卜　　帶

siɔng⁵⁻³ki¹ boʔ⁷⁻⁸ tua⁵
camera   want   take
'Do you want to take the camera?'

In (32), the last word *tua⁵* 'take' immediately follows its preceding word *boʔ⁷* 'want' with a shorter pause between *boʔ⁷* and *tua⁵* than that in a declarative sentence. In addition, *tua⁵* has a higher pitch with a more prominent stress without any obvious change of its tone contour.[2]

Note that this intonation pattern is also used in echo questions (a special type of question) to indicate surprise, as in (33).

(33) A: 今日　　蜀　　日　　刣　　四　　隻　　其　　鴨
　　　kiã¹let⁸ tsit⁸⁻⁴ let⁸ thai² si⁵⁻³ tsiaʔ⁷ e⁰ aʔ⁷
　　　today   one   day   kill   four   CL   FOC duck
　　　'(I) killed four ducks within one day today.'
　　B: 刣　　去　　四　　隻？
　　　thai² khɯ⁵⁻³ si⁵⁻³ tsiaʔ⁷
　　　kill   RVC   four   CL
　　　'(You) killed four (ducks)?'

In (33), the last word *tsiaʔ⁷* in turn B immediately follows its preceding word *si⁴* 'four' with a shorter pause between *si⁴* and *tsiaʔ⁷* than in a declarative sentence. In addition, *tsiaʔ⁷* is in a higher pitch than in its declarative counterpart, with a more prominent stress but no obvious change of its tone contour (which is high falling checked in this case).

19.3.3 Tag questions

Tag questions refer to those expressions which syntactically follow a declarative statement or an imperative to turn them into questions (i.e. declarative statement/imperative + tag question > question), and are semantically often used to invite confirmation or ask for agreement. In Hui'an, there are mainly three types of tag question: (a) simple particle interrogatives involving the particles m^0 呣 and

---

[2] This description of the features of question intonation is based on my analysis and observations as a native speaker. Of course, an acoustic study would be necessary to provide a detailed account of the associated features of prominence and stress etc.

bo^0 無; (b) a sentence-final particle, e.g. hau^0; and (c) a fused form of the tag question si^4 m^0 是唔 (consisting of the copular verb si^4 and the particle m^0) and the particle a^0 啊 (i.e. $siã^0 < si^4$ $m^0 + a^0$).

Examples of simple particle interrogatives involving the particle m^0 are given in (34) and (35).

(34) 恁   食   蜀   碗,   卜   唔
     len^3 $tsia?^8$ $tsit^{8\text{-}4}$ $uã^3$ $\underline{bo?^7}$ $\underline{m^0}$
     2PL   eat   one   bowl   want   SFP
     'You eat one bowl (of noodles), OK?'

(35) 懷   是   滾水,   是   唔
     $huai^2$ si^4 $kun^{3\text{-}2}\text{-}tsui^3$ $\underline{si^4}$ $\underline{m^0}$
     those   be   boil-water   be   SFP
     'That is boiled water, right?'

In (34), $bo?^7$ m^0 is used to invite agreement to the suggestion put forward by the speaker. In (35), si^4 m^0 is used to ask for confirmation.

An example of a simple particle interrogative involving bo^0 無 is given in (36), where u^4 bo^0 有無 is used to ask for confirmation.

(36) 迄擺   我   共   汝   (才罪)   迄本   冊,
     $hit^{7\text{-}8}\text{-}pai^3$ gua^3 $ka^{5\text{-}4}$ $lu^{3\text{-}2}$ $tshə^{5\text{-}4}$ $hit^{7\text{-}8}\text{-}pun^{3\text{-}2}$ $tshe?^7$
     that-time   1SG   BEN   2SG   look.for   that-CL   book
     有   無
     u^4 bo^0
     have SFP
     'I looked for that book for you last time, right?'

The following are examples of tag questions encoded by the sentence-final particle hau^0 and the fused form $siã^0$.

(37) 我   佫   煮   口
     gua^3 $ko?^{7\text{-}8}$ tsu^3 $\underline{hau^0}$
     1SG   again   cook   SFP
     'I cook again, OK?'

(38) 無　　椅　　口
    bo²⁻⁴　i³　siã⁰
    not.have　chair　SFP
    'There are no chairs, right?'

In (37), by using the sentence-final particle hau^0, the speaker asks for agreement from the addressee about her suggestion. In (38), the sentence-final particle $siã^0$ is used to ask for confirmation of an assumption. In origin, the particle $siã^0$ is probably a fused form of $si^4\ m^0\ a^0$ 是呣啊, which is formed by the tag question $si^4\ m^0$ as in (35) and the sentence-final particle a^0. The fusion process can be represented as $si^4\ m^0 + a^0 \rightarrow siã^0$ (see §2.5).

19.4 Constituent interrogatives

Constituent interrogatives can also be called question-word interrogatives, WH-interrogatives, special interrogatives, information questions or content interrogatives (cf. Siemund 2001:1011; Wu 2008:3, among others). They differ from polar Yes-No questions in that they are used to obtain new information rather than a simple affirmation or negation of a proposition. In this section, we focus on the question words which are used in constituent interrogatives. Like other Chinese varieties, the questions words in Hui'an are *in-situ*, simply taking the place of the linguistic form being questioned, without any syntactic re-arrangement. This is different from many other languages such as English where the question words (or interrogative phrases) occur obligatorily in clause-initial position (cf. Dryer 2011).

The paradigm for questions words in Hui'an is shown in Table 19-1.

Tab. 19-1: The question words in the Hui'an dialect

English	The Hui'an dialect	Mandarin Chinese
'what'	$siəm^{3\text{-}2}bĩʔ^7$ 甚物 $siã^2$ 啥	$shénme$ 什麼
'who'	$siã^2laŋ^2$ 啥儂 $siaŋ^2$	$shuí$ 誰
'when'	ti^4si^2 (or tu^4si^2) 底時 $siəm^{3\text{-}2}bĩʔ^{7\text{-}8}\ si^{2\text{-}4}tsam^4$ 甚物時站	$shénme\ shíhou$ 什麼時候
'which'	to^3 底	$nǎ$ 哪
'where'	to^3 底	$nǎr$ 哪兒

English	The Hui'an dialect	Mandarin Chinese
	$to^{3\text{-}2}ta\textipa{P}^7$ 底搭	
'how many/much'	kui^3 幾 (small quantities)	$jǐ$ 幾 (small quantities)
	lua^4tsue^5 偌儕	$duōshao$ 多少
	lua^4 偌	$duō$ 多
'how'	$tsiũ^5(\text{-}^3ai^3)$障(仔)	$zěnme$ 怎麼
	$kŋ^5(\text{-}^3le^3)$	
'why'	$lã^5$ 哪	$wèishénme$ 為什麼
	$ui^{5\text{-}4}siəm^{3\text{-}2}bĩ\textipa{P}^7$ 為甚物	

19.4.1 $siəm^{3\text{-}2}bĩ\textipa{P}^7$ and $siã^2$ 'what'

The question words $siəm^{3\text{-}2}bĩ\textipa{P}^7$ 甚物 and $siã^2$ 啥 are both used for 'what' questions. $Siəm^{3\text{-}2}bĩ\textipa{P}^7$ is mainly used alone as a predicate, as in (39), or to modify a noun, as in (40).

(39) 撮　　　甚物　　　啊
　　 $tsuai^2$　$siəm^{3\text{-}2}bĩ\textipa{P}^7$　a^0
　　 these　 what　　　 SFP
　　 'What are these?'

(40) 甚物　　　　　問題
　　 $siəm^{3\text{-}2}bĩ\textipa{P}^{7\text{-}8}$　$bun^{5\text{-}4}tue^2$
　　 what　　　　　question
　　 'what question?'

In (39), the plural demonstrative $tsuai^2$ 'these' and the question word $siəm^{3\text{-}2}bĩ\textipa{P}^7$ 'what' serve as the subject and the predicate, respectively. In other words, example (39) takes the form of 'Subject + Q-word + SFP', unlike 'what' questions in English such as *What are these*, in which the question word is moved into clause-initial position. In (40), the question word $siəm^{3\text{-}2}bĩ\textipa{P}^7$ functions as an attributive modifier of the noun $bun^{5\text{-}4}tue^2$ 'question'.

The following example suggests that $siəm^{3\text{-}2}bĩ\textipa{P}^7$ can also function as a direct object of a verb.

(41) 汝　口　卜　洗　甚物　啊
　　 lu³　tse⁵　bo?⁷⁻⁸　sue³⁻²　siəm³⁻²bĩ?⁷　a⁰
　　 2SG　now　want　wash　what　SFP
　　 'What do you want to wash now?'

In (41), the question word *siəm³⁻²bĩ?⁷* is used as an object of the verb *sue³* 'wash'. Note that the question word in this example is also *in-situ*, rather than occurring in clause-initial position.

Unlike *siəm³⁻²bĩ?⁷*, the question word *siã²* is mainly used in object position. In other words, it does not pose any difficulties to substitute *sue³⁻² siã²* for *sue³⁻² siəm³⁻²bĩ?⁷* 'wash what' in (41) above. Another example of *siã²* in object position is given in (42), where *siã²* serves as an object of the verb *sə?⁷* 'say'.

(42) 伊　說　啥
　　 i¹　sə?⁷⁻⁸　siã²
　　 3SG　say　what
　　 'What did he say?'

The question word *siã²* can also be used alone as a predicate, like *siəm³⁻²bĩ?⁷* in (39) above. An example of *siã²* is given in (43), where the demonstrative *tsat⁸* 'this' and the question word *siã²* function as the subject and the predicate, respectively.

(43) 口　啥　啊
　　 tsat⁸　siã²　a⁰
　　 this　what　SFP
　　 'What is this?'

The question words *siã²* and *siəm³⁻²bĩ?⁷* can only refer to things (inanimates or non-human animates), but not to persons, when they are used alone. However, they can be used to refer to a person, when co-occurring with the noun *laŋ²* 儂 'person': *siəm³⁻²bĩ?⁷⁻⁸ laŋ²*, literally 'what person'. Two examples are given in (44) and (45).

(44) 迄孤　甚物　儂
　　 hit⁷⁻⁸-kɔ¹　siəm³⁻²bĩ?⁷⁻⁸　laŋ²
　　 that-CL　what　person
　　 'What is that (person)?'

(45) 迄孤　　啥儂
　　 hit⁷⁻⁸-kɔ¹　siã²-laŋ²
　　 that-CL　what-person
　　 'Who is that (person)?'

Example (44) is typically used to ask for a description of someone with respect to his/her occupation and social status, whereas (45) is often used when the addressee is asked to identify someone (see the following section for more details).

Two questions arise. What are the sources/etymologies of these two question words? Is there any relationship between these two question words? According to the pronunciation, the question word *siəm*³⁻²*bĩʔ*⁷ seems to be a cognate of the question word *shénme* 什麼 in Mandarin Chinese. As suggested in Lǚ (1985:128-130), *shénme* is derived from *shìwù* 是物 'what' in earlier Chinese, while *shìwù* 是物 'what' is a contracted form of *shì héwù* 是何物, in which *shì* 是 is a copular verb and *héwù* 何物, a commonly used question word for 'what' since the Wei-Jin period (AD 220-420), as shown in (i).
(i) *shì héwù* 是何物 'be what' -> *shìwù* 是物 '(be) what' -> *shénme* 什麼 'what'

Following this line of reasoning, we can hypothesize that the question word *siəm*³⁻²*bĩʔ*⁷ in Hui'an may also be traced back to *shì héwù* 'be what' in earlier Chinese.

The question words for 'what' in some other Southern Min varieties such as Xiamen and Taiwan share similar pronunciations with those in Hui'an, e.g. *sim miʔ*, *siã* and *siã miʔ* in Xiamen (Zhou & Ouyang 1998:360; Zhou 2006:522), and *siã* and *siã bĩʔ* in Taiwan (Yang 1991:219). The question word *siã* in Hui'an (also Xiamen and Taiwan) may be the fused form of *siəm bĩʔ* (or *sim miʔ*), as in (ii), while *siã miʔ* in Xiamen (or *siã bĩʔ* in Taiwan) may be formed by adding *miʔ* (or *bĩʔ*) after the fused form *siã*, as shown by (iii).
(ii) *siəm bĩʔ*/ *sim miʔ* 甚物 'what' -> *siã* 啥 'what'
(iii) *siã* + *miʔ*/*bĩʔ* -> *siã miʔ*/*siã bĩʔ*

Syllable fusion seems also to be attested in the emergence of the question word ṣa/sa 啥 'what' in most Mandarin and Wu varieties: Lǚ (1985:127) suggests that this question word may be a fused form of *shénme* 什麼.

19.4.2 *siã²laŋ²* and *siaŋ²* 'who'

As mentioned in §19.4.1, the question word *siã²* 啥 'what' can be used in 'who' questions when followed by the noun *laŋ²* 'person'. Two more examples are given in (46) and (47).

(46) 即領　　啥儂　　　其
　　 tsit⁷⁻⁸-liã³　*siã²-laŋ²*　e²
　　 this-CL　what-person　GEN
　　 'Whose is this piece (of clothing)?'

(47) 送　　啥儂　　　啊
　　 saŋ⁵⁻³　*siã²-laŋ²*　a⁰
　　 send　what-person　SFP
　　 'Whom (would you like to) give (it) to?'

In (46), *siã²laŋ²* is followed by the genitive marker *e²* 其 to express 'whose'. In (47), *siã²laŋ²* functions an indirect object of the verb *saŋ⁵* 'send'.

The question word *siã²laŋ²* has undergone syllable fusion and the fused form is *siaŋ²*, as in (48), where *siaŋ²* functions as the subject of the verb phrase *boʔ⁷⁻⁸ tshiŋ⁵* 卜穿 'want to wear (it)'.

(48) （啥儂）　卜　　　穿
　　 siaŋ²　boʔ⁷⁻⁸　tshiŋ⁵
　　 who　want　wear
　　 'Who wants to wear (it)?'

The fusion process can be represented as *siã²* + *laŋ²* -> *siaŋ²*. Both *siã²laŋ²* and *siaŋ²* are commonly used in the contemporary Hui'an dialect. These two question words are also attested in some other Southern Min varieties such as Quanzhou, Xiamen, Zhangzhou and Taiwan (Zhou 2006:522; Yang 1991:219). Note that there is no special form for 'who' questions in Hui'an, unlike Mandarin Chinese in which *shuí* 誰 serves as a specific form for this function and is not associated with *shénme* 'what'. However, the question word for 'who' consisting of WHAT and PERSON such as *siã²laŋ²* in Hui'an is not uncommon: it is also attested in Wu varieties such as the Suzhou 蘇州 variety and a small number of Gan varieties such as Duchang 都昌 and Yanshan 鉛山 (Wang & Chappell 2012).

19.4.3 ti^4si^2/tu^4si^2 and $siəm^{3\text{-}2}bi\text{ʔ}^{7\text{-}8}\ si^{2\text{-}4}tsam^4$ 'when'

The question words ti^4si^2 (or tu^4si^2) 底時 and $siəm^{3\text{-}2}bi\text{ʔ}^{7\text{-}8}\ si^{2\text{-}4}tsam^4$ 甚物時站 are both used for 'when', of which, $siəm^{3\text{-}2}bi\text{ʔ}^{7\text{-}8}\ si^{2\text{-}4}tsam^4$ is formed by 'what' and 'time'. Examples are given in (49) and (50).

(49) 個　　　底時　　　　　來
     en^1　ti^4si^2/tu^4si^2　lai^2
     3PL　when　　　　 come
     'When did they come?'

(50) 甚物　　　　　　時站　　　　　著　　　　去
     $siəm^{3\text{-}2}\text{-}bi\text{ʔ}^{7\text{-}8}$　$si^{2\text{-}4}\text{-}tsam^4$　$tio\text{ʔ}^{8\text{-}4}$　khu^5
     what　　　　　　 time　　　　 have.to　 go
     'When (do you) have to go?'

The question word 底時 'when' is pronounced only as ti^4si^2 in some other Southern Min varieties such as Quanzhou and Xiamen (Zhou 2006:6). However, both ti^4si^2 and tu^4si^2 are attested in Hui'an. The reconstructed form for DI 底 has been regarded as the etymology of ti^4/tu^4 in previous works such as Li (1999:282), where he mentions that DI 底 functioning as 'what' is common during the period between the Southern and Northern Dynasties (A.D. 420-589) and the Tang and Song Dynasties (A.D. 618-1279). However, Yang (2002) argues that ti^4si^2 (or tu^4si^2) in Southern Min is derived from 著時 in earlier Chinese in which 著 is originally a verb/preposition meaning '(be) at'.

In Hui'an, ti^4si^2 (or tu^4si^2) is much more widely used than $siəm^{3\text{-}2}bi\text{ʔ}^{7\text{-}8}\ si^{2\text{-}4}tsam^4$. In addition, $siəm^{3\text{-}2}bi\text{ʔ}^{7\text{-}8}\ si^{2\text{-}4}tsam^4$ is mainly attested via elicitation, and is thus probably modeled on *shénme shíhou* 什麼時候 'when' in Mandarin Chinese.

19.4.4 to^3 'which'

In Hui'an, the complex [to^3 底 + numeral + classifier] is used for 'which' questions, asking for specific one(s) from a certain number of options, as in (51) and (52).

(51) 底　　　蜀　　　間　　　學堂
     $to^{3\text{-}2}$　$tsit^{8\text{-}4}$　$kuin^1$　$o\text{ʔ}^{8\text{-}4}tŋ^2$
     which　one　　 CL　　 school
     'Which school?'

(52) 汝　　卜拺　　　底　　蜀　　領
　　 lu³　*boʔ⁷⁻⁸tiʔ⁸⁻⁴*　*to³⁻²*　*tsit⁸⁻⁴*　*liã³*
　　 2SG　want　　　which　one　CL
　　 'Which piece (of clothing) do you want?'

In (51), *to³* is followed by the numeral *tsit⁸* 'one' and then the classifier *kuin¹*, and the complex *to³⁻² tsit⁸⁻⁴ kuin¹* serves as a modifier of the noun *oʔ⁸⁻⁴tŋ²* 'school'. In (52), the complex *to³⁻² tsit⁸⁻⁴ liã³* 'which piece' functions as an object of the verb *boʔ⁷⁻⁸tiʔ⁸* 'want'.

19.4.5　*to³* and *to³⁻²taʔ⁷* 'where'

Besides being used in 'which' questions, *to³* 底 can also be used in 'where' questions, as in (53), where the question word *to³* alone functions as a predicate.

(53) 汝　　郵箱　　　底
　　 lu³　*iu²⁻⁴-siũ¹*　*to³*
　　 2SG　email-box　where
　　 'Where is your email box?'

Another common question word for 'where' in Hui'an is *to³⁻²taʔ⁷* 底搭, as in (54), where *to³⁻²taʔ⁷* functions as an object of the verb *ti⁴* 伫 'be at'.

(54) 恁　　厝裡　　　　伫　　底搭
　　 len³　*tshu⁵⁻³-lai⁴*　*ti⁴*　*to³⁻²-taʔ⁷*
　　 2PL　house-inside　be.at　where-LOC
　　 'Where is your home?'

The numeral *tsit⁸* 蜀 'one' can be inserted between *to³* and *taʔ⁷* to ask for a specific place, as in (55).

(55) 底蜀搭　　　　　　咧　　　賣
　　 to³⁻²-tsit⁸⁻⁴-taʔ⁷　*leʔ⁷⁻⁸*　*bue⁴*
　　 which-one-LOC　HAB　sell
　　 'Where can (I) get (this)?'

It is clear that question words for 'which' and 'where' in Hui'an are similar in form, like some other Southern Min varieties such as Quanzhou and Xiamen (cf. Li

1999:276-279; Zhou 2006:131, among others). In fact, this phenomenon is not uncommon in Chinese (cf. Li & Chang 1999).

In addition, previous studies such as Li (1999:282) and Yang (2002:161) have suggested that the question word *to* for 'which' and 'where' in Southern Min is derived from the question word DI 底 'what' in earlier Chinese, like the question word *ti⁴/tuɪ⁴* 底 for 'what' mentioned in §19.4.3.

19.4.6 *kuiˀ³*, *lua⁴tsue⁵* and *lua⁴* 'how many/much'

The question words *kuiˀ³* 幾 and *lua⁴tsue⁵* 偌儕 are both used to ask for a quantity, as shown by (56) - (58).

(56) 汝　　卜　　　買　　幾　　　個　　啊
　　 luˀ³　*boʔ⁷⁻⁸*　*bue³*　*kuiˀ³⁻²*　*e²*　*a⁰*
　　 2SG　want　buy　how.many　CL　SFP
　　 'How many do you want to buy?'

(57) 汝　　卜　　　買　　偌儕　　　啊
　　 luˀ³　*boʔ⁷⁻⁸*　*bue³*　*lua⁴tsue⁵*　*a⁰*
　　 2SG　want　buy　how.many　SFP
　　 'How many do you want to buy?'

(58) 偌儕　　　　錢
　　 lua⁴tsue⁵⁻⁴　*tsin²*
　　 how.much　money
　　 'How much (is it)?'

The question word *kuiˀ³* is typically used when the quantity is supposed to be a small one. For example, (56) is usually used when the speaker supposes that the addressee will buy something in a small amount. When larger quantities are involved, the question word *lua⁴tsue⁵* is used, as illustrated by (57). The question word *kuiˀ³* normally occurs with a classifier such as *e²* in (56), while *lua⁴tsue⁵* can be immediately followed by a noun such as *tsin²* 'money' in (58). Similar distinctions are also attested in other Chinese varieties such as Mandarin Chinese, as shown in Table 19-1 above.

Unlike *kuiˀ³* and *lua⁴tsue⁵*, the question word *lua⁴* 偌 is usually followed by an adjective to ask for a degree, as in (59), where *lua⁴* precedes the adjective *kuˀ³* 久 'long' to ask about duration.

(59) 恁　　去　　佪　　　　久
　　 len³ khu⁵ lua⁴　　 ku³
　　 2PL　go　 how.much long
　　 'How long have you been away?'

19.4.7 *tsiũ⁵* and *kŋ⁵* 'how'

Both *tsiũ⁵* 障 and *kŋ⁵* are used for manner interrogatives, as illustrated by (60), where the question words *tsiũ⁵* and *kŋ⁵* precede the verb *pha?⁷* 拍 'hit' to ask how the two persons fought each other.

(60) 兩　　個　　障/口　　　　拍
　　 lŋ⁴　 e²　 tsiũ⁵⁻³/kŋ⁵⁻³　pha?⁷
　　 two　CL　 how/how　　　 hit
　　 'How did the two (persons) fight (with each other)?'

The following two examples show that *tsiũ⁵⁻³ai³* 障仔 and *kŋ⁵⁻³le³* are used for expressing 'how is...?', 'what about...', or 'why'.

(61) 汝　　收入　　　 障仔/口口
　　 lu³　 siu¹liəp⁸　tsiũ⁵⁻³ai³/ kŋ⁵⁻³le³
　　 2SG　salary　　 how/how
　　 'How is your salary?'

(62) 汝　　障仔/口口　　　　卜　　　創　　　　口
　　 lu³　 tsiũ⁵⁻³ai³/kŋ⁵⁻³le³　bo?⁷⁻⁸　tshɔŋ⁵⁻³　tse²
　　 2SG　why/why　　　　　 want　　do　　　　this
　　 'Why did you want to do this?'

In (61), the question words *tsiũ⁵⁻³ai³* and *kŋ⁵⁻³le³* function as a predicate, asking how the addressee's salary is. In (62), *tsiũ⁵⁻³ai³* and *kŋ⁵⁻³le³* are placed between the subject *lu³* 'you' and the predicate *bo?⁷⁻⁸ tshɔŋ⁵⁻³ tse²* 'want to do this' to ask the reason why the addressee wants to do something.

According to Zhou (2006:387, 548, 1095), the question words for manner interrogatives and expressing 'how is...' and 'why' in Quanzhou can be *an⁵⁻³tsuã³* 安怎, *tsai⁵iũ⁵* 怎樣, *tsiũ⁵* 障 and *tsiũ⁵⁻³a³* 障仔, of which *tsiũ⁵* is a contracted form of *tsai⁵iũ⁵*. The *ai³* following *tsiũ⁵* in Hui'an is probably the counterpart of the diminutive suffix *a³* in Quanzhou. As for the question word *kŋ⁵⁻³le³*, we have been unable to find a similar form in other Southern Min varieties. Thus, at this stage, its origin remains unclear.

19.4.8 $l\tilde{a}^5$ and $ui^{5\text{-}4}si\partial m^{3\text{-}2}bĩʔ^7$ 'why'

Besides $tsi\tilde{u}^{5\text{-}3}ai^3$ and $kŋ^{5\text{-}3}le^3$, there are another two question words indicating 'why' questions, i.e. $l\tilde{a}^5$ 哪 and $ui^{5\text{-}4}si\partial m^{3\text{-}2}bĩʔ^7$ 為甚物 as in (63) and (64), respectively.

(63) 汝　　哪　　　講　　口　　　儕　　　話
    lu^3　<u>$l\tilde{a}^{5\text{-}3}$</u>　$kaŋ^3$　$tsuaʔ^{7\text{-}8}$　$tsue^{5\text{-}4}$　ue^5
    2SG　why　say　this　　many　word
    'Why do you talk so much?'

(64) 為甚物　　　　　無　　　儂　　　讓座
    <u>$ui^{5\text{-}4}\text{-}si\partial m^{3\text{-}2}bĩʔ^7$</u>　$bo^{2\text{-}4}$　$laŋ^{2\text{-}4}$　$li\tilde{u}^{5\text{-}4}\text{-}ts\partial^4$
    for-what　　　not.have　person　offer-seat
    'Why did no one offer his/her seat?'

Lǚ (1985:137) points out that the question word for 'why' formed by 'for' and 'what' can be found in documents from the Tang Dynasty (AD 618-907), which corresponds to the period of Late Medieval Chinese, and is still used in contemporary Chinese, e.g. *wèishénme* 為什麼 in Mandarin Chinese. The counterpart of *wèi shénme* in Mandarin Chinese in Hui'an is $ui^{5\text{-}4}si\partial m^{3\text{-}2}bĩʔ^7$ which is probably recently borrowed from Mandarin Chinese, since it is only used by the younger generation and not reported in the literature of Southern Min.

19.5 Summary

This chapter has examined three types of interrogative in Hui'an: alternative, polar and constituent interrogatives.

    The disjuncts of alternative interrogatives are typically connected by the alternative marker $aʔ^{8\text{-}4}si^4$ 抑是 or $aʔ^8$ 抑. In other words, the alternative interrogative typically takes the form of [A + $aʔ^{8\text{-}4}si^4/aʔ^8$ + B]. The first adjunct may be further preceded by the copular verb si^4 是, i.e. forming [si^4 + A + $aʔ^{8\text{-}4}si^4/aʔ^8$ + B].

    Polar interrogatives can be marked by a series of strategies such as interrogative particles, interrogative intonation, disjunctive structures and the addition of tags. Polar interrogatives with disjunctive structures typically consist of an affirmative sentence followed by its negative counterpart, with or without the alternative marker $a\mathit{?}^8$ 抑 'or', more specifically, taking the form of VP-or-NEG-VP, VP-NEG-VP and VP-or-NEG. All these three forms semantically convey an interrogative meaning which is neutral in assumption, that is, expectations regarding the answer to the interrogative on the part of the addressee are neither overtly coded nor implied.

The 'VP-NEG' pattern (without an alternative marker), which is widely used in Chinese, especially Southern Chinese, is not attested in Hui'an, since negative markers in the 'VP-NEG' pattern of the Hui'an dialect (m^5 唔, $bə^5$ 未, bo^2 無 and bue^4 燴) have developed into interrogative particles undergoing tonal reduction (m^0 唔, $bə^0$ 未, bo^0 無 and bue^0 燴), though they show different degrees of grammaticalization. Another important interrogative particle is a^0 啊.

There are three main types of tag question: (a) simple particle interrogatives involving the particles m^0 唔 and bo^0 無; (b) a sentence-final particle, e.g. hau^0; and (c) a fused form of the tag question si^4 m^0 是唔 (consisting of the copular verb si^4 and the particle m^0) and the particle a^0 啊 (i.e. $siã^0 < si^4$ $m^0 + a^0$).

We also examined the paradigm of the in-situ question words in Hui'an that are used to form constituent interrogatives.

20 Topic-comment constructions

20.1 Introduction

Topic-comment constructions play an important role in the grammar of some Chinese varieties such as Mandarin Chinese, Wu and Min (see Li & Thompson 1976, 1981; Xu & Liu 2007; Liu 2001, inter alia). On the discourse level, the topic of a sentence basically tells us what the rest of the sentence (called the comment) is about, or it can be seen as providing the frame of reference for the rest of the sentence (see Barry 1975; Li & Thompson 1981; Lambrecht 1994, inter alia). In other words, unlike the notion of subject which typically has a direct semantic relationship ('doing' or 'being' relationship) with the verb, the topic need not be an argument of the main verb in a sentence (see also Chao 1968; Li & Thompson 1976, 1981). As suggested by previous studies such as Li & Thompson (1981), due to its function in the sentence, the topic normally refers to something that is identifiable for both the speaker and the addressee, being typically either definite or generic.

Unlike Mandarin Chinese in which the topic, if overt, always occurs in sentence-initial position, the topic, especially the patient topic, in Wu and Min branches of Chinese often occurs between the subject and the main verb in the comment (Liu 2001). To distinguish the topic in these two different positions, the terms 'main topic' and 'subtopic' have been created by Xu & Liu (2007). More specifically, the main topic refers to the topic that occurs before the subject, while the subtopic is the topic occurring between the subject and the main verb in the comment. What needs to be noted is that in daily Hui'an conversation, the subject is often omitted and more than one topic may occur before the main verb in the comment, as will be shown in the following examples. As with Mandarin Chinese, the topic in Hui'an can be separated from the comment by a pause, though the use of a pause is optional.

In the remainder of this chapter, topic-comment constructions in Hui'an will be examined in terms of the following aspects: (a) forms of topics (§20.2); (b) semantic relations between topic and comment (§20.3); (c) positions of topics (§20.4); (d) patient topicalization (§20.5); (e) topic markers (§20.6); and (f) contrastive function of topic (§20.7). Note that we focus on the topic that does not simultaneously function as a subject.

https://doi.org/10.1515/9781501511868-020

20.2 Forms of topics

Topics can be a personal pronoun, as in (1) and (2).

(1) NP_{PRO} TOPIC NP_{SUBJECT} VP
    伲   路頭   遠
    lan³ *lɔ⁵⁻⁴thau²* *hŋ⁴*
    1PL   distance   far
    'We are far away (from there).' (lit. As for us, the distance is far.)

(2) NP_{PRO} TOPIC NP_{SUBJECT} VP
    伊   骹   蠻   大雙
    i¹   *kha¹*   *ban²⁻⁴* *tua⁵⁻⁴-saŋ¹*
    3SG   foot   rather   big-pair
    'His feet are rather big.' (lit. As for him, the feet are rather big.)

In (1), the noun *lɔ⁵⁻⁴thau²* 'distance', rather than the inclusive first person plural pronoun *lan³*, functions as a subject, since the predicative adjective *hŋ⁴* 'far' describes the noun *lɔ⁵⁻⁴thau²* 'distance', rather than the pronoun *lan³* 'we'. In this case, the pronoun *lan³* functions as the topic, indicating the frame of reference for the comment *lɔ⁵⁻⁴thau² hŋ⁴* 'the distance is far'. A pause can be used after the pronoun *lan³*, though it is not necessary. The pronoun *lan³* and the noun *lɔ⁵⁻⁴thau²* cannot form a genitive noun phrase meaning 'our distance'. Similarly, the third person singular pronoun *i¹* in (2) functions as a topic, coding what the comment *kha¹ ban²⁻⁴ tua⁵⁻⁴saŋ¹* 'the feet are rather big' is about, while the noun *kha¹* 'foot' in the comment serves as a subject, described by the adjectival phrase *ban²⁻⁴ tua⁵⁻⁴saŋ¹* 'rather big'. The topic *i¹* can be optionally followed by a pause. In addition, *i¹ kha¹* cannot be regarded as a genitive noun phrase, since the genitive marker *e²* is usually required when the possessee is encoded by a body part (see §8.2.4). Sentences like these two examples are traditionally called 'double subject sentences' in the literature of Chinese linguistics, and later regarded as prototypical topic-comment constructions (see Li & Thompson 1976, 1981).

The demonstratives and the [demonstrative + classifier] complexes often function as a topic, as in (3) and (4).

(3) NP_{DEM} TOPIC VP
    口   抾   去   送   儂
    tsat⁸ *thueʔ⁸* *khu⁵⁻³* *saŋ⁵*   *laŋ⁴*
    this   take   go   send   other
    'As for this, give (it) to someone as a gift.'

(4) NP$_{\text{DEM+CL}}$ TOPIC NP$_{\text{SUBJECT}}$ VP
即領　　（啥儂）　卜　　穿　　啊
tsit$^{7\text{-}8}$-liã^3　siaŋ$^{2\text{-}4}$　bo?$^{7\text{-}8}$　tshiŋ^5　a^0
this-CL　who　　　want　wear　SFP
'This piece (of clothing), who wants to wear it?'

In (3), the demonstrative *tsat^8* 'this', being semantically a patient of the verb *thue?^{8}* 'take', syntactically functions as a topic. Similarly, the [demonstrative + classifier] complex *tsit$^{7\text{-}8}$liã^3* 'this piece' in (4) syntactically functions as a topic, and is semantically a patient of the main verb *tshiŋ^5* 'wear' in the comment *siaŋ$^{2\text{-}4}$ bo?$^{7\text{-}8}$ tshiŋ^5 a^0* 'who wants to wear'.

Topics are also often encoded by a noun (phrase), as in (5) – (8), which all involve topicalization of a patient or direct object noun (see §20.5 below).

(5) NP$_{\text{TOPIC}}$ VP
厝租　　　加　　挅　　　蠻儕
tshu$^{5\text{-}3}$-tsɔ^1　ke^1　thue?^{8}　ban$^{2\text{-}4}$tsue^5
house-rent　more　take　　much
'As for the house rent, (they) have paid much more.'

(6) NP$_{\text{GEN}}$ TOPIC NP$_{\text{SUBJECT}}$ VP
阮　　其　　　課　　　伊　也　　上
gun^3　e$^{2\text{-}4}$　khɔ^5　i^1　a^4　siɔŋ^5
1PL　GEN　　lecture　3SG　also　take
'Our classes, she also attended them.'

(7) NP$_{\text{RC+NP}}$ TOPIC VP
翕　　懷　　相　　　與　　恁　　爸仔　　　看
hiəp^7　huai^2　siɔŋ^5　khɔ$^{5\text{-}4}$　len$^{3\text{-}2}$　pa^2-a^0　khuã^5
take　those　picture　give　2PL　father-NM　look
'The pictures that (you) took, let your father look at (them).'

(8) NP$_{\text{DEM+CL+N}}$ TOPIC VP
迄領　　　　衫　　　唔通　　　褪　　（起來）
hit$^{7\text{-}8}$-liã$^{3\text{-}2}$　sã^1　m$^{5\text{-}4}$-thaŋ^1　thŋ^5　khai^0
that-CL　　clothes　not-can　　take.off　RVC
'That piece of clothing, don't take off (if).'

In (5), the bare noun *tshu⁵⁻³tsɔ¹* 'house rent' functions as a topic. In (6), the topic is encoded by the possessive construction *gun³ e²⁻⁴ khɔ⁵* 'our classes'. In (7), the topic *hiəp⁷ huaĩ²siɔŋ⁵* 'those pictures that (you) took' is a noun phrase consisting of the relative clause *hiəp⁷* '(you) took' and the head noun *huaĩ² siɔŋ⁵* 'those pictures'. In (8), the noun phrase *hit⁷⁻⁸liã³⁻²sã¹* 'that piece of clothing', functioning as a topic, involves a [demonstrative + classifier] complex (*hit⁷⁻⁸liã³*) and a head noun (*sã¹* 'clothes').

Numerals and 'numeral + classifier + noun' constructions can sometimes function on their own as a topic, as in (9) and (10).

(9) NP_SUBJECT V_SAY [NP_TOPIC ADV NP_NUM TOPIC VP]
　　佴　　說　　東南　　　懷
　　en¹　*səʔ⁷⁻⁸*　*taŋ¹lam²*　*huaĩ²*
　　3PL　say　southeast　those
　　(唔攏)　蜀半　　唔　　佫　　租　　儂
　　bɔŋ³⁻²　*tsit⁸⁻⁴puã⁵*　*m⁵⁻⁴*　*koʔ⁷⁻⁸*　*tsɔ¹*　*laŋ⁴*
　　perhaps　half　　not　again　rent　other
　　'They said perhaps half (of the houses) in the southeast region are no longer for rent.' (lit. They say those (houses) in the southeast region perhaps half no longer rent out people)

(10) NP_NUM+CL+N TOPIC VP
　　兩　　間　　房　　鋪　　者　　就　　好看
　　lŋ⁴　*kuin¹*　*paŋ²*　*phɔ¹*　*tse⁰*　*tsiu⁵⁻⁴*　*ho³⁻²-khuã⁵*
　　two　CL　room　lay　DELIM　then　good-look
　　'Those two rooms will look good after laying (wooden floors).' (lit. two rooms lay (wooden floors) DELIM then good-looking)

In (9), there are two instances of topic in the complement clause of the utterance verb *səʔ⁷* 'say': (a) the topic *taŋ¹lam² huaĩ²* 'those (houses) in the southeast region' designates what the comment *bɔŋ³⁻² tsit⁸⁻⁴puã⁵ m⁵⁻⁴ koʔ⁷⁻⁸ tsɔ¹ laŋ⁴* 'perhaps half are no longer for rent' is about; and (b) the topic *tsit⁸⁻⁴puã⁵* 'half' (encoded by a numeral) indicates what the comment *m⁵⁻⁴ koʔ⁷⁻⁸ tsɔ¹laŋ⁴* 'no longer for rent' is about. Note that these two topics are in a part-whole relationship with each other: the first topic (*taŋ¹lam² huaĩ²*) is the whole of which the second topic (*tsit⁸⁻⁴puã⁵*) is a part. In (10), the noun phrase *lŋ⁴ kuin¹ paŋ²* 'two rooms', with the structure of 'numeral + classifier + noun', functions as a topic, indicating what the comment *phɔ¹tse⁰ tsiu⁵⁻⁴ ho³⁻²khuã⁵* 'look good after laying (wooden floors)' is about.

The topic can also be encoded by a nominalization construction, as in (11) and (12), both of which involve topicalization of a patient.

(11) NP_{NOMINALIZATION TOPIC} NP_{SUBJECT} VP
    阮   厝裡   剩   其
    gun^3 $tshu^{5\text{-}3}\text{-}lai^4$ $tshun^4$ e^0
    1PL   house-inside   remain   NMLZ
    伊   從來   唔   食
    i^1 $tsiɔŋ^{2\text{-}4}lai^2$ $m^{5\text{-}4}$ $tsia?^8$
    3SG   always   not   eat
    'As for the leftovers at home, he never eats (them).'

(12) NP_{NOMINALIZATION TOPIC} VP
    否其   去   挽   揀
    $phai^3\text{-}e^0$ $khu^{5\text{-}3}$ $ban^{3\text{-}2}$ sak^7
    bad-NMLZ   go   pull   RVC
    'As for the bad (tooth), have it extracted.'

In (11), the nominalization construction $gun^3\ tshu^{5\text{-}3}lai^4\ tshun^4\ e^0$ 'the leftovers at home' functions as a topic. This sentence cannot be directly turned into a SVO construction unless the first person pronoun gun^3 is deleted, that is, forming $i^1\ tsiɔŋ^{2\text{-}4}lai^2\ m^{5\text{-}4}\ tsia?^{8\text{-}4}\ tshu^{5\text{-}3}\text{-}lai^4\ tshun^4 e^0$ 'He never eats the leftovers at home'. Though this SVO construction is acceptable, it is less natural than the topic-comment construction. The topic in (12) is the nominalization construction $phai^3\ e^0$ 'the bad (tooth)'. This sentence cannot be turned into a SVO construction.

Time and location words also often function as a topic, as in (13) and (14).

(13) NP_{TEMPORAL TOPIC} VP
    下日   會   恰   無   儂   租
    e^4let^8 e^4 $kha?^{7\text{-}8}$ $bo^{2\text{-}4}$ $laŋ^{2\text{-}4}$ $tsɔ^1$
    future   will   comparatively   not.have   person   rent
    'In the future, there will be fewer people renting (the house).'

(14) NP_{LOCATIVE TOPIC} NP_{SUBJECT} VP
    北京   梨仔   恰   俗
    $pak^{7\text{-}8}kiã^1$ $lai^{2\text{-}4}\text{-}a^3$ $kha?^{7\text{-}8}$ $siɔk^8$
    PN   pear-NM   comparatively   cheap
    'In Beijing, pears are cheaper.'

In (13), the time word e^4let^8 'future' functions as a topic, providing a time frame for the event encoded by the comment $e^4 khaʔ^{7-8} bo^{2-4} laŋ^{2-4} tsɔ^1$ 'there will be fewer people renting (the house)'. In (14), the location word $pak^{7-8}kiã^1$ 'Beijing' functions as a topic, providing a location frame for the comment $lai^{2-4}a^3 khaʔ^{7-8} siɔk^8$ 'pears are cheaper', in which the noun $lai^{2-4}a^3$ 'pear' serves as a subject, described by the predicative adjectival phrase $khaʔ^{7-8} siɔk^8$.

The following three examples illustrate that a topic can also be a verb or clause.

(15) VP$_{TOPIC}$ VP

調	獪	調	呀
tiau²	*bue⁴*	*tiau²*	*ia⁰*
adjust	can.not	adjust	SFP

'Concerning adjustment, (it) cannot be adjusted.'

(16) VP$_{TOPIC}$ VP

卜	食	煮	兩	三	碗
boʔ⁷⁻⁸	*tsiaʔ⁸*	*tsu³*	*lŋ⁴*	*sã¹*	*uã³*
want	eat	cook	two	three	bowl

'If (you) want to eat (it), (I'll) cook two or three bowls of (it).'

(17) S$_{TOPIC}$ NP$_{SUBJECT}$ VP

阿明	28		歲	伊	會記得
a¹biŋ²	*liəp⁸⁻⁴pueʔ⁷⁻⁸*		*hə⁵*	*i¹*	*e⁴ki⁵let⁰*
PN	twenty.eight		year	3SG	remember

'As for the fact that Ah-Ming is 28 years old, she remembers (it).'

In (15), the verb *tiau²* 'adjust' functions as a topic. Note that *tiau²* is repeated in the comment, which shows that this is an example of identical topic construction (see §20.3.3 for details). In (16), the conditional clause encoded by the verb phrase *boʔ⁷⁻⁸ tsiaʔ⁸* 'want to eat' functions as a topic, providing a conditional frame for the event encoded by the comment *tsu³ lŋ⁴ sã¹ uã³* 'cook two or three bowls'. In (17), the clause *a¹biŋ² liəp⁸⁻⁴pueʔ⁷⁻⁸ hə⁵* 'Ah-Ming is 28 years old' functions as a topic, indicating what the comment *i¹ e⁴ki⁵let⁰* 'she remembers' is about, in which the third person singular pronoun *i¹* is a subject.

Adjectives can sometimes also function as a topic, as in (18).

(18) VP$_{\text{ADJ TOPIC}}$ VP
  好 也 好 無 儕
  ho³ *a⁴* *ho³* *bo²⁻⁴* *tsue⁵*
  good also good not.have much
  'Even though (it) is good, (it) is not much better either.'

In (18), the adjective *ho³* 'good' functions as a topic, providing the frame of reference for the comment *a⁴ ho³ bo²⁻⁴ tsue⁵* 'it is not much better either'. This is also an example of the identical topic construction.

  As shown by the examples so far, the topic in Hui'an can be encoded by different categories of words, phrases and clauses. Among these, the topics encoded by noun phrases, verb phrases and clauses are equally common in Mandarin Chinese and other Chinese varieties such as the Shanghai variety of Wu (cf. Xu & Liu 2007). However, topics encoded by adjectives and numerals have been much less described in the relevant literature.

20.3 Semantic relations between topic and comment

According to Xu & Liu (2007:104), the topics can be classified into four types in terms of the semantic relations between topic and comment, i.e. coreferential (pseudo-)argument topic, frame-setting topic, identical topic, and clause topic. Liu (2003b[2001]) identifies another type: split-argument topic.

20.3.1 Coreferential (pseudo-)argument topic

The coreferential argument topic is co-referential with an overt argument or a gap in the comment (Xu & Liu 2007:104), as in (19) below, where the topic *Wú Xiānsheng* 吳先生 'Mr. Wu' is coreferential with the third person singular pronoun *tā* 他, which is the subject of the verb *rènshi* 認識 'know' in the comment *tā rènshi wǒ* 'he knows me'.

(19) NP$_{\text{TOPIC i}}$ NP$_{\text{SUBJECT i}}$ VP
  吳先生， 他 認識 我 (Mandarin Chinese)
  Wú Xiānsheng *tā* *rènshi* *wǒ*
  Mr. Wu   3SG know 1SG
  'Mr. Wu, he knows me.'

In Hui'an, this type of topic is often coreferential with the ellipsed patient of the verb in the comment, as illustrated by examples (11) and (12) above. The following examples show that the topic can also be coreferential with the agent, beneficiary/maleficiary, goal or recipient of the verb in the comment.

(20) NP$_{TOPIC\ i}$ NP$_{SUBJECT(AGENT)\ i}$ VP
男其　　　　伊　　無　　　　抹
lam²-e⁰　　*i¹*　*bo²⁻⁴*　　*bua?⁷*
male-NMLZ　3SG　not.have　smear
'As for men, they don't use (skin products).'

(21) NP$_{PRO\ TOPIC\ i}$ NP$_{SUBJECT}$ [PREPOSITION NP$_{PRO\ i}$ VP]
汝　　啥儂　　　　共　　　汝　　　挽　　其
lu³　*siã²-laŋ²*　　*ka⁵⁻⁴*　*lu³⁻²*　*ban³*　*e⁰*
2SG　what-person　MAL　　2SG　　pluck　NMLZ
'Who plucks your (eyebrows) on you?' (lit. you who on you pluck)

(22) NP$_{TOPIC}$ NP$_{SUBJECT}$ VP [ ]$_t$
深圳　　　　　　無　　　　　儂　　　　卜　　　去
tshiəm¹tsun⁵　*bo²⁻⁴*　　*laŋ²⁻⁴*　*bo?⁷⁻⁸*　*khu⁵*
PN　　　　　　not.have　person　want　go
'Shenzhen, no one wants to go there.'

(23) NP$_{TOPIC}$ [V [ ]$_t$ DO]
蜀　　　　個　　分　　　　　五　　千
tsit⁸⁻⁴　*e²*　*pun¹*　　*gɔ⁴*　*tshiŋ¹*
one　　　CL　　distribute　five　thousand
'Five thousand was given to each (person).'(lit. one distribute five thousand)

In (20), the topic *lam²e⁰* 'men' is coreferential with the agent *i¹* 'he' of the verb phrase *bo²⁻⁴ bua?⁷* 'don't use' in the comment. In (21), the first occurrence of *lu³* 'you' functions as a topic, being coreferential with the second occurrence of *lu³*, the maleficiary of the verb *ban³* 'pluck' in the comment. In (22), the topic *tshiəm¹tsun⁵* 'Shenzhen' is coreferential with the goal of the motion verb *khu⁵* 'go' in the comment (syntactically, it is the gap of the locative object for the verb *khu⁵*). In (23), the topic *tsit⁸⁻⁴ e²* 'one' is coreferential with the recipient of the ditransitive verb *pun¹* 'distribute' in the comment (syntactically, the indirect object gap of the verb *pun¹*).

In the examples above, the topic is coreferential with an argument in the comment composed of a simple clause. It may be overt or covert in the comment clause as we have explained.

As shown by the following example, the topic can also be coreferential with an ellipsed argument of the verb in an embedded clause of the comment.

(24) NP$_{TOPIC}$ NP$_{SUBJECT}$ V$_{FEEL}$ [[]$_t$ VP]

迄種	戶型	我	感覺	也	繪	否
hit$^{7-8}$-tsiɔŋ$^{3-2}$	hɔ^4-hiŋ^2	gua^3	kam$^{3-2}$kak$^{7-8}$	a^4	bue^4	phai^3
that-kind	house-style	1SG	feel	also	cannot	bad

'That kind of house style, I feel it's not so bad.'

In (24), the topic hit$^{7-8}$tsiɔŋ$^{3-2}$ hɔ^{4}hiŋ^2 迄種戶型 'that kind of house style' in the sentence-initial position is coreferential with the subject gap of the embedded clause a^4 bue^4 phai^3 也繪否 'also not bad'. However, this is not common, partly because sentences with an embedded clause are themselves not common in daily conversation. In addition, when it is coreferential with a non-subject argument in an embedded clause such as in example (9) above and example (25) below, the topic is often placed within the embedded clause and just after the main clause verb rather than in the sentence-initial position.

(25) NP$_{SUBJECT}$ V$_{SAY}$ [NP$_{TEMPORAL\ TOPIC}$ NP$_{TOPIC}$ VP]

我	說	明年	存摺	著	交	來	咯
gua^3	sə?$^{7-8}$	buã$^{2-4}$-lin^2	tsun$^{2-4}$tsi?^{7}	tio?$^{8-4}$	kau^1	lai^0	lɔ^0
1SG	say	next-year	bankbook	should	hand.in	come	SFP

'I said, next year, the bankbook should be handed in.'

In (25), there are two instances of different topics in the complement clause of the utterance verb sə?^{7} 'say': (a) the topic buã$^{2-4}$lin^2 'next year', providing the time frame for the comment tsun$^{2-4}$tsi?^{7} tio?$^{8-4}$ kau^1 lai^0 lɔ^0 'the handbook should be handed in'; and (b) the topic tsun$^{2-4}$tsi?^{7} 'bankbook', being coreferential with the patient gap of the comment tio?$^{8-4}$ kau^1 lai^0 'should hand in'. The second topic tsun$^{2-4}$tsi?^{7} appears right before the verb phrase tio?$^{8-4}$ kau^1 lai^0 (and is still part of the embedded clause), rather than in the sentence-initial position (i.e. before the main clause beginning with gua^3 'I').

In subject-prominent languages such as English, the topic is normally in sentence-initial position. This could also be one of the reasons why earlier studies tend to restrict the position of topic to the sentence-initial one, also because given information generally precedes new in terms of information structure. In some topic-prominent languages, however, such as those belonging to the Min and Wu branches of Chinese, the topic can also appear in positions other than sentence-initial ones. In Min and Wu, the topic in sentence-initial position tends to be the same as that of the surrounding discourse context and is not syntacticized, whereas the topic in other positions (e.g. the subtopic position between the subject and the main verb in the comment) may have undergone syntacticization, or has a higher degree of syntacticization. This is consistent with what is mentioned in Xu & Liu (2007) and, similarly, that the use of a subtopic can be regarded as another manifestation of topic prominence.

Cross-linguistically, the coreferential argument topic is very common, while the coreferential pseudo-argument topic seems to be a characteristic of Chinese (Xu & Liu 2007:104). The pseudo-argument is used by Xu & Liu (2007:104, 106) to refer to those constituents that are not typical arguments but share some syntactic characteristics of arguments, such as the copular complement of a copular verb and the verb phrase appearing after a modal verb in a non-topic-comment sentence. An example of coreferential pseudo-argument topic from Hui'an is given in (26).

(26) VP $_{\text{TOPIC}}$ VP$_{\text{MODAL}}$
　　　啉　　燒酒　　會
　　　liəm^1　sio^{1}tsiu^3　e^4
　　　drink　alcohol　can
　　　'As for drinking mulled wine, he can.'

In (26), the topic is encoded by the verb phrase *liəm^1 sio^{1}tsiu^3* 'drink alcohol', and the modal verb *e^4* 'can' alone constitutes the comment.

In Hui'an, the coreferential (pseudo-)argument topic normally takes the form of a gap in the comment, as illustrated by examples (22) - (24) above. However, a resumptive form is used instead in some cases. For example, when the topic functions as an agent of the comment, a resumptive form can occur in the comment, as in (20), where the third person singular pronoun *i^1* serves as a resumptive form. In addition, when the topic is coreferential with the object of an adposition in the comment, the position after the adposition usually involves a resumptive form, as illustrated by (21), where the second person singular pronoun *lu^3* introduced by the malefactive marker *ka^5* in the comment functions as a resumptive form, being coreferential with the the topic *lu^3* in the sentence-initial position. Generally speaking, in terms of the encoding of coreferential (pseudo-)argument topics in the comment, the Hui'an dialect is more like Mandarin Chinese than the

Shanghai variety of Wu. According to Xu & Liu (2007:111-112), compared to Mandarin Chinese, the coreferential (pseudo-)argument topics in Shanghai tend to use a resumptive form in the comment. In addition, quite a few of examples given in Xu & Liu (2007) involve a patient topic. In Hui'an, however, the coreferential patient topic normally takes the form of a gap in the comment, except when the patient marker ka^5 is involved, as in (27) (see also §16.4.2 above on this construction).

(27) NP$_{SUBJECT}$ NP$_{TOPIC i}$ [PREPOSITION NP$_{PRO i}$ VP]
    汝   桌   共   伊   擦擦   者
    lu^3 $to?^7$ $ka^{5\text{-}4}$ i^1 $tshet^{7\text{-}8}$~$tshet^7$ tse^0
    2SG   table   OM   3SG   wipe~wipe   DELIM
    'You, the table, clean it.'

In (27), the third person singular pronun i^1 serves as a resumptive form, being co-referential with the patient subtopic $to?^7$ 'table'. Note that the complex $ka^{5\text{-}4}$ i^1 is often omitted in daily conversation, that is, the construction lu^3 $to?^7$ $tshet^{7\text{-}8}tshet^7$ tse^0 (without the complex $ka^{5\text{-}4}$ i^1) is normally used.

20.3.2 Frame-setting topic

The frame-setting topic provides the domain or framework within which the comment holds and falls into four subtypes: time/location frame-setting topic, possession frame-setting topic, superordinate frame-setting topic and background frame-setting topic (Xu & Liu 2007:113-121). Among these, the superordinate frame-setting topic constitutes a superordinate concept of an argument in the comment, as in (28), an example from Mandarin Chinese.

(28) NP$_{TOPIC}$ NP$_{SUBJECT}$ VP
    動物,   老虎   最   兇猛 (Mandarin Chinese)
    dòngwù   lǎohǔ   zuì   xiōngměng
    animal   tiger   most   fierce
    'As for animals, the tiger is most fierce.'

As mentioned in Xu & Liu (2007:117), the superordinate frame-setting topic as in (28), is a common type of topic in Chinese such as Mandarin Chinese. However, it is not common in daily conversation for the Hui'an dialect. Thus, this section focuses on the other three types of frame-setting topic.

20.3.2.1 Time/location frame-setting topic

The time/location frame-setting topic provides a time/location frame of the comment (Xu & Liu 2007:114). This type of topic, especially the topic encoded by a time word, is very common in Hui'an. Two examples have been given in (13) and (14), where the time frame-setting topic $e^4 let^8$ 'future' and the location frame-setting topic $pak^{7-8}kiã^1$ 'Beijing' both occur in the sentence-initial position. The following is an example of non-sentence-initial position.

(29) NP_{SUBJECT} NP_{TEMPORAL TOPIC} VP
汝　　　明日　　　　合　　　小妹　　　兩　　個
lu^3　$biã^{2-4}let^8$　$ka?^{7-8}$　$sio^{3-2}bə^5$　$lŋ^4$　e^2
2SG　tomorrow　COMT　Y.sister　two　CL
著　　　　去　　買　　衫
$tio?^{8-4}$　khu^{5-3}　bue^{3-2}　$sã^1$
should　go　buy　clothes
'You should go shopping tomorrow with your young sister.'

In (29), the time word $biã^{2-4}let^8$ 'tomorrow' functions as a time frame-setting topic, establishing the time frame of the comment. In addition, the topic $biã^{2-4}let^8$ appears after the subject lu^3 'you', rather than in the sentence-initial position.

Note that, time and location words, no matter whether they appear in sentence-initial or sentence-medial position, tend to be used alone, rather than follow an adposition. Two more examples of the time/location frame-setting topic in sentence-medial position (subtopic position) are given in (30) and (31).

(30) NP_{SUBJECT} NP_{TEMPORAL TOPIC} VP
我　　　年兜　　　　就　　　　卜　　　徙
gua^3　$lin^{2-4}tau^1$　$tsiu^{5-4}$　$bo?^{7-8}$　sua^3
1SG　end.of.year　as.early.as　want　move
'I would like, at the end of the year, to make a move.'

(31) NP_{SUBJECT} ADV NP_{LOCATIVE TOPIC} VP
汝　　　(唔攏)　　　學堂　　　　計　　無　　　　讀冊
lu^3　$boŋ^{3-2}$　$o?^{8-4}tŋ^2$　ke^{5-3}　bo^{2-4}　$thak^{8-4}tshe?^7$
2SG　perhaps　school　all　not.have　study
'You, perhaps, have not been studying (at) school.'

In (30), the time word $lin^{2-4}tau^1$ 'end of the year' functions as a subtopic (appearing after the subject gua^3 'I'). In (31), the subtopic encoded by the location word $o?^{8-}$

^{4}tŋ^2 'school' appears after the subject luɯ^3 'you' and the modal adverb boŋ^3 'perhaps'.

20.3.2.2 Possession frame-setting topic

The possession frame-setting topic semantically involves a possessive relation with an argument of the verb in the comment, as in the Mandarin Chinese example in (32), where the topic lǎowáng 老王 'Mr. Wang' is semantically the possessor of the subject érzi 兒子 'son' in the comment (cf. Xu & Liu 2007:115).

(32) NP$_{TOPIC}$ NP$_{SUBJECT}$ VP
老王， 兒子 考 上 了 大學 (Mandarin Chinese)
lǎowáng *érzi* *kǎo* *shàng* *le* *dàxué*
Mr. Wang son take.exam RVC PFV university
'As for Mr. Wang, his son has been admitted to a university.'

This type of topic is not very common in daily conversation of the Hui'an dialect. In addition, this type of topic is often followed by a body-part noun, as in (33) and (34).

(33) NP$_{TOPIC}$ NP$_{TOPIC}$ VP
阮 爸 喙齒 挽 遘 澈澈
gun$^{3-2}$ *pa*^{2} *tshui*$^{5-3}$-*khi*^{3} *ban*^{3} *a*$^{5-3}$ *theʔ*$^{7-8}$~*theʔ*^{7}
1PL father mouth-tooth pull CM finished~finished
'My father's teeth were all pulled out.'

(34) NP$_{TOPIC}$ NP$_{TOPIC}$ VP
汝 目眉 呣免 去 挽
luɯ^3 *bak*$^{8-4}$*bai*^{2} *m*$^{5-4}$*ben*$^{3-2}$ *khu*$^{5-3}$ *ban*^{3}
2SG eyebrow no.need go pluck
'You don't need to pluck your eyebrows.' (lit. you eyebrows no need go pluck)

In (33), the noun *tshui*$^{5-3}$*khi*^{3} 'tooth' is semantically a patient of of the verb *ban*^{3} 'pull' in the comment *ban*^{3} *a*$^{5-3}$ *theʔ*$^{7-8}$*theʔ*^{7} 'be all pulled out', while *gun*$^{3-2}$ *pa*^{2} 'my father' is semantically the possessor of the patient noun *tshui*$^{5-3}$*khi*^{3}. Note that *gun*$^{3-2}$ *pa*^{2} 'my father' is not the agent of the verb *ban*^{3}, and thus *tshui*$^{5-3}$*khi*^{3} 'tooth' and *gun*$^{3-2}$ *pa*^{2} 'my father' can be regarded as two independent topics. In other words, the possession frame-setting topic *gun*$^{3-2}$ *pa*^{2} 'my father' is the possessor of its following topic *tshui*$^{5-3}$*khi*^{3}. Similarly, the possession frame-setting topic *luɯ*^{3}

'you' in (34) is the possessor of the second topic bak$^{8\text{-}4}$bai^2 'eyebrow', which is a patient argument of the verb ban^3 'pull' in the comment m$^{5\text{-}4}$ben$^{3\text{-}2}$ khu$^{5\text{-}3}$ ban^3 'no need to pluck'.

Two more examples of possession frame-setting topic in Hui'an are given in (35) and (36).

(35) NP$_{\text{TOPIC}}$ NP$_{\text{SUBJECT}}$ VP
    伊   本性   是   繪   改   其
    i^1 pun$^{3\text{-}2}$siŋ^5 si^4 bue^4 kue^3 e^0
    3SG   nature   be   cannot   change   SFP
    'His nature cannot be changed.' (lit. he nature be cannot change)

(36) NP$_{\text{TOPIC}}$ NP$_{\text{SUBJECT}}$ VP
    恁   媽   身體   無   好
    len$^{3\text{-}2}$ bã^2 sen^{1}the^3 bo$^{2\text{-}4}$ ho^3
    2PL   mother   body   not.have   good
    'Your mother is in poor health.' (lit. your mother body not good)

In (35), the noun pun$^{3\text{-}2}$siŋ^5 'nature' can be regarded as the subject of the copular verb si^4 'be', and the third person singular pronoun i^1 'he', being a topic, involves a possessive relation with the noun pun$^{3\text{-}2}$siŋ^5. Similarly, the noun sen^{1}the^3 'body' in (36) is the subject of the verb phrase bo$^{2\text{-}4}$ ho^3 'not good', while len$^{3\text{-}2}$ bã^2 'your mother', involving a possessive relation with the noun sen^{1}the^3, functions as a topic.

20.3.2.3 Background frame-setting topic

The connection between the background frame-setting topic and the comment is typically based on background information or the context in which the conversation occurs, rather than a syntactic-semantic relation such as those mentioned above (Xu & Liu 2007:119). A famous example of this type from Mandarin Chinese is reproduced in (37), where the relationship created between the topic nà chǎng huǒ 那場火 'that fire' and the comment xìngkuī xiāofángduì lái de kuài 幸虧消防隊來得快 'fortunately the fire brigade came quickly' is based on common sense about the fire and the role of a fire brigade.

(37) NP_TOPIC ADV NP_SUBJECT VP
那　　場　　火，　幸虧　　消防隊　　　來　　得　　快
nà　　chǎng　huǒ　xìngkuī　xiāofángduì　lái　de　kuài
that　CL　　fire　luckily　fire.brigade　come　CM　quick
'That fire, fortunately the fire brigade came quickly.'

This type of topic is not uncommon in daily conversation of the Hui'an dialect. Examples are given in (38) – (40).

(38) NP_SUBJECT NP_TOPIC VP
阿山　　　蜀　　　垺　　　雞腿　　　　食　　　去　　蜀　　　碗　　　飯
a¹san¹　tsit⁸⁻⁴　tə⁵⁻³　kue¹-thui³　tsiaʔ⁸⁻⁴　khu⁵⁻³　tsit⁸⁻⁴　uã³⁻²　bãi¹
PN　　　one　　　CL　　chicken-leg　eat　　　RVC　　one　　　bowl　rice
'Ah-Shan, with only a chicken leg, ate a bowl of rice.'

(39) NP_SUBJECT NP_TOPIC VP
後生家　　　　迄碗　　　　　　面　　　行　　　者　　　枵　　　咯
hau⁴sin¹ke¹　hit⁷⁻⁸-uã³⁻²　bin⁵　kiã²　tse⁰　iau¹　lɔ⁰
young.man　that-bowl　　　noodle　walk　DELIM　hungry　SFP
'Young man, (take) that bowl of noodles, as you must be hungry after a short walk.'

(40) NP_SUBJECT NP_TOPIC VP
儂　　伊　　迄領　　　　　　佫　　　去　　做工
laŋ⁴　i¹　hit⁷⁻⁸-liã³　koʔ⁷⁻⁸　khu⁵⁻³　tsue⁵⁻³-kaŋ¹
other　3SG　that-CL　　　also　　go　　do-work
'He also (wore) that piece (of clothing) to work.' (lit. he that piece also go work)

In (38), the speaker aims to express that the subject *a¹san¹* 'Ah-Shan' finishes eating a bowl of rice with only a chicken leg, rather than with more vegetables or meat. In this case, the noun *a¹ san¹* 'Ah-Shan' and the noun phrase *tsit⁸⁻⁴ uã³⁻² bãi¹* 'a bowl of rice' respectively function as an agent and a patient of the transitive verb phrase *tsiaʔ⁸⁻⁴ khu⁵* 'eat'. There is no clear semantic relation between the noun phrase *tsit⁸⁻⁴ tə⁵⁻³ kue¹thui³* 'a chicken leg' and the verb phrase *tsiaʔ⁸⁻⁴ khu⁵⁻³ tsit⁸⁻⁴ uã³⁻² bãi¹* 'eat a bowl of rice'. Thus, the noun phrase *tsit⁸⁻⁴ tə⁵⁻³ kue¹thui³* here can be regarded as a background frame-setting topic.

The context of (39) is that the addressee, who has just come back from outside, does not feel hungry since he already ate a bowl of noodles before going out, while the speaker insists on asking the addressee to have lunch, since she thinks that he must be hungry after a short walk. In this case, the noun *hau^{4}sin^{1}ke^1* 'young man' is the subject of the clause *kiã^2 tse^0 iau^0 lɔ^0* 'being hungry after a short walk'. The noun phrase *hit$^{7\text{-}8}$ uã$^{3\text{-}2}$ bin^5* 'that bowl of noodles', however, does not involve a clear semantic relation with the clause *kiã^2 tse^0 iau^0 lɔ^0*, and thus can be interpreted as a background frame-setting topic.

Example (40) literally means 'he that piece (of clothing) also go to work'. Human beings can go to work, while clothes cannot. The context of this example is that Mother told her daughter that the shirt her father happened to be wearing was very dirty, since he had been to work in it. In this case, the complex *hit$^{7\text{-}8}$liã^3* 'that piece (of clothing)' can also be regarded as a background frame-setting topic.

20.3.3 Identical topic

Identical topic shares the same form with (part of) the subject, object or even the verb in the comment (Xu & Liu 2007:121), as illustrated by the Mandarin Chinese example in (41).

(41) NP$_{\text{SUBJECT}}$ VP$_{\text{ADJ TOPIC}}$ VP

他	兒子	聰明	倒	挺	聰明,
tā	*érzi*	*cōngmíng*	*dào*	*tǐng*	*cōngmíng*
3SG	Son	clever	ADV	rather	clever
就	是	寫	作業	太	粗心
jiù	*shì*	*xiě*	*zuòyè*	*tài*	*cūxīn*
only	Be	write	homework	too	careless

'Clever, his son is certainly clever, but is too careless in doing his homework.'

In (41), the first occurrence of *cōngmíng* 聰明 'clever' functions as a topic, sharing the same form with part of the comment *dào tǐng cōngmíng* 倒挺聰明 'rather clever', where *dào* is an adverb indicating concession.

As with Mandarin Chinese (also the Shanghai variety), this type of topic in Hui'an can be either nominal or verbal. However, in daily conversation, the identical verbal topic is more common than the nominal one. Examples of identical nominal topic are given in (42) and (43).

(42) NP_TOPIC NP_SUBJECT VP
班車,　　　伊　　有　　幾　　　　條　　　班車線　　　　　嘛
pan¹tshia¹　*i¹*　*u⁴*　*kui³⁻²*　*tiau²⁻⁴*　*pan¹tshia¹-suã⁵*　*bã⁰*
shuttle.bus　3SG　have　several　CL　shuttle.bus-line　SFP
'As for the shuttle bus, it has several shuttle bus lines.'

(43) NP_TOPIC NP
各　　　儂,　　　各　　　儂　　　其　　　習慣
kɔk⁷⁻⁸　*laŋ²*　*kɔk⁷⁻⁸*　*laŋ²*　*e²⁻⁴*　*siəp⁸⁻⁴kuan⁵*
each　person　each　person　GEN　habit
'For everybody – we each have our own habits.'

In (42), the topic *pan¹tshia¹* 'shuttle bus' shares the same form with part of the noun phrase *pan¹tshia¹suã⁵* 'shuttle bus line' in the comment. In (43), the comment is encoded by the possessive noun phrase *kɔk⁷⁻⁸ laŋ² e²⁻⁴ siəp⁸⁻⁴kuan⁵* 'each person's habits', and the topic *kɔk⁷⁻⁸ laŋ²* 'each person' shares the same form with the possessor *kɔk⁷⁻⁸ laŋ²* in the nominal comment.

When encoded by a verb (phrase), the identical topics in Hui'an are typically not separated: they are neither followed by an adverb (e.g. *dào* in (41)) nor by a pause particle, as shown in (44) and (45).

(44) NP_TEMPORAL TOPIC VP_TOPIC VP
年兜　　　　愛　　　倒來　　　　倒來,
lin²⁻⁴tau¹　*ai⁵⁻³*　*to⁵lai⁰*　*to⁵lai⁰*
New.Year　like　come.back　come.back
唔愛　　　　倒來　　　　口　　　　倒來
m⁵⁻⁴-ai⁵⁻³　*to⁵lai⁰*　*buan³⁻²*　*to⁵lai⁰*
not-like　come.back　do.not　come.back
'The New Year, if (you) want to come back, then come back; if not, then don't come back.'

(45) VP_TOPIC [V + DUR]
愛　　　口　　　口　　　咧
ai⁵⁻³　*hio⁴*　*hio⁴*　*leʔ⁰*
like　keep　keep　DUR
'If (you) would like to keep (it), then keep (it).'

Example (44) involves two juxtaposed topic-comment constructions, where the topics are encoded by the verb phrase *ai⁵⁻³ to⁵lai⁰* 'want to come back' and *m⁵⁻⁴ai⁵⁻³*

to^5lai^0 'don't want to come back' respectively, while the comment in both constructions is encoded by the verb phrase to^5lai^0 'come back'. In other words, in this case, the comment shares the same form with part of the topic. In (45), the topic and comment are encoded by the verb phrase $ai^{5-3}hio^4$ 'want to keep (it)' and $hio^4le?^0$ 'keep (it)', respectively. In this case, part of the topic shares the same form with part of the comment. In addition, the topic-comment constructions in these two examples can also be interpreted as involving topics encoded by a conditional clause. In both cases, the identical topic is neither followed by an adverb nor by a pause particle.

The identical topic is also often encoded by a bare verb such as tsu^3 煮 'cook' in (46) and $sion^{5-4}kho^5$ 上課 'take lectures' in (47).

(46) VP$_{TOPIC}$ NP$_{SUBJECT}$ VP
 煮， 我 煮
 tsu^3 gua^3 tsu^3
 cook 1SG cook
 'Cooking, let me do it.'

(47) VP$_{TOPIC}$ [ADV + V]
 上課 做做 上
 $sion^{5-4}kho^5$ $tsue^{5-3}tsue^5$ $sion^5$
 take.lectures together take
 'Take lectures, (we) did it together.'

The identical topic can sometimes be followed by an adverb such as $tsiu^5$ 就 'then' in (48) and a^4 也 'also' in (49).

(48) VP$_{TOPIC}$ [$tsiu^5$ + V + SFP]
 來 就 來 嘍
 lai^2 $tsiu^{5-4}$ lai^2 lo^0
 come then come SFP
 '(They) may come (if they wish).'

(49) S, NP_LOCATIVE TOPIC VP_TOPIC [a^4 + V + RVC]
　　　四界　　　　看　　　無，
　　　siak$^{7-8}$kue^5　khuã$^{5-3}$　bo^2
　　　everywhere　look　　not.have
　　　佫　　　房咧　　　看　　也　　看　　　　無
　　　koʔ$^{7-8}$　paŋ^2-leʔ^0　khuã^5　a^4　khuã$^{5-3}$　bo^2
　　　and　　room-LOC　look　also　look　　not.have
　　　'(I) didn't find (it) anywhere, nor did (I) find (it) in the room.'

The identical topic and the main part of the comment can also be connected by the concessive marker *khɔ^5* 與 (< 'give'), as in (50).

(50) VP_ADJ TOPIC [*khɔ$^{5-1}$* (or *khɔ$^{5-4}$ i^1*) + VP_ADJ]
　　　否看　　　　　　與　　　　否看
　　　phai$^{3-2}$-khuã^5　khɔ$^{5-1}$　phai$^{3-2}$-khuã^5
　　　bad-look　　　give　　bad-look
　　　'Ugly though it may be.'

In (50), the topic is encoded by the adjective *phai$^{3-2}$khuã^5* 'ugly', and *khɔ^5* here is a concessive marker (see §18.6 above).

20.3.4 Clause topic

The clause topic, taking the form of an entire clause, involves a logical-semantic relation with the comment, rather than a syntactic relation with the comment (Xu & Liu 2007:205). This type of topic in Hui'an normally expresses the protasis in a conditional relation, as in (51) and (52).

(51) S_TOPIC, S_COMMENT
　　　卜　　　　知，　　直接　　　　　叫　　　即個　　　　來　　　　做
　　　boʔ$^{7-8}$　tsai^1　tet$^{8-4}$tsiəp^7　kio$^{5-3}$　tsit$^{7-8}$-e$^{2-4}$　lai$^{2-4}$　tsue^5
　　　want　know　directly　　　call　　this-CL　come　do
　　　'If (we) had known (it), (we) would've contacted him directly for the job.'

(52) S_TOPIC, S_COMMENT
有 代志， 明日 則 商量
u^4 $tai^{5\text{-}4}tsi^5$ $biã^{2\text{-}4}let^8$ $tsia?^{7\text{-}8}$ $siɔŋ^1liɔŋ^2$
have thing tomorrow only.then discuss
'Let's talk about it tomorrow, if necessary.'

An adverb may be used to connect the topic and the main part of the comment, as in (53).

(53) S_TOPIC, S_COMMENT
做做 來， 就 包 蜀 個 與 伊
$tsue^{5\text{-}3}tsue^5$ lai^2 $tsiu^{5\text{-}4}$ pau^1 $tsit^{8\text{-}4}$ $e^{2\text{-}4}$ $khɔ^5$ i^0
together come then wrap one CL give 3SG
'If (they) come together, then wrap one to give him.'

The clause topic is also often in a negative form, as in (54).

(54) S_TOPIC, S_COMMENT
無 燙， 會 否 去
$bo^{2\text{-}4}$ $thŋ^5$ e^4 $phai^3$ khu^0
not.have heat would bad PVC
'If (we) don't heat (it), (it) would turn bad.'

20.3.5 Split argument topic

According to Liu (2003b[2001]), the patient argument can be split into two syntactic constitutents: one occurs before the main verb functioning as a topic, and the other occurs after the main verb functioning as an object, as in (55), an example from Mandarin Chinese.

(55) NP_SUBJECT NP_TOPIC, [VP + NUM + CL]
他 襯衫 買 了 三 件 (Mandarin Chinese)
tā chènshān mǎi le sān jiàn
3SG shirt buy PFV three CL
'The shirts, he bought three of them.' (lit. he shirt bought three)

In (55), the patient argument *sān jiàn chènshān* 'three shirts' is split into two syntactic constituents: (a) *chènshān* 'shirt' occurs after the subject *tā* 'he' but before the main verb *mǎi* 'buy', functioning as a subtopic, and (b) the complex *sān jiàn* 'three pieces' occurs after the main verb *mǎi*, functioning as its object. The topic *chènshān* is thus named the 'split argument topic' in Liu (2003b[2001]) since it is separated from its classifier phrase *sānjiàn*.

This type of topic in Hui'an is normally encoded by a bare noun phrase, especially a bare noun, as in (56).

(56) NP$_{TOPIC}$ [V + NUM + MW]
菜花　　　炒　　蜀　　簇
tshai$^{5\text{-}3}$hue^1　*tsha^3*　*tsit$^{8\text{-}4}$*　*tshiɔk^7*
cauliflower　fry　one　MW
'The cauliflower, fry a little of it.'

The split argument topic can also be encoded by a demonstrative indicating a category of object, as in (57).

(57) NP$_{DEM\,TOPIC}$ [V + MUM + MW]
口　　買　　蜀　　瓶
tse^2　*bue^3*　*tsit$^{8\text{-}4}$*　*pan^2*
this　buy　one　bottle
'This kind (of cafe), buy a bottle.'

The object in the comment is normally encoded by a [numeral + classifier] complex, as shown in (56) and (57) above. The following example shows that the comment can also be encoded by a demonstrative phrase or a nominalization.

(58) NP$_{SUBJECT}$ NP$_{TOPIC}$ [VP + DEM + CL + SFP]
汝　　口褲　　　　著　　　去　　穿　　迄領　　　咯,
lu^3　*khau$^{3\text{-}2}$khɔ^5*　*tioʔ$^{8\text{-}4}$*　*khu$^{5\text{-}3}$*　*tshiŋ$^{5\text{-}4}$*　*hit$^{7\text{-}8}$-liã^3*　*lɔ^0*
2SG　trousers　should　go　wear　that-CL　SFP
[V + NP$_{NOMINALIZATION}$ + SFP]
穿　　迄領　　　黃色　　　其　　咯
tshiŋ$^{5\text{-}4}$　*hit$^{7\text{-}8}$-liã^3*　*ŋ$^{2\text{-}4}$siak^7*　*e^0*　*lɔ^0*
wear　that-CL　yellow　NMLZ　SFP
'As for the trousers, you should wear that pair, the yellow ones.' (lit. You, as for the trousers, (you) should wear that pair, wear that yellow pair.)

In (58), the noun *khau$^{3\text{-}2}$khɔ^5* 'trousers' occurs after the subject 'you', functioning as a subtopic, and the classifier phrase *hit$^{7\text{-}8}$liã^3* 'that piece' functions as the object of the verb *tshiŋ⁵* 'wear' in the first clause. The nominalization construction *ŋ²⁻⁴siak⁷ e⁰* 'the yellow one' also serves as the object of the verb *tshiŋ⁵* 'wear' in the second clause.

The object in the comment is often followed by a verb phrase, as in (59).

(59) NP_{TOPIC} NP_{TEMPORAL TOPIC} [VP + NUM + CL + VP]
    口   下日   加   買   蜀   領   去   穿
    tse² *e⁴let⁸* *ke¹* *bue³* *tsit⁸⁻⁴* *liã³* *khuɨ⁵⁻³* *tshiŋ⁵*
    this future more buy one CL go wear
    'As for this kind, in future buy one more pair to wear.' (lit. This, in the future, buy one more to wear.)

20.4 The position of topic

The topic in Hui'an can occur before the subject, functioning as main topic, as in (60), where the topic *kha¹liau³* 骹爪 'claw' is placed before the subject *luɨ³* 'you'.

(60) NP_{TOPIC} NP_{SUBJECT} VP
    骹爪   汝   卜   唔
    kha¹liau³ *luɨ³* *bo?⁷* *m⁰*
    claw 2SG want SFP
    'The (chicken) claw, do you want (it)?'

However, examples like (60) are not common in daily conversation of the Hui'an dialect. When the topic and the subject are both overt in the sentence, the topic is typically placed after the subject and before the main verb in the comment, if not directly before the verb phrase (the comment), i.e. the subtopic position according to Xu & Liu (1998). An example is given in (61), where the topic *tɔ²⁻⁴tsua³* 圖紙 'drawing' can be regarded as a subtopic, since it is placed after the subject *en¹* 㑑 'they' and before the verb phrase *ke⁵⁻³ bue⁴hiau³⁻² khuã⁵* 計繪曉看 'all do not understand'.

(61) NP_{SUBJECT} NP_{TOPIC} VP
    㑑   圖紙   計   繪曉   看
    en¹ *tɔ²⁻⁴tsua³* *ke⁵⁻³* *bue⁴hiau³⁻²* *khuã⁵*
    3PL drawing all can.not look
    'As for them – and the drawing, none understand it at all.' (lit. they the drawing all cannot look)

The topic can also occur between an auxiliary verb (or an adverb) and the verb (phrase), as in (62) and (63).

(62) NP$_{SUBJECT}$ AUX NP$_{TOPIC}$ VP
汝　　著　　　蠟燭油　　　　　上
lui³　tioʔ⁸⁻⁴　laʔ⁸⁻⁴tsiak⁷⁻⁸-iu²　siɔŋ⁵
2SG　should　candle-oil　　　apply
'You should use the candle oil.' (lit. you should the candle oil use)

(63) NP$_{SUBJECT}$ ADV NP$_{TOPIC}$ VP
我　　佮　　骹　　去　與　儂　　按摩
gua³　koʔ⁷⁻⁸　khaౖ¹　khu⁵⁻³　khɔ⁵⁻⁴　laŋ⁴　an⁵⁻³bɜ̃²
1SG　also　foot　go　give　other　massage
'I also had a foot massage.' (lit. I also foot go let other people give massage)

In (62), the topic *laʔ⁸⁻⁴tsiak⁷⁻⁸iu²* 'candle oil' occurs between the auxiliary verb *tioʔ⁸* 'should' and the main verb *siɔŋ⁵* 'apply'. In (63), the topic *kha¹* 'foot' is placed between the adverb *koʔ⁷* 'also' and the verb phrase *khu⁵⁻³ khɔ⁵⁻⁴ laŋ⁴ an⁵⁻³bɜ̃²* 'go to let other people give a massage'.

In contrast to this, the subject is often omitted in daily conversation, particularly when it is a speech act participant. In other words, the topic, especially the patient topic, often occurs in the sentence-initial position, followed by the comment, as in (64).

(64) NP$_{TOPIC}$ VP
相機　　　卜　　　帶
siɔŋ⁵⁻³ki¹　boʔ⁷⁻⁸　tua⁵
camera　want　take
'Do (you) want to take the camera (with you)?' (lit. camera want take)

In (64), the subject *lui³* 'you' is omitted, and the patient topic *siɔŋ⁵⁻³ki¹* 'camera' is placed in the sentence-initial position. The subject *lui³* tends to occur before the patient topic *siɔŋ⁵⁻³ki¹*, if it is overtly expressed. Hence, the topic *siɔŋ⁵⁻³ki¹* may be regarded as a subtopic with an ellipsed subject in the sentence-initial position. This kind of patient topicalization is discussed directly below in §20.5.

Examples so far in this section involve only one topic in the same sentence. As mentioned above, more than one topic can occur in the same sentence. Two more examples are given in (65) and (66).

(65) NP_SUBJECT NP_TEMPORAL TOPIC NP_TOPIC VP
    汝   今日   衫   無   換   者
    lu³   kiã¹let⁸   sã¹   bo²⁻⁴   uã⁵   tse⁰
    2SG   today   clothes not.have change DELIM
    'You have not changed clothes today.' (lit. you today clothes not change)

(66) VP_TOPIC [VP [NP_SUBJECT NP_TOPIC VP]]
    啊   倚,   看   汝   厝   卜   泉州   買
    a⁰   khia⁴   khuã⁵⁻³ lu³   tshu⁵ boʔ⁷⁻⁸   tsuan²⁻⁴tsiu¹ bue³
    DM   live   look   2SG   house want   PN   buy
    抑   廈門   買   嘍
    aʔ⁸   e⁵⁻⁴bŋ²   bue³   lɔ⁰
    or   PN   buy   SFP
    'As for the residence, this depends on whether you want to buy a house in Quanzhou or Xiamen.'

In (65), the subject lu^3 'you' occurs at the sentence-initial position, followed by the temporal subtopic $kiã^1let^8$ 'today' and the patient subtopic $sã^1$ 'clothes'. In (66), the verb $khia^4$ 'live' functions as a topic in the main clause, while the noun $tshu^5$ 'house', being semantically the patient of the verb bue^3 'buy', functions as a subtopic in the embedded clause.

20.5 Patient topicalization

As shown by the examples given in the preceding sections, the object, especially patient objects, that typically occur after the verb in SVO languages, are often preposed directly before the verb (but less frequently before the subject, if present) and, in this position, they functions as a (sub)topic in Hui'an. This section aims to focus on this issue, especially the constructions where patient topicalization is involved, as well as the topicalization of locative objects.

In Hui'an, the patient in imperative sentences is normally placed before the verb, functioning as a topic, as in (67), where the patient noun $sã^1$ 衫 'clothes' occurs before the verb $tshiŋ^5$ 穿 'wear' functioning as a topic.

(67) NP_TOPIC VP
    衫   穿
    sã¹   tshiŋ⁵
    clothes   wear
    'Put on the clothes!'

Note that an imperative with the patient postposed after the verb is possible too in Hui'an. However, imperatives with the patient preposed before the verb as a (sub)topic, as in (68), are much more natural and common.

The patient constituent in double object constructions also typically occurs before the verb functioning as a topic, as in (69), where the noun kue^1set^8 雞翼 'chicken wing' is placed before the ditransitive verb $khɔ^5$ 與 'give', functioning as a topic.

(68) NP$_{TOPIC}$ VP

雞翼	與	恁	爸仔	咯
kue^1-set^8	$khɔ^{5\text{-}4}$	$len^{3\text{-}2}$	pa^2-a^0	$lɔ^0$
chicken-wing	give	2PL	father-NM	SFP

'The chicken wing has been given to your father.'

The patient in verb-complement constructions is also often preposed to function as a topic, as in (69), where the noun $phiŋ^{2\text{-}4}kɔ^3$ 蘋果 'apple', semantically the patient of the resultative verb complement construction $tsiaʔ^{8\text{-}4}$ $liau^3$ 食了 'eat up', occurs at the sentence-initial position to function as a topic. Note that the noun $phiŋ^{2\text{-}4}kɔ^3$ cannot occur after the resultative verb complement construction.

(69) NP$_{TOPIC}$ VP

蘋果	食	了	咯
$phiŋ^{2\text{-}4}kɔ^3$	$tsiaʔ^{8\text{-}4}$	$liau^3$	$lɔ^0$
apple	eat	RVC	SFP

'The apple has been eaten up.'

The patient of the first verb phrase in serial verb constructions also often occurs before the verb functioning as a topic, as in (70), where the noun te^2 茶 'tea', being the patient of the first verb $phaŋ^2$ 捧 'hold' in the serial verb construction $phaŋ^2$ $khɔ^{5\text{-}4}$ i^1 $liəm^1$ 捧與伊啉 'hold in both hands for him to drink', is preposed before the verb $phaŋ^2$ to function as a subtopic.

(70) NP$_{SUBJECT}$ ADV NP$_{TOPIC}$ VP

汝	著	茶	捧	與	伊	啉
lu	$tioʔ^{8\text{-}4}$	te^2	$phaŋ^2$	$khɔ^{5\text{-}4}$	i^1	$liəm^1$
2SG	should	tea	hold	give	3SG	drink

'You should hold the tea in both hands for him to drink.'

As mentioned in §20.1 and illustrated by many previous examples, the topic usually refers to something that is identifiable for both the speaker and the addressee, being typically either definite or generic. However, an indefinite patient topic is also found in Hui'an, as in (71).

(71) QW   NP_TOPIC   VP
　　 哪   蜀   張   相   創   咧   搭
　　 lã⁵⁻³ tsit⁸⁻⁴ tiũ¹ siɔŋ⁵   tshɔŋ⁵   leʔ⁷⁻⁸ taʔ⁷
　　 how   one   CL   picture do   at   here
　　 'Why has a picture been put here?'

In (71), the indefinite noun phrase *tsit⁸⁻⁴ tiũ¹ siɔŋ⁵* 'a picture', semantically the patient of the verb phrase *tshɔŋ⁵ leʔ⁷⁻⁸ taʔ⁷* 'put here', occurs before this verb phrase and functions as a topic. Even though it is encoded by an indefinite noun phrase, the topic *tsit⁸⁻⁴ tiũ¹ siɔŋ⁵* refers to a specific entity and can be identified by both the speaker and the addressee. The indefinite noun phrase *tsit⁸⁻⁴ tiũ¹ siɔŋ⁵* may occur after the verb *tshɔŋ⁵*, though it is less natural than the pre-verbal position.

It is quite common in Chinese for locative nouns to act as the direct objects of motion verbs, that is, in syntactically transitive constructions (see Chao 1968). For this reason, locative nouns are included under this discussion of patient topicalization.

Some locative constituents which normally occur after the verb in SVO languages such as Mandarin and Hakka are preferentially preposed however in Hui'an, as in (72) and (73).

(72) NP_LOCATIVE TOPIC   VP, S
　　 門   未   入,   電話   已經   到   咯
　　 bŋ²   bə⁵⁻⁴   liəp⁸   ten⁵⁻⁴ue⁵   i³⁻²kiŋ¹   kau⁵   lɔ⁰
　　 door not.yet enter   telephone   already   arrive   SFP
　　 'Before I entered the door, the telephone rang.'

(73) NP_LOCATIVE TOPIC   VP
　　 迄搭   呣   八   去   著
　　 hit⁷⁻⁸-taʔ⁷ m⁵⁻⁴   pat⁷⁻⁸   khuɨ⁵   tioʔ⁰
　　 that-LOC   not   EXP   go   EXP
　　 'I have not been there.'

In (72), *bŋ²* 'door' occurs before the verb phrase *bə⁵⁻⁴ liəp⁸* 'have not entered'. Similarly, *hit⁷⁻⁸taʔ⁷* 'there' in (73) is placed before the verb phrase *m⁵⁻⁴pat⁷⁻⁸ khu⁵ tioʔ⁰* 'have not been to'.

20.6 Topic markers

Topic markers in Chinese commonly include pause and pause particles, among which, pause particles, roughly equivalent to sentence-medial particles, are commonly used in some Chinese varieties such as the Shanghai variety. A similar case can be found in Hui'an, as in (74), where the clause topic *lã⁴ si⁴ siu¹liəp⁸* 若是收入 'as for the salary' is followed by the particle *hau⁰*.

(74) NP$_{\text{TOPIC}}$ TM VP

若 是 收入 口, 算 野 低 咯
lã⁴ si⁴ siu¹liəp⁸ hau⁰ sŋ⁵⁻³ ia³⁻² ke⁴ lɔ⁰
if be salary SFP count quite low SFP
'As for the salary, it is quite low.'

However, this is not common in Hui'an. Note also that the particle *hau⁰* in (74) is not exclusively used as a topic marker, since it can also be used in a different position as a sentence-final particle, as in (75), where the particle *hau⁰* is used to ask for confirmation.

(75) 汝 坐 搭 口
lu³ tsə⁴ taʔ⁷ hau⁰
2SG sit here SFP
'Sit here, OK?'

The topic in Hui'an is basically not followed by any obviously audible pause.[1] The lack of a prominent pause means that any pause between the topic and the comment, if there is one, is the same as that to be had between the subject and the predicate, or between other sentence constituents. In all the examples given so far, except example (66) (reproduced in (76) below), there is no audible pause between the topic and the comment that can be detected in the recordings.

---

[1] We have carefully checked our recordings and transcriptions and there is no audible pause.

(76) VP_TOPIC [VP [NP_SUBJECT NP_TOPIC VP]]
　　啊　　倚，　　看　　汝　　厝　　卜　　泉州　　　　買
　　a⁰　　khia⁴　khuã⁵⁻³　lu³　tshu⁵　bo?⁷⁻⁸　tsuan²⁻⁴tsiu¹　bue³
　　DM　　live　　look　2SG　house　want　PN　　　　　　buy
　　抑　　廈門　　買　　嘍
　　a?⁸　　e⁵⁻⁴bŋ²　bue³　lɔ⁰
　　or　　PN　　　buy　SFP
　　'As for the residence, this depends on whether you want to buy a house in Quanzhou or Xiamen.'

In this case, when the topic *khia⁴* 'live' is uttered, the speaker is still thinking about what she is going to say. In other words, the pause following the topic *khia⁴* is more like a pause for thought, though it may highlight the topic *khia⁴* in some way.

In other words, the main method for identifying a topic in Hui'an is the word order of a given structure: the topic is always placed before the main verb, though it may occupy a range of positions in the different types of topic constructions discussed in the preceding sections (e.g. occurring between the auxiliary verb and the main verb). This may also show that topic in Hui'an is more like an unmarked constituent, in not being signalled by a formal marker. In fact, this is consonant with Liu (2001)'s viewpoint of topic-comment forming a common construction type in Wu and Min.

20.7 Contrastive function of topic

According to Xu & Liu (2007:195), one of the main functions of topic is for contrast. In Hui'an, however, topic constructions are rarely used in this way. Consider the example of patient topicalization in (77) which is not however contrastive in Hui'an:

(77)　我　　錢　　　交　　　蠻儕
　　　gua³　tsin²　　kau¹　ban²⁻⁴tsue⁵
　　　1SG　money　pay　　much
　　　'I have paid a lot of money.'

In (77), the noun *tsin²* 'money', semantically the patient of the verb *kau¹* 'pay', occurs immediately after the subject *gua³* 'I' to function as a subtopic. This example is used to express 'I have paid a lot of money', rather than to contrast with other situations.

As mentioned above, the topic in the Shanghai variety is often followed by a pause particle, which is the main way to express contrastive topic in this variety. Similarly, the topic markers in Japanese and Korean often involve a contrastive function. This may explain why the topic in Hui'an is normally not used with – and does not need - a pause particle.

All these features - lack of a contrastive function, lack of a formal topic marker, and prevalence of object topicalization -may show that the topic in Hui'an tends to be an unmarked constituent in the sentence, with a less pragmatic and, consequently, a more syntactic function.

20.8 Summary

This chapter has examined the topic-comment construction in Hui'an from six aspects: (a) forms of topics; (b) semantic relations between topic and comment; (c) positions of topics; (d) patient topicalization including locative objects; (e) topic markers; and (f) the contrastive function of topic.

The topic in Hui'an can be encoded by different categories of words, phrases and clauses, including personal pronouns, demonstratives, noun phrases, numerals, time and location words, verb, adjective and clause.

Following Xu & Liu (2007) and Liu (2003b[2001]), the topics in Hui'an can be classified into five types in terms of the semantic relations between topic and comment: (a) coreferential (pseudo-)argument topic; (b) frame-setting topic; (c) identical topic; (d) clause topic; and (e) split-argument topic.

Unlike Mandarin Chinese in which the topic always occurs in sentence-initial position, the topic in Hui'an normally occurs after the subject and before the main verb in the comment (i.e. constituting a subtopic in Xu & Liu (2007)'s term), especially when both the topic and the subject are present in the sentence. The topic may occur between the subject and the verb phrase, or occur after both the subject and an auxiliary verb (or an adverb), but always before the main verb in the comment. In daily conversation, the subject is often omitted, particularly when it is a speech act participant. In other words, the topic often occurs at the sentence-initial position with an omitted preceding subject. More than one topic may occur in the same sentence.

The object, especially the patient object, that typically occurs after the verb in SVO languages is often found preposed before the verb functioning as a (sub)topic in Hui'an. Patient topicalization typically occurs with imperative sentences, double object constructions, verb-complement constructions, and serial verb constructions. The topic usually refers to something that is identifiable for both speaker and the addressee, being typically either definite or generic. In

Hui'an, an indefinite patient topic is also attested, although, even then, it usually refers to a specific referent. Some locative constituents acting as direct objects of motion verbs and which would normally occur after the verb in SVO languages are preferentially preposed in Hui'an.

Unlike some Chinese varieties such as Wu, the topic in Hui'an is basically not followed by either an obvious pause or a pause particle. In other words, the main method for identifying a topic in Hui'an is the word order of a given structure, i.e. the topic is always placed before the verb. In additon, the topic in Hui'an is rarely used for contrast. All these suggest that the topic in Hui'an is more like an unmarked constituent.

Part IV: complex sentences

The term 'complex sentences' traditionally refers to grammatical constructions consisting of multiple clauses, which include two categories: one involving coordinate clauses, and the other involving a matrix clause and a subordinate clause (cf. Frajzyngier 1996; Diessel 2004, among others). Subordinate clauses are traditionally further classified into three subtypes: complement clauses, relative clauses, and adverbial clauses (cf. Cristofaro 2003; Diessel 2004; Longacre 2007; Thompson, Longacre & Hwang 2007, among others).

This part examines these four types of complex sentence in Hui'an: coordination (chapter 21), relative clauses (chapter 22), adverbial clauses (chapter 23) and complement clauses (chapter 24). Chapter 21 focuses on three main semantic types of coordination, i.e. conjunction, disjunction and adversative coordination. For comparison, coordination involving non-clausal units is also mentioned. In chapter 22, we discuss restrictive relative clauses based on four parameters: (a) the relativization marker used; (b) the position of the head noun in relation to the relative clause; (c) the role and encoding of the head noun in the relative clause; and (d) the role and encoding of the head noun in the main clause. Chapter 23 focuses on how four types of adverbial clauses are encoded in Hui'an: time, cause, purpose and conditional clauses. Chapter 24 examines complement clauses, which typically function as an object of the main clause, as well as their use with complementizers.

21 Coordination

21.1 Introduction

Coordination and subordination serve as two important clause linkage strategies. Unlike subordination, however, coordination may also function as a strategy linking two non-clausal units, such as words and phrases. More specifically, the term 'coordination' is traditionally used to refer to 'syntactic constructions in which two or more units of the same type are combined into a larger unit and still have the same semantic relations with other surrounding elements', while the units involved include words, phrases, subordinate clauses and full sentences (cf. Haspelmath 2007:1). Four English examples of coordination are given in (1).

(1) a. *Mary is tall and beautiful.*
    b. *A boy or two girls are at home.*
    c. *He likes to play basketball and to sing popular songs.*
    d. *I like going to the zoo, and I like bringing my friends to the zoo.*

In (1a), two adjectives, i.e. *tall* and *beautiful*, are combined into a larger unit (i.e. tall and beautiful). Example (1b) involves two noun phrases, i.e. *A boy* and *two girls*. The two units connected by the morpheme *and* in (1c), i.e. *to play basketball* and *to sing popular songs*, are subordinate clauses. In (1d), the morpheme *and* is used to link two full sentences, i.e. *I like going to the zoo* and *I like bringing my friends to the zoo*.

The units of a coordinate coordination such as *tall* and *beautiful* in (1a) are called coordinands, while the particle or affix used to link the coordinands such as English *and* and *or* in (1) are labeled the coordinator (cf. Haspelmath 2004, 2007), or the coordinating conjunction (cf. Schachter & Shopen 2007:45). Different coordinators may be used according to the different syntactic types of coordinand, depending on the language (Haspelmath 2007:3). This is also true for the Hui'an dialect. Thus, in this chapter, coordination involving non-clausal units will also be examined for comparison.

According to Haspelmath (2004, 2007), there are three main semantic types of coordination, i.e. conjunction, disjunction and adversative coordination. Conjunction as in example (1a) above is also called 'conjunctive coordination', or "'and'-coordination" in which 'and' refers to English *and* and its equivalents in other languages. Similarly, disjunction is also called 'disjunctive coordination', or "'or' -coordination", as in (1b). Adversative coordination also goes under the name of "'but' -coordination", as in example (2) below.

(2) *The dwarfs were ugly but kind.* (Haspelmath 2007:2)

In the following sections, we will examine how these three semantic types of coordination are encoded in Hui'an.

21.2 Conjunction

As with Mandarin Chinese, different coordinators are required for nominal and verbal/clausal conjunction in Hui'an. Either *kaʔ⁷* 合 'and' or *kiau¹* 交 'and', being counterparts of Mandarin coordinators such as *hé* 和 and *gēn* 跟, is used in nominal conjunction, as exemplified by (3) – (5).

(3) 糖　　合/交　　　　鹽
    thŋ²　*kaʔ⁷⁻⁸/kiau¹*　*iəm²*
    sugar　and　　　　 salt
    'sugar and salt'

(4) 我　　合/交　　　　伊
    gua³　*kaʔ⁷⁻⁸/kiau¹*　*i¹*
    1SG　and　　　　 3SG
    'he and I'

(5) 聽　　合/交　　　　寫　　繪　　　否
    thiã¹　*kaʔ⁷⁻⁸/kiau¹*　*sia³*　*bue⁴*　*phai³*
    listen　and　　　　 write　can.not　bad
    '(He is) good at both listening and writing.'

In (3), the coordinators *kaʔ⁷* and *kiau¹* are used to connect the nouns *thŋ²* 'sugar' and *iəm²* 'salt'. In (4), *kaʔ⁷* and *kiau¹* connect the first person singular pronoun *gua³* and the third person singular pronoun *i¹*. The morphemes *thiã¹* 'listen' and *sia³* 'write' are originally verbs denoting actions. In (5), however, *thiã¹* and *sia³* both denote skills, rather than actions. In addition, *thiã¹ kaʔ⁷⁻⁸/kiau¹ sia³* 'listening and writing' in (5) functions as a complex noun phrase to be used as a subject. In other words, the status of *thiã¹* and *sia³* in (5) probably reflects a process of nominalization, thereby creating deverbal nouns in Hui'an. Comparatively speaking, the coordinator *kiau¹* is less used than *kaʔ⁷* in daily conversation in the contemporary Hui'an dialect.

    Similar to Mandarin Chinese, the coordinands in nominal conjunction in Hui'an can be juxtaposed without a coordinator, as in (6).

(6) 灶骹、　　兩　　間　　浴室　　計　　有
　　 tsau⁵⁻³kha¹　lŋ⁴　kuin¹　iɔk⁸⁻⁴siak⁷　ke⁵⁻³　u⁴
　　 kitchen　　two　CL　　bathroom　　all　　have
　　 'The kitchen and two bathrooms all have (hot water).'

In (6), the noun *tsau⁵⁻³kha¹* 'kitchen' and the noun phrase *lŋ⁴ kuin¹ iɔk⁸⁻⁴siak⁷* 'two bathrooms' are connected without any coordinator such as *kaʔ⁷* and *kiau¹*. However, a pause is normally audible between the coordinands, reflected in the transcription by the punctuation mark "、" in (6).

The coordinands in nominal conjunction may be followed by a particle such as *lɔ⁰* 咯 in (7).

(7) 蘋果　　　　咯、　梨仔　　　咯
　　 phiŋ²⁻⁴kɔ³　lɔ⁰　lai²⁻⁴-a³　lɔ⁰
　　 apple　　　PRT　pear-NM　　PRT
　　 'apples and pears'

Similar particles used in nominal conjunction in Mandarin Chinese involve *a* 啊 and *la* 啦 (Zhu 1982:156).

These coordinative structures should be compared with nouns that have been juxtaposed without either a coordinator or a pause when they form a conceptual unit, i.e. constituting a compound word, as in (8).

(8) 糖仔餅
　　 thŋ²⁻⁴-a³⁻²-piã³
　　 sugar-NM-biscuit
　　 'snacks (like candy and biscuit)'

In (8), *thŋ²⁻⁴a³* and *piã³* are originally nouns meaning 'candy' and 'biscuit' respectively, while the compounding of *thŋ²⁻⁴a³* and *piã³* forms a conceptual unit denoting 'snacks'.

The coordinator *koʔ⁷* 佫 'and' is used in both verbal and clausal conjunction. Two examples of verbal conjunction are given in (9) and (10).

(9) 伊　　走　　　佫　　　跳
　　 i¹　tsau³　koʔ⁷⁻⁸　thiau⁵
　　 3SG　run　　and　　jump
　　 'He runs and jumps.'

(10) 糖仔　　　芳　　　佮　　　甜
　　　thŋ²⁻⁴-a³　phaŋ¹　koʔ⁷⁻⁸　tin¹
　　　sugar-NM　fragrant　and　sweet
　　　'The candy is both fragrant and sweet.'

In (9), the coordinator *koʔ⁷* is used to connect two actions encoded by the verbs *tsau³* 'run' and *thiau⁵* 'jump'. In (10), the coordinator *koʔ⁷* conjoins two states which are expressed by the adjectives (stative verbs) *phaŋ¹* 'fragrant' and *tin¹* 'sweet'. In addition, *tsau³ koʔ⁷⁻⁸ thiau⁵* 'run and jump' and *phaŋ¹ koʔ⁷⁻⁸ tin¹* 'fragrant and sweet' are both verb phrases used as predicates. Both these two examples would be marked by the adverb *yòu* 又 in Mandarin Chinese, as in *tā yòu pǎo yòu tiào* 他又跑又跳 'he runs and jumps'.

The following is an example of *koʔ⁷* connecting two clauses.

(11) 兩　　　個　　　出門　　　　咯,
　　　lŋ⁴　　e²　　tshut⁷⁻⁸-bŋ²　lɔ⁰
　　　two　　CL　　out-door　　　SFP
　　　佮　　　　遘　　　伯搭　　　　無　　　　　利便
　　　koʔ⁷⁻⁸　kau⁵⁻³　lan³-taʔ⁷　bo²⁻⁴　li⁵⁻⁴pen⁵
　　　and　　　arrive　1PL-LOC　not.have　convenient
　　　'Those two don't live at home, and it is not convenient to come here.'

In (11), the speaker is giving two reasons why he suggests a simple rather than a grand wedding ceremony. In this instance, the two units connected by *koʔ⁷* are both independent clauses. Note that, in Mandarin Chinese, clausal conjunction is usually marked by a conjunction such as *érqiě* 而且, as in (12).

(12) 他們　　兩　　　個　　都　　不　　在　　　家，(Mandarin Chinese)
　　　tāmen　liǎng　ge　　dōu　bù　　zài　　jiā
　　　3PL　　two　　CL　　all　　not　be.at　home
　　　而且　　到　　　我們　　這兒　　也　　不　　方便
　　　érqiě　dào　　wǒmen　zhèr　　yě　　bù　　fāngbiàn
　　　and　　arrive　1PL　　here　　also　not　convenient
　　　'Those two don't live at home, and it is not convenient to come here.'

As with Mandarin Chinese, verbal and clausal conjunction in Hui'an may be marked by the adverb *a⁴* 也 'also', as in (13) - (15).

(13) 伊　　也　　無　　　　歁　　　也　　無　　　　恁
    i¹　　a⁴　　bo²⁻⁴　　kham³　 a⁴　 bo²⁻⁴　　gɔŋ⁵
    3SG　also　not.have　stupid　also　not.have　dull
    'He is neither stupid nor dull.'

(14) 汝　　也　　卜　　　　買　　　厝　　　也　　卜　　　　創　　　甚物
    lu³　　a⁴　　boʔ⁷⁻⁸　　bue³⁻²　tshu⁵　a⁴　　boʔ⁷⁻⁸　tshɔŋ⁵⁻³　siəm³⁻²bĩʔ⁷
    2SG　also　want　　　buy　　house　also　want　　do　　　what
    'You want to buy a house, and also want to do other things.'

(15) 阮　　　老師　　也　　姓　　　　　陳，
    gun³⁻²　lau⁴suɪ¹　a⁴　sin⁵⁻³　　　tan²
    1PL　　teacher　also　one's　surname.is　TAN
    阮　　　領導　　　也　　姓　　　　　陳
    gun³⁻²　liŋ³⁻²tɔ⁵　a⁴　sin⁵⁻³　　　tan²
    1PL　　leader　　also　one's　surname.is　TAN
    'The surname of my teacher is Tan, and the surname of my boss is also Tan.'

In (13), the adjectival phrases $bo^{2-4}\,kham^3$ 'not stupid' and $bo^{2-4}\,gɔŋ^5$ 'not dull' are both preceded by the adverb a^4 'also'. Similarly, the verb phrases $boʔ^{7-8}\,bue^{3-2}\,tshu^5$ 'want to buy a house' and $boʔ^{7-8}\,tshɔŋ^{5-3}\,siəm^{3-2}bĩʔ^7$ 'want to do something' in (14) both follow the adverb a^4. As is clear from these two examples, when a verbal conjunction is marked by the adverb a^4 'also', the coordinands are typically encoded by a verb phrase, rather than a bare verb such as $tsau^3$ 'run' and $thiau^5$ 'jump' in example (9) above. In (15), both clauses involve the adverb a^4 'also', which is placed between the subject (i.e. $gun^{3-2}\,lau^4suɪ^1$ 'my teacher' and $gun^{3-2}\,liŋ^{3-2}tɔ^5$ 'my boss', respectively) and the verb phrase (i.e. $sin^{5-3}\,tan^2$ 'one's surname is Tan').

In examples (13) – (15), the adverb a^4 'also' is used in each coordinand in verbal and clausal conjunction. In fact, as illustrated by the following two examples, the first coordinand can occur without the adverb a^4 'also'.

(16) 伊　　唔　　愛　　聽　　　也　　唔　　愛　　應
    i¹　　m⁵⁻⁴　ai⁵⁻³　thiã¹　a⁴　　m⁵⁻⁴　ai⁵⁻³　en⁵
    3SG　not　　like　listen　also　not　　like　answer
    'He neither likes listening nor answering.'

(17) 伊　　嗯　　食，　　我　　也　　嗯　　食
　　　i^1　　$m^{5\text{-}4}$　　$tsia\textipa{P}^8$　　gua^3　　a^4　　$m^{5\text{-}4}$　　$tsia\textipa{P}^8$
　　　3SG　not　eat　　1SG　also　not　eat
　　　'He didn't want to eat (it), and neither did I.'

The second coordinand in verbal conjunction in (16) $m^{5\text{-}4}$ $ai^{5\text{-}3}$ en^5 'doesn't like answering' is preceded by the adverb a^4 'also', while the first coordinand $m^{5\text{-}4}$ $ai^{5\text{-}3}$ $thi\tilde{a}^1$ 'doesn't like listening' is not. Similarly, in clausal conjunction in (17), only the second clause gua^3 a^4 $m^{5\text{-}4}$ $tsia\textipa{P}^8$ 'I also didn't want to eat (it)' involves the adverb a^4 'also'.

The coordinands in verbal and clausal conjunction can also be juxtaposed without overt marking of a coordinator, as in (18) and (19).

(18) 伊　　規日　　　　陪　　　　儂　　食　　陪　　　　儂　　啉
　　　i^1　$kui^1\text{-}let^8$　$pue^{2\text{-}4}$　$la\eta^4$　$tsia\textipa{P}^8$　$pue^{2\text{-}4}$　$la\eta^4$　$liəm^1$
　　　3SG　whole-day　accompany　other　eat　accompany　other　drink
　　　'He eats and drinks with other people all the time.'

(19) 蜀　　　隻　　　伯　　其，　蜀　　　隻　　　佢　　同事　　　　其
　　　$tsit^{8\text{-}4}$　$tsia\textipa{P}^{7\text{-}8}$　lan^3　e^2　$tsit^{8\text{-}4}$　$tsia\textipa{P}^{7\text{-}8}$　en^1　$tɔŋ^{2\text{-}4}sɯ^5$　e^2
　　　one　CL　1PL　GEN　one　CL　3PL　colleague　GEN
　　　'One (duck) is ours, and the other one belongs to his colleague.'

In (18), the verb phrases $pue^{2\text{-}4}$ $la\eta^4$ $tsia\textipa{P}^8$ 'eat with other people' and $pue^{2\text{-}4}$ $la\eta^4$ $liəm^1$ 'drink with other people' are connected without a coordinator, as too in (19) for the two clauses $tsit^{8\text{-}4}$ $tsia\textipa{P}^{7\text{-}8}$ lan^3 e^2 'one is ours' and $tsit^{8\text{-}4}$ $tsia\textipa{P}^{7\text{-}8}en^1$ $tɔŋ^{2\text{-}4}sɯ^5$ e^2 'one belongs to his colleague'. As shown by these two examples, when a coordinator is not used, the coordinands in verbal and clausal conjunction usually have similar structures, though this is not obligatory.

To summarize, the forms which these coordinate structures take, according to the constituency, is as follows:
(i)   NP (Coord.) NP
(ii) VP (Coord.) VP
(iii) Clause (Coord.) Clause
(iv) NP (ADV) Clause, (NP) ADV Clause

21.3 Disjunction

In Hui'an, the coordinators $aʔ^8$ 抑/$aʔ^{8\text{-}4}si^4$ 抑是 'or' are used for all syntactic types of coordinand in the case of disjunctive coordination. Examples are given in (20) – (22).

(20) 阿姨　　　抑(是)　　阿舅　　　卜　　　來
　　　a^1-i^2　　　$aʔ^{8\text{-}4}(si^4)$　　a^1-ku^4　　$boʔ^{7\text{-}8}$　lai^2
　　　PREF-aunt　or　　　PREF-uncle　want　come
　　　(a) 'Aunt or uncle will come.'
　　　(b) 'Will aunt or uncle come?'

(21) 澹　　　抑(是)　　無　　　　澹
　　　tam^2　$aʔ^{8\text{-}4}(si^4)$　$bo^{2\text{-}4}$　tam^2
　　　wet　　or　　　　not.have　wet
　　　'wet or not'

(22) 汝　　過來　　　　抑(是)　　我　　過去
　　　lu^3　$kə^{5\text{-}3}lai^2$　$aʔ^{8\text{-}4}(si^4)$　gua^3　$kə^{5\text{-}3}khu^5$
　　　2SG　come.over　or　　　　1SG　go.over
　　　'Do you want to come to my place, or I go to your place?'

In (20), the coordinators $aʔ^8(^{\text{-}4}si^4)$ are used to connect the nouns a^1i^2 'aunt' and a^1ku^4 'uncle', and there are two possible interpretations for the whole sentence: on the one hand, it can be regarded as a declarative sentence as in (20a); on the other hand, it can serve as an alternative interrogative, as in (20b). It should be mentioned, however, that the interpretation for (20b) is more common than the one for (20a). In (21), the coordinators $aʔ^8(^{\text{-}4}si^4)$ connect the adjective tam^2 'wet' and its negative form $bo^{2\text{-}4}$ tam^2 'not wet'. In (22), the two coordinands connected by $aʔ^8(^{\text{-}4}si^4)$ are represented by two clauses, i.e. lu^3 $kə^{5\text{-}3}lai^2$ 'you come to my place' and gua^3 $kə^{5\text{-}3}khu^5$ 'I go to your place'. As illustrated by these examples, a coordinator is always required for disjunction in Hui'an, unlike conjunctive coordination examined in §21.2 above.

Another way to express (20a) in Hui'an is shown in example (23) below.

(23) 阿姨　　　　卜　　　來，
　　 a¹-i²　　　 *boʔ⁷⁻⁸*　 *lai²*
　　 PREF-aunt　want　come
　　 無　　　就(是)　　　　阿舅　　　卜　　　來
　　 bo²　　 *tsiu⁵⁻⁴(si⁴)*　 *a¹-ku⁴*　 *boʔ⁷⁻⁸*　 *lai²*
　　 not.have　then(be)　 PREF-uncle　want　come
　　 'Aunt or uncle will come.' (lit. Aunt will come, if not, then uncle will come)

In (23), *bo²*, originally a verb meaning 'not have, not possess', is used here as a conjunction to mean 'if not, otherwise'.

21.4 Adversative coordination

In Hui'an, the typical adversative coordinator is *m⁵⁻⁴koʔ⁸* 'but', which is used to link two clauses, as in (24).

(24) 伊　 也　 會　 洗，
　　 i¹　 *a⁴*　 *e⁴*　 *sue³*
　　 3SG　also　can　wash
　　 唔口　　　伊　 也　 無　　　　清氣
　　 m⁵⁻⁴koʔ⁸　 *i¹*　 *a⁴*　 *bo²⁻⁴*　 *tshiŋ¹khi⁵*
　　 but　　　　3SG　also　not.have　clean
　　 'He is also willing to wash (the dishes), but he doesn't get them clean.'

In (24), the coordinator *m⁵⁻⁴koʔ⁸* is used to introduce the statement *i¹ a⁴ bo²⁻⁴ tshiŋ¹khi⁵* 'he doesn't get them clean' (lit. he also not clean), which is in contrast to the preceding statement *i¹ a⁴ e⁴ sue³* 'he is also willing to wash (the dishes)'.

　　The coordinator for adversative coordination in Mandarin Chinese, i.e. *dànshì* 但是 'but', can also be found in daily conversation in the contemporary Hui'an dialect, as in (25). However, it is confined to the younger generation and much less used in general than *m⁵⁻⁴koʔ⁸*.

(25) 伊　 無　　　　說　　　　是，
　　 i¹　 *bo²⁻⁴*　 *səʔ⁷⁻⁸*　 *si⁴*
　　 3SG　not.have　say　　　be
　　 但是　　　　逐個　　　　禮　　　知影　　　　咯
　　 tan⁵⁻⁴si⁴　 *tak⁸⁻⁴-e²*　 *tsau²⁻⁴*　 *tsai¹iã³*　 *lo⁰*
　　 but　　　　 every-CL　　all　　　know　　　SFP
　　 'She didn't admit (it), but everyone knew (it).'

In most cases, however, the two clauses are juxtaposed without a coordinator, as in (26).

(26) 開始　　懷　　野　　緊,　後尾　　等　　遘　　蠻　　久
　　　khai¹si³　huai²　ia³⁻²　ken³　au⁴bə³　tan³　a⁵⁻³　ban²⁻⁴　ku³
　　　begin　　those　quite　fast　back　　wait　CM　rather　long
　　　'The things went quite fast at the beginning, but later (I) waited for a long time.'

When the coordinands in adversative coordination are encoded by a structurally equivalent verb phrase, as in (27), the coordinator is not required.

(27) 汝　　有　　房　　　無　　　　車
　　　lu³　u⁴　paŋ²　bo²⁻⁴　tshia¹
　　　2SG　have　room　not.have　vehicle
　　　'You have a house, but don't have a car.'

In (27), the two verb phrases u^4 $paŋ^2$ 'have a house' and bo^{2-4} $tshia^1$ 'don't have a car' are connected without a coordinator. Semantically speaking, the second one is in contrast to the first one.

21.5 Summary

This chapter has examined three main semantic types of coordination, i.e. conjunction, disjunction and adversative coordination. Coordination involving non-clausal units has also been touched upon for the purposes of comparison.

Different coordinators are required for nominal and verbal/clausal conjunction. Either $kaʔ^7$ 合 'and' or $kiau^1$ 交 'and' is used in nominal conjunction, while the coordinator $koʔ^7$ 佮 'and' is used in both verbal and clausal conjunction. Verbal and clausal conjunction may also be marked by the adverb a^4 也 'also'. Nonetheless, the coordinands in both nominal and verbal/clausal conjunction can be juxtaposed without a coordinator.

The coordinators $aʔ^8$ 抑/$aʔ^{8-4}si^4$ 抑是 'or' are used for all syntactic types of coordinand in the case of disjunctive coordination.

The typical adversative coordinator is $m^{5-4}koʔ^8$ 'but', which is used to link two clauses. The coordinator for adversative coordination in Mandarin Chinese, i.e. dànshì 但是 'but', can also be found in daily conversation in the contemporary Hui'an dialect, but is confined to the younger generation and much less used in general than $m^{5-4}koʔ^8$. In most cases, however, the two clauses are juxtaposed without a coordinator. When the coordinands in adversative coordination are encoded by a structurally equivalent verb phrase, the coordinator is not required.

22 Relative clauses

22.1 Introduction

Early studies on relative clauses focus on English. The term 'relative clause' in English refers to a clause that modifies a noun (phrase) and which involves the following characteristics: (a) contains a finite verb; (b) delimits the potential referents of the noun modified, or presents new information about an already identified entity, i.e. a distinction between respectively a restrictive relative clause and a non-restrictive relative clause; and (c) the noun modified (i.e. the head noun) is coreferential with an argument of the relative clause (cf. Comrie 1989; Tang 2005). This definition of relative clause tends to be syntactically based, and thus is inadequate to identify the relative clause in other languages or even to investigate the relative clause from a cross-linguistic perspective. Due to this limitation, a semantically-based definition of relative clause, such as that put forward by Song (2001), is required. According to Song (2001:211), the relative clause 'consists of two components: the head noun and the restricting clause. The semantic function of the head noun is to establish a set of entities, which may be called the domain of relativization...whereas that of the restricting clause is to identify a subset of the domain...by imposing a semantic condition on the domain of relativization referred to by the head noun'. The following is an example of the relative clause provided by Song (2001:211).

(1) *The girl whom Miss Edge coached won the game.*

The domain of relativization "is denoted by the head noun *the girl*. This domain of relativization is then 'narrowed down'...to the only entity that can satisfy the condition expressed by the restricting clause *whom Miss Edge coached*".

Similar definitions for the relative clause can also be found in some early and important studies on relative clauses, e.g. Keenan & Comrie (1977), Keenan (1985) and Comrie (1981, 1989) which all focus mainly on this restrictive type and only marginally discuss the less common non-restrictive types. In fact, the term 'relative clause' is more often used to refer to the restricting clause, as indicated by the traditional syntactically based definition of the English relative clause and more recent studies on the relative clause such as Givón (1990) and Dryer (2013). Take (1) as an example. The term 'relative clause' nowadays usually refers to the

---

Note: A preliminary version of this chapter also appeared in Chen (2017).

https://doi.org/10.1515/9781501511868-022

restricting clause *whom Miss Edge coached*, while the nominal construction consisting of the head noun and the relative clause, i.e. *the girl whom Miss Edge coached*, is regarded as the relative clause construction.

Note that the definition of the relative clause as proposed by Song (2001) is a definition of the restrictive relative clause, which is our focus in this chapter. For the purposes of comparison, an example of a non-restrictive relative clause is given in (2).

(2) *The man, who had arrived yesterday, left this morning.* (Comrie 1989:138)

In example (1) above, the restrictive relative clause (RC) *whom Miss Edge coached* is used to help the addressee identify the girl in question. In (2), however, the speaker assumes that the addressee can identify, this time, the man in question, and the non-restrictive relative clause *who had arrived yesterday* is only used to give the addressee an added piece of information about an already identified entity, rather than help identify that entity (Comrie 1989:138).

Some nice work has been done on relative clauses in Chinese, e.g. Matthews & Yip (2011), Fang (2004), Liu (2005a), Tang (2005) and Xu (2007) (see Fang (2004) and Tang (2005) for a review of studies on relative clauses in Chinese). These studies focus on several Chinese varieties such as Beijing Mandarin, Guanzhong Mandarin, Hong Kong Cantonese and Suzhou Wu. There are, however, still several important questions that need further research and discussion, as revealed by the following set.

(i) It has been argued that the basic relative clause in Beijing Mandarin and Suzhou Wu is the relative clause marked by the general attributive marker (i.e. *de* 的 and *kəʔ*葛, respectively) and the basic relative clause in Yue is the one marked by a demonstrative–classifier phrase, while Guanzhong Mandarin tends to use the relative clause marked by a demonstrative (or both a demonstrative and the attributive marker *de* 的) (Liu 2005a; Tang 2005). Can these three types cover all the possibilities in Chinese? Can the basic relative clause in other branches of Chinese belong to a different type? In fact, we will show that there are also zero-marked relative clause constructions in Hui'an, not to mention postnominal ones (see Matthews & Yip 2011 as well on zero-marked relative clauses in Cantonese).

(ii) According to previous typological studies, SVO languages have a distinct preference to use the head-initial type of relative clause, while Chinese (exemplified by Chinese varieties such as Mandarin, Hakka and Yue) is one of the few SVO languages that uses the head-final type of relative clause (see

Dryer 2005a). Fang (2004) found that there exists a non-restrictive head-initial type of relative clause in Beijing Mandarin which is introduced by the relative pronoun *tā* 他 (< 3SG). The question to ask in this case is whether the restrictive head-initial type of relative clause in Chinese also exists, especially for those varieties involving a greater number of characteristics typical of SOV languages such as Min and Wu? In addition, is there a head-internal type of relative clause in Chinese?

(iii) Traditional syntactically-based definitions of the relative clause require the head noun being coreferential with an argument in the relative clause, and thus the relative clause is termed 'argument relative clause'. When the semantically-based definition of relative clause is used, what other kinds of relative clause can be attested in Chinese, besides the argument relative clause?

(iv) The demonstrative elements in Guanzhong Mandarin can constitute a head-less relative clause [relative clause (*de* 的) – demonstrative element] (Tang 2005). The question to ask is whether demonstrative elements in other Chinese varieties can have a similar function. In other words, can similar constructions be found that can be regarded as head-less relative clause constructions?

In this chapter, we attempt to answer some of these questions by examining the restrictive relative clause in Hui'an in terms of the following four parameters: (a) the relativization marker used (§22.2); (b) the position of the head noun relative to the relative clause (§22.3); (c) the role and encoding of the head noun in the relative clause (§22.4); and (d) the role and encoding of the head noun in the main clause (§22.5).

22.2 The relativization markers

Liu (2005) has put forward two syntactic criteria for identifying relativization markers which involve a substitution test: (a) if a relativization marker is used which does not belong to the attributive DE type as in Mandarin, the latter will not be necessary; and (b) once a relativization marker is deleted which does not belong to the attributive DE type, another relativization marker such as the attributive DE type is needed to replace it. We will apply these two criteria to our Hui'an data in the discussion below. Liu also states that relativization markers in Chinese include the *de* 的-type general attributive marker, demonstratives (e.g. in

Beijing Mandarin and Yue), demonstrative complexes[1] (e.g. in Beijing Mandarin and Yue), classifiers (e.g. in Wu), and pre-postpositional compounds (e.g. in Wu) (see Liu 2005 for more details). All these types of relativization marker except pre-postpositional compounds can be attested in Hui'an. In addition, relative clauses in Hui'an can be zero-marked in that there is no special relativization marker to indicate that the constituent is a relative clause. Comparatively speaking, relative clauses marked by demonstratives (or demonstrative complexes) and zero-marked relative clauses are more common than the other types. This section will focus on relativization markers.

In terms of relativization markers (whether a relativization marker is used (i.e. zero-marked or not), and which one), relative clauses in Hui'an fall into five sub-types (following the syntactic criteria put forward by Liu (2005)):
(a) relative clauses marked by the attributive marker e^2 其 (i.e. §22.2.1)
 [VP + e^2 其 $_{RM}$]$_{RC}$ - NP$_{HEAD}$
 e^2 其 is a typical relativization marker
(b) relative clauses marked by demonstratives (i.e. §22.2.2)
 RC - [DEM$_{RM}$ + NP]$_{HEAD}$
 Unlike e^2 其, DEM constitutes a part of the head noun and simultaneously functions as a relativization marker.
(c) relative clauses marked by demonstrative complexes (i.e. §22.2.3)
 RC - [[DEM + CL]$_{RM}$ + NP]$_{HEAD}$
 'DEM + CL' constitutes a part of the head noun and simultaneously functions as a relativization marker.
(d) relative clauses marked by classifiers (i.e. §22.2.4)
 RC - [CL$_{RM}$ + NP]$_{HEAD}$
 CL constitutes a part of the head noun and simultaneously functions as a relativization marker.
(e) zero-marked relative clauses (i.e. §22.2.5)
 Zero-marked relative clauses structurally fall into three subtypes:
 (i) RC - DEM$_{HEAD}$
 (ii) RC - [DEM + CL]$_{HEAD}$
 (iii) RC - COMMON NOUN$_{HEAD}$

In §22.2.5, we explain why (e-i) and (e-ii) are regarded as zero-marked relative clauses. Why has it proved necessary to give an explanation here? Because similar structures in Guanzhong Mandarin are regarded as headless relative clauses

---

[1] The term 'demonstrative complexes' here is used to refer to the Chinese term *zhǐliàng duǎnyǔ* 指量短語 (lit. demonstrative classifier(or measure word) phrases) in Liu (2005).

in Tang (2005), where Tang argues that demonstratives (or demonstrative complexes) in (e-i) and (e-ii) are relativization markers as they are found in structures like (b) and (c). We are not in agreement with Tang, at least for the data from the Hui'an dialect.

In §22.5.2, we focus on the encoding of the head noun in the main clause. In terms of the encoding of the head noun in the main clause, relative clauses are usually divided into headed and headless types. Citko (2004) identifies another type, i.e. light-headed relatives. In this section (§22.5.2), we point out that some of the zero-marked relative clauses in (e) above, more specifically, the types (i) and (ii), are light-headed relative clauses. Based on this, we give more examples of light-headed relatives in Hui'an, followed by examples of headed and headless relatives.

22.2.1 Attributive marker *e² 其*

As with Mandarin Chinese and other Chinese dialects, the attributive marker in Hui'an (i.e. *e²* 其, the counterpart of Mandarin *de* 的) can be used as a relativization marker. When functioning as a relativization marker, *e²* is in neutral tone, i.e. *e⁰*. The relative clause construction with *e⁰* typically indicates a general referent with its head noun encoded by a generic noun. This can be exemplified by (3) below.

(3) 租　其　厝
   tsɔ¹　e⁰　tshu⁵
   rent　RM　house
   'rented houses'

In (3), *e⁰* functions as a relativization marker, and the bare noun *tshu⁵* 'house' functions as the head noun. This example usually refers to a subset of houses (i.e. rented houses) in general, rather than a specific entity.

In a certain context, however, the relative clause construction with *e⁰* may refer to a specific entity, as in (4).

(4) 口　是　伵　租　其　厝
   tse²　si⁴　en¹　tsɔ¹　e⁰　tshu⁵
   this　be　3PL　rent　RM　house
   'This is the house they rented.'

Example (4) is a copular construction, in which the predicate is encoded by the relative clause construction en^1 $tsɔ^1$ e^0 $tshu^5$ 'the house they rented'. In this example, the speaker is talking about a specific house that someone rented. In other words, the relative clause construction can refer here to a specific entity, rather than a subset of houses.

22.2.2 Demonstratives

In this type of relative clause construction, the head noun consists of a demonstrative and a noun, in which the demonstrative simultaneously functions as a relativization marker, according to the criteria in Liu (2005). The structure is as follows: RC - [DEM$_{RM}$ + NP]$_{HEAD}$.

First of all, before treating this type in more depth, the five sets of nominal demonstratives used in Hui'an are given in the following table, reproduced from chapter 5.

Tab. 22-1: Nominal demonstratives in the Hui'an dialect

	Proximal	Distal
1	$tsit^7$ 即 (this)	hit^7 迄 (that)
2	$tsat^8$ (this one)	hat^8 (that one)
3	$tsuai^2$ 撮 (these) (this)	$huai^2$ 懷 (those) (that)
4	tse^2 (this kind of) (generic)	$hə^2$ (that kind of) (generic)
5	$tsiɔŋ^{3\text{-}2}e^2$ 種其 (this kind of) (generic)	$hiɔŋ^{3\text{-}2}e^2$ 向其 (that kind of) (generic)

The demonstratives $tsit^7$ and hit^7 require a classifier (or a measure word, sometimes also a numeral) to form demonstrative complexes (see the following section for their uses as a relativization marker). This section focuses on the other four sets of demonstratives, which can directly modify a noun, and function as a relativization marker, as illustrated by (5) – (7).

(5) [VP + IO + DO]$_{RC}$ - [DEM$_{RM}$ + NP]$_{HEAD}$
 教 汝 語文 口 老師
 $ka^{5\text{-}3}$ $lɯ^3$ $gu^{3\text{-}2}bun$ $\underline{hat^{8\text{-}4}}$ lau^4su^1
 teach 2SG Chinese that teacher
 'the teacher who teaches you Chinese'

(6) a. [VP]$_{RC}$ - [DEM$_{RM}$ + NP]$_{HEAD}$ - VP
　　　[翕]　　[懷　　相]　　與　　恁　　爸仔　　　看
　　　hiəp^7　 huai^2　siɔŋ^5　khɔ$^{5-4}$　len$^{3-2}$　pa^2-a^0　 khuã^5
　　　take　　 those　picture　give　 2PL　father-NM　look
　　　'Have your father look at the pictures that (you) took.'

　　b. VP - [DEM + NP]$_{OBJECT}$
　　　翕　　　懷　　相　　　用　　　蠻儕　　　　時間
　　　hiəp$^{7-8}$　huai^2　siɔŋ^5　iŋ$^{5-4}$　ban$^{2-4}$tsue$^{5-4}$　si$^{2-4}$ kan^1
　　　take　　those　picture　use　　much　　　　time
　　　'It takes a lot of time to take those pictures.'

(7) a. [NP + VP]$_{RC}$ - [DEM$_{RM}$ + NP]$_{HEAD}$
　　　[佢　　買]　　[口　　桌]　　恰　　　　　　貴
　　　en^1　bue^3　 hə^2　 toʔ^7　 khaʔ$^{7-8}$　　　kui^5
　　　3PL　buy　　that　table　comparatively　expensive
　　　'The kind of table they bought is more expensive.'

　　b. NP - VP - [DEM + NP]$_{OBJECT}$
　　　佢　　買　　　口　　桌　　真　　　闇
　　　en^1　bue$^{3-2}$　hə^2　toʔ^7　tsen^1　am^1
　　　3PL　buy　　　that　table　really　stupid
　　　'They are really stupid to buy that kind of table.'

In (5), the relative clause *ka$^{5-3}$ lɯ^3 gɯ$^{3-2}$bun^2* 'teach you Chinese' precedes the head noun *hat$^{8-4}$ lau^{4}sɯ^1* 'that teacher', which consists of the demonstrative *hat^8* 'that' and the bare noun *lau^{4}sɯ^1* 'teacher'. If the demonstrative *hat^8* is deleted, this example is no longer a relative clause construction, unless another relativization marker (e.g. the attributive marker *e^2*) is added. In other words, the demonstrative *hat^8* here simultaneously functions as a relativization marker, as well as being part of the head noun. This is different from the attributive marker *e^2* in (3) and (4) above, which is used only as a relativization marker, but not as part of the head noun.

The verb *hiəp^7* followed by the noun phrase *huai^2 siɔŋ^5* in example (6) also has two possible interpretations. In (6a), the noun phrase *huai^2 siɔŋ^5* 'those pictures' serves as a head noun, following the relative clause encoded by the bare verb *hiəp^7* 'take'. When deleting the demonstrative *huai^2* 'those', *hiəp$^{7-8}$ siɔŋ^5* only expresses 'take pictures', but not 'the pictures taken', unless another relativization marker such as *e^2* 其 is used. In other words, the demonstrative *huai^2* here, just like *hat⁸* in (5), simultaneously functions as a relativization marker, besides being part of the head noun. In (6b), however, the noun phrase *huai² siɔŋ⁵* 'those pictures' functions as an object of the verb *hiəp⁷* 'take'.

Comparatively speaking, the first interpretation (i.e. as a relative clause construction) is more common. This can be supported by the fact that the utterance in (6a) is a real recorded example from our spoken data, while that in (6b) is elicited. One of the reasons is that the definite object of a verb in Hui'an tends to occur before the verb functioning as a topic. The difference between these two interpretations relies on the presence or absence of tone sandhi on the verb *hiəp⁷* 'take': the verb is realized in its citation tone in (6a), but realized in its sandhi tone in (6b) (see chapter 2). This difference in tone is also applicable to other similar constructions (see also §22.2.3 and §22.3.2).

The verb *bue³* followed by the noun phrase *hə² toʔ⁷* in example (7) also tends to be interpreted as a relative clause construction, as in (7a). The demonstrative *hə²* 'that kind of' is a part of the head noun *hə² toʔ⁷* 'that kind of table', and simultaneously serves as a relativization marker. In contrast to this, the noun phrase *hə² toʔ⁷* functions as an object of the verb *bue³* 'buy', as in (7b), shown by the tone sandhi in operation.

The relative clause construction expresses different referential meanings according to the demonstrative used. For example, the relative clause construction refers to a specific entity (i.e. that teacher) in (5), plural entities (i.e. those pictures) in (6), and a category (i.e. that kind of table) in (7).

In all these three examples, the relativization marker is encoded by a distal demonstrative. In fact, the distal demonstratives are more commonly used as a relativization marker than the proximal demonstratives, though the proximal ones are also possible, as illustrated by example (8), where the proximal demonstrative *tsat⁸* 'this' constitutes part of the head noun *tsat⁸⁻⁴ lau⁴suɯ¹* 'this teacher' and simultaneously functions as a relativization marker. Note that proximal demonstratives (both singular and plural ones) as relativization markers are also attested in some other Chinese varieties such as Beijing Mandarin (cf. Liu 2005).

(8) [VP + IO + DO]$_{RC}$ - [DEM$_{RM}$ + NP]$_{HEAD}$
 教   我   語文   口   老師
 ka⁵⁻³ gua³ guɯ³⁻²bun² tsat⁸⁻⁴ lau⁴suɯ¹
 teach 1SG   Chinese   this   Teacher
 'the teacher who teaches me Chinese'

In this type of relative clause construction (RC - [DEM$_{RM}$ + NP]$_{HEAD}$), such as (5) – (8) above, the attributive marker e^2 cannot be inserted between the relative clause and the head noun (see the following section for details).

22.2.3 Demonstrative complexes

As mentioned above, demonstrative complexes in Hui'an can also simultaneously function as relativization markers. Two examples are given in (9) and (10).

(9) a. [NP + VP]$_{RC}$ - [[DEM + CL]$_{RM}$ + NP]$_{HEAD}$
　　　[汝　　買]　　迄本　　　　冊
　　　lu^3　bue^3　hit$^{7\text{-}8}$-pun$^{3\text{-}2}$　tshe?^{7}
　　　2SG　buy　　that-CL　　book
　　　'that book you bought'

　　b. NP - [VP - [DEM + CL + NP]$_{OBJECT}$]
　　　汝　　[買　　迄本　　　　冊]
　　　lu^3　bue$^{3\text{-}2}$　hit$^{7\text{-}8}$-pun$^{3\text{-}2}$　tshe?^{7}
　　　2SG　buy　　that-CL　　book
　　　'You buy that book.'

(10) [NP + VP + O]$_{RC}$ - [[DEM + CL]$_{RM}$ + NP]$_{HEAD}$
　　阮　　下　　電視　　　迄坲　　　桌
　　gun^3　khe^4　ten$^{5\text{-}4}$si^4　hit$^{7\text{-}8}$-tə$^{5\text{-}3}$　to?^{7}
　　1PL　put　television　that-CL　table
　　'that table where we put the television'

As with example (6) above, example (9) has two possible interpretations. In (9a), the noun phrase hit$^{7\text{-}8}$pun$^{3\text{-}2}$ tshe?^{7} 'that book' serves as a head noun, following the relative clause lu^3 bue^3 'you buy'. In (9b), the noun phrase hit$^{7\text{-}8}$pun$^{3\text{-}2}$ tshe?^{7} 'that book' functions as an object of the verb bue^3 'buy'. In (10), the relative clause gun^3 khe^4 ten$^{5\text{-}4}$si^4 'we put the television' precedes the head noun hit$^{7\text{-}8}$tə$^{5\text{-}3}$ to?^{7} 'that table'. In both examples (9a) and (10), the demonstrative complexes (i.e. hit$^{7\text{-}8}$pun^3 and hit$^{7\text{-}8}$tə^5) constitute part of the head noun, and simultaneously function as a relativization marker.

In the function of a relativization marker, the demonstrative in demonstrative complexes is typically a distal one, as in (9) and (10) above. However, we also find examples of the proximal demonstrative tsit^7 即 'this', as in (11).

(11) A1: 伊　　迄個　　　　水空　　　　　仩咧　　　　半中間
　　　　i^1　　hit$^{7\text{-}8}$-e$^{2\text{-}4}$　tsui$^{3\text{-}2}$khaŋ^1　tu^{4}le$ʔ^{7\text{-}8}$　puã$^{5\text{-}3}$-tiɔŋ^{1}uin^1
　　　　3SG　　that-CL　　drain　　　　be.at　　　half-middle
　　　　'That drain is in the middle.'
　　B:　汝　　　說　　　房　　　裡腹　　　迄個
　　　　lu^3　　sə$ʔ^{7\text{-}8}$　paŋ^2　lai^{4}pak^7　hit$^{7\text{-}8}$-e^2
　　　　2SG　　say　　　room　　inside　　that-CL
　　　　'Are you talking about that (drain) inside the room?'
　　A2: AUX - COP - [[VP]$_{RC}$ - [[DEM + CL]$_{RM}$ + NP]$_{HEAD}$ - OM - VP
　　　　應該　　　　是　　洗身　　　　　即個　　　　　空　　　共　　　圍　　　　（起來）
　　　　iŋ^{1}kai^1　si^4　sue$^{3\text{-}2}$-sen^1　tsit$^{7\text{-}8}$-e$^{2\text{-}4}$　khaŋ^1　ka$^{5\text{-}1}$　ui^2　　khai^0
　　　　should　　be　　wash-body　this-CL　　drain　　OM　　enclose　RVC
　　　　'This drain for taking a shower should be enclosed.'

In (11), speaker A is talking about a drain inside the room in A1, but addressee B is not sure which drain this is. Thus, in A2, speaker A uses a relative clause construction (i.e. sue$^{3\text{-}2}$sen^1 tsit$^{7\text{-}8}$e$^{2\text{-}4}$ khaŋ^1 'this drain for taking a shower') to make the referent identifiable. In this case, the proximal demonstrative complex tsit$^{7\text{-}8}$e^2 'this' constitutes part of the head noun tsit$^{7\text{-}8}$e$^{2\text{-}4}$ khaŋ^1 'this drain', and is simultaneously used as a relativization marker. This example differs from the examples above in that the referent encoded by the relative clause construction has been mentioned in the previous discourse. We suggest that this is one reason why a proximal demonstrative (rather than a distal demonstrative) is used.

Relative clause constructions in (9) – (11) all refer to a specific entity, that is, 'that book', 'that table' and 'this drain'. These three examples involve two specific classifiers (pun^3 and tə^5) and the general classifier e^2. The following is an example of the classifier tsiɔŋ^3 種 'kind'.

(12)　[VP + O]$_{RC}$ - [[DEM + CL]$_{RM}$ + NP]$_{HEAD}$
　　　下　　　　電腦　　　　　迄種　　　　　　桌
　　　khe^4　ten$^{5\text{-}4}$lo^3　hit$^{7\text{-}8}$-tsiɔŋ$^{3\text{-}2}$　toʔ^7
　　　put　　　computer　　that-kind　　　table
　　　'that kind of table where we put a computer'

This example refers to a category, that is, 'that kind of table', rather than a specific entity.

A numeral (> 1) can be inserted between the demonstrative and the classifier, as in (13) below. In this case, the relative clause construction refers to plural entities.

(13) [VP + O]_RC - [[DEM + NUM + CL]_RM + NP]_HEAD
今日　　來　　看　　厝　　即三個　　儂
kiã¹let⁸ lai²⁻⁴ khuã⁵⁻³ tshu⁵ tsit⁷⁻⁸-sã¹-e²⁻⁴ laŋ²
today　 come　 look　 house　 this-three-CL　 person
'these three persons who came to look at the apartment today'

In Mandarin Chinese, the relativization marker *de* 的 can be followed by a demonstrative (complex) as shown by (14) and (15) below.

(14) [NP + VP + *de* _RM]_RC - [DEM + NP]_HEAD
我們　　住　　的　　那　　胡同兒
wŏmen　 zhù　 <u>de</u>　 nà　 hútòngr
1PL　　 live　 RM　 that　 alley
'that alley we live in'

(15) [NP + VP + *de* _RM]_RC - [DEM + CL + NP]_HEAD
我　　看到　　的　　那　　個　　學生
wŏ　 kàn-dào　 <u>de</u>　 nà　 ge　 xuéshēng
1SG　 look-PVC　 RM　 that　 CL　 student
'that student I saw'

In both these two examples, the relativization marker *de* and the demonstrative *nà* 'that' co-occur in the same string. In (14), the demonstrative *nà* constitutes a part of the head noun *nà hútòngr* 'that alley'. In this case, the demonstrative *nà* does not function as a relativization marker, due to the presence of the common relativization marker *de*. Similarly, the demonstrative *nà* with the general classifier *ge* in (15) serves as a modifier of the noun *xuéshēng* 'student', and does not function as a relativization marker.

Now, several questions arise. Can the relativization marker *e²* in Hui'an, the counterpart of Mandarin *de*, also be followed by a demonstrative? Can relative clause constructions in Hui'an take the form of [[NP + VP + *e²*_RM]_RC - [DEM(+CL) + NP]_HEAD], like Mandarin examples (14) and (15) above? If yes, is it the source of the relative clause construction marked by demonstratives or demonstrative complexes such as (5) – (13) in Hui'an, i.e. [[NP + VP + *e²*_RM]_RC - [DEM(+CL) + NP]_HEAD] > [[NP + VP]_RC - [[DEM(+CL)]_RM + NP]_HEAD]?

Generally speaking, unlike Mandarin Chinese, the Hui'an dialect does not use such relative clause constructions as in (14) and (15), where the relativization marker *de* is followed by a noun phrase which consists of a demonstrative (complex) and a noun. In other words, in Hui'an, when the relative clause is marked by the attributive marker e^2 其, the head noun is not encoded by a demonstrative (complex) and a noun. As mentioned in §22.2.1 above, in this type of relative clause construction in Hui'an, the head noun is typically encoded by a bare noun expressing a generic meaning. When the head noun involves a demonstrative (complex) and a noun, such as (5) – (13), the demonstrative (complex) simultaneously functions as a relativization marker, and thus the relative clause construction does not require another marker such as the attributive e^2. It would be unnatural to add an e^2 before the demonstrative in (5) - (13).

In fact, we do find examples of relative clause constructions in which the relativization marker e^2 is followed by a demonstrative, as shown in (16) below. However, the demonstrative such as the plural demonstrative $huai^2$ in (16) is itself used as the head noun, that is, it is not followed by a noun like those given in Mandarin Chinese in (14) and (15) (see also chapter 5 on demonstratives and their pronominal use).

(16) [VP + $e^0{}_{RM}$]$_{RC}$ - DEM$_{HEAD}$
　　　扣　　　其　　懷
　　　khio⁵　　e⁰　 huai²
　　　deduct　RM　those
　　　'those that were deducted'

In (16), e^0 serves as a relativization marker, and the plural demonstrative $huai^2$ alone functions as the head noun, rather than constitutes a part of the head noun. Such an example is actually not common in daily conversation. Typically, even when the head noun is encoded only by a demonstrative, the relativization marker e^0 is not required. In other words, the relativization marker e^0 in (16) can be deleted, that is, forming $khio^5\ huai^2$, which can also express 'those that were deducted' (see also §22.5). Furthermore, this example was produced by a younger speaker, and thus may involve influence from the use of de in Mandarin Chinese. The emergence of such a type as in (16) may be due to the simple syntactic structure involved here. In this example, both the relative clause and the head noun are encoded by a monosyllabic word, i.e. $khio^5$ 'deduct' and $huai^2$ 'those', respectively, and the form without the marker e^0 (i.e. $khio^5\ huai^2$) involves two possible interpretations. In other words, the marker e^0 here shows that a relative clause construction, rather than a verb-object construction, is involved.

22.2.4 Classifiers

In some Chinese varieties such as Wu and Yue, the claim has been made that classifiers can be used alone as relativization markers (see Matthews & Yip 2011; Liu 2005). In this section, we will provide arguments in favor of the very same use of classifiers in Hui'an. First, an example from Cantonese Yue is given in (17).

(17) [[NP + VP]$_{RC}$ - [CL$_{RM}$ + NP]$_{HEAD}$]NP - VP

我哋	喺	法國	食	啲	嘢
ngóhdeih	hái	Faatgwok	sihk	dī	yéh
we	in	France	eat	CL	stuff

幾	好食	㗎
géi	hóu-sihk	ga
quite	good-eat	SFP

'The food we ate in France was pretty good.' (Matthews & Yip 2011:329)

In (17), the relative clause *ngóhdeih hái Faatgwok sihk* 'we ate in France' modifies the noun phrase *dī yéh* 'the food', in which the classifier *dī* can be regarded as a relativization marker.

The Hui'an dialect can also use a classifier as a relativization marker, as in (18).

(18) [[NP + VP]$_{RC}$ - [CL$_{RM}$ + NP]$_{HEAD}$]NP - SFP

我	看	本	冊	咧
gua³	khuã⁵	pun³⁻²	tshe˩⁷	le˨⁰
1SG	look	CL	book	SFP

'Where is the book I was reading?'

In (18), the relative clause *gua³ khuã⁵* 'I read' modifies the noun phrase *pun³⁻² tshe˩⁷* 'the book', which consists of the classifier *pun³* and the noun *tshe˩⁷* 'book'. Semantically speaking, the classifier *pun³* is used to express definite reference akin to English 'the' in the head noun 'the book'. There is an audible pause between the verb *khuã⁵* 'look' and the classifier *pun³*, rather than between the classifier *pun³* and the noun *tshe˩⁷* 'book'. This is consistent with the fact that the verb *khuã⁵* does not undergo tone sandhi, whereas the classifier *pun³* does clearly undergo tone sandhi. All these go to show that the classifier *pun³* constitutes a part of the head noun *pun³⁻² tshe˩⁷* 'the book'. Like demonstratives (or demonstrative complexes) mentioned above, the classifier *pun³* here can be regarded as simultaneously functioning as a relativization marker.

This type of relative clause construction normally refers to a specific and singular entity. For example, the relative clause construction *gua³ khuã⁵ pun³⁻² tsheʔ⁷* 'the book I was reading' in (18) refers to a specific book. Classifiers used as relativization markers generally code singular number in Hui'an. In addition, this type of relative clause construction is not common in daily conversation in Hui'an, unlike in other Chinese varieties such as Wu and Yue.

22.2.5 Zero-marked

As mentioned above, in Hui'an, a relativization marker such as *e²* is not required, when the head noun is encoded by a demonstrative, as in *khio⁵ huai²* 'those that were deducted', where the verb *khio⁵* 'deduct' and the demonstrative *huai²* 'those' can be regarded as the relative clause and the head noun respectively, without a relativization marker. More examples are given in (19) and (20).

(19) [VP$_{RC}$ - DEM$_{HEAD}$]$_{NP}$ - VP

（才罪）	口	咧	五中	咧	教册
tshə⁵	*hat⁸*	*leʔ⁷⁻⁸*	*gɔ⁴-tiɔŋ¹*	*leʔ⁷⁻⁸*	*ka⁵⁻³tsheʔ⁷*
look.for	that	at	five-middle.school	HAB	teach

'The one that (she) found (as her spouse) is a teacher at No. 5 Middle School.'

(20) [VP$_{RC}$ - [DEM + CL]$_{HEAD}$]$_{NP}$ - VP

恁	爸	掠	迄隻	加	珍	遘
len³⁻²	*pa²*	*liaʔ⁸*	*hit⁷⁻⁸-tsiaʔ⁷*	*ke¹*	*tin¹*	*a³*
2PL	father	catch	that-CL	more	sweet	EVC

'That (duck) that your father took (home) is tastier (than this one).'

In (19), the relative clause construction *tshə⁵ hat⁸* means 'the one that (she) found (as her spouse)'. In this case, the bare verb *tshə⁵* 'look for' functions as a relative clause, while the demonstrative *hat⁸* 'that' serves as a head noun. In (20), *len³⁻² pa² liaʔ⁸ hit⁷⁻⁸tsiaʔ⁷* is also a relative clause construction, literally meaning 'that (duck) your father caught'. In this case, *len³⁻² pa² liaʔ⁸* 'your father caught' functions as a relative clause, while the demonstrative complex *hit⁷⁻⁸tsiaʔ⁷* 'that one' is used as a head noun. In both cases, the relative clause and the head noun are combined together without a relativization marker, and thus the relative clause can be regarded as a zero-marked one.

In the following, we would like to explain why the relative clauses in (19) and (20) are regarded as zero-marked, and the demonstrative (or demonstrative-classifier phrase) is regarded as a head noun. First, it is not the case that the head noun has always to be a bare noun. Instead, the head noun is usually encoded by a noun phrase, as in (21) and (22), two examples from English.

(21) Do you know **the tall girl** who is standing by the gate?

(22) **My relatives** who came from France in the 19th century love pizza.

In (21), the head noun is *the tall girl*, consisting of the determiner *the*, the adjective *tall* and the bare noun *girl*. In (22), *my relatives*, formed by the possessive determiner *my* and the plural bare noun *relatives*, function as a head noun.

That the nominal demonstratives (and demonstrative complexes) in Hui'an can constitute a NP is shown by the fact that they are able to substitute for a noun (phrase), and thus can qualify as a head noun in a relative clause construction. This is different from attributive markers such as Mandarin *de* 的 and Hui'an e^2 其. Unlike the demonstratives (or demonstrative complexes), these attributive markers can neither be used alone, for example, nor substitute for a noun (phrase) as an argument in, for example, a simple declarative sentence. They are bound forms. In fact, in certain other languages, demonstratives can be used alone as a head noun, as in (23), an example from English (see also §22.5).

(23) Please send this message to those people who mean something to you, to **those** who have touched your life in one way or another.

In (23), there are two relative clause constructions. In the first relative clause construction, the head noun is *those people*, consisting of the plural demonstrative *those*, and the bare noun *people*. In the second relative clause construction, the head noun is encoded by the plural demonstrative *those*, due to the omission of the bare noun *people*. In both cases, *who* functions as a relativization marker.

Second, the demonstrative in this type of relative clause construction in Hui'an does not change or reduce its original grammatical meanings. For example, both the demonstrative hat^8 in (19) and the demonstrative complex $hit^{7\text{-}8}tsia\text{?}^7$ in (20) are still used to refer to a specific entity. When followed by a noun, the demonstrative (complex), due to the position in which it occurs, can be regarded as a relativization marker besides constituting a part of a head noun. However, when it is used alone as a pronominal demonstrative (that is, when it is an argument of the clause itself), the demonstrative (complex) is better regarded as a head noun, rather than as a relativization marker similar to Mandarin *de* 的 and Hui'an *e⁰*.

Third, in terms of prosody, in this type of relative clause construction in Hui'an, there is an obvious pause between the relative clause and the demonstrative (complex), while the last word of the relative clause retains its citation tone, rather than undergoing tone sandhi. These show that the relative clause and the demonstrative (complex) can be regarded as two independent parts of the relative clause construction as a whole. The relativization marker *e⁰* can nevertheless be regarded as a part of the relative clause, as shown by the fact that there is no obvious pause between the marker *e⁰* and its preceding verb phrase or clause.

Fourth, cross-linguistically speaking, other languages can be cited where the relative clause is clearly zero-marked, as in (24), an example from Japanese.

(24) [watasi   ga   kinoo   katta]   bon
     I   NOM   yesterday bought   book
     'the book I bought yesterday' (Matsumoto 2007:132)

Example (24) is a relative clause construction expressing 'the book I bought yesterday'. In this example, *watasi ga kinoo katta* 'I bought yesterday' functions as a relative clause, while *bon* 'book' serves as a head noun. There is no a relativization marker such as English *that/which*, or Mandarin *de*.

Thus, we tend to regard the two relative clause constructions in (19) and (20) in Hui'an as zero-marked relative clause constructions, in which the verb (or clause) functions as a relative clause, while the demonstrative (complex) functions as a head noun, but does not simultaneously serve as a relativization marker.

In zero-marked relative clause constructions, the head noun can also be encoded by a common noun, as in (25), rather than a demonstrative (complex).

(25) NP - [VP$_{RC}$ - NP$_{HEAD}$]$_{NP}$
     家己   艱苦   家庭   出來   囝仔
     kai$^{5-4}$ki^5   *kan^{1}khɔ$^{3-2}$*   *ke^{1}tiŋ^2*   *tshut^{7}lai^0*   *ken$^{3-2}$a^3*
     self   indigent   family   come.out   child
     '(He) himself is a poor child.'

In (25), the reflexive pronoun *kai$^{5-4}$ki^5* 'oneself' functions as a subject, while the relative clause construction *kan^{1}khɔ$^{3-2}$ ke^{1}tiŋ^2 tshut^{7}lai^0 ken$^{3-2}$a^3* 'the child that comes from a poor family' functions as a predicate. In this relative clause construction, the head noun is encoded by the common noun *ken$^{3-2}$a^3* 'child', and *kan¹khɔ³⁻² ke¹tiŋ² tshut⁷lai⁰* 'comes from a poor family' serves as a relative clause modifying the head noun *ken³⁻²a³*. It is clear that there is no relativization marker between the relative clause and the head noun.

22.2.6 Interim summary

In Hui'an, when a lexical head noun is present, the relativization marker can be encoded by the attributive marker e^2, a demonstrative, a demonstrative complex (DEM-CL), or a classifier, among which the demonstrative, demonstrative complex or classifier constitute a part of the head noun, while simultaneously serving as a relativization marker. The relative clause construction marked by e^0 typically expresses a generic meaning, and, in this type, the head noun is often encoded by a generic bare noun. The relative clause construction identified by the use of a demonstrative (complex) can refer to a specific entity, plural entities or a category of entity, according to the demonstrative or classifier used. In contrast to the demonstrative relative clause type, the construction identified by the presence of a classifier refers to a specific entity, which is typically singular.

The relative clause in Hui'an can also be zero-marked, that is, the relative clause and the head noun are combined together without any kind of relativization marker. The zero-marked relative clause construction is relatively unrestricted in referring to a specific entity, plural entities, a category of entity, and can even express a generic meaning.

In daily conversation, the relative clause constructions marked by a demonstrative (complex) and the zero-marked relative clause construction are very common, while those marked by e^0 or a classifier alone are less common. In other words, the relative clause marked by a demonstrative (complex) and the zero-marked relative clause represent the basic relative clause types in Hui'an. This is somewhat different from certain other Chinese varieties as mentioned in §22.1 above.

Unlike Tang (2005), the construction [relative clause + demonstrative (complex)] in Hui'an, as in (19) and (20) above, is regarded as a zero-marked relative clause construction in which the demonstrative (complex) alone functions as a head noun.

22.3 Position of the head noun

There are three possibilities for the position of the head noun in relation to the relative clause: (a) head-initial, i.e. the relative clause follows the head noun; (b) head-final, i.e. the relative clause precedes the head noun; and (c) head-internal, i.e. the head noun is inside the relative clause. As mentioned above, typologically, SVO languages have a distinct preference to use the head-initial type of relative clause, i.e. [head noun + relative clause]. Chinese, however, tends to use head-final type of relative clause, i.e. [relative clause + head noun]. This is also true of the Hui'an dialect. However, the head-initial type of relative clause can also be attested in daily conversation in Hui'an. In the following, we first examine head-final and head-initial types of relative clauses (§22.3.1), and then discuss whether there is a head-internal type of relative clause in Hui'an (§22.3.2).

22.3.1 Head-final and head-initial types

Relative clauses in Hui'an mainly belong to the head-final type, as in (26) and (27).

(26) 趁　　其　　錢
  than⁵ *e⁰* *tsin²*
  earn RM money
  'the money earned'

(27) 伊　　傳　　汝　　懷
  i¹ *tŋ²* *lu⁰* *huai²*
  3SG give 2SG those
  'those he gave you'

In (26), the relative clause *than⁵ e⁰* precedes the head noun *tsin²* 'money'. In (27), the relative clause *i¹ tŋ² lu⁰* 'he gave you' precedes the head noun *huai²* 'those'.

  Based on a study on naturally occurring spoken data, Fang (2004) found that head-initial type of relative clause can be attested in colloquial Northern Mandarin, which has a descriptive function and is used to provide new information. In other words, the head-initial type of relative clause discussed in Fang (2004) belongs to non-restrictive relative clauses. In Hui'an, however, we find examples of the restrictive head-initial type of relative clause, as in (28).

(28) 阮　　買　　蜀　　個　　口　　蜀　　百　　口
　　　gun³　bue³⁻²　tsit⁸⁻⁴　e²⁻⁴　hə²　tsit⁸⁻⁴　paʔ⁷⁻⁸　khɔ¹
　　　1PL　buy　one　CL　that　One　hundred　YUAN
　　　會　　燃火　　　煮菜
　　　e⁴　liã²⁻⁴-hə³　tsɯ³⁻²-tshai⁵
　　　can　burn-fire　cook-dish
　　　'We bought one (utensil) that costs one hundred and can be used for cooking.' (lit. we buy one that kind (of utensil) (which) cost one hundred can cook)

In (28), the speaker is introducing a utensil they bought, which is mentioned for the first time. In other words, the addressee does not know anything about the utensil. The demonstrative *hə²* functions as a head noun, referring to the utensil, and the following relative clause *tsit⁸⁻⁴ paʔ⁷⁻⁸ khɔ¹ e⁴ liã²⁻⁴ hə³ tsɯ³⁻² tshai⁵* 'one hundred and can be used for cooking' is used to help the addressee identify what type of utensil the speaker is talking about. In other words, this is a restrictive head-initial type of relative clause, rather than a non-restrictive one. In this example, the relative clause is somewhat complicated, which may be one reason why a head-initial type of relative clause is chosen.

The following are two examples where a demonstrative and *e⁰* 其 co-occur in the same string.

(29)　儂　　口　　新　　工作　　其
　　　laŋ⁴　hə²　sen¹　kaŋ¹tsɔk⁷　e⁰
　　　other　that　new　work　NMLZ
　　　'people who just started working'

(30)　儂　　口　　西裝　　規身　　其
　　　laŋ⁴　hə²　se¹tsɔŋ¹　kui¹-sen¹　e⁰
　　　other　that　business.suit　whole-body　NMLZ
　　　'the entire set of a suit' (lit. other that the suit complete)

In Hui'an, when followed by a noun (phrase), the pronoun *laŋ⁴* 'other' can be interpreted as being coreferential with the following noun (phrase) (see §4.5). In (29), the noun phrase *hə² sen¹ kaŋ¹tsɔk⁷ e⁰* 'people who just started working' is a relative clause construction, in which the demonstrative *hə²* functions as a head noun. In this case, the relative clause *sen¹ kaŋ¹tsɔk⁷ e⁰*, encoded by the verb phrase *sen¹ kaŋ¹tsɔk⁷* 'just start working' and the relativization marker *e⁰*, is used to help the addressee identify which type of people the speaker is talking about. In (30), the noun phrase *hə² se¹tsɔŋ¹ kui¹sen¹ e⁰* 'the entire set of a suit', literally meaning 'the suit which is complete', is also a relative clause construction, in which the head noun is encoded by the noun phrase *hə² se¹tsɔŋ¹* 'the suit'. In this case, the relative clause *kui¹sen¹ e⁰* is used to help identify that the speaker is talking about the entire set of garments that make up a suit, rather than just the upper garment. Both (29) and (30) are examples of the restrictive head-initial type of relative clause.

In this type of relative clause, the head noun can also be encoded by a demonstrative complex, as in (31).

(31) 汝　　口褲　　　　著　　　　去　　穿　　　迄領　　　　　黃色　　　　其
　　 luɯ³　*khau³⁻²khɔ⁵*　*tioʔ⁸⁻⁴*　*khuɯ⁵⁻³*　*tshiŋ⁵⁻⁴*　*hit⁷⁻⁸-liã³⁻²*　*ŋ²⁻⁴siak⁷*　*e⁰*
　　 2SG　trouser　　　should　　 go　　wear　　 that-CL　　　yellow　　　NMLZ
　　 'As for the trouser, you should wear the one that is yellow.'

In Hui'an, in order to express 'those yellow trousers', people often use the head-final type of relative clause construction *ŋ²⁻⁴siak⁷ hit⁷⁻⁸liã³(⁻²khau³⁻²khɔ⁵)*, in which *ŋ²⁻⁴siak⁷* 'yellow' functions as a relative clause, and the demonstrative complex *hit⁷⁻⁸liã³* 'that piece' (derived from the noun phrase *hit⁷⁻⁸liã³⁻² khau³⁻²khɔ⁵* 'those trousers') serves as a head noun. In (31), however, *hit⁷⁻⁸liã³ ŋ²⁻⁴siak⁷ e⁰* constitutes a head-initial type of relative clause construction, in which the demonstrative complex *hit⁷⁻⁸liã³* serves as a head noun, and the clause *ŋ²⁻⁴siak⁷ e⁰* is a relative clause modifying the head noun *hit⁷⁻⁸liã³*. In this case, 'those trousers which are yellow' is mentioned for the first time, and the relative clause *ŋ²⁻⁴siak⁷ e⁰* is used to help the addressee identify the entity.

In examples (28) – (31) above, the demonstrative *hə²* and the demonstrative complex *hit⁷⁻⁸liã³* either function as a head noun, or function as a part of the head noun. In the following example, however, the first occurrence of the demonstrative *hə²* may function like the English relative pronoun *that*.

(32) (a) NP - [DEM$_{HEAD}$ - [VP + *e⁰*]$_{RC}$]$_{NP}$ or (b) NP$_{HEAD}$ - [DEM$_{RP}$ + VP + *e⁰*]$_{RC}$
　　　有其　　　儂　　　口　　（才罪）　　口　　　別搭　　　　儂　　　其
　　　u⁴e⁰　　*laŋ²*　*hə²*　*tshə⁵⁻⁴*　　*hə²*　*pat⁸⁻⁴-taʔ⁷⁻⁸*　*laŋ²*　*e⁰*
　　　some　　person　that　look.for　　that　other-LOC　　person　RM
　　　'some people whose partner comes from another place' (lit. (a) some people, that kind (of person) (who) look for other.place people; (b) some people that look for other.place people)

Example (32) is used to refer to a type of person, i.e. the person whose partner comes from another place. This example has two possible interpretations. Firstly, it can be interpreted as an appositive construction consisting of two noun phrases: the initial noun phrase $u^4e^0\ laŋ^2$ 'some people' and the subsequent noun phrase $hə^2\ tshə^{5\text{-}4}\ hə^2\ pat^{8\text{-}4}taʔ^{7\text{-}8}\ laŋ^2\ e^0$ 'those (i.e. the people) whose partner comes from another place'. The second noun phrase is by itself a relative clause construction, in which the first demonstrative $hə^2$ functions as the head noun, referring to 'the people', while $tshə^{5\text{-}4}\ hə^2\ pat^{8\text{-}4}taʔ^{7\text{-}8}\ laŋ^2\ e^0$, literally meaning 'look for people that come from another place' serves as a relative clause. Secondly, the whole utterance can be regarded as a relative clause construction. In this case, $u^4e^0\ laŋ^2$ 'some people' functions as a head noun, while $hə^2\ tshə^{5\text{-}4}\ hə^2\ pat^{8\text{-}4}taʔ^{7\text{-}8}\ laŋ^2\ e^0$, literally meaning 'that (=relative pronoun) look for a partner that comes from another place', serves as a relative clause, in which the first demonstrative $hə^2$ functions like the English relative pronoun *that*. No matter which interpretation, the type of person referred to by example (32) is mentioned for the first time in the given context, and thus the head-initial type of relative clause construction, in both cases is used to help the addressee identify the type of person that the speaker is talking about.

22.3.2 Is there a head-internal type?

The head-internal type is a form of relative clause which presents a domain noun internal to the relative clause and is thus syntactically headless (Keenan 1985:161). The following are examples of internally headed relative clauses and headed relative clauses in Ancash Quechua from Cole (1987:279).

(33) a. Headed Relative Clause
[NP [S nuna ø$_i$ ranti-shqa-n] bestya$_i$] allli
man   buy-PERFECT-3   horse(NOM) good
bestya-m   ka-rqo-n
horse-EVIDENTIAL   be-PAST-3
The horse the man bought was a good horse.

b. Internally Headed Relative Clause
   [NP nuna   bestya-ta   ranti-shqa-n]   alli
   man   horse-ACC   buy-PERFECT-3   good
   bestya-m   ka-rqo-n
   horse-EVIDENTIAL   be-PAST-3
   The horse the man bought was a good horse.

As Basilico (1996:499) points out, the difference between these two examples above is that "in the externally headed relative clause, the noun *bestya* 'horse' is not a constituent of the clause *nuna ranti-shaq-n* 'that the man bought', while in the internally headed relative clause, the noun is a constituent of the clause".

Matthews and Yip (2007) propose that the object classifier relative in Cantonese has two possible analyses: head-final type and head-internal type, as shown in (34).

(34) a. Head-final
        [[keoi   maai $_S$]   go   cang   lau $_{NP}$]   hou   leng
        3SG   buy   that   CL   flat   very   nice
        'The flat she's buying is really nice.'

   b. Head-internal
      [$_{S/NP}$ keoi   maai   go   cang   lau]   hou   leng
      3SG   buy   that   CL   flat   very   nice
      'The flat she's buying is really nice.'

In (34a), the noun phrase *go cang lau* 'the flat' functions as a head noun, following the relative clause *keoi maai* 'she is buying'. In this case, the head noun *go cang lau* is not regarded as a constitutent of the relative clause *keoi maai*. In (34b), however, the head noun *go cang lau* is regarded as a constituent of the clause *keoi maai go cang lau* 'she is buying the flat'. As mentioned by Matthews & Yip (2007), however, it is not easy to distinguish the head-internal type from head-final type of relative clause in Cantonese.

As with Cantonese, classifier relatives can also be found in the Jieyang variety of Southern Min. However, the object classifier relative in Jieyang can be shown to belong to the head-final type. This is illustrated by example (35) from Xu (2007:118).

(35) [[ku⁵⁵⁻¹¹-ni⁵⁵ ua⁵³   poi⁵³ₛ] t'au²¹³⁻⁵³ ts'u²¹³_NP] ho?² tua¹¹
     last-year   1SG   buy   CL   house   very   big
     The house which I bought last year is very big.

The tone of the verb *poi⁵³* 'buy' must be a sandhi tone when followed by an object *t'au²¹³⁻⁵³ ts'u²¹³* 'house'. In (35), however, *poi⁵³* does not undergo tone sandhi, which suggests that *t'au²¹³⁻⁵³ ts'u²¹³* is not a constituent of the clause *ku⁵⁵⁻¹¹ni⁵⁵ ua⁵³ poi⁵³* 'I bought last year', as it would be under the head-internal analysis in (34b).

Now, let's look at the relative clause in Hui'an. In fact, similar structures in Hui'an are also clearly of the head-final type, like the Jieyang variety. This can be illustrated by a comparison between (36) and (37) below.

(36) 我   借   迄本   冊
     gua³   tsio?⁷⁻⁸   hit⁷⁻⁸-pun³⁻²   tshe?⁷
     1SG   borrow   that-CL   book
     'I borrowed that book.'

(37) [[我   借 s]   迄本   冊 NP]   野   好看
     gua³   tsio?⁷   hit⁷⁻⁸-pun³⁻²   tshe?⁷   ia³⁻²   ho³⁻²-khuã⁵
     1SG   borrow   that-CL   book   quite   good-look
     'That book I borrowed is quite good.'

In the main clause of (36), *hit⁷⁻⁸pun³⁻² tshe?⁷* 'that book' is an object of the verb *tsio?⁷* 'borrow', and the verb undergoes tone sandhi accordingly. While in the object relative clause (37), *tsio?⁷* does not undergo tone sandhi, which indicates that *hit⁷⁻⁸pun³⁻² tshe?⁷* is not a constituent of the clause *gua³ tsio?⁷* 'I borrowed'. Instead, the citation tone of *tsio?⁷* indicates a prosodic boundary at the end of the relative clause. Thus, we can conclude that (37) is an example of head-final type, and we have no evidence for a head-internal type of relative clause in Hui'an.

22.3.3 Interim summary

As with Mandarin Chinese, the Hui'an dialect tends to use the head-final type of relative clause. In daily conversation, however, we also find examples of the restrictive head-initial type of relative clause. In the head-initial type, the head noun is often encoded by the demonstrative *hə²* (expressing a generic meaning), a noun phrase (consisting of the demonstrative *hə²* and a noun), or a demonstrative complex. In this type of relative clause, the demonstrative *hə²* seems to have developed a function like the English relative pronoun *that*. In Hui'an, we have not yet found typical examples of the head-internal type of relative clause. The object relative clause in Cantonese may be interpreted as a head-final or head-internal type of relative clause, while similar structures in Hui'an belong to the head-final type.

22.4 The role and encoding of the head noun in the relative clause

As mentioned above, the relative clause, as syntactically defined in earlier studies, requires the head noun being coreferential with an argument in the relative clause, and for this reason is termed 'argument relative clause'. In their study on Mandarin relative clauses, Cheng & Sybesma (2005) mention another two types of relative clause: (a) adjunct relative clauses: the head noun takes an adjunct position in the relative clause; and (b) aboutness relative clauses: the head noun takes neither an argument nor a typical adjunct position in the relative clause, but involves the 'aboutness' semantics with the relative clause. In other words, according to the role of the head noun in the relative clause, relative clauses can be classified into three types: argument relative clauses, adjunct relative clauses and aboutness relative clauses. Examples from Mandarin Chinese are given in (38) – (40) (cf. Cheng & Sybesma 2005:69-70).

(38) 他　　剛　　買　　的　　房子 (argument relative clause)
　　　tā　　gāng　mǎi　de　　fángzi
　　　3SG　just　buy　DE　　house
　　　'the house he just bought'

(39) 他　　修　　車　　的　　車庫 (adjunct relative clause)
　　　tā　　xiū　　chē　de　　chēkù
　　　3SG　fix　　car　DE　　garage
　　　'the garage where he fixes his car'

(40) 他　　唱　　歌　　的　　聲音 (aboutness relative clause)
　　　tā　　chàng　gē　　de　　shēngyīn
　　　3SG　sing　　song　DE　　voice
　　　'the voice that he has while singing'

In (38), the head noun *fángzi* 'house' is coreferential with the understood direct object of the main verb *mǎi* 'buy' in the relative clause. Previous studies suggest that there is a syntactic gap after the verb *mǎi* where the direct object would occur in a declarative sentence. In contrast to this, in (39), the main verb *xiū* 'fix' in the relative clause is a transitive verb, with two arguments, i.e. *tā* 'he' and *chē* 'car'. The head noun *chēkù* 'garage' can be regarded as having the role of a locative adjunct with respect to its use in a declarative, rather than an argument of the verb *xiū*. In (40), the head noun *shēngyīn* 'voice' functions neither as an argument nor as a typical adjunct that expresses location, time or reason. In this case, *shēngyīn* 'voice' is a concept that only involves the aboutness semantics with 'singing' in the cognitive framework of the main verb *chàng gē* 'sing' (a similar interpretation can also be found in Tang (2005)).

Traditional relative clauses typically refer to argument relative clauses. This has likely been determined by the characteristics of relative clauses in European languages such as English. In European languages, the head noun is extracted from an argument position of the main clause, and, as a consequence, the identification of which constituents can be relativized is essentially syntactically constrained: different NP positions show different degrees of relativizability. Based on this, Keenan and Comrie (1977) put forward the 'Noun Phrase Accessibility Hierarchy', as shown in (41).

(41) SU > DO > IO > OBL > GEN > OCOMP

This hierarchy expresses the relative accessibility to relativization of NP positions in simplex main clauses: it predicts that the possibility of relativizing decreases when moving to the right along the accessibility hierarchy.

In some other languages such as Japanese, it seems that there are no syntactic constraints on the relation between the head noun and the covert coreferential noun in the subordinate clause: the acceptability of relations between the head noun and the coreferential noun in the subordinate clause is determined by pragmatic factors, that is, according to whether a native speaker can establish a plausible relation (Comrie 1996). Thus, many non-traditional relative clauses can be attested in Japanese, as in (42).

(42) [[tabeta] nokori], reezooko ni ireta?
 ate remainder refrigerator LOC put.in
 Did (you) put the remainder of (your) eating in a refrigerator?' (Matsumoto 2007:133)

In (42), the clause encoded by the verb *tabeta* 'eat' functions as a relative clause modifying the noun *nokori* 'remainder' to express 'what is remaining'. In this case, the noun *nokori* is neither an argument of the verb *tabeta*, nor its adjunct. In addition, there is no traditional syntactic gap in the relative clause that can be coreferential with the noun *nokori*. In other words, this example can be regarded as an instance of aboutness relative clauses, as mentioned at the beginning of this section. Note that the head noun *nokori* (also the relative clause construction *tabeta nokori*) is the direct object of the verb *ireta* 'put in'.

Similar phenomena are also attested in many other languages in Asia such as Korean, Mandarin and some other Sino-Tibetan languages (Comrie 1996). In other words, both adjuncts and aboutness relative clauses are not peculiar to Mandarin, as illustrated by Mandarin examples (39) and (40) above, but probably reflect an areal feature.

What is the case in Hui'an? Can argument, adjunct and aboutness relative clauses all be attested in Hui'an? Do relative clauses in Hui'an show some distinct features, compared with those in Mandarin? Generally speaking, all three types of relative clause can be attested in Hui'an, and we also find examples of 'aboutness' relative clauses that are different from those given in Cheng & Sybesma (2005). In the following, we will examine these three types one by one.

In this section, we also examine the encoding of the head noun in the relative clause. The ways in which the head noun is encoded in the relative clause are also called relativization strategies. Keenan (1985) and Comrie (1989) both recognize that there are at least four different relativization strategies, according to the following syntactic features: (i) gapping or obliteration; (ii) pronoun-retention; (iii) relative-pronoun; and (iv) non-reduction. However, the issue of whether there is a 'gap' in the relative clause in languages such as Japanese, Korean and Mandarin remains controversial. Comrie (1996) suggests that 'aboutness' relative clauses are gapless, and argument relative clauses in languages such as Japanese are also gapless since these languages have a high use of zero anaphora. For practical reasons, we maintain the use of the term 'gap'.

Thus, for ease of presentation, we use 'relative clauses with a resumptive pronoun' and 'relative clauses with a gap' to refer to those using a 'pronoun-retention' strategy and those without any resumptive pronoun, respectively. This enables us to classify the relative clause in Hui'an as follows.

(i) A. argument relative clauses
   (a) argument relative clauses with a gap
   (b) argument relative clauses with a resumptive pronoun
 B. adjunct relative clauses
   (a) adjunct relative clauses with a gap
   (b) adjunct relative clauses with a resumptive pronoun
 C. 'aboutness' relative clauses

22.4.1 Argument relative clauses

In Hui'an, argument relative clauses are usually subject relative clauses, direct object relative clauses or indirect object relative clauses. In other words, the head noun functions as a subject or direct object, or an indirect object, in argument relative clauses. When the head noun is the subject, as in (43), or direct object of the relative clause, as in (44), the 'gap' strategy is used.

(43) [[ ] + VP + e^0 其 RM]RC - NP_HEAD
　　　無　　　　讀冊　　　　其　　儂
　　　bo^{2-4}　　$thak^{8-4}tshe?^7$　e^0　lan^2
　　　not.have　study　　　　RM　person
　　　'people who have not studied'

(44) [NP + VP + [ ] + e^0 其 RM]RC - NP_HEAD
　　　伊　　看　　　其　　冊
　　　i^1　$khuã^5$　e^0　$tshe?^7$
　　　3SG　look　　RM　Book
　　　'the books he read'

In (43), the head noun lan^2 'person' is the subject in the relative clause bo^{2-4} $thak^{8-4}tshe?^7$ 'have not studied'. In (44), the head noun $tshe?^7$ 'book' is the object in the relative clause i^1 $khuã^5$ 'he reads'. We do not see any resumptive pronoun bound to the head noun in the relative clause in either (43) or (44), both of which belong to the general type using the marker e^0.

The 'pronoun-retention' strategy has to be used when the head noun functions as an indirect object in the relative clause. This is exemplified by (45) below.

(45)　我　　　送　　　伊　　賀卡　　　　　迄個　　　　老師
　　　gua^3　san^{5-3}　i^1　$ho^{5-4}kha^3$　hit^{7-8}-e^{2-4}　lau^4su^1
　　　1SG　send　　3SG　card　　　that-CL　　teacher
　　　'that teacher to whom I sent a card'

In (45), the head noun $hit^{7-8}e^{2-4}$ lau^4su^1 'that teacher' is co-referential with the indirect object in the relative clause, i.e. the third-person singular pronoun i^1.

As evident from the examples above, the indirect object in Hui'an shows lower accessibility to relativization than the subject and direct object due to the required presence of a resumptive pronoun in the relative clause in (45). This is entirely compatible with the Noun Phrase Accessibility Hierarchy put forward by

Keenan & Comrie (1977), where the indirect object is located at a lower position than either the subject or the direct object.

22.4.2 Adjunct relative clauses

When the head noun serves an adjunct function to express concepts in the domains of time, location, instrument or possessor in the relative clause, the 'gap' strategy can also be used. The following are relative clauses that have temporal and locative head nouns.

(46) 伊 倒來 迄日
 i^1 to^5lai^0 $hit^{7\text{-}8}\text{-}let^8$
 3SG come.back that-day
 'the day he came back'

(47) 阮 昨日 買 衫褲 迄間 店
 gun^3 tsa^4let^8 $bue^{3\text{-}2}$ $sã^1khɔ^5$ $hit^{7\text{-}8}\text{-}kuin^1$ $tuin^5$
 1PL yesterday buy clothes that-CL shop
 'the shop where we bought clothes yesterday'

In (46), the verb to^5lai^0 'come back' in the relative clause is an intransitive verb, requiring only an agentive argument. The head noun $hit^{7\text{-}8}let^8$ 'that day' would function as a temporal adjunct in the corresponding declarative clause, rather than as an obligatory constituent. In (47), the verb bue^3 'buy' in the relative clause is transitive, requiring two arguments, that is, the subject gun^3 'we' and the object $sã^1khɔ^5$ 'clothes' in the relative clause. The head noun $hit^{7\text{-}8}kuin^1$ $tuin^5$ 'that shop', however, functions as a locative adjunct in the related declarative clause.

When the head noun functions as another type of adjunct such as the standard of comparison or the comitative in a relative clause, a resumptive pronoun is typically required after the preposition in the relative clause, as in (48) and (49).

(48) 阮 媽 比 伊 恰 大 迄孤 女其
 $gun^{3\text{-}2}$ $bã^2$ $pi^{3\text{-}2}$ i^1 $khaʔ^{7\text{-}8}$ tua^5 $hit^{7\text{-}8}\text{-}kɔ^1$ $lu^3\text{-}e^0$
 1PL mother DMC 3SG HMC big that-CL female-NMLZ
 'that woman whom my mother is older than'

(49) 我   合   伊   去   看   電影   迄孤   儂
    gua³ ka⁷⁻⁸   i¹   khu⁵⁻³ khuã⁵⁻³ ten⁵⁻⁴iã³ hit⁷⁻⁸-kɔ¹ laŋ²
    1SG   COMT   3SG go   look   film   that-CL   person
    'that person with whom I went to the cinema'

In (48), the head noun *hit⁷⁻⁸kɔ¹ lu³ e⁰* 'that woman' is co-referential with the standard of comparison in the relative clause, i.e. *i¹* 'her'. In (49), the head noun *hit⁷⁻⁸kɔ¹ laŋ²* 'that person' is co-referential with the comitative *i¹* 'him' in the relative clause. In these two examples, the resumptive pronoun *i¹* occurs after the prepositions *pi³* 'compare' and *ka⁷* 'with'.

22.4.3 'aboutness' relative clauses

In the Mandarin examples of 'aboutness' relative clauses given in Cheng & Sybesma (2005), the head noun is encoded by a bare noun, such as *shēngyīn* 聲音 'voice' in (40) above. Similar examples are also found in Hui'an, as in (50) with the general relative clause construction.

(50) 見面   其   時間   恰   少
    kin⁵⁻³ben⁵   e⁰   si²⁻⁴kan¹   kha⁷⁻⁸   tsio³
    meet   RM   time   comparatively little
    'The time for meeting (each other) is less (than before).'

In (50), the head noun is encoded by the bare noun *si²⁻⁴kan¹* 'time'. This head noun is neither an argument of the verb *kin⁵⁻³ben⁵* 'meet' in the relative clause, nor a temporal adjunct. Rather, it can only be regarded as a concept that expresses 'aboutness' semantics with the verb *kin⁵⁻³ben⁵* in the cognitive framework of the verb.

In Hui'an, the head noun of the 'aboutness' relative clause construction can also be a noun phrase referring to a specific entity, as in the relative clause of (51).

(51) 汝   買   機票   迄孤   男其
    lu³   bue³⁻² ki¹phio⁵   hit⁷⁻⁸-kɔ¹   lam²-e⁰
    2SG   buy   air.ticket that-CL   male-NMLZ
    'the man whom (we met when) you bought your plane ticket'

In (51), people are talking about a man whom they come across when the speaker accompanies the addressee to buy a plane ticket. In this case, the head noun *hit⁷⁻*

⁸kɔ¹ lam² e⁰ 'the man' functions neither as an argument of the verb bue³ 'buy' nor as an adjunct in the relative clause, and, as such, the correct interpretation requires the shared experience of the speaker and the addressee. As with argument relative clauses marked by a demonstrative complex, the aboutness relative clause in (51) is also used to help identify a specific entity, i.e. a specific person.

The following is another example of an 'aboutness' relative clause with the general marker e⁰.

(52) 口　是　阮　厝裡　　　看　出去　　　其　早上
tse² si⁴ gun³ tshu⁵⁻³-lai⁴ khuã⁵ tshutºkhuº e⁰ tsai³⁻²i³
this be 1PL house-inside look go.out RM morning
'This is (a view of) morning (when we) look towards the outside from our house.'

In (52), the head noun tsai³⁻²i³ 'morning' is neither an argument of the verb khuã⁵ 'look', nor a temporal adjunct. In this case, the speaker is introducing a picture, and the relative clause is used to indicate that this is a view of the morning when looking outside from the house of the speaker, rather than a view of morning from the vantage point of other places. In other words, the relative clause is used to help identify a view of the morning in a certain place shown by the picture.

22.5 The role and encoding of the head noun in the main clause

22.5.1 The role of the head noun in the main clause

In Hui'an, the head noun of the relative clause mainly functions as topic, subject, object and predicate nominal[2] in the main clause. Examples of topic and subject are given in (53) and (54), respectively.

---

[2] 'Predicate nominal' is put forward by Fox & Thompson (1990:298) who show that the role of the head noun in the main clause can be subject, object, prepositional phrase object, predicate nominal and existential.

(53) 攑　　懷　　相　　與　　恁　　爸仔　　　看
　　　hiəp⁷　huai²　siɔŋ⁵　khɔ⁵⁻⁴　len³⁻²　pa²-a⁰　khuã⁵
　　　take　those　picture　give　2PL　father-NM　look
　　　'Those pictures you took, let your father have a look at them.'

(54) 伊　　趁　　其　　錢　　野　　少
　　　i¹　than⁵　e⁰　tsin²　ia³⁻²　tsio³
　　　3SG　earn　RM　money　quite　little
　　　'The money he earns is not much.'

The head noun *huai² siɔŋ⁵* 'those pictures' in (53) functions as a topic in the main clause, while the head noun *tsin²* 'money' in (54) serves as a subject in the main clause.

The following are examples of object and predicate nominal, respectively.

(55) 看　　　　伊　　攑　　其　　相
　　　khuã⁵⁻³　en¹　hiəp⁷　e⁰　siɔŋ⁵
　　　look　3PL　snap　RM　picture
　　　'Look at the pictures they took.'

(56) 即領　　　是　　頂　　禮拜　　　買　　迄領
　　　tsit⁷⁻⁸-liã³　si⁴　tiŋ³⁻²　le³⁻²pai⁵　bue³　hit⁷⁻⁸-liã³
　　　this-CL　be　up　week　buy　that-CL
　　　'These (clothes) are those bought last week.'

In (55), the head noun *siɔŋ⁵* 'picture' functions as an object of the verb *khuã⁵* 'look' in the main clause. In (56), the head noun *hit⁷⁻⁸liã³* 'that piece' functions as a predicate nominal of the copular verb *si⁴* in the main clause.

22.5.2 The encoding of the head noun in the main clause

According to the encoding of the head noun in the main clause, relative clauses are usually divided into headed and headless types. Citko (2004), however, proposes another type of relative clause, i.e. light-headed relatives. In Citko (2004:95), the terms 'headed' and 'headless' are used to refer to relatives 'involving an external nominal head', and those 'lacking an overt nominal head', respectively; the term 'light-headed' refers to relatives which are "headed by morphologically 'light' elements". These 'light' elements can be demonstratives, indefinites, negative indefinites and universals such as 'everything'. The following is an example of the demonstrative light head in Polish from Citko (2004:96).

(57) Jan czyta <u>to</u>, co   Maria czyta.
     Jan reads this what Maria reads
     'John reads what Maria reads.'

The Hui'an examples of relative clause given above involve different types of head noun. In the section on relativization markers (§22.2), we briefly described relative clause constructions with a demonstrative (complex) as the head noun. In Hui'an, the light-headed type is in fact mainly encoded by the demonstrative and the [DEM (+NUM) + CL] complex. More examples are given in (58) – (60).

(58) RC - DEM$_{HEAD}$
     汝   買   懷   無算   貴
     lu^3 bue^3 <u>$huai^2$</u> $bo^{2\text{-}4}\text{-}sŋ^{5\text{-}3}$ kui^5
     2SG   buy   those   not.have-count   expensive
     'Those you bought are not expensive.'

(59) RC - [DEM + NUM + CL]$_{HEAD}$
     汝   攑   迄兩垛
     lu^3 kia^2 $hit^{7\text{-}8}\text{-}lŋ^4\text{-}tə^5$
     2SG   take   that-two-CL
     'two (chairs) that you took'

(60) RC - [DEM + CL]$_{HEAD}$
     恁   爸   掠   迄隻
     $len^{3\text{-}2}$ pa^2 $liaʔ^8$ <u>$hit^{7\text{-}8}\text{-}tsiaʔ^7$</u>
     2PL   father catch   that-CL
     'that (duck) that your father took (home)'

In (58), the head noun is encoded by the plural demonstrative $huai^2$ 'those'. In (59), the head noun $hit^{7\text{-}8}lŋ^4tə^5$ 'two (chairs)' is formed by a demonstrative, a numeral and a classifier. In (60), the head noun is encoded by the demonstrative complex $hit^{7\text{-}8}tsiaʔ^7$ 'that (one)', which consists of the demonstrative hit^7 'that' and the classifier $tsiaʔ^7$. All these three examples can thus be considered as light-headed relative clause constructions.

Examples of headed and head-less relatives are given in (61) and (62), respectively.

(61) 今日　　買　　迄領　　　衫
　　 kiã¹let⁸　bue³　hit⁷⁻⁸-liã³⁻²　sã¹
　　 today　 buy　 that-CL　 clothes
　　 'the clothes/clothing bought today'

(62) 阮　　 厝裡　　　　 剩　　 其　　伊　　 從來　　　　 唔　　食
　　 gun³　tshu⁵⁻³-lai⁴　tshun⁵　e⁰　i¹　tsiɔŋ⁴lai²　m⁵⁻⁴　tsiaʔ⁸
　　 1PL　 house-inside　leave　RM　3SG　always　　 not　 eat
　　 'He never eats the leftovers at home.'

In (61), the head noun is encoded by the noun phrase $hit^{7-8}liã^{3-2}$ $sã^1$ 'the clothing'. By way of contrast, in the relative clause construction gun^3 $tshu^{5-3}$-lai^4 $tshun^5$ e^0 'the leftovers at home' in (62), the head noun is covert.

22.6 Summary

In this chapter, we have examined the restrictive relative clause based on four parameters: (a) the relativization marker used; (b) the position of the head noun in relation to the restricting clause; (c) the role and encoding of the head noun in the restricting clause; and (d) the role and encoding of the head noun in the main clause.

The relativization marker in Hui'an can be the attributive marker e^2, a demonstrative, a demonstrative complex, or a classifier, among which, the attributive marker e^2 functions only as a relativization marker, whereas the demonstrative, demonstrative complex or classifier all constitute part of the head noun while simultaneously serving as relativization markers when there is an overt lexical head noun. The relative clause construction marked by e^0 typically expresses a generic meaning, and the head noun is often encoded by a generic bare noun. The relative clause construction identified by the use of a demonstrative (complex) can refer to a specific entity, plural entities or a category of entity, according to the demonstrative or classifier used. The construction identified by the presence of a classifier only refers to a specific entity which is typically singular. Their structures are:

[VP + e^2 其 $_{RM}$]$_{RC}$ - NP$_{HEAD}$
RC - [DEM$_{RM}$ + NP]$_{HEAD}$
RC - [[DEM + CL]$_{RM}$ + NP]$_{HEAD}$
RC - [CL$_{RM}$ + NP]$_{HEAD}$

The relative clause can also be zero-marked, that is, the relative clause and the head noun are juxtaposed together without any relativization marker. The zero-marked relative clause construction is relatively unrestricted in referring to a specific entity, plural entities, a category of entity, and may even express a generic meaning. Distinct from the overtly marked ones above, the three main structures are the following:

RC - DEM$_{\text{HEAD}}$
RC - [DEM + CL]$_{\text{HEAD}}$
RC - COMMON NOUN$_{\text{HEAD}}$

Comparatively speaking, relative clauses marked by demonstratives (or demonstrative complexes) and zero-marked relative clauses are more common than the other types.

As with Mandarin Chinese, the relative clause in Hui'an mainly belongs to the head-final type, however, the head-initial type can also be used. There is, however, no evidence for any head-internal type of relative clause.

According to the role of the head noun in the relative clause, relative clauses can be classified into three types: argument relative clauses, adjunct relative clauses and 'aboutness' relative clauses. The 'gap' strategy is used when the head noun serves as an argument such as subject and object or as an adjunct for the temporal, locative, causal, instrumental and agentive domains in the relative clause. The 'pronoun-retention' strategy has to be used when the head noun functions as an indirect object or the object of a preposition in the relative clause, coding the comitative or the comparative, for example.

The head noun of the relative clause mainly functions as a topic, subject, object and predicate nominal in the main clause. According to the encoding of the head noun in the main clause, relative clauses can be divided into headed relatives, headless relatives and light-headed relatives. The light-headed type is mainly encoded by the demonstrative and the [DEM (+NUM) + CL] complex.

23 Adverbial clauses

23.1 Introduction

Adverbial clauses are subordinate clauses that function as modifiers of verb phrases or entire clauses (cf. Thompson, Longacre & Hwang 2007; Longacre 2007, *inter alia*). An adverbial clause modifies the matrix clause in a similar way to those where an adverb modifies a predicate. In some European languages such as English, adverbial clauses are marked by subordinating morphemes. For example, English subordinating conjunctions *before*, *where*, and *if* can be used to mark a temporal, locative and conditional adverbial clause, respectively. Similar semantic relations (except conditionals) in Hui'an, however, tend not to be marked by subordinating conjunctions. Comparatively speaking, the Hui'an dialect tends to juxtapose the clauses, with the semantic relation between the clauses inferred, or else an adverb is used in the main clause to mark the semantic relation between the clauses. Other forms are also attested, as will be shown in the following sections. In this chapter, we focus on how the equivalents to adverbial clauses in European languages such as English would be encoded in Hui'an.

23.2 Time clauses

In Hui'an, time clauses can be zero-marked, in the sense that no overt forms (such as the English conjunction *when*) are used, as in (1) and (2).

(1) Time clause + Matrix clause
讀　　蜀　　年，　去　　　下鄉
thak^{8}　tsit$^{8\text{-}4}$　lin^{2}　khɯ$^{5\text{-}3}$　ha^{4}hiɔŋ^{1}
study　one　year　go　go.to.countryside
'I went to the countryside, after studying for a year.'

(2) Time clause + Matrix clause
下日　　（才罪）　　工作，　　著　　　懷　　　證書
e^{4}let^{8}　tshə$^{5\text{-}4}$　kaŋ^{1}tsɔk^{7}　tioʔ$^{8\text{-}4}$　huai^{2}　tsiŋ$^{5\text{-}3}$tsɯ^{1}
future　look.for　job　　need　those　certificate
'(You) need those certificates, when (you) look for a job in the future.'

The two verb phrases in (1) describe two events that happen in succession. More specifically, the event encoded by *khɯ$^{5\text{-}3}$ ha^{4}hiɔŋ^{1}* 'go to the countryside' happens after the event encoded by *thak⁸ tsit⁸⁻⁴lin²* 'study for a year'. These two verb phrases are juxtaposed together, without any marker indicating the temporal sequence relationship between two events, apart from their order. In terms of meaning, the first clause in (2), *e⁴let⁸ tshə⁵⁻⁴ kaŋ¹tsɔk⁷* 'look for a job in the future', denotes the time when the event encoded by *tioʔ⁸⁻⁴ huai² tsiŋ⁵⁻³tsui¹* 'need those certificates' should happen. The temporal word *e⁴let⁸* 'future' is used to indicate that a potential future event is involved, simultaneous with the event denoted by the second clause. As with (1), example (2) does not use a formal marker to indicate the temporal semantic relation between the two events.

The temporal semantic relation between two events or states is also often marked by an adverb such as *tsiu⁵* 就 in (3) and (4).

(3) Time clause + [*tsiu⁵* 就 + VP]_{MATRIX CLAUSE}

伊	看	著	我
i¹	khuã⁵⁻³	tioʔ⁸⁻⁴	gua³
3SG	look	PVC	1SG

就	共	我	說	無	票
tsiu⁵⁻⁴	ka⁵⁻⁴	gua³⁻²	səʔ⁷⁻⁸	bo²⁻⁴	phio⁵
then	to	1SG	say	not.have	ticket

'He told me that the tickets have been sold out, when/after he saw me.'

(4) Time clause + [*tsiu⁵* 就 + ADJ]_{MATRIX CLAUSE}

兩	間	房	鋪	者	就	好看
lŋ⁴	kuin¹	paŋ²	phɔ¹	tse⁰	tsiu⁵⁻⁴	ho³⁻²-khuã⁵
two	CL	room	pave	DELIM	then	good-look

'(The house) will be nice after laying the flooring in the two rooms.'

In (3), the first event *i¹ khuã⁵⁻³tioʔ⁸⁻⁴ gua³* 'he saw me' indicates the time when the second event *ka⁵⁻⁴ gua³⁻² səʔ⁷⁻⁸ bo²⁻⁴ phio⁵* 'tell me that the tickets have been sold out' happens. The adverb *tsiu⁵* is used to denote that these two events happen in succession. Unlike English subordinating conjunctions such as *when* and *(right) after*, the adverb *tsiu⁵* in Hui'an is used in the main clause, rather than used to introduce the temporal adverbial clause *i¹ khuã⁵⁻³tioʔ⁸⁻⁴ gua³* 'he saw me'. In (4), *ho³⁻²khuã⁵* 'good looking' denotes the envisaged state after the event encoded by *lŋ⁴ kuin¹ paŋ² phɔ¹ tse⁰* 'lay the floor in the two rooms'. The adverb *tsiu⁵* here indicates the temporal sequence relation between the event 'lay the floor in the two rooms' and the state 'good looking'. In addition, the event 'lay the floor in the two rooms' can also be interpreted as a cause of the state 'good looking'. In other words, the adverb *tsiu*⁵ in (4) not only denotes a temporal sequence relation, but also signals a cause-consequence relation.

Similarly, the following example denotes not only a temporal relation, but also a conditional relation.

(5) Time clause + [*tsiu*⁵ 就 + VP]ₘₐₜᵣᵢₓ ₒₗₐᵤₛₑ
 拜六　　　拜日，　　我　　　有　　　閑，
 *pai*⁵⁻³*lak*⁸　*pai*⁵⁻³*let*⁸　*gua*³　*u*⁴　*uin*²
 Saturday　Sunday　1SG　have　Leisure
 就　　　　著　　　　開始　　　掃　　　塗骹　　　　洗　　　塗骹
 *tsiu*⁵⁻⁴　*tioʔ*⁸⁻⁴　*khai*¹*si*³⁻²　*sau*⁵⁻³　*thɔ*²⁻⁴*kha*¹　*sue*³⁻²　*thɔ*²⁻⁴*kha*¹
 then　should　begin　sweep　floor　wash　floor
 'At the weekends, when/if I have time, I need to do some cleaning.'

Example (5) has two possible interpretations: firstly, the situation coded by the first clause *gua*³ *u*⁴ *uin*² 'I have time' can indicate the time when the event in the second clause, *tioʔ*⁸⁻⁴ *khai*¹*si*³⁻² *sau*⁵⁻³*thɔ*²⁻⁴*kha*¹ *sue*³⁻²*thɔ*²⁻⁴*kha*¹ 'need to begin doing some cleaning' will happen; and, secondly, the same first clause *gua*³ *u*⁴ *uin*² can also indicate the necessary condition for the event 'need to begin doing some cleaning' to take place. In other words, the adverb *tsiu*⁵ denotes the temporal relation between the two events in the first interpretation, but signals the conditional relation between the two events in the second interpretation.

The adverb *tsiu*⁵ can co-occur with *tsit*⁸ 蜀 'one' as in (6), or with *tu*³ 拄 'just' as in (7), to express that two events happen in succession and emphasizes a short time interval between the events.

(6) [*tsit*⁸ 蜀 + VP]ₜᵢₘₑ ₒₗₐᵤₛₑ + [*tsiu*⁵ 就 + VP]ₘₐₜᵣᵢₓ ₒₗₐᵤₛₑ
 蜀　　　去　　　就　　　可以　　　申請　　　　　副教授
 *tsit*⁸⁻⁴　*khuɩ*⁵　*tsiu*⁵⁻⁴　*khɔ*³⁻²*iʔ*³　*sen*¹*tshiŋ*³⁻²　*hu*⁵⁻³*kau*⁵⁻³*siu*⁵
 one　go　then　can　apply　associate.professor
 '(He) can apply for associate professor as soon as (he) goes there.'

(7) [*tu*³ 拄 + VP]ₜᵢₘₑ ₒₗₐᵤₛₑ + [*tsiu*⁵ 就 + VP]ₘₐₜᵣᵢₓ ₒₗₐᵤₛₑ
 我　　　拄　　　出　　　蜀仔久　　　　　就　　　拍　　　電話
 *gua*³　*tu*³⁻²　*tshut*⁷　*tsit*⁸⁻⁴-*a*³⁻²-*ku*³　*tsiu*⁵⁻⁴　*phaʔ*⁷⁻⁸　*ten*⁵⁻⁴*ue*⁵
 1SG　just　go.out　one-DIM-long　then　hit　telephone
 '(They) phoned me right after I went out for a short while.'

In (6), the adverb *tsiu⁵* co-occurs with *tsit⁸* 'one' to indicate that the event *khɔ³⁻²i³ sen¹tshiŋ³⁻² hu⁵⁻³kau⁵⁻³siu⁵* 'can apply for associate professor' will happen right after the event of his going there, encoded by the verb *khɯ⁵* 'go'. In (7), the adverb *tsiu⁵* is used with *tu³* 'just' to show that the event *phaʔ⁷⁻⁸ ten⁵⁻⁴ue⁵* 'phone (me)' happened right after the event of my going out for a short while, encoded by the clause *gua³ tu³⁻² tshut⁷ tsit⁸⁻⁴a³⁻²ku³*.

Besides the adverb *tsiu⁵*, the adverbs *tsiaʔ⁷* 則 'then' and *koʔ⁷* 佫 'again' can also be used to signal the relation of a temporal sequence between two events. Examples are given in (8) and (9), respectively.

(8) Time clause + [*tsiaʔ⁷* 則 + VP]_{MATRIX CLAUSE}
    泉州   教   幾   年   則   調   過來
    tsuan²⁻⁴tsiu¹ *ka⁵* *kui³⁻²* *lin²* *tsiaʔ⁷⁻⁸* *tiau⁵* *kəᵒlaiᵒ*
    PN teach several year then transfer come.over
    '(I) was transferred here after teaching for several years in Quanzhou.'

(9) Time clause + [*koʔ⁷* 佫 + VP]_{MATRIX CLAUSE}
    幾   垛   落去   交,   佫   去   燙
    kui³⁻² *tə⁵* *loʔ⁸⁻⁴khɯ⁵⁻³* *kiau¹* *koʔ⁷⁻⁸* *khɯ⁵⁻³* *thŋ⁵*
    several CL go.down add.in again go heat
    '(The duck meat) can be heated after putting several pieces into (the noodles).'

In (8), the adverb *tsiaʔ⁷* indicates that the event *tiau⁵ kəᵒlaiᵒ* 'transfer here' happens after the event *tsuan²⁻⁴tsiu¹ ka⁵ kui³⁻²lin²* 'teach for several years in Quanzhou'. The context of (9) is that people are talking about some duck meat, and the speaker suggests putting several pieces of duck meat into the noodles, and then heating the rest of duck meat. In this case, the adverb *koʔ⁷* is used to indicate that one event takes place after another event. In other words, the event *kui³⁻² tə⁵ loʔ⁸⁻⁴khɯ⁵⁻³ kiau¹* 'put several pieces of (duck meat) into (the noodles)' happens before the event *khɯ⁵⁻³ thŋ⁵* 'go to heat (the duck meat)'.

Besides the adverbs such as *tsiu⁵*, *tsiaʔ⁷* and *koʔ⁷*, the verbal complement *liau³* 了 'finish' is also often used to signal the temporal relation between two events or states. An example is given in (10).

(10) [VP + *liau³* 了]ₜᵢₘₑ ᴄʟᴀᴜsᴇ + Matrix clause
　　成家　　　　了，　彎　　艱苦　　　哦
　　siŋ²⁻⁴ke¹　　*liau³*　*ban²⁻⁴*　*kan¹khɔ³*　*o⁰*
　　get.married　finish　rather　tough　　SFP
　　'Life is rather tough after getting married.'

In (10), the verbal complement *liau³*, originally being a verb meaning 'finish', occurs after the verb *siŋ²⁻⁴ke¹* 'get married', indicating the realization of the event 'get married'. At the same time, *liau³* has a sequencing function in signaling that the situation *ban²⁻⁴ kan¹khɔ³* 'rather tough' happens after the event of getting married. In other words, the verbal complement *liau³* in (10) denotes the temporal relation between an event and a state in coding the anteriority of the first event with respect to the second (see Bybee et al. 1994 for 'finish' as a common lexical source of anteriors). Unlike adverbs such as *tsiu⁵*, the verbal complement *liau³* is always used in clause-final position of the temporal adverbial clause, rather than in the main clause.

The verbal complement *liau³* is also often used with the adverbs such as *tsiu⁵* and *tsiaʔ⁷*, as in (11) and (12).

(11) [NP + VP + *liau³* 了]ₜᵢₘₑ ᴄʟᴀᴜsᴇ + [NP + *tsiu⁵* 就+ VP]ᴍᴀᴛʀɪx ᴄʟᴀᴜsᴇ
　　我　　讀　　　中學　　　　了，
　　gua³　*thak⁸⁻⁴*　*tiɔŋ¹oʔ⁸*　*liau³*
　　1SG　study　middle.school　finish
　　媽仔　　　就　　　唔八　　　　罵　　我
　　bã²-a⁰　*tsiu⁵⁻⁴*　*m⁵⁻⁴paʔ⁷⁻⁸*　*bã⁵⁻⁴*　*gua³*
　　mother-NM　then　never　　scold　1SG
　　'Mother never scolded me after I entered middle school.'

(12) [NP + VP + *liau³* 了]ₜᵢₘₑ ᴄʟᴀᴜsᴇ + [NP + *tsiaʔ⁷* 則+ VP]ᴍᴀᴛʀɪx ᴄʟᴀᴜsᴇ
　　個　　背　　　了，　我　　則　　　會做　　　斡來
　　en¹　*pue⁵⁻⁴*　*liau³*　*gua³*　*tsiaʔ⁷⁻⁸*　*e⁴tsue⁵⁻³*　*uat⁷lai⁰*
　　3PL　recite　finish　1SG　only.then　can　come.back
　　'I cannot come back until they finish reciting.'

In (11), the verbal complement *liau³* is preceded by the verb phrase *thak⁸⁻⁴ tiɔŋ¹oʔ⁸* 'study in a middle school', indicating the achievement of the event 'enter into study at middle school'. In addition, the verbal complement *liau³* and the adverb *tsiu⁵* together signal the temporal sequence between the event 'I study in middle school' and the event 'Mother never scolds me'. Similarly, *liau³* in (12) occurs after the verb *pue⁵* 'recite' to denote the completion of the event 'recite'. In addition, *liau³* and the adverb *tsiaʔ⁷* together signal that the event 'they finish reciting' happens before the event 'I can come back'.

The clause with the verb *tan³* 等 'wait' as in (13), or with *kau⁵* 遘 'arrive' as in (14), can also be used to indicate the time of an event or state.

(13) [*tan³* 等 + NP + VP]_{TIME CLAUSE} + [*tsiaʔ⁷* 則 + VP]_{MATRIX CLAUSE}
 等 伊 來 則 與 伊
 tan³⁻² *i¹* *lai²* *tsiaʔ⁷⁻⁸* *khɔ⁵* *i⁰*
 wait 3SG come then give 3SG
 'Give (it) to him when he comes.'

(14) [*kau⁵* 遘 + NP + VP]_{TIME CLAUSE} + Matrix clause
 遘 我 會曉得， 都 中年 咯
 kau⁵⁻³ *gua³* *e⁴hiau³let⁰* *tɔ¹* *tiɔŋ¹len²* *lɔ⁰*
 arrive 1SG know already middle.age SFP
 '(She) was already a middle-aged woman when I was old enough to know better.'

In (13), the clause introduced by the verb *tan³* 'wait', i.e. *tan³⁻² i¹ lai²* (literally means 'wait him come'), indicates the time when the event *khɔ⁵ i⁰* 'give him' happens. In (14), the clause introduced by the verb *kau⁵* 'arrive', i.e. *kau⁵⁻³ gua³ e⁴hiau³let⁰* 'when I was old enough to know better', provides a reference time, when the person referred to was already a middle-aged woman.

The Hui'an dialect also uses the form of relative clause to express the time of an event or a state, as in (15).

(15) 恁 搬厝 其 時站， 我 無 倒來
 len³ *puã¹-tshu⁵* *e²⁻⁴* *si²⁻⁴tsam⁴* *gua³* *bo²⁻⁴* *tɔ⁵lai⁰*
 2PL move-house RM time 1SG not.have come.back
 'I didn't come back when you moved house.'

In (15), the noun *si²⁻⁴tsam⁴* 'time' functions as the head noun of the relative clause *len³ puã¹tshu⁵* 'you move house'. The whole construction *len³ puã¹tshu⁵ e²⁻⁴ si²⁻⁴tsam⁴* 'when you moved house' provides a reference time for when the event *gua³ bo²⁻⁴ tɔ⁵lai⁰* 'I didn't come back' happens.

As shown by the examples so far, the Hui'an dialect basically does not use subordinating conjunctions (such as English *when*, *before* and *after*) to mark a temporal adverbial clause. In Hui'an, there is a preference for the use of adverbs and a variety of sequencing markers, including *tsit⁸* + Verb 'as soon as' and clause-final *liau³*, as has been shown. However, the clause introduced by *tak⁸⁻⁴kiŋ³* 'every time' as in (16) below seems to be similar to English temporal adverbial clauses marked by *every time* or *whenever*.

(16) 逐口　　　買　　物件，　　計　　無　　　　算　　錢
　　 tak⁸⁻⁴kiŋ³　*bue³⁻²*　*bŋʔ⁸⁻⁴kiã⁴*　*ke⁵⁻³*　*bo²⁻⁴*　*sŋ⁵⁻³*　*tsin²*
　　 every.time　buy　thing　　all　not.have　count　money
　　 '(I) don't count money every time (I) buy something.'

23.3 Cause clauses

Cause clauses indicate the cause or reason of an action, event or a state. In Hui'an, the cause clause is typically zero-marked. The cause clause and the consequence clause are juxtaposed together, without any overt marker. Generally speaking, the cause clause iconically precedes the consequence clause, as in (17).

(17) Cause clause + Consequence clause
　　 過　　早　　落去，　　　　過　　　布
　　 kə⁵⁻³　*tsa³*　*loʔ⁸khɯ⁰*　*kə⁵⁻³*　*pɔ⁵*
　　 too　early　go.down　too　tough
　　 '(The meat) is too tough, since (it) was put into the pot too early.'

In (17), the first clause *kə⁵⁻³ tsa³ loʔ⁸khɯ⁰* '(it) was put into the pot too early' serves as a cause of the second clause *kə⁵⁻³ pɔ⁵* '(the meat) is too tough'.

The cause clause can also occur after the consequence clause, as in (18). This is used for further explanation.

(18) Consequence clause + Cause clause
　　 去　　　哦，　迄搭　　　　坐　　恰　　　　　　　燒　　呀
　　 khɯ⁵　*o⁰*　*hit⁷⁻⁸-taʔ⁷*　*tsə⁴*　*khaʔ⁷⁻⁸*　*sio¹*　*ia⁰*
　　 go　SFP　that-LOC　sit　comparatively　warm　SFP
　　 'Go ahead, since it is warmer sitting there.'

In (18), the speaker suggests to the addressee to sit at another place, since it is warmer there. The first clause *khɯ⁵ o⁰* 'go ahead' is the suggestion of the speaker, and the second clause *hit⁷⁻⁸taʔ⁷ tsə⁴ khaʔ⁷⁻⁸ sio¹ ia⁰* 'it is warmer sitting there' is used to explain why the suggestion has been made.

The clauses with subordinating conjunctions en^1ui^5 因為 'because' or $sɔ^{3\text{-}2}i^3$ 所以 'so' can also be attested in daily conversations. Two examples are given in (19) and (20).

(19) [en^1ui^5 因為 + NP + VP]_{CAUSE CLAUSE} + Consequence clause

因為	伊	呣	知	伯	障	想,
en^1ui^5	i^1	$m^{5\text{-}4}$	$tsai^1$	lan^3	$tsiũ^{5\text{-}3}$	$siũ^4$
because	3SG	not	know	1PL	how	think

伊	就	按	伊	的	風俗	來	辦
i^1	$tsiu^{5\text{-}4}$	$an^{5\text{-}3}$	i^1	$e^{2\text{-}4}$	$hɔŋ^1sioʔ^8$	$lai^{2\text{-}4}$	pan^5
3SG	then	follow	3SG	GEN	custom	come	do

'Since they don't know what we think about (the ceremony), they're preparing for it according to their custom.'

(20) Cause clause + [$sɔ^{3\text{-}2}i^3$ 所以 + NP + VP]_{CONSEQUENCE CLAUSE}

小妹	也	會	拵,
$sio^{3\text{-}2}bə^5$	a^4	e^4	$thueʔ^8$
Y.sister	also	would	take

所以,	恁	該	用	著	用
$sɔ^{3\text{-}2}i^3$	len^3	kai^1	$iŋ^5$	$tioʔ^{8\text{-}4}$	$iŋ^5$
so	2PL	should	use	should	use

'The younger sister will also give you (money), so, you should use (it) when you need.'

In (19), the clause introduced by the subordinating conjunction en^1ui^5 'because' semantically functions as a cause of the second clause. In (20), the second clause, i.e. the consequence clause introduced by the subordinating conjunction $sɔ^{3\text{-}2}i^3$ 'so', occurs after the first clause (i.e. the cause clause).

Note, however, that the clauses with the subordinating conjunctions en^1ui^5 'because' or $sɔ^{3\text{-}2}i^3$ 'so', as in (19) and (20), are not commonly used in daily conversations, and are essentially restricted to the speech of the younger generation. The use of this type of clause is probably a result of influence from Mandarin Chinese.

As mentioned above, some complex sentences that denote a temporal sequence relation may also signal cause, especially those involving an adverb such as $tsiu^5$, as in example (4) above. Similar clauses may only signal cause, bearing no relation to temporality, as illustrated by (21) and (22).

(21) Cause clause + [siã² + VP]₍CONSEQUENCE CLAUSE₎
合　　我　　其　　骹　　遘，
hap⁸⁻⁴　gua³　e²⁻⁴　khaⁱ　a³
suit　1SG　GEN　foot　EVC
口　　共　　伊　　買　　來
siã²　ka⁵⁻⁴　i¹　bue³　laiº
then　KA　3SG　buy　come
'(It) fits my feet well, so I bought it.'

(22) Cause clause + [NP + tsiaʔ⁷ 則 + VP]₍CONSEQUENCE CLAUSE₎
我　　驚　　　起　　遘　　暗摸摸，
gua³　kiã¹　　khi³　a⁵⁻³　am⁵⁻³bɔ̃¹bɔ̃¹
1SG　be.afraid　build　CM　dark
我　　則　　　唔　　敢　　訂
gua³　tsiaʔ⁷⁻⁸　m⁵⁻⁴　kã³⁻²　tiã⁵
1SG　Then　　not　dare　reserve
'I was afraid that (it) would be dark, so I didn't dare to reserve (the storage room).'

In (21), the first clause *hap⁸⁻⁴ gua³ e²⁻⁴ khaⁱ a³* 'it fits my feet well' serves as a cause of the event 'I bought it', encoded by the second clause. The adverb *siã²* 'then', used in this second, consequence clause, is used to signal a causal relation between the two events. Similarly, in (22), the first clause *gua³ kiã¹ khi³ a⁵⁻³ am⁵⁻³bɔ̃¹bɔ̃¹* 'I was afraid that (it) would be dark' is the cause of the event 'I didn't dare to reserve (the storage room)', encoded by the second clause. In this case, it is the adverb *tsiaʔ⁷* that indicates a causal relation between the two events. As with the adverb *siã²*, the adverb *tsiaʔ⁷* is also used in the consequence clause, rather than in the cause clause.

23.4 Purpose clauses

In Hui'an, purpose clauses often take the form of a serial verb construction, especially those using the verb *khuɯ⁵* 去 'go' to link two verb phrases, as in (23).

(23) VP + [khuɯ⁵ 去 + VP]₍PURPOSE CLAUSE₎
我　　行　　遘　　南門　　　去　　（才罪）　伊
gua³　kiã²　a³　kau⁵⁻³　lam²⁻⁴-bŋ²　khuɯ⁵⁻³　tshə⁵　iº
1SG　walk　EVC　arrive　south-gate　go　look.for　3SG
'I walked to South Gate (in order) to see her.'

In (23), $tshə^5 i^0$ 'see her' (lit. look for her) serves as a purpose of the event 'I walked to South Gate', encoded by the clause $gua^3 kia^2 a^3 kau^{5\text{-}3} lam^{2\text{-}4} bŋ^2$. The verb $khuɨ^5$ is used here to link the two clauses, and thus can be regarded as a purpose marker.

The auxiliary verb $thaŋ^1$ 啯 'can' seems to have similar functions, as in (24) and (25).

(24) VP + [NP + $thaŋ^1$ 啯 + VP]$_{\text{PURPOSE CLAUSE}}$

口	恰	過,	阮	啯	摒	衫褲
$tshau^2$	$khaʔ^{7\text{-}8}$	$kə^5$	gun^3	$thaŋ^1$	$piã^{5\text{-}3}$	$sã^1 khɔ^5$
move	a.bit	over	1PL	can	pack	clothes

'Move over a little bit, so that we can pack the clothes.'

(25) VP + [$thaŋ^1$ 啯 + VP]$_{\text{PURPOSE CLAUSE}}$

蜀	日	衫褲	共	摒摒	啯	搬家
$tsit^{8\text{-}4}$	$let^{8\text{-}4}$	$sã^1 khɔ^5$	$ka^{5\text{-}1}$	$piã^{5\text{-}3}{\sim}piã^5$	$thaŋ^1$	$puã^1\text{-}ke^1$
one	day	clothes	OM	pack~pack	can	move-home

'Pack the clothes one day (in order) to move house.'

In (24), the clause $gun^3 thaŋ^1 piã^{5\text{-}3} sã^1 khɔ^5$ 'we can pack the clothes' denotes the purpose of the speaker's suggestion 'move over a little bit', encoded by the first clause. Similarly, in (25), $puã^1 ke^1$ 'move-home' is the purpose of the suggestion 'pack the clothes one day', encoded by the clause $tsit^{8\text{-}4} let^{8\text{-}4} sã^1 khɔ^5 ka^{5\text{-}1} piã^{5\text{-}3} piã^5$. In both examples, $thaŋ^1$ occurs in the purpose clause. The morpheme $thaŋ^1$ is originally a modal auxiliary verb (see chapter 12). It is possibly the semantic component of enabling that 'can' verbs possess which allows this development into a quasi-marker of purpose, that is, of one event enabling another to be realized.

23.5 Conditional clauses

Conditional clauses provide the condition for the realization of an event. The conditional clause in Hui'an is often marked by a subordinating conjunction such as $lã^4$ 若 'if', especially when the conditional clause is used to predicate what it will be, as in (26), or express counterfactuals, as in (27).

(26) [Temporal + NP + *lã⁴* 若 + VP]CONDITIONAL CLAUSE + VP

下日	伯	若	洗	碗箸，
e⁴let⁸	*lan³*	*lã⁴*	*sue³⁻²*	*uã³⁻²-tu⁵*
future	1PL	if	wash	bowl-chopsticks

就	燒水	放	（起來）	洗
tsiu⁵⁻⁴	*sio¹-tsui³*	*paŋ⁵⁻³*	*khai⁴*	*sue³*
just	hot-water	release	RVC	wash

'In the future, if we need to wash the dishes, we can just use the hot water.'

(27) [NP + *lã⁴* 若 + VP]CONDITIONAL CLAUSE + VP

我	若	無	倒來，	驚	汝	看
gua³	*lã⁴*	*bo²⁻⁴*	*to⁵lai⁰*	*kiã¹*	*lɯ³⁻²*	*khuã⁵*
1SG	if	not.have	come.back	be.afraid	2SG	look

'If I didn't come back, I'd be afraid that you would be expecting me anyway.'

In (26), the time word *e⁴let⁸* 'future' indicates that a potential future event is involved. The clause introduced by the subordinating conjunction *lã⁴* 'if', i.e. *e⁴let⁸ lan³ lã⁴ sue³⁻² uã³⁻²tu⁵* 'in the future, if we need to wash the dishes', functions as a conditional adverbial clause. This example may also be interpreted as a future time clause. Cross-linguistically, it is not uncommon that there is no distinction between predicative conditionals and future time clauses (cf. Thompson, Longacre & Hwang 2007:257). The context of (27) is that the speaker goes back home every weekend during the periods when she is studying in another city, since she does not want her mother to keep expecting her in vain. In this case, *bo²⁻⁴ to⁵lai⁰* 'not come back' is not a fact but purely hypothetical. This is a case of the counterfactual. The first conditional clause has also been marked by the subordinating conjunction *lã⁴* 'if'. In terms of position, in both these examples, the subordinating conjunction *lã⁴* 'if' occurs between the subject and the verb phrase. For example, *lã⁴* in (26) is placed between the subject *lan³* 'we' and the verb phrase *sue³⁻² uã³⁻²tu⁵* 'wash the dishes'.

The conditional clause marked by the conjunction *lã⁴* 'if' can also be used for the situations that might happen, as in (28), or for the present or past situations in the real world, as in (29).

(28) [NP + *lã⁴* 若+ VP]_{CONDITIONAL CLAUSE} + VP
 伊　　若　　聽　　繪　　　　落,
 i¹　　*lã⁴*　 *thiã¹*　*bue⁴*　　 *lɔʔ⁸*
 3SG　 if　　listen　can.not　down
 也　　繪　　　來　　　佮搭　　　　坐　　咯
 a⁴　 *bue⁴*　 *lai²⁻⁴*　 *lan³-taʔ⁷*　 *tsə⁴*　 *lɔ⁰*
 also　 can.not　come　 1PL-LOC　　 sit　　SFP
 'If he couldn't listen to us, he wouldn't come to our place.'

(29) [Locative + *lã⁴* 若+ VP]_{CONDITIONAL CLAUSE} + VP
 口面　　　　 若　　落雨,
 khau³⁻²ben²　 *lã⁴*　 *lɔʔ⁸⁻⁴-hɔ⁴*
 outside　　　 if　　 fall-rain
 衫褲　　 共　　　口　　　入來
 sã¹khɔ⁵　 *ka⁵⁻¹*　 *hiãʔ⁷*　 *liəp⁰lai⁰*
 clothes　 OM　　take　 come.into
 'If it is raining outside, take the clothes in.'

The context of (28) is that people are giving advice to their friend, and the speaker is sure that their friend does not mind what they are telling him. In other words, the conditional clause *i¹ lã⁴ thiã¹ bue⁴ lɔʔ⁸* 'if he couldn't listen to us' in (28) involves a situation that might happen (i.e. a hypothetical situation). In (29), however, the conditional clause *khau³⁻²ben² lã⁴ lɔʔ⁸ho³* 'if it is raining outside' involves a possible present situation outside the house at the time of speech.

Besides the conjunction *lã⁴*, other formal markers for conditional clauses are also attested in daily conversations. For example, the subordinating conjunction *lã⁴si⁴* 若是 'if' is typically used to express counterfactuals, as in (30), but can also be used for the present or past situations, as in (31).

(30) [NP + *lã⁴si⁴* 若是+ VP]_{CONDITIONAL CLAUSE} + VP
 阮　　　 老　　 若　　是　　 卜　　　 捒　　　 我　　 錢　　 去
 gun³⁻²　 *lau⁴*　 *lã⁴*　 *si⁴*　 *bɔʔ⁷⁻⁸*　 *thueʔ⁸⁻⁴*　 *gua³*　 *tsin²*　 *khu⁵*
 1PL　　 old　　 if　　 be　　 want　　 take　　　 1SG　　 money　go
 蜀　　 個　　 月　　 會　　 㵾㵾㵾
 tsit⁸⁻⁴　 *ko⁵⁻³*　 *gəʔ⁸*　 *e⁴*　 *theʔ⁷⁻⁸~theʔ⁷⁻⁸~theʔ⁷*
 one　 CL　　 month　can　 finished~finished~finished
 'If my father had wanted to take my money, I would be absolutely broke by the end of each month.'

(31) [lã⁴si⁴ 若是 + VP]CONDITIONAL CLAUSE + [NP + VP]

若	是	遘	拜五	暗頭,	我	是	發呆,
lã⁴	si⁴	kau⁵⁻³	pai⁵⁻³gɔ⁴	am⁵⁻³thau²	gua³	si⁴	huat⁷⁻⁸tai¹
if	be	arrive	week.five	dusk	1SG	be	stare.blankly

計	無	心	哃	做	生理
ke⁵⁻³	bo²⁻⁴	siəm¹	thaŋ¹	tsue⁵⁻³	siŋ¹li³
all	not.have	heart	can	do	business

'If Friday evening arrived with me in a daze, I wasn't always in the mood for doing business.'

In (30), the fact is that the speaker's father does not want to take his money, and thus the conditional clause *gun³⁻² lau⁴ lã⁴ si⁴ boʔ⁷⁻⁸ thueʔ⁸⁻⁴ gua³ tsin² khuĩ⁵* 'if my father wanted to take my money' is a case of a counterfactual conditional, used to show that the salary of the speaker is not very high. In (31), the speaker is recalling past memories, and thus the conditional clause *lã⁴ si⁴ kau⁵⁻³ pai⁵⁻³gɔ⁴* 'if Friday evening arrived' is used for a past situation.

The expression *boʔ⁷⁻⁸ khɔ⁵⁻⁴ gua³* 卜與我, literally meaning 'if give me', can be used in a hypothetical situation, meaning 'if it were me', as in (32).

(32) [boʔ⁷⁻⁸ khɔ⁵⁻⁴ gua³ 卜與我]CONDITIONAL CLAUSE + [NP + VP]

卜	與	我,	我	唔	愛	去
boʔ⁷⁻⁸	khɔ⁵⁻⁴	gua³	gua³	m⁵⁻⁴	ai⁵⁻³	khuĩ⁵
want	give	1SG	1SG	not	like	go

'If it were me, I wouldn't want to go there.'

The context of (32) is that people are talking about living and working in the City of Shenzhen, and the speaker points out that if it were him, he would avoid moving there.

Other forms involving the verb *boʔ⁷* that can be used in a conditional clause include *boʔ⁷⁻⁸ si⁴* 卜是 'if' (lit. want be), as in (33), and *boʔ⁷⁻⁸ tsai¹* 卜知 'if (I) knew (it)' (lit. want know), as in (34). Both are typically used to express counterfactuals.

(33) [*boʔ⁷⁻⁸ si⁴* 卜是 + NP + VP]_{CONDITIONAL CLAUSE} + [NP + *a⁴* 也 + VP]
　　 卜　　　是　　我　　當時　　　無　　　　說　　汝,
　　 boʔ⁷⁻⁸　si⁴　gua³　tŋ¹si²　bo²⁻⁴　səʔ⁷　lu⁰
　　 want　be　1SG　then　not.have　say　2SG
　　 伯　　也　　　儶　　　　冤家
　　 lan³　a⁴　bue⁴　uan¹ke¹
　　 1PL　also　can.not　quarrel
　　 'If I hadn't scolded you, we wouldn't have quarreled.'

(34) [DM + VP] + [*boʔ⁷* 卜 + V] + VP
　　 啊　　　唔　　　知,　　　卜　　　　知,
　　 a⁰　m⁵⁻⁴　tsai¹　boʔ⁷⁻⁸　tsai¹
　　 DM　not　know　want　know
　　 直接　　　　　叫　　　即個　　　　來　　　做
　　 tet⁸⁻⁴tsiəp⁷　kio⁵⁻³　tsit⁷⁻⁸-e²　lai²⁻⁴　tsue⁵
　　 directly　call　this-CL　come　do
　　 '(I) didn't know (it), if (I) had known (it), (I) would've contacted him directly for the job.'

In (33), the interlocutors are looking back at what happened, and the speaker is regretting that she scolded the addressee, which led to a quarrel between them. In other words, the speaker is imagining a possible world in which the event of scolding encoded by the first clause did not happen, and consequently nor did the ensuing quarrel, coded by the second clause. Thus, a case of the counterfactual is involved in this example. In (34), the speaker is talking about what he would have done if he knew something before. The fact is that he did not know it beforehand, as shown by the first clause *a⁰ m⁵⁻⁴ tsai¹* '(I) didn't know (it)'. This is also a case of a counterfactual conditional.

Conditional clauses without a subordinating conjunction are also commonly used in Hui'an, especially those used for present situations, as in (35).

(35) VP_{CONDITIONAL CLAUSE} + VP
　　 愛　　　　睏,　　　去　　　　睏
　　 ai⁵⁻³　khun⁵　khɯ⁵⁻³　khun⁵
　　 like　sleep　go　sleep
　　 'Go to sleep, if (you) are sleepy.'

In (35), the speaker finds that the addressee looks sleepy, and thus suggests to the addressee to go to bed, if he feels sleepy.

Conditional clauses without a subordinating conjunction are also attested in other contexts, as in (36) and (37).

(36) VP_{CONDITIONAL CLAUSE} + VP

做做	來，	就	包	蜀	個	與	伊
tsue$^{5\text{-}3}$tsue^5	lai^2	tsiu$^{5\text{-}4}$	pau^1	tsit$^{8\text{-}4}$	e$^{2\text{-}4}$	khɔ^5	i^0
together	come	then	wrap	one	CL	give	3SG

'If (they) come together, then give him a (red envelope).'

(37) [NP + VP]_{CONDITIONAL CLAUSE} + [NP + VP]

汝	卜	褪剝潡，		
lu^3	bɔʔ$^{7\text{-}8}$	thŋ$^{5\text{-}3}$-pak$^{7\text{-}8}$-theʔ^7		
2SG	want	take.off-peel.off-nothing.left		
阮	也	無	法	
gun^3	a^4	bo$^{2\text{-}4}$	huat^7	
1PL	also	not.have	method	

'If you had wanted to be naked to the waist, I still could do nothing for you.'

Example (36) is used to predict what will happen if something takes place in the future. The conditional clause *tsue$^{5\text{-}3}$tsue^5 lai^2* 'come together' refers to a potential future event. In (37), the speaker wishes to express that she is not able to look after her daughter (i.e. the addressee), since her daughter is living and working in another city, which is far away from home. In this case, *lu^3 bɔʔ$^{7\text{-}8}$ thŋ$^{5\text{-}3}$pak$^{7\text{-}8}$theʔ^7* 'you want to be naked to the waist' involves an impossible event, since it is basically impossible for a Chinese girl to move around naked to the waist even at home. In other words, this example shows a case of the counterfactual.

Conditional clauses in a negative form (i.e. involving a negator) typically do not use a subordinating conjunction, and can be found in present, past or future situations in real world contexts. Examples are given in (38) – (40).

(38) [NEG + V]_{CONDITIONAL CLAUSE} + [NP + VP]

唔	穿，	我	穿
m$^{5\text{-}4}$	tshiŋ^5	gua^3	tshiŋ^5
not	wear	1SG	wear

'If (you) don't want to wear (it), then I will.'

(39) [NEG + VP]_{CONDITIONAL CLAUSE} + VP

呣　　與　　伊　　食，　　驚　　　伊　　吼
$m^{5\text{-}4}$　$kh\mathfrak{o}^{5\text{-}4}$　i^1　$tsia\text{?}^8$　$kia\!\tilde{\,}^1$　i^1　hau^3
not　give　3SG　eat　be.afraid　3SG　cry
'If (I) didn't let him eat (it), (I) was afraid that he would cry.'

(40) [NEG + V]_{CONDITIONAL CLAUSE} + VP

呣　　來，　　明日　　　　掠　　去　　賣　　　揀
$m^{5\text{-}4}$　lai^2　$bi\tilde{a}^{2\text{-}4}let^8$　$lia\text{?}^{8\text{-}4}$　$khu^{5\text{-}3}$　bue^4　sak^7
not　come　tomorrow　catch　go　sell　RVC
'If (he) doesn't come, let's sell (it) tomorrow.'

In (38), people are talking about a piece of clothing which is in front of them at the speech time. In (39), the speaker is looking back at what has just happened with a child. Example (40) involves a potential future event of selling a chicken.

As with the conditional clauses in a negative form as in (38) – (40), concessive conditionals in Hui'an usually do not co-occur with a subordinating conjunction. However, as illustrated by the following example, the adverb a^4 也 'also' is typically used in the main clause of this type of complex sentence.

(41) VP_{CONDITIONAL CLAUSE} + [a^4 也 + VP]

佫　　　買，　　也　　無　　　　即垛　　　　口
$ko\text{?}^{7\text{-}8}$　bue^3　a^4　$bo^{2\text{-}4}$　$tsit^{7\text{-}8}\text{-}t\mathfrak{\text{ə}}^5$　$thiak^7$
again　buy　also　not.have　this-CL　beautiful
'Even if (we) buy (one) again, (we) would not find a better one.'

23.6 Summary

This chapter focuses on how adverbial clauses are encoded in Hui'an. Generally speaking, unlike some European languages such as English where adverbial clauses are usually marked by subordinating conjunctions, the Hui'an dialect tends to juxtapose the clauses with the semantic relation between the clauses inferred, or use an adverb in the main clause to mark the semantic relation between the clauses, though other types of marker are also attested.

Besides being zero-marked, time clauses are also often marked by an adverb such as $tsiu^5$ 就 'then', $tsia\text{?}^7$ 則 'then' and $ko\text{?}^7$ 佫 'again', among which $tsiu^5$ can also co-occur with $tsit^8$ 蜀 'one' or tu^3 拄 'just' to mean 'as soon as...then'. Other temporal markers include the clause-final $liau^3$ 了 (< 'finish'), the verbs tan^3 等

'wait' and *kau⁵* 遘 'arrive', the relative clause with *si²⁻⁴tsam⁴* 時站 'time' as the head noun, and *tak⁸⁻⁴kiŋ³* 'every time'.

The cause clause normally precedes the consequence clause, though it can also occur after the consequence clause for providing further explanation. The cause clause tends to be zero-marked. However, the subordinating conjunctions *en¹ui⁵* 因為 'because' and *sɔ³⁻²i³* 所以 'so' can be attested in the speech of the younger generation, probably due to the influence from Mandarin Chinese. The cause clause can also be marked by an adverb such as *siã²* 'then' and *tsiaʔ⁷* 則 'then'.

Purpose clauses often take the form of a serial verb construction, especially those using the verb *khu⁵* 去 'go' to link two verb phrases. The auxiliary verb *thaŋ¹* 嗵 'can' is also used to mark this construction type.

The conditional clause is often marked by a subordinating conjunction such as *lã⁴* 若 'if' and *lã⁴si⁴* 若是 'if'. The expression *boʔ⁷⁻⁸ khɔ⁵⁻⁴ gua³* 卜與我, literally meaning 'if-give-me', can be used in a hypothetical situation, meaning 'if it were me'. Other forms involving the verb *boʔ⁷* that can be used in a conditional clause include *boʔ⁷⁻⁸ si⁴* 卜是 'if' (lit. want-be) and *boʔ⁷⁻⁸ tsai¹* 卜知 'if (I) knew (it)' (lit. want-know), both of which are used to express counterfactuals. Conditional clauses without any subordinating conjunction are also commonly used.

24 Complement clauses

24.1 Introduction

Complement clauses refer to the clauses which function as a core argument of a higher clause (cf. Noonan 1985; Dixon 2006). Little systematic research has been conducted on this topic for Chinese. To our knowledge, several papers (Cheng 1997e; Xu & Matthews 2007; Chappell 2008) examined the complementizers developed from the 'say' verb and/or the 'see' verb, among which Cheng (1997e) focuses on both the 'say' verb and the 'see' verb in Taiwan Southern Min and Taiwan Mandarin, Xu & Matthews (2007) examine the 'say' verb and the 'see' verb in two varieties of Southern Min (Taiwan and Chaozhou), while Chappell (2008) gives a discussion of the 'say' verb used as a complementizer in Chinese in general. In Hui'an, complement clauses typically function as an object of the main clause, and thus can be referred to as object clauses.

The main semantic classes of verbs that can take an object clause in Hui'an include (a) utterance verbs, such as $sə\textipa{P}^7$ 說 'say', $kaŋ^3$ 講 'say' and $bŋ^5$ 問 'ask'; (b) verbs of perception and cognition, such as $khuã^5$ 看 'look', $thiã^1$ 聽 'listen to, hear', $kam^{3\text{-}2}kak^7$ 感覺 'feel', $siũ^4$ 想 'think', ai^5 愛 'like', $kiã^1$ 驚 'be afraid', $tsai^i(iã^3)$知(影) 'know', $e^4ki^5(let^0)$會記(得) 'remember', and $huat^{7\text{-}8}hen^5$ 發現 'find'; (c) modal verbs of volition, such as $bo\textipa{P}^7$ ト 'want', $siũ^4bo\textipa{P}^7$ 想ト 'want' and ai^5 愛 'want'; and (d) causative (or manipulative) verbs, such as $khɔ^5$ 與 'give', kio^5 叫 'call, ask' and $tshiã^3$ 請 'invite, hire'. As shown in the following table, utterance verbs and some verbs of perception and cognition such as $kam^{3\text{-}2}kak^7$ 'feel' and $siũ^4$ 'think' can be followed by the complementizer $sə\textipa{P}^7$ (< 'say') and/or $khuã^5$ 看 (< 'look'), among which the complementizer $khuã^5$ is typically used to introduce an interrogative complement clause and is used in the context which inquires about something or looks for an answer. Note, however, that the utterance verb $sə\textipa{P}^7$ 'say' cannot co-occur with the complementizer $sə\textipa{P}^7$ (< 'say'), unlike some other Southern Min varieties such as Taiwan.

Tab. 24-1: The main semantic classes of verbs that can take an object clause in the Hui'an dialect

		+complementizer *səʔ⁷* 說 (< 'say')	+complementizer *khuā⁵* 看 (< 'look')
Utterance verbs	*səʔ⁷* 說 'say'	−	+
	kaŋ³ 講 'say'	+	+
	bŋ⁵ 問 'ask'	+	+
Verbs of perception and cognition	*khuā⁵* 看 'look'	−	−
	thiā¹ 聽 'listen to, hear'	−	+
	kam³⁻²kak⁷ 感覺 'feel'	+	+
	siū⁴ 想 'think'	+	+
	ai⁵ 愛 'like'	−	−
	kiā¹ 驚 'be afraid'	−	−
	tsai¹(iā³) 知(影) 'know'	−	−
	e⁴ki⁵(let⁰) 會記(得) 'remember'	+	−
	huat⁷⁻⁸hen⁵ 發現 'find'	+	−
Modal verbs of volition	*boʔ⁷* 卜 'want'	−	−
	siū⁴boʔ⁷ 想卜 'want'	−	−
	ai⁵ 愛 'want'	−	−
Causative (or manipulative) verbs	*khɔ⁵* 與 'give'	−	−
	kio⁵ 叫 'call, ask'	−	−
	tshiā³ 請 'invite, hire'	−	−

24.2 Utterance verbs

Utterance verbs describe the manner of information transfer, and the object clause they take represents the transferred information. The subject of utterance verbs, i.e. the subject of the main clause, is the agent who transfers the information. As mentioned above, utterance verbs in Hui'an include *səʔ⁷* 'say', *kaŋ³* 'say' and *bŋ⁵* 'ask', of which, *səʔ⁷* is the most basic and common one. Note that this differs from Taiwan Southern Min where *kóng* 講 is the main speech act verb of saying (cf. Chappell 2008).

Compared to other semantic classes, an important feature of utterance verbs is that they can introduce what was said by the speaker or other people, i.e. the object clause they take can be a quotation: either a direct quotation, as in (1), or an indirect quotation, as in (2).

(1) 我　　　說　　　"汝　　著　　　問　　清楚"
　　 gua^3　$sa?^{7-8}$　lu^3　$tio?^{8-4}$　$bŋ^{5-4}$　$tshiŋ^1tshɔ^3$
　　 1SG　　say　　　2SG　　should　　ask　　clear
　　 'I said, "You should clarify it".'

(2) 伊　　　說　　　伊　　卜　　　過來
　　 i^1　$sa?^{7-8}$　i^1　$bo?^{7-8}$　$kə^5lai^0$
　　 3SG　　say　　　3SG　　want　　come.over
　　 'He said that he wanted to come over.'

The direct quotation gives the actual words of the speaker, and even often imitates the intonation and body language, while the indirect quotation needs to be adapted to the viewpoint of the speaker, especially those deictic expressions such as personal pronouns and demonstratives (cf. Noonan 1985:121; Givón 2001:155). In (1), the speaker quotes what she herself said before. The clause $lu^3\ tio?^{8-4}\ bŋ^{5-4}\ tshiŋ^1tshɔ^3$ 'you should clarify it' is the direct quotation, functioning as an object of the utterance verb $sa?^7$ 'say' in the main clause. Note that the object clause in (1) may not necessarily be a word-for-word quotation, albeit its purported character. In fact, most direct quotations in Hui'an such as (1) keep the meanings of what was said and the original perspective of the expression, but do not necessarily represent the exact words or intonation, even though the speaker intends for the addressee to understand that it is a verbatim reproduction. In (2), however, the speaker reports, rather than quotes directly, what was said by another person. The clause $i^1\ bo?^{7-8}\ kə^5lai^0$ 'he wanted to come over', which also functions as an object of the verb $sa?^7$, is an indirect, rather than a direct, quotation. This fact is evident in the second occurrence of the third person singular pronoun i^1 'he', i.e. the subject of the object clause, which substitutes for the original first person singular pronoun gua^3 'I', and is thus used to report.

Both (1) and (2) are used to quote different declarative sentences. The following are two examples of quoting an interrogative.

(3) 我　　說　　"我　　　　通　　去　　唔"
    gua³　saʔ⁷⁻⁸　gua³　thaŋ¹　khuɨ⁵　m⁰
    1SG　say　　1SG　　can　　go　　SFP
    'I said, "Can I go there?".'

(4) NP + V_UTTERANCE + khuã⁵_COMP + [VP]_COMPLEMENT CLAUSE
    伊　　說　　　看　　　通　　共　　伊　　囝
    i¹　　saʔ⁷⁻⁸　khuã⁵⁻³　thaŋ¹　ka⁵⁻⁴　en¹　kã³
    3SG　say　　COMP　　can　　to　　3PL　child
    買　　　電腦　　　　　唔
    bue³⁻²　ten⁵⁻⁴lo³　　m⁰
    buy　　computer　　SFP
    'She asked whether (she) could buy her son a computer.'

As with (1), (3) is an example of direct quotation: the speaker directly quotes what she herself said before. Unlike (1), however, the object clause *gua³ thaŋ¹ khuɨ⁵ m⁰* 'can I go there' is an interrogative clause, rather than a declarative clause. When people report an interrogative clause in indirect speech, a complementizer is usually placed after the utterance verb. For example, in (4), the speaker reports what was said by another person, and the complementizer *khuã⁵* (derived from the verb *khuã⁵* 'look') is inserted between the verb *saʔ⁷* 'say' and the object clause *thaŋ¹ ka⁵⁻⁴ en¹ kã³ bue³⁻² ten⁵⁻⁴lo³ m⁰* 'can (she) buy her son a computer'.

When the verb in the main clause is encoded by the verb *saʔ⁷* 'say', the addressee is often covert, as illustrated by (1) – (4) above. The following example, however, shows that the addressee can also be overt, and is typically introduced by the preposition *ka⁵* 共.

(5) NP + ka⁵_GOAL MARKER + NP_GOAL + V_UTTERANCE + [NP + VP]_COMPLEMENT CLAUSE
    我　　共　　伊　　說　　　我　　咧　　　洗　　　衫褲
    gua³　ka⁵⁻⁴　i¹　　saʔ⁷⁻⁸　gua³　leʔ⁷⁻⁸　sue³⁻²　sã¹khɔ⁵
    1SG　to　　3SG　say　　　1SG　PROG　　wash　　clothes
    (a) 'I said to him, "I am washing the clothes".'
    (b) 'I said to him I was washing the clothes.'

In (5), the third person singular pronoun *i¹* 'he', preceded by the preposition *ka⁵*, is the addressee of the verb *saʔ⁷* 'say'. The declarative clause *gua³ leʔ⁷⁻⁸ sue³⁻² sã¹khɔ⁵* 'I am washing the clothes' functions as an object of the verb *saʔ⁷* 'say'. Unlike examples (1) – (4) above, example (5) has two possible interpretations due to the presence of a first person pronoun: (a) the object clause is a direct quotation, as in (5a); and (b) the object clause is an indirect quotation, as in (5b). The subject of the object clause (the second occurrence of the pronoun gua^3 'I') is co-referential with the subject of the main clause (the first occurrence of gua^3 'I'). In other words, the differences in the use of pronouns, which help distinguish direct quotations from indirect quotations in (1) and (2), do not work in the case of example (5). In this case, the speaker may use a pause after the verb $sə\textipa{P}^7$ 'say' and imitate the intonation of the original utterance to distinguish a direct quotation such as (5a) from an indirect quotation such as (5b). However, we cannot rule out the possibility that examples which use neither a pause nor imitate the intonation could also be direct quotations. It is obvious that the distinction between direct and indirect quotations in (5) is not as explicit as that in (1) – (4), where it is made more clearly through the use of pronouns and also in (4) by the presence of an overt complementizer. This may suggest that, in daily conversation, not all object clauses of utterance verbs can be clearly grouped into direct or indirect quotations, independent of their context.

Note, furthermore, that not all the languages in the world use indirect quotations, though direct quotations are claimed to exist in all languages (Noonan 1985:122). In Hui'an, however, both direct and indirect quotations are common in daily conversation, as reflected in our texts.

The object clause of the verb $sə\textipa{P}^7$ 'say' is itself normally an independent clause, and can be used alone as a main clause, as illustrated by examples (1) – (3) and (5). However, when the subject of the object clause, which functions as an indirect quotation, is co-referential with the subject of the main clause, the subject of the object clause is usually omitted, as in (4), where the subject of the object clause ($thaŋ^1\ ka^{5\text{-}4}\ en^1\ kã^3\ bue^{3\text{-}2}\ ten^{5\text{-}4}lo^3\ m^0$ 'can (she) buy her son a computer') is covert, since it is co-referential with the subject of the main clause i^1 'she'. This is a case of an interrogative clause. The following is an example of a declarative one.

(6) 伊   說   暗暝   倒來
    i^1 $sə\textipa{P}^{7\text{-}8}$ $am^{5\text{-}3}bin^2$ to^5lai^0
    3SG   say   evening   come.back
    'He said he would come back tonight.'

In (6), the declarative clause $am^{5\text{-}3}bin^2\ to^5lai^0$ 'come back tonight' is an indirect quotation, and functions as an object of the verb $sə\textipa{P}^7$ 'say'. The subject of the object clause is omitted, since it is co-referential with the subject of the main clause i^1 'he'.

All the examples given so far quote or report what was said by the speaker or other people. This, however, cannot cover all the instances of object clauses of the verb *səʔ⁷* 'say', as illustrated by (7) and (8).

(7) 汝　　共　　伊　　說　　"我　　　無　　　　錢"
　　 luˀ³　*ka⁵⁻⁴*　*iˀ¹*　*səʔ⁷⁻⁸*　*gua³*　*bo²⁻⁴*　*tsin²*
　　 2SG　 to　　3SG　say　 1SG　 not.have　money
　　 'Tell him, "I have no money".'

(8) 汝　　共　　伊　　說　　汝　　　無　　　　閒
　　 luˀ³　*ka⁵⁻⁴*　*iˀ¹*　*səʔ⁷⁻⁸*　*luˀ³*　*bo²⁻⁴*　*uin²*
　　 2SG　 to　　3SG　say　 2SG　 not.have　leisure
　　 'Tell him that you don't have time.'

In (7), the clause *gua³ bo²⁻⁴ tsin²* 'I have no money' functions as an object of the verb *səʔ⁷* 'say'. In (8), the clause *luˀ³ bo²⁻⁴ uin²* 'you don't have time' also functions as an object of the verb *səʔ⁷* 'say'. Unlike those in examples (1) – (6), the object clauses in (7) and (8) are not instances of what has been said previously by the speaker (or other people). They do not involve a past event, but involve suggestions made by the speaker for the addressee, that is, the speaker suggests to the addressee how to talk to another person (i.e. *iˀ¹* 'he', the addressee of the verb *səʔ⁷* 'say') in a potential future event. Interestingly, these two examples show differences in terms of their use of personal pronouns: the first person singular pronoun *gua³* is used in (7), while the second person singular pronoun *luˀ³* is used in (8), though they are both used to refer to the addressee *luˀ³* 'you'. In other words, a similar distinction between direct and indirect quotations is also attested in examples (7) and (8), that is, the suggested information can be transferred from different viewpoints (the viewpoint of the addressee, or the viewpoint of the speaker).

The verb *səʔ⁷* 'say' can also take other types of object clause, as illustrated by (9) and (10).

(9) 阿三　　　心裡　　　　說　　阮　　　無　　　　愛　　去
　　 a¹sã¹　*siəm¹-lai⁴*　*səʔ⁷⁻⁸*　*gun³*　*bo²⁻⁴*　*ai⁵⁻³*　*khuˀ⁵*
　　 PN　　 heart-inside　say　 1PL　 not.have　like　 go
　　 'Ah-San said in his heart, "I don't want to go".'

(10) 我　　說　　恁　　蜀　　個　　啉　　半　　碗
　　　gua³　səʔ⁷⁻⁸　len³　tsit⁸⁻⁴　e²　liəm¹　puã⁵⁻³　uã³
　　　1SG　say　　2PL　one　　CL　drink　half　　bowl
　　　'I suggest that each of you drink half a bowl of (soup).'

In (9), the object clause *gun³ bo²⁻⁴ ai⁵⁻³ khɯ⁵* 'I don't want to go' does not represent what is said by the subject of the main clause (i.e. *aˡsã¹* 'Ah-San') in the real world, but is rather a conjecture of the speaker about Ah-san's innermost feelings. In (10), the object clause *len³ tsit⁸⁻⁴ e² liəm¹ puã⁵⁻³ uã³* 'each of you drink half a bowl of (soup)' does not represent what is said by the speaker, but is rather a suggestion of the speaker at the speech time. Unlike (7) and (8) above where the speaker suggests to the addressee how to talk to another person, example (10) is used by the speaker to suggest a certain course of action to the addressees.

As with the verb *səʔ⁷* 'say', object clauses of the utterance verb *kaŋ³* 講 'say' can be a quotation or a non-quotation. Unlike *səʔ⁷* 'say', however, when the verb *kaŋ³* 'say' takes an object clause, it tends to be understood as an indirect quotation, as illustrated by (11).

(11) 共　　阮　　　傷害　　　咯,
　　　ka⁵⁻⁴　gun³⁻²　siɔŋ¹hai⁵　lɔ⁰
　　　OM　　1PL　　hurt　　　SFP
　　　佫　　　共　　阮　　　講　　　心　　是　　好　　其
　　　koʔ⁷⁻⁸　ka⁵⁻⁴　gun³⁻²　kaŋ³⁻²　siəm¹　si⁴　ho³　e⁰
　　　still　　to　　1PL　　say　　　heart　be　　good　SFP
　　　'(He) has hurt us, yet still told us that (he) is good-hearted.'

In (11), the speaker is reporting what was done and said by another person. The clause *siəm¹ si⁴ ho³ e⁰* (literally meaning 'the heart is good') functions as an object of the verb *kaŋ³* 'say', reporting what was said. This is a case of indirect quotation. To form a direct quotation, at least the first-person singular pronoun *gua³* should occur before the noun *siəm¹* 'heart' in the object clause. As with the verb *səʔ⁷* 'say', the addressee of the verb *kaŋ³* 'say' is introduced by the preposition *ka⁵*, when it is overt in the main clause. The complementizer *səʔ⁷* (derived from the verb *səʔ⁷* 'say') can be added after the verb *kaŋ³* 'say'. This is different from the verb *səʔ⁷* 'say', which cannot co-occur with its grammaticalized use in the form of complementizer *səʔ⁷*. This is also different from Taiwan Southern Min where *kóng*, as the main speech act verb of saying as mentioned above, can be used with the complementizer *kóng*.

The object clause in (11) is a declarative clause. An example of interrogative use is given in (12).

(12) V$_{\text{UTTERANCE}}$ + [sə$ʔ^7_{\text{COMP}}$ + VP]$_{\text{COMPLEMENT CLAUSE}}$
  講   說   下日   卜   障   辦
  kaŋ$^{3\text{-}2}$ sə$ʔ^{7\text{-}8}$ e^{4}let^8 boʔ$^{7\text{-}8}$ tsiũ$^{5\text{-}3}$ pan^5
  say   COMP   future want   how   do
  '(We) can talk about what (we) can do in the future.'

The context of (12) is that the speaker suggests that two families can get together and discuss what they can do in the future. This is a case of non-quotation. The clause 'how it can be done in the future' functions as an object of the verb kaŋ^3 'say', while sə$ʔ^7$ functions as a complementizer. In this case, the complementizer khuã^5 can also be used.

Comparatively speaking, kaŋ^3 with an object clause is less common than sə$ʔ^7$ used with the same in daily conversations. The verb kaŋ^3 in (11) and (12) can be substituted by the verb sə$ʔ^7$ 'say', if the complementizer sə$ʔ^7$ is not present.

The verb bŋ^5 問 'ask' is often followed by a quotation, as illustrated by (13) – (15).

(13) NP + V$_{\text{UTTERANCE}}$ + [sə$ʔ^7_{\text{COMP}}$ + NP + VP]$_{\text{COMPLEMENT CLAUSE}}$
  伊   問   說   "汝   底時   卜   倒來"
  i^1 bŋ$^{5\text{-}4}$ sə$ʔ^{7\text{-}8}$ lɯ^3 ti^{4}si^2 boʔ$^{7\text{-}8}$ to^{5}lai^0
  3SG   ask   COMP   2SG   when   want   come.back
  'He asked, "When will you come back?".'

(14) 伊   問   我   "汝   咧   創   啥"
  i^1 bŋ$^{5\text{-}4}$ gua^3 lɯ^3 leʔ$^{7\text{-}8}$ tshɔŋ$^{5\text{-}3}$ siã^2
  3SG   ask   1SG   2SG   PROG   do   what
  'He asked, "What are you doing?".'

(15) V$_{\text{UTTERANCE}}$ + [khuã$^5_{\text{COMP}}$ + NP + VP]$_{\text{COMPLEMENT CLAUSE}}$
  問   看   汝   口   仵   底   呀
  bŋ$^{5\text{-}4}$ khuã$^{5\text{-}3}$ lɯ^3 tse^5 ti^4 to^3 ia^0
  ask   COMP   2SG   now   be.at   where   SFP
  '(He) asked where you are now.'

In (13), the speaker directly quotes what was said by the subject of the main clause (i^1 'he'). The interrogative clause lɯ^3 ti^{4}si^2 boʔ$^{7\text{-}8}$ to^{5}lai^0 'when will you come back' functions as an object of the verb *bŋ⁵* 'ask', and *səʔ⁷* functions as a complementizer. As with (13), example (14) is also a case of direct quotation. As illustrated by this example, the addressee of the verb *bŋ⁵* 'ask', *gua³* 'I', is not introduced by the preposition *ka⁵*, but directly follows the verb *bŋ⁵*. This example also shows that a complementizer such as *səʔ⁷* in (13) is not obligatory. The context of (15) is that the father is reporting to his daughter what was said by one of the classmates of his daughter. In other words, this is a case of indirect quotation. This example shows that the complementizer occurring with the verb *bŋ⁵* can also be *khuã⁵*. Note also that, unlike the verbs *səʔ⁷* 'say' and *kaŋ³* 'say', the verb *bŋ⁵* 'ask' is followed by an interrogative clause (rather than a declarative clause), predictable from its lexical meaning, as illustrated by (13) – (15).

24.3 Verbs of perception and cognition

As mentioned above, verbs of perception and cognition that can take an object clause in Hui'an include *khuã⁵* 看 'look', *thiã¹* 聽 'listen to, hear', *kam³⁻²kak⁷* 感覺 'feel', *siũ⁴* 想 'think', *ai⁵* 愛 'like', *kiã¹* 驚 'be afraid', *tsai¹(iã³)*知(影) 'know', *e⁴kì⁵(let⁰)* 會記(得) 'remember', and *huat⁷⁻⁸hen⁵* 發現 'find'. This type of verb describes a mental state or event. Unlike utterance verbs examined in §24.2, the subject of verbs of perception and cognition is usually an experiencer, rather than an agent.

Among the verbs listed above, the most commonly used in daily conversations is the verb *khuã⁵* 'look'. This, however, does not mean that *khuã⁵* as a visual perception verb is most often followed by an object clause. In fact, the verb *khuã⁵* involves a series of non-perception meanings, some of which can take an object clause, as will be illustrated in the following. Note that this verb does not take a complementizer, including itself as a complementizer.

Two examples of *khuã⁵* as a visual perception verb followed by an object clause are given in (16) and (17).

(16) 阮　　昨日　　　去　　　看　　　佤　　拍　　　球
　　　gun³　*tsa⁴let⁸*　*khw⁵⁻³*　*khuã⁵⁻³*　*en¹*　*phaʔ⁷⁻⁸*　*kiu²*
　　　1PL　yesterday　go　　look　　3PL　hit　　　ball
　　'Yesterday we went to watch them play ball.'

(17) 我　　八　　　看　　　著　　　汝　　穿
　　　gua³　*pat⁷⁻⁸*　*khuã⁵⁻³*　*tioʔ⁸⁻⁴*　*lw³*　*tshiŋ⁵*
　　　1SG　EXP　　look　　PVC　　2SG　wear
　　'I have seen you wearing (those clothes) before.'

In (16), the clause en^1 $pha\textipa{P}^{7\text{-}8}kiu^2$ 'they play ball' functions as an object of the verb $khuã^5$ 'look'. This example emphasizes the action of watching. In (17), the verb $khuã^5$ 'look' is followed by the phase complement $tio\textipa{P}^8$, indicating achievement of the action encoded by the verb $khuã^5$. The clause lu^3 $tshiŋ^5$ 'you wear (those clothes)' functions as an object of the verb phrase $khuã^{5\text{-}3} tio\textipa{P}^8$ 'see'. Due to the use of the phase complement $tio\textipa{P}^8$, example (17) emphasizes the achievement and result of the action encoded by the verb $khuã^5$, rather than emphasizing the action itself.

Examples of $khuã^5$ as a non-perception verb are given in (18) and (19).

(18) 啊   倚,   看   汝   厝   卜   泉州   買
    a^0 $khia^4$ $khuã^{5\text{-}3}$ lu^3 $tshu^5$ $bo\textipa{P}^{7\text{-}8}$ $tsuan^{2\text{-}4}tsiu^1$ bue^3
    DM   live   look   2SG   house   want   PN   buy
    抑   廈門   買   咯
    $a\textipa{P}^8$ $e^{5\text{-}4}bŋ^2$ bue^3 $lɔ^0$
    or   PN   buy   SFP
    'As for the residence, this depends on whether you want to buy a house in Quanzhou or Xiamen.'

(19) 伊   說   看   汝   過   得   蠻   辛苦
    i^1 $sə\textipa{P}^{7\text{-}8}$ $khuã^{5\text{-}3}$ lu^3 $kə^5$ $le\textipa{P}^{7\text{-}8}$ $ban^{2\text{-}4}$ $sen^1khɔ^3$
    3SG   say   look   2SG   live   CM   rather   hard
    'He says that he thinks you have a hard life.'

In (18), $khia^4$ 'live' functions as a topic, and $khuã^5$ (meaning approximately 'depend on' in this context) is the verb in the main clause. The complement clause lu^3 $tshu^5$ $bo\textipa{P}^{7\text{-}8}$ $tsuan^{2\text{-}4}tsiu^1$ bue^3 $a\textipa{P}^8$ $e^{5\text{-}4}bŋ^2$ bue^3 'you want to buy a house in Quanzhou or Xiamen' functions as an object of the verb $khuã^5$ 'depend on'. In (19), the clause $khuã^{5\text{-}3}$ lu^3 $kə^5$ $le\textipa{P}^{7\text{-}8}$ $ban^{2\text{-}4}$ $sen^1khɔ^3$ '(he) thinks you have a hard life' functions as an object of the utterance verb $sə\textipa{P}^7$ 'say', while the clause lu^3 $kə^5$ $le\textipa{P}^{7\text{-}8}$ $ban^{2\text{-}4}$ $sen^1khɔ^3$ 'you have a hard life' functions as an object of the verb $khuã^5$ 'think'. The use of the verb $khuã^5$ in (19) can be regarded as an instance of indirect perception, with 'look' understood in its extended cognition sense of 'consider' or 'judge'. Note that the subject of the verb $khuã^5$ in (19) is covert, since it is co-referential with the subject of the verb $sə\textipa{P}^7$ 'say' (i.e. i^1 'he').

Unlike the verb $khuã^5$ 'look', the verb $thiã^1$ 聽 'listen to, hear' with an object clause is not commonly used in daily conversation. In addition, the verb $thiã^1$ is mainly used in the sense of immediate perception. An example is given (20), where the clause *laŋ⁴ tsiũ⁵⁻³ səʔ⁷* 儂障說 'how other people say' functions as an object of the verb *thiã¹* 'listen to'.

(20) 先　　聽　　　儂　　障　　　說
　　 suin¹　thiã¹　　laŋ⁴　tsiũ⁵⁻³　səʔ⁷
　　 first　listen.to　other　how　　say
　　 'first listen to what other people say'

In this example, the verb *thiã¹* can be followed by the complementzier *khuã⁵*, i.e. forming *suin¹ thiã¹ khuã⁵ laŋ⁴ tsiũ⁵⁻³ səʔ⁷* 先聽看儂障說. In general, this verb is not used with the complementizer *səʔ⁷*, since *thiã¹səʔ⁷* is a compound verb meaning 'hear of'.

The verb *kam³⁻²kak⁷* 感覺 'feel' with an object clause can be illustrated by (21) – (23).

(21) 我　　感覺　　　　即領　　　　質量　　　　　　艙　　　　否
　　 gua³　kam³⁻²kak⁷⁻⁸　tsit⁷⁻⁸-liã³　tset⁷⁻⁸liɔŋ⁵　bue⁴　phai³
　　 1SG　feel　　　　　this-CL　　 quality　　　can.not　bad
　　 'I think that this item (of clothing) is of good quality.'

(22) 伊　　感覺　　　　說　　　迄個　　　　學堂　　　　也佫　　　　好
　　 i¹　　kam³⁻²kak⁷⁻⁸　səʔ⁷⁻⁸　hit⁷⁻⁸-e²⁻⁴　oʔ⁸⁻⁴tŋ²　a⁴koʔ⁷⁻⁸　ho³
　　 3SG　feel　　　　　COMP　 that-CL　　 school　　 fairly　　　good
　　 'He thinks that that school is fairly good.'

(23) 恁　　感覺　　　　看　　　即垛　　　　會挃得　　　　艙
　　 len³　kam³⁻²kak⁷⁻⁸　khuã⁵³　tsit⁷⁻⁸-tə⁵　e⁴tiʔ⁸let⁰　bue⁰
　　 2PL　feel　　　　　COMP　 this-CL　　 OK　　　　　SFP
　　 'Do you think this (table) is OK?'

In (21), the clause *tsit⁷⁻⁸liã³ tset⁷⁻⁸liɔŋ⁵ bue⁴ phai³* 'this item (of clothing) is of good quality' functions as an object of the verb *kam³⁻²kak⁷*. In this case, the speaker describes her judgment about some clothes after touching them. This can be interpreted as the speaker expressing her opinion, which is associated with tactile perception in some way. In daily conversations, however, the verb *kam³⁻²kak⁷* tends to be used to express an opinion, which bears no relation to tactile perception. For example, the verb *kam³⁻²kak⁷* in (22) has nothing to do with tactile perception. This example also shows that the verb *kam³⁻²kak⁷* can co-occur with the complementizer *səʔ⁷*, unlike the verbs *khuã⁵* 'look' and *thiã¹* 'listen to, hear'. As shown by example (23), the verb *kam³⁻²kak⁷* followed by the complementizer *khuã⁵* is acceptable, though it is uncommon in daily conversation, compared to the complementizer *səʔ⁷*.

As with the verb *khuã⁵* 'look', the verb *siũ⁴* 想 is also a polysemous word. The verb *siũ⁴* can mean 'think, think about', as its basic sense, describing a mental activity. This use of *siũ⁴* can take an object clause, as in (24).

(24) 我　　　想　　　說　　　恁　　　唔知　　　會　　　來　　　燴
　　　gua³　　siũ⁴　　səʔ⁷⁻⁸　len³　　m⁵⁻⁴-tsai¹　　e⁴　　lai²　　bue⁰
　　　1SG　　think　COMP　2PL　　not-know　　can　　come　SFP
　　　'I was wondering whether you would come.'

In (24), the clause *len³ m⁵⁻⁴tsai¹ e⁴ lai² bue⁰* 'whether you would come' functions as an object of the verb *siũ⁴* 'think, think about', indicating what the subject *gua³* 'I' was thinking about. In addition, *səʔ⁷* functions as a complementizer. The complementizer *khuã⁵* can be used to substitute the complementizer *səʔ⁷*, though it is less natural than *səʔ⁷*.

Other examples of the verb *siũ⁴* with an object clause are given in (25) – (27).

(25) 我　　　想　　　說　　　囝仔　　已經　　出門　　　咯
　　　gua³　　siũ⁴　　səʔ⁷⁻⁸　ken³⁻²a³　i³⁻²kiŋ¹　tshut⁷⁻⁸-bŋ²　lɔ⁰
　　　1SG　　think　COMP　child　　already　out-door　　SFP
　　　'I meant that the children are away from home.'

(26) 我　　　想　　　說　　　票　　　好　　　拆　　　遘
　　　gua³　　siũ⁴　　səʔ⁷⁻⁸　phio⁵　ho³⁻²　thiaʔ⁷　a³
　　　1SG　　think　COMP　ticket　good　　tear　　EVC
　　　'I thought that it was quite easy to get a ticket.'

(27) 阮　　　想　　　汝　　　倒來
　　　gun³　　siũ⁴　　lw³⁻²　to⁵lai⁰
　　　1PL　　think　2SG　come.back
　　　'We hope you come back.'

The context of (25) is that the speaker explains that he prefers a simple wedding, due to the situation that the children are away from home. In other words, the verb *siũ⁴* indicates the speaker's thoughts on a particular situation or fact. In (26), the clause *phio⁵ ho³⁻² thiaʔ⁷ a³* 'it is easy to get a ticket' functions as an object of the verb *siũ⁴*. In this case, *siũ⁴* is used by the speaker to express an opinion on getting a ticket. In (27), the clause $luɯ^{3-2}$ to^5lai^0 'you come back' functions as an object of the verb $siũ^4$. In this case, the verb $siũ^4$ expresses the meaning of 'hope, want'. Note that the verb $siũ^4$ is typically followed by the complementizer $səʔ^7$ when taking an object clause, as illustrated by (25) and (26), but can also occur without a complementizer, as in (27).

The verb $siũ^4$ in (24) – (27) is followed by a clause, while the following example shows that $siũ^4$ can also be followed by a verb phrase such as m^{5-4} $phɔ^1$ 唔鋪 'not pave'.

(28) 阮　　想　　說　　唔　　鋪
     gun^3　$siũ^4$　$səʔ^{7-8}$　m^{5-4}　$phɔ^1$
     1PL　think　COMP　not　pave
     'We plan not to use (wooden floors).'

When followed by a verb phrase, the verb $siũ^4$ often expresses the meaning of 'plan to do something'. In this context, the complementizer $səʔ^7$ can also added after the verb $siũ^4$, as in (28).

The verb $siũ^4$ may also be followed by the phase complement $tioʔ^8$ 著, as in (29).

(29) 想　　　著　　　說,　　有影,　　著　　　拾　　　口面
     $siũ^4$　$tioʔ^{8-4}$　$səʔ^{7-8}$　$u^4iã^3$　$tioʔ^{8-4}$　$khioʔ^{7-8}$　$khau^{3-2}ben^2$
     think　PVC　COMP　right　should　pick　outside
     '(We) realized that it is true that (we) should choose (the house) that is close to the street.'

In (29), the verb $siũ^4$ preceding the phase complement $tioʔ^8$ combines to express the meaning of 'realize', while $səʔ^7$ following the verb phrase $siũ^4$ $tioʔ^8$ 'realize' functions as its complementizer.

The verb ai^5 愛 'like' is normally followed by a verb phrase such as $tshiŋ^{5-4}$ $tsit^{7-8}liã^3$ 穿即領 'wear this piece (of clothing)' in (30). Note that this verb usually does not co-occur with a complementizer.

(30) 我　　愛　　穿　　即領
     gua^3　ai^{5-3}　$tshiŋ^{5-4}$　$tsit^{7-8}$-$liã^3$
     1SG　like　wear　this-CL
     'I like wearing this piece (of clothing).'

The verb *kiã¹* 驚 means 'be afraid' and describes a mental state. An example of *kiã¹* with an object clause is given in (31).

(31) 我   驚   迄領   無   夠   燒
      gua³   kiã¹   hit⁷⁻⁸-liã³ bo²⁻⁴   kau⁵⁻³   sio¹
      1SG   be.afraid that-CL   not.have enough   Warm
      'I am afraid that piece (of clothing) is not warm enough.'

In (31), the clause *hit⁷⁻⁸liã³ bo²⁻⁴ khau⁵⁻³ sio¹* 'that piece (of clothing) is not warm enough' is the object clause of the verb *kiã¹* 'be afraid'. As with the verb *ai⁵* 'like', the verb *kiã¹* tends not to be followed by a complementizer.

The verbs *tsai¹(iã³)* 知(影) 'know', *e⁴ki⁵(let⁰)* 會記(得) 'remember' and *huat⁷⁻⁸hen⁵* 發現 'find' are all concerned with knowledge or acquisition of knowledge. The verb *tsai¹* 'know' can be used alone to take an object clause, as illustrated by (32).

(32) 我   知   超市   咧   賣
      gua³   tsai¹   tshiau¹tshi⁴   leʔ⁷⁻⁸   bue⁴
      1SG   know   supermarket   PROG   sell
      'I know that the supermarket is selling (this).'

Comparatively speaking, the negative form of the verb *tsai¹*, i.e. *m⁵⁻⁴ tsai¹* 唔知 'not know', is more often used with an object clause, as in (33) and (34).

(33) 我   唔   知   伊   甚物   學堂
      gua³   m⁵⁻⁴   tsai¹   i¹   siəm³⁻²biʔ⁷⁻⁸   oʔ⁸⁻⁴tŋ²
      1SG   not   know   3SG   what   school
      'I don't know where he is studying.'

(34) 唔   知   好用   抑   否用
      m⁵⁻⁴   tsai¹   hoˀ³⁻²-iŋ⁵   aʔ⁸⁻⁴   phai³⁻²-iŋ⁵
      not   know   good-use   or   bad-use
      '(I) don't know whether (it) is useful.'

As illustrated by these two examples, the object clause of *m⁵⁻⁴ tsai¹* 'not know' is typically an interrogative such as a constituent interrogative in (33) and an alternative interrogative in (34).

The object clause of the verb *tsai¹* 'know' is often placed at the sentence-initial position, functioning as a topic, as in (35).

(35) 伯搭　　　有，　汝　　知　　唔
　　 lan³-ta?⁷　u⁴　 lu³　 tsai¹　 m⁰
　　 1PL-LOC　have　2SG　know　SFP
　　 'Do you know that we have (this) at home?'

In (35), the clause *lan³ta?⁷ u⁴* 'we have (this) at home' occurs at the sentence-initial position, functioning as a topic. The comment in this type of topic-comment construction often takes the form of *lu³ tsai¹ m⁰* 'do you know', as in (35).

The meaning of 'know' can also be encoded by the compound verb *tsai¹iã³* 知影. This compound verb and its negative form *m⁵⁻⁴ tsai¹iã³* 唔知影 'not know' often also take an object clause, as in (36) and (37).

(36) 伊　 　知影　 　汝　　倒來
　　 i¹　 tsai¹iã³　 lu³　 to⁵lai⁰
　　 3SG　know　　2SG　come.back
　　 'He knows that you have come back.'

(37) 我　 也　 唔　　知影　　伊　　障　　　想
　　 gua³　a⁴　m⁵⁻⁴　tsai¹iã³　i¹　　tsiũ⁵⁻³　siũ⁴
　　 1SG　also　not　know　　3SG　how　　think
　　 'I also don't know what he thinks.'

In (36), the clause *lu³ to⁵lai⁰* 'you come back' functions as an object of the verb *tsai¹iã³* 'know'. In (37), the clause *i¹ tsiũ⁵⁻³ siũ⁴* 'what does he think' functions as an object of *m⁵⁻⁴ tsai¹iã³* 'not know'. As with *m⁵⁻⁴ tsai¹* 'not know', the negative form *m⁵⁻⁴ tsai¹iã³* 'not know' is also often followed by an interrogative clause, as in (37). Note that the verb *tsai¹(iã³)* and its negative form are usually not used with a complementizer.

An example of the verb *e⁴ki⁵* 會記 'remember' with an object clause is given in (38), where the verb *e⁴ki⁵* is immediately followed by its object clause *gua³ bue³⁻² tsaŋ²⁻⁴ tshiŋ⁵* 我買叢銃 'I buy a gun'. The complementizer *sə?⁷* may be added after the verb *e⁴ki⁵*.

(38) 我　　　會記　　　　我　　買　　叢　　　銃
　　 gua³　e⁴ki⁵⁻³　　gua³　bue³⁻²　tsaŋ²⁻⁴　tshiŋ⁵
　　 1SG　remember　1SG　buy　　CL　　　gun
　　 'I remember that I bought a gun.'

The preference for the object clause of $e^4ki^5let^0$ 會記得 'remember' is to be placed in the sentence-initial position functioning as a topic, as in (39), where the clause $a^1sã^1\ liəp^{8\text{-}4}tshet^{7\text{-}8}\ hə^5$ 阿三廿七歲 'Ah-San is twenty seven years old' occurs in the sentence-initial position, functioning as a topic.

(39) 阿三　廿七　　　　歲，　伊　　會記得
　　　$a^1sã^1$　$liəp^{8\text{-}4}\text{-}tshet^{7\text{-}8}$　$hə^5$　i^1　$e^4ki^5let^0$
　　　PN　　twenty-seven　year　3SG　remember
　　　'She remembers that Ah-San is twenty seven years old.'

The following is an example of the verb $huat^{7\text{-}8}hen^5$ 發現 'find' taking an object clause.

(40) 我　　發現　　　　伊　無　　　　來
　　　gua^3　$huat^{7\text{-}8}hen^{5\text{-}4}$　i^1　$bo^{2\text{-}4}$　lai^2
　　　1SG　find　　　　3SG　not.have　come
　　　'I found out that he didn't come.'

In (40), the verb $huat^{7\text{-}8}hen^5$ is followed by the object clause 伊無來 'he didn't come'. The complementizer $səʔ^7$ can be inserted after the verb $huat^{7\text{-}8}hen^5$. Note however that this verb is not commonly used in daily conversation, and tends to be used by the younger generation.

24.4 Modal verbs of volition

Modal verbs of volition that can take an object clause in Hui'an include $boʔ^7$ 卜, $siũ^4boʔ^7$ 想卜 and ai^3 愛. This type of verb has an experiencer subject, and does not co-occur with a complementizer, as will be shown by the following examples.

The verbs $boʔ^7$ and $siũ^4boʔ^7$ tend to be followed by a verb phrase, as in (41) and (42).

(41) 我　　卜　　　食　　　蘋果
　　　gua^3　$boʔ^{7\text{-}8}$　$tsiaʔ^{8\text{-}4}$　$phiŋ^{2\text{-}4}kɔ^3$
　　　1SG　want　eat　　　apple
　　　'I want to eat an apple.'

(42) 伊　　想卜　　　　買　　　第二垺　　　　　厝
　　　i¹　　siũ⁴boʔ⁷⁻⁸　bue³⁻²　teˤ⁵⁻⁴-li⁵⁻⁴-tə⁵⁻³　tshu⁵
　　　3SG　want　　　　buy　　PREF-two-CL　　　house
　　　'He wants to buy his second house.'

In (41), *boʔ⁷* is followed by the verb phrase *tsiaʔ⁸⁻⁴ phiŋ²⁻⁴kɔ³* 'eat an apple', indicating the subject's intention to eat an apple. Similarly, *siũ⁴boʔ⁷* in (42) is followed by the verb phrase *bue⁵⁻⁴li⁵⁻⁴tə⁵⁻³ tshu⁵* 'buy the second house' to express the subject's desire to buy his second house. In these two cases, the subject of the verb phrase in the complement clause is covert, since it is co-referential with the subject of the verbs *boʔ⁷* and *siũ⁴boʔ⁷*, i.e. *gua³* 'I' in (41) and *i¹* 'he' in (42).

As shown by the following two examples, the verb *ai⁵* can be followed by either a verb phrase or a clause.

(43) 伊　　愛　　　與　　　　儂　　　知
　　　i¹　　ai⁵⁻³　khɔ⁵⁻⁴　laŋ⁴　tsai¹
　　　3SG　want　give　　　other　know
　　　'She wants other people to know (it).'

(44) 伊　　愛　　　佢　　小妹　　　　倒來
　　　i¹　　ai⁵⁻³　en¹　sio³⁻²bə⁵　to⁵lai⁰
　　　3SG　want　3PL　Y.sister　　come.back
　　　'She wants her younger sister to come back.'

In (43), *ai⁵* is followed by the verb phrase *khɔ⁵⁻⁴ laŋ⁴ tsai¹* 'let other people know', indicating the subject's desire to let other people know something. In this case, the subject of the verb phrase *khɔ⁵⁻⁴ laŋ⁴ tsai¹* is co-referential with the subject of the verb *ai⁵*, and is thus covert as in the two previous examples. Example (44), however, shows that *ai⁵* can be followed by a clause such as *en¹ sio³⁻²bə⁵ to⁵lai⁰* 'her younger sister comes back', and the subject of the clause (*en¹ sio³⁻²bə⁵* 'her younger sister') is not co-referential with the subject of the verb *ai⁵* (*i¹* 'she').

24.5 Causative (or manipulative) verbs

Causative (or manipulative) verbs that can take an object clause in Hui'an include *khɔ⁵* 與 'give, let', *kio⁵* 叫 'call, ask' and *tshiã³* 請 'invite, hire', among which, *khɔ⁵* 'give' is the most common one. As with verbs of volition mentioned in the preceding section, causative verbs also do not co-occur with a complementizer. Unlike verbs of volition, however, causative verbs generally require an agent subject, rather than an experiencer subject. In addition, this type of verb tends to be followed by a clause, whose subject is not co-referential with the subject of the main clause. Examples are given in (45) – (47).

(45) 與　　爸仔　　坐　　迄搭
　　 khɔ⁵⁻⁴　pa²-a⁰　tsə⁴　hit⁷⁻⁸-taʔ⁷
　　 give　father-NM　sit　that-LOC
　　 'Let father sit there.'

(46) 汝　　叫　　伊　　過來
　　 luˀ³　kio⁵⁻³　iˀ¹　kə⁵laiˀ⁰
　　 2SG　call　3SG　come.over
　　 'Ask him to come over.'

(47) 伊　　請　　別儂　　做
　　 iˀ¹　tshiã³⁻²　pat⁸⁻⁴-laŋ²　tsue⁵
　　 3SG　hire　other-person　do
　　 'He hired other people to do (it).'

24.6 Summary

This chapter has examined complement clauses in Hui'an, which typically function as an object of the main clause, i.e. constitute object clauses. Complement-taking verbs in Hui'an fall into four main semantic types: (a) utterance verbs such as səʔ⁷ 說 'say'; (b) verbs of perception and cognition such as khuã⁵ 看 'look', thiã¹ 聽 'listen to, hear' and kam³⁻²kak⁷ 感覺 'feel'; (c) modal verbs of volition such as boʔ⁷ 卜 'want'; and (d) causative verbs such as khɔ⁵ 與 'give'. Complement clauses of utterance verbs and some perception and cognition verbs (e.g. kam³⁻²kak⁷ 'feel' and siũ⁴ 'think') can be marked by the complementizer səʔ⁷ (< 'say') and/or khuã⁵ 看 (< 'look'). The complementizer khuã⁵ is typically used to introduce an interrogative complement clause and used in the context which inquires about something or looks for an answer. Note also that the utterance verb səʔ⁷ 'say' cannot co-occur with its grammaticalized use in the form of complementizer səʔ⁷.

25 Conclusion

This volume has presented a detailed description of the Hui'an dialect, a variety of Southern Min spoken in the Hui'an County, in Fujian province of China. The description is given within the framework of linguistic typology, mainly based on data collected via naturally occurring conversation. Besides the Introduction (chapter 1), a brief overview of phonology (chapter 2), and this concluding chapter, the grammar is presented in four parts: nominal structure (part I), predicate structure (part II), clause structure (part III) and complex sentences (part IV). Part I has examined the following six aspects of nominal structure: affixation and compounding, pronouns, nominal demonstratives, numerals and quantifiers, classifiers, and possessive constructions. Part II has focused on reduplication, verb complement constructions, aspect, modality, negation, adpositions and adverbs. Reduplication is included in the part on predicate structure, since it constitutes an important aspect of verbal morphology in the Hui'an dialect. In Part III, we have discussed the $ka\textipa{P}^7$-construction and the ka^5-construction, comparative constructions of inequality, the 'give' construction, interrogatives, and topic-comment constructions. A description of four types of complex sentence, that is, coordination, relative clauses, adverbial clauses and complement clauses, is given in Part IV.

Though our description shows that the Hui'an dialect shares much in common with other Southern Min varieties in Fujian and Taiwan, especially the Quanzhou variety, differences are also identified in our grammar. More significantly, this volume sheds some new and important light on the grammar of Southern Min, especially those varieties in Fujian, by examining in depth a series of topics, including those that have not yet attracted sufficient attention, such as possessive constructions, topic-comment constructions, relative clauses, and complement clauses. Our findings also show, in general, that the Hui'an dialect, on the one hand, preserves some conservative features, and on the other hand, reflects influence from Mandarin Chinese.

References

Aikhenvald, Alexandra Y. 2000. Classifiers: A Typology of Noun Categorization Devices. Oxford: Oxford University Press.
Aikhenvald, Alexandra Y. 2006. Serial verb constructions in typological perspective. In Serial Verb Constructions: A Cross-linguistic Typology, Alexandra Y. Aikhenvald and R. M. W. Dixon (eds.), 1-68. Oxford: Oxford University Press.
Aikhenvald, Alexandra Y. and R. M. W. Dixon (eds.) 2006. Serial Verb Constructions: A Cross-linguistic Typology. Oxford: Oxford University Press.
Allan, Keith. 1977. Classifiers. Language 53: 285-311.
Ameka, Felix. 1996. Body parts in Ewe grammar. In The Grammar of Inalienability: A typological perspective on body part terms and the part-whole relation, Hilary Chappell and William McGregor (eds.), 783-840. Berlin; New York: Mouton de Gruyter.
Ansaldo, Umberto. 1999. Comparative Constructions in Sinitic: Areal typology and patterns of grammaticalization. Ph. D. diss., Stockholm University at Sweden.
Ansaldo, Umberto and Lisa Lim. 2004. Phonetic absence as syntactic prominence: Grammaticalization in isolating tonal languages. In Up and Down the Cline: The Nature of Grammaticalization, Olga Fischer, Muriel Norde, and Harry Perridon (eds.), 345-362. (Typological Studies in Language 59.) Amsterdam/Philadelphia: John Benjamins.
Barry, Roberta. 1975. Topic in Chinese: An overlap of meaning, grammar, and discourse function. In Papers from the Parasession on Functionalism, Robin E. Grossman, L. James San, Timothy J. Vance (eds.), 1-9. Chicago: Chicago Linguistic Society.
Basilico, David. 1996. Head position and internally headed relative clauses. Language 72.3: 498-532.
Bhat, D.N.S. 2004. Pronouns. Oxford: Oxford University Press.
Bisang, Walter. 1999. Classifiers in East and Southeast Asian languages: Counting and beyond. In Numeral Types and Changes Worldwide, Jadranka Gvozdanovic (ed.), 113-185. Berlin: Mouton de Gruyter.
Bodomo, Adams B. 2006. The structure of ideophones in African and Asian languages: The case of Dagaare and Cantonese. In Selected Proceedings of the 35th Annual Conference on African Linguistics: African Languages and Linguistics in Broad Perspectives, John Mugane, John P. Hutchison, and Dee A. Worman (eds.), 203-213. Somerville, MA: Cascadilla Proceedings Project.
Bybee, Joan. 2003. Mechanisms of change in grammaticization: The role of frequency. In The Handbook of Historical Linguistics, Brian D. Joseph and Richard D. Janda (eds.), 602-623. Oxford: Blackwell.
Bybee, Joan and William Pagliuca. 1985. Cross linguistic comparison and the development of grammatical meaning. In Historical Semantics, Historical Word Formation, Jacek Fisiak (ed.), 59-83. (Trends in Linguistics, Studies and Monographs 20.) Berlin: Mouton de Gruyter.
Bybee, Joan, Revere Perkins and William Pagliuca. 1994. The Evolution of Grammar: Tense, Aspect, and Modality in the Languages of the World. Chicago & London: The University of Chicago Press.
Bybee, Joan and Joanne Scheibman. 1999. The effect of usage on degrees of constituency: the reduction of don't in English. Linguistics 37.4:575-596.

Cai, Junming (ed.) 1991. Chaozhou Fangyan Cihui: Putonghua Duizhao [Lexicon of the Chaozhou Dialect: A Comparison with Putonghua]. Hong Kong: T. T. Ng Chinese Language Research Centre Institute of Chinese Studies, The Chinese University of Hong Kong.

Chang, Miao-Hsia. 1996. The grammaticalization of *beh* in Taiwanese Hokkian. Studies in the Linguistic Sciences 26:39-59.

Chang, Miao-Hsia. 2002. Discourse functions of *Anne* in Taiwanese Southern Min. Concentric: Studies in English Literature and Linguistics 28.2:85-115.

Chang, Miao-Hsia. 2009. Metaphorization and metonymization: diachronic development of verbs of volition in Southern Min. Taiwan Journal of Linguistics 7.1:53-84.

Chang, Miao-Hsia and Hsin-Yi Su. 2012. To mark or not to mark the cause, that is the question: causal marking in Taiwanese conversation. Journal of Pragmatics 44:1743-1763.

Chao, Yuenren. 1968. A Grammar of Spoken Chinese. Berkeley: University of California Press.

Chappell, Hilary. 1992. Towards a typology of aspect in Sinitic languages. In Zhongguo Jingnei Yuyan ji Yuyanxue: Hanyu Fangyan [Languages and Linguistics in China: Chinese Dialects] 1.1, 67-106. Taipei: Academia Sinica.

Chappell, Hilary. 1996. Inalienability and the personal domain in Mandarin Chinese discourse. In The Grammar of Inalienability: A typological perspective on body part terms and the part-whole relation, Hilary Chappell and William McGregor (eds.), 465-528. Berlin; New York: Mouton de Gruyter.

Chappell, Hilary. 1999. The double unaccusative construction in Sinitic languages. In External Possession, Doris L. Payne and Immanuel Barshi (eds.), 195-228. Amsterdam/Philadelphia: John Benjamins Publishing Company.

Chappell, Hilary. 2000. Dialect grammar in two early modern Southern Min texts: a comparative study of dative *kit*, comitative *cang* and diminutive *–guia*. Journal of Chinese Linguistics 28. 2:247-302.

Chappell, Hilary (ed.) 2001a. Sinitic Grammar: Synchronic and Diachronic Perspectives. Oxford: Oxford University Press.

Chappell, Hilary. 2001b. A typology of evidential markers in Sinitic languages. In Hilary Chappell (ed.), 56-84.

Chappell, Hilary. 2007. Hanyu fangyan de chuzhi biaoji de leixing [Typology of disposal markers in Chinese dialects]. Yuyanxue Luncong 36:183-209.

Chappell, Hilary. 2008. Variation in the grammaticalization of complementizers from *verba dicendi* in Sinitic languages. Linguistic Typology 12:45-98.

Chappell, Hilary. 2013. Pan-Sinitic object markers: Morphology and syntax. In Breaking down the barriers: Interdisciplinary studies in Chinese linguistics and beyond, Guangshun Cao, Hilary Chappell, R. Djamouri and Thekla Wiebusch (eds.), 785-816. Taipei: Academia Sinica.

Chappell, Hilary. 2015. Linguistic areas in China for differential object marking, passive and comparative constructions. In Diversity in Sinitic Languages, Hilary Chappell (ed.), 13-52. Oxford: Oxford University Press.

Chappell, Hilary and Alain Peyraube. 2007. Jindai zaoqi minnanhua fenxixing zhishi jiegou de lishi tantao [A diachronic exploration of analytic causatives in early modern Southern Min]. Fangyan 1:52-59.

Chappell, Hilary and Alain Peyraube. 2008. Chinese localizers: diachrony and some typological considerations. In Dan Xu (ed.), 15-37.

Chappell, Hilary and Alain Peyraube. 2016a. Mood and modality in Sinitic languages. In The Oxford Handbook of Mood and Modality, Jan Nuyts and Johan van der Auwera (eds.), 296-329. Oxford: Oxford University Press.

Chappell, Hilary and Alain Peyraube. 2016b. A typological study of negation in Sinitic languages: Synchronic and diachronic views. In New Horizons in the Study of Chinese: Dialectology, Grammar, and Philology - Studies in Honor of Professor Anne Yue, Pang-hsin Ting, Samuel Hung-nin Cheung, Sze-Wing Tang and Andy Chin (eds.), 483-534. Hong Kong: T.T. Ng Chinese Language Research Center, Chinese University of Hong Kong.

Chappell, Hilary, Alain Peyraube and Na Song. Forthc. Comparatives of inequality in Southern Min: A study in diachronic change from 15th to 21st centuries.

Chappell, Hilary, Ming Li and Alain Peyraube. 2007. Chinese linguistics and typology: The state of the art. Linguistic Typology 11.1:187-211.

Chappell, Hilary and Sandra Thompson. 1992. The semantics and pragmatics of associative DE in Mandarin discourse. Cahiers de linguistique – Asie orientale 21.2: 199-229.

Chappell, Hilary and William McGregor. 1989. Alienability, inalienability and nominal classification. In Proceedings of the Fifteenth Annual Meeting of the Berkeley Linguistics Society 15, K. Hall, M. Meacham and R. Shapiro (eds.), 24-36. Berkeley: Berkeley Linguistics Society.

Chen, Chuanjia. 1997. Chaoshan fangyan de "jian" ["Jian" in the Chaoshan dialect]. Hanshan Shifan Xueyuan Xuebao 3:84-91.

Chen, Chuimin. 1992. Minnanhua de "qu"ziju [Sentences with the word "qu" in Southern Min]. In Donghan Liang, Lunlun Lin and Yongkai Zhu (eds.), 97-103.

Chen, Chuimin. 2001. Chen Chuimin Yufa Fangyan Lunji [Papers of Chen Chuimin on Grammar and Dialects]. Lanzhou: Lanzhou Daxue Chubanshe.

Chen, Ee-San. 2002. 'You Play with Me, Then I Friend You': Development of conditional constructions in Chinese-English bilingual preschool children in Singapore. Ph. D. diss., The University of Hong Kong.

Chen, Fajin. 1982. Minnan fangyan de liangzhong bijiaoju [Two kinds of comparative sentences in Southern Min]. Zhongguo Yuwen 1: 62-65.

Chen, Fajin. 1984. Minnan fangyan de pingbiju [Comparison of Equality in Southern Min]. Zhongguo Yuwen 1:71-76.

Chen, Fajin. 1985. Minnanhua de "会" "(勿会)"ziju [Sentences with the words "会" and "(勿会)" in Southern Min]. Huaqiao Daxue Xuebao 1:82-92.

Chen, Fajin. 1988. Minnanhua de "hu"ziju [Sentences with the word "hu" in Southern Min]. Huaqiao Daxue Xuebao 2:96-103.

Chen, Fajin. 1989. Minnanhua de zhishi daici [Demonstrative pronouns in Southern Min]. Huaqiao Daxue Xuebao 1:101-109.

Chen, Fajin. 1991. Fujian Hui'anhua de dongtai zhuci "者、(目卖)、咧" [Dynamic auxiliaries "者、(目卖)、咧" in the Hui'an dialect in Fujian]. Zhongguo Yuwen 5:363-365.

Chen, Fajin. 1992. Quanzhou fangyan de shubu jiegou [Verb complement constructions in the Quanzhou dialect]. Fangyan 3:181-185.

Chen, Fajin. 1993. Quanzhouhua dongbu duanyu fujia dongtai zhuci [Verb complement constructions with dynamic auxiliaries in the Quanzhou dialect]. Huaqiao Daxue Xuebao 3:102-109.

Chen, Fajin. 1994. Quanzhouhua "唔"zi juwei gongneng [The sentential function of the word "唔" in the Quanzhou dialect]. Huaqiao Daxue Xuebao 1:99-106.

Chen, Haizhong. 2003. Chaoshan fangyan jieci lishi [A study on some adpositions in the Chaoshan dialect]. Shantou Daxue Xuebao 19:77-80.

Chen, Manjun. 2004. Minnanhua zhudongci "tong" de juwei gongneng [Sentential functions of the auxiliary verb "tong" in Southern Min]. Yuwen Yanjiu 3:61-63.
Chen, Manjun. 2005. Hui'an Fangyan Dongci Weiyuju Yanjiu [A Study of the Verb Predicate Sentence of the Hui'an Dialect]. Ph. D. diss., Ji'nan University.
Chen, Manjun. 2006. Hui'an fangyan dai dongtai zhuci de danbinju [Single object sentences with verbal particles in the Hui'an dialect]. Paper presented at the 3rd International Conference on Chinese Dialects, Guangzhou.
Chen, Manjun. 2008. Hui'an fangyan teshu jianyuju [Special pivotal sentences in the Hui'an dialect]. Ji'mei Daxue Xuebao 1:71-77.
Chen, Manjun. 2011. Mintai minnan fangyan de fanfu wenju [A-not-A questions in Southern Min in Fujian and Taiwan]. Fangyan 2:153-163.
Chen, Manjun. 2013. Hui'an Minnan Fangyan Dongci Weiyuju Yanjiu [Sentences with Verbal Predicates in Hui'an Southern Min]. Beijing: Zhongguo Shehui Kexue Chubanshe.
Chen, Manjun. 2017. Minnan fangyan chixuti biaoji "lie" de layuan jiqi yufahua [The origin and grammaticalization of the durative aspect marker "lie" in Southern Min]. Yuyan Kexue 4:384-405.
Chen, Matthew Y. 2000. Tone Sandhi: Patterns Across Chinese Dialects. Cambridge: Cambridge University Press.
Chen, Wanli and Chunlai Wang. 1998. Hui'an Xianzhi [Hui'an County Annals]. Beijing: Fangzhi Chubanshe.
Chen, Weirong. 2008. Comparative sentences in Hui'an Southern Min. In Proceedings of the 2007 Mid-America Linguistics Conference, Kansas Working papers in Linguistics, Vol.30, Emily Tummons and Stephanie Lux (eds.), 31-39. https://kuscholarworks.ku.edu/handle/1808/276.
Chen, Weirong. 2013. Nominal demonstratives in the Southern Min dialect of Hui'an. The Cahiers de Linguistique – Asie Orientale 42.2: 118-162.
Chen, Weirong. 2015. Comparative constructions of inequality in the Southern Min dialect of Hui'an. In Diversity in Sinitic Languages, Hilary Chappell (ed.), 248-272. Oxford: Oxford University Press.
Chen, Weirong. 2017. Fujian Hui'an minnan fangyan de guanxi congju biaoji [Relativization markers in the Hui'an variety of Southern Min in Fujian]. Fangyan 3: 352-359.
Chen, Weirong and Foong Ha Yap. 2018. Pathways to adversity and speaker affectedness: On the emergence of unaccusative 'give' constructions in Chinese. Linguistics 56.1: 19-68.
Chen, Weirong and Fuxiang Wu. 2015. Phonological reduction and grammaticalization: examples from the Southern Min dialect of Hui'an. Faits de Langues 46: 165-186.
Chen, Weirong and Stephen Matthews. 2009. The grammaticalization of khɔ5 'give' in Hui'an Southern Min. In Selected Papers from the 2007 Annual Research Forum of the Linguistic Society of Hong Kong, Vicky Man (ed.), 1-16. The Linguistic Society of Hong Kong.
Chen, Zhangtai. 1991a. Datianxiannei de fangyan [Dialects of the Datian County]. In Minyu Yanjiu [Studies on Min Dialect], Zhangtai Chen and Rulong Li (eds.), 266-303. Beijing: Yuwen Chubanshe.
Chen, Zhangtai. 1991b. Shunchangxian pushing minnan fangyandao [Southern Min Island in Pushang of Shunchang County]. In Minyu Yanjiu [Studies on Min Dialect], Zhangtai Chen and Rulong Li (eds.), 421-458. Beijing: Yuwen Chubanshe.
Chen, Zhangtai and Rulong Li (eds.) 1991. Minyu Yanjiu [Studies on Min Dialect]. Beijing: Yuwen Chubanshe.

Chen, Zeping. 1996. Fuzhou fangyan dongci de ti he mao [Aspects in the Fuzhou dialect]. In Shuangqing Zhang (ed.), 225-253.
Chen, Zeping. 1999. Fuzhou fangyan de daici [Pronouns in the Fuzhou dialect]. In Daici [Pronouns], Rulong Li and Shuangqing Zhang (eds.), 247-262.
Chen, Zeping. 2000. Fuzhou fangyan de jieci [Adpositions of the Fuzhou dialect]. In Jieci [Adpositions], Rulong Li and Shuangqing Zhang (eds.), 101-121.
Chen, Zeping. 2001. Fuzhou fangyan de jiegou zhuci jiqi xiangguan de jufa jiegou [Structural particles and related syntactic constructions in the Fuzhou dialect]. Yuyan Yanjiu 2:57-64.
Chen, Zhengtong (ed.) 2007. Minnanhua Zhangqiang Cidian [A Dictionary of the Zhangzhou Variety of Southern Min]. Beijing: Zhonghua Shuju.
Cheng, Gong. 1998. Cong kuayuyan de jiaodu kan hanyu zhong de xingrongci [Adjectives in Chinese from a cross-linguistic perspective]. Xiandai Waiyu 2:17-26.
Cheng, Lisa L. S., James C. T. Huang, Audrey Y. H. Li, and Jane C. C. Tang. 1999. Hoo, hoo, hoo: syntax of the causative, dative and passive construction in Taiwanese. In Contemporary Studies on the Min Dialects, Pang-Hsin Ting (ed.), 146-203. JCL Monograph Series 14.
Cheng, Lisa and Rint Sybesma. 2005. A Chinese relative. In Organizing Grammar: Linguistic studies in honor of Henk van Riemsdijk, Hans Broekhuis, Norbert Corver, Riny Huybregts, Ursula Kleinhenz and Jan Koster (eds.), 69-76. Berlin: Mouton.
Cheng, Robert L. 1977. Taiwanese Question Particles. Journal of Chinese Linguistics 5:153-185.
Cheng, Robert L. (ed.) 1997a. Taiyu, Huayu de Jiegou ji Dongxiang [Taiwan Southern Min and Mandarin Structures and Their Development Trends], 4 Vols. Taipei: Yuan-Liou Publishing Co., Ltd.
Cheng, Robert L. 1997b. Taiyu yuyin guilv dagang ji yuli [An outline and examples of phonological rules in Taiwan Southern Min]. In Robert L. Cheng (ed.), I: taiyu de yuyin yu cifa [phonology and morphology in Taiwan Southern Min], 3-171.
Cheng, Robert L. 1997c. A comparison of neutralization of tonal contrasts in Taiwanese and Peking dialects. In Robert L. Cheng (ed.), I: taiyu de yuyin yu cifa [phonology and morphology in Taiwan Southern Min], 231-242.
Cheng, Robert L. 1997d. Huayu ji Taiyu de shengdong chongdie [Vivid reduplication in Mandarin and Taiwan Southern Min]. In Robert L. Cheng (ed.), I: taiyu de yuyin yu cifa [phonology and morphology in Taiwan Southern Min], 303-320.
Cheng, Robert L. 1997e. Taiyu yu Taiwan huayu li de ziju jiegou biaozhi "讲" yu "看" [The complementizer "讲" and "看" in Taiwan Southern Min and Taiwan Mandarin]. In Robert L. Cheng (ed.), II: tai, huayu de jiechu yu tongyiyu de hudong [contacts between Taiwan Southern Min and Mandarin and restructuring of their synonyms], 105-132.
Cheng, Robert L. 1997f. Xiandairen benwei de taiyu yufa yanjiu: *beh* de tongyiyu ji yuyan yanbian Dongxiang tantao [A study of Taiwan Southern Min grammar on the basis of modern people: synonym of *beh* and the direction of language change]. In Robert L. Cheng (ed.), III: tai, huayu de shikong, yiwen yu fouding [temporal and spatial relations, questions and negatives in Taiwan Southern Min and Mandarin], 3-17.
Cheng, Robert L. 1997g. Taiwanese 'U' and Mandarin 'YOU'. In Robert L. Cheng (ed.), III: tai, huayu de shikong, yiwen yu fouding [temporal and spatial relations, questions and negatives in Taiwan Southern Min and Mandarin], 191-230.
Cheng, Robert L. 1997h. Cong Lin Yukeng jiaoshou "zanmen yingyu zhongxin" tanqi: beijingyu de "咱们" he taiyu de "咱" [A study on "咱们" in Peking dialect and "咱" in Taiwan Southern Min beginning with 'our English center' of Prof. Yukeng Lin]. In Robert L. Cheng (ed.),

IV: tai, huayu de daici, jiaodian yu fanwei [pro-forms, focus and scope in Taiwan Southern Min and Mandarin], 3-10.
Cheng, Robert L. and Susie S. Cheng. 1994. Taiwan Fujianhua de Yuyin Jiegou ji Biaoyinfa [Phonological Structure and Romanization of Taiwan Hokkien]. Revised edition. Taipei: Xuesheng Shuju.
Cheng, Robert L. and Shuanfan Huang (eds.) 1988. The Structure of Taiwanese: A modern synthesis. Taipei: Crane Publishing Co., Ltd.
Cheng, Robert L. and Jinjin Zeng. 1997. Zhongyin zai shengdiao yuyan zhong de xingshi、gongneng、hudong ji zhenghe [Forms, functions, interaction and integration of stress in tone languages]. In Robert L. Cheng (ed.), I: taiyu de yuyin yu cifa [phonology and morphology in Taiwan Southern Min], 243-273. Taipei: Yuanliu Chuban Gongsi.
Cheng, Ying and Fengfu Tsao. 1995. Minnanyu 'ka' yongfa zhijian de guanxi [The relationship among the uses of 'ka' in Southern Min]. In Fengfu Tsao and Meihui Tsai (eds.), 23-45.
Chiu, Bienming. 1931. The phonetic structure and tone behavior in Hagu and their relation to certain questions in Chinese linguistics. T'oung Pao, Vol. 28, 3/5:245-342.
Citko, Barbara. 2004. On headed, headless, and light-headed relatives. Natural Language and Linguistic Theory 22.1:95-126.
Cole, Peter. 1987. The structure of internally headed relative clauses. Natural Language and Linguistic Theory 5.2:277-302.
Comrie, Bernard. 1976. Aspect: An Introduction to the Study of Verbal Aspect and Related Problems. Cambridge: Cambridge University Press.
Comrie, Bernard. 1989. Language Universals and Linguistic Typology: Syntax and Morphology. Second edition. Oxford: Blackwell.
Comrie, Bernard. 1996. The unity of noun-modifying clauses in Asian languages. In Proceedings of the Fourth International Symposium on Languages and Linguistics: Pan-Asiatic linguistics, 1077-1088. Salaya, Thailand: Institute of Language and Culture for Rural Development, Mahidol University at Salaya.
Comrie, Bernard. 2008. Pronominal relative clauses in verb-object languages. Language and Linguistics 9.4:723-733.
Croft, William. 1991. Syntactic Categories and Grammatical Relations: The Cognitive Organization of Information. Chicago; London: University of Chicago Press.
Crystal, David. 2008. A Dictionary of Linguistics and Phonetics, 6th edition. Oxford: Blackwell Publishing.
Cuyckens, Hubert, Kristin Davidese and Lieven Vandelanotte. 2010. Introduction. In Subjectification, Intersubjectification and Grammaticalization, Kristin Davidse, Lieven Vandelanotte and Hubert Cuyckens (eds.), 1-26. Berlin; New York: De Gruyter Mouton.
de Sousa, Hilário. 2015. Language contact in Nanning-from the point of view of Nanning Pinghua and Nanning Cantonese. In Diversity in Sinitic Languages, Hilary Chappell (ed.), 157-189. Oxford: Oxford University Press.
Diessel, Holger. 1999. Demonstratives: Form, Function, and Grammaticalization. Amsterdam: Benjamins.
Ding, Shengshu, et al. 1961. Xiandai Hanyu Yufa Jianghua [Introductions to Modern Chinese Grammar]. Beijing: Shangwu Yinshuguan.
Dixon, R. M. W. 1977. Where have all the adjectives gone? Studies in Language 1.1:19-80.
Dixon, R. M. W. 2003. Demonstratives: A cross-linguistic typology. Studies in Language 27.1:61-112.

Dixon, R. M. W. 2004. Adjective classes in typological perspective. In Adjective Classes: A cross-linguistic typology, R. M. W. Dixon & Alexandra Y. Aikhenvald (eds.), 1-49. Oxford: Oxford University Press.

Dixon, R. M. W. 2006. Complement clauses and complementation strategies: in typological perspective. In Complementation: A cross-linguistic typology, R. M. W. Dixon & Alexandra Y. Aikhenvald (eds.), 1-48. Oxford: Oxford University Press.

Dixon, R. M. W. 2012. Basic Linguistic Theory, Vol.3: Further grammatical topics. Oxford: Oxford University Press.

Dixon, R. M. W. and Alexandra Y. Aikhenvald. 2006. Complementation: A cross-linguistic typology. Oxford: Oxford University Press.

Djamouri, Redouane, Waltraud Paul and John Whitman. 2013. Postpositions vs prepositions in Mandairn Chinese: Thhe articulation of disharmony. In Theoretical Approaches to Disharmonic Word Orders, Theresa Biberauer and Michelle Sheehan (eds.), 74-105. Oxford: Oxford University Press.

Dong, Tonghe. 1974. Xiamen fangyan de yinyun [Phonology of the Xiamen dialect]. In Dong Tonghe Xiansheng Yuyanxue Lunwen Xuanji [The Collected Essays of Dong Tonghe on Linguistics], Pang-Hsin Ting (ed.), 275-297. Taipei: Shihuo Chubanshe.

Donohue, Mark. 2008. Covert word classes: seeking your own syntax in Tukang Besi. Studies in Language 32.3:590-609.

Douglas, Carstairs. 1873. Chinese-English Dictionary of the Vernacular or Spoken Language of Amoy with the Principal Variations of the Chang-chew and Chin-chew Dialects. London: Trubner and Co.

Downing, Angela and Philip Locke. 2006. English Grammar: A University Course. Second edition. London; New York: Routledge.

Downing, Pamela. 1996. Numeral Classifier Systems: The Case of Japanese. Amsterdam: John Benjamins Publishing Co.

Dryer, Matthew S. 2005a. Order of relative clause and noun. In The World Atlas of Language Structures, Martin Haspelmath, Matthew S. Dryer, David Gil and Bernard Comrie (eds.), 366-367. Oxford: Oxford University Press.

Dryer, Matthew S. 2005b. Polar questions. In The World Atlas of Language Structures, Martin Haspelmath, Matthew S. Dryer, David Gil and Bernard Comrie (eds.), 470-471. Oxford: Oxford University Press.

Dryer, Matthew S. 2013. Order of relative clause and noun. In Matthew S. Dryer and Martin Haspelmath (eds.), The World Atlas of Language Structures Online. Leipzig: Max Plank Institute for Evolutionary Anthropology. (Available online at http://wals.info/chapter/90)

Embree, Bernard L. M. 1973. A Dictionary of Southern Min. Hong Kong: Hong Kong Language Institute.

Ernst, Thomas. 1994. Conditions on Chinese A-not-A questions. Journal of East Asian Linguistics 3:241-264.

Evans, Nicholas. 2007. Insubordination and its uses. In Finiteness: theoretical and empirical foundations, Irina Nikolaeva (ed.), 366-431. Oxford: Oxford University Press.

Evans, Nicholas. 2009. Insubordinatoin and the grammaticalization of interactive presuppositions. Paper presented at Methodologies in Determining Morphosyntactic Change: case studies and cross-linguistic applications, 5-6 March 2009, Osaka, Japan.

Fan, Xiaolei. 2011. Yi hanyu fangyan wei ben de nengxing qingtai yuyi ditu [The semantic map of possibility modality based on comparative evidence from Chinese dialects]. Yuyanxue Luncong Vol. 43. Beijing: Commercial Press.

Feng, Aizhen. 1993. Fuqing Fangyan Yanjiu [A Study of the Fuqing Dialect]. Beijing: Shehui Kexue Wenxian Chubanshe.
Feng, Aizhen. 1998. Fuzhou Fangyan Cidian [A Dictionary of the Fuzhou Dialect]. Jiangsu: Jiangsu Jiaoyu Chubanshe.
Fillmore, Charles. 1971. Santa Cruz Lectures on Deixis. Bloomington: Indiana University.
Finegan, Edward J. 1995. Subjectivity and subjectivisation: An introduction. In Subjectivity and Subjectivisation: Linguistic Perspectives, Dieter Stein and Susan Wright (eds.), 1-15. Cambridge: Cambridge University Press.
Fischer, Olga, Muriel Norde and Harry Perridon. 2004. Up and Down the Cline: The nature of grammaticalization. (Typological Studies in Language 59) Amsterdam/Philadelphia: John Benjamins.
Fox, Barbara A. and Sandra A. Thompson. 1990. A discourse explanation of the grammar of relative clauses in English conversation. Language 66.2:297-316.
Gao, Mingkai. 1990. Gao Mingkai Yuyanxue Lunwenji [Selected Papers on Linguistics by Gao Mingkai]. Beijing: Shangwu Yinshuguan.
Givón, Talmy. 1975. Serial verbs and syntactic change: Niger-Congo. In Word Order and Word Order Change, Charles N. Li (ed.), 47-112. Austin: University of Texas Press.
Givón, Talmy. 1990. Syntax: A Functional-typological Introduction, Vol.2. Amsterdam: Benjamins.
Givón, Talmy. 2001. Syntax: an introduction, Vol.1. Amsterdam/Philadelphia: John Benjamins Publishing Company.
Greenbaum, Sidney. 1996. The Oxford English Grammar. Oxford: Oxford University Press.
Greenberg, Joseph H. 1966. Some universals of grammar with particular reference to the order of meaningful elements. In Universals of Language, Joseph H. Greenberg (ed.), 73-113. Cambridge, Masachusets, and London, England: MIT Press.
Haiman, John. 1978. Conditionals are topics. Language 54.3:564-589.
Haiman, John. 1985. Natural Syntax. Cambridge: Cambridge University Press.
Hajek, John. 2004. Adjective classes: What can we conclude? In Adjective Classes: A cross-linguistic typology, R. M. W. Dixon and Alexandra Y. Aikhenvald (eds.), 348-361. Oxford: Oxford University Press.
Haspelmath, Martin. 2001. Word classes/parts of speech. In Internal Encyclopedia of the Social and Behavioral Sciences, Paul B. Baltes and Neil J. Smelser (eds.), 16538-16545. Amsterdam: Pergamon.
Heine, Bernd. 1997a. Possession: Cognitive Sources, Forces, and Grammaticalization. Cambridge: Cambridge University Press.
Heine, Bernd. 1997b. Cognitive Foundations of Grammar. Oxford: Oxford University Press.
Heine, Bernd. 2002. On the role of context in grammaticalization. In New Reflections on Grammaticalization, Ilse Wischer and Gabriele Diewald (eds.), 83-101. Amsterdam: John Benjamins.
Heine, Bernd and Tania Kuteva. 2002. World Lexicon of Grammaticalization. Cambridge: Cambridge University Press.
Heine, Bernd and Tania Kuteva. 2003. On contact-induced grammaticalization. Studies in Language 27.3:529-572.
Heine, Bernd, Ulrike Claudi and Friederike Hunnemeyer. 1991. Grammaticalization: A Conceptual Framework. Chicago: University of Chicago Press.
Heine, Bernd and Mechthild Reh. 1984. Grammaticalization and Reanalysis in African Languages. Hamburg: Helmut Buske.

Hopper, Paul J. 1991. On some principles of grammaticization. In Elizabeth Closs Traugott and Bernd Heine (eds.), Vol.1:17-36.
Hopper, Paul J. and Sandra A. Thompson. 1984. The discourse basis for lexical categories in universal grammar. Language 60.4:703-752.
Hopper, Paul J. and Elizabeth Closs Traugott. 1993. Grammaticalization. Cambridge: Cambridge University Press.
Hopper, Paul J. and Elizabeth Closs Traugott. 2003. Grammaticalization. Second edition. Cambridge: Cambridge University Press.
Ho, Dah-an (ed.) 2002. Papers from the Third International Conference on Sinology: Linguistic section. Dialect variations in Chinese. Institute of Linguistics, Preparatory Office. Academia Sinica, Taipei, Taiwan.
Hong, Yifang. 2004. Dunhuang Shehui Jingji Wenshu zhong zhi Liangci Yanjiu [Classifiers in the Dunhuang Documents on Society and Economy]. Beijing: Wenjin Chubanshe.
Hu, Yushu and Xiao Fan. 1985. Shilun yufa yanjiu sange pingmian [On three levels of grammar studies]. Xinjiang Shifan Daxue Xuebao 2:7-15, 30.
Huang, Churen and Kathleen Ahrens. 2003. Individuals, kinds and events: Classifier coercion of nouns. Language Sciences 25:353-373.
Huang, C.-T. James. 2003. The distribution of negative NPs and some typological correlates. In Functional Structure(s), Form and Interpretation, Yun-hui Audrey Li and Andrew Simpson (eds.), 262-280. Routledge: Taylor and Francis.
Huang, C.-T. James. 2013. Variations in non-canonical passives. In Non-canonical Passives, Artemis Alexiadou and Florian Schäfer (eds.), 95-114. Amsterdam: John Benjamins.
Huang, Dinghua. 1961. Minnan fangyan li de zhishi daici [Demonstrative pronouns in Southern Min]. Zhongguo Yuwen 12:23-29.
Huang, Dinghua. 1963. Minnan fangyan de yiwen daici [Interrogative pronouns in Southern Min]. Zhongguo Yuwen 4:298-308.
Huang, Han-chun and Chinfa Lien. 2007. Wanli ben Lizhi Ji zhishici yanjiu [Demonstratives in the Wanli Version of Lizhi Ji]. Tsing Hua Journal of Chinese Studies, New Series 37.2: 561-577.
Huang, Huiyu. 2007. Ambiguity in the negative V + *bo* NP construction in Taiwanese Southern Min. In Proceedings of the 21st Pacific Asia Conference on Language, Information, and Computation, 163-172. The Korean Society for Language and Information.
Hui'an County. 2010. Retrieved from http://baike.baidu.com/view/40995.htm.
Huddleston, Rodney and Geoffrey K. Pullum. 2002. The Cambridge Grammar of the English Language. Cambridge: Cambridge University Press.
Iwasaki, Shoichi and Preeya Ingkaphirom. 2005. A Reference Grammar of Thai. Cambridge: Cambridge University Press.
Jackendoff, Ray. 1972. Semantic Interpretation in Generative Grammar. MIT press.
Jackendoff, Ray. 1987. The status of thematic relations in linguistic theory. Linguistic Inquiry 18.3:369-412.
Jackendoff, Ray. 1990. Semantic Structures. Cambridge: MIT Press.
Jiang, Lansheng and Guangshun Cao (eds.) 1997. Tang Wudai Yuyan Cidian [Dictionary of the Language of Tang and Five Dynasties]. Shanghai: Shanghai Jiaoyu Chubanshe.
Jurafsky, Daniel. 1996. Universal tendencies in the semantics of the diminutive. Language 72.3:533-578.
Kearns, Kate. 2000. Semantics. New York: St. Martin's Press.

Keenan, Edward L. 1985. Relative clauses. In Language Typology and Syntactic Description, Vol. II: Complex constructions, Timothy Shopen (ed.), 141-170. Cambridge: Cambridge University Press.
Keenan, Edward L. and Bernard Comrie. 1977. Noun phrase accessibility and universal grammar. Linguistic Inquiry 8:63-99.
König, Ekkehard and Volker Gast. 2002. Reflexive pronouns and other uses of *self*-forms in English. Zeitschrift für Anglistik und Amerikanistik 50.3:1-14.
Krug, Manfred. 1998. String frequency: a cognitive motivating factor in coalescence, language processing and linguistic change. Journal of English Linguistics 26.4:286-320.
Kuryłowicz, Jerzy. 1965. The evolution of grammatical categories. Diogenes 51. Reprinted in his Esquisses linguistiques, Vol.2:38-54. Munich: Wilhelm Fink Verlag.
Lai, Hueiling. 2001. On Hakka BUN: a case of polygrammaticalization. Language and Linguistics 2.2:137-153.
Lai, Hueiling. 2003. The semantic extension of LAU. Language and Linguistics 4.3:533-561.
Lai, Yunfan. 2019. The polysemous *liah* 力 in Early Modern Southern Min and its contemporary fate. Journal of Chinese Linguistics 47.1:193-226.
Lamarre, Christine. 2001. Verb complement constructions in Chinese dialects: types and markers. In Hilary Chappell (ed.), 85-120.
Lambrecht, Knud. 1994. Information Structure and Sentence Form: Topic, Focus and the Mental Representations of Discourse Referents. Cambridge: Cambridge University Press.
Langacker, Ronald W. 1977. Syntactic reanalysis. In Mechanisms of Syntactic Change, Charles N. Li (ed.), 57-139. Austin: University of Texas Press.
Langacker, Ronald W. 1987. Nouns and verbs. Language 63:53-94.
LaPolla, Randy J. 1990. Grammatical Relations in Chinese: synchronic and diachronic considerations. Ph. D. diss., UC Berkeley.
LaPolla, Randy J. and Chenglong Huang. 2003. A Grammar of Qiang: with annotated texts and glossary. Berlin; New York; Mouton de Gruyter.
Lee, Hui-chi. 2009. *KA...HOO* constructions in Taiwan Southern Min. Taiwan Journal of Linguistics 7.2:25-48.
Lee, Hui-chi. 2010. Taiwan Southern Min denominal verbs. Language and Linguistics 11.3:503-526.
Lee, Hui-chi. 2012. Applicatives in Taiwan Southern Min: benefactives and malefactives. Journal of East Asian Linguistics 21.4:367-386.
Lehmann, Christian. 1982. Thoughts on Grammaticalization: A Programmatic Sketch. Vol.1. Arbeiten des Kölner Universalien-Projekts 48. Cologne: Universität zu Köln, Institut für Sprachwissenschaft.
Lehmann, Christian. 1985. Grammaticalization: synchronic variation and diachronic change. Lingua e Stile 20.3:303-318.
Li, Charles N. and Sandra A. Thompson. 1976. Subject and topic: a new typology of language. In Subject and Topic, Charles N. Li (ed.), 457-489. New York: Academic Press.
Li, Charles N. and Sandra A. Thompson. 1981. Mandarin Chinese: A Functional Reference Grammar. Berkeley: University of California Press.
Li, Charles N., Sandra A. Thompson and R. McMillan Thompson. 1982. The discourse motivation for the perfect aspect. In Tense-Aspect: Between semantics and pragmatics, Paul J. Hopper (ed.), 19-44. Amsterdam/Philadelphia: John Benjamins Publishing Company.
Li, Cherry Ing and Leslie Fu-mei Wang. 2003. Conceptual mapping and functional shift: the case of Taiwanese Southern Min *Cit-e*. Language and Linguistics 4.2:403-428.

Li, Jen-Kuei. 1971. Two negative markers in Taiwanese. Bulletin of the Institute of History and Philology Academia Sinica XLIII:201-220.
Li, Jiachun and Chinfa Lien.1995. Lun Minnanyu bijiaoshi ---- leixing ji lishi de tantao [A discussion on comparatives in Southern Min ---- types and history]. In Taiwan Minnanyu Lunwenji [Collections of Theses on Taiwan Southern Min], Fengfu Tsao and Meihui Tsai (eds.), 71-85. Taipei: Wenhe Chuban Gongsi.
Li, Lan. 2003. Xiandai hanyu fangyan chabiju de yuxu leixing [Word order types of comparative construction in modern Chinese dialects]. Fangyan 3:214-232.
Li, Rulong.1986.Minnanhua de "you" he "wu" ["You" and "wu" in Southern Min]. Fujian Shifan Daxue Xuebao 2:76-83.
Li, Rulong. 1996a. Preface. In Shuangqing Zhang (ed.), 1-8.
Li, Rulong. 1996b.Quanzhou fangyan de ti [Aspects in the Quanzhou dialect]. In Shuangqing Zhang (ed.), 195-224.
Li, Rulong. 1997. Quanzhou fangyan de dongci weiyuju [Verb predicate sentences in the Quanzhou dialect]. In Rulong Li and Shuangqing Zhang (eds.), 121-135. Ji'nan: Ji'nan Daxue Chubanshe.
Li, Rulong. 1999. Minnan fangyan de daici [Pronouns in Southern Min]. In Rulong Li and Shuangqing Zhang (eds.), 263-288.
Li, Rulong. 2000.Minnan fangyan de jieci [Adpositions in Southern Min]. In Rulong Li and Shuangqing Zhang (eds.), 126-143.
Li, Rulong. 2001. Minnan fangyan de jiegou zhuci [Structural particles in Southern Min]. Yuyan Yanjiu 2: 48-56.
Li, Rulong. 2003.Minnan fangyan de foudingci he foudingshi [The negative words and negative constructions in Southern Min]. Zhongguo Yuwen Yanjiu 2:24-34.
Li, Rulong. 2005a.Minyu de "囥" jiqi yufahua ["囥" in Min dialects and its grammaticalization]. Nankai Yuyan Xuekan 1:1-8.
Li, Rulong.2005b. Guanyu fangyan yu diyu wenhua de yanjiu [A study on dialect and regional culture]. Quanzhou Shifan Xueyuan Xuebao 23.1:48-56.
Li, Rulong. 2007a. Minnan Fangyan Yufa Yanjiu [A Study of Southern Min Grammar]. Fuzhou: Fujian Renmin Chubanshe.
Li, Rulong.2007b. Minnanhua de jige xuziyaner [Several function words in Southern Min]. In Rulong Li, 164-172.
Li, Rulong and Shuangqing Zhang (eds.) 1997. Dongci Weiyuju [Verb Predicate Sentences]. Ji'nan: Ji'nan Daxue Chubanshe.
Li, Rulong and Shuangqing Zhang (eds.) 1999.Daici [Pronouns]. Ji'nan: Ji'nan Daxue Chubanshe.
Li, Rulong and Shuangqing Zhang (eds.) 2000. Jieci [Adpositions]. Ji'nan: Ji'nan Daxue Chubanshe.
Li, Xinkui. 1994.Guangdong de Fangyan [Dialects of Guangdong]. Guangzhou: Guangdong Renmin Chubanshe.
Li, Ying-che.1992.Aspects of comparative syntax between Mandarin and Taiwanese: Use of negatives in questions. In Proceedings of the 1st International Symposium on Chinese Languages and Linguistics, 437-448. Taipei : Academia Sinica.
Li, Ziling and Peter Cole. 1996.Xinjiapo chaozhou fangyan zhong de sanzhong zhengfan wenju [Three kinds of neutral questions in the Chaozhou dialect in Singapore]. Yuyan Yanjiu 2:65-73.

Li, Zongche. 2004. Shiji Liangci Yanjiu [A Study on the Quantifiers in Shiji]. Ph. D. diss., Fudan University.

Liang, Donghan, Lunlun Lin and Yongkai Zhu (eds.) 1992. Dierjie Minfangyan Xueshu Yantaohui Lunwenji [Proceeding of the 2nd Symposium on Min Dialect]. Ji'nan: Ji'nan Daxue Chubanshe.

Lien, Chinfa. 1988. Taiwanese sentence-final particles. In Robert L. Cheng and Shuanfan Huang (eds.), 209-234.

Lien, Chinfa. 1992. Taiwan minnanyu de quxiang buyu – fangyan leixing he lishi de yanjiu [Directional complements in Taiwan Southern Min – a dialectal typology and a historical perspective]. In Zhongguo Jingnei Yuyan ji Yuyanxue [Languages and Linguistics in China] IV: typological studies of languages in China, Qiuyu Zheng (ed.), 379-404. Taipei: Zhongyang Yanjiuyuan Lishi Yuyan Yanjiusuo.

Lien, Chinfa. 1994. The order of 'Verb-complement' constructions in Taiwan Southern Min. Tsing Hua Journal of Chinese Studies. New Series. 24:345-369.

Lien, Chinfa. 1995. Taiwan Minnanyu Wanjie Shixiangci Shilun [Phase words in Taiwan Southern Min]. In Fengfu Tsao and Meihui Tsai (eds.), 121-140.

Lien, Chinfa. 1998. Taiwan Minnanyu cizhui zai de yanjiu [A study of the affix 'a' in Taiwan Southern Min]. In Dierjie Taiwan Yuyan Guoji Yantaohui Lunwen Xuanji [Selected Papers from the Second International Symposium on Languages in Taiwan], Xuanfan Huang (ed.), 465-483. Taipei: The Crane Publishing Co., Ltd.

Lien, Chinfa. 1999a. Sociolinguistic dimensions of comparative constructions in Taiwan Southern Min: a preliminary report. In Contemporary Studies on the Min Dialects. Journal of Chinese Linguistics Monograph 14, Pang-Hsin Ting (ed.), 204-224. Project on Linguistic Analysis, University of California at Berkeley.

Lien, Chinfa. 1999b. A typological study of causatives in Taiwan Southern Min. Tsing Hua Journal of Chinese Studies 29:395-422.

Lien, Chinfa. 1999. Place deixis in Taiwan Southern Min. In In Honor of Professor Mei Tsu-lin on Chinese Syntax and Morphology, Alain Peyraube and Chaofen Sun (eds.), 73-88. Paris: Centre de Recherches Linguistiques sure l'Asie Orientale, Ecole des Hautes Etudes en Sciences Sociales.

Lien, Chinfa. 2001. The semantic extension of *Tioh*^{8} 著 in Taiwanese Southern Min: an interactive approach. Language and Linguistics 2.2:173-202.

Lien, Chinfa. 2002. Grammatical function words 乞，度，共，甲，將 and 力 in Li4 Jing4 Ji4 荔镜记 and their development in Southern Min. In Dah-an Ho (ed.), 179-216.

Lien, Chinfa. 2003a. Exploring multiple functions of *choe*^{3} 做 and its interaction with constructional meanings in Taiwanese Southern Min. Language and Linguistics 4.1:85-104.

Lien, Chinfa. 2003b. In search of covert grammatical categories in Taiwanese Southern Min: a cognitive approach to verb semantics. Language and Linguistics 4:379-402.

Lien, Chinfa. 2003c. Coding causatives and putatives in a diachronic perspective. Taiwan Journal of Linguistics 1:1-28.

Lien, Chinfa. 2005a. Verbs of visual perception in Taiwanese Southern Min: a cognitive approach to shift of semantic domains. Language and Linguistics 6.1:109-132.

Lien, Chinfa. 2005b. Families of ditransitive constructions in Li Jing Ji. Language and Linguistics 6.4:707-737.

Lien, Chinfa. 2006a. Verb classification, aktionsart and constructions in Li Jing Ji. Language and Linguistics 7.1:27-61.

Lien, Chinfa. 2006b. Lijingji quxiangshi tansuo [Directional constructions in Li Jing Ji]. Language and Linguistics 7.4:755-798.

Lien, Chinfa. 2007. Grammaticalization of *pat4* in Southern Min: a cognitive perspective. Language and Linguistics 8.3:723-742.

Lien, Chinfa. 2008. Special types of passive and causative constructions in TSM. In Redouane Djamouri, Barbara Meisteremst and Rint Sybesma (eds.), Chinese Linguistics in Leipzig. Chinese Linguistics in Europe CLE n°2, 223-237. Paris: Centre de Recherches Linguistiques sure l'Asie Orientale. École des hautes Études en Sciences Sociales.

Lien, Chinfa. 2010. Middles in Taiwanese Southern Min: the interface of lexical maning and event structure. Lingua 120:1273-1287.

Lien, Chinfa. 2013. 'Why' and 'How' WH-words in earlier Southern Min texts: interface of inherent properties of 'why/how' WH-words and their syntactic positions. Language and Linguistics 14.4:633-661.

Lien, Chinfa. 2014. The development of Southern Min demonstratives + type classifier/quantifier construction in the late Ming and early Qing texts: from demonstratives to intensifiers. Language and Linguistics 15.4:495-512.

Lien, Chinfa. 2015. Imperative negatives in earlier Southern Min and their later development. Faits de Langues 46:187-200.

Lien, Chinfa and Pengying Wang. 1999. Shape classifiers in Mandarin and Taiwanese: a psycholinguistic perspective. In Ovid J. L. Tzeng (ed.), The Biological Bases of Language. Journal of Chinese Linguistics Monograph 13: 189-221. Project on Linguistic Analysis, University of California at Berkeley.

Lin, Baoqing. 1998. Minnan Fangyan yu Guhanyu Tongyuan Cidan [A Dictionary of Cognates in Southern Min and Ancient Chinese]. Xiamen: Xiamen Daxue Chubanshe.

Lin, Huadong. 2007. Minnan fangyan yuqici yanjiu [A Study on modal particles in Southern Min]. Quanzhou Shifan Xueyuan Xuebao 5:47-54.

Lin, Huei-Ling. 2011. Pure unaccusatives with *HOO I* in Taiwan Southern Min. Lingua 121:2035-2047.

Lin, Huei-Ling. 2016. Non-disposal *KA* in Taiwan Southern Min. Taiwan Journal of Linguistics 14.1:1-27.

Lin, Lifang. 1996. Meixian fangyan dongci de ti [Aspects in the Meixian dialect]. In Shuangqing Zhang (ed.), 34-47.

Lin, Lifang. 1999. Meixian fangyan de daici [Pronouns in the Meixian dialect]. In Rulong Li and Shuangqing Zhang (ed.), 176-200.

Lin, Liantong. 1995. Fujian Yongchun fangyan de shubushi [Verb complement constructions in the Yongchun dialect in Fujian]. Zhongguo Yuwen 6:455-460.

Lin, Lunlun. 1996. Chenghai Fangyan Yanjiu [A Study of the Chenghai Dialect]. Shantou University Press.

Lin, Lunlun. 1997. Xinbian Chaozhouyin Zidian [New Chaozhou Pronunciation Dictionary]. Shantou: Shantou Daxue Chubanshe.

Lin, Lunlun and Xiaofeng Chen. 1996. Guangdong Minfangyan Yuyin Yanjiu [A Phonetic Study of Min Dialects in Guangdong]. Shantou: Shantou Daxue Chubanshe.

Lin, Shuangfu. 1974. Reduction in Taiwanese A-not-A question. Journal of Chinese Linguistics 2.1:37-78.

Lin, Tiansong. 2012. Fujian Jinjianghua de zhishici [Demonstratives in the Jinjiang dialect in Fujian]. Fangyan 1:32-39.

Lin, Yenhwei. 1989. An Autosegmental Treament of Chinese Segments. Ph. D. diss., University of Texas, Austin.
Lin, Yongxiang. 2005. Minnan Yongchun Fangyan Yuqici Yanjiu [A Study on Modal Particles in Southern Min of Yongchun]. M.A. thesis. Fujian Normal University.
Liu, Chen-Sheng. 2010. Dimension-denoting classifiers in Taiwanese compound adjectives. Journal of East Asian Linguistics 19.2: 181-205.
Liu, Danqing. 1996. Dongnan fangyan de timao biaoji [Aspect markers in Southeastern dialects]. In Shuangqing Zhang (ed.), 9-33.
Liu, Danqing. 1998. Putonghua yu shanghaihua zhong de kaobeishi huati jiegou [Identical topic constructions in Putonghua and the Shanghai dialect]. Yuyan Jiaoxue yu Yanjiu 1:85-103.
Liu, Danqing. 2000. Yueyu de jufa leixing tedian [Typological characteristics of Yue Syntax]. Yatai Yuyan Jiaoyu Xuebao 2:1-30.
Liu, Danqing. 2001. Hanyu fangyan yuxu leixing bijiao [A comparison of word order types of Chinese dialects]. Xiandai Zhongguoyu Yanjiu 2:24-37.
Liu, Danqing. 2003a. Yuxu Leixingxue yu Jieci Lilun [Word Order Typology and a Theory of Adposition]. Beijing: Shangwu Yinshuguan.
Liu, Danqing. 2003b[2011]. Lunyun fenlieshi huati jiegou chutan [Split argument topic constructions]. In Huati yu Jiaodian Xinlun [New Ideas about Topic and Focus], Xu, Liejiong and Danqing Liu (eds.), 220-241. Shanghai: Shanghai Jiaoyu Chubanshe.
Liu, Danqing. 2003c. Chabiju de diaocha kuangjia yu yanjiu silu [The investigation framework and research ideas of comparative sentences]. In Xiandai Yuyanxue Lilun yu Zhongguo Shaoshu Minzu Yuyan Yanjiu [Modern Linguistic Theory and the Study of Minority Languages in China], Qingxia Dai and Yang Gu (eds.), 1-21. Beijing: Minzu Chubanshe.
Liu, Danqing. 2005. Hanyu guanxi congju biaoji leixing chutan [A typology of relativizers in Chinese]. Zhongguo Yuwen 1:3-15.
Liu, Danqing. 2008. Syntax of space across Chinese dialects: conspiring and competing principles and factors. In Dan Xu (ed.), 39-67.
Liu, Danqing and Zhengda Tang. 2003. Xiandai Hanyu Fangyan Yufa Yuliaoku Diaocha Fang'an [Investigation Scheme of Chinese Dialects Corpus]. (Unpublished).
Liu, Jian and Alain Peyraube. 1994. History of some coordinative conjunctions in Chinese. Journal of Chinese Linguistics 22.2:179-201.
Liu, Lili. 2002. Ershi shiji hanyu qingsheng yanjiu zongshu [A review of studies on Chinese Qingsheng in 20th century]. Yuwen Yanjiu 3:43-47.
Liu, Xiaomei and Rulong Li. 2004. Dongnan fangyan yufa dui Putonghua de yingxiang sizhong [Four kinds of influences on Putonghua by grammar of the southeastern Chinese dialects]. Yuyan Yanjiu 24.4:61-64.
Liu, Xiuxue. 2005. Qionglin fangyan de zhishi daici – gouci, yuyi he yuyong tanxi [Place-deixis in the Qionglin dialect]. Language and Linguistics 6.1:133-152.
Liu, Yuehua (ed.) 1998. Quxiang Buyu Tongshi [A General Explanation of Directional Complements]. Beijing : Beijing Yuyan Daxue Chubanshe.
Liu, Ziyu. 1998. Hanyu fanfu wenju de lishi fazhan [The historical development of Chinese A-not-A question]. In Guhanyu Yufa Lunji [The Proceeding of Ancient Chinese Grammar], Xiliang Guo (ed.), 566-582. Beijing: Yuwen Chubanshe.
Liu, Ziyu. 2006. Shilun yuefangyan "V dao C" shubu jiegou de yufahua jiqi yu 'V de C' shubu jiegou de hubu fenbu [The grammaticalization of the V*dao* 到 C verb-complement construction in Yue dialect and the complementary distribution between the V*dao* 到 C

verb-complement construction and the V *de* 得 C verb-complement construction]. Yuyan Yanjiu 3:50-56.
Liu, Ziyu. 2008. Zhuzi Yulei Shubu Jiegou Yanjiu [A Study of Verb Complement Constructions in Zhuzi Yulei]. Beijing: Shangwu Yinshuguan.
Liu, Zhenfa and Huiling Xu. 2002. Chaozhouhua he Guangzhouhua、kejiahua de fangyan gongtongci [Cognate words of the Chaozhou dialect, the Guangzhou dialect and Hakka. In Pang-Hsin Ting and Shuangqing Zhang (eds.), Minyu Yanjiu jiqi yu Zhoubian Fangyan de Guanxi [The Study of Min Dialects and its Relationship with Peripheral Dialects], 173-180. Hong Kong: Chinese University Press.
Longacre, Robert E. 2007. Senteces as combinations of clauses. In Language Typology and Syntactic Description, vol. 2: complex constructions, Timothy Shopen (ed.), 372-420.
Lord, Carol, Foong-Ha Yap and Shoichi Iwasaki. 2002. Grammaticalization of 'give': African and Asian perspectives. In New Reflections on Grammaticalization (Typological Studies in Language 49), Ilse Wischer and Gabriele Diewald (eds.), 217-235. Amsterdam/Philadelphia: John Benjamins.
Lu, Guangcheng. 1999. Taiwan Minnanyu Cihui Yanjiu [A Study on Taiwan Southern Min Lexicon]. Taipei: Nantian Shuju.
Lu, Guangcheng. 2003. Taiwan Minnanyu Gaiyao [An Introduction to Taiwan Southern Min]. Taipei: Nantian Shuju.
Lu, Jilun and Jialing Wang. 2005. Guanyu qingsheng de jieding [On defining 'qingsheng']. Dangdai Yuyanxue 2:107-112.
Luo, Changpei. 1956[1930]. Xiamen Yinxi [The Phonology of the Xiamen Dialect]. Beijing: Kexue Chubanshe.
Luo, Haiyan. 2002. Hainan huangliu fangyan de yiwen daici [Interrogative pronouns of the Huangliu dialect in Hainan]. Qiongzhou Daxue Xuebao 1.1:62-64.
Lv, Shuxiang. 1984. Shi Jingdechuandenglu zhong 在、著 erzhuci [Two Particles 在、著 in Jingdechuandenglu]. In Hanyu Yufa Lunwenji [Papers on Chinese Grammar] (enlarged edition), 58-72. Beijing: Shangwu Yinshuguan.
Lv, Shuxiang. 1985. Jindai Hanyu Zhidaici [Modern Chinese Pronouns]. Shanghai: Xuelin Press.
Lv, Shuxiang. 1990. Lv Shuxiang Wenji [Selected Papers of Lv Shuxiang], Vol.1. Beijing: Shangwu Yinshuguan.
Lv, Shuxiang. 1999. Xiandai Hanyu Babaici [800 Words in Modern Chinese]. Enlarged edition. Beijing: Shangwu Yinshuguan.
Lyons, John. 1977. Semantics. Volume 2. Cambridge: Cambridge University Press.
Lyons, John. 1982. Deixis and subjectivity: *loquor, ergo sum*? In Speech, Place and Action: studies in deixis and related topics, Robert J. Jarvella and Wolfgang Klein (eds.), 101-124. New York: Wiley.
Ma, Chongqi. 1994. Zhangzhou Fangyan Yanjiu [A Study of the Zhangzhou Dialect]. Hong Kong: Hong Kong Zongheng Press.
Ma, Chongqi. 2002. Mintai Fangyan de Yuanliu yu Shanbian [The History and Evolution of Southern Min in Fujian and Taiwan]. Fuzhou: Fujian Renmin Chubanshe.
Matsumoto, Yoshiko. 2007. Integrating frames: complex noun phrase constructions in Japanese. In Susumu Kuno, Seiichi Makino and Susan Strauss (eds.), Aspects of Linguistics: in honor of Noriko Akatsuka, 131-154. Tokyo: Kurosio Publishers.
Matthews, Stephen. 2003. Verb-fronting in French and Sinitic vernaculars: a comparative study inspired by Chris Corne. Te Reo: Joural of the Linguistic Society of New Zealand 46:3-17.

Matthews, Stephen. 2006. On serial verb constructions in Cantonese. In Alexandra Y. Aikhenvald and R. M. W. Dixon (eds.), 69-87.
Matthews, Stephen and Virginia Yip. 2001.Aspects of contemporary Cantonese grammar: the structure and stratification of relative clauses. In Hilary Chappell (ed.), 266-281.
Matthews, Stephen and Virginia Yip. 2007.Are there internally headed relative clauses in Cantonese? Paper presented at the LSHK 2007 Annual Research Forum, 8-9 December 2007, Hong Kong.
Matthews, Stephen and Virginia Yip. 2008. Passive, unaccusative and pretransitive constructions in Chaozhou. In Redouane Djamouri, Barbara Meisterernst and Rint Sybesma (eds.), Chinese Linguistics in Leipzig, 163-174. Centre de Recherches Linguistiques sur l'Asie Orientale, Paris.
Matthews, Stephen and Virginia Yip. 2009. Contact-induced grammaticalization: evidence from bilingual acquisition. Studies in Language 33.2:366-395.
Matthews, Stephen and Virginia Yip. 2011. Cantonese: a comprehensive grammar. 2nd edition. London: Routledge.
Matthews, Stephen, Huiling Xu and Virginia Yip. 1999.Passives of the Chaozhou dialect: syntactic properties and grammaticalization. Paper presented at the Eighth Annual Conference of the International Association of Chinese Lin*guistics*, Melbourne, Australia.
Matthews, Stephen, Huiling Xu and Virginia Yip. 2005.Passive and unaccusative in Jieyang dialect of Chaozhou. Journal of East Asian Linguistics 4.4:267-298.
Matthews, Stephen, Virginia Yip and Huiling Xu. 2004. Causative constructions in Chaozhou and the causative continuum in Southern Min. Paper presented at the 36th International Conference on Sino-Tibetan Languages and Linguistics, La Trobe University, Melbourne.
McCawley, James.1992.Justifying part-of-speech assignments in Mandarin Chinese. Journal of Chinese Linguistics 20.2:211-246.
Mei, Tsu-Lin. 1999. Jige Taiwan Minnanhua changyong xuci de laiyuan [The etymologies of some grammatical particles in Taiwan Southern Min]. In Contemporary Studies on the Min dialects. Journal of Chinese Linguistics Monograph No. 13, TING Pang-hsin (ed.), 1-41.
Mei, Tsu-Lin. 2002. Jige Minyu xuci zai wenxianshang he fangyanzhong chuxian de niandai [The time of emergence of some Min function words in documents and the dialects]. In Dah-an Ho (ed.), 1-21.
Mei, Tsu-Lin and Xiufang Yang. 1995. Jige Minyu yufa chengfen de shijian cengci [The chronological levels of several grammatical constituents in Min dialect]. Bulletin of the Institute of History and Philology of the Academia Sinica 66.1:1-21.
Meillet, Antoine. 1921. Linguistique historique et linguistique générale. Paris: La société linguistique de Paris.
Modini, Paul. 1981. Inalienable possession and the 'double subject' constructions in East Asian. Cahiers de Linguistique Asie Orientale 9:5-15.
Mok, Sui-Sang. 1998.Cantonese Exceed Comparatives. Ph. D. diss., University of California, San Diego.
Moravcsik, Edith A. 1978.Reduplicative constructions. In Joseph H. Greenberg (ed.), Universals of Human Language, Vol.3: word structure, 297-334. Stanford, CA: Stanford University Press.
Nadarajan, Shanthi. 2006. A crosslinguistic study of reduplication. In Arizona Working Papers in SLAT, vol. 13:39-53.
Newman, John. 1996.Give: A cognitive linguistic study. Berlin and New York: Mouton de Gruyter.

Nichols, Johanna. 1986. Head-marking and dependent-marking grammar. Language 62:56-119.
Ning, Chunyan. 1993. The Overt Syntax of Relativization and Topicalization in Chinese. Ph. D. diss., University of California, Irvine.
Noonan, Michael. 2007. Complementation. In Language Typology and Syntactic Description, vol. 2: Complex Constructions, Shopen, Timothy. (ed.), 42-140. Canbridge: Cambridge University Press.
Palmer, F. R. 2001. Mood and Modality. Cambridge: Cambridge University Press.
Pan, Maoding, Rulong Li, Yuzhang Liang, Shengyu Zhang and Zhangtai Chen. 1963. Fujian hanyu fangyan fenqu lueshuo [A brief introduction to classification of Chinese dialects in Fujian]. Zhongguo Yuwen 6:475-495.
Pan, Wuyun. 1996. Wenzhou fangyan de ti he mao [Aspects in the Wenzhou dialect]. In Shuangqing Zhang (ed.), 254-284.
Pan, Wuyun and Huan Tao. 1999. Wuyu de zhidaici [Demonstratives in Wu dialect]. In Rulong Li and Shuangqing Zhang (eds.), 25-67.
Payne, Doris L. and Immanuel Barshi (eds.) 1999. External Possession. Amsterdam/Philadelphia: John Benjamines.
Pe, Hla. 1965. A re-examinaiton of Burmese 'classifiers'. Lingua 15:163-185.
Pingtian, Changsi and Wei Wu. 1996. Xiuning fangyan de ti [Aspects in the Xiuning dialect]. In Shuangqing Zhang (ed.), 130-142.
Piñol, Francisco.1928. *Gram*ática China del dialecto de Amoy. Imprenta de Nazaret, Hong Kong.
Qi, Huyang. 2002. Yuqici yu Yuqi Xitong [Modal Particles and Mood System]. Hefei: Anhui Jiaoyu Chubanshe.
Qian, Dianxiang. 2000. Tunchang fangyan de jieci [Adpositions of the Tunchang dialect]. In Rulong Li and Shuangqing Zhang (eds.), 173-184.
Qian, Dianxiang. 2002. Hainan Tunchang Minyu Yufa Yanjiu [A Study of Grammar in the Min Dialect of Tunchang in Hainan]. Kunming: Yunnan Daxue Chubanshe.
Rubino, Carl. 2005. Reduplication: form, function and distribution. In Bernhard Hurch (ed.), Studies on Reduplication, 11-29. Berlin: Mouton de Gruyter.
Saeed, John I. 2003. Semantics. Oxford: Blackwell Publishers.
Schachter, Paul and Timothy Shopen. 2007. Parts-of-speech systems. In Language Typology and Syntactic Description, Vol.1: clause structure, Timothy Shopen (ed.), 1-60. Second edition. Cambridge: Cambridge University Press.
Schiffrin, Deborah. 1992. Conditionals as topics in discourse. Linguistics 30:165-197.
Shen, Jiaxuan. 1987. Subject function and double subject construction in Mandarin Chinese. Cahiers de Linguistique Asie Orientale 16.2:195-211.
Shen, Jiaxuan. 1989. Yuyan Gongxing he Yuyan Leixing (B. Comrie: Language Universals and Linguistic Typology). Beijing: Huaxia Chubanshe.
Shen, Jiaxuan. 2003. Xiandai hanyu 'dongbu jiegou' de leixingxue kaocha [The resultative construction in modern Chinese: a typological perspective]. Shijie Hanyu Jiaoxue 3:17-23.
Shi, Qisheng. 1984. Shantou fangyan de chixu qingmao [Continuous aspect in the Shantou dialect]. Zhongshan Daxue Xuebao 3:127-136.
Shi, Qisheng. 1985. Min Wu fangyan chixumao xingshi de gongtong tedian [Common characteristics of continuous aspect in Min and Wu]. Zhongshan Daxue Xuebao 4:132-141, 131.
Shi, Qisheng. 1990. Shantou fangyan de fanfu wenju [A-not-A questions in the Shantou dialect]. Zhongguo Yuwen 3:182-185.
Shi, Qisheng. 1995. Shantou fangyan de zhishi daici [Demonstrative pronouns in the Shantou dialect]. Fangyan 3:201-207.

Shi, Qisheng. 1996a. Fangyan Lungao [Papers on Dialects]. Guangzhou: Guangdong Renmin Chubanshe.
Shi, Qisheng. 1996b. Lun "有"ziju [A study on existential "有"-sentences]. In Qisheng Shi, 48-59.
Shi, Qisheng. 1996c. Shantou fangyan de jizhong jushi [Several sentence patterns in the Shantou dialect]. In Qisheng Shi, 152-162.
Shi, Qisheng. 1996d. Shantou fangyan de ti [Aspects in the Shantou dialect]. In Qisheng Shi, 163-199.
Shi, Qisheng. 1996e. Shantou fangyan de yiwen daici [Interrogative pronouns in the Shantou dialect]. In Qisheng Shi, 250-258.
Shi, Qisheng. 1997. Lun Shantou fangyan zhong de chongdie [A study on redulplication in the Shantou dialect]. Yuyan Yanjiu 1:72-85.
Shi, Qisheng. 1999. Shantou fangyan de daici [Pronouns in the Shantou dialect]. In Rulong Li and Shuangqing Zhang (eds.), 289-324.
Shi, Qisheng. 2000. Shantou fangyan de jieci [Adpositions of the Shantou dialect]. In Rulong Li and Shuangqing Zhang (eds.), 163-179.
Shi, Qisheng. 2012. Minnan fangyan de bijiaoju [Comparative constructions in Southern Min]. Fangyan 1:12-22.
Shi, Qisheng. 2013. Minnan fangyan de chixu timao [On the durative aspect of Southern Min]. Fangyan 4:289-306.
Shi, Rujie. 1999. Suzhou fangyan de daici xitong [The pronoun system in the Suzhou dialect]. In Rulong Li and Shuangqing Zhang (eds.), 85-101.
Shibatani, Masayoshi and Prashant Pardeshi. 2002. The causative continuum. In Masayoshi Shibatani (ed.), The Grammar of Causation and Interpersonal Manipulation, 85-126. Amsterdam: John Benjamins.
Siemund, Peter. 2001. Interrogative constructions. In Language Typology and Language Universals: an international handbook, Vol.2, Martin Haspeimath, Ekkehard König, Wulf Oesterreicher and Wolfgang Raibe (eds.), 1010-1028. Berlin; New York: Walter de Gruyter.
Siewierska, Anna. Person. Cambridge: Cambridge University Press.
Smith, Carlota S. 1997. The Parameter of Aspect. Second edition. Springer Science+Business Media.
Song, Jae Jung. 2001. Linguistic Typology: Morphology and Syntax. New York: Longman.
Stassen, Leon. 1985. Comparison and Universal Grammar. Oxford: Blackwell.
Stassen, Leon. 2009. Predicative Possession. Oxford: Oxford University Press.
Sun, Chaofen. 2008. Two conditions and grammaticalization of the Chinese locative. In Dan Xu (ed.), 199-228.
Sun, Xixin. 1999. Jindai Hanyu Yuqici [Modal Particles in Modern Chinese]. Beijing: Yuwen Chubanshe.
Sun, Yan. 2005. Rutang Qiufa Xunli Xingji de Liangci [Classifiers in Ennins Travels in Tang China]. In Jinfang Li (ed.), Hanzang Yuxi Liangci Yanjiu [Classifiers of Sino-Tibetan Languages], 387-408. Beijing: Zhongyang Minzu Daxue Chubanshe.
Sweetser, Eve Eliot. 1988. Grammaticalization and semantic bleaching. Berkeley Linguistics Society 14:389-405.
Tai, James. H-Y. 1985. Temporal sequence and Chinese word order. In John Haiman (ed.), Iconicity in Syntax, 49-72. Amsterdam: John Benjamins.

Tai, James. H-Y. 1994. Chinese classifier systems and human categorization. In Matthew Chen and Ovid Tseng (eds.), Honor of Professor William S-Y. Wang: Interdisciplinary Studies on Language and Language Change, 479-494. Taipei: Pyramid Publishing Company.
Tai, James H-Y. and Fangyi Chao. 1994. A semantic study of the classifier *zhang*. Journal of Chinese Language Teachers Association 29.3:67-78.
Tai, James H-Y. and Lianqing Wang. 1990. A semantic study of the classifier tiao. Journal of the Chinese Language Teachers Association 25.1:35-56.
Tang, Tingchi. 1999a. Minnanyu Yufa Yanjiu Shilun [A Tentative Study on Southern Min Grammar]. Taipei: Xuesheng Shuju.
Tang, Tingchi. 1999b. Hanyu dongcizu buyu de jufa jiegou yu yuyi gongneng: beipinghua yu minnanhua de bijiaofenxi [The syntax and semantics of resultative complements in Chinese: a comparative study of Beijing Mandarin and Southern Min]. In Tingchi Tang, 1-134.
Tang, Tingchi. 1999c. Minnanhua foudingci de yuyi neihan yu jufa biaoxian [On the semantics and syntax of negatives in Southern Min]. In Tingchi Tang, 135-185.
Taylor, J. R. 1989a. Possessive genitives in English. Linguistics 27: 663–86.
Taylor, J. R. 1989b. Linguistic Categorization: Prototypes in linguistic theory. Oxford: Clarendon Press.
Teng, Shou-hsin. 1974. Double nominatives in Chinese. Language 50.3: 455-473.
Teng, Shou-hsin. 1982. Disposal structures in Amoy. Bulletin of the Institute of History and Philology 53.2: 331-352.
Teng, Shou-hsin. 1990. Diversification and unification of negation in Taiwanese. In Hwang-Cherng Gong and Dah-an Ho (eds.), Proceedings of the First International Symposium on Chinese Languages and Linguistics, 335-351.
Thomason, Sarah G. 2001. Language Contact: an introduction. Edinburgh: EUP.
Thompson, Sandra A. Robert E. Longacre and Shin Ja J. Hwang. 2007. Adverbial clauses. In Language Typology and Syntactic Description, vol. 2: complex construction, Timothy Shopen (ed.), 237-300.
Thomson A. J. 1986. A Practical English Grammar. Oxford: Oxford University Press.
Trask, R. L. 1996. Historical Linguistics. London: Arnold.
Traugott, Elizabeth Closs. 1989. On the rise of epistemic meanings in English: an example of subjectificaton in semantic change. Language 57:33-65.
Traugott, Elizabeth Closs. 1995. Subjectification in grammaticalization. In Dieter Stein and Susan Wright (eds.), Subjectivity and Subjectivisation, 31-54. Cambridge: Cambridge University Press.
Traugott, Elizabeth Closs. 1996. Grammaticalization and lexicalization. In Keith Brown and Jim Miller (eds.), Concise Encyclopedia of Syntactic Theories. Oxford/New York: Pergamon.
Traugott, Elizabeth Closs. 2003. From subjectification to intersubjectification. In Raymond Hickey (ed.), Motives for Language Change, 124-139. Cambridge: Cambridge University Press.
Traugott, Elizabeth Closs. 2010. (Inter)subjectivity and (inter)subjectificatoin: a reassessment. In Kristin Davidse, Lieven Vandelanotte and Hubert Cuyckens (eds.), Subjectification, Intersubjectification and Grammaticalization, 29-71. Berlin; New York: De Gruyter Mouton.
Traugott, Elizabeth Closs and Bernd Heine (eds.) 1991. Approaches to Grammaticalization, 2 Vols. Amsterdam: Benjamins.
Traugott, Elizabeth Closs and Ekkehard König. 1991. The semantics-pragmatics of grammaticalization revisited. In Elizabeth Closs Traugott and Bernd Heine (eds.), Vol.1:189-218.

Tsao, Fengfu. 1977. A Functional Study of Topic in Chinese: the first step towards discourse analysis. Ph. D. diss., University of Southern California.
Tsao, Fengfu. 1987. A topic-comment approach to the BA construction. Journal of Chinese Linguistics 15.1:1-53.
Tsao, Fengfu. 1988. The function of Mandarin *gei* and Taiwanese *hou* in the double object and the passive construction. In Robert L. Cheng and Shuanfan Huang (eds.), 165-208.
Tsao, Fengfu. 2005. Taiwan Minnanyu de *ka7* yu binyu de qianzhi [*Ka7* in Taiwan Southern Min and the proposing of the object]. Hanyu Xuebao 1:21-30.
Tsao, Fengfu and Meihui Tsai (eds.)1995. Papers from the 1994 Conference on Language Teaching and Linguistics in Taiwan, Vol. I: Southern Min. Taipei: The Crane Publishing Co., Ltd.
T'sou, Benjamin K. 1976. The structure of nominal classifier systems. Oceanic Linguistics Special Publications 13:1215-1247. Honolulu: University of Hawai'i Press.
Ultan, Russell. 1978. Some general characteristics of interrogative systems. In Joseph H. Greenberg (ed.), Universals of Human Languages, Vol.4:211-248. Stanford: Stanford University Press.
van der Auwera, J. and D. P. O'Baoill (eds.) 1998. Adverbial Constructions in the Languages of Europe. Berlin and New York: Mouton de Gruyter.
Van der Auwera, Johan and Vladimir A. Plungian. 1998. Modality's semantic map. Linguistic Typology 2:79-124.
Vogel, Petra M. and Bernard Comrie (eds.)2000. Approaches to the Typology of Word Classes. Berlin; New York: Mouton de Gruyter.
Wan, Bo. 1996. Anyi fangyan de ti [Aspects in the Anyi dialect]. In Shuangqing Zhang (ed.), 79-96.
Wang, Benying and Chinfa Lien. 1995. Taiwan minnanyu zhong de fanfu wenju [A-not-A questions in Taiwan Southern Min]. In Fengfu Tsao and Meihui Tsai (eds.), 47-69.
Wang, Dejie and Shiguang Wang. 2007. Fanfu wenju de lishi tantao [A historical study of A-not-A question]. Xiandai Yuwen 6:31-33.
Wang, Jian. 2013. Leixingxue shiyexia de hanyu fangyan "liang ming" jiegou yanjiu [Bare classifier phrases in Chinese dialects: A typological perspective]. Yuyan Kexue 4:383-393.
Wang, Jian. 2015. Bare classifier phrases in Sinitic languages: A typological perspective. In Hilary Chappell (ed.), Diversity in Sinitic Languages, 110-133. Oxford: Oxford University Press.
Wang, Jian and Hilary Chappell. 2012. How to ask for who without who. Ms.
Wang, Jianshe. 1992. Cong kouyu daici xitong de bijiao kan Shishuoxinyu yu Minnanhua de yizhixing [The consistency between Shishuoxinyu and Minnanhua from the comparison of pronouns system in spoken language]. In Donghan Liang, Lunlun Lin and Yongkai Zhu (eds.), 82-89.
Wang, Jianshe. 1996. Quanzhouhua zhong de qingsheng xianxiang [Qingsheng of the Quanzhou dialect]. In Bohui Zhan, Rulong Li and Shuangqing Zhang (eds.), 101-114.
Wang, Jianshe and Ganli Zhang. 1994. Quanzhou Fangyan yu Wenhua [The Dialect and Culture of Quanzhou]. Xiamen: Lujiang Press.
Wang, Li. 1984a. Cilei [Word Classes]. Ji'nan: Shanghai Jiaoyu Chubanshe.
Wang, Li. 1984b. Wangli Wenji [Collected Works of Wang Li], Vol.1. Ji'nan: Shandong Jiaoyu Chubanshe.
Wang, Shaoxin. 1992. Tangdai Shiwen Xiaoshuo zhong Mingliangci de Yunyong [The usage of nominal classifiers within poems, literatures and novels in Tang Dynasty]. In Xiangqing

Cheng (ed.), Suitang Wudai Hanyu Yanjiu [Studies of the Chinese Language of the Sui, Tang and Five Dynasties (581-960 A.D.)], 327-386. Ji'nan: Shandong Jiaoyu Chubanshe.
Wang, Yude. 1993. Taiwanhua Jiangzuo [Lectures on Taiwan Southern Min]. Taipei: Zili Wanbaoshe Wenhua Chubanshe.
Wei, Desheng. 2000. Dunhuang hanjian zhong de liangci [Classifiers in bamboo slips of the Han Dynasty from Dunhuang]. Guhanyu Yanjiu 2:74-78.
Wei, Qingwen and Guosheng Qin (eds.) 1980. Zhuangyu Jianzhi [A Brief Description of the Zhuang Language]. Beijing: Minzu Chubanshe.
Wen, Duanzheng. 1994. Cong Zhenan minnanhua xingrongci chengdu biaoshi fangshi de yanbian kan youshi fangyan dui lieshi fangyan de yingxiang [A study on strong dialects' impact on weak dialects based on the development of the expressions of degree of adjectives in Zhenan Southern Min]. Yuwen Yanjiu 1:43-49.
Winford, Donald. 2003. An Introduction to Contact Linguistics. Oxford: Blackwell.
Wu, Fuxiang. 1996. Dunhuang Bianwen Yufa Yanjiu [A Study of Grammar in Dunhuang Bianwen]. Changsha: Yuelu Shushe.
Wu, Fuxiang. 1997. Cong 'VP-neg'shi fanfu wenju de fenhua tan yuqici 'me' de chansheng [The appearance of particle 'me' from polarization of VP-neg interrogatives]. Zhongguo Yuwen 1:44-54.
Wu, Fuxiang. 1998. Chongtan 'dong+le+bin' geshi de laiyuan he wanchengti zhuci le de chansheng [Rethinking the source of the configuration 'verb+le+object' and the emergence of the aspect marker le]. Zhongguo Yuwen 6:452-462.
Wu, Fuxiang. 2001. Nanfang fangyan jige zhuangtai buyu biaoji de laiyuan (yi) [Origin of some markers of stative complements in the Southern Chinese dialects (I)]. Fangyan 4:344-354.
Wu, Fuxiang. 2002. Nengxing shubu jiegou suoyi [Some remarks on the potential verb-complement construction in Chinese]. Yuyan Jiaoxue yu Yanjiu 5:19-27.
Wu, Fuxiang. 2008. Nanfang yuyan zhengfan wenju de laiyuan [Origins of A-not-A in the languages of Southern China]. Minzu Yuwen 1:3-18.
Wu, Fuxiang. 2009. Yufahua de xinshiye: jiechu yinfa de yufahua [A new perspective of grammaticalization: contact-induced grammaticalization]. Dangdai Yuyanxue 3:193-206.
Wu, Fuxiang. 2011. Minyu Chabishi de Lishi Cengci [The Historical Stratum of Comparative Constructions in Min Dialect]. Unpublished manuscript.
Wu, Jianfeng. 2006. Yanyu xingwei yu xiandai hanyu julei yanjiu [Speech Acts and Chinese Sentece Types]. Ph. D. diss., Huadong Normal University.
Wu, Yunji (ed.) 1999. Hanyu Fangyan Gongshi yu Lishi de Yufa Yantao Lunwenji [Synchronic and Diachronic Perspectives on the Grammar of Chinese dialects]. Guangzhou: Ji'nan University Press.
Xiamen Daxue Zhongguo Yuyan Wenxue Yanjiusuo Hanyu Fangyan Yanjiushi. 1982. Putonghua Minnan Fangyan Cidian [Putonghua-Southern Min Dictionary]. Fuzhou: Fujian Renmin Chubanshe.
Xiang, Mengbing. 1996. Liancheng (Xinquan) fangyan de ti [Aspects in the Liancheng (Xinquan) dialect]. In Shuangqing Zhang (ed.), 48-78.
Xiao, Richard and McEnery, Tony. 2004. Aspect in Mandarin Chinese: a corpus-based study. Amsterdam; Philadelphia: J. Benjamins Pub.
Xing, Fuyi. 1995. Cong Hainan Huangliuhua de 'yi、er、san' kan xiandai hanyu shuci xitong [A study of numeral system in modern Chinese based on 'one, two, three' of the Huangliu dialect in Hai'nan]. Fangyan 3:188-196.

Xu, Dan (ed.) 2008. Space in Languages of China: cross-linguistic, synchronic and diachronic perspectives. Dordrecht: Springer.
Xu, Huiling. 2001. On the demonstrative system of the Jieyang dialect: a comparative study with Mandarin. In Language Research Institute of Shenzhen and Hong Kong (ed.), Bilingualism (7), Proceedings 2001 Seventh International Conference on Bilingualism and Bidialect, 187-205. Shenzhen: Chinese Studies Publishing House.
Xu, Huiling. 2004. Comparative constructions in Jieyang. Paper presented at the Research Centre of Linguistic Typology Workshop on the Comparative Constructions, La Trobe University.
Xu, Huiling. 2005. Clausal negation in the Jieyang dialect: internation of negators with verb types, temporal reference, aspect and modality. Interventions, Interactions and Interrelations. School of Languages Postgraduate Research Papers on Language and Literature 5:175-207. School of Languages, the University of Melbourne, Australia.
Xu, Huiling. 2006. The aspect marking of the Jieyang dialect. Journal of Chinese Language Teaching 3.1:45-81.
Xu, Huiling. 2007. Aspects of Chaozhou Grammar: a synchronic description of the Jieyang variety. Journal of Chinese Linguistics. Monograph series, no. 22.
Xu, Huiling and Stephen Matthews. 2007. Cong dongci dao ziju jiegou biaoji: Chaozhou fangyan he Taiwan minnanyu "说" he "看" de xuhua guocheng [The grammaticalization of the words for "say" and "see" in the Chaozhou dialect and Taiwan Southern Min]. Zhongguo Yuwen Yanjiu 23:61-72. T. T. Ng Chinese Language Research Center, The Chinese University of Hong Kong.
Xu, Huiling and Stephen Matthews. 2011. On the polyfunctionality and grammaticalization of the morpheme kai in the Chaozhou dialect. In Nominalization in Asian Languages: Diachronic and typological perspectives, Foong Ha YAP, K. Grunow-Harsta and J. Wrona (eds.), 109-124. Amsterdam: John Benjamins Publishing Company.
Xu, Jie. 2003. Zhuyu chengfen、huati tezheng ji xiangying yuyan leixing [Subject as a constituent, topic as a feature and their respective typologies]. Yuyan Kexue 2.1:3-22.
Xu, Liejiong and Danqing Liu. 2007. Huati de Jiegou yu Gongneng [Topic: structural and functional analysis]. Enlarged edtion. Shanghai: Shanghai Jiaoyu Chubanshe.
Xu, Ruirong. 2000. Minfangyan "囝" de ciyi yanbian [Semantic changes of "囝" in Min dialects]. Yuwen Yanjiu 2:54-58.
Xu, Ruiyuan. 2017. Chuanjiaoshi cailiao zhong de Fujian Xiamen fangyan changyong danyin foudingci [Monosyllabic negative words of Xiamen dialect in Fujian province in materials written by missionaries]. Fangyan 3:360-367.
Xu, Shirong. 1980. Putonghua Yuyin Zhishi [Phonetics and Phonology in Putonghua]. Beijing: Wenzi Gaige Chubanshe.
Xu, Zhaohong. 2016. Binglie lianci 'he' de yuyi yanbian licheng [The semantic change of the coordinative conjunction 'he']. Hunan Keji Daxue Xuebao 5:149-151.
Yang, Barry Chung-Yu. 2006. Syntactic structure of ka-construction in Taiwanese Southern Min. UST working Papers in Linguistics, Vol.2:141-171.
Yang, Xiufang. 1991. Taiwan Minnanyu Yufagao [Taiwan Southern Min Grammar]. Taipei: Da'an Press.
Yang, Xiufang. 2000. Fangyan benzi yanjiu de guannian yu fangfa [Concepts and methods in the study of original characters of dialects]. Hanxue Yanjiu 18:111-146.
Yang, Xiufang. 2002. Lun Minnanyu yiwendaici '当时' '著时' '底位' [On Southern Min $ta\eta1\ si2$, $ti4\ si2$, and $tai3\ ui6$]. In Dah-an Ho (ed.), 155-178.

Yang, Yonglong. 2003. Juwei yuqici "ma" de yufahua [On the grammaticalization of sentence-final particle "ma"]. Yuyan Kexue 1:29-38.
Yap, Foong-Ha, Karen Grunow-Hårsta and Janick Wrona (eds.) 2011. Nominalization in Asian Languages: diachronic and typological perspectives (Typological Studies in Language 96). Amsterdam: John Benjamins Publishing Company.
Yap, Foong-Ha and Shoichi Iwasaki. 1998. 'Give' constructions in Malay, Thai and Mandarin Chinese: polygrammaticalization perspective. In M. C. Gruber, D. Higins, K. S. Olson and T. Wysocki (eds.), Papers from the 34th Meeting of the Chicago Linguistic Society, Part I: papers from the main session, 421-437. Chicago, IL: the Chicago Linguistic Society.
Yap, Foong-Ha and Shoichi Iwasaki. 2003. From causative to passive: a passage in some East and Southeast Asian languages. In Eugene H. Casad and Gary B. Palmer (eds.), Cognitive Linguistics and Non-Indo-European Languages (Cognitive Linguistics Research 18), 419-446. Berlin: Mouton de gruyter.
Yap, Foong-Ha and Shoichi Iwasaki.2007. The emergence of 'give' passives in East and Southeast Asian languages. In Mark Alves, Paul Sidwell and David Gil (eds.), Proceedings of the Eighth Annual Meeting of the Southeast Asian Linguistics Society, 193-208. Canberra: Pacific Linguistics.
Ye, Guichen. 2005.Liushizhong Qu he Mingdai Wenxian de Liangci [Classifiers in Liushizhong Qu and Documents of Ming Dynasty]. Ph. D. diss., Hu'nan Normal University.
Yin, Wei. 2006. Wu Deng Hui Yuan Fanfu Wenju ji Xuanze Wenju Yanjiu [A Study of A-not-A Questions and Alternative Questions in Wu Deng Hui Yuan]. MA. thesis. Nanjing Normal University.
Yip, Virginia and Stephen Matthews. 2007. Relative clauses in Cantonese-English bilingual children: typological challenges and processing motivations. Studies in Second Language Acquisition 29.2:277-300.
Yuan, Jiahua.1989. Hanyu Fangyan Gaiyao [An Introduction to Chinese Dialects]. Beijing: Wenzi Gaige Chubanshe.
Yuan, Yulin. 1996. Huatihua ji xiangguan de yufa guocheng [Topicalization and related grammatical processes]. Zhongguo Yuwen 4:241-254.
Yue-Hashimoto, Anne. 1991. Stratification in comparative dialectal grammar. Journal of Chinese Linguistics 19.2:172-201.
Yue-Hashimoto, Anne. 1993. Comparative Chinese Dialectal Grammar. Paris: École des hautes etudes en sciences sociales, Centre de recherches linguistiques sur l'Asie orientale.
Yue-Hashimoto, Anne. 2001. The verb complement construction in historical perspective with special reference to Cantonese. In Hilary Chappell (ed.), 232-265.
Zeng, Nanyi and Xiaofan Li. 2013. Cong Mingqing xiwen kan Quanzhou fangyan tibiaoji "lie" de yufahua [Grammaticalization of the aspect marker "lie" in the Quanzhou dialect based on Ming and Qing play scripts]. Zhongguo Yuwen 3:205-214.
Zeng, Xiantong. 1991. Mingben Chaozhou xiwen suojian Chaozhou fangyan shulue [The Chaozhou dialect in stage play scripts of the Min Dynasty]. Fangyan 1:10-29.
Zhan, Bohui, Rulong Li and Shuangqing Zhang (eds.)1996. Disijie Guoji Minfangyan Yantaohui Lunwenji [Proceeding of the 4th International Symposium on Min Dialect]. Shantou: Shantou Daxue Chubanshe.
Zhang, Bojiang. 1997. Xingzhi xingrongci de fanwei he cengci [The scope and stratification of adjectives]. Yufa Yanjiu he Tansuo 8: 50-61. Beijing: Shangwu Yinshuguan.
Zhang, Bojiang and Mei Fang. 1996. Hanyu Gongneng Yufa Yanjiu [A Functional Study of Chinese Grammar]. Nanchang: Jiangxi Jiaoyu Chubanshe.

Zhang, Cheng. 2012. Leixingxue Shiye de Hanyu Mingliangci Yanbianshi [The Evolutional History of Chinese Classifiers in Typological Perspective]. Peking University Press.

Zhang, Hongnian. 2007 Xianggang Yueyu Yufa Yanjiu [A Grammar of Yue Spoken in Hong Kong]. Revised edition. The Chinese University of Hong Kong Press.

Zhang, Junru, Min Liang, Jueya Ouyang, Yiqing Zheng, Jianyou Xie, Xulian Li. 1999. Zhuangyu Fangyan Yanjiu[A Study of Zhuang Dialects]. Chengdu: Sichuan Minzu Chubanshe.

Zhang, Meilan. 2003. Zutangji Yufa Yanjiu [A Study of Grammar in Zutangji]. Beijing: Shangwu Yinshuguan.

Zhang, Min. 1999. Hanyu fangyan tici chongdieshi yuyi moshi de bijiao yanjiu [A comparative study on semantic models of reduplicative forms across Chinese dialects] In Yunji Wu (ed.), 1-33.

Zhang, Shuangqing (ed.) 1996a. Dongci de Ti [Verbal Aspects]. T. T. Ng Chinese Language Research Centre Institute of Chinese Studies, The Chinese University of Hong Kong.

Zhang, Shuangqing. 1996b. Xianggang yueyu dongci de ti [Aspects in Hong Kong Cantonese]. In Shuangqing Zhang (ed.), 143-160.

Zhang, Shuangqing. 1999. Xianggang yueyu de daici [Pronouns in Hong Kong Cantonese]. In Rulong Li and Shuangqing Zhang (eds.), 345-360.

Zhang, Xiaoshan. 1996. Chaozhouhua de foudingci "wu" [The negative word "wu" in the Chaozhou dialect]. In Bohui Zhan, Rulong Li, and Shuangqing Zhang (eds.), 271-290.

Zhang, Xiaoshan. 1999. Chaozhouhua de foudingci "未" [The negative word "未" in the Chaozhou dialect]. Hanshan Shifan Xueyuan Xuebao 1:118-122.

Zhang, Zhenxing. 1983. Taiwan Minnan Fangyan Jilue [An Outline of Taiwan Southern Min]. Fuzhou: Fujian Renmin Chubanshe.

Zhang, Zhenxing. 1992. Zhangping Fangyan Yanjiu [A Study of the Zhangping Dialect]. Beijing: Zhongguo Shehui Kexue Chubanshe.

Zhao, Jinming. 2002. Hanyu chabiju de nanbei chayi jiqi lishi shanbian [Variation and historical development of comparative sentence in Chinese]. Yuyan Yanjiu 3:49-55.

Zhao, Rixin. 2000. Jixi fangyan de jieci [Adpositions of the Jixi dialect]. In Rulong Li and Shuangqing Zhang (eds.), 78-93.

Zheng, Ying and Chen, Yawen. 2005.Taiwan Minnanyu ziyici jian nan zai er de bijiao [Comparison of words meaning 'son' in Taiwan Southern Min: *jian*, *nan*, *zai* and *er*]. Taiwan Yuyan Jiaoxue yu Yanjiu 6:202-219.

Zhongguo Shehui Kexueyuan Yuyan Yanjiusuo [Institute of Lingusitics, The Chinese Academy of Social Sciences], Zhongguo Shehui Kexueyuan Minzuxue yu Renleixue Yanjiusuo [Institute of Ethnology and Anthropology, The Chinese Academy of Social Sciences], and Xianggang Chengshi Daxue Yuyan Zixun Kexue Yanjiu Zhongxin [Language Information Sciences Research Centre, City University of Hong Kong] (eds.)2012. Zhongguo Yuyan Dituji [Language Atlas of China]. Second edition. Beijing: Shangwu Yinshuguan.

Zhong, Rongfu. 2002. Taiyu de Yuyin Jichu [Basic Phonology of Taiwan Southern Min]. Taipei: Crane Publishing Co. Ltd.

Zhou, Changji. 1991. Minnanhua yu Putonghua [Southern Min and Putonghua]. Yuwen Chubanshe.

Zhou, Changji. 1995.Xiamenhua jieci "互"、"共" jiqi xiangguan jushi [The adposiitons "互" and "共" and related constructions in the Xiamen dialect]. Zhongguo Yuwen Yanjiu, Vol.11: the proceeding of the third international conference on Min dialects, 169-176. The Chinese University of Hong Kong Press.

Zhou, Changji. 1996. Xiamenhua dai "了去着" buyu de shubujiegou [Verb-complement constructions with the complements "了去着" in the Xiamen dialect]. In Bohui Zhan, Rulong Li and Shuangqing Zhang (eds.), 250-257.
Zhou, Changji (ed.) 1998. Xiamen Fangyan Cidian [A Dictionary of the Xiamen Dialect]. Nanjing: Jiangsu Jiaoyu Chubanshe.
Zhou, Changji. 1999. Xiamenhua de chabiju [Comparative sentences in the Xiamen dialect]. In Yunji Wu (ed.), 217-223.
Zhou, Changji (ed.) 2006. Minnan Fangyan Da Cidian [A Dictionary of Southern Min Dialect]. Fuzhou: Fujian Renmin Chubanshe.
Zhou, Changji and Yiyun Ouyang. 1998. Xiamen Fangyan Yanjiu [A Study of the Xiamen Dialect]. Fuzhou: Fujian Renmin Chubanshe.
Zhou, Changji and Qinghai Zhou. 2000. Xinjiapo Minnanhua Gaishuo [An Introduction to Southern Min in Singapore]. Xiamen: Xiamen Daxue Chubanshe.
Zhou, Changji and Qinghai Zhou (eds.) 2002. Xinjiapo Minnanhua Cidian [A Dictionary of Southern Min in Singapore]. Beijing: Zhongguo Shehui Kexue Chubanshe.
Zhu, Dexi. 1956. Xiandai hanyu xingrongci yanjiu [A study on adjectives in Modern Chinese]. Yuyan Yanjiu 1:83-111.
Zhu, Dexi. 1982. Yufa Jiangyi [Grammar Issues]. Beijing: Shangwu Yinshuguan.
Zhu, Dexi. 1985. Yufa Dawen [The Questions and Answers on Grammar]. Beijing: Shangwu Yinshuguan.
Zhu, Dexi. 1991. "V-neg-VO" yu "VO-neg-V" liangzhong fanfu wenju zai hanyu fangyan li de fenbu [The dialectal distribution of the interrogative sentence patterns V-neg-VO and VO-neg-V in Chinese]. Zhongguo Yuwen 5:321-332.
Zhu, Minche. 1995. Hanyu xuanzewen、zhengfanwen de lishi fazhan [The historical development of Chinese alternative questions and V-not-V questions]. Yuyan Yanjiu 2:117-122.
Zhu, Xiaonong. 2010. Yuyin Xue [Phonetics]. Beijing: Shangwu Yinshuguan.
Zhuang, Chusheng. 2000. Minyu Pinghe fangyan de jieci [Adpositions of the Pinghe variety of Min dialect]. In Rulong Li and Shuangqing Zhang (eds.), 139-156.

Index

adposition
- agent 274, 275, 280
- basis 262, 278
- benefactive 275, 276, 280, 297, 298, 299, 301, 302, 303, 304, 305, 306, 308, 309, 310, 311, 74
- comitative 276, 277, 280, 297, 299, 300, 301, 306, 311, 444, 77
- goal 262, 268, 269, 270, 280, 297, 298, 299, 301, 302, 303, 304, 305, 306, 308, 311
- instrument 267, 278, 279, 280
- location 262, 263, 264, 265, 268, 269, 280
- patient 224, 270, 271, 272, 273, 279, 280, 297, 298, 299, 304, 305, 306, 307
- perlative 269, 280
- source 262, 264, 266, 267, 269, 270, 273, 278, 280, 297, 298, 299, 301, 302, 305, 306, 308, 311
- standard of comparison 277, 278, 444, 66
adverbial clauses
- cause clauses 457
- conditional clauses 460, 464, 465, 466
- purpose clauses 459
- time clauses 451, 461, 466
adverbs 454, 455
- adverbs of quantity and scope 288
- attitude and epistemic adverbs 238, 240, 241, 242, 293
- degree adverbs 283, 294, 126
- manner adverbs 282, 294
- time adverbs 287, 294
affixation
- prefix 25, 26, 27, 28, 29, 30, 32, 33, 37, 120
- suffix 26, 27, 28, 29, 30, 31, 32, 33, 34, 35, 37
aspect
- durative 215, 222, 224, 225, 228
- experiential 215, 226, 227, 228, 248
- habitual 215, 222, 225, 226, 228
- perfective 215, 216, 218, 219, 220, 222, 228
- progressive 215, 222, 223, 224, 225, 228, 263

causative constructions 344, 345, 483
classifiers 368, 370, 376, 378, 395, 420, 426, 428, 30, 31, 43, 46, 61, 62, 64, 65, 66, 67, 68, 69, 70, 71, 72, 73, 76, 79, 80, 81, 83, 84, 87, 94, 97, 98, 103, 111, 112, 113, 114, 115, 116, 117, 124, 127, 129, 130, 134, 135, 137, 139, 140, 141, 142, 160, 169, 177
comparative constructions of inequality
- absolute comparatives 321, 322, 324, 337
- comparatives with the marker $khɯ^5$ 316, 332
- dependent-marking comparatives with pi^3 336
- double-marking/hybridized comparatives 322, 337
- head-marking comparatives with kha^{7} 277, 322
- zero-marked comparatives 332, 337
complement clauses
- causative (or manipulative) verbs 468, 483
- modal verbs of volition 468, 482
- utterance verbs 378, 383, 468
- verbs of perception and cognition 467, 475, 484
coordination
- adversative coordination 407, 414, 415
- conjunction 407, 408, 409, 410, 411, 412, 413, 415
- disjunction 407, 413, 415

demonstratives 327, 332, 364, 365, 376, 403, 419, 420, 422, 424, 427, 428, 429, 431, 447, 449, 469, 120, 122, 123, 124, 138, 142
- basic adnominal demonstratives 64
- generic demonstratives 63, 81, 86
- plural demonstratives 76, 80, 81
- singular demonstratives 73

'give' constructions
- (permissive) causative verb 274, 343, 348
- concessive marker 339, 347, 348
- dative marker 274, 339, 341, 342, 348

https://doi.org/10.1515/9781501511868-027

– ditransitive verb 339, 340, 341, 343, 348
– perspective marker 339, 340, 341, 348
– purposive marker 339, 345, 348
– speaker-affectedness marker 274, 339, 346, 348

Hui'an dialect
– location 3
– previous studies 7

interrogatives 469, 470, 471, 474
– alternative interrogatives 349, 350, 355, 372, 413, 480
– constituent interrogatives 363, 480
– polar interrogatives 349, 351, 354, 355, 357, 359, 360

modality
– ability 229, 230, 231, 232, 233, 234, 235, 236, 241
– epistemic possibility 230, 231, 233, 237, 238, 241, 251, 293
– necessity 229, 230, 239, 240, 241, 242, 293
– non-deontic possibility 230, 231, 236, 241
– permission 229, 230, 231, 233, 237, 241, 251, 256
– possibility 229, 230, 231, 234, 235, 236, 237, 241, 359
– root possibility 230, 231, 234, 235, 236, 241, 251, 256
– volition 229, 230, 240, 241, 242, 244, 245

negation
– 'lack of necessity' negatives 244, 259
– general and volitional negatives 243, 244
– general prohibitive 244, 259
– imminent negative 259
– injunctive negative 244, 258, 259, 260
– irrealis negative 244, 259
– perfective negative 244, 251, 252, 255, 259
numerals 28, 30, 31, 43, 46, 61, 62, 64, 65, 66, 67, 68, 69, 70, 71, 72, 73, 83, 84, 98, 101, 103, 105, 106, 115, 117, 120
– approximate numbers 110
– cardinal numbers 101
– ordinal numbers 106, 116

object marking constructions 270, 271, 273, 280, 297, 306, 307, 312, 125

passive constructions 346
phoneme inventory 11, 13
possessive constructions
– attributive possessive construction 146, 147, 163, 164, 165
– predicative possessive construction 146, 163, 164, 165, 166
pronoun
– demonstrative pronouns 39, 40, 59, 60, 62
– interrogative pronouns 349, 363, 364, 366, 367, 369, 371, 372, 60
– 'other, other people' 39, 56
– personal pronouns 469, 39, 40, 41, 42, 43, 44, 46, 47, 49, 53, 56
– reciprocal pronouns 39, 56
– reflexive pronouns 432, 39, 50, 51, 56

quantifiers 101, 114, 115, 117, 121

reduplication 282, 25, 169, 171, 172, 173, 176
relative clauses 456, 40, 66, 67, 74, 75, 78, 83, 124, 138
– 'aboutness' relative clauses 441, 442, 444, 449
– adjunct relative clauses 439, 442, 449
– argument relative clauses 439, 440, 442, 445, 449
– light-headed relatives 421, 447, 450
– position of the head noun 419, 433, 448
– relativization markers 419, 420, 424, 425, 428, 429, 447, 449

tone system 15, 16, 18
topic-comment constructions
– clause topic 381, 393, 400, 403
– contrastive function of topic 402
– coreferential argument topic 381, 384
– coreferential pseudo-argument topic 384
– forms of topics 376
– frame-setting topic 381, 385, 386, 387, 388, 389, 390, 403
– identical topic 390
– patient topicalization 375, 397, 398, 400, 402

- position of topic 383, 395
- split argument topic 394
- topic marker 400

verb complement construction
- directional verb complement construction 179, 182, 189, 190, 211
- potential verb complement construction 180, 197, 199, 208, 209, 210, 211, 213
- resultative verb complement construction 179, 197, 198, 199, 202, 208, 212, 252, 399
- verb-extent complement construction 180, 205, 206
- verb-manner complement construction 179, 202, 203, 205, 213
- verb-phase complement construction 179
- verb-quantitative complement construction 180

Appendix

Story

北風　　合　日頭
pak⁷⁻⁸huaŋ¹　kaʔ⁷⁻⁸　letˣ⁻⁴thau²
The North Wind and the Sun

有　　蜀　　日，　北風　　　合　　日頭
u⁴　　tsit⁸⁻⁴　let⁸　pak⁷⁻⁸-huaŋ¹　kaʔ⁷⁻⁸　let⁸⁻⁴thau²
have　one　　day　north-wind　　and　　sun
為　　啥儂　　　其　　本領　　　恰　　　　大　　相諍。
ui⁵⁻⁴　siã³⁻²-laŋ²　e²⁻⁴　pun³⁻²liŋ³　khaʔ⁷⁻⁸　　tua⁵　saˈtsĩ⁵
for　what-person　GEN　capability　comparatively　big　RECP-argue
'One day, the North Wind and the Sun had a quarrel about which of them was the stronger.'

拄好　　　　路咧　　　　有　　蜀　　　個　　儂　　　咧　　　　行。
tu³⁻²ho³　lɔ⁵-leʔ⁰　u⁴　　tsit⁸⁻⁴　e²⁻⁴　laŋ²　leʔ⁸⁻⁴　kiã²
just　　　road-LOC　have　one　　CL　person　PROG　walk
'Just then, a person was walking along the road.'

日頭　　　　　共　　　　北風　　　　説　　"伯　　來　　比　　者，
let⁸⁻⁴thau²　ka⁵⁻⁴　pak⁷⁻⁸-huaŋ¹　səʔ⁷　lan³　lai²⁻⁴　pi³　tse⁰
Sun　　　　to　　north-wind　say　　1PL　come　compare　DELIM
看　　　(啥儂)　　有法嗵　　　　　　將　　即個　　　　儂　　　其　　　衫
khuã⁵⁻³　siaŋ²　u⁴huat⁷⁻⁸-thaŋ¹　tsiɔŋ¹　tsit⁷⁻⁸e²⁻⁴　laŋ²　e²⁻⁴　sã¹
look　　who　have.method-can　OM　　this-CL　person　GEN　clothes
褪　　　　落來。"
thŋ⁵　　loʔ⁰lai⁰
take.off　come.down
'The Sun talked to the North Wind, 'Let's see who can make the person take off his coat'.'

北風　　　　　説　　"好勢，　　與　　我　　先　　來。"
pak⁷⁻⁸-huaŋ¹　səʔ⁷⁻⁸　hɔ³⁻²se⁵　khɔ⁵⁻⁴　gua³　suin¹　lai²
north-wind　Say　　good　　　give　　1SG　first　come
'The North Wind said, 'OK, let me try first'.'

北風　　　吸　　　蜀　　　口　　　氣　　　口　　　出去。
pak⁷⁻⁸-huaŋ¹　khiəp⁷⁻⁸　tsit⁸⁻⁴　khau³⁻²　khi⁵　pun²　tshut⁰khɯ⁰
north-wind　inhale　one　mouth　air　blow　go.out
'The North Wind took a breath and blew it out.'

迄個　　　儂　　　無　　　褪　　　衫,
hit⁷⁻⁸-e²⁻⁴　laŋ²　bo²⁻⁴　thŋ⁵⁻³　sã¹
that-CL　Person　not.have　take.off　clothes
反而　　　將　　　衫　　　裹　　　得　　　佫恰　　　　口。
huan³⁻²li²⁻⁴　tsiɔŋ¹　sã¹　kɔ³⁻²　leʔ⁷⁻⁸　koʔ⁷⁻⁸khaʔ⁷⁻⁸　an²
Instead　OM　clothes　Wrap　CM　even.more　tight
'That person did not take off his coat, but wrapped it more closely around himself instead.'

北風　　　氣　　　迄,　　　出　　　全力　　　口　　　蜀　　　下。
pak⁷⁻⁸-huaŋ¹　khi⁵⁻³　a³　tshut⁷⁻⁸　tsuan²⁻⁴-lat⁸　pun²　tsit⁸⁻⁴　e⁵
north-wind　angry　EVC　Use　full-force　blow　one　time
'The North Wind was so angry that he used all his strength to blow.'

迄個　　　儂　　　寒　　　迄,　　　將　　　衫　　　裹　　　迄　　　佫恰　　口。
hit⁷⁻⁸-e²⁻⁴　laŋ²　kuã²　a³　tsiɔŋ¹　sã¹　kɔ³⁻²　a⁵⁻³　koʔ⁷⁻⁸khaʔ⁷⁻⁸　an²
that-CL　person　cold　EVC　OM　clothes　wrap　CM　even.more　tight
'That person was so cold that he held his coat much more tightly around himself.'

日頭　　　說　　　"啊　　　即陣　　　　著　　　看　　　我　　　咯。"
let⁸⁻⁴thau²　səʔ⁷　aº　tsit⁷⁻⁸tsun⁵　tioʔ⁸⁻⁴　khuã⁵⁻³　gua³　lɔº
Sun　say　DM　this.time　should　look　1SG　SFP
'The sun said, 'Now, let me have a try'.'

拄　　　說　　　了,　　　日頭　　　出力　　　　燿　　　者。
tu³⁻²　səʔ⁷⁻⁸　liau³　let⁸⁻⁴thau²　tshut⁷⁻⁸-lat⁸　tshio⁵　tseº
just　say　finish　sun　use-force　shine　DELIM
'No sooner had the sun finished what he said than he used his strength to shine.'

迄個　　　儂　　　感覺　　　　燒晴　　　起來,　　　將　　　紐　　　褪　　　揀。
hit⁷⁻⁸-e²⁻⁴　laŋ²　kam³⁻²kak⁷⁻⁸　sio¹tsin⁴　khiºlaiº　tsiɔŋ¹　liu³　thŋ⁵⁻³　sak⁷
that-CL　person　feel　warm　PVC　OM　button　take.off　RVC
'That person felt warm and unbuttoned his coat.'

日頭　佫　出　蜀　個　力。
let⁸⁻⁴thau²　koʔ⁷　tshut⁷⁻⁸　tsit⁸⁻⁴　e²⁻⁴　lat⁸
Sun　again　use　one　CL　force
'The sun used his strength (to shine) again.'

迄個　儂　熱　邁　規身　大汗,
hit⁷⁻⁸-e²⁻⁴　laŋ²　luaʔ⁸　a⁵⁻³　kui¹-sen¹　tua⁵⁻⁴-kuã⁵
that-CL　person　hot　CM　whole-body　big-sweat
將　外衫　褪　挷。
tsiɔŋ¹　gua⁵⁻⁴-sã¹　thŋ⁵⁻³　sak⁷
OM　outside-clothes　take.off　RVC
'That person was hot and sweaty, and so took off his coat.'

北風　對　日頭　其　本領　誠　欽佩。
pak⁷⁻⁸-huaŋ¹　tui⁵⁻³　let⁸⁻⁴thau²　e²⁻⁴　pun³⁻²liŋ³　tsiã²⁻⁴　khiəm¹phue⁵
north-wind　for　sun　GEN　capability　rather　admire
'The North Wind admired the capability of the Sun.'

日頭　說　"其實　伫　兩　個
let⁸⁻⁴thau²　səʔ⁷　ki²⁻⁴setˀ⁸　lan³　lŋ⁴　e²
sun　say　in.fact　1PL　two　CL
汝　有　汝　其　本事，我　有　我　其　本事。"
lɯ³　u⁴　lɯ³　e²⁻⁴　pun³⁻²sɯ⁵　gua³　u⁴　gua³　e²⁻⁴　pun³⁻²sɯ⁵
2SG　have　2SG　GEN　capability　1SG　have　1SG　GEN　capability
'The Sun said, 'Actually, we both have our own capabilities.''

Conversations I

Context: This conversation covers various topics, beginning with a banana joke, followed by an inquiry about the need to make a call to a friend, and then talking about what happened the night before and in the morning, which is interrupted by someone else's coming in.

A:　食　弓蕉　哦，家己　食　哦,
　　tsiaʔ⁸⁻⁴　kiŋ¹tsio¹　o⁰　kai⁵⁻⁴ki⁵　tsiaʔ⁸　o⁰
　　eat　banana　SFP　self　eat　SFP
　　啊　無　與　別儂　食　啊
　　a⁰　bo²⁻⁴　khɔ⁵⁻⁴　pat⁸⁻⁴-laŋ²　tsiaʔ⁸　a⁰
　　DM　not.have　give　other-person　eat　SFP

'(You are) eating a banana, but (you are) eating (it) by (your)self, you didn't give (it) to anyone else to eat.'

B: 想　　　說　　　醃臢，　　唔　　　敢　　　與　　　儂　　　食，
　　siũ⁴　　sə↷⁷⁻⁸　　a¹ tsam¹　m⁵⁻⁴　kã³⁻²　khɔ⁵⁻⁴　laŋ⁴　tsia↷⁸
　　think　COMP　　Dirty　　Not　dare　give　other　eat
　　家　　　食
　　kai⁵⁻⁴　tsia↷⁸
　　Self　　Eat
'(I) thought that (it) was dirty. (I) dared not give (it) to anyone else to eat, and that's why (I'm) eating (it) by myself.'

A: 啊　　汝　　著　　　共　　　美麗　　　　拍　　　　電話　　　　　唔？
　　a⁰　　lɯ³　tio↷⁸⁻⁴　ka⁵⁻⁴　bi³⁻²le⁵　pha↷⁷⁻⁸　ten⁵⁻⁴ue⁵　m⁰
　　DM　2SG　need　　to　　　PN　　　　hit　　　telephone　SFP
'Do you need to call Bi-le?'

C: 唔免
　　m⁵⁻⁴ben³
　　no.need
'No.'

A: 唔免　　　啊
　　m⁵⁻⁴ben³　a⁰
　　no.need　SFP
'No?'

A: 伊　　　咋暝　　　　合　　　我　　　說話……
　　i¹　　tsa⁴bĩ²　　ka↷⁷⁻⁸　gua³　sə↷⁷⁻⁸-ue⁵
　　3SG　last.night　COM　　1SG　say-word
'She talked with me last night…'
　　倒來　　　　咯？　　（才罪）　　無　　　　　啊？
　　to⁵lai⁰　　lɔ⁰　　tshə⁵⁻⁴　　bo²　　　a⁰
　　come.back　SFP　look.for　　not.have　SFP
'(You) came back? (You) didn't find (it)?'

D: （才罪）　　無
　　tshə⁵⁻⁴　　bo²
　　look.for　not.have

'(I) didn't find (it).'

A: 伊　　昨暝　　　合　　　我　　說話，
　　 i^1　tsa^4bi^2　$ka?^{7-8}$　gua^3　$sə?^{7-8}$-ue^5
　　 3SG　last.night　COM　1SG　say-word
　　 說　　　遘　　我　　最後　　　睏　　　去。
　　 $sə?^{7-8}$　a^{5-3}　gua^3　$tsue^{5-3}au^4$　$khun^5$　khu^0
　　 say　CM　1SG　last　　　　sleep　PVC
　　 'She talked with me last night until I fell asleep.'

　　 啊　　睏睏睏，　　　　　　俉　　　聽　　　著　　伊　　咧　　　說話，
　　 a^0　$khun^5khun^5khun^5$　$ko?^{7-8}$　$thiã^1$　$tio?^{8-4}$　i^1　$le?^{8-4}$　$sə?^{7-8}$-ue^5
　　 DM　sleep~sleep~sleep　again　listen　PVC　3SG　PROG　say-word
　　 俉　　　醒　　　（起來），　醒　　　（起來）　也　　嘸　　　知
　　 $ko?^{7-8}$　$tshi^3$　$khai^0$　$tshi^3$　$khai^0$　a^4　m^{5-4}　$tsai^1$
　　 still　wake.up　PVC　wake.up　PVC　also　not　know
　　 伊　　咧　　　講　　　啥
　　 i^1　$le?^{8-4}$　$kaŋ^{3-2}$　$siã^2$
　　 3SG　PROG　Say　what
　　 'Then I heard that she was talking and woke up, but I didn't know what she was talking about even though I was awake.'

B: 口　　　愛睏　　　去　　　咯
　　 $siã^2$　$ai^{5-3}khun^5$　khu^0　$lɔ^0$
　　 then　Sleep　　　PVC　　SFP
　　 'Then (you) got sleepy.'

A: 老儂　　　　　咯
　　 lau^4-$laŋ^2$　$lɔ^0$
　　 old-person　SFP
　　 'I am already old.'

A: 驚儂，　　　　老儂　　　　　咯。
　　 $kiã^1laŋ^0$　lau^4-$laŋ^2$　$lɔ^0$
　　 frightened　old-person　SFP
　　 'It's terrible. I am already old.'
　　 阿三　　儂　　　也　　三十　　　　　幾　　　　歲，　　卜　　　　四十　　　　　歲
　　 $a^1sã^1$　$laŋ^4$　a^4　$sã^1tsap^{8-4}$　kui^{3-2}　$hə^5$　$bo?^{7-8}$　$si^{5-3}tsap^{8-4}$　$Hə$
　　 PN　other　also　Thirty　several　year　FUT　forty　year
　　 'Ah-San is in his thirties, and is going to be forty years old.'

M: 阿三　伫咧？
　　$a^1sã^1$　$tuɯ^4le\text{ʔ}^0$
　　PN　　be.at
　　'Was Ah-San there?'

A: 無　　　伫
　　$bo^{2\text{-}4}$　$tuɯ^4$
　　not.have　be.at
　　'(He) was not there.'

Conversations II

Context: Three persons are mainly talking about an item of clothing, whose owner originally planned to keep, only for killing a duck the next day.

A: 迄領　　換　　來　　換，
　　$hit^{7\text{-}8}\text{-}liã^3$　$uã^5$　$lai^{2\text{-}4}$　$uã^5$
　　that-CL　change　come　change
　　迄領　　手䘼　　　換　　揀，驚儂　　　遘
　　$hit^{7\text{-}8}\text{-}liã^3$　$tshiu^{3\text{-}2}\text{-}\eta^3$　$uã^{5\text{-}4}$　sak^7　$kiã^1laŋ^{2\text{-}4}$　a^3
　　that-CL　hand-sleeve　Change　RVC　frightened　EVC
　　迄領　　口……
　　$hit^{7\text{-}8}\text{-}liã^3$　$siã^2$
　　that-CL　then
　　反正　　　汝　　即領　　　都　　卜　　　唔　　捭
　　$huan^{3\text{-}2}tsiŋ^5$　$lɯ^3$　$tsit^{7\text{-}8}\text{-}liã^3$　$tɔ^1$　$boʔ^{7\text{-}8}$　$m^{5\text{-}4}$　$tiʔ^8$
　　anyway　　2SG　this-CL　already　want　not　want
　　'Come and change that item (of clothing). Change that item (of clothing). (It looks) terrible. That item (of clothing) then... Anyway you don't want this item (of clothing) anymore.'

B: 驚儂，　　驚儂
　　$kiã^1laŋ^0$　$kiã^1laŋ^0$
　　frightened　frightened
　　'Terrible, terrible.'

C: 底　　蜀　　領　　唔　　捭　　啊？
　　$to^{3\text{-}2}$　$tsit^{8\text{-}4}$　$liã^3$　$m^{5\text{-}4}$　$tiʔ^8$　a^0
　　which　one　CL　not　Want　SFP

'Which one doesn't (he) want?'

A: 即領　　伊　　卜　　唔　　挃　　呀
　　tsit⁷⁻⁸-liã³　i¹　boʔ⁷⁻⁸　m⁵⁻⁴　tiʔ⁸　ia⁰
　　this-CL　3SG　Want　Not　want　SFP
　'He doesn't want this one (item of clothing).'

C: 即領　　唔　　挃　　啊？
　　tsit⁷⁻⁸-liã³　m⁵⁻⁴　tiʔ⁸　a⁰
　　this-CL　not　want　SFP
　'(He) doesn't want these clothes?'

A: 口　　口　　咧　　口面，
　　siã²　hio⁴　leʔ⁷⁻⁸　khau³⁻²ben²
　　just　place　at　Outside
　明日　　　　　㓂　　　刣　　　鴨。
　　biã²⁻⁴leʔ⁸　thaŋ¹　thai²⁻⁴　aʔ⁷
　　tomorrow　can　kill　Duck
　明日　　　　　汝　　說　　卜　　刣　　抑　　唔免　　　刣　　啊
　　biã²⁻⁴leʔ⁸　lɯ³　səʔ⁷⁻⁸　boʔ⁷⁻⁸　thai²　aʔ⁸⁻⁴　m⁵⁻⁴ben³⁻²　thai²　a⁰
　　tomorrow　2SG　say　want　Kill　Or　no.need　kill　SFP
　'Just put (it) outside. (You) can kill the duck (wearing it) tomorrow. Do you think we shall kill the duck tomorrow or not?'

B: 明日　　　　　刣　　　揀　　哦。
　　biã²⁻⁴leʔ⁸　thai²⁻⁴　sak⁷　o⁰
　　tomorrow　kill　RVC　SFP
　抑　　　卜　　　遘　　　年兜日　　　　則　　　刣　　啊？
　　aʔ⁸⁻⁴　boʔ⁷⁻⁸　kau⁵⁻³　lin²⁻⁴tau¹leʔ⁸　tsiaʔ⁷⁻⁸　thai²　a⁰
　　or　want　arrive　New Year's Eve　Then　kill　SFP
　下　　遘　　臭臭臭
　　khe⁴　a⁵⁻³　tshau⁵⁻¹~tshau⁵⁻⁴~tshau⁵
　　put　CM　smelly~smelly~smelly
　'Let's kill (the duck) tomorrow. Or wait until the New Year's Eve to kill (it)? (It) would smell bad (if we) keep (it).'

A: 下　　遘　　臭臭臭
　　khe⁴　a⁵⁻³　tshau⁵⁻¹~tshau⁵⁻⁴~tshau⁵
　　put　CM　smelly~smelly~smelly

'(It) would smell bad (if we) keep (it).'

B: 刣　　揀　　共　　□　　者。
　　thai²⁻⁴　sak⁷　ka⁵⁻¹　kun²　tse⁰
　　kill　　RVC　OM　　Cook　DELIM
　　啊　　蜀　　身　　衫褲　　　　噸　　　換,
　　a⁰　　tsit⁸⁻⁴　sen¹　sã¹khɔ⁵　thaŋ¹　uã⁵
　　DM　　one　　MW　clothes　　can　　change
　　噸　　　洗洗　　　　　者
　　thaŋ¹　sue³⁻²~sue³　tse⁰
　　can　　wash~wash　　DELIM
'Kill and cook (it), then the clothes can be changed and given a wash.'